Indigenising Anthropology
with Guattari and Deleuze

Plateaus – New Directions in Deleuze Studies

'It's not a matter of bringing all sorts of things together under a single concept but rather of relating each concept to variables that explain its mutations.'
Gilles Deleuze, *Negotiations*

Series Editors
Ian Buchanan, University of Wollongong
Claire Colebrook, Penn State University

Editorial Advisory Board
Keith Ansell Pearson, Ronald Bogue, Constantin V. Boundas, Rosi Braidotti, Eugene Holland, Gregg Lambert, Dorothea Olkowski, Paul Patton, Daniel Smith, James Williams

Titles available in the series
Christian Kerslake, *Immanence and the Vertigo of Philosophy: From Kant to Deleuze*
Jean-Clet Martin, *Variations: The Philosophy of Gilles Deleuze*, translated by Constantin V. Boundas and Susan Dyrkton
Simone Bignall, *Postcolonial Agency: Critique and Constructivism*
Miguel de Beistegui, *Immanence – Deleuze and Philosophy*
Jean-Jacques Lecercle, *Badiou and Deleuze Read Literature*
Ronald Bogue, *Deleuzian Fabulation and the Scars of History*
Sean Bowden, *The Priority of Events: Deleuze's Logic of Sense*
Craig Lundy, *History and Becoming: Deleuze's Philosophy of Creativity*
Aidan Tynan, *Deleuze's Literary Clinic: Criticism and the Politics of Symptoms*
Thomas Nail, *Returning to Revolution: Deleuze, Guattari and Zapatismo*
François Zourabichvili, *Deleuze: A Philosophy of the Event* with *The Vocabulary of Deleuze* edited by Gregg Lambert and Daniel W. Smith, translated by Kieran Aarons
Frida Beckman, *Between Desire and Pleasure: A Deleuzian Theory of Sexuality*
Nadine Boljkovac, *Untimely Affects: Gilles Deleuze and an Ethics of Cinema*
Daniela Voss, *Conditions of Thought: Deleuze and Transcendental Ideas*
Daniel Barber, *Deleuze and the Naming of God: Post-Secularism and the Future of Immanence*
F. LeRon Shults, *Iconoclastic Theology: Gilles Deleuze and the Secretion of Atheism*
Janae Sholtz, *The Invention of a People: Heidegger and Deleuze on Art and the Political*
Marco Altamirano, *Time, Technology and Environment: An Essay on the Philosophy of Nature*
Sean McQueen, *Deleuze and Baudrillard: From Cyberpunk to Biopunk*
Ridvan Askin, *Narrative and Becoming*
Marc Rölli, *Gilles Deleuze's Transcendental Empiricism: From Tradition to Difference* translated by Peter Hertz-Ohmes
Guillaume Collett, *The Psychoanalysis of Sense: Deleuze and the Lacanian School*
Ryan J. Johnson, *The Deleuze-Lucretius Encounter*
Allan James Thomas, *Deleuze, Cinema and the Thought of the World*
Cheri Lynne Carr, *Deleuze's Kantian Ethos: Critique as a Way of Life*
Alex Tissandier, *Affirming Divergence: Deleuze's Reading of Leibniz*
Barbara Glowczewski, *Indigenising Anthropology with Guattari and Deleuze*

Forthcoming volumes
Justin Litaker, *Deleuze and Guattari's Political Economy*
Nir Kedem, *A Deleuzian Critique of Queer Thought: Overcoming Sexuality*
Felice Cimatti, *Becoming-animal: Philosophy of Animality After Deleuze*, translated by Fabio Gironi
Ryan J. Johnson, *Deleuze, A Stoic*

Visit the Plateaus website at edinburghuniversitypress.com/series/plat

INDIGENISING ANTHROPOLOGY WITH GUATTARI AND DELEUZE

Barbara Glowczewski

EDINBURGH
University Press

Edinburgh University Press is one of the leading university presses in the UK. We publish academic books and journals in our selected subject areas across the humanities and social sciences, combining cutting-edge scholarship with high editorial and production values to produce academic works of lasting importance. For more information visit our website: edinburghuniversitypress.com

© Barbara Glowczewski, 2020, 2021

Edinburgh University Press Ltd
The Tun – Holyrood Road
12(2f) Jackson's Entry
Edinburgh EH8 8PJ

First published in hardback by Edinburgh University Press 2020

Typeset in 11/13 Sabon LT Std by
Servis Filmsetting Ltd, Stockport, Cheshire

A CIP record for this book is available from the British Library

ISBN 978 1 4744 5030 0 (hardback)
ISBN 978 1 4744 5031 7 (paperback)
ISBN 978 1 4744 5032 4 (webready PDF)
ISBN 978 1 4744 5033 1 (epub)

The right of Barbara Glowczewski to be identified as the author of this work has been asserted in accordance with the Copyright, Designs and Patents Act 1988, and the Copyright and Related Rights Regulations 2003 (SI No. 2498).

Contents

Acknowledgements ... vii

Prelude: The Wooden Egg Made Me Sick
    by Nakakut Barbara Gibson Nakamarra ... 1

1 Becoming Land ... 5

Part I: *The Indigenous Australian Experience of the Rhizome*

2 Warlpiri Dreaming Spaces: 1983 and 1985 Seminars with
  Félix Guattari ... 81
3 Guattari and Anthropology: Existential Territories among
  Indigenous Australians ... 114

Part II: *Totem, Taboo and the Women's Law*

4 Doing and Becoming: Warlpiri Rituals and Myths ... 131
5 Forbidding and Enjoying: Warlpiri Taboos ... 171
6 A Topological Approach to Australian Cosmology and
  Social Organisation ... 202

Part III: *The Aboriginal Practice of Transversality and Dissensus*

7 In Australia, it's 'Aboriginal' with a Capital 'A':
  Aboriginality, Politics and Identity ... 225
8 Culture Cult: Ritual Circulation of Inalienable Knowledge
  and Appropriation of Cultural Knowledge (Central and
  NW Australia) ... 257
9 Lines and Criss-Crossings: Hyperlinks in Australian
  Indigenous Narratives ... 281

Part IV: *Micropolitics of Hope and De-Essentialisation*

10 Myths of 'Superiority' and How to De-Essentialise Social
   and Historical Conflicts ... 299

11 Resisting the Disaster: Between Exhaustion and Creation   321
12 Standing with the Earth: From Cosmopolitical Exhaustion
 to Indigenous Solidarities   340

Part V: *Dancing with the Spirits of the Land*

13 *Cosmocolours*: A Filmed Performance of Incorporation
 and a Conversation with the Preta Velha Vó Cirina   359
14 The *ngangkari* Healing Power: Conversation with Lance
 Sullivan, Yalarrnga Healer   377

Bibliography   410
Index   439

Acknowledgements

All my gratitude to the Indigenous Australian multitude who taught me over the years: first the Warlpiri Law women and men from Lajamanu, especially Nakakut Barbara Gibson Nakamarra, Janjiya Herbert Nakamarra, Jimmy Robertson Jampijinpa and Wanta Steve Patrick Jampijinpa for sharing their challenging knowledge of *Jukurrpa*; the Yolngu Burrarwanga family for their filmic collaboration in Bawaka and Joe Neparrnga Gumbula for his vision of trans-Pacific flows; Lex Wotton, his mother, Agnes, sister Fleur and wife Cecilia in Palm Island for their exemplary struggle to defend social justice; David Mowaljarlai, Ngarrinyin visionary, for his testimonies; Lance Sullivan, Yalarrnga Law man from Boulia, for his trust in sharing with me in Townsville and in France his *ngangkari* healing gift that allowed the last chapter of this book. I would not have been able to keep battling against eurocentrism without the support of my daughters, Milari and Nidala, and their Djugun family, their father Jowandi Wayne Barker, auntie Pat Torres Mamanyjun, grandmother Theresa Barker, grand-uncle Brian Bin Saaban and others in Broome. My commitment to Indigenous cosmopolitics is continuously nurtured by many Aboriginal activists and scholars: great thanks to Shorty O'Neil and Djon Mundine for their early seminars in Paris; Ralf Rigby for editing the Palm film; Marcia Langton, Chair of Indigenous Australians Studies in Melbourne, for our collaborations, Brook Andrew for his artistic reclaim of colonial history; Max Lenoy, professor at JCU, and all the Guarani, Kaingang and Laklano students of the Indigenous *licentiatura* who welcomed him at UFSC in Brazil; Bouaza Benachir for his pioneer philosophy of Berber knowledge; Hawad for the impact of his Touareg furigraphic poems and paintings; Chantal Spitz for the intransigence of her writing and fight for Ma'ohi justice in Polynesia, Tokai Devatine and his mother Flora Devatine for their welcome in Tahiti, Viri Taimana, Vaite Devatine, and Hinanui Simon from Papeete, for sharing their healing skills at the French festival of Genac; Alex Tiouka, Maurice Tiouka, Jean Apollinaire, Christophe Yanuwana Pierre and Ludovic Pierre for sharing their Kali'na heritage and struggles in France, Felix Tiouka for his invitation to the Awala-Yalimapo Games, Linia Opoya and Tasikele Alupki for their hospitality in the Wayana village of Taluen, Aïma Opoya, Alain Mindjouk, Fabio Léon-Akati, for their political lesson in French Guiana.

This book would not exist without the rhizomatic world-wide connections generated by Guattari and Deleuze studies. I am very grateful to Félix Guattari for his enthusiasm and to his 1980s seminar accomplices, Eric Alliez, Jean-Claude Pollack, Anne Querrien; to Mayette Viltard for 35 years of topological and ecosophical supportive exchanges; Erin Manning and Brian Massumi for their micropolitical analysis of Aboriginal art; Maurizio Lazzarato and Angela Melitopoulos for their *Assemblages* film installation; Claude Mercier for inspiring transversalities between Lacan and Deleuze; Abrahao Oliveira de Santos for translating my Guattari seminars in Portugese to use in his collective dream workshop at the University of Fluminense and Peter Pal Pelbart for publishing them with n-1 in Brazil; Anne Sauvagnargues for stimulating schizoanalysis at ENS in Lyon, Paris, and at Cerisy; Emine Gorgul for her warm hospitality conveying a Deleuze conference in Istanbul; George Varghese and Manoj N.Y. for their formidable Deleuze and Guattari in India collective, allowing passionate debates with Patricia Pisters, Paul Patton and many others. I owe to Ian Buchanan the invitation to join this network after two enriching Guattari workshops at the University of Wollongong, and to imagine a book for his collection at EUP. Special thanks to Geraldine Lyons for editing the typescript, and all EUP staff for their caring assistance. My sincere appreciation to Andrew Burk for translating the first chapter; John Angell for chapter 2, Itsuki Kurihara and Shinichi Nakazawa for the Japanese version in *Gendai-Shiso*; Andrew Goffey for chapter 3 and Continuum for authorising its republication; Pat Lowe for working with me in Broome on the translation of extracts from *Du Rêve à la Loi* published here as chapters 4 et 5; Kenneth Maddock for editing my paper for *Mankind,* here chapter 6; Nora Scott for translating chap 7 and 8, one edited by Françoise Douaire-Marsaudon and Serge Tcherkezoff for ANU, the other by Monique Jeudy-Ballini and Bernard Juillerat for Carolina University Press; Christiane Senn for translating German archives; Hart Cohen for editing chapter 9 for *MIA* journal; Mariquian Kpédetin Ahouansou for her doctoral research on French Black people that inspired my keynote at the Cairns Institute, published here as chapter 10. My profound recognition to Tiécoura Traoré for showing me the

Acknowledgements

disastrous effect of globalisation in Mali and Sénégal, Henri Courau for his pioneer work on the 'camp-form' in Sangatte, Peter Stuart for his update on the NT Intervention, Alexandre Soucaille for our seminar and conference on disaster, who all inspired chapter 10, the team of editors who translated it for the *Spheres* online journal, and Gary Genosko for his published comments. I thank Christophe Bonneuil and Frédéric Neyrat for challenging me to speak and think "with" the earth at their workshop, Toni Pape and Adam Szymanski for translating for *Inflexions* this paper republished here as chapter 12; Pai Abilio Noé da Silveira for his welcome at the Tenda Spirita Vo Cirina in Florianopolis, Kabila Aruanda for the rehearsal at his *terreiro*, Clarissa Alcantara for cowriting in Portugese about our performance experience in Geneva, and Paula Morgado for editing the paper for the GIS Brazilian journal that authorised its republication as chapter 13. Special thanks to the Warnayaka Art Centre for their welcome, particularly Kitty Simon Napanangka for her Mina Mina painting on the cover, and Bertrand Estrangin in Bruxelles for providing the photo.

I am much obliged to many colleagues and institutions for their support: the Laboratory of Social Anthropology and the CNRS for funding my fieldwork over thirty years and the translation of the first and second chapter of this book; Annette Hamilton from Macquarie University who encouraged me to finish my PhD; Charles-Henry Pradelles de Latour and Bertrand Gérard for initiating me to topology, John Stanton and the Berndt museum in WA for our collaboration with Unesco; Laurent Dousset from the CREDO for setting up my Warlpiri and Djugun audiovisual archives on odsas.net; Mary Laughren, linguist in Warlpiri, for our joint regular fieldwork; Rosita Henry and the James Cook University for the establishment of our TransOceanik international Laboratory, and all its Australian, French and Brazilian members, for the joy and creativity we shared over the years, especially Miriam Grossi for organising a six months invitation at UFSC where she hosted a great symposium. I am very thankful to Irène Bellier for our indigenous seminars at EHESS, Florence Brunois-Pasina for enlightening our students, Jean-Christophe Goddard and Eduardo Viveiros de Castro for the decolonial meetings at the University of Toulouse; Radek Przedpelski and Steve Wilmer for the Deleuze art and multiplicity stimulating conference in Dublin; Nadia Wadori-Gauthier for sharing her One minute dance; Elisabeth Povinelli for our laughs and debates during events at Khiasma and the Paris Columbia Global Centre.

Sincere indebtedness to all my other friends for their intellectual nurturing, especially Michel Potage for *Le rire dans le désert*, a magnificent artistic homage to Aboriginal Land-Rights; Laurence Vale for her constant care since our 1970's films; Beriou for the cataphile network; Elisabeth D. Inandiak for the serenity of her engagement in Indonesia; Estelle Castro-Koshy for her commitment to Aboriginal and Polynesian writers; Jessica De Largy Healy for her Yolngu research and our intense collaborations, Lise Garond for her sound ethnography dedicated to Palm Island, Géraldine Le Roux for her innovative projects in art and ecology, Arnaud Morvan for his Kija research and Indigenous art curatorial work, Martin Préaud for his engaged analysis of the Kimberley Aboriginal Law and Culture Centre. I am deeply grateful to Yoann Moreau for thinking the multiversal, Elie Kong, Natura and the inhabitants of the Plateau de Millevaches for their écoles de la terre, Dénétem Touam Bona for his marooning lessons, Josep Rafanell i Orra for his creative dedication to mutual aid, Christophe Laurens for his entropic critique and supportive commitment towards Notre-Dame-des-Landes. Warmest gratitude to the inhabitants of this *ZAD*, Jojo, Uma, Nico, Agate, Christian, Marion, John, Isa, Mél, Maia, Jean-Marie, and many others whose struggle opens new hope for the future.

Prelude: The Wooden Egg Made Me Sick
By Nakakut Barbara Gibson Nakamarra

The other night, after Yakiriya told you the Emu Dreaming, I dreamt I was sitting with her and some ancestral women. We were getting ready for a ceremony and a crowd of white people were taking a photo of us! My mother-in-law called me, very angry, and said she did not want to be photographed by all these white people. But I answered, 'Don't worry, they are going to give us a truck!'

The next day I had to go to Yuendumu for a royalty meeting where I was intending to claim compensation from the mining company for my traditional land-rights over the Granites area!

My dream continued by revealing to me two new Dreaming songs, one for Emu and one for Rain. They were given to me by the female egg. Poor fellow, he is alone now that Yakiriya gave you the male one. I made them both years ago for her that is why the egg sang for me, making me sick even before my dream. I was cold and I did not know why. When I took the plane, I was feeling worse.

When I came back from the meeting, I told Yakiriya, 'It is Yankirri, emu, the cracking foot, who made me feel so sick in my stomach! I was carrying his two songs in the plane!'

Yakiriya was in the dream with two other Nangala who were singing the new Emu song: '*Karnanganja nangu nangu mangurrularna mangurrungurru.*'

Karnanganja means the parents of the egg, *nangu nangu* is the waterhole they saw, and the rest means that they had a rest there. All the singing women of my dream, me included, were painted with the Rain Dreaming.

Two Napanangka, Betty and Nyilirpina, erected the *mangaya* stick, right in the spot where Emu and his wife brooded their eggs. I was dancing with the other women and we were singing the new Rain song: '*Muraninginti kutakuta jurrdungku jurrdungku luwarninya.*'

Muraninginti means the other side, that is, west from the Emu trail; *kutakuta* is the storm; and *jurrdujurrdu*, the sand whirlwind. Finally, *luwarni*, throwing, refers to the bolt of lightning.

Suddenly, a cloud of sand rushed upon us. A very strong wind lifted the sand. We were covered with dust. And it started to rain. Because we were singing the Rain Dreaming, he was sending us the sand storm and the lightning.

All the women ran to the bush shelters which formed a circle around the dancing ground. *'Come here, there is too much dust!'* I shouted to the two Napanangka. But they continued to dance to get the sacred stick they had previously erected. And they joined us to hide it.

This is when I woke up, in the middle of the night. I thought about our old Rain and Emu yawulyu. I thought about two Nangala now deceased. They used to be the bosses of these rituals, being custodians of the Rain Dreaming from Kulpulunu and the Emu Dreaming in that region where the couple discovered the miyaka nuts. These two women taught me, like in school. All the Kulpulunu mob was my family because my father-clan would visit them every dry season. Thinking about these two elders, I felt very sad.

Falling asleep again, I went back into the same dream. The sand storm was over. There was only a small group of women now, two Nakamarra, my sister Beryl and myself, Yakiriya and another Nangala, one Nampijinpa and Betty Napanangka who was leading. We danced up to the Kuraja swamp, near Katherine. All around there, black stones called 'black clouds' are the trace of the Rain Dreaming. They also refer to the salt water, the sea further north (Darwin).

The Rain Dreaming paintings we had on our chests turned into Emu paintings. 'Now you are going to track the Emu Dreaming up to the salt water', Napanangka said. She took a big wooden dish that she painted with the Emu Dreaming. We danced far away to Jikaya, a place with many small waterholes. Each of us was dancing and dipping her foot into the holes, pulling it out as soon as the water was coming up. It was fun we tasted the water of all the holes with our feet!

We danced all night. At dawn, just before the day rose, we saw the sea, the huge black salt water. *'This is where you have to finish because the Emu brother and sister disappeared here'*, Napanangka said. So each of us tasted the sea with a foot like we had done in Jikaya. Gigantic waves lifted up and I got scared. Suddenly we found ourselves back in the 'black clouds' waterhole near Katherine (200 km south of the sea). I saw a ring place there and a crowd of ancestral women whose faces I could not recognise.

I woke up. The sun was rising. The Dreaming women had shown me the whole Ancestral Dreaming for Rain and Emu right up to where the two trails finish far away from the Warlpiri country. We dance and sing all this trail during the man-making Law (initiation). We dance all day and night. Before dark we sing Kulpulunu, a site crossed by Rain and Emu. Around midnight the songs bring us to Jikaya. And at dawn we sing and dance the arrival to the sea where the two Emu children bodies are resting for ever.

Prelude, with Nakakut Nakamarra

We paint all this journey on the ritual parraja dish. We dance with the dish and in the ground we erect the *mangaya* stick painted with black and white lines, representing, as on the dish, the sea and the clouds.[1]

Nakakut Barbara Nakamarra Gibson, who told me that dream in 1984, was born just before the Second World War on the land of her Warlpiri father in the Tanami Desert. Her mother was from a neighbouring tribe, the Mudpura. Nakakut grew up living a semi-nomadic life of hunting and gathering. A severe drought forced her family to seek refuge near the sacred site of the Granites which was occupied by goldminers. There, the government had situated a ration depot for all the Warlpiri people who were chased away from their land and shot while trying to get rid of the settlers' cattle that were spoiling their waterholes. Nakakut's father was the ritual custodian of that region, but the family was forcibly moved to Yuendumu, a reserve built in the late 1940s. Hundreds of Warlpiri were forced to live there and the pressure of such miserable cohabitation with so many people led to the eruption of regular conflicts. In the 1950s the government built another reserve on the northern edge of the Tanami Desert where some families, including Nakakut's, were forced to move. The early conditions were horrific. In the 1960s the Warlpiri people and other Aboriginal people across the continent saw their struggles recognised by a series of new laws. The reserve became the Lajamanu self-managed community. The Warlpiri won a huge land claim in 1978 which allowed them to negotiate with mining companies and receive royalties for explorations that they authorised. If any elders expressed concern about the destruction of their land, including the risk of spoiling the underground network of water, other Warlpiri signed and continue to sign various agreements, which generated constant conflicts.

Ten years after that dream, Nakakut came for the birth of my second daughter, Nidala, when I was living in Broome, on the Indian Ocean. I took her to Gantheaume Point, which the local Aboriginal custodians, the Djugun ancestors of my daughters' father, associate with the Giant Emeu Dreaming, Karnanganja, whose trail is shared with the desert tribes. On the bottom part of the big red cliff, there are many little pools that are filled with water after the tide goes

---

[1] Recorded in Lajamanu, NT, Australia in 1984 in Warlpiri, translated by Nakakut Barbara Nakamarra Gibson and edited in 1995 for the CD-ROM *Dream Trackers* (Glowczewski 2000). A French version was published with a commentary (Glowczewski and Nakamarra Gibson 2002).

out. When we 'tasted' that salt water with our bare feet, I suddenly felt transported to the desert, while Nakakut who was carrying my baby backed away a few steps from what she called the power of the place. I felt a sense of *déjà vu* in relation to her dream where she travelled on the tracks of the ancestral Emu and 'tasted' a Rain Dreaming sacred waterhole with her feet. Feeling the water and the earth with my feet and accessing a different experience of time-space was one of the many ways in which I have been invited by her people and other Indigenous people that I met over the past forty years to share with them a becoming land, to decolonise my mind, and through their lessons to indigenise anthropology.

Figure I.1 Nakakut Barbara Nakamarra Gibson leads her Nakamarra sisters (Perilpa, Jenny, Beryl) and Melody Napurrurla during the ritual dance for her Black Plum Dreaming. Lajamanu © B. G. (1984)

1
Becoming Land

I was eighteen, when, during a stimulating course on the history of philosophy ranging from Heraclitus to Foucault, our young professor invited us to read *Anti-Oedipus*.[1] I devoured it with a passion. In those post-1968 days, an education scheme had been established in high schools to fund creative activities. So seven other classmates and I wrote a script and acted in a film which we called *Angoisse* (1974: Anguish). Our professor agreed to play the role of the king fool in this strange film which questioned both religion and power:

> Our faces covered with psychedelic designs, disguised in a neo-ancient Greek style, we took turns placing an object at the bottom of a hill of sand in a huge quarry (in the forest). Every offering throughout the procession was interspliced with a scene of the person making the offering that depicted, within their daily life, some sort of anguish or anxiety that was crystallised into the object he or she provided as offering. As for me, I offered an empty (painting) frame since during my filmed sequence I tried to draw the contours of my reflection, starting with my left hand placed on the mirror, going all the way to my right hand which held the marker and which couldn't draw its own contour: the impossibility of representing this movement was an allusion to Escher's famous piece where a hand emerges from off the page of a drawing in order to draw another hand, creating the optical illusion of a Moebius strip. The film ended with a banquet in the quarry where one of us, covered in white sheets, was carried onto a table to be be painted using the food from the feast.[2]

The following year, enrolled at the University of Jussieu-Paris 7 (now known as Université Paris Diderot) to study economic and social administration, I drafted a short commentary around *Anti-Oedipus* that consisted of systematically pointing out every time the

---

[1] Special thanks to Drew Burk for translating and commenting this introductory chapter, and to the Laboratory of Social Anthropology (CNRS/EHESS/Collège de France) for the translation grant.
[2] Glowczewski (2012); see film on: https://vimeo.com/315628049

authors mentioned Marx. It was my way of validating a course criticising capitalist development throughout the countries of the Third World. At first rather sceptical upon receiving the text, the professor ended up thanking me the following week for having prompted him to read Deleuze and Guattari since his Marxist circle of economists viewed *Anti-Oedipus* with suspicion. It was quite a different story for all the fans who packed themselves into the lecture hall at the University of Vincennes Paris 8 where Deleuze presented his lectures in constant dialogue with Guattari. I ended up enrolling there in 1977 for a masters in cinema with a minor in philosophy. This was long before Deleuze's publication on *The Movement-Image* ([1983] 2003). But he had just released the essay 'Rhizome' with Guattari and its proposition for an anti-hierarchical conception of things was very exciting to me. I was not one of those students or attendees who arrived way before the course began in order to grab a seat within the crammed lecture hall. I preferred the margins, in every sense of the term.

There were so many creative things happening inside this experimental university located at the edge of the woods of Vincennes. In particular, the meetings organised by the MLF (Movement for the Liberation of Women), the seminars held by the group Psyche & Po organised by Antoinette Fouque and, not to be forgotten, the courses held by Hélène Cixous (1976) who, in 1974, founded the first Centre for Women's and Gender Studies in Europe in the university's new Department of Texts and Societies. I happened to film and document a truly remarkable feast reserved specifically for women only and which gathered together hundreds of women dancing on the esplanade around a fire of joy.[3] It was under the direction and supervision of Claudine Eizykman, author of experimental films and creator of the Paris film co-op, that I completed my masters presenting one of the experimental films I had made with a tiny spring-loaded, hand-cranked webo camera. For this experimental film, *Picturelure*, I ended up creating all sorts of visual effects based on little drawings and animation techniques, using no sound and working frame by frame. All my other experimental films focused on the exploration of the female body. Many women in those days discovered their bodies through a variety of experiences, both private and public, through love, writing, political action and artistic performances. I was

---

[3] 1977: http://www.cinedoc.org/film-1958-fete-de-femmes-a-l-universite-de-vincennes-html

fortunate to have benefited from a summer workshop in women's studies at the University of California, Santa Cruz in 1974, followed by a course taught by the American feminist anthropologist Judith Brown at the University of Jussieu-Paris 7. She provided us with a synthesis of the male bias found in all anthropological literature that was being thoroughly criticised at that time, mostly notably by certain female anthropologists who systematically reinterpreted anthropological history, especially in the United States.[4] One could also see this feminist movement in anthropology begin to take place in France under prominent figures such as the anthropologist Nicole-Claude Mathieu (1985) at the EHESS who co-founded the journal *Questions féministes* in 1977.

While *Anti-Oedipus* and *A Thousand Plateaus* are both brimming with anthropological references, they contain hardly any critique of masculine domination and debates concerning gender. Certainly, the 'becoming-woman' is posited as of one of the rhizomatic virtualities traversing both sexes, which to a certain extent calls into question the duality of gender, but the exacting work and findings questioning male bias found within the interpretations of the social and human sciences, including within psychoanalysis, are in no way mobilised within either of the two volumes on *Capitalism and Schizophrenia*. Guattari, nevertheless, supported a number of minoritarian struggles, including the movement of the FHAR (Front homosexuel d'action révolutionnaire) created in 1971 by the writer Guy Hocquenghem along with Françoise d'Eaubonne, co-founder of MLF. The FHAR would later split into a number of homosexual liberation groups in particular in response to the rise and spread of AIDS. D'Eaubonne would eventually create the Ecology-Feminism association in 1978 and propose the concepts of ecofeminism and phallocracy.[5]

Guattari was a friend to several anthropologists, most notably Pierre Clastres, who had become rather well known for his *Society Against The State* inspired by Amerindians from Paraguay and Brazil, along with Robert Jaulin, author of *La mort Sara* and *La Paix Blanche*, two books criticising colonisation, one focusing on Africa and the other on the Amazon Rainforest. Jaulin denounced the ethnocide taking place among Indigenous people, a concept created

---

[4] Rosaldo and Lamphere (1974); Rubin (1975); Ortner and Whitehead (1981); Moore (1988).
[5] See documentary: Alessandro Avellis, *La Révolution du désir* (2006); Albistur and Armogathe (1977: 458).

by the anthropologist and Vietnam specialist Georges Condominas ([1957]1977). In the aftermath of May 1968, Jaulin was also responsible for creating the Department of Ethnology at Jussieu-Paris 7. Michel de Certeau who also taught there, would end up becoming the supervisor of my masters thesis, 'Anthropologie des 5 sens' (Anthropology of the Five Senses) whose final page, like the preceding sixty-three, was typed on a tiny typewriter and punctuated with a myriad of elipses:

> If I had to undertake this work again starting from the very beginning, I would not take myths as my starting point so as to attempt discerning the sensorial apprehension of different cultures, but rather, I would create and take as my mode of research what has become known as ethnographic documentary films. And this doesn't mean that I consider information to be more objective: there is just as much subjectivity in the visual transcription of human behavior as can be found in writings and the interpretation of a myth. But in finally arriving at a hypothesis – having initially endeavored to accumulate the necessary 'matter', the required 'material' from other cultures' philosophies for demonstrating the relativisation of our confined Western perception – I realised that the act of 'demonstration' is metaphysical whereas my goal was precisely an attempt to escape this metaphysics ... throughout this long process and journey, it's as if everything that could suggest itself as being matter ended up systematically evaporating, thereby satisfying the principle of permanent metaphorphosis that I had evoked throughout the entirety of my work: I had become ensnared in the logic of my own reasoning ... what's important to retain from this text is the sensation of a voyage that is no more physical than metaphysical but rather alchimical ... it's a feeling of *jouissance*, of joy that I in no way regret, even if it already has fallen into the schema of an old dream (which doesn't take away the initial premonition!): the past of others can be our future ...
>
> My desire for images of (felt) presence today corresponds to a new need perhaps awakened by this bath of intemporal images, of so many myths ... It's certainly with new eyes that I view an Aboriginal person carefully preparing flour or a Fulani shepherd watching over and minding his cattle, or an Indian who paints himself in traditional guise or a Polynesian who traditionally burns portions of the land ... the rhythm of these gestures, their complexity within space. What seems to be suggested by these acts besides a certain automatism, besides an extreme sense of contemplation, is the living presence of a specific kind of sensuality that escapes our grasp. These rhythms and rituals have taught me, in a much more immediate and indelible way, about a sensuality that is always personal and cultural, and complicit with a certain relation of love with specific objects, plants, animals or more generally a

relation with regions above or below the earth, a relation similar to that which we have sadly reduced to only being accessible by humankind and unfortunately oftentimes not considered accessible to all of humankind or everything else that exists ...

I have often had the impression that magic is a way of being surprised in allowing ourselves to see something new that we had not allowed ourselves to encounter in what we were already looking at, to hear something within what we are listening to that we didn't know was there, to detect and smell an odor which we were sure wasn't really present, to allow ourselves to be swept up in the throes of ectasy upon eating a sliver of chocolate where we no longer recognise the limit point between one's skin and what we touch ... We could all therefore be sorcerer apprentices and the magic wand would be nothing more than our thousand and one senses ... (Glowczewski 1978)

This excerpt represented a myriad of diffuse ideas which, during that time period, directly nourished themselves off writings and images derived from other cultures but also from personal experimentation of the senses, such as my practice of experimental films that had strived to elicit feelings, a kind of optical music, to affect perception without attempting to represent some sort of symbolic intention. I was also imbued with the struggles of women that, throughout every corner of the world, began to seriously question masculine domination, and with the creative responses of various peoples oppressed by colonisation, most notably the Indigenous populations who were organising themselves so as to affirm their own sovereignty. Bringing along my tiny 16 mm camera to Australia, I tried to continue the experimental technic by filming the rituals of Warlpiri women frame by frame[6] but, after reviewing the special effects of acceleration and superimposition of their movements that I used in the first developed rolls of film, the Warlpiri women dissuaded me from continuing to film in this experimental way. They simply asked for me to stick to the rhythms of their dances and to not show the films to the men of my country as their rituals were restricted to women only. This trip would completely change my life and every layer of my existence specifically regarding questions of gender.

---

[6] In a 16 mm film as I used it there were twenty-four frames per second but the mechanism of the camera allowed one to imprint each frame separately or as short sequences of two to twelve frames in a row and then to wind back the film strip to film again frame by frame, creating superimpositions.

The Indigenous Australian Experience of the Rhizome

For the Indigenous people of Australia, a manner of wandering, of movement, situated along earthbound pathways (called Dreamings) of mythic heroes, defines a specific space-time. The 'Dreaming' voyages of mythic ancestors (whether as anthromorphic incarnations, as plants or animals, or incarnated in the forces of nature themselves) have all left their marks on the earth which shows itself today as proof of what has also been called the Dreamtime. The land with its mountains, caves, creeks, and water sources, its freshwater springs, its minerals, and vegetation and its animals is therefore the space of the Dreaming and can be read as a network of signs in intimate correspondence: the earth, by 'incarnating' the Dreaming, materialises the human's memory and, as such, guarantees in a certain way their connection to the land as well as with the Dreaming.

The Dreaming is not a space-time of creation but of the transformations of pre-exising conditions that are never completely explained within the myths. The Dreaming rids itself of the question of the origin of things. It is an active principle of various metamorphoses and, as we shall see, metamorphosis is the image of social dynamics particular to the Aboriginal people. It's through the Dreaming that everything takes on a life and a meaning, but throughout all that exists, it's the earth itself, the land, that is the source of power or the force that makes of the Dreaming this force which passes throughout all the inherent 'energies' found within matter, the so-called vital forces of the species that constitute the Dreaming and life.

The term 'Dreaming' – 'to be in the middle of dreaming', 'the activity of dreaming', – has been the translation used by ethnologists to encompass the Aboriginal terms that the 500 different Indigenous Australian ethnic groups (language groups) use in order to speak about both their mythic histories, of the time referring to these stories and histories, and to the earthly pathways corresponding to the voyages of the heroes of these stories, linked with the natural species with which the Indigenous Australians identify themselves. For the Aboriginal people, 'Dreaming' is the Law. The present continuous grammatical form in English, 'being in the middle of', doesn't have an equivalent in French, but this English way of translating the term clearly indicates the notion of becoming that is unique to the Aboriginal people, that of the 'Dreaming'. We thus posit the problem of exactly knowing just what is supposed to be in becoming within this formulation since, a priori, nothing allows us to postulate that there is a subject 'in the process of dreaming'. Out of convenience and utility, we will use the term Dreaming to speak of stories, of time and the mythic pathways that make up what the Aboriginal people call their Law.[7]

---

[7] In French, the progressive form of 'dream', dreaming, literally 'rêvant', is not used as a noun which is why the author has translated 'Dreaming' to *Rêve* (Dream with

Becoming Land

The Dreaming, as Law, is the principle of adaptation par excellence at both the symbolic and social level. We will see how fluctuating can be for each Aboriginal man or woman his or her identification with the mythic heroes defined as his/her ancestors, for whom he or she inherits the responsibility as spiritual custodian of the specific terrestrial pathways corresponding to their mythic voyages. We will see that the spiritual control of the earth and land, to a certain degree, corresponds to a specific Aboriginal identity and, on the other hand, to a specific political functioning where women play a very active role. (Glowczewski 1981a)

So began my PhD dissertation in anthropology, 'Le Rêve et la Terre – Rapports au temps et à l'espace des Aborigènes d'Australie' (The Dreaming and the Land – Relations to time and space of Aboriginal Australians) that Félix Guattari had just finished reading when he called me up one day to invite me to come speak at his apartment Rue de Condé. On that day, 18 January 1983, after a number of hours of questions, he asked me to stay in order to continue our discussion in public since it was time for his weekly seminar (there were no students, mostly scholars and people working in mental health, activists, etc. ...). The seminar was recorded and four years later it was published in the first issue of *Chimères*, the journal that Félix Guattari would create with Gilles Deleuze in 1987. A second seminar that we did together in 1985 was also recorded, still at his same apartment on Rue de Condé. The transcription of these two seminars 'Warlpiri Dreaming Spaces' constitutes the opening of Part I of this present book, entitled 'The Indigenous Australian Experience of the Rhizome'.

Guattari met twelve Warlpiri men from Lajamanu (the community I spoke about in my dissertation) when they were invited by the organisers of the festival d'Automne [The Autumn Festival] in 1983 to paint a ground painting made on a ton of sand covering an entire room of the Museum of Modern Art in Paris. They were also invited to dance a ritual dreamed by a Warlpiri woman, Janjiya Nakamarra (see Figure 4.1), at Peter Brook's theatre, Théâtre des Bouffes du Nord (see Figure 4.2). We then attempted to organise – within the framework of the transcultural foundation that he had initiated with Jean-Pierre Faye – an encounter with healers coming from what we then called the Fifth World – to differentiate it from the First World (Western capitalist countries, including Japan and South Korea), the

---

a capital). But in the reverse translation here, all 'Rêves' are retranslated using the Aboriginal English term, Dreaming.

Second World (the Soviet Union and the Communist Bloc), the Third World ('undevelopped' countries from the Southern Hemisphere) or the Fourth World (designating people suffering from poverty in rich countries). The Fifth World for Guattari brought together Indigenous peoples who had been colonised by different states but who resisted within their affirmation of an existential sovereignty alongside other groups proclaiming their autonomy in such regions as Corsica, the Basque Country or Palestine. For Guattari ([1985] 1986), these sorts of movements were 'nationalitary' (*nationalitaires*) and not 'nationalistic'. We were unable to secure the proper funding to organise the event that Félix wanted to call the Rainbow Gathering. The colours of the Rainbow ended up later becoming a flag of recognition used both by Indigenous peoples along with the Gay Pride and equal marriage rights' movements. Rainbow colours became a sign of recognition for a collective call against homophobia but also against the homogenisation of the world so as to affirm the multiplicities emerging throughout the globe within transnational cultural gatherings, shamanic or other neo-pagan festivals.

My thesis in anthropology was supervised by Maurice Godelier, a specialist of Papua New Guinea, who analysed the purported universal domination of women through a Marxist lens. I did not agree with him, as both my own personal experience and my enlightening time on the ground in Australia in 1979 convinced me that recognising feminine singularity does not necessarily induce a domination of women by men. As I explain in Chapter 2, 'Warlpiri Dreaming Spaces', the women custodians of the rituals – who call themselves 'businesswomen', business being the Aboriginal English translation of their ritual activities – helped me to live my very own feminine subjectivity from the inside out. Along with the Warlpiri women, I experienced a troubling and overwhelming experience of a complete dissolution into a collective body that couldn't be captured by any essentialisation of the feminine but rather affirmed a cosmological singularity of a becoming feminine traversing all forms of life. The Warlpiri people who during the 1950s had forcefully and unwillingly been made to adapt to a sedentary lifestyle had just reacquired their rights to a vast territory (600 km N/S × 300 km E/W) and had begun to invent new forms for self-managing the old reservation and reoccupation of their sacred ancestral sites. The opportunity to partake in the community life of these Warlpiri families, who had to learn to re-nomadise themselves in automobiles, gave me reason to believe and imagine a future world where Aboriginal peoples would perhaps be capable of helping us respond to numerous questions regarding gender as well as the impasses we were experiencing in relation to consumption caught within destructive forms of development and living environments of the current social fabric and mentalities.

> In the 1970s, some alternative or 'underground' media, like the French magazine *Actuel*, were promoting a postmodern collusion between Indigenous tribes and hightech science fiction. Arriving in Lajamanu in 1979, I was struck with an apocalyptic vision: the entrance of the old Hooker Creek reserve, established on the edge of the Tanami Desert hundreds of kilometres from the first petrol station, had piles of old cars, fridges, and other Western waste, spread in the bush as a parody of our consumption society but also like a spare parts shop for the Warlpiri people who would pick up what they needed from there to build shanty camps or repair their cars. I was attracted to this oneiric end of the world landscape, which would later resonate with the 'Zone' of *Stalker* (1979) by Tarkovski. The minimalist mental and physical resistance of the 'Zone' was a forbidden, 'dangerous' place to cross. In a way, during the many months I spent each time in Lajamanu – as well as in other Aboriginal places – I also learned how to manoeuvre through forbidden spaces of knowledge, embodied in the landscape: zones of information and ritual camps were restricted either to men or women and to different levels/classes/groups of initiates, camping spots and pathways to be avoided because of a death, sacred sites that could not be attended or that needed a ritual protocol of introduction to the spirits. The landscape was full of spirits crossing time in a perpendicular way but leaving traces and symptoms of disease. The language was constantly fragmented with taboo words to be replaced by whispers and gestures evoking the deceased, synonyms, or simply left as holes 'without name', a punctuation of memorial vacuums, the space also for virtual re-emergence through new dream revelations after the lifting of the mourning period. (Glowczewski 2014)

Upon returning from my initial fieldwork in Australia, I dreamed of places of refuge that would allow for drifting into the imaginary of futurist disaster and survival like the Warlpiri attempted in the desert, having themselves already experienced colonisation and its violent impact starting at the beginning of the twentieth century through to the 1960s. A collective research group that I led in urban anthropology introduced me to various clandestine groups, amateurs of a network of some 300 km of tunnels cut in old Parisian underground stone quarries whose access was forbidden to the public. With them, I explored their nocturnal practices of walking through the subterranean world beneath Paris as well as their different motivations for investing their time in doing so (Glowczewski et al. 1983). Félix agreed to write a preface for our book *La cité des Cataphiles* (The city of Cataphiles) which was subtitled 'Anthropological mission in the Paris underground':

> What's the purpose of these vertigenous implosions within the lower beyond [endeça] of the day and night? To reinitiate the battle between Eros and Thanatos one more time, both of them exhausted by decades of psychoanalytic abuse? It's certainly not into this area of research that our authors guide us! Their viewpoint of the underbelly of the city is not some sounding of a death knell. Quite the opposite: the rhizome of catacomb-intensities they lead us to discover constitutes a mega-machine of desire, a bearer of incadescant life or, at the very least, the most maddening 'revivals', as the suprising and 'addictive' character of the book bears witness to. (Guattari [1983] 1986: 242)

Chapter 3, 'Guattari and Anthropology: Existential Territories among Indigenous Australians' was first published in the collective book *The Guattari Effect* (Alliez and Goffey 2011) derived from the conference hosted by the Department of Philosophy at Middlesex University in 2007. In this chapter, I discuss the various debates around the notion of a rhizome of intensities proposed by Deleuze and Guattari. For those peoples who sustain themselves through gathering yams that grow as underground rhizomes, this term is not a mere poetic metaphor, but a daily reality, a figure of thought that in turn becomes simultaneously a model of social, environmental and mental organisation. This encounter between the form of a plant, a way of behaving collectively and thinking, is one among many other ways of interweaving what Guattari called the three ecologies at the core of his ecosophy: an ecology of the environmental (the natural and cultural environment, including any additional machinic overlays), a social ecology (of both the local and the global) and a mental ecology (of processes of subjectivation concerning the individual as much as the collective).

Many Indigenous Australians define the space-time of their Dreamings – Yam Dreaming, Kangaroo Dreaming or Rain Dreaming – as their Law, where the life of human beings is intimately linked with all forms of living beings be they animals, plants, the rain or the stars, but also with a multitude of sites that they are connected to and consider to be sacred. This simultaneous oneiric and geologic geography made a lasting impression on Félix and would end up leading him to orient his common work with Deleuze a bit differently. In his *Schizoanalytic Cartographies,* Guattari ([1989] 2013) will develop a way of thinking his concept of existential territories and the refrain [*la ritournelle*][8] that is simultaneously more multi-situational and oneiric. For the Warlpiri and their desert neighbours, each named thing has its specific Dreaming, its dream as image-force, a becoming of a model of thought and a way of acting that concerns human as much as some other living beings, including places in the land which are also imbued with life. Consequently, the Yam Dreaming is the Dreaming of a network opened up to an infinite number of unpredictable lines that etch the earth from above and below, that crack the earth open when the tubers grow large and the liana cling onto the trees they encounter that cross their paths. The Yam Dreaming is also a series of relations between generations and local groups, the simultaneous singular and common experience of a spirit that becomes incarnated within certain people at the same time as it places them in resonance, throughout waking-life and the space-time of the Dreaming, with an infinite multiverse.

> *Puurda* (Yam) came from the East, from Yawulawulu and he travelled to Talala. The vines were coming up and the roots were shooting underground, many of them, going towards Lajamanu. Small yams came out. These yams, the Japanangka, Napanangka, Japangardi and Napangardi[9] saw all the *Wirntiki* Stone Curlew, and they went down in the ground. As they were going, the ground became soft.
>
> They went to Munju. The food was spreading everywhere. The Yam people looked back at their country. My Dreaming, my *Jukurrpa* had grown everywhere, the Yam from Yawulawulu that belongs to the Japanangka, Napanangka, Japangardi and Napangardi.
>
> My *Jukurrpa* also went to Yumurrpa. Not really the yam, but the *yuparli* leaves that gave birth to new yams. The root grew underground and went to Jukakarinya. Yam looked at the other one from far. He went on. The people from Yawulawulu continued their way, crossing Talala. Then they stopped for ever. They were tired from trying to go

---

[8] The refrain (*ritournelle*) first appears in one of Guattari's clinical summaries titled, 'Monographie sur R. A.' which was written in 1956 – when he was only twenty-six years old – then, ten years later in 'Réflexions pour des philosophes à propos de la psychothérapie institutionnelle' (*Cahiers de philosophie de la Sorbonne* 1, 1966). These are referenced by Guattari (1972: 18–22, 86–97), as indicated by Guesdon (2016: 18–19).

[9] Classificatory names called 'skin-names' by Aboriginal people or 'subsections' in anthropology. Warlpiri have eight skin-names, each having a female version (starting with N) and a male version (starting with J). The eight (× 2) names form a system of relations that has the mathematical properties of a diedric group that can be diagrammatised by two interconnected circles (see Figure 1.4) and also a cube (see Figure 6.1).

all over, everywhere. Our fathers Japanangka and Japangardi stopped. That is why Yumurrpa is not owned by us but by Jupurrurla, Jakamarra, Napurrurla and Nakamarra. (Nelly Morrison Napanangka)[10]

Such is one of the mythic narratives of the ancestors of the Yam Dreaming common to the yams of today and the men and women who bear the Dreaming's name and its totemic becoming, i.e., the obligation to take care of the yams so they may continue to grow. If the ancient, semi-nomadic hunter-gatherer peoples didn't farm anything, they sang, danced and made paintings to ensure the reproduction of the species, that is, by way of these ritual activities (that for us are also artistic), they re-actualised the memory of the relations of interdependence that allow for the proper continuation of the species. For example, one had to transmit, by way of songs, tales, cartographic paintings and the dances that perform them, the so-called sites of the multiplication of the species. For the Yams, it has to do with a particular sacred cave where the very ancient roots must not be disturbed at the risk of placing the entire network in danger. For the Warlpiri and their desert neighbours, it's with the help of the stars in the night sky that they know when it's ok to begin digging into the soil in order to dig up the yams. The season is indicated when the so-called 'pointer' stars of the Southern Cross constellation touch the horizon, it's 'feeding time' for the yams that are exchanged for beef. The women are the ones who provide the yams to the men in exchange for the kangaroos they hunt, and this exchange is more about the exchange between genders: the men must give the game to their mothers-in-law, who, following ritual obligation, must in turn give them the yams. This ritual of exchange, reminding everyone of the alliance between the sexes, is at the heart of the Fire ceremonies and conflict resolution, Jardiwanpa, that must specifically be performed at the moment when the two stars of the Southern Cross shine on the horizon.[11]

The sung versions of the myths are encrypted or coded into some sort of minimalist code in order to memorise important and vital landmarks, as beacons or markers in the terrestrial and celestial landscape integrated into the songlines that become interconnected on the continent into a multitude of superimposed networks punctuated by sacred sites.

---

[10] Recorded in Lajamanu, 1984, translated from Warlpiri with B. Nakamarra Gibson (Glowczewski 2000).

[11] See *Lajamanu* (60'), documentary by B. Glowczewski, 2018: https://vimeo.com/289440509; see also Laughren et al. (2014).

Becoming Land

Miyikampi kampi yarlaangka warlawuru
The Yam Dreaming from Miyikampi takes different roads between Mt Theo and Yawulawulu.

ngamarna nguluna marimari pijarra ngulu
Root one walks around and small one come along.

warlawurulu Talalapungu wirlimpangulu Talalapungu
Warlawuru the leafy vine go up the tree and that is the mother one (yam) *wirlimpangu* big one making young ones in Talala.

mardi mardila jutajutarla
When the yam makes the soil crack because mardi is a big yam and *jutajuta* mean they dig it out.

mardinya laparparnka ngamarna lapirpunga
Mardi big mob they get from the root everywhere.

yarla pari pari ngamarna pirlpiwangkanya
Yarla is everywhere outside when they get it and leave it.

papirdaji taja wararujuruju
Papirda is *yarla*, the sweet potato.[12]

If the verses of the songs are coded it's because their performativity resides elsewhere than within the narrative contents of the verses. It's about singing the attachments to the land as engrams that simultaneously become inscribed into the earthen soil, body and mind. Moreover, each child is supposed to be an incarnation of one of the verses of the song, sowed into the ground by one of the ancestors of a Dreaming whose name and site of insemination is revealed in a dream to the father, to the mother or to a relative or a close friend of the family in the camp. As Betty Jamanawita Nungarrayi explains:

> *Jukurrpa* (Dreaming) took *Ngarlajiyi* (Yam) from Yarduralinyi. He took the name of my father. My father's spirit went with the Dreaming to Yamakangu. The yam flower talked to the Yam Dreaming. She said *Ngarlajiyi* and the yam grew, the spirit of my father.
>
> *Jukurrpa* went. He went to a *kumanjayi* place. The leaves grew. A new yam was born. The roots spread very far. They took the Dreaming to Ngarrnka. They went in parallel lines. The yam flower talked.

---

[12] Yarla song cycle by Nampiya Judy Jigili Napangardi and Lajamanu women, 1995, translated from Warlpiri by B. Nakamarra Gibson. Recorded and edited by B. Glowczewski (2000).

In Yalingparunyu a new yam was born. The Dreaming made a yam in the wet ground. The leaves lay down. They were shining bright green, fed by the water of the ground. My father's Dreaming took his name. Yam spread his roots. New roots, long, very long, travelled to Yinikimpi. All along they gave tubers which shoot to the top or the bottom.

My father felt the ground, he hit it. The land was hard where the tubers had grown. The roots spread to Lapurrkurra. Tubers were born. My father dug the ground. He found many of them. He dug and dug and followed the roots to Ngarranji. The Dreaming made the roots fall very close, in Yarunkanyi, the place of Napaljarri, Nungarrayi, Japaljarri and Jungarryi skins. This is where my father's name was left. He left him with other *Kurruwalpa* spirit-children. My father's name fell in the Pankulmanu waterhole. My father's conception Dreaming continued to Waputarli, but there the story does not belong to me.

I am from Yarunkanyi. This is where I was conceived. My parents were collecting seeds they made into a damper and they ate. This is how my mother caught me inside her. My father found my spirit-child in the seeds of his country. This spirit was coming from the *Ngarrka* (Initiated Man) Dreaming who lies there. My father and his brother were the custodians of this Dreaming. He organised the dances and the Law ceremonies for this land. I was born and learnt how to dance, sing and paint my Dreaming. (Jamanawita Betty Nungarrayi)[13]

After my fourth long period of fieldwork in Australia in 1984 I found myself without any permanent lodging in Paris. Félix Guattari offered me an empty room in his flat in which to stay for a couple of months, where I began to write down my notes for what would become *Desert Dreamers*. The book garnered some success upon publication in 1989 primarily from the fact that I wrote candidly about my experiences conducting fieldwork with a very critical point of view by expressing my doubts and my disappointments as much as my passions and enthusiasms for the feminine world that I had discovered there. I state in 'Guattari and Anthropology' (Chapter 3) that each morning we would discuss my fieldwork and what I attempted to write. Félix would take notes on some of the passages that I would read to him and played around a bit with the translation of my words from the Warlpiri language. I tried to gain an understanding of where he positioned himself in relation to a non-Freudian reading of the myths and dreams that I had just recorded. He was very excited by the fact that the Warlpiri claimed to travel

---

[13] Translated by B. Nakamarra Gibson in 1995 from original 1984 recording in Warlpiri by Glowczewski (2000).

within the mythic time-space of the Dreaming and at the same time bring back from these voyages oneiric revelations directly connected to what they were living in their daily lives.

Nakakut Barbara Gibson Nakamarra's testimony above bears witness to this (Prelude). Her narrative shows the way in which ancestral women from the Emu and Rain totems – the Warlpiri say *Jukurrpa*, Dreamings – revealed two songs to her, whereas the women of her entourage who she also saw in her dream will take her to task because she will end up having meetings with the Whites in order to negotiate the land rights for an area that a mining company wishes to explore: she could indeed become the beneficiary of royalties that are distributed among the Aboriginal people identified as traditional owners of a specific region. In her dream, this compensation takes the form of a 'truck' since most of the Indigenous Australians who receive royalty compensation often end up buying 4 × 4s (four-wheel-drive vehicles) in order to have a more expedient way to journey through their territories.

In addition to the right for some sort of compensation regarding the minerals mined, the Aboriginal tribes concerned also receive veto power so as to refuse any mining explorations or operations on their lands. These rights have been recognised in the Land Rights Act from 1976 applied to the Northern Territory, and allowed for Indigenous Australians to make land claims on territories where male and female members of each local group had the functions of spiritual and ritual custodians by way of their spiritual connections with sacred sites: sites of their Dreamings. The Warlpiri had won their land claims in 1978, and when I arrived at that time into their territory they had just begun experimenting with this new freedom to agree or to decline any new forms of development proposed by the state or private companies. The debates at that time would include hundreds of people who would discuss whether or not they should accept mining exploration for minerals and, if so, what the conditions would be. Many of the elders were reluctant to accept exploratory mining expeditions that could potentially disturb the already fragile networks of the water table in the desert. Others pushed for the economic autonomy from the state that this mining godsend seemed to offer. Enormous sums of money were injected into Indigenous organisations by way of mining companies which for thirty years drilled holes throughout every part of the continent's desert landscape. Meetings concerning the mining of the lands continued to increase throughout the decades to the point that for some Indigenous members of the community it became almost a full-time job travelling to diverse regions from one meeting to the next in order to listen to traditional landowners make claims to monetary compensation as a result of their Dreamings and songlines that criss-crossed the territories. But with each new permit for mining exploration, the Australian laws force the Aboriginal people once again to establish their sacred ancestral ties to specific sections of the land, through a demonstration of their proprietary totemic regimes as they have been described by the anthropologists of old and those anthropologists who are still recruited today either by the mining company, the state or by the myriad of organisations and lawyers that represent the various members of different Aboriginal families, who can either form alliances or create conflicts between themselves concerning shared interests.

The Aboriginal people in Australia have been able to develop impressive social and ritual strategies in the face of colonisation. While they were initially rather inclusive with their relatives and allies in distributing compensation, so as to prevent any inequalities with regard to resources and the emergence of dominant groups, the rights-holders eventually became more and more exclusive and the resulting conflicts have led to divisions within the community. During each new meeting, the debates become more and more heated, all the more so since today the Warlpiri must not only deal with negotiations regarding oil and gold, but also uranium and fracking. The immediate response to this, by a number of Indigenous groups from the Northern Territory and the rest of the Australian continent, is to come together in solidarity and in opposition to this continuing extraction of fossil fuel energies. The anti-extractivist movement is gaining in popularity particularly with the younger generation which – via social media – has witnessed the struggles of other Indigenous populations around the world who have also experienced first-hand the significant amount of damage that can be done to the environment by certain multinational companies and such extraction processes. Confronted by daily reminders of the mounting evidence and warnings regarding climate change, this younger generation is proud to identify as Aboriginal even if today most of them now have a mixed Indigenous and European-Australian ancestry and no longer live in the countryside but attend schools in the city. The Aboriginal Dreamings and the history of traditional practices and land stewardship (such as bushfire management through controlled burns at the right season) have today become a precious resource that allows for a renewed chance at teaching and maintaining traditions, as well as for providing important opportunities for geologists, astrophysicists and other scientists to learn vital information for the future from the knowledge maintained and passed on through these ancient practices (Glowczewski and Laurens [2015] 2018). As Noam Chomsky (2016) also recently noted:

> I think there have been quite hopeful developments in the last 10 or 15 years, Chomsky said. 'Indigenous communities have begun to find a voice for the first time in countries with large indigenous populations like Bolivia ... Ecuador there are plenty of conflicts between the indigenous people and the governments they initially supported. That's a tremendous step forward for the entire world. It's a kind of incredible irony that all over the world the leading forces in trying to prevent a race to disaster are the indigenous communities (...) Anyone who's not living under a rock knows that we're facing potential environmental catastrophe and not in the distant future. All over the world, it's the indigenous communities trying to hold us back: first nations in Canada, indigenous people in Bolivia, aborigines in Australia, tribal people in India. It's phenomenal all over the world that those who we call 'primitive' are trying to save those of us who we call 'enlightened' from total disaster.

Totem, Taboo and the Women's Law

Why have the Aboriginal concepts which were translated very early on in Australia as 'Dreaming' been discussed throughout the history of anthropology under the name of 'totem'? The term totem is a word inspired by one of the concepts originating from the Algonquin Native Americans but which became generalised to define a form of spirituality common to a variety of peoples the world over in which humans claim to be connected by both the 'body and soul' to animals and other forms of non-human life. Specialists immediately multiplied and presented conflicting arguments striving to come to a unified agreement on the common criteria required to define this form of spirituality or social organisation that would be lived and experienced in the same manner by a multiplicity of societies and cultures that are supposedly 'totemic'.

Durkheim and Mauss (1901–1902), his nephew, combined a myriad of complex variations so as to fit better with the theory they strived to posit as the foundational universal classification system. The totemic debates regarding the existence (or non-existence) of a religion among non-monotheistic people would then inspire Durkheim's *The Elementary Forms of Religious Life* ([1913] 2008) whose arguments rest essentially on his interpretation of the Arrernte (Aranda or Arunta) Central Australian monographs by Spencer and Gillen (1899). I have shown elsewhere (Glowczewski 2014b) that because Durkheim was focusing on the ritual of one clan, he missed in his analysis the importance of men's and women's spiritual attachment to the extensive tracks of land as well as the network interconnecting the different clans and language groups beyond their local lands which extended across the continent. During this same time period, Freud was writing *Totem and Taboo* where, based on practices drawn from similar ethnographic observations of Aboriginal peoples as Durkheim, he projected the supposed universality of the incest taboo on the dawn of humanity and the early childhood of each human being. After Polish anthropologist Bronisław Malinowski dismissed his theory on the basis of his extensive fieldwork with Trobriand Islanders in the Pacific, Freud sent Geza Roheim to verify the Oedipus complex in Australia. Roheim, Freud's disciple and a talented linguist who worked with desert people in the 1930s, developed his own interpretation of the primal scene and a complex of the fusion with the mother. I have shown elsewhere why I do not agree with Roheim's interpretations, nor with Freudian ones (Glowczewski [1991] 2017). Whereas Roheim had a very biased vision of women, I looked at these issues from the perspective of desert women. Neither Roheim nor Freud took into consideration elements present in some ethnographies that would allow them to understand that the major taboo in Australia was not reducible to the Oedipus complex, but was of a much more complex nature that I had strived to posit in my research undertaken in the early 1980s. This of course delighted Guattari.

The well-known taboo common to all Indigenous Australians forbids any man from engaging not only with his mother-in-law, but with any women who are classified as potential mothers-in-law (who could even be the same age as him). It is not, as Freud claims, a metaphor for the mother/son incest taboo but, as I have indicated in my research, a prevention against incest between the father/daughter. The rule against men having any sort of close relations with women (even if only at the level of conversation) whose daughter he might potentially marry has to do with averting the risk that he ends up marrying his own daughter. But the taboo also has another effect: it is so shameful to be approached by one's mother-in-law in public that when two men get into a fight, all it takes is for a real or potential mother-in-law of one of the fighters to step forward for him to flee the scene in shame. I saw this first-hand on several occasions in 1979 and in the early 1980s. Moreover, this taboo grants to any woman the power to intervene with regard to certain men deemed to be classified as their potential son-in-law in order to prevent any spousal abuse or the abuse of other women or young girls. This dispositive had been in place for a long time and was still in use during my fieldwork; it has, however, eventually degraded over time in part because of the forced sedentarisation of Indigenous Australians and in part due to a promiscuity drenched in alcohol that has led to a rise in domestic violence and the disrespect of taboos.

At the time I wrote my first academic article, 'Affaire de femmes ou femmes d'affaires. Les Warlpiri du désert central australien' (Women's business or business women), I put forth the hypothesis that certain masculine rituals consisting of making the penis bleed highlighted the fact that the castration complex in Australia wasn't a question of 'lack' (in the psychoanalytical sense) on the part of women but instead indicated a man's desire to bleed like women. The reviewer for the *Journal de la Société des Océanistes* (Glowczewski 1981b), Bernard Juillerat, recommended that I include the essay, 'Les Blessures Symboliques' by Bruno Bettleheim (1962) to my bibliography, which I did after taking the time to borrow it from the library and read it. Bettleheim's work with suffering adolescents in France who intentionally harmed themselves and made themselves bleed proposed the hypothesis that they did this in a similar fashion as some Aboriginal practices whereby men experience the flow of female menstrual blood that they lack. I felt uneasy asserting a psychoanalytical diagnosis on ritual practices such as this. We spoke a lot about these sorts of issues with Guattari, expecially during the time period in which I did research for the Prevention Committee at the Ministry of Health during the outbreak of AIDS in France in the early 1980s (Glowczewski 1994). From that research I published a book in French, *Adolescence et Sexualité – L'entre-deux* (1995), in which I compared ritual practices and discourses about the relation between love and death, the different cultural ways in which adults transform young people into becoming men and women, the individual, collective and environmental risks in breaking taboos, and the varying and variable recognition of the status of adulthood across the planet. Following that study, it seemed to me that Aboriginal people, rather than pointing to a man's 'lack' in relation to a woman's power of bleeding (or vice versa as is common in the Freudian approach of penis castration), were instead valuing a form of Dreaming androgyny which is encountered among many of the totemic heroes and re-enacted through ritual dance where men and women are separated. Each group enacts in their own way their man-woman or woman-man becomings where is not just about male and female bodies but also about other, different totemic bodies: animal, plant, wind or objects like a digging stick. A Digging Stick, as a Snake-man or a Snake-woman. Similarly a Digging Stick woman is not the same as a Digging Stick man. The Kana (Digging Stick) Dreaming says that these women pierced the penis of a rapist who was detaching his long penis from himself to send it like a snake to penetrate them when they were urinating in the bush, as told by a Warlpiri story-teller in this chapter. When men re-enact this they become Digging Stick men-women but when women re-enact it they become women-men Digging Sticks: each gender here experiments with its transgender Dreaming power in a different way.

In the second part of this book, 'Totem, Taboo and the Women's Law', I propose three essays that deal with the relation between totems, taboos and social organisation compared with the topological modelisation of the hypercube that I developed in my postdoctoral thesis (1988) that was published in 1991 as *Du Rêve à la Loi chez les Aborigènes* (From Dreaming to the Law among Aboriginal Australians). Two chapters are direct excerpts from this book which haven't been translated into English, 'Doing and Becoming: Warlpiri Rituals and Myths' (Chapter 4) and 'Forbidding and Enjoying: Warlpiri Taboos' (Chapter 5). 'A topological Approach to Australian Cosmology and Social Organisation' (Chapter 6) is a synthesis of my ideas as published in the Australian journal *Mankind* (1989) summarising the topological method that I have adopted, in this case in order to compare the Warlpiri society where I worked with the available data about other Indigenous Australian groups.

The hypercube served as an inspiration due to the way that the cube derivation summarises the eight algebraic subsections or *skin-names* – the non-hierarchised classification system interpreted by Claude Lévi-Strauss in his book, *The Elementary Structures of Kinship* ([1947] *1970)*, but which is also used by a number of other mathematicians and anthropologists. My use of the hypercube at the level of kinship structures helped me to visually show how the Aboriginal desert people's system of exchange cannot be reduced or summarised as a restrained exchange (as Lévi-Strauss maintains), the so-called 'Dravidian' model encountered in other regions of the world such as in India or in the Americas where men exchange their sisters as wives. Instead, I focused specifically on the actions of the Warlpiri who claim that they do not exchange their sisters but that two men exchange their nieces as wives: in order for this to happen, logic requires that not simply must two exogamous groups be implicated but at the very mininum four. Starting from here, the exchange is not restrained and reciprocal (A gives to B who in turns gives to A) but 'generalised' and 'asymmetrical', as can be said with regard to kinship studies which I prefer to call unilateral: A gives to B who gives to C who gives to D who gives to A in order for a new cycle that continues following the same order but that can't start again in the reverse order. To sum it up: a minimal equation in order to ally oneself with the multiple.

A hypercube or cube with eight different perspectives was also very useful in that it presents itself as a topological figure where there is no one single point or core perspective but rather, at the very least, eight perspectives with a multitude of others above or below according to the space of reference or depending on how we situate ourselves. In this way, the hypercube, as a pair of eyeglasses, allowed me to see space more clearly as a multiplicity and thus posit an anthropological proposition that also called into question Lévi-Strauss's position that he takes up in his book on *Totemism* ([1962] 1963) where he defines the totemic systems of Australia as a pure form of classificatory nominalism. It's certainly true that naming plays an essential role in Indigenous Australian cosmologies, but as I emphasised in the title of the first part of *Du Rêve à la Loi* (1991), 'Naming and Situating' (*Nommer et localiser*), the stakes of naming are derived from a toponymical dynamics. In other words, the names set about in movement (on voyages and according to the songlines) but they are also anchored in places and linguistic territories. As such, the languages and visions of things change according to the site and the line of the Dreaming according to which we look at the rest of the network. In *The Savage Mind* ([1962] 1966), Lévi-Strauss actually pays homage to Aboriginal sacred objects by recognising that their totemic status is also territorial (something I discuss at length in Chapter 4 of this book). In *The Jealous Potter* ([1985] 1988), Lévi-Strauss uses the topological figure of the Klein Bottle in order to speak about Amerindian myths. In this light, Lévi-Strauss was quite pleased to see that I also used topological figures to place into resonnance the structures of myths, rites, kinship and Aboriginal taboos. But in contrast to what a number of my colleagues in France or elsewhere take as an understanding of my work, my method was neither structuralist in the Lévi-Straussian sense of the term, nor Lacanian.

I was seeking out paradoxical structures which don't posit themselves against opposites, but rather articulate them in complex ways, such as can be found in Stéphane Lupasco's work on the non Aristotelian logic he called 'du contradictoire'[14] – a dynamic non-exclusive logic valuing heterogeneity and complexity that Dominique Temple, who taught at Paris 7, applied to the Amerindians and which Jean-François Matteudi and myself also applied to the cataphiles' practices of the Parisian underground (Glowczewski et al. [1983] 2008). I attempted to deploy an anthropology that was dynamic and not situated outside of history nor even outside the historical continuity of the human. To be perfectly honest, at the time, I was more inspired by the Aboriginal peoples themselves and a number of anthropologists accused me of 'going native'. I think this criticism of my work was based on unsound reasoning that didn't understand to what extent we still needed to decolonise our Western ways of thinking or how our sciences themselves had become too Westernised due to a certain privileging of a history of science, and even sometimes sexually biased in an unconscious manner. I worked from the model of the hypercube by considering it as an Aboriginal 'Dreaming', that is, as an image-force that reorganised my real: I tested it in order to organise the data I gathered in Australia and in comparison with all the other data I could find on the Indigenous peoples of Australia. I was also inspired by science fiction, such as the short story that told the tale of the construction of a hypercube house in which we never knew what outside we would head out into nor through what doorway we would return (Heinlein 1941).

The most important part of my research method at that time was to insist on the fact that, according to the Aboriginal peoples I lived with, men and women were said not to do or see things in the same way and that it was this difference, as with any of the differences among the local languages or customs, that was for them 'same but different'. In other words, they were able to think of heterogeneity

---

[14] Stephane Lupasco (1900–1988) was a Romanian philosopher who lived and worked in France: In *Trois matières* ([1960] 2003), he used 'actual' and 'potential' categories as a process of resolving contradictory elements at a higher level of reality or complexity. The three matters referred to in the title are defined as physical with a logic of homogeneity, biological with a logic of heterogeneity and psychic with a logic of the contradictory and the notion of *tiers-inclus*.

as simultaneously a recognition of irreducible singularities and the condition for a commons that in no way homogenised the whole: this was how the Indigenous Australians had achieved this ingenious way of practising exchange, throughout millenia, from one end of the continent to the other, without for all that becoming a lone people, but rather providing a way for the flourishing of multiple languages, ways of living and unique ways for explaining their world.

When I defended my post-doctoral thesis in 1988, Guattari criticised my topological approach, which he found several reasons to be suspicious of: on the one hand, its seeming rapport with structuralism which he and Deleuze had criticised, and, on the other hand, what appeared to be my use of topology in the same way as Lacan and certain other Lacanians who made use of topological figures such as the Moebius strip, the torus, or knots, to think the unconcious. Three years later, with the publication of my book (Glowczewski 1991), and after having made Deleuze read it, Guattari changed his mind. Having just gotten over a long depression, he now saw the world in a new light. *Schizoanalytic Cartographies* ([1989] 2013) and *The Three Ecologies* ([1989] 2008), as well as a variety of other articles on Guattarian ecosophy, had been published in the interim. But it was after his death in 1992 that Stéphane Nadeau would edit these texts together into one single volume, the 586-page, *Qu'est-ce que l'écosophie?* (2013) which still remains unpublished in an English translation:

> I have baptized one such concatenation of environmental, scientific, economic, urban and social and mental ecologies: ecosophy. Not in order to incorporate all of these heterogeneous ecological approaches in the same totalizing or totalitarian ideology, but, to indicate, on the contrary, the prospect of an ethico-political choice of diversity, creative dissensus, of responsibility concerning difference and alterity. Each segment of life, while continuing to be inserted into the transindividual phylums which exceed it, is fundamentally understood in its uniqueness. Birth, death, desire, love, the relationship to time, to bodies, to both animate and inanimate forms, require a fresh and attentive re-evaluation that is unsullied and receptive. It is incumbent upon us to reproduce continuously this subjectivity that the psychoanalyst and ethologist of childhood, Daniel Stern [1985], calls the 'emergent self.' Recapturing childhood glances and poetry instead, and in the place of, the hard and blind perspective on the meaning of life according to the expert and technocrat [...] We [must] shake free from a false nomadism that in reality leaves us back to where we started from, in the emptiness of a bloodless modernity, in order to access lines of flight where machinic, communicational, and aesthetic

deterritorializations engage us [...] creating the conditions of emergence, on the occasion of a reappropriation of the forces of our world, of an existential nomadism that is as intense as the pre-Columbian American Indians or Australian Aboriginals! (Guattari [1993] 2015: 99)[15]

The Aboriginal Practice of Transversality and Dissensus

In 1985, Claire Parnet (who would later interview Gilles Deleuze in a rare, long-form interview/documentary film about the philosopher, *L'Abécédaire*[16]) created *L'Autre Journal* with Michel Butel, Antoine Dulaure and Nadia Tazi. It was a magazine on recycled paper teeming with enchanted inherited worlds as well as those in the midst of invention. I ended up publishing several articles in the journal including an interview in Polish with the science fiction writer and author of *Solaris*, Stanislaw Lem:

> The theory of evolution that we teach in schools is still too impoverished: we speak of chance mutations due to natural selection, this not enough. Prigogine creates the foundations for a theory that has a place for both order and chaos. (Lem 1984)

Guattari was excited by the propositions published in *Order Out of Chaos: Man's New Dialogue with Nature* ([1979] 1984), a book by Ilya Prigogine co-written with Isabelle Stengers who often participated in Guattari's seminars at Rue de Condé. During that time, she gave me her copy of Deleuze's *Difference and Repetition* ([1968] 1995), brimming with higlighted passages and her notes in the margins. I digested the work very slowly. It was only later on that I understood

---

[15] In Guattari's compilation edited in French by Nadaud (2013: 31–4), two different notes indicate that *le Nouvel Observateur* published a short version of the 'subjective city' on 14 November 1981 without this paragraph and others like this one (p. 55): 'The wild nomadism of contemporary deterritorialisation calls for a 'transversalist' apprehension of the subjectivity in the midst of emergence, a manner of grasping striving to articulate points of singularity (for example, a particular configuration of the environment or landscape), specific existential dimensions (for example, the way a space is viewed by children or those who physically handicapped or who are dealing with mental illness), functional virtual transformations (for example pedagogical innovations), all while affirming a style and an inspiration that help to recognise, at a first glance, the individual or collective signature of a creator.'

[16] 1988–1989; with English sub-titles, *Gilles Deleuze from A to Z*, Pierre André-Boutang, Claire Parnet, Gilles Deleuze, Los Angeles: Semiotext(e) (Deleuze et al. 2011).

to what extent how much of what I wrote could be derived from the articulation of both these notions.

After giving birth to my first daughter, Milari, in Australia, I returned with her to Paris so we could be with my mother in her final weeks as she was dying of cancer. During this same time period, Guattari gave me a copy of his last book, *Chaosmosis* ([1992] 1995). He would die four months later. I continued to live in Broome on the west coast of Australia until 1998 when I finally moved back to Paris with my family which had grown to include another daughter, Nidala, and their father, a film-maker and musician dedicated to the promotion of his Aboriginal culture, Wayne Jowandi Barker (2011, 2016). Those years in the Kimberley led me to discover a new Aboriginal universe that I examine in Part III of this present work, 'The Aboriginal Practice of Transversality and Dissensus', two concepts that were at the heart of Guattari's input during his collaborations with Deleuze.

'In Australia, it's 'Aboriginal' with a Capital 'A': Aboriginality, Politics and Identity' (Chapter 7) was published in a collective book entitled *The Changing South Pacific* (Douaire-Marsaudon and Tcherkezoff [1997] 2005). It discusses the issue of pan-Aboriginality and strategic essentialism in tribal territorial identification. Indeed Aboriginal people had hundreds of names to designate themselves in different regions of Australia. Some names were used to designate neighbours in a different way than the name used by members of this neighbouring group to refer to themselves. Among many Indigenous peoples in the world, the word used to identify as a group means 'human', but it is not systematic. Warlpiri people for instance identify as the Warlpiri tribe with language variations such as Warnayaka in the north-east, the majority of the people living in Lajamanu, and Ngalia in the South where people mostly live in Yuendumu which was the first Warlpiri reserve that was created in the 1940s. It became so overcrowded in the 1950s that a group of families were forcibly deported to a new settlement called Hooker Creek, which became Lajamanu. All the Warlpiri use the word *Yapa* (the Warlpiri term for 'human') to identify themselves with other language groups with whom they practise exchanges across a network that extends for thousand of kilometres to the west on the coast of the Indian Ocean and hundreds of kilometres to the north and south. Other Aboriginal people outside of this network used to be called *yapakarri* 'other (than) human', but today they are recognised as Yapa. Similarly, any Indigenous people or people of colour from other countries can be called Yapa but only if they are seen as sharing a similar situation of colonial history or discrimination. This social identification can also be extended beyond colour: for instance in a film about a US basketball team where the hero was Italian and who, in the film, endured a number of hardships as a migrant, was identified by all the Warlpiri audience with a lot of sympathy as *Yapa*. Similarly a White person is said to be 'like' a *Yapa* when she shares experiences with *Yapa* that are seen as specific to them, like rituals, camping or sharing food and other things.

The word 'Europeans' was commonly used in Australia by non Aboriginal people to identify themselves even if they were descendants of the first generation of settlers. They are called *Kardiya* by the Warlpiri and many other desert groups. Similarly in the North of Australia, among the Yolngu people who also have traditional exchanges with the Warlpiri, the Europeans were called *Balanda*, a Kriol pronunciation of 'Hollanders', who were the colonisers of the Macassar islands. Long before the British colonisation, Macassan fishermen used to sail to the northern coast of Australia to collect trepang and they developed exchange relations with the Aboriginal peoples of the North until the beginning of the twentieth century when the Australian government forbid this trade.[17] Throughout the period of colonisation, hundreds of different Aboriginal language groups had already established ancient networks of ritual exchange across the continent. But it was only in the 1960s that they decided to unite in their struggles for their common recognition.

In 1972, four activists set up a camp which they called the Aboriginal Tent Embassy in front of the Canberra Parliament, a political performance affirming the position of exclusion of the First Nations of Australia treated as foreigners in their own country. The Land Rights Movement then decided to adopt a common flag for the hundreds of different language groups, and this has become a sign of self-determination and Indigenous sovereignty all over Australia in protests as well as at official events. When the famous track and field star, sprinter Cathy Freeman, first raised the Aboriginal flag in celebration of her victory during the 1994 Commonwealth Games, she caused a scandal. However, during the 2000 Olympic Games in Sydney, upon winning the gold medal in the 400 metres, Freeman's decision to take her celebratory lap carrying both the Aboriginal

---

[17] See Glowczewski (2004) and film by Wayne Barker and B. Glowczewski, *Spirit of Anchor* (2002), CNRS Images: http://videotheque.cnrs.fr/doc/980?langue=EN

flag and the Australian flag had by that time become recognised and accepted as a standard practice at sporting events and elsewhere. The word Aboriginality became the signifier of a common identity to help create strategies of pressure for the recognition of Aboriginal peoples as prior occupants of the continent. Chapter 6 discusses two understandings of identity. The chapter begins by exploring an identity of resistance focused primarily around the revision of contact history. The valorisation of a national aboriginal identity – symbolised by a flag, land rights and the denunciation of poor living conditions – is analysed in terms of exclusion and exploitation. The chapter then focuses on an identity of continuity, based on language, religious beliefs and practices. An Aboriginal conception of a pre-contact worldview and lifestyle is shown to be essential in the struggle to affirm the recognition of traditional rights to the land.

Since the beginning of the colonisation of the continent in 1788, Aboriginal peoples have attempted to defend their lands by opposing what the colonial law called *Terra nullius*: a land supposedly 'without inhabitants'. And yet, the inhabitants had lived in Australia for at least the past 60,000 years. The struggle for land rights led to the Northern Territory (NT) Land Rights Act in 1976 which allowed the Aboriginal people of this region – like the Warlpiri – to reclaim their ancestral rights established by way of the distribution of ritual responsibilities along the totemic paths that connect the sites created by their Dreaming ancestors. It was only in 1992, after twelve years of judiciary process against the state for Eddie Mabo, a Torres Strait Islander, that the concept of *Terra nullius* was invalidated at the federal level for the entire continent. Today, alongside some land claims which have been won by way of restitution to local groups for the right to collectively use their ancestral lands, several hundred claims are still at different levels in the judiciary process of the tribunal set up to prove what the Mabo Native Title Law (1993) means by 'native title': the recognition of a native principle of pre-colonial title-holders that must be demonstrated by proving 'the continuity of the occupation of the lands and traditional practices'. This clause is obviously biased by way of a governmental system itself that favours the groups that have survived massacres by staying on the reserves built on their land where they could continue some land usage. The continuity of traditional practice is more difficult to prove for other groups who have been born elsewhere due to the fact that their parents or ancestors had been deported or placed into a position of having to flee. Since the 1990s, the native title process has provoked terrible conflicts that have torn families apart, but this process has also pushed many Aboriginal people to explore their past and revive some aspects of their culture.

The full extent of the ethnocide, which was a veritable genocide, still remains to be properly calculated due to the vast numbers of victims, by way of illnesses contracted through infected clothes, the arsenic injected into their watering holes to poison them, and the large number of massacres, some of which date back to the 1930s, and whose hidden mass graves we still continue to uncover. Forced into a sedentary lifestyle by missionaries, the Indigenous Australians were converted by all the Christian churches – Catholic, Anglican, Baptist or Evangelical – that continue to compete for them, after having prohibited the teaching of Islam to the Aboriginal children of mixed descent whose fathers were Muslims, either camel drivers brought from Pakistan in the 1920s to help with the exloration of the continent, or the pearl divers indentured in their thousands from Malaysia, or other islands, such as Timor, to develop the world's biggest pearling extraction in Broome. In the early days Aboriginal people on the west coast were 'blackbirded' and forced to dive for pearls, but many refused despite risking a paddle to the head if they did not succeed in collecting pearls.

The Indigenous Australians also had to suffer through what became known as a politics of 'whitening'. Starting from the genetic principle that the black colour of skin seemed to disappear within several generations of Aboriginal peoples mixing with Whites, Arabs or the Asian populations, the government had the fantasy – which was also shared in Europe and North America – that it could control Aboriginal reproduction in order to favour the White race as superior to others. Thus, the government decided to segregate the most light-skinned people so as to make sure that their children would be even more 'whitened', first in terms of their psychological mindset (esprit), then by way of their genetic descendence. The government thus created a 'protectorate' whose funciton was to send in its special police (including priests) in order to gather up all the 'light-skinned' children and take them away from their families. Between 1905 and the 1970s, one child out of five – from young babies to adolescents – was kidnapped under the pretext that their biological familes were too 'tribal' and 'savage' and couldn't raise them properly. Even though the children – resulting either from rapes or genuine love affairs with the early European pioneers – lived with their Aboriginal or non-Aboriginal families, it was actually illegal for both to raise their mixed children even if they had the necessary material means to do so. There are hundreds of poignant letters written to the protectorates of different Australian states which bear witness to this. Other Aboriginal children were also taken away if their parents were killed or jailed due to resistance.

The 'Protectors' of the state refused to give the children back to their parents since their mission was to 'civilise' them (in spite of themselves), within boarding schools that functioned like orphanages, where the young children – as with the schoolchildren in the French colonies or Brittany – were punished for speaking their birth language or that of their lost family. The youngest children and babies were told that their parents had abandoned them and the older ones were told that they should never visit their 'tribes' under penalty of prison time or lack of access to the right to work. A sucessful 'whitening' led to educating the children to serve Whites as maids or farmhands, and then marry other young, light-skinned individuals so as to eventually, over time, erase all trace of black skin. In these institutions, as well as others throughout the world, a great number of both girls and boys were raped, and often mistreated again and again by the families of their employers. Some of the children ended up being adopted and properly loved and cared for, but as the recent documentary film, *Servant and Slave*, directed by Hettie Perkins (daughter of the famous boxer and activist, Charlie Perkins), shows through interivews with five Aboriginal women, the status of servant or maid often masked a form of slavery. These children who were forcefully taken away from their Aboriginal families have been called 'The Stolen Generations' – a name given to them by the Royal Commission that carried out its own investigation in the 1990s concerning the historical situation, and produced, as a result of the hundreds of interviews with the victims or their families, what it called the 'Bringing Them Home' report which recommended a variety of programmes. Since then, a number of initiatives for collective care have attempted to palliate past and present traumas, notably those traumas that are passed down through several generations, and the current discriminations that continue to provoke a variety of violent reactions, the improper treatment of young people, and even suicide. Work performed by stolen children, adolescents as well as adults, often was not paid, as was also the case with non-mixed Aboriginal peoples.[18] The servants and sheep herders

---

[18] Between 1963 and 1982, the French state established a similar method of taking very young children away from poor families on the French island of Reunion

only received flour, tea or tobacco, along with a small ration of meat, until they ended up revolting in the different regions of Australia by movements that ended up unsettling the government in place.

'Culture Cult: Ritual Circulation of Inalienable Knowledge and Appropriation of Cultural Knowledge (Central and NW Australia)' (Chapter 8) was published in the collective book *People and Things. Social Mediations in Oceania* (Jeudy-Ballini and Juillerat 2002). It discusses the international context of the contemporary claims to cultural property, and the concept of inalienability which, in Central and North Western Australia, surrounds the ritual circulation of sacred objects and the ceremonial cycles of which they are a part. The expression 'culture cult' in the title refers to an appropriation of the word 'culture' by Aboriginal people from the north and the desert that was not initially used when I first began my fieldwork in Australia. It is as if the popularity of the Western concept in governmental policies and laws relating to land had almost sacralised into 'culture' what before was only referred to by different practices, be they ritual or not. Inalienibility has been conceptualised by the anthropologist Annette Weiner who extended her fieldwork in the Trobriand Islands to other Oceanic societies. In *Inalienable Possessions. The Paradox of Keeping-While-Giving* (1992), she also discusses some Aboriginal cases from Australia, especially my analysis of Warlpiri data. I must say that she was an inspiration to me when in 1980 she came to talk about her theory in a seminar of Maurice Godelier at the School of Social Sciences (EHESS, Paris). Her talk inspired me to extend her notion of inalienable objects produced by women – woven mats in the Trobriand islands – to hairstrings made of women's hair cut during death rituals in Central Australia; one of the chapters of the 1981 thesis that Guattari was struck by. I was advised at that time not to publish it as a book but to translate the specific chapter from my thesis as a paper for the US journal *Ethnology* (Glowczewski 1983a).

Inalienability is also the key to understanding the circulation of rituals, ceremonial objects and other knowledge from tribe to tribe

---

(Indian Ocean) in order to send them to be raised by and work for farmers in the then dying region of central France, the Creuse. Many were mistreated and never returned to their island. The survivors have started a similar movement as the Aboriginal people to ask for reparations. In French Guiana, Wayana and Teko from the Amazonia have been asking for many years to have bilingual secondary schools in their own villages instead of having to send their children to town where, cut off from the practice of their own people's cultural teachings, they face mistreatment and suicide.

across the whole continent. My aim in referencing the Kimberley example is to demonstrate how the circulation of ceremonial objects after colonisation (and continuing up into the 1990s) through the transmission of initiation-related ceremonial cycles was a real machine for producing culture(s), first by regenerating local specificities and second by asserting a common procedure that, beyond language differences, enabled exchange to take place over thousands of kilometres. Each local group's identity is strengthened by this ritual nomadism, which is enriched by new religious forms wherein local variants of what Aboriginal people call their respective Laws nurture those of their neighbours. This is true of men's rituals as well as women's rituals, for both types of rituals help create these exchanges that reinforce the bond between each group and its sacred places, and the inalienable possession of its sacred objects. Similar identity-building can also be seen in the interregional gatherings for traditional mixed dancing, commonly called 'corroborees'. In fact, since the 1980s and up to the present we have been able to detect a similar logic of transmission which has expanded into cultural intertribal regional festivals such as those created by the Kimberley Law and Culture Council that regularly bring people from over thirty-three communities together to dance, sing and share their ideas and common strategies concerning all areas of life, be it culture, health, education, justice, economy and the environment.

In Chapter 8 I also examine the elaboration of a project for a cultural centre in the 1990s involving the representatives of a dozen Aboriginal languages and organisations based in the coastal town of Broome, because of a regional diaspora from the desert, the North and the South. This initiative reflected an attempt to control the representation given for these cultures and to reappropriate their objects and knowledge. To date, as of June 2019, the cultural centre has still not been built, but many other positive things have occurred in Broome, such as the winning of the Yawuru Native Title and the establishment of a big Yawuru language centre that has helped to revive the language. But there are also current conflicts around the issue of the status of Djugun people, who were recognised as a separate tribe in the 1930s but were incorporated in the Yawuru Native Title.[19] Today, Djugun descendants claim their singularity and exclusive relation to the land in order to oppose fracking and

---

[19] Pat Mamanyjun Torres speech during the UN special rapporteur visit, March 2017, film clip by B. Glowczewski: https://vimeo.com/222221650

other gas development in the region. Similarly, other groups which spread across the whole of the Kimberley and further to the North and the South use their ancient tribal affiliation and responsibilities to the land for the same kind of struggle against multinational companies that try to bribe them with a lot of money. Of course, there are always some families who accept the money and sign but the movement of resistance to fossil energies is strong.

'Lines and Criss-Crossings: Hyperlinks in Australian Indigenous Narratives' (Chapter 9) was published with a DVD in the *Media International Australia* journal dedicated in August 2005 to 'Digital Anthropology'. The chapter deals with the issue of ethics, whereby pleasure (and desire) does not imply a religious or moral order but a constant re-evaluation of how each image or representation of any contemporary culture (Indigenous, musical, professional, digital, etc.) impacts on social justice, equity, tolerance and freedom. The chapter narrates two forms of anthropological restitution developed with Aboriginal peoples for a mixed audience. The first project was the CD-ROM, *Dream Trackers: Yapa Art and Knowledge of the Australian Desert*, which I developed with fifty Warlpiri artists and ritual custodians from Lajamanu in the Northern Territory and which was awarded by the 1997 Moebius Awards and eventually published by UNESCO in 2000. The second project was an interactive DVD (*Quest in Aboriginal Land*) based on films by Indigenous film-maker Wayne Jowandi Barker, documenting four regions of Australia (Arnhem Land, Central and Western Deserts, Kimberley, and the Grampians in Victoria). Both projects aimed to explore and enhance the cultural foundations of the reticular way in which many Indigenous people in Australia map their knowledge and experience of the world in a geographical virtual web of narratives, images and performances. The relevance of games for anthropological insights is also discussed in this chapter. Non-linear or reticular thinking mostly stresses the fact that there is no centrality to the whole rather there is a multipolar view from each recomposed network within each singularity – be it a person, a place (or a Dreaming in the case of Aboriginal cultures) – allowing for the emergence of meanings and performances, encounters, creations as well as new original autonomous flows.

The wide array of my multimedia experiments, from the middle of the 1990s to the explosion of the Internet and beyond, have directly transformed my way of writing, making it more reticular and leading me to develop – during my time teaching at Broome (University of Notre Dame, 1995–2000) and then in Paris (Advanced School of Social Sciences, EHESS, 2000–2004)— what I have called an 'Anthropology of Networks' or 'reticular thinking'. As explained in the chapter, this method has allowed me to value the way in which Aboriginal peoples have already been experts in 'hyperlinks' projected into the space and time of their environments and their dream worlds – well before the emergence of these various Internet technologies. I have written extensively about the fact that Aboriginal perception of the Dreaming is not that of a golden age dreamtime but a multifolded dynamic memory that I defined a virtual space-time. I proposed then a conception of time which is neither linear (like the arrow of calendar historical time) nor circular (like the notion of cyclical eternal return).

The fact that computers and the Internet have familiarised us with network connections and the rapid access to ideas and knowledge in a non-linear mode has made it easier to understand the complexity of Aboriginal systems of knowledge that project memory, stories and rituals into entangled pathways activated to become both in geography and the embodiment of living things, as well as mythical and oneirical narratives and performances. The experience anyone can make in his/her dreams of going beyond boundaries of space and time gives an insight into the relativity and synchronicity of Aboriginal cosmological space-time. Aboriginal artists who at an already advanced age began in the 1970s and 1980s to paint on canvas with acrylics went through the traumatic rupture of their nomadic life and various types of violence, dispossession and pressures imposed by the state. But they responded to this ecosophical disaster with an extreme creativity anchored on their reticular perception of land.[20] I think that the originality of what they produced then as well as the success their paintings – and those of the younger generation – encountered among the audience of contemporary art is due to a paradigmatic shift corresponding to the global transversality of technology and economy affecting all aspects of our world including affective and intellectual perception (Glowczewski 2015). From survivors of the Stone Age they have become guardians of a New Age where more and more people aspire to experience, beyond universal rationality, the multiplicity of different parallel logics. Space-time

---

[20] See Le Roux (2016) on Aboriginal and Torres Strait Islander artistic use of ghost nets found in the ocean to fight against this waste that kills fish, dolpins and turtles.

relativity and current use of the notions of 'pluriverse' or 'multiverse' by astrophysicists seem to resonate with the experience of shamans from different cultures, and complex cosmologics like the Warlpiri concept of *Jukurrpa*.

To overcome the impasse of the alleged irrationality of the practices and beliefs of traditional people, the structuralism of Lévi-Strauss has apprehended them as symbolic manifestations of a savage mind hiding structural logics. The reaction to structuralism was two-fold: on one side a call for history, on the other a call to emotion. Today the tension seems to oppose a certain relativism claiming the pluralism of cultural dynamics, and a socio-biology aiming at reducing the symbolic language to a material determination. Philippe Descola has inaugurated the chair of anthropology of nature at the Collège de France by proposing to overcome this opposition with 'relative universalism'. Personally, in every situation I strive to track and locate the singular and the 'affect' at work, while also tirelessly pursuing a comparative interrogation of societies. I look for 'invariants', common but dynamic principles, where the spirit carries the body as much as the body carries the esprit. I believe it is because we have acquired the universal 'habit' of circulating on the Web of the Internet that we can better understand today the very ancient and singular construction of reticular thinking among Aboriginal people. If biodiversity reveals to us everyday the striking capacities of the multiplication of a common language, the DNA, similarly, cultural diversity is a source of access to a common knowledge which articulates the fundaments of life.

History has shown time and time again that systems of knowledge can change their meanings according to their applications. But they can also disappear for lack of transmission. In a long-term time perspective, the content of what transmits itself is partly not under (our) control, but the responsibility falls on all of humanity to prevent places and modes of transmission which were maintained for so long to be swept away by the illusion of modernity of the Western World which believes to have the mission of supplanting everything. Globalisation is understood as a levelling of consumption practices and discourses. Now, parallel to this process of standardisation, we are also bearing witness to a differentiation of the local that flourishes everywhere: in creole tongues, school yards, neighbourhood associations or forums online. From deep in the urban landscape to the most remote places of the outback, calls for identity, symbolic territoriality and spirituality can be heard loudly expressing themselves. Television and primarily the Internet have led to an inflation of discourses and practices in search of a territorial, historical, cultural or religious rooting. With this flow of images and speeches, humans are increasingly confronted with a paradox: the more the world globalises itself, with its markets and means of which seem to bring us together and make us similar, the more differences emerge and the need for a local specificity affirms itself in many different ways. It is not by isolating and forbidding exchange(s) that one preserves differences, it is on the contrary by instituting modes of circulation of peoples and ideas. Even though very few anthropologists have established a link between linguistic diversity and the extent of networks of solidarity and of symbolic equivalences that exist between different Aboriginal groups, I am convinced that their current strength stands in this equation. (Glowczewski 2004)

This text is extracted from the introduction to my French book *Rêves en colère*, literally 'Dreams in anger', not yet translated in English. I wrote it as an experimental form of rhizome connecting fifteen lines of Aboriginal voices from four regions of Australia. It is constructed as a series of sixteen lessons (in history, totemism, psychoanalysis, ecology, etc.) intermingling observations and conversations with Aboriginal men and women from different parts of North Western and Central Australia to show both their local singularities and the commonalities identified by Indigenous people themselves as connecting them across the continent. I argue that reticular or network thinking is a very ancient Indigenous practice – enhancing the way memory and dreams function for all humans – but it gained a striking actuality at the turn of the twenty-first century thanks to the fact that our so-called scientific perception of cognition, Euclidian space and linear time had changed through the use of new technologies. I must admit that I would be less enthusiastic nowadays when the Internet and its algorithms demonstrate everyday their ability to consume all aspects of our life. Nevertheless, I think that there is an ancient art of connection that Aboriginal people have nurtured which resonates with the vision that Deleuze and Guattari were promoting even though some of their readers misunderstood the dangerous impact of some of the logic they described so well. Horizontal reticularity is not just 'good' in itself, as opposed to tree-like vertical bad power: they are poles in tension that need to be analysed and confronted in an ecosophical manner, that takes into account the milieu as around and across our subjectivities. '*Prendre les choses par le milieu*' ... 'To understand things from the middle or the milieu'. The milieu invites us to turn things inside out, to be affected and traversed by the land, the city, people and things. It is not about being lost in nature, as Guattari explains in a text entitled 'The Environment and Humans, Emerging and Returning Values or the Ethics at Stake in Ecology':

Social and mental ecology, which rightfully function as complements to scientific and political ecology, should therefore not be founded upon some sort of feeling of a timeless fusion with nature, but upon the recognition and assumption of finitude, of the individual life as much as collective life, the life of various species as much as that of the planets and the Sun [...] so in order to confront the gigantic stakes of our current era, it is vitally important to radically re-orient its end goals, so as to move on from an backward-looking ecology focused on the defense of already acquired [acquis] knowledge toward an ecology that is completely mobilized toward creation. (Guattari [1989–1990] 2013: 523)

This feeling of existential finitude is also what Guattari became accustomed to calling 'existential territories', defined not from inside as eternity but on the contrary according to external determinations, which he defined as articulated together: a constellation of values or incorporeal universes, a dimension of flows (fluxes), and a machinic phylum or alterity that works as an ontological (autopoïetic) self-affirmation. For Guattari, this ecosophical object was like a meta-model to take into account all kinds of modelisation, whether Marxist or animist. This is why Guattari, when defining 'What is ecosophy?', spoke of ethics in his aesthetical paradigm as being in tension between molecular micropolitics and the molar world of integrated capital. For him:

an ontology could only be cartographic, a metamodelisation of transitory figures of intensive conjunctions. The event resides within this conjunction of an ennunciative cartography and this capturing of the precarious, qualitative, and intensive [...] starting from points of singularity, and allowing for lines of the possible to set off in movement once again. (Guattari [1991] 2013)

Micropolitics of Hope and De-Essentialisation

On 27 November 2008, Brian Massumi and Erin Manning paid me a visit at my office at the Collège de France to conduct an interview that would eventually be published online in their journal, *Inflexions*. Both had spent some time in Australia and wrote stimulating texts about Aboriginal art.[21] To conclude the interview, Erin asked me the following question:

---

[21] Massumi (2002), Manning (2009). See discussion of Massumi's paper in Glowczewski (2016b).

I want to propose three different ways to think about the micropolitical in the context of what you've told us. You might want to comment on one or more. One of them, it seems to me, is an interesting singularity that has to do with the complexity of the collective body that includes 'other bodies,' including your body. It seems to me that in a politics to come that would radically take seriously the kind of political initiatives brought forward by the Aboriginal people, there would also have to be some way of taking the temperature of these new singularities (bodies in process) rather than lumping all Aboriginal people in one box. That would be one singularity. The other singularity would be [would have] to do with the issue of memory. It seems to me that the Aboriginal cultures that I have looked into have a very important way of thinking spacetime where memory is not conceived as a simple linear passageway to a discrete past and a proposed future but is thought instead as a complex nonlinear topological field with transversal linkages. And the third singularity you might comment on would be a gesturing toward the global politics to come through the election of Obama with respect to the fear that I think a lot of left-leaning political groups have that people might perceive that with Obama's election the important work has been done: We have now elected a black president. We have done our work. So there isn't more work to come in any of those registers.'

My reply:

I agree absolutely with what you say and those three levels. Just on Obama, I think the same thing happened in Australia when the new government was elected, last November, from Liberal to Labor. And Kevin Rudd, for the first time after many years of public pressure, accepted to give an official apology to the Aboriginal people. This was done last February. It was like you say, like in USA: a black man is elected and it is done. And here the apology was done, which means the Aboriginal issue is sorted out. Well today, we know it is not the case. (Glowczewski, Manning and Massumi 2009)

'Myths of 'Superiority' and How to De-Essentialise Social and Historical Conflicts' (Chapter 10) was a conference paper I presented at an international conference on racism convened by the James Cook University in Cairns in 2012. It shows that accusations of racism can mask an ontology of superiority in which the victims of racism are themselves accused of being racist. I analyse the example of a famous writer from French Polynesia, Chantal Spitz, who was accused of being racist by a couple of reactionary academics because she promotes her Ma'ohi language and culture. She produces her literature in French (also translated into English) but infuses it with Ma'ohi expressions and social and political local context, including autonomist positions: it is a perfect example of what Deleuze and Guattari called a minor literature that is not simply literature written by someone who belongs to a minority group but rather is a particular form of literary and linguistic resistance. Deleuze and Guattari use the example of Franz Kakfa (whose first language was Czech but who chose to write in German) to show how a writer from a dominated people transforms the dominant language in which he writes.[22] Anti-colonial writers are accused of racism by those who identify with the colonial power. Indigenous people or migrants are accused of racism for laying claim to their history and culture. UNESCO may have proclaimed cultural diversity as a value, but in many social interactions it is not valued. Difference is either reduced to hierarchical models – such as dominant/dominated and primitive/civilised – or denied recognition in the name of universalism as opposed to cultural relativism.

My aim here was to show that a third option is possible. I chose to speak about the French situation between 2005 and 2012, because when in 2005 a historical outburst of anger followed the death of two young French men of colour (aged fifteen and seventeen years old), it made me think about how anthropologically and as a French citizen my duty is to try to compare situations. In 2005, I had just returned to live in Paris after spending two years in Australia where I had followed the process of the inquest after a violent Aboriginal death in custody on Palm Island. In 2008 I published a book in France with Lex Wotton, an Aboriginal man who was accused of a riot that broke out a week after this death in custody. The book was written in agreement with his lawyers, but I never found a publisher in Australia; thus, I uploaded the updated translation *Warriors for Peace* that I paid for on the online library of James Cook University (Glowczewski and Wotton [2008] 2010). In 2017, after serving four years in jail and being released before his time, Wotton, with his sister, mother and wife, won a class action claim against the state of Queensland, which had to pay compensation of AUS$220,000 for 'the acts of unlawful racial discrimination by the police'[23] and which led to a new way for

---

[22] Deleuze and Guattari ([1975] 1986, [1987] 1997); Deleuze ([1989] 2010). See also: http://stl.recherche.univlille3.fr/seminaires/philosophie/macherey/Macherey20022003/Sibertin.html

[23] Federal Court of Australia (2018), class action settlement notice. Palm Island Residents – Queensland Police Class action: http://www.fedcourt.gov.au/__data/assets/pdf_file/0005/49523/24-Apr-2018-Settlment-Notice.pdf

Aboriginal people to question government decisions in Australia. In 2018 Wotton, with 447 Palm inhabitants, won a new class action suit that questioned the intervention on Palm Island by the special emergency police section to arrest the 'rioters', and that led to the payment of AUS$30 million by the Queensland government and an official apology acknowledging the trauma and suffering of the Palm Islanders, with a special mention to Wotton's family.

Today, as we see the global resonance with the Black Lives Matter movement in the United States and the way in which Black people and Indigenous people across the world recognise themselves in each other's struggles, I can only reaffirm, as I did six years ago in that conference paper, that too many countries seem to deny their citizens the right to adopt alternative ways of living; this is true for different historical, constitutional and geopolitical reasons in France and Australia. Indeed, Australia has massive public debates and local confrontations between different Aboriginal leaders in relation to government policies such as the Northern Territory Intervention that had to overrule the Racial Discrimination Act to forcibly intervene in seventy-three communities in 2007 or the dismantling of ATSIC, the Aboriginal-elected national commission and its regional councils. Debates also rage around the change to the Constitution to suppress its racist connotations and to recognise the prior sovereignty over the land of the continent to its Indigenous people, among whom some continue to ask for a treaty to be signed so that they can be empowered with the right to protect their country from environmentally and socially destructive projects as well as to have their own form of governance. A huge body of work has been published on these matters and on what has been called the History Wars, but I would rather not enter into a discussion that would advertise the names of scholars who negate the violence of Australian colonial history or, like some in France, claim that we should not awaken the memories of that conflicted past.

My priority is to value and disseminate information about alternative and experimental solutions that have been attempted in Australia, France or in other countries that face similar problems in the global destiny of our planet. The dissemination of these creative attempts also plays a role in how I understand my own position as a researcher in circulating official criticisms that are made of the Indigenous situation or migrant crisis in Australia or France. For instance, the 2017 report of the UN Special Rapporteur, Victoria Tauli-Corpuz, on the rights of Indigenous peoples, after her visit to Australia, states:

In the report, the Special Rapporteur observes that the policies of the Government do not duly respect the rights to self-determination and effective participation; contribute to the failure to deliver on the targets in the areas of health, education and employment; and fuel the escalating and critical incarceration and child removal rates of Aboriginal and Torres Strait Islanders. A comprehensive revision of those policies needs to be a national priority, and the consequences and prevalence of intergenerational trauma and racism must be acknowledged and addressed.[24]

Similarly, the report prepared by the France Libertés foundation in France denounces the industrial goldmining megaproject by La Montagne d'Or (Gold Mountain, Canadian and Russian multinational consortium) that is opposed by more than 100 collectives in French Guiana: with the assistance of the foundation it was denounced by a young Kali'na Indigenous man, Yanuwana Christophe Pierre, at the Tribunal of the Rights of Earth that took place in Bonn at the COP23 gathering in November 2017. He is now the vice-president of the Big Customary Council created last year to deal with Indigenous land and other issues. The mega-goldmining not only threatens to destroy part of the Amazonian Rainforest and its biodiversity, but also to pollute the water table with cyanide leaching that is planned to replace the old mercury technique. Mercury used by the clandestine goldminers expanding from Brazil and Surinam has already poisoned the forest rivers, with very high levels detected in fish and people – who are asked not eat fish from it. And while this gold industry promises a few jobs, it threatens the very existence of dozens of Indigenous villages that already struggle against drugs and prostitution from the clandestine mafia. The French government has been summoned by the UN to consult with the Indigenous peoples, and it announced early in 2019 that the project so far was not meeting proper environmental conditions.[25]

In the United States the recent change in governments presents similar racist and ecological threats to the future. President Donald Trump (a figure Guattari had already warned against in his *Threes Ecologies*) is ignoring the Black Lives Matter movement and is now

---

[24] Link to the UN report, September 2017: https://digitallibrary.un.org/record/1303201/files/A_HRC_36_46_Add-2-EN.pdf

[25] See: https://www.france-libertes.org/fr/victoire-projet-de-mega-montagne-dor-condamne-tribunal-droits-de-nature/; see in English: https://www.theguardian.com/environment/2018/apr/27/paris-to-decide-fate-of-mega-gold-mine-in-forests-of-french-guiana

cancelling rights over Native American land in favour of big extraction companies. In Brazil, which has its own colonial and postcolonial geopolitics, Michel Temer, now followed by Jair Bolsonaro, opened up the Amazonian rainforest to massive destruction through logging and a variety of extractions while threatening the process of land demarcation for Indigenous people and the Quilombolas (descendants of escaped slaves who in agreement with Indian groups established communities in which to hide; here, their descendants still live today and saw legal recognition by the previous government). Temer also cut the FUNAI funding which aimed at protecting some Indigenous groups in the forest from invasion; these groups are now attacked and sometimes savagely murdered by mercenaries working for private interests. The lives of leaders of other groups are also regularly threatened. Despite this discouraging turn, initiatives emanating from local civil society across the world – and also from transnational alliances of solidarity – continue inventing innovative ways of envisioning a multidimensional society in which the recognition of differences and specific rights is held in the same regard as universal human rights that are respected as well as expanded to better include the realities of our current world. Despite the decision by Temer's government to stop the mega dam projects in the Amazon, Bolsonaro's administration again plans megaprojects in what he calls 'umproductive, desertlike' forest.[26]

In June 2017 the parliament of Victoria, a state in Australia, invited an Aboriginal delegation from the Wurundjeri people whose representative, Alice Kolasa, proposed a bill in front of the assembly (which was eventually confirmed) which granted a river on their lands status as a living entity.[27] According to Alice Kolasa, the fact that this was the first time in Australian history that an official judicial text was written both in English and in one of the hundreds of Aboriginal languages – the Woi Wurrung spoken by one of the

---

[26] See: https://truthout.org/articles/bolsonaro-government-reveals-plan-to-develop-the-unproductive-amazon/; and see also: https://www.businessinsider.fr/us/bolsonaro-plan-to-develop-amazon-rainforest-2019-1

[27] See: https://www.theguardian.com/australia-news/2017/jun/22/the-dream-of-our-ancestors-victorian-bill-gives-indigenous-owners-custodianship-of-yarra; the Fitzroy River declaration in the north of Australia is also aiming at the First Law of the River to 'Secure sustainable and Equitable Futures for the West Kimberley', see Lim et al. (2017), Anne Poelina's call here: https://croakey.org/climate-justice-a-call-to-broaden-science-with-indigenous-knowledge/. See also McDuffie (2016).

clans of the Wurundjeri who go by the same name – provided in law a place for her people as First Nations: the state of Victoria, by way of this parliamentary process, had recognised the Woi Wurrung as the First Nation of the Birrarung River. The name of the legislation, 'Keep Birrarung Alive', can't simply be summed up as an ecological response to prevent any continuing pollution of the river and a call to be good stewards for the ecosystem, the fish, the vegetation, and the humans who live within this environment and live from it. Nor can the legislation be summed up by the new field of 'environmental justice' being taught in Anglo-Saxon universities and which has been put into action by Indigenous peoples (and which can most notably be seen in the inter-American tribunal on human rights and the right to life through the vantage point of the interdependence of humans, society and the environment).[28] The legislation in Victoria resonates in a much larger and important way by redefining the notion itself of life: it affirms the existence of the river as a living entity, in the same spirit as the judicial precedence in New Zealand which in 2017 recognised the official status of the Whanganui River as a living being.

In both cases, it was the Indigenous people, First Nation peoples of colonised countries – the Maori in New Zealand and the Wurundjeri in Australia – who led the campaign for granting the river a juridical personality. This status, which the Te Urewera Park in northern New Zealand had already benefited from, allows for 'the interest of the flow of water' to be protected by two actors: a lawyer for the tribe recognised as the owner of the river and another lawyer for the government. According to certain people, the status of the river ends up being closer to that of a corporation than an individual. However, what's important to retain from this is that the legislation recognises a collective voice that is inseparable from a specific site and its environment. The Indigenous peoples of two different countries didn't need the confirmation of old anthropological debates which relativise the old Western opposition between nature and culture in order to defend their struggle. These debates, which are purported as being very recent (as part of the ontological turn), merely reformulate, albeit in a rather delayed fashion, the multiple forms of transversality practised and thought by Indigenous peoples that we, as anthropologists, are supposed to be studying: they affirm that rivers, like all water sources, are living in the same way as all forms of matter of which humans – alongside animals, plants or minerals – are merely

---

[28] See, for example, Thériault (2015).

particular aspects. At the time I write this piece, New Zealand has also just recognised a mountain as a living being.[29]

'Resisting the Disaster: Between Exhaustion and Creation' (Chapter 11) was translated from French (2011) for a special issue on *Ecologies of Change* for the online journal *Spheres*.[30] In the same issue, I was lucky to have a discussion paper by a specialist of Félix Guattari, Gary Genosko (2002b), who defined me as an 'anthropologist of micropolitical hope'. In the essay, I begin by quoting Chakrabarty about the anthropocene and emphasise the fact that Indigenous people all around the world have always considered themselves as being responsible for any kind of catastrophe that has befallen them. They seek out the blame as tied to some sort of disprespect regarding any of the myriad of taboos that they impose on themselves in the name of ancestral laws. As Genosko (2017) maintains, I deploy Guattari's three registers of ecosophy 'to understand the foliatedness of disaster in the anthropocene' with a range of examples,

> from artists' responses to crises and neoliberal betrayals, collective intelligence marshalled against the violence of privatisation, experimentations leading to micro-social innovations challenging the criminalisation of asylum seekers, and political actions against the endo-colonialist policies of settler states. Eschewing victim discourses traded like stocks by big media, she eviscerates the dehumanising logic of humanitarian care in the form of 'assistancialism' and as some Aboriginals know it, 'sit down money'.

My priority since the 1980s has been to side-step the 'victimisation trap' in order to look at creative forms of resistance.

These are also at the heart of Guattari's ecosophy which articulates four dimensions: (1) existential territories (real but virtual) that can be material or immaterial; (2) fluxes (real but actual) related with the body and the land as well as money and trade; (3) constellations of values (virtual and possible) which are incorporeal universes like the *ritournelles*; and (4) machinic phylums or machines (actual and possible) referring to cybernetic retroaction, or autopoïesis: 'for it is

---

[29] See http://www.newsweek.com/human-rights-mountain-maori-people-mount-tar anaki-757237. For river rights see O'Donnell (2018). In Australia see the Birrarung (Yarra River) case in Victoria and the environmental justice struggle for Martuwarra (Fitzroy River) in Western Australia.

[30] *Spheres – Journal for Digital Cultures 2*: http://spheres-journal.org/2-ecologies-of-change/

precisely about linking the machines of the ecosystems of material fluxes to those of the ecosystems of semiotic fluxes. Therefore, I try to widen the notion of autopoïesis, without limiting it, like Varela does, solely to the living system, and I consider that there are proto-autopoïeses in all other systems: ethnological, social, etc.' (Guattari ([1991] 2013). Francisco Varela proposed the concept of autopoïesis (from the Greek 'autoproduction') in a seminar at the university of Santiago in 1972 to define how a living system can reproduce its organisation even when its composition or structure changes (Maturana and Varela 1980, 1987). Guattari extended the notion of autopoïesis to the analysis of human societies and the reproduction of social organisation, ethnic, cultural, religious, political and other factors in the face of structural transformations imposed by colonisation, and the Integrated World Capitalism. Widely used since, 'the idea of autopoïesis, when applied as an instrument of social analysis, confirms the conclusion already established by other means of investigation – that our societies are self-mutilating, pathologic systems' (Mariotti 1999). But for Guattari, as for me, against this destructive trend there still is a hope for machines of war and new assemblages of creative resistance.

In Chapter 11, I mention that when in 2005, at the court of Townsville, Australia, I attended the investigation of a group of twenty-three Palm Islanders accused of inciting a riot after the death of an Aboriginal man while he was held in custody, one hour after he was arrested for public drunkenness, I was impressed by the inhabitants' capacity to withstand adversity. They had been either deported to the island or were the descendants of the 3,000 Aboriginal people deported there between 1918 and the 1970s, from the respective lands of about forty different language groups spread throughout the state of Queensland. Indigenous Australians call their displaced populations 'historical people'. Their colonial anchoring to the deportation sites is thereby distinguished from the ancestral heritage of the 'traditional owners'; even if both groups argue in opposition for land claims based on the priority of the principle of Native titles, they nevertheless share in part a common history, as it is built on the same place of social belonging and life.

Palm Island has become well known for the workers' strike that took place there in 1957 led by various unions and the Labor Party. The first strike took place in Pilbara in Western Australia, 1 May 1946: 800 Aboriginal farmworkers and cowboys (stockmen) all abandoned their jobs on the same day at hundreds of ranches thanks to an initiative launched four years previously by Dooley Bin Bin and Clancy McKenna in alliance with the White communist activist Don McLeod. The strike paralysed the sheep industry until 1949. Most of the Aboriginal workers never returned to their jobs. They would go on to create their own business for panning for gold in the desert and purchase several cattle farms. It was only much later, in the afermath of the 1966 'Walk off' initiated by the Kurintji, who left the ranch at Wave Hill in the Northern Territory and squatted on their land, that the state, in 1969, finally forced employers to pay Aboriginal workers the same salaries as non-Aboriginal workers. As a result of this ruling, many Aboriginal workers simply lost their jobs.

Beginning in the 1960s, a campaign called 'Stolen Wages' was initiated by an Aboriginal woman, Yvonne Butler from Palm Island, who received the support of pro bono work from a group of lawyers convinced that she would win her case since the state had held onto the archives of the salaries received from employers that it never passed on to the workers: a sum estimated at AUS$500 million. The government proposed a minimal solution: AUS$3,000 of individual compensation granted to the survivors but not to their descendents. Most of the survivors refused. In 2004, the workers' union printed and passed out tiny cards that callled for the civil population to support this campaign and to recognise that, for Australia to have become what it is today, it was in large part thanks to the work of Aboriginal people. Very few Australians are aware of this fact, presupposing that all Aboriginal peoples resemble the small number of the Aboriginal people they see in the streets – homeless and unemployed, drinking. And yet, even those people on the streets, including in France and elsewhere, should be able to have a working life, without even mentioning all the youths who are invited to engage in internships without ever receiving a diploma. As such, despite the myriad of competencies these people acquire in a variety of areas (as auto-mechanics, gardeners, construction workers, electricians, radio broadcasters), administrations prefer to employ supposedly more qualified non-Aboriginal workers who are in fact rarely more efficient at their work out in the field. An official investigation in 2006 concerning 'Stolen Wages' has led to bringing the term 'slavery' back into the current discourse in order to speak about this exploitation of Aboriginal peoples linked to the past institutationalisation of children. But despite the enormous cost of the investigation, only a very small number of Aboriginal people have been compensated and the acceptance of demands for restitution was supposed to expire in September 2017. In 2016, three hundred Aboriginal people from Queensland brought forth a class action suit to continue their claim. The history of justice is not achieved simply through an investigation and official commision nor through the governmental appeal for certain so-called policies of reconciliation. If things change it's because people fight. And in Australia, as in other countries, the people who have suffered through injustices have had to fight before the state began to respond by way of judicially recognised processes.

The recent evolution of Australian politics towards Aboriginal people has aggravated this catastrophic logic throughout various regions of the continent, most notably in the Northern Territory, whose seventy-three Aboriginal communities were placed under the federal 'intervention' (Northern Territory National Emergency Response Act 2007) and a new centralised administrative system of city shires that suppressed Aboriginal councils. The elected Community Councils have been replaced by regional administrators who decide on municipal and individual expenses. The Aboriginal people have received debit cards to access their wages and subsidies, but they can only use them to buy food in some shops and they have to request authorisation for any other expense, such as buying a bus ticket or a plane ticket. This system has been wonderfully criticised in a fiction movie, *Charlie's Country* inspired by the life of the main actor, David Gulpilil.

Chapter 11 also refers to the United Nations' Declaration on the Rights of Indigenous Peoples, adopted on 13 September 2007 by the United Nations General Assembly. Whether among the Maori or other peoples from Oceania who have not gained independence, among Indians from North and South America, Moroccan Berbers, Touareg and Peuls in sub-Saharan states, nomadic peoples from Central Asia, everywhere Indigenous leaders currently analyse their situations by proposing to 'subalternise Indigenous politics' and 'indigenise subaltern politics'. At the time I initially wrote the paper reproduced in Chapter 11 I claimed that the rejection of Indigenous singularities by states like Australia echoed the situation of the Roma and Gipsies, including the 900 settlements that were dismantled in France in the summer of 2010 despite there having been a tradition of travelling and camping in French villages for centuries. I also posed the question regarding asylum and refugee rights for people running away from countries or places affected by natural disasters, such as Hurricane Katrina that devastated New Orleans. Today the issue is even worse as we know very well that we should continue to expect a massive displacement of refugees because of climate change disasters and the mass flooding of entire countries in the Pacific or Indian Oceans. In Europe, we are already confronted with the massive influx of refugees for a variety of reasons, including people fleeing from their countries because of the wars or misery provoked by Western powers who sell weapons or corrupt other governments to capture resources. Recently, laws concerning asylum seekers have been changed nationally and supranationally at the European level so as to close boundaries to the influx of refugees. Meantime, the life of displaced people remains a nightmare despite the presence of those who try to help them but who now, in France, as in Australia, risk jail.

'Standing with the Earth: From Cosmopolitical Exhaustion to Indigenous Solidarities' (Chapter 12) was translated and expanded for *Inflexions* following a paper I presented in June 2016 and which was published in the journal *Multitudes* (Glowczewski 2016b). It is inspired directly by Guattari's ecosophical project which he restated a few weeks before his death on 29 August 1992, as a call for 'Remaking Social Practices'. The translator's choice has been to use the verb 'Remaking' instead of the literal translation of *'Pour une refondation'*: 'For a refoundation'. In the latter sense I would propose using 'regrounding' instead because a 'remake' can be understood as a 'reinvented copy' which is different I think from what Félix Guattari was calling us to do.

> The 'ecosophic cartographies' that must be instituted will have, as their own particularity, that they will not only assume the dimensions of the present, but also those of the future. They will be as preoccupied by what human life on Earth will be thirty years from now, as by what public transit will be three years from now. They imply an assumption of responsibility for future generations, what philosopher Hans Jonas /1984/ calls 'an ethic of responsibility.' It is inevitable that choices for the long term will conflict with the choices of short-term interests. The social groups affected by such problems must be brought to reflect on them, to modify their habits and mental coordinates, to adopt new values and to postulate a human meaning for future technological transformations. In a word, to negotiate the present in the name of the future.
>
> It is not, for all that, a question of falling back into totalitarian and authoritarian visions of history, messianisms that, in the name of 'paradise' or of ecological equilibrium, would claim to rule over the life of each and everyone. Each 'cartography' represents a particular vision of the world that, even when adopted by a large number of individuals, would always harbor an element of uncertainty at its heart. That is, in truth, its most precious capital; on its basis, an authentic hearing of the other

could be established. A hearing of disparity, singularity, marginality, even of madness, does not arise only from the imperatives of tolerance and fraternity. It constitutes an essential preparation, a permanent return to the order of uncertainty, a stripping-bare of the forces of chaos that always haunt structures that are dominant, self-sufficient, and imbued with belief in their own superiority. Such a hearing could overturn or restore direction to these structures, by recharging them with potentiality, by deploying, through them, new lines of creative flow. (Guattari 1992: 26–7)[31]

Chapter 12 concerns the question of the creativity of new ontologies as responses to the worldwide disaster that hovers all around us and that is already affecting the planet. I begin the chapter by referring to a science fiction novel that makes a reference to the four ontologies of the French anthropologist, Philippe Descola, as an archive found in space during a future time when humans no longer live on earth. The nostalgia for terrestrial life aroused by Descola's interpretations of what he named respectively (by pitting each term against the other) the four ontologies of naturalism, animism, totemism and analogicism will provoke within intergalactic space a multiplication of sects that will reinvent practices so as to re-facilitate one of these ontologies. In its own way, the novel shows the limits of the model. The future humans were not capable of imagining how terrestrial societies were able to live since by taking back up certain characteristics examined by Descola, we are still very far from understanding how a given society truly functioned and, more importantly, how it could continue to exist after colonisation.

Invited by Descola to respond to his book *Beyond Nature and Culture* ([2005] 2013) at the Collège de France, I expressed my unease with his totemist ontology that relied on information about Aboriginal cultures that was sort of picked up haphazardly, most notably from my own work, and which in no way demonstrated the complexity of Australian totemism that, according to the context, can also contain characteristics mentioned in Descola's other ontologies: for example animism, which can be seen in the practice of Australian shamanism (which can be viewed in the same way as

---

[31] Translated by Sophie Thomas, revised by Brian Holmes on the basis of the French original, 'Pour une refondation des pratiques sociales', in *Le Monde Diplomatique* (October 1992): http://palimpsestes.fr/ecologie/textes_ecolo/Pour_une_refondation_des_pratiques_sociales.pdf

the shamanism practised in South America or Siberia).[32] One can also detect a pure analogism through the way in which the various totemic entities are placed into relation by way of their form (for example, the ray and the anchor for the Yolngu) and some other contexts can even be considered as naturalist. This last ontology is defined by Descola as the ontology of our Western universe of scientific rationality which has separated the mind (as interiority) from the body (as physicality): the man as a biological entity distinct from his mind which relies on culture being separate from nature. His book was very influential at showing that this separation is not universal since there are a great number of peoples who have not made this rupture between the body and the mind, be that in the ancient past or more recently as with Guattari and his ecosophy. However, there is still one of the aspects of this Western scientific approach that rests on these oppositions that can be seen in certain cognitive operations of totemic hunter-gatherers, for example when they are in the midst of tracking wild game, plants or geological layers. But, as is the case with astrophysics and quantum mechanics, these hunter-gatherers' operations of deduction and perception are much more complex than the mere dualism that guided Western science until our current times. Viveiros de Castro proposed the concept of multinature, I prefer the term multiverse, but the words taken as they are can't truly take into account the complexity hidden within the terms of the Indigenous languages and the mysteries that we are unable to explain.

The way in which Brazilian anthropologist, Eduardo Viveiros de Castro, critiques the Western narcissism present in the history of the sciences by articulating Deleuze and Lévi-Strauss together made me feel as if I was navigating in a boat out in the middle of the ocean where the waves continued to crash against each other. There was something familiar in both Deleuze and Lévi-Strauss that I was capable of digesting in spite of myself, but it was also clear that Viveiros de Castro's *Cannibal Metaphysics* ([2009] 2014) was deeply anchored within the history of South America, so much so that I lost my footing a bit in trying to find 'my' desert and other Australian landscapes. His call for a decolonisation of thought would end up

---

[32] 'The Paradigm of Indigenous Australians: Anthropological Phantasms, Artistic Creations and Political Resistance', in Art catalogue *The Revenge of Genre*, 2007 revised translation (phantasies instead of phantasms), in Glowczewski (2015b: 131–55).

bringing us together in 2012 during a conference organised by philosopher Jean-Christophe Goddard at the University of Toulouse.[33] When Viveiros de Castro was invited to São Paulo to present my Brazilian book, *Totemic Becomings: Cosmopolitics of the Dreaming* (2015), he acknowledged a lack of familiarity with the Australian data but pointed to the fact that we shared a similar allergy for the ontological reductions.

Maurizio Lazaratto and Angela Melitopoulos had taken note of what brings both of our anthropological projects closer together by publishing in the catalogue of the exhibition, *Animism*, our respective interviews partly contained in their film installation, *Assemblages: Félix Guattari and machinic animism*. I said the following, which was filmed in my kitchen in Paris:

> That which appear[s] natural to us – springs, rocks – are loaded with history for the aboriginal peoples, who practice forms of totemism, and are thus cultural and non-natural ... There are those here among us who function this way even more today than in the past, because we have less and less an apprehension regarding what is natural, while the category that philosophy contributed to setting up opposes humans to untouched nature. And the greater the desire was to leave it untouched, the more it was developed. This sort of opposition no longer really makes any sense. The nature/culture opposition nevertheless constricts our thinking a great deal.
>
> It is still our paradigm, since we continue to fantasize about natural peoples, natural environments, about the fact that we must preserve nature. And as much as we think this way, I think we are wrong when it comes to the solutions to be found for the different problems. For example, the question of the environment is not really about protecting nature by stopping pollution. On the contrary, it is necessary to invest it with new forms of assemblages and cultural mechanisms. (Melitopoulos and Lazzarato 2010)

Descola was criticised by a number of South American colleagues and, since the translation of his book into English, *Beyond Nature and Culture*, he has also been criticised by Bessire and Bond (2014):

> As Elizabeth Povinelli (2002) suggests, the figure of radical alterity may organize new regimes of inequality or create the conditions for the hypermarginality of supposedly insufficient or 'deculturated' Indigenous

---

[33] *Décolonisations de la pensée: Anthropologie, philosophie et politique (2). Leçons Deleuzo-guattariennes*, 2012, filmed conference, 12 July 2012, University of Toulouse: http://choplair.com.free.fr/Europhilosophie/FIPS_videos/index.php

populations (Bessire 2014b). Ontological anthropology seems neither able to reflect on this slippage nor able to address the question it begs: Why is the ontological status of radical exteriority still so necessary for politics as well as for our aspirations as a discipline, and how might these projects coincide? (Bessire and Bond 2014: 445)

While I tend to agree with some of the aspects of Bessire and Bond's criticisms regarding the ideal typologies that distance us from a politics of the common or the reification of past forms postulated outside of time, I'm not convinced that a recognition of alterities prevents us from fighting against inequalities and marginalisation. In order to engage in this fight, there are better things worth undertaking than simply continuing to criticise the so-called ontological turn that was sparked much like a marketing campaign that led to a revitalised interest in the discipline of anthropology after focusing only on promoting the work of four men: Bruno Latour, Philippe Descola, Eduardo de Castro and Tim Ingold. All of them having been friends for a great many years, united by way of the success of their ideas, they are however less in agreement with each other than it might seem – to such an extent that a recent criticism made by Tim Ingold (2016) with regard to the work of Philippe Descola led to strong criticism in return (Descola 2016). But these debates hold little interest for me.

Nevertheless, the ontological scene has revealed a more essential problem. It took some time for commentators on the work of this rowdy bunch to recognise that a myriad of complex ontological speculations have already been proposed – long before this sudden resurgence of current interest – by such thinkers as Marilyn Strathern, an anthropologist of complex theories inspired by her interpretation of the Papuan cosmologies in Papua New Guinea. A number of other women thinkers have been writing about the critical subject of the shattering of ontologies and thought regarding immanence, confronting themselves with issues of power and violence in a much more political manner than the masculine figures of the ontological turn. Such has been the case with Elizabeth Povinelli from her early *Labor's Lot* (1993), dealing with the history of an Aboriginal community from Northern Australia, to her most recent geontological project.[34] More recently, the writings of Rosi Braidotti regarding

[34] In a workshop at my laboratory in Paris in February 2016 I was lucky enough to discuss with Elizabeth Povinelli her manuscript, *Geontology* (2016). I must admit that I don't agree with her figure of the desert which, from my point of view,

affirmation have also offered new grounds for social critique in a Deleuzian framework. And Anna Tsing has provided a very rhizomatic work of hope taking into account many complexities in *The Mushroom at the End of the World: On The Possibility of Life in Capitalist Ruins* (2015), even though ruins might be the only space left for living despite the struggle against extractivism to promote another world. We all owe a great deal to Isabelle Stengers's continuous and steadfast elaboration of cosmopolitics, her quest for new enchantments, and the promotion in France of the work of Starhawk, the WICCA activist, as well as Donna Haraway whose string figures inspire speculative gestures (Stengers and Debaise 2015). And then there are the myriad of other women and men emerging everyday, such as the ecofeminists and decolonial thinkers. Many writers and speakers are in the shadows producing works that are reappropriated, certainly as much by men as well as women from various groups across the world who are engaged with current issues with regard to migrants, domestic or racial violence, or climate justice. The environmental activism physicist Vandana Shiva is a clear inspiration, while many Indigenous scholars raise their voices through the planet. For instance Zoe Todd calls for 'Indigenizing the Anthropocene' (2015): when she was a student in anthropology this young Indigenous Canadian criticised Latour and his ontological turn with an online statement 'Ontology is another word for colonialism', based on her surprise of him never referring to Indigenous knowledge and Indigenous lawyers who deconstruct the law system by fighting for new environmental justice laws.[35] Katerina Teaiwa who defines herself as an African-American Pacific Islander (from Banaba Island, part of the Republic of Kiribati) pays homage to the relational archipelic notion of Pacific identity expressed by Epeli Hau'ofa's concept of a 'sea of islands' and analyses the pan-Pacific activism in the following terms:

---

cannot be an empty and lifeless place – as the desert is depicted in fantasies of Western development – but I admire her political and cinematic engagement with the Aboriginal community very much, a community that she has accompanied and followed since 1989.

[35] Todd (2016), published since its 2015 online buzz (see comment by Glowczewki 2015b); on decolonial sensibilities and Indigenous research see Ribeiro and Escobar (2002), Prober et al. (2011), Rose et al. (2012), Gaad (2014), Ribeiro (2014), Whitehouse et al. (2014, 2017), Fraser and Todd (2016), Harrison and Sellwood (2016), Hunt and Stevenson (2016).

> Both Oceania Rising and the Climate Warriors represent post-colonial, antihegemonic movements that are grounded in contemporary customs, realities, and cultural identities, while simultaneously championing broader regional identities and unifying concerns (26) (...) the 'rising' in 'rising sea of islands' references not just the impacts of global warming and Hau'ofa's expansive vision of mobile but grounded islanders but the rising and increased visibility of critical and engaged Oceanians who are thinking, writing, performing, and speaking regionally and globally about a range of important issues including climate change (Steiner 2015). (Teaiwa 2018: 29)

More than anything else, we must be open to listening and truly hearing the words, whether written, filmed or spoken during political protests by populations that have been forgotten for far too long and that have been considered as objects of study whether in an exotic manner or near at hand and that have been *othered* [alterisé] by their colonial origins or due to their social exploitation.[36]

To respond to the twofold question proposed by Povinelli and to Bessire and Bond who cite her: 'Why is the ontological status of radical exteriority still so necessary for politics as well as for our aspirations as a discipline, and how might these projects coincide?' First, I would like to simply state that I see two things at stake here. First, in our present time when culture is devouring nature, in the sense that urbanisation and its extractivist and digital technologies are eroding every territory, and when a number of thinkers claim that there is no longer such a thing as an outside – an exteriority – now more than ever, us humans and non-humans truly need the radical outside of peoples in struggle who affirm that other worlds are possible: whether they are Indigenous or arise from out of what Deleuze and Guattari called 'a people that is missing'[37] by reinvesting in territories worth occupying counter to a hegemonic world that not only doesn't accept the heterogeneity of the multitudes but above all no longer thinks about anything else than benefiting a small minority of transhumanised people. The second stake is that of alliances between all these struggles. And this is where the philosophy of Deleuze and Guattari, and more specifically Guattari's project of ecosophy, continues to inspire younger generations (Querrien and Goffey 2017).

---

[36] See for instance Amilia Telford 'Why I Took a Stand – Climate Justice and the Future of the First Australians', May 2017: https://www.youtube.com/watch?v=45S_v6iaKLA; in Canada, Asselin and Basile (2018).

[37] See also Deleuze, *Cinema 2: The Time-Image* ([1989] 2010: p. 216): 'the people no longer exist, or not yet ... *the people are missing*'. Notice the plural here.

During the 2004 Pacific Arts Festival which gathered in the independent Micronesian state of Palau, with delegations from thirty-three Pacific countries, I attended a workshop that was organised by an association of ethnomusicologists, ICTM. A Japanese Osagawaran islander group demonstrated a dance that in 2000 became the 'intangible cultural treasure' of their island. The dance – inspired by a Micronesian tradition of Palau – was appropriated by Osagawaran settlers when occupied by Japan. The fact that the historical context of the dance's origin was acknowledged by the Japanese dancers seemed to satisfy the Palauans who had invited them to the festival. A young Palauan composer explained with a step demonstration that, since those days of Japanese occupation, the dancers of Palau had changed their own steps to adapt them to the 'groove' of the American soldiers who occupied the island during the Second World War. An Aboriginal Yolngu elder from Arnhem Land, Joe Neparrnga Gumbula, then commented:

> Looking at South Pacific, coconut brought by West wind just float to our land, we pick it up on the beach from the Ocean. Never mind that we are not faring from the sea; there is a chain from Papua New Guinea, and in Cape York Peninsula. That's when we dance the coconut movement [...] We play the part of the Ocean; move underneath the current ...

Gumbula stood to demonstrate his Yolngu dance and explained further:

> [...] this is how the songline works. And actually what we are talking about here is traditional: the song series, the dance and all that. But only the copyright is problematic: somebody talks about 'you don't take my song'. And that's only what I am thinking looking at how I look at the Pacific Ocean here, the current movement.

Katerina Teaiwa, defining herself as an African-American and a Banaban Islander, who was then the Convener of Pacific Studies at the Australian National University, responded with passion:

> [...] So it's not that you stole or borrowed something because it flows to your shores. That's a very important point and it's important to talk about it in that way and not just lump things as identity; or culture or tradition. Like you said, it's a process and there are lines and currents that connect.[38]

---

[38] This exchange between Gumbula and Teaiwa is extracted from Glowczewski and Henry ([2007] 2011); see also De Largy Healy ([2007] 2011, 2009, 2017).

The Aboriginal peoples or Pacific Islanders do not need to be Deleuzo-Guattarians to think through the middle (*milieu*), that is the space they live in, which is made of currents and flows of people and things, songs, or dances, be it the Ocean, the desert, the forest or the city. When people defend values of sharing together but each in their own ways, they can hold on to singularities always in becoming and whose affirmation requires new ways of existing. The Aboriginal peoples in struggle, such as Native Americans in the United States or Canada, or Amerindians of Brazil or French Guiana, impress by way of their creativity that relies simultaneously on an ancestral heritage as well as the specificity of the contemporary globalised world, without forgetting to mention their deserts and forests. For me, they create a hope for the future that parallels the youth in France who stand up to protect another possible world at Notre-Dame-des-Landes,[39] or those youths who want to be recognised as both Black and French. The same can be said for Indigenous peoples, or the Quilombola descendants of slaves and the Black population and majoritarian mixed-race population in Brazil forced into misery and who nevertheless attempt to resist against a state machine that wants to destroy them. As expressed by Brazilian philosopher, Peter Pál Pelbart, a friend of Guattari, coordinator of the Ueinzz Theater *Company*, a schizoscenic project, and also co-publisher of n-1 Publications:

> Maybe we have to consider exhaustion at the heart of this existential intersection, micro- and macropolitical, biopolitical. Does exhaustion signify the end of the world, or the end of a certain world we have to leave behind? Is exhaustion the sign of the end of the subject, or of a certain subjectivation? Of a desubjectivation, or a certain desubjectivation? Is it mortifying or vital? Black hole or opening? (Pál Pelbart 2017)

Dancing with the Spirits of the Land

The final part of the book proposes two texts that attempt to focus on some of the other voices of the multiverse that I strive to explore, first in Brazil and then in Australia.

---

[39] Documentary film subtitled in English, *Notre-Dame-des-Luttes:* https://www.youtube.com/watch?v=_Z0mfkeGp34; the project of building an airport there was cancelled by the government in January 2017 and the activists who had been occupying the land in protest since 2012 now stand for continuing their social experiment of the ZAD 'Zone to defend' as an alternative mode of collective land use: https://www.youtube.com/watch?v=4rh_6j6vIrc

Guattari visited Brazil on a number of occasions before and after 1985, when it was freed from dictatorship thanks to the Workers' Party (PT) of Luiz Inácio Lula da Silva, his friend. His stimulating Brazilian encounters are documented in the *Molecular Revolution in Brazil*, first published in Portugese:

> Yes, I believe that a multiple people exists, a people of mutants, a people of potentialities that appear and disappear, that becomes embodied in social events, literary events, in musical events. It is quite well known that many accuse me of being rather stupidly or almost foolishly optimistic, of not seeing the misery of various peoples. I can see it, but ... I don't know, perhaps I'm delirious, but I also think that we are living in a period of productivity, or proliferation, of creation, of absolutely fabulous revolutions from the viewpoint of the emergence of a people. That's the molecular revolution: it's not some sort of fancy phrase, some sort of program, it's something I feel deep down, that I live within the encounters I make, inside the institutions, in the affects as well as through reflections. (In Guattari and Rolnik ([1986] 2008: 9/preface to the 7th Brazilian edition)

Guattari left an impressive imprint in Brazil on philosophers, psychologists, anthropologists and artists. Several departments of psychology have been training students as 'schizoanalysts' for over ten promotions. Many young therapists of Indigenous or Afro-Brazilian background refer to his writings and practice. '*Cosmocolours*: A Filmed Performance of Incorporation and a Conversation with the Preta Velha Vó Cirina' (Chapter 13) was first written in Portuguese with the help of Brazilian performer and schizoanalyst, Clarissa Alcantara, and translated into English for publication in the bilingual Brazilian journal of visual anthropology *GIS (Gest(ure), Image and Sound)* 2017. The chapter begins with the presentation of an art performance experience I proposed to Clarissa Alcantara, at 'The Beast and Adversity' (BAC) exhibition in Geneva (August 2015), consisting of projecting on her rituals I filmed in an Umbanda terreiro in Florianopolis. Chapter 13 then continues with an interview that I conducted with the spirit of a Black woman, Vó Cirina (August 2016), incorporated in the Umbanda ritual leader, Abilio Noé da Silveira, of that cult. In a way this conversation with a spirit resonates with what was at the heart of Deleuze's and Guattari's call for heterogeneous becomings. In that performance I propose to compare these Brazilian cults with the way Aboriginal people experiment a form of incorporation in their totemic becomings. In my conversation with the spirit of the old African woman, she proposes her own way to recognise 'Indians' in Australia and those of North or South

America as being 'same but different', like the Orixá entities of the African diaspora.[40]

It's an enormous challenge for anthropologists or historians of religion to explain what exactly it is within rituals that actualises and virtualises the heterogeneities within the rites, the persons, objects, places, rocks, etc., that can't be reduced to symbolic 'representations', to the extent that the question of 'presence' is not considered as a support image, but, rather, its lines of flight in becoming. Deleuze and Guattari are a source of inspiration here so as to 'imagine an anthropology that escapes representation' (Goldman 2015), which is what I have attempted to create in my writings since my very first visit to Australia. The text proposed here mixes together genres: the narrative of performance, a film and interview with the Spirit of the Tent (Tenda Espirita) Vó Cirina disturb boundaries, and the languages produce parallel spaces that nevertheless come into contact with each other. This is my proposition for an 'undisciplined' anthropology which allows one to see and feel a multiplicity of lines in becoming; the Warlpiri Dreamings, the Orixás and the spirits of the dead, anthropology, philosophy, sacred art and many other things are composed in the possibility of a singular dance that would superimpose bodies and spirits in *Cosmocolour-becoming*.

This type of intervention – which mixes together writings, film, performance and ritual – in some ways echoes what Félix Guattari was exploring when trying to make a science fiction film that he called *A Love of UIQ* (the Infra-Quark Universe).[41] This quantum and multipolar brain will become externalised in the form of a face that will constantly be in flux, without a fixed identity and without a body, a potential that is somewhat childish and that learns very rapidly by way of interacting with a variety of characters that are more or less delirious, and that ends up becoming madly jealous in falling in love; the emergence of this 'infra-quark' universe, whether it's crazy or not, constitutes the tension of the story, along with the risk of a contamination of the entire universe tuning the film into a thriller of a global conspiracy. The seven years it took Guattari to write the script (1980–1987), and the different versions of it, were for

---

[40] See also Glowczewski (2016c, 2019). Special thanks to Claude Mercier (2019) for his inspiring conversations and writings on Deleuze and Guattari.

[41] Guattari ([2012] 2016) (1980s' scripts, translated and edited by Silvia Maglioni and Graeme Thomson).

him, like so many existential territories and incorporeal universes, a testing machine for transforming, by way of fiction and the staging of the different characters, what he strived to diagrammatise elsewhere in his cartographies. If he wasn't able to make his film, it's perhaps not just because he couldn't find the financial backing from the National Centre of Cinematography (CNC) and the required production, but, as his letters with the American producer Robert Kramer suggest, it was in part due to the fact that the initial 'drive' towards the end of the early 1980s was no longer the same. Félix wanted for his film to connect with the mainstream public following the success of *Blade Runner*. He couldn't have imagined or anticipated to what degree the image – art, installation or cinema – and the critique of its ethnocentric representation would become the object of a reappropriation by the colonised peoples themselves, by those subalternised, and all the other peoples in resistance to an Integrated World Capitalism, but he had the intuition and the hope for this potential creativity at the beginning of the 'winter' years. His hope returned on the eve of his death when, in his own words – and his own eyes – he would claim to have finally gotten over a long depression.[42]

For Guattari, to create cartographies was a very complex practice which evoked a form of diagrammatisation of movements and tensions of space and time, in order to simultaneously grasp and ungrasp subjectivity. His cartographic metamodel constructed from four functors (flux/flow, machinic phylums, universes of values, and existential territories), polarised between a folding of the virtual/actual and real/possible into four layers, was not much used until his *Schizoanalytic Cartographies* was translated. Even though I witnessed the development of this thought tool during Guattari's seminars in the early 1980s, it gained a new applicability for me after I saw Anne Querrien ([2008] 2011) redraw the cartography in a conference and after I read an article by Brian Holmes (2009) that showed how to articulate the functors with situations of our current times. It encouraged me to start drawing different applications of the functors in tension.

I have demonstrated elsewhere that the way in which Guattari articulates his four functors with chaosmosis can be unpacked by the

---

[42] 'Qu'est-ce que la philosophie?' Filmed interview in Greece in 1991 after the publication of *What is Philosophy?* (Deleuze and Guattari ([1992] 1996): https://novom.ru/en/watch/NAahyYZkrAo; about Leros see also Guattari ([1989] 2012).

way in which Wanta Steve Patrick Jampjinpa drew in the sand his five pillars for the Warlpiri system of knowledge:

> I used Felix's cartography to rethink not only Aboriginal totemic cosmology but also its recent translation by an Aboriginal man, Wanta Jampijinpa, who had made a drawing lesson of his cosmo-vision for YouTube. This Warlpiri teacher, who later became an honored researcher at ANU, had selected five Aboriginal concepts that he drew as circles of a web in the shape of the Southern Cross that would collapse if any of these five 'pillars' and their links were broken. It is an Indigenous cosmopolitical model responding to global digital society.
>
> Home (*ngurra*, literally 'land', 'place' and 'camp') is the first Warlpiri concept drawn as a circle in the sand by Wanta, Law (*Kuruwarri*) is the second circle, Ceremony (*Jardiwanpa* for settling dispute, *kurdiji*, the 'man-making' initiation, and other rituals) is the third, followed by Language (*yimi*) and Family (*warlalja* 'my people' as extended kin and classificatory relations between people, Dreamings and places). Law is a common expression used by Aboriginal people to translate concepts of different languages that relate to the Dreaming as the foundation of their cosmopolitics. The Warlpiri word *Kuruwarri* translates literally as 'image', 'mark', 'track' or 'trace'. To suggest its cosmological meaning, I have proposed translating it as the 'image-forces' and 'vital forces' of Dreamings (*Jukurrpa*).
>
> [...] What makes Indigenous Australians resist and insist on claiming a spiritual relationship with the land despite changes in their of mode of existence from semi-nomadic to forced sedentarization with all the current economical and social pressures? How can deterritorialization be the source of their reanchoring in existential territories? Or, on the contrary, threaten their lives with despair, violence, and even death. Wanta, the Warlpiri man, answers in his own way when he says that if one of the five pillars –home, language, law, ceremony or family – is not strong and connected to the others, everything collapses, and there is no Warlpiri anymore. For him the pillars are mirrored as stars in the Southern Cross, with the vertical axis being the Digging stick Dreaming that announces in September the season for *Puurda* yams, a time of the year also called the waking Emu, seen as the black hole in the Milky Way, two other Dreamings which like all things in nature and culture have their songline and pathway on the earth. (Glowczewski 2015)[43]

---

[43] The original *Ngurra-kurlu*, Wanta's filmed sand lesson in Warlpiri (2008) has been integrated into the website Indigenous Governance Toolkit: http://toolkit.aigi.com.au/resource/video-ngurra-kurlu-the-way-yapa-life-is-governed (accessed in October 2018). See Holmes and Jampijinpa (2013); drawings in filmed conference by Glowczewski (2011).

According to my analysis, four of Wanta's five 'pillars' echo Guattari's functors. *Kuruwarri* 'Image-force/Law' operates like an Existential Territory; *yimi* 'Language' refers to an 'Incorporeal Universe/Constellation' especially through the concept of spirit-children *Kuruwalpa* who as song verses wait to be born, that is to be embodied in a new baby; all the Ceremonies are Fluxes, because it is through them that traditional economy operated, a system of exchange between different people (generations, sexes, clans and tribes), with a circulation of goods that does not treat what is traded as objects but as living things including the ceremonial media, that is songs, dances, paintings that travel from place to place; the fourth pillar *warlalja* 'my people', that is Family as a system of extended kinship with complex classificatory relations, corresponding to the mathematical properties of a diedric group (the cube) and the topological properties of an hypercube, are an example of Guattari's Phylums or Abstract Machines. As for the fifth pillar that Wanta drew first in the 'middle', *ngurra* 'place' or 'camp' as home, multiple and different for each person through their life, I understand it as the empty centre that articulates deterritorialisation and reterritorialisation in Guattari's chaosmatic cartography. For the Warlpiri and their desert neighbours, places and their Dreaming connections are at the heart of anchoring in space – and time – their travels as semi-nomads before colonisation. Place is also at the heart of today's resistance against the destruction of land and the affirmation of their cosmovision.

Both Guattari's and Wanta's modes of thought unfold as diagrammatic practice and speculative gestures to approach the collective unconscious as intersubjectivation and as an active force to move the world. During a filmed interview in 2017, Wanta Steve Patrick Jampijinpa explained to me what I understand as the cosmopolitics of an Indigenous philosopher-mediator: from one year to the next, he transliterates his understanding of some Western concepts into Warlpiri values re-adapted to the contemporary world of interactions that pile on top of each other and endlessly create interference.

> 'You can see this one ? (*Wanta opens and closes his hand in a pulsating manner*)
> you learn that one in the Eagle one. It's flying high. The High-flyer.
> He is the high Thunder. And he can come down
> (*Gesture pointing from sky to the earth*)

Mapping Warlpiri concepts of the Dreaming (Jukurrpa) with Guattari's chaosmosis.

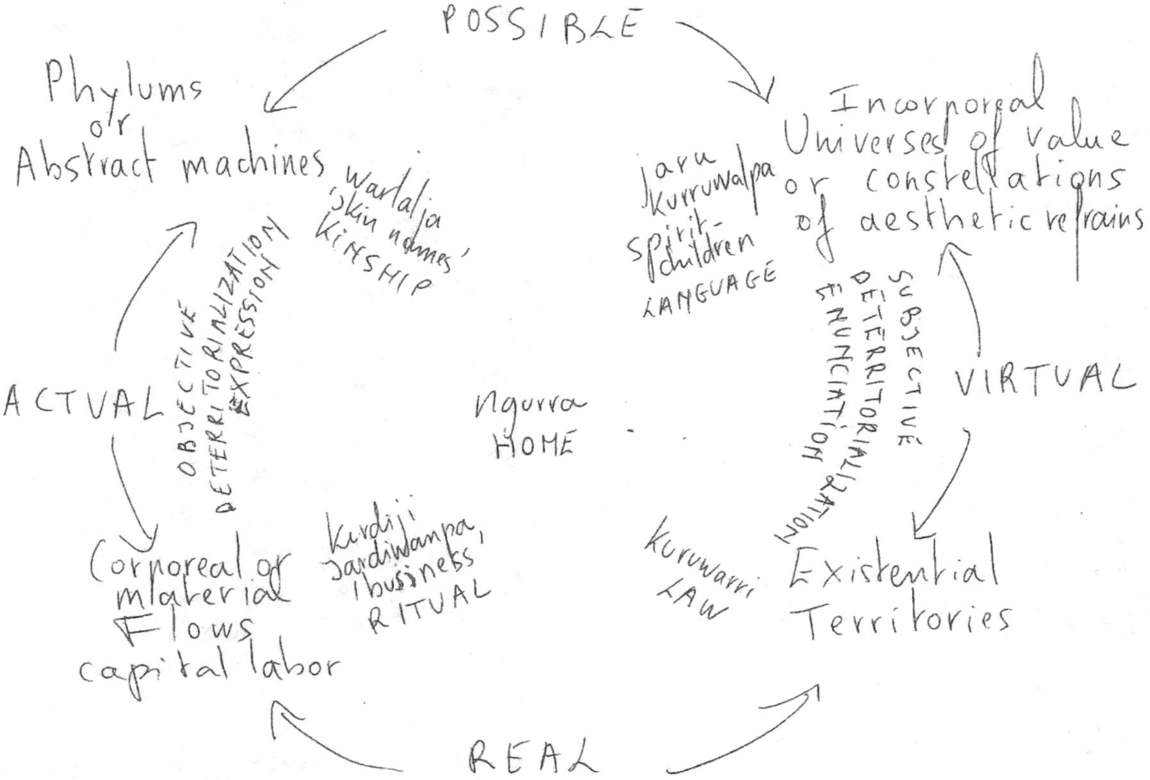

Figure 1.1 Guattari's cartography and Ngurrakurlu system of knowledge by Wanta Jampijinpa © B. G. from Totemic Becomings (2015)

He can make the connection with the clouds or star. That's the
   High-flyer.
That's, sorry to say (*laugh*), penetration I call it
(*Fingers to the ground*)
This one penetration, always try to engage.
(*Hand to the sky and back to the ground*)

That's what we call *malkarri*:
malkarri teaches you how to look at the sky and the earth.
When you do that you already, how I can I say ...
you marry the two and you become a High-flyer
because you got knowledge from here
(*Hand down the ground*)
and you can read the stars, you read country. That's the intercourse, yes.
(*Wanta traces a vertical line runnning from his head down his body*)
It's to marry the two, and you come to existence.'
(*Wanta's line continues up his chest*)

I showed Wanta a photo of an acrylic painting on canvas by Paddy Gibson Japaljarri that I had bought in 1988 in his community, Lajamanu. The Warlpiri artist called it Kurlungalinpa, the name of his sacred place connected with Stars and *Ngarrka*, the Initiated

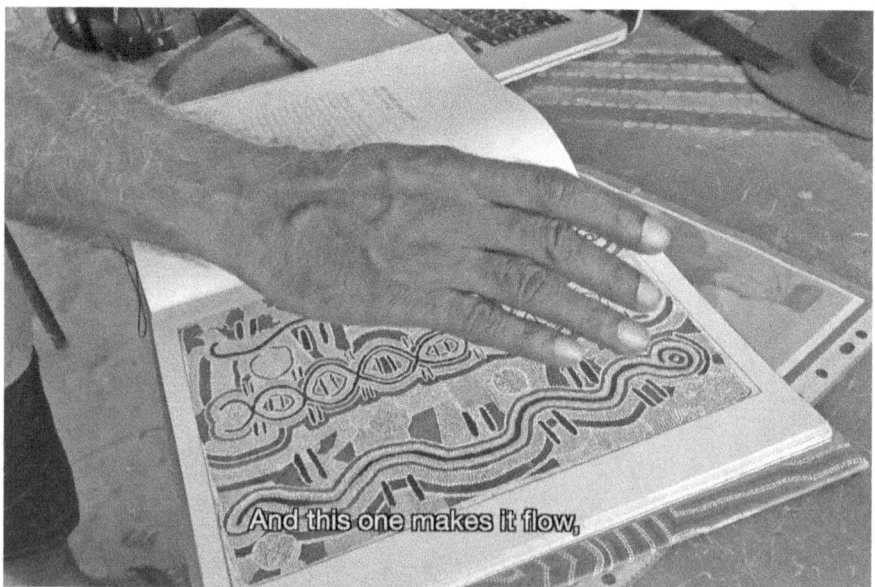

Figure 1.2 *The photo shows the hand of Wanta (the speaker in the book) commenting on the same painting printed in the book that I published in 2007.* © B.G. 2017.

Becoming Land

Men who grew trees at their feet when they came out of the earth while a comet was falling, turning into the sacred hill. The painting is separated by a double helix, the Milky Way. Wanta traced with his finger the double helix that cuts across the middle of the painting, commenting:

'You can see this one? that's always marrying,
always being productive, *yuwayi* (yes), put it that way.

Wanta followed one of the two meandering lines drawn along each side of the double helix:

And this line makes it flow, talks about flow

– But that middle one, I asked, can also be *ngalypi* (Vines) for the *Witi* (Leafy poles) dance?

– Yep, that one talks about the positive and negative consequences.

– My 'father' (*Japaljarri, the artist who I call 'father' because I was given the skin-name Nungarrayi*) was saying this is the Milky Way ...

– Yeah, the Milky, all that *Wantarri*, Gift road, that's the Gift road where people trade ...
   (*Wanta lifts his head up pointing to the sky*)
But that story (*pointing again to the sky*)
reflects that story (*pointing to the ground*)
that why the two 'moities' ...
(*Wanta rolls his hands forward then backward*)
This one ...
(*Wanta lifts with his hand his right breast*)
This 'moiety' for me, for us (*matriline of skin-names:
Jampijinpa (his skin-name), Japanangka, Jakamarra, Jungarrayi,
Nungarrayi (my skin-name), Nampijinpa, Napanangka, Nakamarra*)
This side of breast milk
(*Wanta shows his left breast*)
Other line sky mob
(*matriline of Napangardi, Nangala, Napaljarri, Napurrurla;
Jupurrurla, Japangardi, Jangala, Japaljarri matriline*)[44]
But you know because we're facing that way,
(*Wanta turns his back to the camera to fix the wall of the art centre to the South*)
we got to try to become that star, Southern Cross,
so we can face that way, the North.
(*Wanta opens his arms like the Cross turning back towards the camera*)

---

[44] See Figure 1.3; see also Chapter 6.

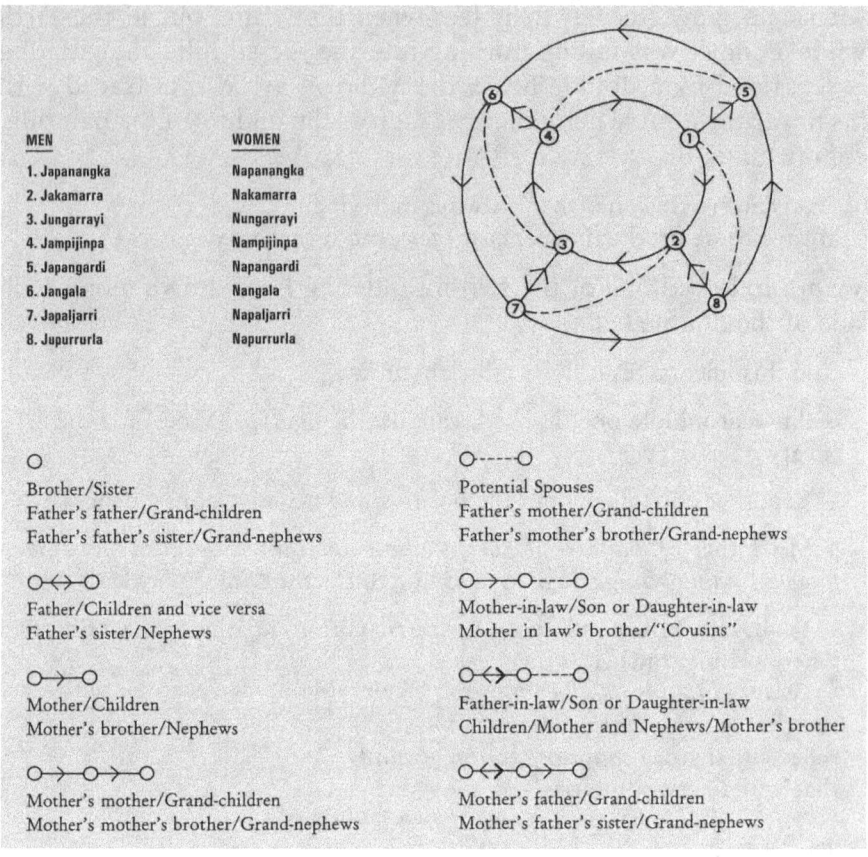

Figure 1.3 Two matriline circles for the Warlpiri 8 subsections or skin-names system © B. G. from Yapa, Art From Balgo and Lajamanu (1991b)

That's saying you are your home when you know your history and knowledge.
Identity really'[45]

Wanta is referring here to many complex things, especially the fact that classificatory kinship (the *skin-name* matrilines) is reproduced through exchange between people and the whole totemic cosmos, 'like' a double helix which figures the Milky Way. Interestingly for geneticians the double helix emerged as a structure when DNA was discovered in the 1950s and more recently it has been modelised

---

[45] See *Lajamanu* (60'), film by B. Glowczewski: https://vimeo.com/289440509

as a structure for the Milky Way galaxy. In Wanta's sand model, four of his pillars – (1) extended kin, (2) rituals of exchange, (3) cosmological Law of totemic lines, (4) language of spirit-children/songs emerging from the Dreaming space-time places on earth – are connected by the Southern Cross, with the 5th pillar *ngurra* 'land, place, camp, home' at the crossing, that is embodied as a human – or any earthling– living being standing on, underneath or above the land, that is *becoming land*.

Wanta's views on totemism are also expressed through the example of one of the personifications of the Emu Dreaming, that is the Giant Emu – whose tracks have been identified by scientists as those of a feather dinosaur species – that travelled East and West of the continent and is said by Aboriginal groups from different parts of Australia to have become the black hole of the Milky Way. Interestingly, among emus it is the male who incubates the eggs and looks after the babies when they hatch while the female hunts to feed them all. In that sense, Emu is one of the 'Dreaming' images for male and female complementarity. For the coastal people, baby emus help healers. For the Warlpiri people, it is Emu who gave them the Jardiwanpa ceremony to settle conflicts. Wanta explains the dependent totemic relationship between humans and non-humans, the earth and the sky, the different Aboriginal groups dispersed around the four corners of Australia, and the founding rituals which are anchored around feminine heroines thought of as pairs of two mothers, matrilines which are reproduced in the form of a double helix within a multitude of totemic forms. Wanta's task is trying to explain a dynamic system of life production in accordance with the mysteries of the cosmos where the multiverse becomes entangled with space-times akin to the craziest questions posed by astrophysics. Such an entanglement is at the heart of the Aboriginal Indigenous practice of healing.

Chapter 14 proposes a conversation with another Aboriginal man, a Yalarrnga healer. Lance Sullivan was born in the southern corner of Queensland, in Boulia, a settlement proclaimed in 1879 as a reserve for his people, the Yalarrnga, who were living a hunting and gathering lifestyle and were hunted down by settlers. One of his great-grandfathers was a Pakistani cameler. Many camel owners brought to Australia by the British to help with the colonisation of the desertic continent had children with Aboriginal women, even though it was forbidden by the government administration and the children of such unions were sought out and taken away from their parents.⁴⁶ But Lance Sullivan's mixed-blood ancestry was hidden by his Aboriginal family, and he grew up learning his Yalarrnga language and became initiated in the rituals of the desert people. After working as a cultural adviser to protect sacred sites from mining, he was offered a grant to study archaeology and anthropology at James Cook University in Townsville where we met at the end of 2004. He had just finished a book on his language (Sullivan 2005).

A few years later, Lance Sullivan was invited to France for an Indigenous workshop in Lyon at which he and Wanta, who was also invited, were asked by the director of the new Musée des Confluences under construction to make a smoking ceremony in the foundations. It was filmed by an Indigenous Peruvian film-maker.⁴⁷ In Townsville, where he lived as a student and a young father, Lance was regularly asked to help people with his healing powers, including for love magic or to cure prisoners caught by panic in jail. He explains here (Chapter 14) how he can see with his *mungan* power (*ngangkari* or *ngangkayi* in Warlpiri) which allows healers, *Cleverman*, like him to see inside the body, through the skin – not just like an x-ray that would show the bones and organs – but beyond the materiality of the body into a vision of many coloured wires where a specific colour indicates the place of pain; he then acts on that 'line' by 'pulling' the pain and the 'wire' inside the body changes colour. This shamanistic gesture of 'pulling' – which can involve the distant imposition of a hand, touching or even going inside the body, is explained by what he calls the parallel glass walls that give access to parallel universes that are all present in the same material place: like a spot of grass, a stone or a wall in my flat in Paris where we talked. To me, his description suggests precisely something of what astrophysicists call multiverse or pluriverse, that is the possibility of heterogeneous assemblage, like the different logics of nanoworlds, molecular worlds, or the galactic macro-worlds, that cannot be reduced to a universal unity. In a book called *Pluriverse: Essay on the End of the World*, Deleuzian philosopher Jean-Clet Martin (2010) describes various divergent worlds that cannot be reduced to a homogenous universe: 'what is first is the place, the strength of the place, this embryonment

---

⁴⁶ Rajkowski (1995).
⁴⁷ *La Terre est notre vie*, 30' documentary, 2009, Musée des Confluences, by Cesar Galindo; filmed during *Paroles autochtones* (Indigenous words), an event organised by the Musée des Confluences in Lyon in collaboration with the UN Human Rights High Commission and Survival International France.

of a space, a topos that is going to concatenate them'. It's all about the emerging of a chaosmosis, just as Guattari was saying.[48]

Guattari would have enjoyed a discussion with Lance about his practice of healing and his cosmovision of parrallel glass walls as invisible folds in places. In my understanding, Guattari's method can be distinguished from those of Gregory Bateson by way of at least two essential points: in relation to memory and the unconscious – which for Guattari were at work in the concepts he created and shared with Deleuze regarding the virtual and the actual as well as the refrain; and, on the other hand, in the ambiguous notion of the subject. Bateson criticises psychoanalysis for its entropic energetic paradigm and proposes to replace it with the systemic and the possibility of negentropy as the creative attitude of the patient in his or her interaction with the analyst. For Bateson, healing is posited as a question of 'communication', most notably in relation to the schizophrenics that he assists. In 1980, in an exposé, 'Men are Grass', Bateson (1991) will state the following about his theory of communication: 'A theory of organisation would perhaps be a better way to put it, or perhaps an even better way would be a theory or resonance.' However, for Guattari, communication is not the primary concern with regard to the cure and any other form of apprehension of relations. It is expression not representation, but self-referential emergence, the possibility of enaction.

> From a Deleuze-Guattarian perspective, it would be better to say that the actual content of expression – what effectively comes to be signified, manifested, designated; its 'object' – emerges from expressive potential through a process of the capture of that potential, and that this emergence into being-determinate necessarily crosses a zone of systemic indeterminacy by virtue of which the whole affair is tinged with a passing element of chance. (Massumi 2002b: 12)

Guattari indeed was attracted to the practical and conceptual method of Fernand Deligny, whose work with autistic children who did not speak at all called into question the notion of the subject and focused its attention more on the concept of the network and the 'us' (nous) of the common created by neither one or the other, but rather a multitude of the 'slightest of gestures', hence Deligny's maps, by avoiding speech and any direct communication with the children. As

---

[48] Translated by the author: http://strassdelaphilosophie.blogspot.com/2012/09/plurivers-et-modalites-dexistence.html#!

the film, *Ce gamin, là* shows, this practice allowed for the children to transform themselves so as to grasp the world and its traces somewhat, allowing for what appears to be a certain joy for life. The year after Guattari's death in 1992, Deleuze published a volume of essays, *Essays Critical and Clinical* ([1993] 1997). Chapter 9 of this volume was entitled 'What Children Say' and discussed the autistic children who lived in the Cévennes region of France under the care of non-specialised volunteer adults who Deligny called 'close presences' (*présences proches*) and who were the ones responsible for making the maps of the children's trajectories. Deleuze reflects on these maps which Deligny called 'wander lines' (*lignes d'erres*) and relates them to the Australian totemic cartographies by citing one of my books:

> The libido does not undergo metamorphoses, but follows world historical trajectories. From this point of view, it does not seem that the real and the imaginary form a pertinent distinction. A real voyage, by itself, lacks the force necessary to be reflected in the imagination; the imaginary voyage, by itself, does not have the force, as Proust says, to be verified in the real. This is why the imaginary and the real must be, rather, like two juxtaposable or superimposable parts of a single trajectory, two faces that ceaselessly interchange with one another, a mobile mirror. Thus the Australian Aborigines link nomadic itineraries to dream voyages, which together compose 'an interstitching of routes,' 'in an immense cut-out [découpe] of space and time that must be read like a map'.[49]
>
> At the limit, the imaginary is a virtual image that is interfused with the real object, and vice versa, thereby constituting a crystal of the unconscious. It is not enough for the real object or the real landscape to evoke similar or related images; it must disengage its own virtual image at the same time that the latter, as an imaginary landscape, makes its entry into the real, following a circuit where each of the two terms pursues the other, is interchanged with the other. 'Vision' is the product of this doubling or splitting in two, this coalescence. It is in such crystals of the unconscious that the trajectories of the libido are made visible.
>
> A cartographic conception is very distinct from the archaeological conception of psychoanalysis (...) from one map to the next, it is not a matter of searching for an origin, but of evaluating displacements. Every map is a redistribution of impasses and breakthroughs, of thresholds and enclosures, which necessarily go from bottom to top. There is not only a reversal of directions, but also a difference in nature: the unconscious no longer

---

[49] Deleuze ([1993] 1997: 61–7); his note 7 (p. 63) refers the quotes to Barbara Glowczewski, *Du Rêve à la Loi chez les Aborigènes* (1991: chapter 1).

deals with persons and objects, but with trajectories and becomings; it is no longer an unconscious of commemoration but one of mobilization, an unconscious whose objects take flight rather than remaining buried in the ground. In this regard, Felix Guattari has defined a schizoanalysis that opposes itself to psychoanalysis. (Deleuze [1993]1997: 62–3)

As much in his common works with Deleuze as in his own writings and practice as an analyst, Guattari distanced himself from Bateson's systemic approach of ecology which he felt to be too closed off, too structuralist, but also too culturalist and behaviouralist. Guattari shared a complicity – animated with heated discussions – with Mony Elkaïm, a Belgian neuropsychiatrist, who, in his family therapy sessions, provoked situations that would propel the actors outside of their enclosure of the double bind of the familial system denounced by Bateson (1972): his method, summarised in *Si tu m'aimes, ne m'aimes pas* (If you like me, don't like me) (1989), renewed interest in systemic therapy by inspiring systems outside of Prigogine's equilibrium, the second wave cybernetics of H. von Foerster or Varela's concept of enaction.

Guattari thought of feedback or self-reference not as a metaphor but, on the contrary, as an action of conscious and unconscious effects and affects of a subjectivation which dissolves within the process, the actualisation of an existential territory, and the deterritorialisation by revirtualisation of a new possible, what he called incorporeal universes of values or refrains. The Warlpiri attracted his interest specifically for the non-metaphorical 'traces' of the Dreamings – materialised by way of the singular sites found throughout the landscape. As we have seen, the rhizome of the Australian Dreaming paths is not a metaphor but a real image of the becoming-yam, which, for the Indigenous Australians, is one form of totemic becoming among others, directly linked to their painting-maps, their repeated gestures and their songs. In the same way as Deleuze and Guattari took their inspiration from birds in order to describe the concept of the refrain as 'any aggregate of matters of expression that draws a territory and develops into territorial motifs and landscapes',[50] the Warlpiri also rely on a multitude of visual and sonic rhythms that turn into painted, sung and danced ritual matters of expression that mark the territories that connect them with the sacred site that they are attempting to define in the name of the well-being of the land and everything that lives

---

[50] Deleuze and Guattari ([1987] 1997: 323); see also Genosko (2002a, 2002b).

there. Interestingly, ethnoastronomy has recently helped to confirm the striking correlations between a series of birds, the dingo, a thorny lizard, a spider and the stars that some Aboriginal groups used to connect with each of them at the beginning of the twentieth century: they have shown that more or less over a period of six weeks the movement of a specific star corresponds to the time when the related bird lays eggs or other animals breed. Signs in the sky were thus used as a calendar for the earth. Today, seasonal indications that connect some birds to stars and some animals to specific plants are being disturbed by the ongoing transformation of the climate. Now more than ever it is wise to listen to Guattari's 'Ecosophical Practices and the Restoration of the 'Subjective City'' for what I call becoming land: 'In this situation, new transcultural, transnational, and transversal earths and universes of value may be formed, unencumbered by the fascination of territorialized power, that can be separated from the outcomes of the current planetary impasse' (Guattari [1993] 2015: 98).

Indeed, since the climate change alert has shaken the planet, especially after the COP21 Paris agreement to reduce emissions, 'new transcultural, transnational and transversal earths and universes of value' have been spreading in various forms. Some, like the struggles against extractivism, advocate to completely change our way of life by stopping the extraction of fossil energies (minerals, petrol, coal, gas by fracking, etc). Ecoactivists, especially women, also struggle against the destruction of the land by so-called renewable energies such as dams, wind farms or underocean gas fields. The struggles of Indigenous people whose food resources and way of life are destroyed by all this industrial predation meet with the claims of other actors of the civil society. As expressed in France by the occupation of 1650 ha of agricultural land and hedgerow (*bocage*) at Notre-Dame-des-Landes, the expelled peasants and new squatters opposed the construction of an airport to fight 'against the airport and its world', that is the acceleration of a worldwide neoliberal economic model that destroys the planet. The airport project was abandoned in February 2018 but, in April 2018, 2,500 policemen were sent to Notre-Dame-des-Landes to evacuate the 200 squatters who since 2012 have been building an alternative life there with annual gatherings for discussions of up to 50,000 people (Mauvaise Troupe Collective 2018). The inhabitants were strongly impacted by the violence of the weapons used by the military police to destroy thirty wooden houses. Despite this destruction they resisted, and some 150 people continue to occupy and work the land, in squatted farms, self-constructed cabins and caravans, looking after cows and sheeps, growing medicinal plants, with two bakeries, a carpentry, various crafts and a library. They hosted two large forums of discussions during the Intergalactic Week in August 2018 and the Common Lands weekend in September 2018, and continue to negotiate innovative land agreements with the support of many people across France and overseas.[51] This ZAD (zone to defend) has spread across France into many other ZAD.

Some authors in settler studies are very cautious of:

> the ways in which Deleuze's (and Guattari's) work has, in many instances, reproduced notions of the frontier or 'rhizomatic West' that erases Indigenous presence and reifies mythic tropes of the so-called 'Great American West'. As Alex Young [2013] writes: Deleuze and Guattari's conception of the rhizomatic West risks reproducing a discourse whereby an account of liberation is imagined at the expense of the indigenous peoples or whom settler colonial deterritorializations constitute a coercive expression of sovereign power rather than an escape from it. (123) [...] While we find Deleuze's articulation useful in its diagnosis of the way the digital may operate today, we are less influenced by his articulations of radical alternatives. (Hunt and Stevenson 2016)

Such critiques could be addressed at the way some people in current colonial situations pretend to use Deleuze and Guattari, for instance the Israeli Army against Palestinians.[52] But Deleuze, like Guattari, was supportive of Palestinians or other dispossessed people.[53] Many Deleuzian thinkers continue to follow suit, including a recent call by *Deleuze Studies* to boycott a Deleuze conference in Israel. Such positions feed other debates about reversed racism, with Deleuze accused of antisemitism (Gleyzon 2015). On the other hand, there have been discussions in France about the environmental social movements and ecoactivism involving mostly White people and not addressing directly issues of racial discrimination. Such a vision forgets the struggle of people colonised by France, from Africa or Asia, Polynesians who fought against nuclear testing,[54] Kanaks in New Caledonia who

---

[51] For comments on both events and also updates as to what happened next, see: https://zadforever.blog/. See also: https://zad.nadir.org/?lang=en (accessed in October 2018); and also see the monthly magazine zadibao.org: https://zadibao.net

[52] See http://www.metamute.org/editorial/articles/art-war-deleuze-guattari-debord-and-israeli-defence-force

[53] Deleuze et al. (1998).

[54] On 2 October 2018, Oscar Temaru, French Polynesian Ma'ohi autonomist and candidate for the presidency, deposited a complaint to the International

Figure 1.4 Three stages of the Yam rhizome Dreaming. Perilpa Nakamarra, Rosy Napurrurla and Lady Nakamarra © B. G. (1984)

try to oppose mining and Native Americans in French Guiana who fight to protect the Amazonian against industrial as well as mafia goldmining. Not all Indigenous people in any country threatened by destruction are militantly against mining. Neverthlesss, the various 'missing people' of today, everywhere in the world, are trying to converge their heterogeneous struggles. New local and transnational alliances emerge between many Indigenous peoples, migrants and African-Americans or Afropeans, descendants of colonisation in Africa or the slavery traffic diaspora and others.

Against the fatality of a homogenous universe which would be predetermined by the global effect of capitalism, many Indigenous people and other collectives of people displaced or excluded who try to build alternatives seem to propose what Argentinian anthropologist Arturo Escobar calls a political pluriversality, the possibility for different worlds and cosmovisions to co-exist on the planet. The title of his 2014 book *Sentipensar con la terra* (Feeling-thinking with the Earth) puts forward an Indigenous Latin American concept[55] that has been guiding activists over decades to struggle against extractivism

---

Criminal Court (ICC/CPI in French) to accuse France of a crime against humanity because of its nuclear testings. See also: https://www.ctbto.org/nuclear-testing/the-effects-of-nuclear-testing/general-overview-of-theeffects-of-nuclear-testing/

[55] The concept *sentipensar* was introduced in academia in 1986 by Colombian researcher Orlando Fals Borda (2009) who promoted action-research practice in the 1970s. See also Cepeda (2017).

and other predations that destroy the land that they share with other non-human inhabitants. Referring to William James's plural universe and the astrophysicist's notion of pluriverse, Escobar calls for a political ontology inspired by an Indigenous concept and practice, an epistemological transformation where pluriversal studies will 'maybe have to walk along with these humans and non humans – with the Dreams of the Land, of peoples and social movements – who in a profound relationality, persist against all odds in imagining and weaving other worlds' (Escobar 2018: 36). In other words, radical alterity is not about exotism and exclusion but about imagination in terms of how to weave different worlds in respect of their singularities always in becoming, how to recreate outsidness in our minds. This is what I call indigenising anthropology.

PART I
The Indigenous Australian Experience of the Rhizome

2

Warlpiri Dreaming Spaces: 1983 and 1985 Seminars with Félix Guattari

Warlpiri Dreaming Spaces (1983)

Félix Guattari[1] — Barbara is an anthropologist specialising in Australian Aboriginal peoples who has written a fascinating piece of work about the dreaming process.[2] I'd like her to tell us a bit about the collective technology of dreams among the Australian Aboriginal people she has studied. In this context, not only do dreams not depend on individual keys, but they are also part of an a posteriori elaboration of the dream that anthropologists have characterised as mythical. But Barbara comes close to refuting that definition. And dreaming is identified with the law, and with the possibility of mapping the itineraries of these people, who circulate all the time since they cover hundreds of kilometers. Barbara, I would like to ask you to try to tell us how the dreaming method functions. My first question is to ask you to explain the relationship between dream, territory, and itinerary.

Barbara Glowczewski – I'll start from a language and translation problem. There are five hundred ethnic groups with different languages in Australia, each with a term that describes something that has been translated into English as *Dreaming*.[3] This word (*Jukurrpa*,

---

[1] Seminar discussion between F. Guattari and B. Glowczewski, 'Les Warlpiri. Espaces de Rêves. Exposé et discussion (18 January 1983)', in *Chimères*, no. 1, Paris: 1987, pp. 1–14. Translation by John Angell first published in Glowczewski (2015), *Totemic Becoming: Cosmopolitics of the Dreaming*, São Paulo: n-1 edições .

[2] Glowczewski (1981) 'Le Rêve et la terre. Rapports à l'espace et au temps chez les Wa(r)lpiri', PhD dissertation, University of Paris 7, 1982.

[3] The original French text contains the word 'dream' in English because the transcriber of the audio recording did not hear the '-ing' ending. French has no equivalent to the English progressive form – the *-ing* – that translates literally as 'dreaming'. The author uses a capital letter to distinguish dreams (*rêves*) from the Aboriginal cosmological concept of the Dreaming(s) (*Rêve/s*), which is also often written with a capital D.

in Warlpiri) corresponds to a mixture of things, referring simultaneously to a mythical time, to a series of itineraries on the ground that criss-cross Australia in a vast web, and also to the heroes (described by anthropologists as totemic) who are thought to have followed these itineraries in their travels. And it also corresponds to what anthrop gists call a totem, i.e., a power of identity stemming from these heroes, who may have taken various forms – human, animal, or plant – to travel throughout Australia and who have transmitted their totemic identity to the clans. So, that's what dreaming is about.

F. G. — When we were chatting a while ago, you said you were not describing an archaic conception of the relationship with dream, but that the notion remains totally contemporary and has even been adapted and transformed via a range of acculturation phenomena. When you were there with them, the people would ask you what you had dreamed in the morning, and it was really conceived as a laborious form of work. Can you try to explain that a little bit?

B. G. — Well actually, today, Aboriginal people refuse the English term *myth* (for their Dreaming stories). They do not accept the classical separation (and I would like to say Anglo-Saxon, because I think the French word *mythe* has a different connotation) between reality and something that would belong to the realm of appearances. Still, markers of difference do exist. A whole series of limits are at work, but the way the boundaries are drawn does not seem the same as our distinction between reality and dreams. But still, it depends on who is speaking.

Whites arrived in Australia two hundred years ago. In the area where I worked, contact took place around forty or fifty years ago, depending on the group, and Aboriginal peoples were forcibly sedentarised. We don't know very much about what happened at that time in Australia. The question of massacres did not come up like it did with Native Americans because of a fairly curious phenomenon – a lot of people just let themselves die. There was a more or less general consensus that they were lost anyway. They weren't traditional warriors, so the confrontations were not particularly violent, although there was fighting in certain areas. The entire period just slid invisibly into history.

The odd thing is that, in the 1960s, people said that Aboriginal people were going to completely disappear, and instead, since 1970 their numbers have grown. People wondered about this increase and how the culture stayed vibrant even though they were forced to lead a sedentary existence, whereas they were nomadic. One answer can be found in their specific vision of space and dreaming, which allows them to keep travelling even when they are sedentarised. Even though they have to stay in one place, they can continue to re-enact their celebrated travels thanks to their ceremonies, songs, and night dreams.

F. G. — And to literally manage the territories of the dream!

B. G. — Yes, and re-experience passages of their itineraries.

F. G. — We need to be specific: They manage territories that are at least two dimensional. Dancing, et cetera, 'mythical' territories, but also real territories in the sense that it is through their dreams that they re-actualise the fact that a given territory – a particular tree or object, or a particular configuration of the landscape – has its own particular function in the dream. And this is even more true because it crosses a series of segments of territory, and men and women do not have the same way of managing the territory.

Anne Querrien — I want to address a question about the notion of 'tracing' (*frayage*), a term often used in discussions about dreams. I am aware of two kinds of *frayage*. The first, in fact, is the dream. You encounter a space that is hostile in the real, you're frozen in fear, and the last thing you want to do is stay there. That said, this hostile space actually has a number of advantages: There are mirrors, cars, good things to eat, wealth, and so there is a dimension that is literally tempting. And in the dream you can enter this space, and little by little, by dint of years of dreaming, create a bridge using this modern space to which they have been forced to adapt. Then of course, there is dancing.

I had a crazy experience in Brittany one winter with children between twelve and eighteen the night of the Saint Sylvester's Day. The church had a nightclub that played reggae and punk and so on for the tourists between ten o'clock to midnight. After that, they played totally cool recordings of old French songs. As 'emigrants,'[4] we adore the old French songs! All the kids do a line dance to the recording. Then the tourists leave, except me, since I'm not a tourist. The recording is very well made because it gives the illusion that it is all coming to an end. And then, right when everybody thinks it's about to stop, the music stops, but the party keeps going and we play cassettes. It's very strange – the music is French, like Renaud.

---

[4] According to Anne Querrien, it is an insiders' joke for some Bretons to call themselves 'emigrants from Brittany', a region of France treated like a colony by the government, where children were punished in schools for using local languages, such as Breton.

At that time in my life, I was a good dancer of punk, Afro, et cetera, but the amazing thing is that they were doing a Breton folk dance! That's what was going on! We spent an absolutely crazy evening doing Breton folk dancing to punk music! It's a pairing that matches dance and music from two spaces that at first glance have nothing to do with each other. And up to that point, these kids had done Breton dancing only as folklore or for tourists in the summer. So it became a modern dance, perfectly dance-able to 'Renaud.' It kept going, and then at three in the morning, I used totally crazy thinking based on Einstein, Zen, and things like that to reinvent the oldest Breton dance-step, which involves hopping from one foot to the other non-stop, like a bouncing ball, for several hours. Because the actual principle of Breton dancing is that you don't stop for thirty-six hours (except for pauses to drink cider and eat *crêpes*) in order to compact the soil floor of a house ... So that was the night we reinvented Breton dancing. For me, dreaming and dancing both provide spaces for technology transfer. And it is these spaces that can allow a so-called 'archaic' culture to communicate with ours. These are 'tracing' or *frayage* spaces.

B. G. — When I was with the Warlpiri in 1979, I was lucky enough to attend an initiation cycle that was performed in a parallel way by men on one side and women on the other.[5] It had been going on for a month when I arrived and continued for another four months. The principle of this kind of cycle is that for two hours almost every day, and sometimes all night, the itineraries of the totemic ancestors who are being celebrated are performed. What I am saying is that we re-travelled hundreds of kilometers in small sequences, a straight itinerary over a five-month period, but gradually; as you advance, it unfolds as a series of sites that intersect with other itineraries that in turn involve other clans that are connected to the guardian-clan of the itinerary being celebrated, and every time, a new scene is played.

F. G. — And that's the moment in the series when they come in?

B. G. — At the time, a certain phase of the itinerary is scheduled for a particular evening. The dance area is essentially like this room, and each step you take is the equivalent of a giant step in the actual itinerary.

F. G. — That kind of tends to confirm what Jean-Claude was saying – recounting the dream using a scenario – because it's ultimately a staging technique.

---

[5] In camps separated by gender.

B. G. — I was also thinking of something else related to this question of hostility in the city that attracts. Maybe it's also the ambiguity of what they call the secret, sacred sites that explains something about the fact that they could not return to their sites for two generations because they were locked up on reservations and not permitted to travel. Ultimately, even prior to contact with Whites, access to their part of the earth was not completely unrestricted; there were places you didn't go, or where you would only go as an exception. So this exceptional, emotional ambiance could be re-enacted in a sedentary space, particularly because those specific sites have become dream places. Regular, physical contact is very important, and that was the first thing the Aboriginal Australians did at different periods. In 1967, a referendum recognising them as citizens[6] was passed that gave them back the right to travel around like everyone else.

x_1 — And what was their status up to that time?

B. G. — They had no status before then. And in 1967 the Warlpiri settled down in their country again, and the first thing they did was to touch the ground, the stones, and the trees in the places that corresponded to their ancestors' sites. There are thousands of similar sites in Australia. You have to picture it as resembling a web of networks with all these little nodes on it. So the contact is important and, as I was saying a little while ago, if it's an effort when we dream at night and we wake up tired, a strong dream is in fact also experienced like a real voyage during which you have touched the time and space of the dream-land (of the Dreamings).

Jean-Claude Polack — Do the Aboriginal people all live a long way from the ocean?

B. G. — There are places in the North and West where they live near the coast. But an extremely confused controversy developed about that, as always in anthropology. In fact, there is a tendency to argue that Europeans were able to colonise the south-east coast because there were no Aboriginal people in the area. And other people have reacted by saying that it was obvious that when they (the Aboriginal people) saw Europeans arriving, they ran away and didn't want to have anything to do with them. In fact, though, there

---

[6] In fact, the referendum entailed counting all Aboriginal people as Australians in the census; some Aboriginal people already possessed citizenship at the time, but many others had no rights.

were massacres.[7] There were numerous attempted exchanges. Which is also fairly interesting, because it continues to be relevant. It's an idea of a symbolic exchange, in a way. In fact, they feel their culture so strongly today that they can assimilate things from Western technology, and they consider that it's their due, because the fact that they exist means giving something to the Whites, while also keeping secret what has to stay secret. As the Aboriginal people see it, it's an exchange: 'If you agree that an entire part of our knowledge remains secret.' There are two irreducible zones, and that's how the exchange is possible.

So, to go back to the question of the ocean, some anthropologists have said they ran away. And after that, a third anthropological wave, rather than justifying the absence of Aboriginal people as a reaction to colonisation, said that there was a life choice to make, they had to walk, and water couldn't be there, next to them.

A number of relatively recent anthropological studies have shown that even in desert areas, hunter-gatherer societies that do not practice agriculture spend less time working to feed themselves than sedentary societies. That's also one of the theories that allow certain researchers to argue that living by the sea was perhaps ultimately an exception. But why were you thinking about that?

J.-C. P. — I just wanted to know if there was an idea of a limit, an external limit, for example, in the cartographies of dreaming or dancing.

B. G. — I think it's not all on just one level. There's overlap between 'it's a long way away' and 'it's here,' and between past and present. An endless back-and-forth between time and space that is explicitly referred to; the sites are caves, and when they plant sticks into the ground in a dancing area (I'm referring to the women here, because the men use different objects), it is said that the two sticks connect two points underground, forming a circle beneath. So I don't think it is perceived as a flat space.

J.-C. P. — But is there a limit somewhere?

---

[7] The new history movement in the 1980s and 1990s revealed violence, massacres and Aboriginal resistance that had been buried for decades. In the 2000s, a revisionist movement began to deny this history, but an excellent documentary series called *First Australians* (2008), produced for Australian Television, provided massive evidence of this hidden Aboriginal history (see Perkins et al. (2009)). The seven episodes of the series are accessible online at: http://www.sbs.com.au/firstaustralians/

Warlpiri Dreaming Spaces with Guattari

B. G. — It is full of limits! But they're not in close proximity. They discuss a separation endlessly. It starts with initiation, when an individual is separated from his or her mother ...

F. G. — There is something I want to remind you about on this subject that I thought seemed extraordinary – the fact that there is no numbering system beyond the number two. That must totally reconfigure the idea of limits from top to bottom, and of the difference between time and space. In effect, once you don't have a numerical system for recording information (which seems to me a theorem in need of examples) ... if I understood correctly, it is numbered 1, 2, and then several. So that's a technique for totally altering how we keep track of coordinates. I mean it already simplifies things a lot for Oedipus! [*Laughter*]

B. G. — On the other hand, there is a difference between the 'us' of two people and the several people's 'us.' And in fact, where the third party comes in, without being expressed explicitly, is in the difference, when I talk to somebody, between enunciating an *'us'* that includes *'you'* (the person I am speaking with) and another *'us'* with others (that excludes *'you,'* the person I am talking to). That's pretty important.

And about this question of borders, I just wanted to give an example of a territory that's about 600 kilometers from North to South and 200 from East to West that has a population of 3,000 people. There are about twenty or so territories defined by circles (see Figure 2.1), but in a completely simplified way in order to facilitate land claims. In truth, each bubble represented here is not a territory in its own right – it's always the same – it's part of a web, and you find ramifications of the bubble in a discontinuous way inside a different bubble. So the same group will have territorial rights over a web within a bubble and also a bit elsewhere, but most importantly it will have a site that establishes the link while also explaining the discontinuity. And the hero, for example, will have travelled underground at that moment.

x_2 — How does time work in dreams?

B. G. — Dreaming is the present, and it's also 'a long time ago.' For me, this present that is also a long time ago is not historical time but a time of metamorphosis. It is a dynamic time, but a time of transformation. So it's a time of the dynamics of transformation, but all of the roles and all of the forms of metamorphoses also exist in the present, except that everything changes form by changing places in this ultimate time of the present. And it's extremely dynamic – in fact, transformation is the main aspect related to the dreamings that is talked about.

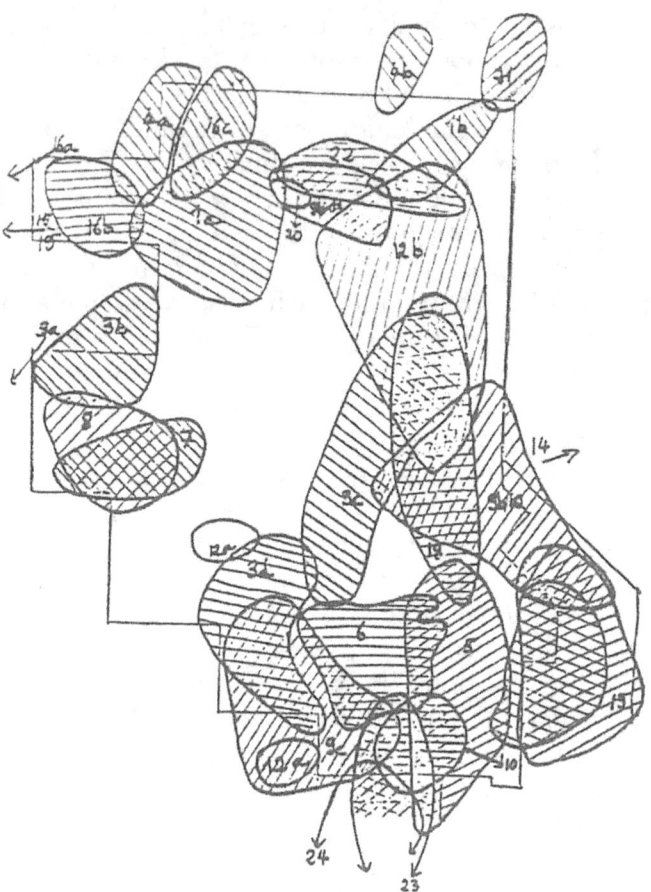

Figure 2.1 Map of Warlpiri land claim, 1978 © CLC, Alice Springs

J.-C. P. — But it's hard to express problems in terms of time, when we are actually dealing with the interplay of territorialities, which is highly spatialising compared to dancing.

B. G. — An Aboriginal person does not say that a territory belongs to him, but that he belongs to the territory.[8] So it isn't so much that a territory is occupied, since the land isn't there to be conquered. It gives meaning to people. It is dynamic and ever changing. It is not

---

[8] Land claims have officialised the legal status of claimants as 'traditional owners'; The Native Title Act 1993 (*Cwlth*) recognised 'Native Title' and invalidated the notion of '*Terra nullius*', which defined the colonisation of Australia as the occupation of a land that belonged to nobody: www.nntt.gov.au/Information-about-native-title/Pages/The-Native-Title-Act.aspx

Warlpiri Dreaming Spaces with Guattari

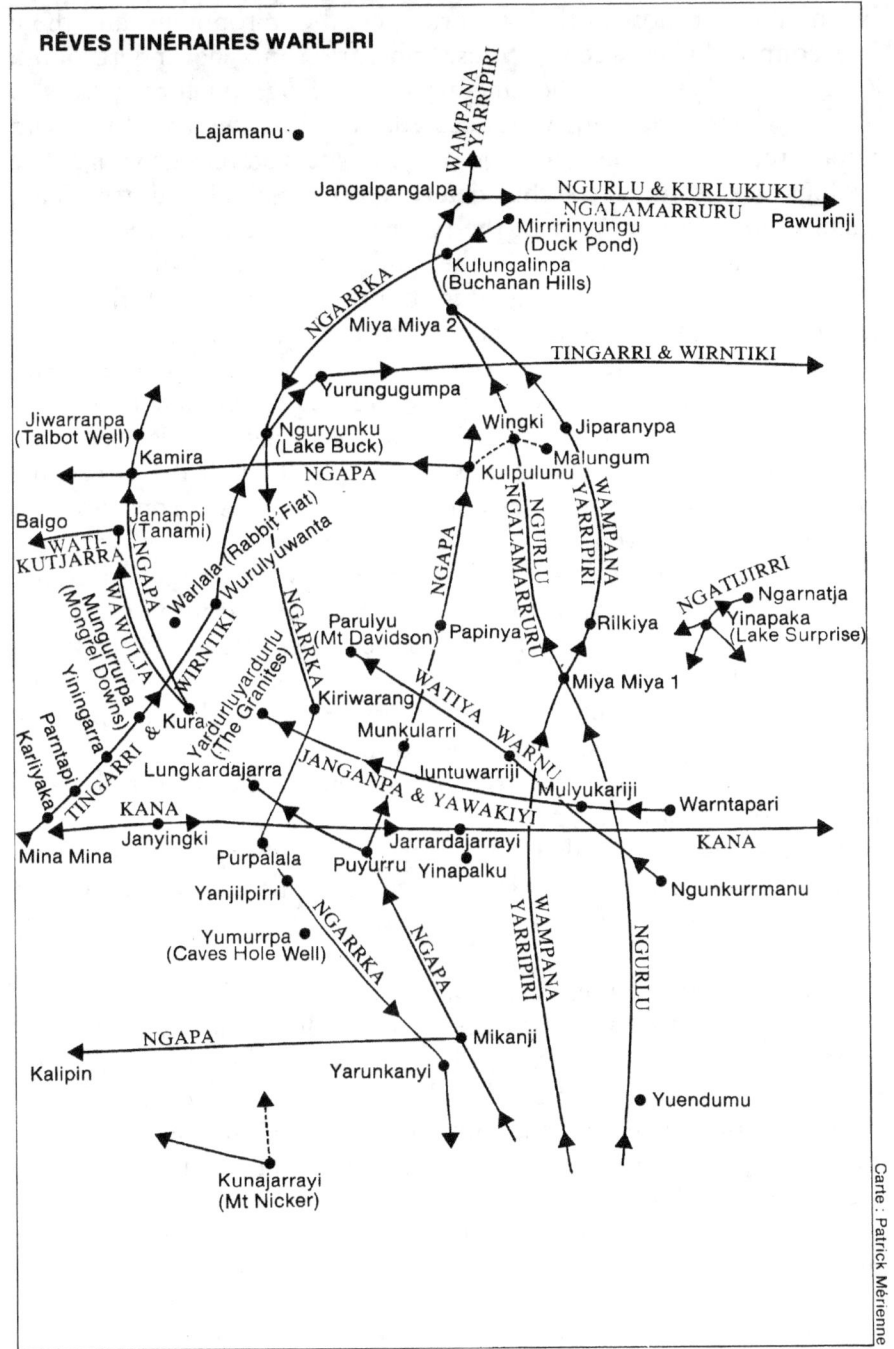

Figure 2.2 Map of some Warlpiri Dreaming lines © B. G. (1991b)

by chance that most of the sites are mineral outcroppings, and there is a connection between all these itineraries and the underground. And also, for example, the itinerary of the kangaroo corresponds to a zone where kangaroos were located, and the itinerary of the wild potato refers to a zone where there were wild potatoes growing. The ecology of this landscape thus determines its general outlines. Then, small events become part of the record from one generation to the next – a hunter goes a little further and finds a place where nobody has been; he comes back and talks about it, and people go there and it gets dreamt about, and somebody in the next generation decides that some child's life force came from that place; and the dream made by one of the child's relatives will determine that that space corresponds to a particular plant or animal species. In this way, there is a multiplication of plants and animals, and small deeds become grafted onto other itineraries and gradually, across generations, it has shifted; you even see the same phenomenon today, meaning that contacts with Whites (and life is riddled with contacts) that are dreamt, interpreted by the groups, and reintegrated into an existing itinerary. And that is how things change. Now what I do not know is what makes it so that something that happens to someone in one generation is retransmitted to the next generation and passes into the dream memory of subsequent generations.

J.-C. P. — Tell me, this really is dream-work they're doing – they're not just storytellers?

B. G. — Everyone is also the storyteller of his/her clan's traditional dreamings and mythical stories. And there are healers, but they have a particular zone.

And the rest ...

F. G. — They are initiates? Non-initiates can ...?

B. G. — Yes, that's it, after a certain age. But what happens is that children become familiar with all of that when they are small. And since every morning people tell each other things, they see it. People tell each other their night dreams using words and their hands, a manual sign language, and by tracing signs in the sand. The word is given meaning like that in the air and ...

F. G. — You need to be specific about a very important point for us, if I may. It relates to the fact that there is a language of the hands that is as elaborate as a real language.

B. G. — So dreams are related using words, the hands, and tracings in the sand. It goes really fast. And children see that from a very young age. Ultimately, it seems like they understand what is traced

Warlpiri Dreaming Spaces with Guattari

in the sand more quickly than the words. So they learn this code quickly. It always resembles cartography, and all of the stories are travel narratives, so it's always – walk, stop, and sit there ...

F. G. — You said that time is conceived of only as the present. Does that mean that from the linguistic point of view, there is no future, no imperfect, no simple past? Does that have a bearing [on life in general – transl. note]?

B. G. — No, that's not it – people do say tomorrow, and they say yesterday ...

F. G. — And verbs? Are they all in the infinitive? How do they work?

B. G. — The forms are totally different ...

A. Q. — Like in Breton. To be doesn't exist, only becoming exists.

x_1 — Is there a notion of time?

B. G. — No, in most [Aboriginal Australian] languages. I have the impression that they refer to time-space in a single word. It doesn't mean privileging space, but that the two are inseparable. That does not mean it's static.

J.-C. P. — It's a way of referencing time that is possible only if using spatial coordinates.

B. G. — I was thinking that the time I spent there was in the middle of a ritual period, but up to 70 percent of every day was related to the Dreamings (dancing, singing ...). And there is something that may be a far more generalised phenomenon, a detachment, that sets in once basic tasks such as finding something to eat and that kind of thing have been taken care of. Going hunting is not the main thing anymore. Of course, they also dream about daily life. I had the impression when I was in the camp that even when there weren't any ceremonies, there was a way of walking, of moving in the zones (to prepare food or a place to sleep ...) as if the people were spaced out, like they had taken acid. Now, it's difficult to know where that effect comes from. Is it sedentarisation? Has it always been this way? I don't know. I was there in 1979. But there's a blend of serenity and total apathy and then, all of a sudden, there's this absolutely extraordinary burst of energy during the ceremonies. In fact, you really have the impression of being in another place and time. I mean, maybe it's subjective ...

J.-C. P. — The work of the dream is to endlessly re-nomadise, to endlessly smooth something out that had a tendency to become striated.

F. G. — Well, if I have understood correctly, it is a re-actualisation, in the sense that Barbara explains in her thesis; there are drought zones that mean that nobody can go to certain places, or else, because of the fact that several tribes find themselves together, or ethnic groups, in the same places. In that case, they have to redefine what the dream territory is. Or, as you were saying a while ago, the definition, a child's essence, will be one of these territories that he is attributed to.

B. G. — There's something I haven't described in detail yet, which is that a child is not truly considered the product of his parents. A woman does not become pregnant because of sexual relations, but because she is penetrated by a spirit-child. There was a whole controversy about that in anthropology and about whether the Aboriginal people knew or did not know how children are made! And now more people say they know. But that's part of the secret. It's something men talk about among themselves, and women among themselves, but it's not something that circulates. Meaning children never hear about it, since it is only spoken of in ceremonial spaces where children are not present. And then it is said that the father, the mother's husband, provides the child with his vital force, but only after the child has been conceived. And, although it is no longer done now but was still practiced fifty years ago, a woman had to have sexual relations with other men so the baby could have more life force, because the father's was not enough.

But what's really significant is that beyond the level of the discourse surrounding the ceremonies, these things are unimportant. In fact, it made them laugh when Whites living in the region said that Aboriginal people didn't know how babies were made. Which is fairly interesting, because like on numerous other subjects, the Aboriginal people do not seem to feel they need to prove anything. I observed scenes in the city where people who are perfectly lucid when they were in the camps passed themselves off as stupid even though privately they were laughing, maybe as a way of keeping their relationship with Whites simple; if you have money, you give me some, you buy me a drink. It's 'I don't know anything.' They don't need to prove who or what they are to Whites, except for land claims, because since 1970 they definitely have to prove that a particular piece of land has been rightfully theirs for generations.

When you think about what is sacred and about religion, at least for me, there is a traditional stereotype, a visual cliché, of something very serious, silent, and somber. But what is really extraordinary is that there is something very powerful during sacred activities, an emotion at the limit of pathos or tragedy. The people are often crying due to particular emotions or contact with an ancestor, but there are also children shouting, dogs barking, people preparing food, laughing, voicing obscenities, all completely blended together. There is a playful quality, but it is play to the bitter end, like in a movie ...

F. G. — In fact, everything is so obvious, there is such widespread sacredness, that there is no need to lay it on too thick, or wear a chasuble, or create some obscure practice. In Africa, I attended a N'Döp ceremony,[9] and it was a little like that at the moment of the sacrifice.

J.-C. P. — I want to know whether what you're saying is totally true, I mean, whether there isn't an increase in things that makes it so that at any given moment, all this agitation is interpreted as a kind of momentary wrinkle in the process. It's like Indian ceremonies, with this music.

B. G. — Well, following up on what you're saying, I was thinking of ... this continuous/discontinuous question. Something has an effect on a small scale, and the same thing on a large scale exerts precisely the opposite effect. Somewhere, there's a discontinuity, but we don't know where it is. On this subject, I'm going to tell you a typical awkward ethnographer's anecdote. Early in my stay, I heard a woman singing one day, and I approached her and said, 'That is so beautiful!' She didn't answer. Some time later, I heard the same song – it wasn't really a song, but something more like a modulated voice – coming from different places in the camp; after that, it went higher and higher, increasing in volume, and it became extremely disquieting. In fact, this song is what people do when they're in mourning, and when the entire camp started doing it, it was totally unbearable ...

---

[9] According to his son, Bruno, in a personal communication with Anne Querrien, Guattari went to Senegal in 1967. He may have attended a N'Döp ceremony as part of his therapeutic experiences at the Fann Psychiatric Hospital in Dakar. The ceremony is described as follows: 'More specifically focused on managing psychiatric disorders, the N'Döp ceremony conducted by Michel Meignant and András Zempleni was intended to show practioners that traditional trance-based rituals should be considered authentic therapeutic approaches that mobilise the social group, making it possible simultaneously to treat the patient and to reinsert them, restoring their place in the community. This second film had even more impact on the profession, because it was focused on the late, much-missed Professor Henri Collomb, Chief of the Neuropsychiatry Department at the Fann Hospital in Dakar. Financed and produced by Sandoz Laboratories, the film was screened in psychiatric services, where it never failed to generate the same questions concerning the singular effectiveness of the treatment, its amazing complexity, and its esoteric character.' Available at: www.ethnopsychiatrie.net/ Pratiquer_1%27ethnopsychiatri.htm

But what's crazy is that the first time I heard it sung by a woman by herself, it seemed quite joyous to me, and in fact, if you break it down, it is a call to the dead and a kind of communication that connects an individual with a particular dead person, a space where people meet and find themselves. It's also a little sad, but above all, it is a successful communication event. So when the whole community turns into this whirl of sound, it is extraordinary. It's an example. What I mean is that these episodes of noise and agitation, with all of it happening at the same time, is perhaps also what sacredness feels like. And it's not like, you stop, you get serious – now it's sacred. But there comes a moment when the accumulation of the same element makes it so that you find yourself absolutely at the opposite extreme. It's as if a line stretched between two opposing poles is crossed ...

F. G. — Asymptote!

x_3 — How do the Aboriginal peoples go about naming each other?

B. G. — Kinship terminology also reflects this history of children with respect to their parents. As in most of these societies, a kinship system implies that you say 'mother' or 'father' to different people, even when you know who is supposed to be your real mother and her husband, and therefore your real father, since in theory he's the one who determines your heritage on a mythical itinerary. But it is so not because the father conceived the child, but because, in crossing the father's territory, the mother became penetrated by the life force of this territory, which is how the child received the life force that made his conception possible.

This type of itinerary, which anthropologists have called a *conception totem*, can be a plant or animal species... It's something the child will keep throughout his life, but it's just about the conception, nothing more, and it doesn't necessarily mean he has any rights over a territory. Although in fact it was usually arranged to coincide with a vaster territory that was the father's or the mother's and that, consequently, provided a new totem, which wasn't the same species but was associated with it. If the mother conceived her child on another territory, he will have that conception totem, but if the father absolutely wants his child to enter his clan, he can transfer the rights to a territory to him at the time of his initiation. In this case, you have two totems. In fact, there are even more, because the child can have a totem from his mother and in addition be adopted by another group.

What is also interesting is that it's not the mother or the husband who determines the conception site – a relative dreams it. So that's the strategy, and you enter into tribal and kinship systems that mean that someone from outside the couple determines where the child was conceived (the location at which the spirit entered the mother and the identity of the spirit), and therefore whom within his generation the child will share rights with. Since they are sedentarised, the conception totem is the one associated with the place where they are settled. But in earlier generations, somebody in the community would wake up one morning and say, 'I know where she conceived her future child ...' It can be linked to the fact that she ate something found only in a particular region, or for example, coming home from the day when she ate that thing, and she was sick the next day. Then everything works backwards from that.

The name of the clan totem coincides with a system of classificatory kinship that defines eight subsections or *skin-names*. Everybody has one of these eight names, and that's what establishes that particular kinship. But it is not given freely to the child; it's a deduction that means that someone from a subsection can only marry someone from one of the seven other subsections. So the child bears a third subsectional name that is the result of the conjunction of the two. That is always determined. So what happens when a couple gets married and aren't in the right subsections? Traditionally, it was only the mother's subsection that counted, meaning that all acted as if she had married a man from the appropriate subsection, and the child bore the correct name. Today, it's the opposite, because in recent years it has been considered urgent to keep the clan territorialised because of land claims, and also because there are more and more marriages that don't respect the subsections. So it's the father's subsection that determines the child's. The term 'no name' (*kumanjayi*) is used when somebody dies and everything associated with the deceased first name is banned from being pronounced for a minimum of a year. You can refer to the name with gestures, but nothing related to it can be uttered. That is how the language became richer. In fact, these names always correspond to plants or animals or other things, and that eliminates a whole cluster of words. So these are replaced by the expression 'no name' or another term, but the taboo word can come back with the next generation.

x_3 — That's how it is with Inuit people.

B. G. — When I arrived there, someone named Francis had just died, so I couldn't say 'France' because it sounded the same. The fact that it's not the same questions that are asked by different generations of ethnographers, even though basically the materials are the same (even more four generations ago), it's because maybe you're not aware here that you see those things, but I think that if you can see them somewhere else, that means in fact that you felt you saw them here. If you see those things in other societies, it means we have the possibility of seeing them here, which functions a little like a reflection.

x_1 — And these interlocking territories, do they sometimes have a city in the middle?

B. G. — The itineraries used to go all over Australia, but now there are cities ...

F. G. — Sometimes there are trash piles, Coca-Cola bottles ... but the itinerary goes over them without any problem.

B. G. — In any case, these itineraries are invisible to us.

x_1 — An important place now is I don't know where ...

B. G. — An important place, that's exactly what is so terrible, that becomes more and more difficult in fact, and I wonder how things are going to be in the future, since there are mineral deposits on sacred sites and real struggles. The curious thing is that a legalistic obsession in Australia allows a zone for the recognition of rights. Since 1976, when Aboriginal peoples were allowed to legally show that their painted boards are like identity cards and geographical maps, they have been recognised by the courts as representing legitimate claims to particular sites. That happened in 1976 at the federal level, and now the authorities do everything they can to reverse directions. Which is fairly easy to do, because the states' legal systems [Australia is a federation of seven states] do not recognise this Act [which applied to the Northern Territory].[10] Which does not prevent the federal government from having the right to question legislation passed by the states. Which has produced interminable trials. That is how it went with uranium mining in Australia. They took ten years to discuss it before beginning to do it, although they might just as well have begun ten years earlier because of this kind of legalistic blockage. In the long run, the Aboriginal people are not at all happy with the results, and they believe they have lost. But after all, they did gain ten years!

And that's the way everything goes. It even becomes absurd, because most mining companies are multinational corporations. And some people get discouraged and are ready to abandon the

---

[10] Aboriginal Land Rights (Northern Territory) Act 1976, available at: www.austlii.edu.au/au/legis/cth/consol_act/ alrta1976444

project, and it's the government that tries to move forward quickly and pushes them. When I came back in 1980, there was a nation-wide protest movement on the front pages for about a month. Aboriginal peoples from every region were protesting in support of a small community of five hundred inhabitants at Noonkanbah, and even Whites participated in marches in every city. Priests got arrested, and there seemed to be a broad consensus, but the problem was oil and a company named Amax. And Amax was leaving, ready to leave, and the government of Western Australia and the miners' and transporters' unions boycotted transportation of the equipment. The government wanted to show its power, so it hired people as a special brigade of a kind of mercenaries to escort convoys of enormous trucks. People were posted along the road everywhere in the desert to try to stop them. They cruised along in huge convoys of about twenty trucks like a sort of freight train. Once they arrived, the Aboriginal people painted themselves and blocked the entrance to the community. And they didn't dare push them out of the way. As a result, after a while things became increasingly tense, and the government passed some laws and arrested a lot of people and started drilling. But the most recent reports say that they had totally overestimated the deposit and that it was not close to worth it! [*Laughter*]

A. Q. — The Aboriginal people tolerate people exploiting certain sites?

B. G. — In general, they share a certain philosophical intransigence that proscribes touching the earth. But some communities accept it on condition that they receive financial compensation for mining activities.

Warlpiri Dreaming Spaces (1985)

Barbara Glowczewski[11] — I have given examples of animal, bird, and plant Dreamings (*Jukurrpa*), along with mythical Dreaming stories of phenomena like water, fire, and the stars, of objects like digging sticks and initiation poles as well as Dreaming roles, like Initiated men, Single women, and Invincible, the incestuous patriarch.

---

[11] Second seminar discussion between F. Guattari and B. Glowczewski, 'Les Warlpiri. Espaces de Rêves. Exposé et discussion (26 February 1985)', in *Chimères*, no. 1, op. cit., pp. 15–28. Translated by John Angell for *Totemic Becomings* (Glowczewski 2015). Thanks to a grant from the Laboratory of Social Anthropology.

In fact, everything in nature and culture has its Dreaming, but not every Dreaming element is actualised in the same way. Only about a hundred elements are used to identify the approximately forty Warlpiri clans. They correspond to very long invisible trails or itineraries that can extend for several hundred kilometers, crossing the territory of the clans that carry the corresponding name. The other elements of a Dreaming form a kind of reservoir, which is the point at which sleeping dreams become relevant. They can draw on this reservoir to provide a new child who is going to be born with an individual identity. This transpires as follows: The conception of every child is announced by a dream experienced by the mother, the father, or another relative. The dream indicates the site where the mother was penetrated by a spirit-child, the pre-condition for making a child. The dream also indicates which specific element of the site provides the spirit-child's identity. It is possible to dream that the child was conceived on the father's land, in which case the child is the incarnation of his clan's Dreaming. But they usually dream that the child is the incarnation of a different Dreaming. This other dreaming, i.e., the element that identifies it, can sometimes be the one that gives another clan its identity, in which case, as the child grows up he or she will have individual rights to the territory and rituals corresponding to that clan, which is not his birth clan. But it is also possible to dream that the child's dream-element doesn't correspond to any particular clan but comes instead from the reservoir of plants, animals, and objects not already celebrated by the clans.

A child who receives this kind of Dreaming has options: If his or her clan is too big, in the past, instead of staying in the father's territory as is customary, he or she establishes his/her own clan based on this new Dreaming. In a sense, this could be perceived as a new creation, but the Warlpiri just perceive it as the reactivation of the Dreaming memory, because the dream-element that the new clan is based on was always part of the dream reservoir and thus present in the environment. The only thing human beings did was to remember the dream-element and bring it into being by connecting it to existing, well-known itineraries.

This is why it's important to emphasise that the notions of Dreaming and of a Dreaming's ancestors – of Dreamtime – do not just refer to the distant, original past. Instead, it is a time-space that simultaneously encompasses the present, the past, and the future, and in which every possible combination of the elements of existence is stored. There is no notion of new elements, because every element already exists even before it has taken shape, as each element is itself a composite of other elements. In other words, the dreaming includes everything that is possible; it has no specifiable beginning point or ending point. It is the condition of life and of every transformation.

Any element can be a dreaming, but that element is also connected to other elements, and together they form what I call a constellation. For example, the Sand Dreaming is connected to the Dreamings of honey, bees, green parrots, and owls. Why? Because the myth – what we call the myth, but the Warlpiri call a Dreaming – recounts that the sand dunes were formed at the Dreaming sites when honey was flowing in the trees and under the ground and the bees carried it to another land, and the owls, birds of the night, and the green parrots, and the daytime birds, were the witnesses. The story is far too long and complicated to relate in detail here.[12]

So every Dreaming constellation is said to have sown the earth with first names. And these names are the spirit-children – the dream children – who are reincarnated from one human generation to the next. But an individual is not just the result of the incarnation of a spirit-child. If he remains alive, it is because he is the recipient of the life force of his clan's Dreaming, in other words, of a force transmitted from mother to daughter. The same Dreaming constellation – the clan's Dreamings – is always transmitted from father to son; they are therefore always the same names. Because of the obligation to marry outside of one's clan, the wife's dreaming constellation is always different. What is handed down from mother to daughter results from the fusion of the mother and father's Dreamings; they are therefore combinations of different dreamings from generation to generation. Which is why this force has no name.

But even all of this is not sufficient to make a full human being because the spirit-energy is still missing. Spirit-energy, which is a specific property of an individual, resembles our concept of the soul, and it resides in the individual's belly. It is this spirit that leaves the body to travel at night in the Dreaming. It is possible for it not ever to return to the body, in which case the individual will be sickly and extremely weak and therefore run-down like an electrical battery that he can die from it. If the spirit-energy returns, it can return to inhabit a different part of the body than the belly where it normally

---

[12] *Du Rêve à la Loi*, op. cit., pp. 329–32. Story by May Yiripanta Napaljarri; Warlpiri audio accessible at: www.odsas.net

resides. In this case, the individual is always in poor health, although a shaman can help.

When a person dies, these various vital elements become redistributed. The child-spirit returns to the site where it emerged to await reincarnation. The father's and the clan's life force are dissipated throughout the length of the itinerary of the clan's Dreaming, or rather the constellation of clan Dreamings. The nameless life force transmitted from mother to daughter must be conjured for funeral rites, and it circulates among the clans in the form of the dead person's hair and, after several years, returns to the mother's clan. The dead person's spirit-energy is carried away into the cosmos, beyond the Milky Way and the two galaxies, the Big and Small Magellanic Clouds, but only if the man or woman died of old age and not of illness or accident. If the cause of death was illness or accident, the spirit-energy behaves as if it was short-circuited and disappears; no one knows where it goes. Once these forces have departed, there is still not an empty void in the place of the dead person, however. An image rises from him or her – a shadow, a double, or a ghost – that is the image of the body emptied of every other element, and it arises from the dead person. It wanders and haunts people, appearing particularly in the dreams of the dead person's relatives while they are sleeping. This is the downside of memory. People go to great lengths to avoid invoking this image or even remembering it. No one in the tribe is allowed to pronounce dead people's names, and no one can sing their Dreaming-songs for two years; no one can return to their territory. But nothing can really be done to totally prevent the image from returning to haunt them.

This is a very important point, because it is in fact the only thing that humans create. Everything else comes from and goes back to the Dreamings. Once all of the elements of the Dreaming that combined to form the individual have decomposed, however, the dead person's image becomes an indivisible residue. The only difference between the Dreaming and life is that living people produce images of the dead that they reinsert into the Dreaming. Once the images are reinserted into the Dreaming, they become part of the limitless possible re-combinations. In summary, it is possible to assert that the Dreaming is responsible for making the possible, while humans are responsible for making the past. There is an essential point of discontinuity between the Dreaming and humans, however, based on the discontinuity implied by the transformations proper to the dream itself. This raises the problem of defining the concept of

Dreaming. If you imagine Dreaming as a space (a dreamscape) in which everything combines with everything else, it can be envisioned in a sense as a continuum. The Dreaming is also the myth, though, or rather the myths, meaning it is the sum of all of the stories that arrange the elements among themselves and that create order from the disorder of every possible combination. Such narrative sequences produce permanent discontinuities, because mankind is capable of making dreams that reveal narrative sequences that people had forgotten. These new sequences can be integrated into the corpus of myths, but only on condition that they are accepted by the group, which is by no means a given and which triggers all kinds of 'payback' as the Warlpiri and their neighbours call it. In a way, then, myths create order among the different elements. The question then is whether there is order or disorder among the myths. If one is looking for order, I think the structural process of isolating the poles and articulating the constellations among themselves is stimulating but ultimately is a highly sterile mental undertaking. It cannot be argued, though, that disorder reigns among the myths. The Warlpiri express very specific connections, either when several Dreaming myths cross paths at a single site, or when two Dreamings are connected via a third Dreaming. It would be pointless to inventory all of the connections, though – that isn't what preoccupies the Warlpiri. They do not try to attribute meaning to these connections, but on the contrary to experience them by making them non-signifying. This is the power of the rituals. Compositions between Dreamings are executed through dance, and what connects the Dreamings must not be said but lived by every individual and by the entire group. A man or woman, after years of ritual activity, can be unable to explain why a particular Dreaming is connected to another. It is not his or her concern, because it has become a part of the secret that is negotiated with age. The important thing in this process is not that the secret conceals a missing meaning but that, on the contrary, it is indispensible to have experienced the connections. A Warlpiri would say that what is important is to have lived the land in a different way but also in a way that can be aligned with others and within the body. Only then does the meaning find a receptacle, only on condition that the body exists can the meaning of the connection take shape, and only then can it become a revelation. And the body only exists through dancing and singing, and through being painted with the elements that transcend the senses.

Based on these observations, I thought it was necessary to build a model in which the organisation of the myths and the rituals was un-dissociated and that would be articulated around what I will call cores, a kind of black hole that represents the absence of meaning, the condition of existence and of meaning. This model would be used to analyse not only myths between themselves but also the elements that compose every myth. Because beyond signifying interpretations of why a particular element is part of a constellation of Dreamings, there is the same phenomenon of gravitation around a core, where in order for the magic of the story to work, you have to *not* look for meaning.

We had a discussion with Félix to prepare this presentation, so I'm going to read what Félix said in relation to what I was just explaining, unless he would rather tell you himself!

Félix Guattari — What is this core that you see as traversing all of these ritual modifications, body tracings, and so on? Is it another structuralist key?

B. G. — First, there is not just one core – there are several – and I was also talking about axes or lines. I perceive them to resemble black holes, as though all of mythology were a sky, a cosmos that is beyond our galaxy, and the myths form inter-connected galaxies among themselves. Every core or axis forms a black hole because it's something that exists, and there are forms around but it cannot be named. In order to continue to exist without being named, it would have to remain unchanged and not be able to metamorphose; it has no shape. Concretely, inside the group this corresponds to a secret that must always be transmitted in the same way. What is important, the only meaning of this thing, is that it remains unchanged, even though everything else shifts.

F. G. — In your earlier talk you clearly stated that the thing had to exist as it is, as an existential repetition, as I was translating, then, that it couldn't only subsist in a paradigmatic field of significations. In my current preoccupations, not only is it not a matter of a structural key for the interpretation of different mythic components, it is a matter of a certain use of the semantic material put into play which has to be actively rendered non-signifying. It is not only the fact that there is, in a contingent fashion, a fact of non-sense or a rupture of signification, but that it has to be actively rendered non-signifying so as to function as a means for what I call existential territorialisation. And it is precisely these non-signifying elements which will constitute what I call the transversality of assemblages: They are what will traverse heterogeneous modes of expression from the point of view of their means of expression, or from the point of view of their content, mythical content, for example. Because what will function from one register to another is not axiomatic, a structure articulating signifying poles, but what I will call an ontological logic, a fashion of constructing existence in different registers, what, with Eric (Alliez), I call ordology, in opposition to a cardology.

B. G. — When you say transversality, that's the way I use the word to connect, things connect themselves among themselves, but you can't do an analysis of how they connect in a general sense, or designate particular meanings that connect things. That's not how it works. It is not, for example, a structural opposition that makes it so that things are connected; it's a whole dynamic process that causes the mythology and the society to exist and that makes it so they're inter-connected.

We have seen the constitution of existential territories through dreams, and also as mythical stories and rituals. Let's look more closely at what happens with body painting. In the Warlpiri sense, painting involves identifying the body with the life force of the dreaming that is being represented, or else as an element in general, or a particular site, or in a constellation of elements. We have seen how every design corresponds to one or several names that refer to a dreaming or a site. But that does not mean there is an equivalency between a particular design and the name assigned to it. It happens that the same design can be used for different dreamings. What matters is what the group has decided to do in a particular situation. If a certain woman is painted and certain songs are sung, the design is called a particular dreaming, and not some other dreaming. Félix would say that the pragmatic dimension takes precedence over the semiotic dimension. So when the women no longer recalled under what conditions a particular photograph was taken, they were refusing to give the name of the design. For that reason, I systematically made sketches along with their identification, while the women were painting themselves, which I later matched with the photographs. There are designs that always come back for the same dreaming; or rather, a type of design, because the variations are infinite, within the principle of white outlines or the number of tiny little features. The important thing is the freedom of the women who paint to improvise once they know the subject. When the painting is finished, it is possible to decompose the elements, or some of the elements, to attribute meaning to them. An animal footprint, a woman seated, a camp, a cloud. This is what I did with certain photographs. Most of the time the women do not like doing this kind of interpretative 'pulling apart' (*décortiquage*). Sometimes they offer different interpretations. It is not a problem as long as the elements are part of the dreaming.

What happens at the moment of painting is highly ambiguous. It seems as though the laying out of the basic elements to be outlined is not done with a meaning attached to each element. But sometimes a woman painter intervenes, or even the one who is being painted says what isn't right and that they have to start over, that they're not going to do, for example, vines, but instead the river. The vines and the river refer to the same dreaming. And so they erase everything and start over.

It's fairly complicated. There is not a particular vine design or river design. But there are certain designs that cannot be either vines or rivers. This may need to be thought of in terms of its relationship to Aboriginal people's memory. Nothing is invented since everything is already part of the dreaming. It suffices to remember it. On the one hand, there is no copying, but you always start at zero, you crystallise your own dream memory. I have heard women say that they copied a motif drawn, for example, by a man on a card board and then do something completely different with it – for them it was the 'same' thing. All these Warlpiri notions about same and different seem to me more crucial than trying to identify iconographic codes. In fact, since there is basically an alphabet of four elements – a straight or a curved line (like an arc), a circle or a meandering line – all possible meanings are necessarily distributed among these four elements. What counts is not how these elements are combined, but what is the context attached to the combination. This is how recognition functions. It's interesting that some Whites – teachers or missionaries – have tried to use these four iconographic elements to get their messages across. Unlike Whites, though, the Warlpiri only understand the messages if they remember what the individual who drew them told them.

Although they often use small arcs to represent seated people in both body painting and sand-drawing on sand to tell stories to children, it would never occur to anybody to systematically interpret the small arcs in a missionary's drawing representing the community of the Church as people, because the arcs could just as easily represent animal footprints, or – why not – animals in the church? I'm going to read what Félix said about these questions of iconography:

Warlpiri Dreaming Spaces with Guattari

So there is this signified landscape that corresponds to a particular signifying tracing (picture), a variation between these two elements – signified/signifier, based on an array, that we could call discrete, of asignifying expressive figures. But what seems equally important to me to consider is the following movement: First, the fact that there is a composition of an array of asignifying expressive figures and of signifying landscapes, in the passage from a motivated landscape to a non-motivated expression, what I will call an arbitrarisation. Second is the fact that these arbitrarised elements are formed among themselves so that they in turn form a certain type of asignifying landscape. What is the benefit, and I would say, the sense of pleasure or fulfillment (*jouissance*) to be gained from this operation? It's the fact that in the first situation, you are under a system of constraints, which is that you take the landscape as it presents itself, you have to adapt yourself to it in one way or another, you have to take responsibility for one mythical sequence or another, for a particular relationship between people, groups, or elements. By passing along a chain of asignifying expression, you acquire considerable degrees of freedom.

You still have denotation or signified landscapes, and you compose an asignifying landscape about which you yourself say that it offers a quasi-infinite variety of compositions of elements. So in principle, there are two ways to view the result. A general semiological way that would consist of saying that you have developed a code, a means of expression that is involved in a relationship of dependency with its contents. This is not what seems to me the most interesting path to take. If I am talking specifically about the asignifying landscape, it is because – independently of or in parallel with the promotion of this code – there is a phenomenon of pragmatic fulfillment, of pleasure via the constitution of existential territories. It's more than the recognition of something that resembles content, it's a simultaneous self-appropriation of this content, which is therefore determined, and a self-appropriation of the coefficients of freedom introduced by these signifying chains. It is the fact that, now that I have fabricated an asignifying existential territory for myself, I am mastering something in terms of content but I am enjoying my own freedom, managing my own space (*mon aménagement*). I am in my territory and I can play with it, just as I can play with a range of discursive elements.

I have often asked myself questions about individual freedom relative to the group among the Warlpiri. Félix says, and I quote, that 'individuated enunciation can be perfectly homogeneous with collective enunciation. Conversely, a group enunciation can be perfectly personological, capitalistic.'

I objected with the example of Warlpiri dreamers who dream new body designs or songs and, unlike what might be expected, it's actually fairly common, the group does not take up these designs and songs at all. To that, Félix replied:

> What the individuated enunciator does is maybe a kind of prospective work that could be taken up by the group. Like a researcher or a mystic, he is working based on the idea that somebody else might take up his idea. And this repetition translates the fact that he is participating as a collective enunciator.

So I objected, citing the case of a mother who dreams her child was not conceived on his clan's land. Before he was even born, she gives the specific identity of the other land she dreamt of to the child. The group will have to accept this as a fact. The child will be initiated into his clan's Dreaming-totem, but he will always have the protection of this individual dreaming that his mother, or another relative, gave him through his own Dreaming-totem. You might say this is how the dreamer expresses his/her freedom relative to the group. Félix answered that you can see it as an individual choice that is opposed to the group consensus. But for the subjective economy of groups, it is more helpful to say that the most enriching aspect is specifically the existence of singularisation processes, whether or not they are taken up by the group.

Instead of saying that 'the creative process is generated by the cut of the individual in the group,' the proposition is 'the creative process emerges with the entrance of a singularity that can come from an individual but also from a sub-group, or from something else that has nothing to do with the group but that comes from an esthetic conjunction, an external intrusion, a cosmic assemblage that begins to speak, a voice from elsewhere.' I agree with this, on the condition that in our societies we also think about the alignment of the individual in a collective enunciation. But what was bothering me is that Félix is talking about individuated subjectivity in the context of capitalistic subjectivity. I quote:

> It is no longer existential territories constituted through collective enunciators that produce subjectivity. It is collective equipment – machines – that produce subjective individuation. In other words, subjectivity is normed to function in the context of abstract equivalent – money, work, and all the systems that are involved in machinic production. This production needs to deny the existential logics which are operating in territorialised subjectivity; but in order not to produce robots, the machinic production must produce its antidote, territorial subjective equivalents, i.e., new nationalities, new family types, of new kinds of ego.

Warlpiri Dreaming Spaces with Guattari

I witnessed a phenomenon among the Warlpiri that is both specific to their culture and perfectly reflects this definition of capitalistic subjectivity. The problem is to find out whether the elaboration of this phenomenon corresponds to anticipation of the threat of the Whites' arrival or to the independent evolution of an aspect of Aboriginal culture. The phenomenon in question began a hundred years ago, well before White people arrived in the region, and also before rumors of their arrival began to circulate. The Warlpiri and the other tribes of Central Australia experienced a kind of intellectual epidemic. One after the other, they began adopting a new kinship system that gave them brothers and cousins and uncles in all of the clans and every tribe. At the same time, marriage choices for all of them opened up enormously. Still, they followed a kinship model, but not using a genealogy based on blood kinship – the genealogy was expanded into a classifying system. For instance, the Warlpiri previously could only marry second-degree cross cousins, but under the new system a sixteenth of the tribe, and of all the tribes that had adopted the system, became marriageable 'cousins.' Around two hundred different kinship relationships, each designated by a different word, were distributed within a system of equivalence. This system was so successful that more isolated tribes are currently in the process of adopting it.

I was lucky enough to observe this adoption process, because a tribe that did not use this system had invited the Warlpiri to visit them to bring them a ceremony. The Warlpiri themselves had adopted the ceremony a hundred years ago; at the same time they adopted the kinship system. The new system gives everyone names that Aboriginal peoples call *skin-names* and that anthropologists call 'subsections.' The Warlpiri not only distributed these names to every man and woman, but also to all of their ancestors – the heroes of their dreamings, their myths.

And so the two ancestral heroines, celebrated in the new ceremony that the Warlpiri were adopting at the time of the new kinship system, were assigned the *skin-name* that corresponds to 'mothers' of the paternal clan; in other words, the name of a woman from outside the clan, because the Warlpiri are exogamous (i.e., they marry outside of their clan). In this ancestral story, the two women were sisters, and under the new system, sisters share the same skin-name. So they received the same *skin-name* in addition to their two ancestral first names. This was a new ceremony because it came from a northern tribe, but it became 'Warlpirised,' with a new dream-myth-itinerary (Dreaming) called *Kajirri* that the Warlpiri elaborated for the occasion. The ceremony was originally linked with a specific dream-myth. But here is a good example of how, in a space of fifty years, the Warlpiri conceived other ceremonies also called *Kajirri*. They expanded the initial *Kajirri* model: two sisters, mothers from the clan and from outside, from other dream-myths. This process of equivalency could be seen as parallel to that of the new kinship system. Nevertheless, it is hard to say that these equivalency models become implanted against the existential territories, as Félix says about the capitalistic subjectivity of equivalency. On the contrary, it seems like the existential territories are reaffirmed and clan identities are maintained via these assemblages of models. Even if people don't return to their lands, they continue to celebrate them. But how can you distinguish between what an Aboriginal person experiences now and what his or her ancestors experienced?

What I was saying to Félix is that even in the 1940s some isolated groups had never seen or heard of Whites. There were bomb tests in the south-western deserts in the 1950s and 1960s, and un-sedentarised groups would see an explosion and not know where it came from. And when the Whites came looking for them, they had never heard of them before ... And groups that had never seen Whites didn't even bother with describing them, but they did organise a camel and horn ceremony, because another group had seen camels. The word that went around wasn't 'we saw some camels,' it was dancing, and that's very important because, as I said earlier, the important thing is not that there are rituals, or knowing what they mean, it's that the rituals take place.

So they danced the camel, but they didn't call them camels ... Maybe the Whites were camels with horns![13]

F. G. — What seems to come out of all this is a series of activities with multiple entry points, through body paintings, dancing, singing, dreaming, and so on, but approached with a certain pragmatism that says well, if we don't get there one way, we'll get there by a different one, which explains the relativity of the entry points and the impossibility of an analytical coding system. What seems to be the objective is an abstract, machinic fulfillment *(jouissance)*,

---

[13] The horns imitated bulls and other cattle that had been introduced by settlers. When Europeans started to cross Australia on camels (with Pakistani guides), Aboriginal peoples first viewed them as new creatures, half-man, half-animal. The dance was circulated as both news and entertainment (see Rosy Napangardi's first contact story at: www.odsas.net).

and gaining a certain possibility of playing with the coefficients of freedom such that one has an array of asignifying expressive figures, which are in fact supported by all kinds of correspondences. For that reason, the various territorialised semiologicial economies have that finality on every level, including in terms of kinship ties, preferential marriages, and so on. And as a matter of fact, it makes me think of the finality of the child, who also has this objective of being able to create increasingly abstract games. We could demonstrate that the goal of children's games is to master articulations at an abstract level via a similar entry point. Moreover, the difference between this and capitalistic abstraction is that the abstract quantities involved are in fact regulated, and they don't factor into the coefficients of freedom because the economy of abstraction is literally colonised, literally articulated, and because there's this notion of a coefficient of libertarian fulfillment (*jouissance*) of abstraction that is a goal, whereas the activities of abstraction in capitalistic subjectivity are highly regulated.

Jean-Claude Polack — The ways the people you are talking about express themselves are very close to the discourse of one of my patients who tells me similar things, where I get especially lost ... There are dreams, and there are stories, objects, phenomena, substances, and materials, all of which enters into extremely complex articulations with body parts and with moments in the story. What strikes me, too, is that she tells stories to me today that are not so different from those she was telling me twenty years ago. It's at the same time somewhat enriching and yet impoverishing in certain ways, but something has remained constant – it can't be said that she constantly invents new things, there's a transmission. What her case shares with this one is this kind of enormous effort that she continues to make, even though we are working in an Assistance Centre through work[14] and she lives in specially-provided housing; and she continues doing her cartographic work, which at the same time takes elements of her story, events she refers to, and that I am sometimes involved in ('In Egypt, three hundred years ago, when we met outside the mosque ...'). It's very complicated, but when she said that three or four times in a row in ten years, it compels me to think she's not simply dazzling me on purpose so that I get confused, there's something more important going on. It always consists of creating a kind of continuum between these stories and the system

---

[14] Regarding this organisation, see Polack and Sivadon (2013).

of involvement of her body, which is in a state of dispersal and is unbelievably complex, in which I am trying to gradually ... It is astonishingly difficult, and I have realised a certain number of things: Her syntax is so bizarrely put together that if I don't understand what she's telling me, I am incapable of remembering how she said things after she leaves, to the point that I asked her if she would allow me to record our sessions ... What I find striking was when you said 'It's not the same thing,' which introduces a shade of meaning, starting from when we short-circuit the phenomena of signification between semblance or identity and analogy; I mean there's something that only goes into formal levels of presentation, drawings, etc., and you have the impression of a transposition of multiple effects in a trajectory onto the field and in traits to, on the skin, and even still there is this continuity – but there is this permanent flow consisting of always deciphering the maps and identifying the tracings, in fact there is an inscription. There might not be signification, but there are tracings, there is an ongoing cartographic effort, and it may be that pragmatic process ... what is very interesting in the case of my patient is what you say about the benefits of fulfillment (*jouissance*), she talks about them: She has things with her urethra, for example, or her asshole, when there is a certain kind of event happens that can interact with what she calls, in her words, the little skin there on the groin, there are special moments when one has the impression that she has a real orgasm, a partial organ-pleasure, and so there is something that can be referenced on the map. That way we know that it works. When she noticed connections like that, you get the impression they are ongoing, and that's what I find so striking: Ten years later, it's always the same story, I mean the meeting with Ho Chi Minh at the Château de Langeais who made her a child up her ass ... So there are in any case things that hold up amid all that, it's precisely these localisable fragmented productions of fulfillment (*jouissance*) that are not very numerous – perhaps five or six – that are very precise on her body, and they are the only points around which one has the impression that one can try to get something stable to stay in place. And in addition, it is articulated in a very complex manner, that I have not been able to understand, with her medications. And her prescriptions. Because medicine is one thing, but prescriptions are totally different! They have to be written in a particular way ...

x_1 — I have the impression that these people travel so they can make history. Ultimately it's through travelling that this history is made; it doesn't need to be made by seizing power.

B. G. — In New Caledonia, too, stories of land distribution are complicated, not because there are Dreaming stories like for Aboriginal peoples, but there is a historical memory about the itineraries, the pathways that people from previous generations moved along/walked through ...

J.-C. P. — There's also something else ... Potocki's novel, *Le manuscrit trouvé à Saragosse* (The Manuscript Found at Saragossa), where numerous trajectories are also told by different personalities, because each of them discovers his buddy, who tells a story, and after a certain number of pages you no longer know who is saying what. What's extraordinary is that, no matter how varied the adventures of the different participants are, there are matrices and constants that regularly return, like the hero of every story who always ends up meeting two women who are sisters, very beautiful; he wants to sleep with them, he falls asleep in their arms and wakes up under a gallows with two hanged men. There are many variations on the appearance of the two sisters, and on the hanged men, too, but what is never missing, I mean, what is in every variation of the story, is always there, even though the variations are multiple, there are the two sisters, the hanged men too – they vary, but they're never missing. Which means that the multivariate nature of the story is still connected through a kind of structure ...

F. G. — Oh yeah! That's where we reconnect with our debate with Eric (Alliez)! Is it a structure? It seems to me very interesting in Barbara's description that you can't talk in terms of structure. Because she presents series of variations that are in fact infinite variations; she says there are four fundamental semiotic elements – the circle, the half-circle, the straight line, and the meandering line – but that the system is ultimately open. In fact, how can you reconcile the fact that there are these open variations with the fact that there is this rigorous individual or collective apperception: That, what you did there, it's OK! But that isn't OK! It is unacceptable!

So there are imperative judgments. It's this knowledge of a composition of intensive traits that, unlike the cohesion that might occur between discursive elements, have no referent, or in any event, whose references are, shall we say, self-referential in nature and that only refer to their own environment within a specific context, but they aren't translatable in the way that you might be able to situate various local referents that belonged to a whole to create a general structural map. I am trying to distinguish between two kinds of logic – a logic of discursive wholes from an ordological logic,

Figure 2.3 Abe Jangala, one of the Warlpiri artists from Lajamanu who was in Paris in 1983 © B. G. (1984).

meaning that its procedures and purposes are totally different from the cardological logic, which is the logic of articulated wholes, even though these two logics are not entirely unrelated. In a certain way, ordology expresses itself through languages constituted via cardology, the logic of wholes, in which there are relationships between the signifier and the signified, but in fact, it puts them to a different use, because it is a use that targets an existential effect, with thresholds, meaning that this effect is more or less traversed, it is crossed, it is not crossed, but it is incontestably either crossed or not crossed.

I have the impression that what Australian Aboriginal peoples contribute to us is a high degree of ease that worries us a lot, not so much as participants in a capitalistic kind of subjectivity, but because this subjectivity relies on vast disorganisation, an immense crushing of every other mode of existentialisation – in dream, in desire, in daily life, in every way.

3

Guattari and Anthropology: Existential Territories among Indigenous Australians

Palestinians, Armenians, Basques, Irish, Corsicans, Lithuanians, Uyghur, Gypsies, Native Americans, Australian Aborigines ... all in their own way and in very different contexts, appear as so many leftovers of history ... In fact this nebula with fuzzy contours is called on to play a growing role at the heart of the international relations that it is already 'parasiting' considerably. And for our part we consider that, in the future, the nationalitarian fifth world will no longer be simply passive and defensive, but will bring a decisive renewal to the cultural values, social practices and models of society of our times. (Guattari ([1985] 1986), *Les Années d'Hiver*)[1]

In the early 1980s, the decade Guattari called *Les Années d'Hiver* (The Winter Years), when he was testing the concepts, graphs and machines of his *Schizoanalytic Cartographies*, in his seminar it was sometimes difficult to understand what was happening in his intellectual garage, full of spare parts and oil.[2] But a very tangible flux regularly emerged, like an illumination that sketched out a route, onto which everyone would graft certain of their own questions. We had the impression that the brain, the heart, the body with or without organs, disconnected us from our individual identity through diverse crystallisations of subjectivity, while reinforcing our existential bedding in a flux of collective desire. It was a passionate subjectification, shared with Guattari through a multitude of singularities: a vocalisation of ideas, as Deleuze put it. I would like

---

[1] This is taken from the text of a lecture that Guattari gave in Bilbao on 26 March 1985 to the International Congress 'Los derechos colectivos de las nacionesminorizadas en Europa'. It was republished in Guattari (2013). It is worth noting that Guattari's neologism 'nationalitarian' does not mean the same thing as 'nationalist'[TN]. Some French references were suppressed in the 2011 translation.

[2] This essay first appeared in French in the journal *Multitudes* 34 under the title 'Guattari et l'anthropologie: Aborigènes et territoires existentiels', in 2008. It was translated by Andrew Goffey for the collective work, *The Guattari Effect*, E. Alliez and A. Goffey (eds), London and New York: Continuum, 2011.

to emphasise here my debt with regard to Guattari's thinking by tracking some steps in the exchanges that we had about my fieldwork with Warlpiri people in Central Australia, notably on the occasion of two seminars published in the first issue of *Chimères*.[3] Guattari is often quoted – with Deleuze – by Anglophone anthropologists (particularly in Oceania) and ignored – even rejected – by a generation of French anthropologists.

It seems that most of them have missed the anthropological potential of his writings, whether by ignorance or incomprehension of the evolution of his concepts. That of 'collective assemblages of enunciation', for example, in the debates on the subject, agency and modes of subjectification. Or the linking together of the three ecologies (environmental, social and mental) in relation to the systemism of Gregory Bateson's ecology of the mind:

> in my own modelling system, I try to advance the notion of an ecosophical object which would go further than the ecosystemic object. I conceptualize the ecosophical object as articulated across four dimensions: those of flux, machine, value and existential territory [...] it is really a matter of producing the junction between the machines of ecosystems of material fluxes and those of ecosystems of semiotic fluxes. I am trying, then, to enlarge the notion of autopoïesis, without restricting it to the living system, as Varela does, and I consider that there are proto-autopoïeses in all other systems: ethnological, social, etc. (Guattari [1991] 2013)

The articulation of existential territories with different systems of valorisation and ontological self-affirmation is, in my opinion, an essential key for the anthropological analysis of any process of resingularisation of the relation to place in the contemporary universe of globalised interactions.

Anthropology, Kinship and Politics

When Robert Jaulin tried to mobilise public opinion against the ethnocide of Amazonian Indians, George Balandier replied (in a discussion filmed in 1967)[4] that such societies were condemned to disappear, because their cultures did not have any 'images', which – as in the case of Japan – would allow them to adapt to the changes of modernity. The last fifty years have shown, on the contrary, that

---

[3] 1987, see Chapters 1 and 2, this volume.
[4] In an interview with Max Pol Fouchet in the film by Julien Papée (dir.) (1967), *Mort et Métamorphoses des Civilisations*, Paris: INA.

despite the killings, the dispossessions and the destruction of their environment, the Indigenous peoples of the Amazonian rain forest – like others in Australia or in the Pacific – had, precisely, trusted in 'images', whether in their shamanic visions, or their political use of art and media (Glowczewski and Soucaille 2007). Guattari was convinced by Jaulin's arguments and by the alternative model presented by the Amazon Indians, such as it was described by another of his anthropologist friends, Pierre Clastres. The latter's essays *Society Against the State* ([1974] 1987) had provoked a sort of scandal in the arena of French anthropology, by calling into question, among other things, Lévi-Strauss's postulation about war as the effect of failed exchanges. The conflict worsened to the point that Clastres and Jaulin quit the Laboratory of Social Anthropology founded by Lévi-Strauss.

In the Department of Ethnology that Jaulin ran at the University of Paris 7 (Jussieu) in the 1970s, we were told to turn our backs on structuralism: rather, it was a matter of urgency to analyse the critique of past orders carried out by feminism, countries in the process of decolonising, and Indigenous peoples. Alongside Jean Monad, we had the opportunity of listening to Native Americans explain their resistance. I was a witness to the impressive creativity of the Aboriginal Australians who, in the name of their ancestral value systems had – after decades of struggle – succeeded in getting a law passed (Northern Territory Land Rights Act 1976) that allowed them to make legal claims for the partial restitution of their traditional lands. They had been dispossessed of these lands by their forced settlement on reserves in the 1950s, when they had had to abandon their lives as semi-nomadic hunter-gatherers.

In the 1980s, the Aboriginal people of the desert reappropriated their lands by car, establishing 'outstations', solar-powered camps, with windmills for water. Both men and women were involved in sacred rituals, painting their bodies with designs that symbolised the geographic journeys of their totemic ancestors, called, in the languages of Central Australia, *Jukurrpa*, Dreamings. Night after night, they celebrated these Dreaming pathways so as to initiate the younger generations by dancing and singing their links to sacred sites marked with traces of the Rain, Lizard or Yam Beings. In some communities, the men and women began to paint their totemic maps on canvas, in order to get their territorial rights – founded on their spiritual links with places – legally recognised. Their success was stunning, and painting became a tool for political claims and an economic resource.

Guattari and Anthropology

Within twenty years, the profusion of artists, of their works, and their growing popularity among collectors from all four corners of the world would challenge the categories of art history, getting this Aboriginal art out of primitivism and into the global contemporary art market.[5] The message that I brought back from Australia after my first field trips in 1979 and 1980 related to the ancestral connections with the land, which Aboriginal people experienced as a moving network: a real ontology in which humans, animals, plants, water and the whole of social life are thought of as the actualisation of virtualities that are constantly in feedback with the space-time of *Jukurrpa*, the itineraries of ancestral travellers called Kangaroo, Plum or Digging Stick Dreaming. These beings and the tracks of their voyages are effectively defined as being in becoming: sleeping in hundreds of places, springs, rocks, and interacting with humans in their own dreams and rituals, which aim to reinforce the links between all living things. Dreaming was practised as a means of regenerating life.

My 1981 thesis, 'Le Rêve et la Terre – Rapports au temps et à l'espace des Aborigènes d'Australie' (The Dreaming and the Land – Relations to time and space of Aboriginal Australians) (1981a), aimed to demonstrate that this dynamic process – mistakenly described by most anthropologists as 'out of time' – was intrinsic to the traditional vision of the world. I also demonstrated the active role of women – whose power had been denied (and continues to be denied) – in these societies. I utilised Guattari's conception of the flux of desires to account for the mythic networks and to analyse numerous rituals: including the circulation among allies of hairstrings as women's non-alienable possessions, or a secret cult which, dreamed following the wrecking in 1912 of a ship (Koombana) deporting Aboriginal people, had journeyed among different language groups as a symbolic form of economic transformation producing a double law, including that of the White men.[6]

Two years after I defended my thesis, I received a surprise phone call from Guattari, whom I hadn't yet met. He invited me to his

---

[5] Glowczewski, B., 'The Paradigm of Indigenous Australians: Anthropological Phantasms, Artistic Creations and Political Resistance' [2007] (retranslated in Glowczewski 2015), discusses, among other things, the matrix of four ontologies proposed by Philipe Descola in Descola ([2005] 2013).

[6] I was inspired by Annette Weiner who, in Maurice Godelier's seminar in 1980, described the circulation of mats among Trobriand Islanders as an inalienable possession of women that thus affirmed their power. She went on to develop this notion of inalienability in Weiner (1992).

seminar to discuss my thesis, a copy of which he had received from his friend, the video-maker François Pain, and which he had just read in one sitting.[7] Guattari's enthusiasm for the totemic paths and the use of dreams by the Warlpiri was stimulated, by, among other things, the fact that the kinship system – which extends to all the totems (Dreamings) and their associated places – seems to favour social strategies that prevent centralised structures of domination, a situation that echoes Clastres's 'society against the state'. For the latter, it was the recourse to war among the Amazonians that seemed to maintain the autonomy and dispersion of each group, preventing the centralising of power and its seizure by some, over others. Many specialists of the Amazon region have criticised Clastres's extreme position, but they recognised the non-hierarchical structure, based on kinship, of the social reproduction of these groups.

A certain resistance of the Warlpiri (and other Aboriginal peoples living in the desert or in the North) to the accumulation of goods and to Western-style management speaks in favour of the fact that in diverse ways they refuse the logic of the state imposed by colonisation and by current bureaucracy. The refusal of a central power seems to me to be founded not on war, but on a particular way of extending kinship (in the form of symbolic filiations and alliances) to the management of land, of its resources and associated systems of knowledge. Men and women use the English terms 'boss' and 'worker' to translate the ritual roles and duties according to which everyone is the 'boss' (*kirda* in Warlpiri) of the land of his/her father and the 'worker' (*kurdungurlu* – also 'manager','lawyer') of the land of his/her mother and of his/her spouse. This description of meta-kinship so fascinated Guattari that he invited me to talk about it to the patients at La Borde. It was an extraordinary experience, because the residents seemed to have a surprisingly intuitive understanding of the Aboriginal aims and workings of these social games and rituals. The rules for the ritual management of the land and of the knowledge of stories, songs, dances and paintings invert the roles of men and women according to the place in which each action takes place: the land of the father, the mother or the spouse. It is not just a matter of biological parents or of true marriage alliances, but of classificatory parents.

Everyone in the group as well as every stranger who works with the group is automatically classified as the *skin* brother or sister of

---

[7] Glowczewski (1981a), see Chapter 1 of this book. See also Ales (2006: 129, 131, 134), and Viveiros de Castro (1998), Alliez (2005), Sibertin-Blanc (2005).

certain group members. Thus, all social relations are expressed with kinship terms as one big family. This system has inspired numerous anthropologists and mathematicians, but the literature on this subject – including the sections Lévi-Strauss devoted to Australians in his *The Elementary Structures of Kinship* ([1947] 1970) – is a little lacking in flesh and in soul. This posed a real problem for anthropology which, at the time, had difficulty in transposing into the same books both theoretical speculations and the performativity of life.

In my experience, the *skin-names* kinship system is a brilliant type of role-playing (which in its simplest form corresponds to what is called in mathematics a dihedral group, combining reversible and irreversible cycles of relations between eight poles). At the time though, most anthropologists rejected the analogy with games to explain ritual or political activities. The patients at La Borde, however, immediately said that the 'family game' was essential for mental and social survival and for that of the environment. In other words, they saw in the Australian kinship game an entwined dynamic similar to the three ecologies Guattari was later to theorise.

Totemism, Structuralism, Onirism and Deterritorialisation

Since everything that is named in nature and culture is associated, in the desert and in the North, with series of toponyms whose links are deployed in stories (Dreamings) that act as 'totems', I have emphasised that there was no opposition between nature and culture in totemism (an opposition which is the basis of Lévi-Strauss's nominalist interpretation of totemism) from the moment that concepts from more than 200 different languages, like *Jukurrpa*, translate individual or collective totemic identity (animal, plant, fire or digging stick) and geographic tracks, which – nourished by mythic stories and rites – can be renewed in dreams in the form of new episodes, recounted, sung, danced and painted. The guardians of the Warlpiri law say that they invent nothing, but rather uncover and reveal what is virtually already there in memory, the matrix of the Dreaming, anchored in places associated with totemic beings. This dynamic use of the notion of the Dreaming space-time, which identifies each being with places inhabited by multiple totemic becomings, offers an alternative to Freud's *Totem and Taboo* and to the nominalism of Lévi-Strauss's *Totemism*.

The creative survival and linguistic diversity of Aboriginal people, who have been present in Australia for at least 60,000 years, challenge all forms of evolutionism, whether Darwinian, Marxist or Deleuzo-Guattarian, such as the primitive/barbarian/capitalist model in Anti-Oedipus. Deterritorialisation is certainly a very handy notion for talking about the mental, social and ecological disaster provoked by the colonial violence of the displacement of Aboriginal people into reserves, and the physical and ontological dispossession that the forced settling of these former semi-nomadic hunters constituted. Contrary to the use that some make of it, deterritorialisation here is not a metaphor but the expression of the becoming of the contemporary unconscious as machinic deterritorialisation of living fluxes. As Anne Querrien says, the latter 'is coiled around colonial deterritorialization' and enables the social, economic and environmental disaster that colonisation has engendered to be survived.

Because deterritorialising, in the sense of Anti-Oedipus, is the human capacity to make up imaginary, symbolic and real territory (the three aspects of desire in Lacan), it doesn't coincide with everyday territory, the territory of animal reproduction, but refers to the capacity to dream territory, to modify it, and not simply to submit to it, to pass beyond the death drive, the drive of maximal reterritorialisation. What struck Félix in my work with the Warlpiri was to discover that this capacity for deterritorialisation is not restricted to Westerners. Even if their enforced entry into modernity, with the welfare state and integration, has destroyed some Aboriginal people even more, others resisted, not ably with the tour de force of their artistic production, which metabolises the territories of their totemic Dreamings.

For Guattari, the creation which reassembles (*réagence*) through the desiring machine without Lacan's imaginary/symbolic/real triangle is a revolutionary position provided that one moves away from the psychiatric position, in which the object a is a pathology to be resorbed. The apparent absence of any taking into account of the strength of the assemblage and of the agency (*agencéité*) of desire in the structuralism of Lacan or that of Lévi-Strauss perhaps explains the fixed aspect of a certain analysis of myths and of kinship, which justified the pursuit of the deterritorialisation of anthropology without taking into account the possible deterritorialisation of the peoples concerned.

It remains the case that for many readers of Anti-Oedipus the category of the nomad as landless is problematic. Aboriginal people in the desert and elsewhere in Australia have an extremely strong attachment to diverse places, while nevertheless being nomadic. The particularity of Australia is that land is perceived not as a juxtaposition of limited parcels but as an open network of places linked together by narratives and songs in the form of virtual tracks forming a network that is both unlimited and 'boundless'.

It is open in all the cardinal directions but also according to the principle of an infinite interior. One can always add a narrative place, with its geographical basis, between two others, and a subterranean historical level as a series of superposed strata or layers of events into which one 'digs' (via rituals and dreams). These additions are produced by the interpretation of dreams, which seems to follow certain cultural patterns, to legitimate such and such a vision as authentic.

One requires the approval of other groups for a dream vision to be certified as 'real', it has to be linked to pictorial and narrative forms transmitted for hundreds of generations, the Warlpiri man Maurice Luther Jupurrurla explained when invited to Paris with eleven other law men from Lajamanu to recreate a ritual sand painting at the ARC[8] and to dance in Peter Brook's Théâtre des Bouffes du Nord (see Figure 4.2). The demonstration of authenticity here is an exercise in tracking, just as with a hunter who has to recognise a print on the ground. A dream must reveal a sign of the ancestral principle that is said to sleep actively in different sacred places of a territory. These places – rocks, springs, creeks, trees – which seem natural to us, are cultural places, in the sense that events are attached to them: mythical episodes, oniric interpretations and re-enacted historical and everyday experiences. All these events are constantly re-stratified by rituals and the everyday experience of the people who journey in these places, by physically camping in them or by visiting them mentally in dance performances or dreams.

In his intellectual fight against the reductionism of certain applications of psychoanalysis and structuralism (in Lévi-Strauss or Lacan), Guattari was very touched by this Australian practice of dreams and above all by their integration into much more complex Indigenous concepts accounting for the links between the productions of the unconscious (songs, narratives, dances) and the reterritorialisation of their referents in extended networks of exchange:

> Archaic societies, in particular [those of] Australian Aboriginals, are customary in that each oneiric performance refers not only to a diachronic

---

[8] See Glowczewski ([1989] 2016). Created in 1967, ARC is a department of the Museum of Modern Art of the city of Paris.

series of individual dreams but, furthermore, to dreams with a collective reference, playing a fundamental role in the establishment of filiative relations, ritual itineraries and the fixation of transactions of all kinds.[9]

Aboriginal people presented Félix with an example of his 'logic of archaic intensities',[10] which made evident the role of dreams as a cartographic assemblage, 'the mythic Aboriginal cartographies, which "endeavour to localize the transformative potentials of their real and/ or incorporeal Universes"'.[11] He referred again to the Indigenous Australians in *Chaosmosis*, writing 'in archaic societies, it is through rhythms, songs, dances, masks, marks on the body, ground and totems, on ritual occasions and with mythical references that other kinds of collective existential Territories are circumscribed'.[12]

Colonisation underestimated the Indigenous Australians' relation to place. On the pretext that they didn't practise agriculture or construct houses (with the exception of the groups established along the Murray River in the south-east), Australia was supposed to be a *Terra nullius*, an 'uninhabited land'. It was only in 1992 that this Western colonial notion was challenged by the successful land claim of Eddie Mabo, a Torres Strait Islander, which led to a change of Australian law (the Native Title Act of 1993). Hitherto it had been commonly claimed that Aboriginal people could not be 'owners' of the land, since they said they 'belonged to it', a reasoning that in the colonial era even legitimated their relegation by some to 'non-humans' with the status of animals. However, by claiming a totemic continuity between humans, animals, plants, rain and the land, Aboriginal people (made up by more than 200 different languages and fifteen linguistic families) also insist on the fact that they have always acted on the land: singing, dancing, painting are literally their means of 'looking after the country', in the same way as burning the scrub to 'clean' the land of spinifex grass or even to practise a semi-nomadism to manage the seasonal irregularity of the sourcing of waterholes. Without ritual activities and seasonal practices, the elders say, no species of flora or fauna would be able to reproduce, and the climatic balance would be disturbed. Droughts and cyclones can thus be a human responsibility and threaten the reproduction

---

[9] Guattari ([1989] 2013), *Schizoanalytic Cartographies*, p. 240 in French version (pagination in English version not known).
[10] Ibid., p. 92 in French version.
[11] Ibid., p. 92 in French version.
[12] Guattari ([1992] 1995), *Chaosmosis*, p. 15.

of humans, because everything is linked on the earth, in the sea and the sky. From the Aboriginal point of view, every human action is responsible for the balance between the forces of nature and the health of people and all other living beings. This is not a holism but a singular responsibility for each gesture accomplished individually or collectively, in everyday life, during specific events and also in dreams. It is properly a matter of collective assemblages of enunciation as defined by Guattari: 'collective must not just be understood in the sense of a social group: it also implies the entry of diverse collections of technical objects, material and energetic fluxes, incorporeal entities, mathematical and aesthetic idealities, etc'.[13]

Ontologies and Topologies

When I went back to the desert in 1984, I sent Guattari carbon copies of the transcriptions of translations of the narratives in Warlpiri that I was recording and typing out on a little typewriter. On my return, I lived in his flat, which gave me a wonderful opportunity to discuss the first outlines of my book *Les rêveurs du désert* (*Desert Dreamers*) with him on a daily basis. Sometimes he copied out phrases of mine that pleased him in a notebook, such as: 'what is a word? In Warlpiri it is *yirdi*, which also serves to designate a proper name and a songline. The etymology refers to *yirdiyi*, which condenses the indissociable connections between words, itineraries, the flesh and the dream.' 'The status of the word is to be a place or an itinerary. As names of places and heroes correspond to things, it is essential to understand that these are neither poetic analogies nor metaphors.' 'In other words, there is no relation between signifier and signified, between a hero and his name. The hero is nothing other than the power of his name.' 'To say the name of a place, to dance a place or paint a place, is not necessarily an identification with this place, but a manner of being, simultaneously in the places of this Dreaming.' Another remark that caught Félix's attention comes from my Warlpiri friend, Barbara Gibson: 'Just as the Voice of the Nights [*mungamunga*] can make us ill because it shows us too many things in dreams, so we are hit by "stones" when we are too weak in our heads.'[14] These phrases have everything to do with the materiality of thought: the Warlpiri

---

[13] Guattari (1986), *Les Années d'hiver*, p. 289.
[14] Glowczewski and Nakamarra Gibson (2002) is a joint analysis of the dream which opens this book.

enunciation of apparently abstract procedures that are conceived in the form of tangible traces seems to escape from structural and linguistic oppositions. Our conversations were continued in public in his seminar on 15 February 1985, published in the first issue of *Chimères*, with our discussion of 1983.

Being in the grip of my year-long immersion in an experience in the field which had me journeying with the Warlpiri to their sacred sites, I was finding it difficult to translate the complexity of their concepts. I spoke of black holes and of energy to try to depict these knots of recognition of secret connections localised in sacred sites that are unchanging, while everything around them can change. Félix told me to replace the notion of energy with those of 'singularity' and of the 'a-signifying':

> [I]n my current preoccupations, I would translate what you say in the following fashion: not only is it not a matter of a structural key for the interpretation of different mythic components, but it is a matter of a certain use of the semantic material put into play which has to be actively rendered non-signifying. It is not only the fact that there is, in a contingent fashion, a fact of non-sense or a rupture of signification, but that it has to be actively rendered non-signifying so as to function as a means for what I call existential territorialisation. And it is precisely these non-signifying elements which will constitute what I call the transversality of assemblages: they are what will traverse heterogeneous modes of expression from the point of view of their means of expression, or from the point of view of their content, mythical content, for example. Because what will function from one register to another, is not axiomatic, a structure articulating signifying poles, but what I will call an ontological logic, a fashion of constructing existence in different registers, what, with Eric Alliez, I call ordology, in opposition to a cardology.[15]

In 1988, Guattari became angry when he read my Thèse d'État, 'Le Rêve et la Loi. Approche topologique de l'organisation sociale et des cosmologies aborigènes' (Dreaming and the Law. A topological approach to Aboriginal social organisation and cosmologies), which was subsequently published.[16] It was an attempt to compare different kinship systems, myths and ritual taboos (of the Warlpiri

---

[15] Guattari and Glowczewski, see Chapter 2 of this book. On the opposition of ordinal/cardinal, Viveiros de Castro (2004: 13) wrote: 'When prices describe cardinal relations of value in transactions between things, the kinship terms describe the ordinal rank between the exchange partners' (author's translation).

[16] Glowczewski (1991): see extracts in Chapters 3 and 4 of this book.

and other Aboriginal groups) by deploying them differently on a hypercube, according to several levels of relational complexity. Why use topology? he asked. Was this a return to the structuralism of Lévi-Strauss and Lacan? Lévi-Strauss had indeed been very pleased with this work, which articulated on the Australian continent what he had proposed for Native American myths with the Klein Bottle in *The Jealous Potter* (Lévi-Strauss [1985] 1988). But my inspiration came above all from science fiction that speculated about the fourth dimension. My true judges were the Warlpiri: when I showed them the hypercube as a tool to account for the kinship logic of their Dreamings, the elders, custodians of the culture thought it was a 'good game'! The famous acrylic canvases that the desert Aboriginals had begun to paint in the 1970s in Papunya (in 1985 in Lajamanu)[17] show structural tendencies in the network compositions of the Dreamings, as too the kinetic effects of the continuities between the above and below characteristic of their cosmological concepts and ritual procedures. According to the Warlpiri, these consist in transforming the *kanunju* (below/virtual/totemic beings and spirit-children of the Dreamings) in *kankarlu* (above/manifest/human and all those who give them their totemic names), and vice versa: this is the topology which had encouraged me to propose the hypothesis according to which there is a 'topologic' (illustrated by the properties of the hypercube) common to kinship, ritual taboos and myths.

Discussing recently the question that Deleuze and Guattari pose in *Rhizome* – 'Does not the East, Oceania in particular, offer something like a rhizomatic model, opposed in every respect to the Western model of the tree?' – the Australian anthropologist Alan Rumsey (2001) refers to the drawing 'The Body of Australia' published in the book *Yorro-Yorro* by David Mowaljarlai. This visionary initiate, with a Ngarrinyin father and Wororra mother, came to Paris in 1996 to call on the scientific community to protect the rock paintings of his people, threatened as they were by diamond mining.[18] His drawing showed a map of Australia and its surrounding waters, entirely covered by a network of intersecting lines connecting places distributed at their intersections in a regular manner like a net. Rumsey, who worked for years with the Ngarrinyin, recognises the

---

[17] Myers (1986, 2002), Glowczewski (1991b), Glowczewski and De Largy Healy (2005).
[18] See conversations with Mowaljarlai in Glowczewski (2004).

'rhizomatic' nature of the cartographies of Aboriginal Dreamings, but he opposes to them more ambiguous examples from Oceania, in which the rhizome model cohabits with arborescent models, notably in Papua New Guinea and on the island of Tanna in Vanuatu (studied by the geographer Joël Bonnemaison). Thomas Reuter (2006: 25) has underlined the fact that numerous researchers have shown that in Oceania botanical metaphors are most common for expressing social relations in the Austronesian world; they 'generally suggest a segmentary process of spatial expansion due to organic growth from within, but can and are applied also within local societies featuring a population with multiple origins'. Corporeal metaphors are also present for imagining social space, but the most important of all the metaphors in the Austronesian world to 'conceptualize socio-territorial unities is the path or the journey, a trajectory of human movement through space and time'.[19] Like others, Rumsey (2001) contests the absence of arborescent systems in Oceania but admits that the rhizome is 'good for thinking with' on condition that it is experienced by the people of Oceania as 'emplaced' and not 'nomadic'.

In the 1980s, particularly after contact with my Aboriginal data, Guattari reformulated his understanding of the rhizome in the ethnographic context of the production of existential territories anchored in places, the space-time of myth and dream, the body and kinship, extended to all becomings, human and non-human. The Yam Dreaming, whose rhizomes weave through the desert and other regions of Australia, is explicitly used by the Aboriginal people of these regions not as a simple metaphor but as a model for thought: the vines where the yams grow extended in a subterranean manner, coming to the surface (notably when they are stimulated by a little adder), and creep to the surface of the ground, coiling around trees in multiple branches that are sometimes broken. Vines at the surface lead to hidden tubers and they supply the Aboriginal people with a rhizomatic machine for thinking alliances and the circulation of tangible or intangible goods for exchange, goods for which the ownership is inalienable.

---

[19] 'In Palau the metaphor of the turmeric rhizome is used to explicate relations between kin and between villages. Traditionally people of Palau, the westernmost and largest of the Caroline Islands, made sense of kin relations through matrilineal decent. To explain these relations they used what has been termed the "turmeric metaphor".' See Rainbird (2001: 112).

Elsewhere I have compared this paradox of 'keeping-while-giving'[20] to the copyleft advocated by the creators of software for which the author's ownership would be better recognised by circulation than by forms of copyright that transform knowledges into monopolised commodities. This thought encounter, between local traditions of the putting into circulation of non-alienable goods across Australia and between groups in the Pacific, and the community of Internauts who advocate Creative Commons licensing, is one of many examples of a transversal – and, here, transhistorical – attractor. It sides with the knotting together of the three ecologies – mental, social and environmental – of Guattari's ecosophical project.

---

[20] Title of Weiner (1992) – see footnote 9 above. See Chapter 8.

PART II
Totem, Taboo and the Women's Law

Figure 4.1 Janjiya Liddy Nakamarra Herbert, painted with her Dreaming Pirlala Bush Bean on the breast and the Yumurrpa cave on the belly. Lajamanu.
© B. G. 1984

4
Doing and Becoming: Warlpiri Rituals and Myths

It is by dancing, singing and painting that Warlpiri men and women (learn how to) memorise the complex network of their *Jukurrpa* trails. They discover progressively the epics of the relevant eternal beings. For their own *Jukurrpa* and the ones owned by their relatives or allies, they have to remember, without knowing at first their full meaning, dozens of designs to be painted on the body or on ritual objects and songlines accompanied by dancing steps. Through regular ritual activity, a man or a woman in their forties should be able to decipher, by inference or with the elders' help, various symbolic connections: how to interpret a verse related to a given narrative episode and Dreaming site, or how to recognise a gesture in a dance that mimes that ancestral action. The content and the scope of this type of knowledge give prestige, so everybody is cautious about exchanging his or her ritual and mythical information. Some excel more than others in making wide networks of alliances that give them access to a larger body of knowledge related to the sacred geography. However, no one person holds the whole of the tribal heritage.

During totemic rites, visits to the ancestral sites, ceremonies for initiations, mournings or settling dispute, all ritual life is marked by the circulation of goods (*kunari* or *palwa*) between people of different clans, between men and women, and always according to specific kinship. Today, wheatflour dampers, or even commercial bread wrapped in plastic, replace the acacia seedcakes made by women in the old days. Similarly, hairstrings, ritual goods exchanged intra- and extra-tribally become rarer and are replaced by cloth, blankets, clothes and even money. Some male ritual objects are made with these hairstrings as are the female ritual ropes used, among other things, for therapeutic operations performed by women for people of both genders. Traditionally, headbands, belts and tassels, the only clothes of the desert people, were made with human or possum hair. By replacing ritual gifts of hairstring with cloth, blankets and clothes, Aborigines retain a dress function in the objects exchanged. The economic importance of this ritual circulation of goods and services has led the Warlpiri and their neighbours to call everything that is connected with the ritual activities *business*, and those in charge *businessmen* and *businesswomen*. In the absence of specialised priests, the majority of people in their late forties have this status.

Yawulyu: *Female Rituals*

In 1979, then in 1984, at the Warlpiri settlement of Lajamanu and a few bush sites, I witnessed some 200 *yawulyu* rituals performed by women.[1] The performers identified their songs, dances and paintings on bodies and objects, with totemic heroes, their paths of travel and special sites. These were often the identical sites recorded among the men thirty years earlier by Mervyn Meggitt (1962). Men recognise that women are *kirda*, owner-custodians of their fathers' land, rituals and *Kuruwarri* (image-forces), and that they are *kurdungurlu*, manager-custodians responsible for the organisation of rituals associated with the land and *Kuruwarri* of their mothers or spouses. This recognition contradicts Mervyn Meggitt, and Nancy Munn (1973), according to whom *kirda* (*girda*) and *kurdungurlu* (*gudungulu*) land responsibilities and the concept *Kuruwarri* (*guruwari*) are an exclusive prerogative of the men. For Munn, who worked in Yuendumu in the late 1950s, female ritual activities were centred on private business, love magic and healing; women had no territorial and cosmological impact at a community level, with the exception of their participation, also noted by Meggitt, in some stages of the circumcision ceremonies.

My own observations of the role of women, parallel to that of the men, as custodians of lands and totemic rituals, confirmed what had already been recorded in the 1970s, during surveys for the Warlpiri land claims (Peterson et al. 1978; Maddock 1981). Should we conclude that the (Warlpiri) ideology concerning women has changed during this decade, or that the first observers were biased by the assumption that women are excluded from any symbolic sphere

---

[1] And many more since, everytime I came back (1988, 1991–1997, 2000, 2004). In 2010, my two daughters were painted on the chest by the Lajamanu ladies, who by then had replaced their ochres with acrylic paint. Since the women's business camp has been replaced by housing, very few such rituals take place except during initiations and the Milpirri Festival I was lucky to witness on 3 November 2018. But women also paint their bodies and dance for art events, as they did in Paris for the Feast of Music on 21 June 2012 and at the Brave Festival in Poland just after that. Chapter translated from Glowczewski 1991.

involving social control, and that consequently they neglected the political impact of the female ritual activities?

Warlpiri people themselves say that women's rituals related to the paths of travel and *Kuruwarri* of their diferent local groups were performed well before the time of the fieldwork of both Meggitt and Munn. Nevertheless, the dream activity of the women, noticed by Munn to be prolific in Yuendumu, seems to have considerably increased its repertoire of songs, dances, graphic designs since the women came to lead a sedentary life. Local *yawulyu* were extended to women of other clans and sometimes modified, while other *yawulyu* were dropped in favour of new ones acquired through dreams. It is possible that the development of female rituals as an effect of sedentarisation, far from being something new, simply reactivated and accelerated a traditional process that used to be restricted to every clan and its affines, and not generalised to the whole of the tribe as it is today.

Whatever *Jukurrpa* trail is celebrated, a female *yawulyu* always unfolds according to the same series of actions. First, the women who today wear tee-shirts or dresses uncover their chests. They coat their breasts and shoulders with cooking oil or butter – in the olden days they used animal fat – mixed with a little red ochre. The ochres are ground on a flat stone which is then used as a palette. They are reduced to a powder, which a few drops of oil give the consistancy of a thick paint. Agreement about the choice of the *Jukurrpa* to paint is reached tacitly: by the group taking up the songs started by some women, by others coming close to them if they want to be painted, or by the initiative of one woman who draws the basic symbols on the chest of another woman with her finger coated in red paint. Once these signs are traced – circles, arcs, horizontal, vertical or meander lines – the design is identified as belonging to a particular Dreaming, still allowing several painters to add variations of their choice so as to cover the whole chest and shoulders; one holds an arm while she draws small arcs behind the first one centred on the shoulder; another does the same with the other arm; a third woman paints dots around a big circle drawn on the solar plexus.

Symbols in red are only the first step. The real freedom of the painters comes when they outline these with white paint, obtained from rocks such as kaolin. Flat sticks, narrower than a finger, at the end of which a string is wound tightly, are used as brushes. The more imposing a woman's breast, the better it is appreciated because more white lines can be drawn in the space left between the red ones. Outlined in white, the red symbols seem to come closer. Shiny black skin progressively disappears under white lines, and what is left in between is now painted with even narrower red lines. Once the painting is finished, the underlying symbols are difficult to see: they seem to melt into their outlines. The effect is kinetic, a many-coloured substance, a transfigured body.

For some Dreamings, such as Lizard (*liwirrinki, lerista* or *lygosoma* sp.) or Yam (*purrda* or *yarla*), the colours are reversed: the basic symbols are traced in white and outlined with red. For others, such as Tree Honey (*ngarlu*) or Stone Curlew (*wirntiki*), yellow ochre replaces or is added to the red, and for Black Plum (*yawakiyi*) black charcoal is used. In addition to the chest, women paint designs around the navel during the growing up or healing rituals, and on the back when treating a persistent disease. All these painting sessions, which generally take place in the late afternoon, last for a minimum of two to three hours. Several women are painted at the same time, and they then take their turn decorating others also wanting to be painted.

Sitting apart from the group of women painting, another group prepares ritual objects, especially the wooden boards, ten to fifteen centimetres wide, twenty to sixty centimetres long, called *yukurrukurru*. Munn translates this word as 'ancestral women' without mentioning the existence of the boards.[2] The boards are painted reverently on one side with designs of the Dreaming to be celebrated. This is said to awake the living image that inhabits them; in this sense the totemic female or male heroes are materialised in the boards. Some carry engraved designs, which are painted afresh at every ritual. The *yukurrukurru* boards are made by the men, often the husbands of the depositary women. Every woman should have her own board, but sometimes sisters or co-wives share one.

Men also give women smooth flat stones, elongated or oval in shape, called by various names, or simply called *Jukurrpa* or *Kuruwarri*, because they are believed to contain through their shape and their substance the living force of the relevant Dreaming: these stones are eminently sacred and always manipulated with great reverence and emotion. They come from totemic sites, and the power of those places is concentrated in them.

In some rituals, such as Acacia Seed (*ngurlu*) or Emu (*yankirri*), women also paint one or two wooden dishes of the same shape and name, *parraja*, as the ones used to carry babies on the hip or

---

[2] She does not mention the female boards but she uses the same word (*julguruguru*) for the male boards (Munn 1970: 154).

Doing and Becoming

food collected in the bush. In Yuendumu, they also paint smaller and deeper dishes, *ngami*. All these vessels are made by men but when they are designated for *yawulyu*, they may not be used for any other purpose. Some women have little boomerangs they use to stage a fight between the Yams (*yarla* and *wapirti*), a ritual that was dreamed by a Lajamanu woman in the 1960s:

> Long time ago I received a *yawulyu* for the Yam *Jukurrpa* that belongs to the Nakamarra and Napurrurla *skins*. *Mungamunga*, my mother gave me in dream four designs to paint on the body. Since then in Lajamanu and Yuendumu, women always dance decorated with these paintings to celebrate the land of Yumurrpa. The first design is the *jijardu* yam flower we call 'father'. From there run the *wapirti* roots we call 'mothers'. On these mother roots, young roots *ngamarna* develop, the 'children' who give the yams. The last design is *mardi*, the 'old man', the edible yam which terminates the young roots that spread everywhere.

> I saw these paintings for the first time when we performed, here in Lajamanu, the Rain Dreaming ceremony. The Nangala and Nampijinpa were dancing their land from Kulpulunu. And us, Nakamarra and Napurrurla, we danced with them for Wingki. It was formed by a cloud that came underground from Kulpulunu, was caught by a bushfire and choked, leaving a salty waterhole.

> We were dancing for weeks when I got this dream for Yam. In the morning I called the *kirda* women, 'Hey you, Nakamarra and Napurrurla! *Mungamunga* gave me a *yawulyu*. But it's not for my country Yiningarra. It is for your country Yumurrpa. It comes from your Yam Dreaming, so I give it to you, I can't keep it.'

> 'No', they said, 'you must make the paintings and look after this *yawulyu*, until we learn it properly. Then only you can give it to us.'

> *Mungamunga* had told me in my dream, 'Look at these yam leaves. Look well! Don't give them too fast, you must learn first!'

> All night the spirit of my mother helped me to learn. So in the morning I was able to teach and paint on the chest the four designs, 'father', 'mothers', 'children' and 'old man'. I also painted a *yukurrukurru* board with the *pilkardi* design, the adder that blocks the way to the roots and forces them to go up the surface. In my dream I saw the adder and heard her singing for the yams. She was going west. I dreamt I was painting a board with her design. The adder was rolling in the grass and calling the 'old man' to make many 'children'.

> After the adder, I saw two Yam men leave Yumurrpa to attack two other Yam men from Waputarli. The Yumurrpa men were big *Yarla* yams and

the Waputarli men were small *Wapirti* yams. The men fought, the big Yams killed the little ones. Going back to Yumurrpa, the victors put their roots in the ground and I saw new young roots and yams fall from the mother root.

This story is told in one of the songs I dreamt, 'In Yumurrpa, the young roots fell ... In Waputarli, the little Yams were evicted for ever.'

In the Dreaming the two *miyi* food were fighting, but since the groups custodians of the two Yams live in ritual company and cannot fight. After the fight, the roots spread everywhere in the plain. The 'father' went underground in a spring. His roots still come across the Yumurrpa cave.

When our elders lived in this site, they never touched these roots nor the yams from the cave. They would always go further away in the plain to find their food. When I was young, I camped with my family at Yumurrpa and used to go down in the cave to get water. I could feel the roots in the dark, and we took the water without hurting them. I had to push them gently to fill my water carrier, just like the *Kajirri* sisters.

In my sleep, *mungamunga* showed me Yurnkunjurru, the place where the 'old man' multiply himself so much that the ground cracked on the surface. I could see the grass becoming green with the growth of new yams. Two women were cooking and digging out yams. They were the *Kajirri* sisters. Seeing the cave, they bent over to see and shouted, 'Oh, but there's lots of women here!'

They continued to cook the yams. Then they erected two kuturu sticks in the ground. Then all the women came out of the cave and danced towards the two sticks. There was a lot of women. After the dance, they sat and the two sisters gave them yams to eat. They took out young men from the cave where they kept them in seclusion. It was midday.
'Where are we going to find some water?', asked one.
'We'll have to go down in the cave', said the other one.

So they lit little *yirriwurrunyu* firesticks. They needed light to see the roots, so not to hurt them. Very carefully they pushed the roots and they filled their *ngami* dishes in the spring. The other women of my dream were waiting outside to pick up the dishes the two sisters were filling, one after the other. (Janjiya Liddy Nakamarra Herbert, 1979)[3]

---

[3] This revelation recorded in 1979 was in the appendix of Glowczewski (1991), with an oral version in the CD-ROM (Glowczewski 2000). Janjiya Nakamarra also dreamt the Jurntu *purlapa* danced by the twelve men in Paris. See her portrait in Figure 4.1.

Doing and Becoming

For the Dreamings of the Initiated Man (*ngarrka*), the Digging Stick (*kana*) or the Honey Eater Bird (*manirtirrpitirrpi*) which sees the souls of the dead, women sometimes cut thin branches (*wurparri*) a metre or more long that represent spears. In everyday life, boomerangs and spears are restricted to men and should not be touched by women.

Of all the objects commonly used by women, the only one they make themselves is the hunting stick, *kana* or *karlangu*, about one metre long, sharp at both ends, which they used traditionally to dig out wild tubers, lizards or small marsupials, and for fighting. Today, although crowbars have replaced them for hunting, wooden sticks are still essential ritual objects, commonly called *kuturru*, fighting stick, and ceremonially *mangaya*, a term designating a female secret power. We will discuss this power more fully later. For dancing, women traditionally made headbands from hairstrings tinted in white or ochre and embellished with bandicoot tails that hung over on their forehead. Nowadays they wear a cloth ribbon to which they sometimes sew white feathers to form a peak.

A *yawulyu* can entail only painting up and singing, but usually when women dance a *kuturru* stick, coated with red ochre and decorated at one end with the design of the Dreaming being celebrated, is driven into the ground. It is said that the participants in the ritual are thus brought into contact with the *Jukurrpa* space-time and beings. Sometimes the stick is erected in the morning, with or without a dance performed by only one woman, and this gives the signal that a ritual will take place in the evening. For the Honey Ant (*yunkuranyi*), a circle is sometimes drawn around the stick on the ground and filled in with the appropriate designs.

At Lajamanu, ritual objects are always painted by the *kurdungurlu* women, the managers, that is members of clans allied to the one called *kirda*, owner of the Dreaming which is being celebrated. The distinction *kirda/kurdungurlu* is also operational among the women of Yuendumu, but it does not apply in the painting of objects[4] (Dussart 1988–1989). Every woman is owner of some Dreamings – hers and those of her 'brother' clans – and she is manager of other Dreamings, especially those of her mother's and her husband's clans.

Several Dreamings may be celebrated at the same time, especially if their paths of travel have crossed at the same site. Different sequences

---

[4] Dussart (1988–1989), this PhD thesis has since been published (Dussart 2000).

of dancing succeed one to another, in which the custodial functions are reversed. In principle, women dance a Dreaming as owners, and they play the role of choreographers as managers. They then surround the dancers, reminding them with many gestures and shouted orders the path they have to follow on the dancing ground. They are the ones who place the painted boards or other ritual objects there and give them to the dancers at the right moment. When the dance is accompanied by songs, some *kurdungurlu* stay sitting, and sing with the owners who do not dance.

On the ground, the trace of the naked feet of the dancers, who usually move along in Indian file, jumping with their legs straight and slightly apart, form meanders superimposed on one another. So they imprint in the sand, in a cloud of red dust, the geography of one or several ancestral Dreaming track. A good *yawulyu* ritual should raise a lot of sand. For some Dreamings, such as that of the Acacia Seed, a dancer picks up a handful of sand which she puts in a ritual dish carried under her arm and, as she jumps, she scatters this sand along her way. The same dish may be held with both hands, lifted to the sky, passed from one dancer to another and put on the ground, the unpainted concave side facing down. Sometimes women move forwards on their knees, close up against one other, and form a circle around a dish, a *kuturru* stick or the boards, on which the design is always turned towards the sky. They are then believed to catch the *Kuruwarri* concentrated in their painted bodies and these objects. With their palms open towards the sky, and shaken in a staccato manner, they lift the *Kuruwarri* to spread them on the earth. Then, their palms turned towards the earth, singing and beating the same beat, they send them back underground.

Sometimes two women make a more figurative pantomime of a specific ancestral event; often the managers perform this rather than the owners of this Dreaming. It usually happens during the night *yawulyu*.[5] All dancing terminates when the boards are deposited in front of the spectators or the erect stick, and a handful of sand is thrown to close the ritual by interrupting the link with the *Jukurrpa* space-time.

When another *yawulyu* is not planned for the next day, one or two women dance and take away the stick. The dances rarely last more than half an hour, except in the nocturnal vigils or initiation cycles. As soon as the dancing is finished, the managers hide the

---

[5] Or in the bush, that is when men cannot see what is going on.

Doing and Becoming

objects in suitcases, or slide them between the leaves of the roof of the boughshade in the women's ceremonial camp. Before every ritual, the designs painted on the objects during the previous ritual are erased then the objects are painted again, with the same or different designs. The painted women get dressed and usually sleep still painted. If during a new ritual traces of the old designs persist they wash them away before they are repainted.

Male Rituals

Male elders meet every day on the ceremonial ground, but they complain that young people do not join them and that, for this reason, they are unable to perform their rituals as often as women. To summarise Meggitt: like women, men paint their bodies and ritual objects, they perform dances or pantomimes which stage ancestral epics, and they share the ritual functions between *kirda* and *kurdungurlu*. The musicologist Wild (1977) has noted that both men and women are painted on their chest, belly, thighs and face, but only managers are painted on the back. Preparation for male rituals takes longer and is more elaborate than for female rituals, especially when men use bid down or wilf cotton to cover their bodies and faces. They dye it white or red and glue it to their skin. In the most secret rituals, blood is drawn from their arms and used as a fixative.

Among the ritual objects, *juju*, are wooden boards with different names that are often connected to particular Dreamings, beings or trails. They may be engraved, painted or both. Some are pierced at one end, to which a string is attached, which allows the board to be whirled round to produce the humming sound typical of a bullroarer. Women, who are supposed not to know of the bullroarer's existence,[6] attribute the sound to a Dreaming bird *kuyupardukuyupardu*, which protects the initiates; its name, which incorporates the word *kuyu*, flesh or game, alludes to the bird always calling out for meat, its hunger like that of the young initiate who is prohibited from eating meat during his retreat.[7] In their rituals, men decorate their

---

[6] Most women do know, but they pretend not to for the sake of the young girls and boys (see Glowczewski [1989] 2016).

[7] When the bullroarer (like other boards) is materialising a female being, it also alludes to the hunger of the novice's future mother-in-law who is waiting for him to be initiated, to get the game he will hunt for her (see the ritual at the end of the initiation).

Figure 4.2 Warlpiri men performing Jurntu purlapa, Théâtre des Bouffes du Nord, Paris © B. G. 1983

shields, which are similar in shape to the women's dishes, and they build emblems, headdresses or poles – structures made with hair-strings covered with down and painted – characterising a particular Dreaming.

For Dreamings such as Python (*pirntina*) or Emu (*yankirri*) men sometimes paint large ground paintings, always with the same technique, using glued bird down to fill the space between designs traced in red. Women may not see the making of these frescos, except in some rain-making rituals that do not take place nowadays, in which men and women used to sing together for hours. Invited to Paris for the Festival d'Automne 1983, twelve Warlpiri men from Lajamanu agreed to produce such a fresco associated with the Jurntu site for the Python Dreaming on condition that it would be destroyed afterwards. At the Théâtre des Bouffes du Nord they also performed a dance associated with the same site that was revealed in a dream to Janjiya Nakamarra, a prolific woman dreamer.

The dance depicted the spirits of three deceased male custodians of the Rain Dreaming, who had gone to join their *Jukurrpa* to give this dream to their descendants through the medium of the woman, who belonged to another clan.

Doing and Becoming

All started with the bough shade where I kept my business things in a case. Especially the *yukurrukurru* painted with the Yam Dreaming I dreamt earlier on. My bough shade was very close to the one of the Nampijinpa and Nangala.

One day, as I was coming back from work at the mission kitchen, a Napanangka called out
'All your things are burnt!'

When I was away some flames came out from my bough shade. She tried to stop the fire with two other women, but the fire stopped only after burning my case. I started to wonder
'Is it a Fire spirit that lit a fire in my case? But why?'

I was very sad and went to sleep. That night, I dreamt about two Nangala each coming to me with a *yukurrukurru* board. They were dancing and shaking them and put them in front of me when they sat. Then a crowd of Dreamtime women came to dance. I did not recognise their faces. But the Nangala had the face of Yakiriya and Miyangula. I was in the dream too, and I was feeling sick every time I saw the boards in their hands. They were painted with new designs, and to see them made me weak.

When I woke up in the morning, I was so weak that I had to go to the clinic. The sister said she might have to send me to the Darwin hospital. I knew I was not really sick, it was only the dream that had hit me too strong. My mother's spirit and all these Dreaming women had caught my spirit, making me *warungka* (mad). I slept at the clinic and had the same dream again.

The next day some women came to visit me. I recognised Yakiriya et Miyangula and shouted
'I always see you two dancing!'

I was delirious but the two Nangala in my dream had their faces. The nurse kept me at the clinic for a month. Night after night, I was dreaming the same dream or new things connected with it.

Finally I was better and I asked all the women and men to gather. They came to the camp where my things had burnt near Kuwinyi. I told them, 'I'll give a new *yawulyu* to the Nampijinpa and Nangala women for the Fire Dreaming. And to the Jampijinpa and Jangala men, I'll give a new *purlapa* dance for Jurntu.'

Women and men listened to me. They had recognised in my long sickness the message of *mungamunga*, the Voice of the Night who had brought me a new yawulyu to dance, to sing and to paint. The Fire spirit had burnt my things to give me these dreams.

I know now that I dreamt of Yakiriya and Miyangula because it was the spirit of their deceased fathers who was using them to teach me the new way to celebrate their Dreaming. I saw the two men, Yunkugarna, Miyangula's father, and Munkurturru, Yakiriya's father. It was his spirit who lit the fire, my mother's spirit told me so.

The two men were custodians of the Rain Dreaming at Lungkardajarra. I saw them with a third Jampijinpa, Werrilwerrilpa, custodian of the Fire Dreaming at Jurntu, who was killed by his uncles when I was little.

These three spirits brought me the *purlapa* for the men. The dance and the songs tell about the chasing and the killing of Werrilwerrilpa. The purlapa celebrates Jurntu with the Fire and *pirntina* Python Dreaming.

I saw the spirits of the three men making a big fire as they were travelling. It happened in Kartarlda, a *Ngatijirri* budgerigar place. The three men continued to travel, flying to the North until they got to Lajamanu.

I could hear the music from the boomerangs. I came close to the big hollow log at Kuwinyi and said
'They sing a purlapa!'

So, in my dream, all the Warlpiri men from Lajamanu came to sit near a ceremonial ground that was not cleared there yet. The three spirits came out of the hollow log. They were carrying *kutari* headdresses, very high with feathers on the top. Their whole body was covered with white fluff. And the Fire and Python Dreaming was drawn in red on their chests, thighs and faces.

Same time, I saw big white clouds carrying rain. A fourth spirit was travelling with them, but he did not stop at Lajamanu. He continued his flight further north to the sea. I saw him jumping in the ocean, and coming out with lots of splashes. He looked at the open space, the sky and said
'I went too far!'

So he landed back in Lajamanu on the plane ground! He carried a spear and danced with it towards the other three Jampijinpa. Munkurturru, who had brunt my things, shouted then
'Look! Mangurlpa!'

It was the spirit's name and also the name of that spear. The four spirits went then to Palwa, a *Wampana* Wallaby place. Women can't go to this place, but in my dream, this is where I saw the spirits show the new purlapa to the Lajamanu men.

'You have to train for the purlapa just as I heard it and saw it in my dream', I said to the men and asked my niece's husband to cut leaves to make a bough shade just like in my dream.

Doing and Becoming

'Where should I put the shade?'

'Just there. It must be opened to the South because the spirits came from there to sit.'

The message was passed from camp to camp, and when the shade was built, all the women came to sit there and sang the new *purlapa* songs with me. Then the men repeated verse after verse what *mungamunga* had taught me. All night we sang.

The next day, the women learnt the new yawulyu. They were happy to receive a new way to celebrate Jurntu. They painted their bodies with the new designs and sang with me the new songs that I had dreamt.

I painted them with the *jingi jingi* 'across' design that shows the plucking of the fire. I also painted the yinti 'sparks' design. These were the designs I had seen on the *yukurrukurru* boards, red for the fire and white for the smoke. The women copied the designs and I also showed them the new dancing steps and how to mime the sparks with their hands and the fire being plucked. It is how *mungamunga* showed me the wind taking the sparks. The women danced. And we've been dancing this yawulyu everywhere ever since.

Meantime in another place men were decorating themselves. When they finished they came to us. Other men sat down to sing the new *purlapa* with the boomerang percussion.

Women join them legs straight in front of them, beating the rhythm, two hands on top of each other, palms hitting the thighs. The men started to dance, the same dance they took to your country (Paris). *Mungamunga* took us even further than the salt water where the spirit dove in!

Our men are proud of the *purlapa* I gave them. Every time they dance it, they have to pay me kunari, a ritual gift. But when I gave them the *purlapa* for the first time, I had to pay the *kunari*. The Nangala and Nampijinpa women helped me to pay. We made two big dampers. One for the kirda, Jangala and Jampijinpa, the other for the *kurdungurlu* of the Fire Dreaming, Japaljarri and Japanangka. Each group also received a pile of cloth.

After this ritual, the kirda men made new *yukurrukurru* boards for me. I painted on them the Fire designs I had seen in my dream. At every *yawulyu*, these designs are swept away and painted again. The boards are used only for the Fire Dreaming and the Rain Dreaming. (Janjiya Liddy Nakamarra Herbert, 1979)[8]

---

[8] See Figure 4.1. This story by Janjiya was not in the original book (1991) but it was published in the *Dream Trackers* CD-ROM (with audio extracts, Glowczewski 2000) and is commented upon in Glowczewski (1989).

Figure 4.3 Men and boys during marlulu *initiation* © B. G. 1984

The type of male dances that women can attend is called *purlapa*, a name also given to the mixed-gender singing sessions. After the trip to Paris, the Jurntu *purlapa* became a sort of emblem. The men made all the little boys dance it at the end of school in 1984, and they performed it in Katherine in July when they marched there with other Aboriginal people for the celebration of National Aboriginal Day.[9] The *purlapa* dancers are always accompanied by a group of seated singers who give the beat by striking together two boomerangs or small sticks, or sometimes one stick against a shield lying on the ground. These percussion instruments are the only musical instruments of the desert tribes, who do not have the didgeridoo (horns) or the drums hollowed from logs of the Arnhem land tribes.

Wild (1977–1978) distinguishes two dancing styles among the Warlpiri, mimetic (*walaparini*) and non-mimetic (*mirli-mirli* or *wintimi*). The men mostly practise the first style, which includes four categories. *Wapantja-kura*, the walking dance, consists of raising the

---

[9] Corresponding to the anniversary of the death, in 1876, of Trucanini, called the 'last' survivor of the massacre of the Tasmanians; since the 1980s, thousands of descendants of the original inhabitants have been claiming their ancestry in Tasmania. NAD became NAIDOC.

Doing and Becoming

knees high and stamping the feet hard on the ground. It is the style used in *purlapa*. But in the rituals restricted to men they can dance running, *pangkatja-kura*, crawling on on all fours, *kiripikanji*, or sitting down, *nyinantja-kura*. Only the sitting or kneeling dances are accompanied by songs, directly translating words into gestures. These dances, which identify the performers with ancestral heroes, often imitate the associated totemic animals. The 'non-mimetic' dances consist in jumping with legs slightly apart in the women's style; they may also be miming female behaviour.

Although at present it is rare for the men to decide (as women do) to celebrate a particular *Jukurrpa*, they are extremely active as soon as an initiation cycle is to begin. The initiation process means that young males from twelve to twenty, sometimes up to thirty, according to the age group concerned, have to be caught and put into seclusion far from women during the whole length of the ceremonial period, which may take from a week to several months. This is the occasion nowadays when men display their various territorial rituals for the younger men.

Kurdiji: *The Boys' First Initiation*

At least once a year, and sometimes more often, a ceremony called *kurdiji*, shield, takes place to prepare one, two or, unusually, three boys for circumcision. Meggitt (1962) gives a detailed account and I have described part of the ceremony elsewhere (Glowczewski 1989b). Some ritual innovations have been introduced since the 1950s, but until recently the issue was still the same: to ally the young initiate to his future father-in-law, his circumciser and his future mother-in-law. This mother-in-law is usually a girl of his own age, whose daughter, already born or yet to be born, is to become his wife.

On the day of his capture by the elders, the novice is called *marlulu* (from *marlu*, kangaroo), and for the first time he attends a ritual male dance. Then he is brought back to the middle of the group which is waiting on ground specially prepared for a nocturnal gathering, *marnakurrawarnu* (from *marna*, grass), during which men sing and women dance (see Figure 4.3). The novice is separated from the men by the women and the children. He sits at the back and is made to stand up at regular intervals by two guardians, his brothers-in-law, who make him look at the sky where the morning star will appear. The most active role in the singing and dancing is taken by men and women called *yulpuwanulurlu* (from *yulpu*, red), the novice's 'fathers' (father's clanic brothers), the maternal uncles, the 'mothers' (mother's sisters and co-wives) and the paternal aunts. These women have their chests painted, wear a *minyeri* headband and dance handing a firestick from one to the other. The novice's clanic sisters and brothers, who in this context are called *jarrawarnulu* (from *jarra*, fat), also participate: the former to dance and the latter to sing until daybreak. At dawn, the novice passes through the assembly with his guardians, who take him to the seclusion camp where he receives the firestick that passed between the women dancers, and with which he lights his first fire, becoming thus *warluwarnu* (from *warlu*, fire).

The firestick is given back to the women, who light it a week later, on the day before circumcision, during a second nocturnal mixed gathering on new ceremonial ground, *kirrirdikirrawarnu* (from *kirrirdi*, big camp). This time, the ground is formed into two big circles linked by a wide path and surrounded by two bough windbreaks, *yunta*,[10] located to the East and the West. Women dance using the stick from the previous gathering, until the mother of the novice hands it to the mother of the girl who has been chosen as the boy's future mother-in-law. This is how the alliance made by the women of the boy's matriline with another matriline is unveiled, a decision that has been secret until now, and should not be commented on or even mentioned until the boy comes out from seclusion. At the end of the night, the brother-in-law guardians of the boy erect a spear next to him on which they fix ropes made of hairstring and many pieces of cloth, presents for the clanic mothers and aunts of the boy. At daybreak, the novice's mothers and aunts, accompanied by his sisters and one or two women of his promised wife's matriline, take him into the bush for a long smoking ritual, *jurnku* (see Figure 4.4). When they bring the boy back to the ceremonial ground, his mothers receive from their sons-in-law the ropes and cloths that have been taken off the spear: they give some back to their brothers and some to their husbands before disappearing with the rest.

At sunset, women and children come back to the night ground to attend the *witi* dance. *Witi* are leafy poles which male dancers fasten to their ankles in remembrance of the Initiated Man people who saw such poles grow from their feet. The dancers perform, one after the other, a curious motion, shaking all their body and rustling the leaves on the poles, which extend almost two metres above them. Men encourage the dancers with shouts while women extend their arms

---

[10] The same name as for windbreaks used in camp.

Doing and Becoming

Figure 4.4 Women carrying boys for a smoking ritual before handing them to men
© B. G. 1984

or pinch each other in excitement. At the end of the dance, at a signal from the elders, most women have to put their heads down. The very old women, or those who have already participated as *yulpuwarnurlu* in several *kurdiji*, see then the arrival of the circumciser, whose identity has to stay secret. He dances to the rhythm of songs broken with very sudden silences, then he lies on top of the boy. Straight away, at a new signal from the elders, the women run away, except for a few who may see the presentation of some emblems before also disappearing to let the men proceed with the circumcision.

Before he is to be circumcised, the boy is covered with a large cross the branches of which are stretched with hairstrings painted with Dreaming designs. This sacred object is shaped like a kite and is called the Southern Cross, *waniki*. It may not be seen by women. It animates the boy's *pirlirrpa*, soul, by making the *Kuruwarri* forces of his clan enter him. In the esoteric knowledge, when at death the soul is drawn up towards the Magellanic Clouds, the smaller galaxy refers to *the* circumciser. The circumciser chosen by the men of the boy's matriline is expected to give one or more of his daughters to the future circumcised when the latter reaches a marriageable age. If the operator is not the husband of the mother-in-law chosen by the women, the circumcised can then claim simultaneously a daughter from his mother-in-law and another from his circumciser, on condition that he satisfies his in-laws by regularly providing them with a share of the products of his hunt. Although all men and women have their 'promised' husband or wife, actual marriages may cancel ritual promises, especially if the chosen mother-in-law does not produce a daughter.

Traditionally, the period between the first gathering and the second extended from one to several months, during which time the novice, guided by his brothers-in-law, travelled a long initiation circuit to visit different clans, who would perform their respective territorial rituals for him. On this journey, all the boy's potential fathers-in-law gave him hairstrings to present to his father. Nowadays, such a trip is sometimes done by car, and the boy may be initiated in another settlement, even in another tribe. Thus, in 1979, a boy was brought to Lajamanu from Noonkanbah, located more than 1,000 km to the West in the Kimberley, to be initiated at the same time as two Warlpiri boys.[11]

After circumcision, the newly initiated youth must remain in seclusion for at least another week for his convalescence. Unlike the period between the two nocturnal gatherings, a week during which the men staged for him a series of territorial rituals, now he stays alone, and is only visited by his brothers-in-law and uninitiated boys, to whom he must not tell anything about what has happened to him. In Meggitt's (1962) time, the post-convalescence ritual, marking the return of the boy to society with the status of a man, was as follows: he ate a vegetable dish prepared by his future mother-in-law, the wife of the circumciser. The latter sat back to back with the boy and ate a portion of the big offering of game that was given to him in the boy's name. As a sign of exchange, the circumciser also ate some of the vegetable dish, and he rubbed the lips of his future son-in-law with a piece of meat before they separated. This gesture allowed the initiate to eat meat, and at the same time to speak, two activities controlled during his seclusion. The game offered to the circumciser and future father-in-law had been caught and cooked by members of the boy's patriline and matriline, with the help of his direct brothers-in-law. This gift, to which were eventually added red ochre, hairstrings, boomerangs, spears, shields and even Western clothes represented payment for the ritual service of the circumciser, and the bride price.

[11] In 1992/1993 a Lajamanu boy was taken even further to Bidyadanga on the north-west coast.

Today, payment in game is replaced by a present of clothes and blankets, and it is not the male relatives of the circumcised youth who provide it but the female: the mother, helped by her sisters, co-wives and sisters-in-law (paternal aunts of the boy). The day after the circumcision, these women, their faces painted white as if in mourning, deposit on the ground a big pile of clothes for the circumciser. These are women's clothes: the gift to the circumciser is for his wife, the future mother-in-law; similarly, the return gift made by her is intended for the circumcised youth's mother. This ritual is called *palkajarri*, 'become body' that is to be born. The paint on the women's faces symbolises the death of the boy, who will be born again as an initiate of his clan, which has contracted an alliance with the respective clans of his future father-in-law and mother-in-law.

Women's Secret: Mangaya

For girls, the initiation process is less formal because natural transformations (growing of breasts and pubic hair, menarche, pregnancy) accompany the practices that ritualise them. The assignment of a girl as a novice's mother-in-law is a type of initiation, as it foreshadows her separation from the daughter she is to bear. In the old days, at the time when the boy was being circumcised, in another camp his sisters and female paternal cousins were enduring ritual scarifications: two arcs between the breasts, or on the belly if they were pregnant or breastfeeding a child, so that the milk would not be contaminated by blood. This was a way to mark, on the body, the separation between brothers and sisters totemically united but destined to marry outside of the clan. The taking of a girl's virginity was also ritualised: it was done with two fingers bound by a hairstring, or by an introcision of the entry to a girl's vagina 'to help a girl to give birth'. We will come back to this later (Chapter 5: p. 174).

The purpose of the female initiation process is to change the girl into a woman, that is to allow her, as she grows older, to gain the *mangaya* power that will give her a privileged relationship with the space-time of the Dreaming. She will then be able to communicate with the ancestral beings and to receive revelations in her dreams. When a woman dreams a new *yawulyu* ritual, it is said that she receives the dream through the intermediary of *yiniwurru* or *mungamunga*, terms that designate generically all the ancestral women associated with totems and sites. But it is also that which resides underground, and talks in dreams to women, and sometimes to children to help them to find their way if they get lost in the bush. Finally, it reveals to the older women new designs to paint on their bodies, new verses to sing, and gestures for dances associated with totemic sites and heroes. A woman usually starts to have such dreams only after she has participated as a 'mother' in a male initiation, that is, once she has experienced the ritual separation of a son she grew up with – her own, her co-wife's or her sister's.[12]

According to Meggitt (1966), the term *mungamunga* used by the northern tribes, such as the Mudbura and Warumungu, was not used at Lajamanu in the 1950s. Ten years later at Yuendumu, Munn found the word *yiniwurru* restricted to women and meaning 'spirit-child'. Today, the Lajamanu women identify *mungamunga* with *yiniwurru*; they also sometimes speak of *tiyatiya*. Dussart (1988) noted, in Yuendumu, that *tiyatiya* denotes ancestral beings of any gender. At Lajamanu, *tiyatiya* denotes pubic depilation, a ritual inaugurated by ancestral women, which entails the women being rubbed before and after the depilation with yellow ochre, *karntawarra* (from *karnta*, woman), which is believed to prevent burns. By this secret ritual, performed during initiations, dispute settling ceremonies or mourning, women reinforce their *mangaya* power. But men also practise ritual depilation. According to the elders, this practice used to characterise the eastern Warlpiri in the eyes of their neighbours, who sometimes called them *tiyatiya*. Many concepts are polyvalent in Aboriginal languages.

Munn noticed that women dreamers, after giving the location of (the protagonists) of their dreams, refer to spirit-children or to ancestral beings in the first person. This apparent amalgam between the dreamer and what she dreams about – spirit-children and ancestral beings – implies not a confusion of the three, but a conceptual identity as expressed in the word *yiniwurru*. Therefore, *yiniwurru* defines the Dreaming generative process, which allows dreamers to see the spirit-children they embody or the ones that will be embodied in children to be born, and to communicate with the ancestral principles from which these spirit-children come. Some women call *yiniwurru* '*ngati*', mother, which suggests the idea of a generative matrix. Symbolised in relation to the female body, *yiniwurru* cannot

---

[12] Actual separation from a daughter when she gets married also marks a formal access to dreams: officially confirmed as a mother-in-law, a woman often dreams about her son-in-law's Dreamings. We will see that the mother-in-law/son-in-law relationship is central to many Dreaming stories.

be reduced to a womb image. Like the infinite night, this matrix takes the form of each thing it generates: images of nocturnal dreams, spirit-children and totemic figures. Inseparable from *yiniwurru* is its intrinsic power, *mangaya*, which is defined as masculine. In this sense, the generative matrix is two-gendered.

In contemporary settlements, female rituals are generally celebrated near a *jilimi*, a camp reserved to women, some divorced, some widows and some married women who wish to be away temporarily from their husband's camp. During the day other married women come to join the others to discuss, to rest, to pick lice from one another's hair, to play cards or to participate in the eventual *yawulyu* on the ceremonial ground. Men must not trespass across the limit of a *jilimi* nor watch what is happening there; nevertheless, as the camp is often surrounded by the family camps, its feminine activities are not hidden. When women camp in the bush, a *jilimi* is any sleeping space for women, old or young, who want to stay away from the men. *Jilimi* is also the name given to places at sacred sites which are reserved to women: rocks, springs, rockholes, or even hills, whose shapes sometimes explicitly evoke a female organ. These markers are associated with episodes from female versions of the mythical trails or songlines and women can perform their ritual dances there.

Men's Secret: Maralypi

To explain their dreams, men do not refer to *yiniwurru* or *mangaya*. On the other hand, they, like the women, say that they split in two: their *pirlirrpa* soul sees and hears the spirit-child they embody and that leads them on the track of the ancestral heroes in *Jukurrpa*. According to Meggitt (1962), they have in their shoulder a little lizard that guides their spirit. Thus, the dream experience is different for each gender.

While women have special places in the sacred sites, men have others which are absolutely forbidden to women. This is where, traditionally, the sacred rites were performed to perpetuate clans and related species; at the Rain Dreaming sites, rain-making rituals took place. Men used to go into some desert caves to paint designs on the walls or to repaint them. Cave paintings are not only associated with specific ancestral heroes but are also considered to be their trace which, generation after generation, the initiates renovate. In this context, *Kuruwarri* as a human drawing is, like the images seen in dreams, a pure copy of an ancestral imprint. If women come close to the cave, say the Warlpiri, they would put in great peril themselves, the men and the future of the clan. This demarcation implies that 'men's business is not women's business' and vice versa but 'without one or the other there is no business ...'.

Each clan, among all the sites on its path of travel, has just one which corresponds to the place in which are concentrated all the *Kuruwarri* scattered inside the other sites, the members of the clan and all the things bearing the same name. This singularity, which condenses all the living images, is called *maralypi*, the power of generation of the clan and the species associated with its path of travel. Reported by the linguist Hale (1974), *maralypi* is not mentioned by Meggitt, who only speaks of the 'concentrated expression' of the *Kuruwarri*, present in a clanic site, and at the same time in all the men under the form of the patriclanic and matriclanic spirit, *bilirba* (Meggitt 1962: 207, 192). According to my data, rather than a patriclanic or matriclanic spirit and a 'concentrated expression' of the *Kuruwarri, pirlirrpa* (*bilirba*) is the individual spirit, a person's soul which is animated by the *Kuruwarri* of the father's clan and the mother's clan, and which is also the medium for men and women to attain *maralypi*, the singularity which concentrates the *Kuruwarri*.[13]

Maralypi, even more than the concentrated expression of the *Kuruwarri* is the driving principle of all the forms the *Kuruwarri* can take (totems, people, places). In this sense, *maralypi* is the secret of life, a business restricted to men. That is why women only whisper the word, and so refer to what is unmentionable because ineffable. There are many clanic sites designated by the term *maralypi*, as many as there are different clans or local groups. In other words, there is no one *maralypi* centre for everybody. Nor is there any hierarchy between the diverse totems characterised by *maralypi* places: they

---

[13] Swain (1993) finding a 'contradiction' in Warlpiri spirit beleifs, assumes the theory of *pirlirrpa* going in the sky as inspired by Christianity versus the traditional belief of the *Kuruwarri* going into the ground of the sites. From the Warlpiri point of view I do not see any contradiction between the fact that the *Kuruwarri* (the forces one shares with one's group, places and totemic species) and the *Kurruwalpa* (spirit-child) go into the land while the *pirlirrpa* (individual soul) is taken away by the Magellanic Clouds. In fact I do not agree with Swain's systematic interpretation of any sky belief as being of Christian influence: to me the presence of multi-components in a person and their separate destiny after death (earth and interstellar space) is in accordance with the Warlpiri complex cosmology expressed in the opposition *kanunju/kankarlu* (below/above) (see end of Chapter 3; for a review of Swain, see Glowczewski 1996).

participate together in the mystery of life. Hale (1974) remarked that men use the word *tarnnga*, always, as an antonym to *maralypi*; thus, *maralypi* is opposed to eternity as process (coming into being). *Jukurrpa* is at the same time eternity and process, but these two attributes are distinguished one from the other as the two inseparable faces of permanence.

In a generic way, as a secret and spatial reference, the term *maralypi* designates male territorial rituals. On the other hand, when the death of an important ritual custodian, man or woman, is not just followed by the usual taboos on using the name and the songline associated with the deceased but by a general prohibition extending to the celebration of his or her whole Dreaming path of travel and the approach to its *maralypi* place, this word is used to designate the ceremony that marks the end of mourning. It is said that *maralypi* 'opens' the *Jukurrpa* that was 'closed' during mourning.[14] In the context of sedentary life, the Warlpiri can perform this ceremony without going to the *maralypi* site; they simply retrace the songline through their ritual acting. The men dance in order to put back into circulation the *maralypi* source of life, and occasionally some older women witness it so that they can catch what is liberated from the ground and the *Kuruwarri* living forces can propagate again on the earth. But women say that they can also harness this generative power at a distance, on their ground where they perform, parallel to the men, the *yawulyu* ritual associated with the same Dreaming. Once open, it allows them to lift all the taboos and to name again people and things who were referrred to as *kumanjayi*, 'no name'.

In 1984 at Lajamanu, I witnessed the female ritual activities accompanying the male *maralypi* ceremony opening the Digging Stick Dreaming, which is connected to a site called Janyingki. Women, after having erected the sacred stick for this *Jukurrpa*, which has not been used during the two years of mourning, put a pile of cloth at its foot and a bag containing hairstring ropes and sacred stones. One after the other, widows, mothers and mothers-in-law of the deceased touched the stick, then sat among the other women. Then, contrary to the normal rule, men, nephews and cousins of the deceased were invited into the women's camp to touch in their turn the stick, the stones and the ropes. At a woman's signal, they took the cloths away with them, then one man was called back to pull out the stick and to put it on the bag with the stones and the ropes. Soon afterwards

---

[14] A *Jukurrpa* that is 'closed' has 'no room' for singing, dancing and painting it.

the women hid everything. Through touching these objects everybody is impregnated with the *Kuruwarri* contained in them, and transfers into the objects part of his or her own living image that will strengthen the people who will touch the objects later. All become relays of a circuit through which the *Jukurrpa* power will actualise the *maralypi* singularity. The intervention of the men on the women's ground works in two ways: through the medium of the objects the men receive the *Kuruwarri* of the women, to whom they give the *Kuruwarri* they actualise in their secret activities. The first stage of the opening of the Dreaming is completed by entering it.

Two weeks later, around midday, ten young women joined the elders on a new ceremonial ground prepared in the bush, to be painted and to dance. At the foot of the two erected sticks connected by a hairstring rope was a pile of blankets. The managers, members of clans allied to the Digging Stick (*kana*) clan, opened the dance. The elders gave them each a long *wurparri* branch that represented the spears the Digging Stick women gave to the Initiated Men. The dancers criss-crossed each other as they brandished the spears and danced around the two sticks. Then they piled the branches on the ground, and the Digging Stick owners took over from them. They advanced on their knees, one close behind the other, looking around everywhere like animals looking for prey or being tracked by predators. When they got up, they were given the *wurparri* branches in their turn, and also boards painted like their chests, with designs from their Dreaming. They danced forward to meet two new dancers painted with the Goanna (*pilja*) Dreaming and carrying under their arms dishes adorned with the same design. The to-ing and fro-ing that followed staged the meeting of these two Dreamings, at the end of which Goanna tricked the Digging Stick women by making them *minyeri* headbands and *makarra*, matrix, ropes with the hair of the heroes of the Initiated Man Dreaming; he seduced them into giving up their knowledge to the men.

Having left their spear-branches on the ground, the Digging Stick dancers took their boards in two hands. They directed one end towards the ground, moving the boards up and down, as if drawing up and being drawn down by an invisible force. The women I talked to said that even though the myth says that the female ancestors revealed to the men the pleasures of the flesh, this to and fro motion does not refer to human sexuality but to the palpitation of the underground forces, the breathing of the earth as a metamorphosis of the bodies of the ancestral heroes. Putting down their boards, the dancers then performed above them, with their hands spread apart, the same up-and-down movement that generally concludes all *yawulyu*; the image-forces of the Digging Stick Dreaming, liberated by the symbolic opening of this Dreaming and of its *maralypi* site, had just been put back into circulation on the earth and were now returning underground.

The two piles of blankets which, all through the ritual, had stayed at the foot of the two *kuturru* sticks, were taken to the edge of the ceremonial ground, and after finishing their own celebration of the Digging Stick Dreaming on the male ground the men took them away. The *maralypi* ceremony was over. It has been staged simultaneously, in two different places, by the men and the women. The separation in space symbolised this polarity of gender as necessary for actualising *maralypi*. Some Warlpiri use the metaphor of an electric current.

Intermythical Dialogues

How to understand the differentiation of male and female roles in rituals? Some myths offer a first answer. The female version of the Goanna Dreaming tells of mother Goanna, who laid the eggs from which the Goanna people were born. She came back to brood the eggs where she had left them but, later on, her children were afraid of her and ran away because she was less 'human' than they were. Since that time, female goannas abandon their eggs straight after laying them in their burrows: the babies hatch on their own, thanks, say the Warlpiri, to *maralypi*, which the Goanna Dreaming left once and for all in the Goanna totemic site, Yinapalku.[15] The *pilja* goanna species, descending from the Dreaming bearing this name, thus offers a model in which women are excluded from the places of gestation of the *Kuruwarri* forces, while women who are entered by the spirit-children are recognised as producers of children, like the females who lay eggs. This animal model and its mythical interpretation is used to justify the prohibition imposed on women from coming close to places with the secret of life, *maralypi*.

According to the female version of the Digging Stick Dreaming, it is women and not men who used to go down in the caves and perform initiations, until the Goanna Dreaming came and intervened. By using male hair from the Initiated Man Dreaming, Goanna made the objects for which the ancestral women exchanged their ritual, sexual

---

[15] See CD-ROM Glowczewski (2000) and www.odsas.net

and hunting knowledge. The meeting of these three Dreamings institutes the social model that allows women to hunt with digging sticks and not with long spears, that reserves to men access to the special caves, and initiations, during which women have to wear the *minyeri* handbands, like the ones introduced by Goanna; like the ancestral women they receive hairstrings in exchange for the sons they give up to the men.[16]

The male version of the Digging Stick Dreaming given by Meggitt (1966: 131–8) presents itself differently. Here is a summary.

Travelling on their own, the women met some north-westerners who invited them to join the group. They camped together at Kanakurlangu (Ganagulangu) 'belonging to the Digging Stick' where the men went hunting wallabies leaving the boys under the women's care. Furious at being excluded from the hunting, the women took revenge by hitting the boys with their digging sticks, but the men, alerted by one man, came back and beat the women. Entrusting the boys to a male elder, they sent the women to a place with *ngalyipi* vines, which they had to twist into ropes. The women came back to the camp and used wallaby hair to make armlets and headbands, on which they drew love magic designs. Adorned with the handbands, they danced for the men, who forgot their anger, and sang and ate with them. Then, when the women went to urinate in the bush before sleep, the youngest men took their digging sticks and stuck them in the ground with the headbands hanging from them, a sign of their desire to make love with the women. The women accepted, unbeknownst to the elders.

The next day they all took off, and when the women saw a group of wallabies they could not stop themselves from throwing their sticks at them, the way they used to hunt when they were on their own. But, tired from their nocturnal activities, they missed them all and made them run away, provoking again the anger of the men, who attacked them with their throwing sticks (they had no boomerangs or spears). They killed a few women and gave up on the others, saying that hunting was not their domain. The Digging Stick women, happy to get rid of those unpleasant companions, continued their travels singing, dancing and miming the events they had just been through. Some went underground in Warlpiri country, others continued to Yanmadgeri, Aranda and Yalyuwari country. One woman

---

[16] A female version of the Digging Stick myth (*kana*) was published in the art catalogue Glowczewski (1991b) and also in the CD-ROM Glowczewski (2000).

was caught on the way by a perentie coming from Aranda country, who tied her to a tree with hairstring and wanted to seduce her. When she refused, he made a headband adorned with Dreaming designs and sang love magic, *yilpinji*, that turned out to be effective: when he showed himself wearing this headband, the woman gave up; engaging in passionate love, they disappeared underground at Nganingiri, the Dreaming place of Perentie and Tree Honey.

In spite of their differences, the male and female versions of the Digging Stick Dreaming combine the same elements. In both cases, the ancestral women, who had the power to hunt, lose it when they come into contact with men, and the action takes place in a site with *ngalyipi* vines: in Meggitt's version women must prepare these vines, which are used to fix the poles of the Initiated Man Dreaming *witi* ceremony; in the version I collected the place where the Digging Stick women give their initiation knowledge to the heroes of the Initiated Man Dreaming is called Ngalyipimalu, after the vines. The male myth shows the women's failure to look after the boys, just as in the female myth the boys' custody is passed from women to men. Finally, in the male version, the women seduce the men with the headbands they make, and Perentie makes a headband to seduce a woman; in the female version the heroines are seduced by the headbands that Goanna made for them, and they give in to the men.

These three themes, hunting, seduction and initiation, recur in another sequence of the male Digging Stick myth, with the Transgressor, *Wingkingarrka* (from *wingki*, transgression, and *ngarrka*, man, orthographed *Winggingarga* by Meggitt (1966), and *Wadaingula* by Peterson (1967), who gives a slightly different version[17]).

Transgressor was coming from the Pintupi tribe's territory, with the appearance of a man but with such a long penis that he had to coil it around his neck or waist when he walked. This penis ended with a fork like the tongue of a snake, danced ahead of him when he stopped and had an insatiable sexual appetite; the man travelled on the surface of the ground and sometimes underneath (Meggitt, Peterson).

At Djundi, he saw the track of a *wakulyari* wallaby from Kunajarrayi (Gunadjari); he attempted to catch it by lighting a bushfire but failed (Peterson). At Badjanbanda, he met a female wallaby and tried to rape her; she shouted for help and the Digging Stick women who were camping nearby came to help her, hitting the rapist

---

[17] For analysis of the version of Peterson (1967), cf. Glowczewski ([1984] 2009).

and cutting off his penis; he died, but his penis escaped and was transformed into another Trangressor (Meggitt).

At Rearringbunga, Transgressor copulated with a pregnant woman, who died as a result (Peterson). At Ngalbiriwanu, he forced a woman who had just given birth and was, through her Dreaming, in a mother-in-law relationship to him, a taboo relationship in which any sexual intercourse is forbidden. For this transgression, the woman killed him by cutting off his penis with her own clitoris, which was also very long; in doing so she lost a piece of it which turned into the Willy Wagtail (*jintirrjintirrpa*) and flew away. The penis again grew into a man, still called Transgressor (Meggitt).

According to Meggitt, when Transgressor arrived at Kunajarrayi he saw a group of Digging Stick women who were camping there. Identifying him as a son-in-law, out of respect for the taboo they covered their eyes and chased him away. But he managed to take them by surprise at Wiranggulubanda and raped one of them, who conceived immediately. The others killed him and castrated him but, for the third time, his penis became a man. At Wakulpu, he surprised a urinating woman. She managed to kill him by cutting off his penis with a stick.[18] Transgressor and his penis then finally disappeared underground.

According to Peterson, when Transgressor arrived at Kunajarrayi, he found women dancing, he threw himself on them to copulate with them and killed them with his penis, which came out from their mouths. The survivors ran away to Wakulpu, where he caught up with them. Seeing a woman urinating with her legs apart, he sent his penis underground intending to make it come out inside her. But she noticed the soil was being cracked by his advancing, and she called the other women, who hit the soil with their digging sticks until it felt soft, indicating that the intruder was dead.

The figure of Transgessor, which is missing in the female myth of the Digging Stick Dreaming (as told to me by the women),[19] emphasises the ambiguity of what is being played out – hunting, seduction and initiation – between the genders, and is at the core of other female and male versions of episodes of this Dreaming. As an

---

[18] In 2017, Wanta Steven Patrick Jampijinpa told this story: see Chapter 1 this volume, and *Lajamanu* (60'), a film by Glowczewski: https://vimeo.com/289440509

[19] Another public female episode for Kunajarrayi tells of *ngarlkirdi* (witchetty grubs) transforming into a *Warnayarra* (Rainbow Snake) that swallowed a group of women (Glowczewski 1991b).

insatiable man with an uncontrolled desire, made monstrous by the rapacity of his excessively long penis, he is the reverse of seduction, which supposes love magic and mutual consent. As a predator of women, he is beaten by them. He becomes the prey, failing both as a man and as a hunter, a failure shown in the beginning of Peterson's version when he misses the wallaby.

His forked penis represents, according to Peterson, penile subincision, a ritual operation practised by some Australian tribes which takes place after circumcision; his coming from a foreign tribe indicates that this practice was imported into Warlpiri territory. According to Meggitt, other heroes are also considered to be importers of this practice, whose adoption by the Warlpiri cannot be dated. The subincision wound is reopened in some rituals to make the men bleed, in the image of menstruation, a female secret. In the female myth, the knowledge transferred from women to men is suggestive of the mystery of this bleeding, which becomes a secret practice among the men.

The symbols of initiation, sexuality and hunting in the Transgressor are, finally, condensed into a single episode, the one that gives him his name: when he copulates with a forbidden woman, his potential mother-in-law. The mother-in-law, chosen during the boy's initiation, symbolises by definition an alliance implying both sexuality in marriage and hunting, with the obligation on the future son-in-law to provide his mother-in-law regularly with game. Transgressor, by raping his mother-in-law, symbolises the reverse of the social order; he fails to be a man, but neither is he a woman. There is also some ambivalence in the female version of the Digging Stick Dreaming, whose heroines are called *jintikirliwati*, 'men with vaginas': by hunting with spears and initiating boys, they act in a manner that today is reserved for men.[20]

The idea of an androgyne gender is also present in the male myth in which the mother-in-law is raped by Transgressor: her clitoris, being very long, was accidentally cut off and transformed into Willy Wagtail. This bird gives its name to a Dreaming that women associate with Kunajarrayi, the place where – in both Meggitt's and Peterson's male versions – the Digging Stick women were camping. In the female myth, Willy Wagtail secretly kept an adult son in her womb until two sisters discovered her trick in a dream and freed the son from

---

[20] In some other desert groups, for example among the Walmajarri people, women do hunt with spears (Pat Lowe, personal communication).

the mother. Furious, she killed the girls' mother, and the son had to kill her to avenge his mother-in-law. In other words, the woman who, in the male myth, was forced to have sexual intercourse with a son-in-law, and lost her clitoris which turned into a Willy Wagtail, becomes, in the (public) female myth, a mother-bird who refuses to ally her son with a wife, and to give him a mother-in-law. The Willy Wagtail Dreaming is part of the totemic constellation: Acacia Seeds (*ngurlu*), Sowing Man (*Wankilpa*), Wallaby (*wampana*), Giant Snake (*Yarripiri*) and Gecko (*yumarimari*); Gecko (*yumarimari*) also slept with his mother-in-law and left his companions' trail through shame; the *Yarripiri* (*Jarapiri*) Snake's songline comes from South Australia (Mountford 1968) where *yumari*, Gecko, is also the word for mother-in-law (Elkin 1939).

The female version of the Digging Stick Dreaming says that at the moment the heroines were going to initiate the men into lovemaking, they had a dispute about the way the men should be distributed. Some thought the men should be shared, others wanted to have one each, the solution that was finally adopted. Since in the Warlpiri polygynous family a man acquires wives progressively rather than simultaneously, the episode of the formation of couples looks like the institution of marriage. On the other hand, choosing to live as a couple can also be seen as an ideal, a dream of exclusivity not institutionalised by the society, but quite often achieved through de facto monogamy, when a wife refuses to have co-wives. Conversely, the desire manifested by some heroines to access freely any man represents another dream, often fulfilled by those who, married or single, practise love magic.

The Goanna Dreaming is synonymous, for the men as well as for the women, with seductive and flighty behaviour. In the female myth specific to this Dreaming, Goanna is described as constantly roving around looking for females to seduce but, when he wants to reproduce, he settles for a while with two companions, as goannas do today. In this sense, the Dreaming legitimates polygynous marriage, and goannas, who have a double penis, offer a symbolic model of it. Nevertheless, as a seducer, Goanna also represents the batchelor's dream.

A female episode of the Kangaroo Dreaming tells of heroes and heroines of this trail who had an argument because they all copulated promiscuously. Kangaroo intervened by imposing some rules of alliance, such as the promise of a mother-in-law and a wife at the time of a boy's initiation. He told them: 'You, the women, will give your sons to your husbands and your daughters to your sons-in-law, and in exchange, they will hunt my kangaroo flesh for you ...'. The Kangaroo Dreaming is thus simultaneously a dream of promiscuity and the institution of alliance.

Examples could be multiplied: although every Warlpiri Dreaming myth has a specific message that gives it a conceptual singularity, most of them, in both their male and female versions, describe a dream of autonomy opposed to a necessity for alliance, the desire to be independent as opposed to the desire of and for the other. Digging Stick women who are happy without men, Goanna the flighty, Kangaroo people who advocate free sex, heroes of the Initiated Man Dreaming who wander around looking for boys to initiate, that is, for women who can give them boys, in all cases the same drama is constantly replayed. Male, female or of indeterminate gender, ancestral heroes go their way, often separately, are seducers or are seduced in turn, and confront each other in a conflict that fixes them in a gender (and a 'genre') in the proper and figurate sense.

Kanunju/kankarlu, *Below/Above: Ritual Transformations*

To carry out a totemic and territorial ritual is not primarily to represent an ancestral epic. The purpose is rather to identify men and women with what they sing, paint and dance, that is, to give a body to words, drawings and gestures, to fuse *Jukurrpa* names and places into symbols supported and mediated by the participants and the ritual objects, and to transfigure bodies or objects into Jukurrpa places and beings. The Warlpiri say that by painting, singing and dancing, men and women become the *Jukurrpa* ancestral principles and the sites they travelled through and where they sit or sleep for ever. The ritual metamorphoses the actors from agents into those acted upon. While in the initial state the actors paint, are painted, sing and dance, in the final stage it is the dances, the songs and the paintings that make the actors come into being. Does this mean that the actions of painting, singing or dancing transform subjects into objects?

Nancy Munn (1970) has analysed the transformation of subject into object which characterises the Warlpiri and Pitjantjatjara myths: through identification with the sites or the sacred objects – achieved by metamorphosis, imprint or 'externalisation' of their bodies, organs or substances (urine, blood, milk, saliva, tears, faeces, sweat) – the heroes affirm themselves as eternal beings. From a linguistic point of view, in both languages the final state is expressed by the addition of a suffix (respectively *-jarri* and *-(a)rri-*) translating as 'in the process of becoming'. Douglas (Capell 1979) concluded that in the Pitjantjatjara language there is no structural contrast between the metamorphosis and the process. He gives the example of Aborigines who say that they are 'caught' by a game when they catch it. The inversion of subject and object does not signify that the hunter is confused with his game. Regarding the mythical beings' relation to the sites, Nancy Munn writes of a 'bi-directional transformation' because of a tension between the process of separating the subject from the object it creates, and the atemporal identification of the subject with the object. The 'objectification' would then be perceived as a movement linking the subjectivity of a person to the exterior world. But, while the ancestral beings as subjects exist before the objects into which they metamorphose, for humans it is the other way around: in the ritual identification with these beings, movement goes from the object to the subject.

At this point, the notion of identification raises a problem: when Aboriginal people say in English that they '*belong*' to this or this country – it has them – to signify that it belongs to them – they have it – it is not that they confuse themselves with the land. In Warlpiri, just as in Pintupi (Myers 1986), they say that they *hold* the land in the sense that this verb, *kanyi*, is used to talk about adults looking after children. On the other hand, they define themselves as the children of the earth that feeds them. It is not a confusion between subject and object, between being and having, but it is an enunciation that shows two points of view corresponding to different stages of the same process: they *are* the country as its children (coming into being), they *have* it as hunters and ritual custodians (action); they are the land not in order to have it, but, in the process of coming into being through the country, they can act to master it.

Surely, as Munn says, landscape offers to the individual images or fragments of himself (or herself) which are simultaneously exterior to himself (or herself) and intrinsically connected with him (or her). But when a Warlpiri becomes the land and the ancestral beings he is singing, dancing or painting, his human identity is not strictly confused with the identity of the ancestral beings. Contrary to what Munn says, (the construction of) the subject is not predetermined by the objective order represented by the sites, because this order is not a *fait accompli*, fixed once and for all. Just as dream interpretation allows the mythic and totemic configuration of the topography to be modified, so humans are carried by a movement by which they can in their turn become singular entities as subjects objectifying themselves in the landscape.

I prefer to talk of self-reference rather than identification. Through their myths, rituals and their everyday use of language, the Warlpiri people and their neighbours seem to say that the subject is deconstructed in time through actions and comings into being which look like temporary metamorphoses. To understand these processes of transformation, one must follow a three-stage argument. Instead of the 'initial' and 'final' states of a transformation, I would say there is a *before without a beginning* (the desiring subject), a *meantime* (the subject 'imprinting' with the object of his/her desire) and an *after without an ending* (the subject becoming another subject). The objectivation of the subject in the myth or in the ritual is only a temporary final state, a step necessary for the process to be constantly repeated that constructs ancestral heroes as well as men as evolving subjects, becoming another subject.

The inversion of subject into object (and vice versa) in the myth, the ritual or the everyday statement, is not a mirror effect but a self-referential movement that involves a third term. The ancestral being becomes not only a hill or a waterhole but the eternal *Jukurrpa* principle living in this place; the ritual actor becomes not just a painting but the *Jukurrpa* of which, like the site, this painting is a 'trace'; the hunter becomes not a kangaroo but the *Jukurrpa* of which this animal is a manifestation; similarly the Warlpiri person becomes not his land but the *Jukurrpa* that gives him his name. The relationship to different *Jukurrpa* can only be understood in a feedback process: men are fed by the land because they come from *Jukurrpa* but they feed it in their turn when in their rituals they become different *Jukurrpa*. Every Warlpiri person is an aspect of the coming into being or rather becoming of the many *Jukurrpa*, an active form of a living memory, *Jukurrpa*, the Dreaming space-time, which transcends that person and which he or she has to actualise in rituals.

'Men have an *inside* story for this *Jukurrpa*, secret one, I can only tell you the *outside* story ...'. This statement is a reminder of all that can be divulged in public, but also of what women may or may not say. I have heard it many times, but it took me a while before I could understand the Warlpiri dialectics related to the concepts *kanunju* (inside-below) and *kankarlu* (outside-above). First, though (the) above is not secret, neither is it profane and opposed to (the) below as the only sacred realm; on the contrary, they are both ways of refering to ritual life and to the sacred links with the *Jukurrpa* totemic beings and the land. Furthermore, if (the) above is public, what it designates is not necessarily open to everybody; thus *kankarlu* is the name given to both the men's ceremonial camp and to the women's ritual responsibility, but it is forbidden for women to come close to the male camp and it is not conceivable for men to participate in women's rituals. The fact that there are things that men and women exclude each other from does not signify that there is a male secret or a female secret; there is only *a* secret that they approach differently, men from 'below' and women from 'above'.

Nancy Munn (1964), in an elegant structural analysis, identifies the below with the ancestral past, the above with the present. According to her diagram, the land and the *Kuruwarri* forces are the media that ensure the passage from the past, *Jukurrpa*, to the present, *yijardu*. However, the word *yijardu* also signifes 'true', an attribute the Warlpiri use to define *Jukurrpa* as opposed to *warlka*, false, lie, meaningless, without ancestral references. Under the apparent ambiguity of these Warlpiri concepts lies an intentional complexity; it is thus reductive to restrict *Jukurrpa* to the past and to relate it to the present, as Munn does, as a 'discontinuity of repeated contrasts', mediated by the *Kuruwarri*.[21]

In comparing *Jukurrpa* to a living memory (in becoming), I have attempted to show a way of thinking that integrates the past, the present and the future in one movement, not as a progressive or a circular continuity, but as a process of feedback that engenders matter and is engendered by it. I agree there is mediation with the production of *Kuruwarri* forces (as ritual designs, myths or dreams), but for me the Warlpiri categories below/above, rather than being two realms of time, past and present, are two aspects of the living

---

[21] Cf. Munn (1964: 98), quote: 'The temporal model summarized in the diagram formulates the time process in a pattern Leach has characterized as a "discontinuity of repeated contrasts". Distinguishing this kind of temporal model from "circular" and "progressive" models, he suggests that "in some primitive societies (...) time is experienced as something discontinuous, a repetition of repeated reversal, a sequence of oscillations between polar opposites: night and day, winter and summer, drought and flood, age and youth, life and death. In such a scheme the past has no depth to it, all past is equally past; it is simply the opposite of now" (Leach 1961: p. 126).' Contrary to Munn's interpretation, I do not think Leach's model does justice to the concept of time implied by the concepts of *Jukurrpa* and Dreaming of the Warlpiri and other Aboriginal groups. Munn subsequently discussed my criticism (Munn 1992).

memory – the virtual and the actual – described in the previous chapter.

What is at play in Warlpiri rituals is always a double movement: an actualisation (above) when the ancestral forces emerge, and a virtualisation (below) when they are sent back underground and into the cosmic elsewhere of the Dreaming, where different potentialities are emerging waiting to materialise. Women, when they set up their ritual sticks and dance, harness the *Kuruwarri* forces, exteriorise them on the surface of the ground, then send them back underground. Men, on the other hand, when they paint the ground paintings and dance on them say they 'go into' the ground and the Dreaming, then 'come out' depicting the mythical heroes who emerged from the underground to travel along the earth before they reentered it (Munn 1973b). One can say that if men 'go into' and 'come out of' from *Jukurrpa*, women on the contrary 'draw it' to themselves and 'propagate it'. In fact, men and women participate in both movements but in different contexts.

Sexual intercourse offers the model according to which men, as penetrating, are identified with 'below-inside' and women with 'above-outside'. Women in childbirth also embody the movement of externalisation-actualisation (*kankarlu*) relegating men to the opposed movement of interiorisation-virtualisation (*kanunju*). Apart from the physical interaction, the situation is reversed: man's genitals are outside and woman's inside. Nevertheless, the woman also has an external organ, the clitoris. This double aspect of the female gender is related to the myth of the knowledge taken from women and the male ritual of subincision: men symbolically give themselves a 'hole' they are missing to mark their body with a symbolic ambivalence similar to women's (Bettelheim [1962] 1971). As such, they also mimic the act of externalisation peculiar to women, in ritually making the initiates 'born again', or in re-enacting the mythical beings sowing image-forces and spirit-children (which explains the name *kankarlu* 'above' given to their ceremonial ground.)

In other terms, when men and women define themselves in an autonomous way, it is with a bisexual body, related to the 'below' as well as the 'above'. But marriage alliance determines men and women in a gender, opposing them as 'below' and 'above', and conversely enacting the double motion that defines *Jukurrpa*: the externalising of the 'below' (in the image of the sex-hole being an envelope) and the interiorising of the 'above' (in the image of penetration). Separated by their respective rituals, men and women replay this reversibility: men coming into and out from *Jukurrpa* re-enact the above-below-above process while the below-above-below process is played by the women who draw up *Jukurrpa* then send it back underground. The collective destiny of each gender thus concentrates in the body of each individual the autonomous but at the same time dependent destiny that is materialised by every *Jukurrpa*; abolishing for the ritual period the contradiction between gender autonomy and alliance with the other.

The mythical relations between ancestral men and women, and their transposition in the ritual and economic life ruling the genders, symbolises the tension between the differentiation and interdependence of all aspects of the natural and cultural environment. All the *Jukurrpa* are autonomous in their respective paths of travel but they are interdependent through their meetings, which transform both their stories and travels. The clans which identify with these routes are diverse in their identities but interdependent because, being exogamous, they can only marry, and reproduce, in alliance with other clans. Besides, every clan crosses the lands of others and uses their resources; on its own land the clan sustains itself on different species whose totems are owned by other clans who ensure their increase. The aim of rituals is to maintain all that is designated by a clan's totems, but they also benefit other clans, since increased rituals for a plant or an animal concern both the clanic land connected with these totems and the reproduction of the same species on the whole of the tribal land. In exchange, the rituals of the Rain Dreaming clans ensure the annual renewal of all the water reserves. This interdependence always affirms the autonomy of each Dreaming-totem and associated clan.

Since for the Warlpiri everything that reproduces – humans, other species, atmospheric and cultural phenomena – participates in the same generative principles, women as procreators are the symbols of everything that is actualised; it is in this sense that they are finally identified with the 'above', and that the ancestral heroines are the keepers of a knowledge that reproduces both nature and culture. Thus, the mythic theme of a transfer of female knowledge to the men, rather then supporting the hypothesis of a lost matriarchy or nostalgia for the foetal fusion (Roheim 1945, 1974), illustrates above all a situation that is always present. The Digging Stick myth seems to insist that even today it is through women that sexuality is revealed to men, children given to them, and alliances made between clans and tribes. This presents the sexual act as a way for men to return to the world of 'below' without returning to the maternal womb, thus legitimising the postulate that the men are the virtuality that women actualise.

One can see that the 'gendering' of the concepts the Warlpiri use to describe the generation and metamorphosis of all existing things is very ambivalent. The *Kurruwalpa* spirit-children take the gender of the newborn they embody, and when they show themselves in dreams their voice and their shapes are gendered to represent a specific person, living or deceased. As a virtual life without a body, the spirit-children remind one of the question of the gender of angels: the first names that identify the spirit-children (cf. Chapter 1) usually belong to children of one gender; on the other hand, according to Meggitt (1962), for some Warlpiri men, every spirit-child is believed to change gender at each of its reincarnations.

The *Jukurrpa*, understood as ancestral principles and clanic names, are called 'fathers' by their *kirda* (the clans that bear their names and the 'brother' clans); in this sense, they are male even if the heroes are female. But the same *Jukurrpa* become female when they are called 'mothers' by the *kurdungurlu* clans, allies of the *kirda*. The *Kuruwarri*, as living images and forces which animate humans, animals, plants and all other totemic things, are not gendered; they symbolise both genders, therefore they are bisexual or asexual. Finally, *maralypi*, the singularity that concentrates in one site the *Kuruwarri* of each *Jukurrpa* path of travel, is virtually double-gendered but one could just as well say non-gendered. We have seen that *maralypi* designates the men's secret, and *yiniwurru* or *munga-munga* and *mangaya* refer to the women's secret. This does not mean that there are two secrets, but two ways to approach the secret of life: men, approaching it from 'below', define it as double-gendered or non-gendered, *maralypi*, while women, approaching it from 'above', suppose a combined action of the female matrix, *yiniwurru* (generating dream images, mythical *Jukurrpa* and spirit-children), and its intrinsic male power, *mangaya*, the double-gendered aspect of women.

So, for men as for women, masculine and feminine are not conceived as separate but rather as two sides of the same surface, whatever the medium involved: a human, animal or vegetable form which may be male or female, a mythical path of travel which is 'father' for one side of the tribe and 'mother' for the other, or a sacred object which takes the totemic and sexual identity of the ancestral being it embodies in each new ritual context. From this perspective, the

Table 4.1 Sexual ambivalence of 'above/below' concepts (translated by Mary Laughren for review article, Australian Aboriginal Studies, *1993/2: 74–80)*

Kanunju	Kankarlu
'below', interiorised, virtual	'above', exteriorised, actual
underground and cosmos	earth's surface
ancestral past and the future	immediate past and present
space-time of eternal beings	signs of eternal beings in the landscape
virtuals totems: not individualised	actual totems: named and localised
dreaming expriences of men and women	experiences when awake
before birth (spirit-children)	pregnancy and childbirth (incarnate spirit-children)
Secret	*Public*
male social prerogative	female social prerogative
secret male rituals	female rituals inaccessible to men
secret power of women (*mangaya*)	men's ceremonial ground inaccessible to women
secret sites (*maralypi*) reserved for men	sacred sites reserved for the guardians of both sexes
totems reserved for men	mixed totems or those reserved for women
esoteric male versions of myths	public versions of myths or those reserved for women
secret paintings: male or female	public paintings: female or male

binary opposition of the Warlpiri 'above/below' categories is only apparent: they are two points of view of the same things which men and women ritualise between birth and death in a constant exchange (see Table 4.1).

While the existence of all things can be explained by processes of reversal between 'below' and 'above', the fact of death on the contrary marks the irreversible passage of time. Reversibility and irreversibility are like two modes of the *Jukurrpa* space-time. For the 'above' world, a deceased person is lost for ever, and his/her corpse must disappear. But for the 'below' world, the deceased becomes eternal through his/her depersonalised name, that is his/her particular identity is lost. The deceased's *Kuruwarri* image-forces and *Kurruwalpa* spirit-child return to and dissolve into the places they

Doing and Becoming

came from, while the destiny of *pirlirrpa* soul is to accompany the image-forces on the clanic path of travel to fuse with the *maralypi* singularity at the main site: by penetrating the earth, the soul is taken beyond the Milky Way, to be absorbed into the cosmos by the two Magellanic Cloud galaxies, like the ancestral heroes when they finished their travels. We have seen that this destiny only belongs to the very old; the souls of children fuse with the spirit-children they embodied, who will wait in specific places to be embodied again, and the souls of all others are condemned to wander like ghosts, with the risk of becoming vampires if they do not find their way into the cosmic path.[22]

One can note that at a cosmological level 'above' and 'below' are not simply opposites like above and below ground. 'Above' is the land, the world of people as well as ghosts, vampires and various spirits who show themselves to people who are awake, but it is also the visible sky. 'Below' is underground, by definition hidden, and the infinite cosmos whose true shapes are visible to people only in dreams or on shamanic journeys; it is the domain of the ancestral and eternal beings, the deceased, spirit-children and all the virtualities. Some Warlpiri are not surprised that Europeans (*kardiya*) say that the earth is round and surrounded by the sky; they knew it already. But passage from 'above' to 'below' is of a different order from travelling on the surface of the earth: the dead, like the ancestral heroes, do not travel on the surface of the earth to reach down under, but by penetrating the terrestrial surface they pass to another dimension that projects them in the stars.[23]

For the Warlpiri, the coming-and-going between the 'below-virtual' (*kanunju*) to the 'above-actual' (*kankarlu*) is a process of transformations which are mediated by the production of dreams and ritual activities. In other terms, there is not infinite and reversible continuity but irreversible changes (events) which generate a certain reversibility. Virtual and actual are neither continuous nor discontinuous but both: for the virtual to actualise or for the actual to virtualise the two levels have to self-penetrate and produce a third one: the level of dreams and rituals.

---

[22] *Kurdaija* soul stealers. See last chapter.
[23] Modern mythology, represented by science fiction, makes us talk of space-time travels, black holes and a fifth dimension; it is ethnocentric to think that traditional thought, imagination and dream experience had no potential to imagine the transcendance of space and time limitations. See last chapter.

To try to visualise such a space-time journey is disconcerting, because it does not obey to the classical laws of Euclidian geometry. Topology, on the other hand, allows one to conceive such paradoxic journeys, and to formalise properties such as self-penetration and reversal of the inside and outside, which seem to characterise cosmological concepts that lie at the heart of Warlpiri ritual life.

5

Forbidding and Enjoying: Warlpiri Taboos

In the previous chapters, two contexts subject to taboos were mentioned: mourning and the mother-in-law/son-in-law (WM/DH) actual or classificatory relationship. Interestingly, the prohibitions imposed by death and by this relationship, which arise from marriage, divide into the same four domains: space, language, sexuality and goods, especially food.

First, a man has to stay away from women in the 'mother-in-law' category for him, and when they see him, they will cover their face or move out of his way. If he crosses their footprints in the bush, he hastens to erase them. Similarly, the camp of a deceased person has to be abandoned, and this place, and even the totemic site of the deceased, must be avoided. Then, women and men in a mother-in-law/son-in-law relationship may not talk to each other; in the same way, it is forbidden to pronounce the names of the dead or to sing verses evoking them. Mothers-in-law and sons-in-law also have to use a special language, *yikirrinji*, to talk to a third person about topics related to their relationship. For their part, widows are subject to a vow of silence during the mourning period, of up to two years, and they use a sign language, *rdaka-rdaka* 'hand-hand', of which Adam Kendon (1988) collected 1,500 signs. The other members of the tribe have a choice about how they communicate with widows but other women often use this 'deaf-and-dumb' language. Everybody has to replace the words that become taboo with the expression *kumanjayi*, 'no name'.

Sexual intercourse is forbidden for widows until the end of mourning. Between mother-in-law and son-in-law it represents incest *par excellence*. In both cases there is deprivation of goods, a corollary of the gift obligation. During funerals, the deceased's property is destroyed and his hair is cut and passed around: the deceased's mothers, actual or classificatory, have to punctuate the mourning rituals with gifts of impressive quantities of cloth and food – flour, tea, sugar, acacia seedcakes in the old days – for their 'brothers', the dead person's maternal uncles, actual or classificatory. Widows are not allowed to eat meat or to cook; they have to be nurtured by other women.

Similarly, the son-in-law may not keep the products of his hunt for himself; throughout his life he has to give a part of it to the mother of his wife, who in exchange prepares vegetable dishes for him.

Prohibitions related to space, language, sexuality, food or other goods are compensated for by behaviours – sign language, exchanges– specific to the context (death or mother-in-law/son-in-law relationship). In relation to the dead, taboos are confined to the period of mourning, while in the mother-in-law/son-in-law relationship they are permanent. Two other contexts, one temporary – socialisation rituals – the other permanent – totemic relationships – also demonstrate the four domains of prohibition.

Male and Female Socialisation

A male initiate is spatially isolated from the women during his ritual seclusion, which can last for several months. He may not marry, nor have sexual relations until circumcision and subincision have taken place. In the past, this latter operation was performed only at around the age of thirty, but nowadays it is carried out shortly after the first, i.e., around adolescence. During the *kurdiji* or other initiation cycles, such as *Kajirri*, young men may not eat some kinds of food and, until they become mature men, they must hunt for the elders who are training them. Finally, Meggitt (1954) reports that novices have to keep silent and use the same sign language as widows.

During the final phase of their initiation young men use a secret language, which, according to Hale (1971), consists in formulating everything 'upside-down' (*ngudalj-kitji-rni*). All the nouns, pronouns and verbs must be replaced by words that either have the opposite meaning, or are considered antonyms in this context, such as one kin term instead of another. The use of the conventions of this reversed language supposes a gradual apprenticeship and a skill in the manipulation of Warlpiri language. The young novice hears his guardians talk to him back to front, and at around the age of thirty, when he becomes a guardian of those younger than himself, he uses this language, which is part of the repertoire of the 'clown', *jiliwirri*. Wild (1977–1978) sees this ritual role as a re-enactment of sexual ambiguity, in which these youth play the role of women before they become accomplished men.[1]

---

[1] Chapter translated from Glowczewski 1991. *Jiliwirri* is also an important part of the women's ritual activities.

Forbidding and Enjoying

The expression 'upside-down' applied to the language of young initiates evokes the cosmological and sexual opposition between 'below' (virtual and male) and 'above' (actual and female) (cf. Chapter 3). If the novices' language taboo can be interpreted as the marking of the passage from a double sexual identity to a single social gender, so too can the other taboos. The novice is restricted to a diet of vegetable food as opposed to meat, which symbolises the status of man and hunter that he will reach later and that will oblige him to feed not only the male elders but also his mother-in-law.[2] In terms of space, separation from women also marks this change of status, which will place him in the 'below', the symbol of the men, and exclude him from the 'above', which from now on women will represent for him as an opposite social universe. The female behaviour that he will have to mimic in some rituals, and the name of the male ceremonial ground (*kankarlu* 'above'), are features of this transformation, which also unveil the symbolic reversibility between 'below' and 'above'.

Finally, in sexual terms, the two initiation operations consist in engraving in the novice's body the two sides of his metamorphosis: circumcision takes away what is 'above', the foreskin, but subincision opens him 'below', to make him bleed like a woman. Periodically reopened during some rituals, this wound is, according to Wild, compared to menses by the initiates themselves. Ashley-Montagu (1937) saw in the boys' subincision an analogy with the kangaroo whose penis looks naturally incised. The fact that for the Warlpiri the Kangaroo Dreaming is the most sacred secret associated with the circumcision and subincision rituals could support this view. Publicly, women associate with this Dreaming the *liwirringki* lizard which has a double penis. Some Aboriginal people claim that a subincised organ, apart from any ritual implications, is supposed to give more pleasure to women. It can be added that if non-subincised men are admonished not to make love, women participate in this discourse and laugh at such men who dare to approach them. European men who live with Aboriginal women are sometimes required to submit to this operation.

For girls, puberty was traditionally accompanied by a series of rituals marking progress from the status of child to that of woman. At regular intervals, girls were painted and massaged with fat tinted

---

[2] In some cases the diet is bullock meat, and vegetables are forbidden, as if the boy had to wait for the end of his initiation to be allowed to enjoy the value of exchange and the gift from the mother-in-law.

with red ochre so that the *Kuruwarri* images-forces of their respective clans penetrate them and favour their growing up, particularly the development of breasts and the growth of pubic hair. Such painting rituals sometimes take place during the female *yawulyu*, but since the 1980s teachers have been inviting women to paint the girls and make them dance at school.

Other practices of marking the body have definitely disappeared: scarifications (Bjerre 1956), ritual defloration with one or two fingers bound with kangaroo hairstring, performed by an old man assisted by an old woman (Abbie 1969) and introcision. According to Spencer and Gillen ([1899] 1968), the man who incised the vulva with a stone knife was a *kurduna* (*kulkuna*) 'son' of the girl, that is, a man from the subsection of her father-in-law. While for the circumcision and subincision a boy lies down on three men, his brothers-in-law, who are lying down next to each other on the ground, the girl used to lie accross the body of her promised husband and two other men of the same subsection.

Warlpiri people do not admit to having practised introcision.[3] However, the abduction by a man of a young girl who is promised to him is occasionally staged as a violent act witnessed by everybody. Generally, the young girl refuses to follow the older man who claims her. As long as her family judges that she is too young, the mother protects her and stops the impatient future son-in-law from exercising his rights. Once the family group considers it is time for the girl to get married and recognises that the pretender is a legitimate spouse, the mother does not interfere if the girl resists and even adopts an attitude of apparent indifference, manifesting neither indignation nor affliction. When the young girl escapes, nobody will hide her, and she ends up being caught by her future husband.[4]

Young girls nowadays tend to have early intercourse with young men, so the promised husbands try to get access to them as soon as possible in order to be the ones who deflower them. Once the marriage has been consummated, if the wife does not want to stay with

---

[3] A paragraph was suppressed here by the author from her 1991 French book because the description by Spencer and Gillen of girls' collective ritual 'intercourse' is considered as a misinterpretation of what the initiation was about. It is possible that Spencer and Gillen who did their fieldwork at the turn of the century were describing not actual intercourse but symbolic re-enactments.

[4] In the 1990s, mothers became more protective when promised marriages were broken by girls who left the community for bigger towns, where some started drinking.

her husband, he sometimes gives her back to her parents. The important thing is not for the promised girl to stay with her husband but for her to be deflowered by him, so that he is the man who officially separates her from her mother, and through whom she sets off on her woman's destiny. The first child of the young woman belongs to the promised husband, even if he does not keep the mother as his wife: but it also happens that he leaves the responsibility with the family of the girl who refused him and who will eventually marry somebody of her own choosing.

Defloration by the promised husband plays the role of lifting the sexual taboo imposed on the young girl until she is married. If she does not live with the man who deflowered her, she is considered his 'divorced' wife. The man whom she marries later has to accept that she has been through the hands of her promised husband.[5]

Sexual intercourse with a husband's 'brother' could be re-enacted during the couple's life, in the context of the temporary exchange of spouses in which the women's consent was implied. Also, if the husband died, a common occurrence because of the big age difference between the spouses, the widow usually remarried with an actual or classificatory 'brother' of the deceased.

While the operation on genitals marks, for both the girl and the boy, a separation from the mother, the (symbolic) implication is different for each. The boy leaves the mother's world to become identified with the men and to become a father in his turn, while the girl is torn away from her mother by the men, to be identified not with them but with the women, as she is expected to become a mother in her turn.

Women look after young wives and teach them how to sing, dance and paint. It is only when the son of a young woman, her co-wife or her sister, is initiated, that she will really gain the status of a woman. This status will be reinforced through her repeated participation in the initiations of her brothers' sons. Recognised as a mother and a paternal aunt, it is from her early thirties that a woman will start ritually to affirm herself through her roles as *kirda*, depositary of the patriclanic *yawulyu* rituals and lands, and as *kurdungurlu*, custodian of the knowledge, managing the rituals of the patriclan of her mother, her husband's sisters or others. In other terms, her relationship to her mother will be changed by the fact that the ritual role she will gain

---

[5] Another paragraph was suppressed here by the author from her 1991 French book.

towards her mother's Dreaming will be extended to the Dreamings of her husband and his 'brother' clans.

A man too only finishes his initiation around the age of thirty. It is then that he starts to become an initiator and is ready really to intervene as *kirda* of his own patriclan and *kurdungurlu* of others, particularly those of his mother and maternal uncles, or of his wife and brothers-in-law.

While the boy goes from the 'above' (actual, female) to the 'below' (virtual, male) through circumcision, with subincision he finds a new symbolic 'above' – the blood periodically shed from his scar. The girl goes from the 'above' to the 'below' through defloration and actualises her own 'above' as a woman through menstrual flow and pregnancy. The male social body identified with the 'below' thus gains an 'above' and a symbolic androgyny, while the female social body, identified with the 'above', is a priori androgynous, having the potential to give birth to men as well as women.

The symbol of this androgyny is the clitoris, which, among other terms, is called *waninja*, a word meaning both throat and love (Reece 1975). The clitoris, which is left intact, is thus regarded as the locus of pleasure but also as the external sign of an internal organ, the throat, through which food goes one way and speech the other. This symbol combines sexuality, food, language and inside/outside space.[6] Another symbol of such a conjunction is *makara*, which means both the uterus that welcomes the life of a future talking being, and the placenta that feeds him. The word also designates the ritual ropes that connect the women's sacred sticks to place them in contact with the 'below', the virtual space-time of the Dreaming.

Traditionally, when a girl had her first period she was secluded in a special camp, and ate only a small amount of vegetable food. Later on, at each menstruation she shifted to the women's camp, where she could take her children. Meggitt (1962) specifies that when a man had two or three wives, he alternated his sexual relations to the rhythm of their periods. Nevertheless, Aboriginal women's menstrual cycle is rather irregular and such a 'calendar' could not be very precise.[7] Menstruating women are no longer segregated from men. Neither are men strictly excluded from the delivery of a baby: women

---

[6] In Warlpiri myths eating is a common metaphor for sexual intercourse.

[7] Many older women who used to live a semi-nomadic life insist that they could stay months without menstruating; an observation that correlates with the fact that children were not numerous and newborns were precious.

Forbidding and Enjoying

are often sent to give birth at the hospital, where they are attended by male European doctors and even Aboriginal health workers.

In contrast, the food taboos accompanying pregnancy persist, and are explained as preventing harm to the mother and the child.[8] A pregnant woman cannot eat *yinjirri* lizards nor *yinarlingi* echidnas, because the pointed tail of the first and the prickles of the second have the power to make the baby get stuck in the womb in the wrong position, making delivery impossible. A species of wallaby, *jika*, a small marsupial like a rabbit, is forbidden because it is said to provoke a miscarriage. Wild turkeys are also prohibited because their rapid breathing might make the baby consumptive. Snakes should not be eaten either because they can make the foetus sick, and the baby stillborn or weak. The last two prohibitions on the mother remain until the child can walk; the others are lifted at the baby's birth.

The prohibition of some foods during pregnancy and during the first menstruation seems to be the counterpart of the food interdictions imposed upon boys and young men during initiation. Similarly, the segregation of menstruating and delivering women can be seen as the equivalent of the seclusion of initiates.

Finally, equivalent to the speech taboo that imposes silence on young initiates is the learning and the use by women of the 'hand sign' language. Indeed, women master it and use it more often than men, who even call the women's ceremonial shelter the same name as this language, *rdaka-rdaka*, hand-hand (hands). Apart from its use during mourning, the sign language allows women to talk of secret things connected with either the ritual life or sexual matters, or simply to gossip. They often use it when, during an argument, the tone rises and shouts threaten to degenerate into blows from sticks, as sometimes happense. The recourse to hand signs instead of hand fights has a curious effect: the coded movements are very violent, because the women double with the left hand the signs which are usually done only with the right, and they shake their body, grimacing, repeating insulting coded gestures several times; but, slowly, all these outbursts end up by exhausting the anger, and provoking lots of laughter.

For women, the resort to compulsory silence is a means of bringing back the social peace compromised by verbal confrontation; for young initiates it is a means of reminding them that the elders hold

---

[8] Respected in the mid-1980s, such rules have weakened since.

the power of speech and of social order. The sexual rules which forbid sexuality to girls as well as to boys until their genitals are ritually 'opened', are reinstated for each couple at events that are based on a similar symbolism. A man must abstain from sexual intercourse with a menstruating woman, and also during the few months after she gives birth, but not during pregnancy.

Applied to the transformation of boys into men, girls into women and the relations between members of each gender, the taboos on space, speech, sexuality or goods summarise the symbolic acts that socialise each individual. In this context of socialisation, they are by definition temporary, punctuating each rite of passage or test of sociality.

Taboos Relating to Totemic Relations

As far as totemic relations are concerned, prohibitions concerning the four domains – space, language, sexuality, goods – are in some cases permanent. Men of one clan (which is) united by the same totems have no right to marry nor to have sexual relations, except in the case of ritual transgressions, with the women of their clan who bear the same totemic names. Holders of the same totems, women share with men the same *Kuruwarri* living images, and celebrate them in their territorial rituals (*yawulyu*).

As to language, secrecy is compulsory in relation to male ritual activities and mythical stories which may not be revealed to women or the uninitiated, the young or strangers. To a lesser extent, the same applies to the ritual activities and stories restricted to women. As to space, the totemic sites which are defined as secret for men may not be approached by women, who must also keep away from the men's ceremonial ground; neither may men walk into the women's ceremonial ground, although nothing prevents them from going on totemic sites connected with female myths.

Men are subject to restrictions concerning the most sacred clanic sites. There is at least one site – that associated with the *maralypi* singularity that concentrates the image-forces of the clan – which men may not frequent or approach alone. It is men from outside the clan, the *kurdungurlu* – uterine nephews or brothers-in-law of the men of the clan – who have the responsibility of going to these places to do the necessary rituals or those preliminary to the approach of the men of the clan. Often these are not allowed to help themselves to the water that comes from their sites; they may drink it if it is

Forbidding and Enjoying

brought to them by *kurdungurlu*. Similarly, only the *kurdungurlu*, managers, may cut the wood in the vicinity of the site. The men of the clan, as *kirda*, owners of the sites and the totemic forces, must always be asked for the right to use their land, and they may refuse access to outsiders. However, they depend on their relations both uterine and by marriage, who act as mediators, to be able to enjoy the land's resources. As everybody is sumultaneously *kurdungurlu* of sites other than his/her own, in this way everyone benefits from a greater freedom of land usage.

The logic that dictates the regulation of what one possesses and the enjoyment of what one does not possess can be found in the prohibition on eating clanic totems, against having freely at one's disposal what they represent if they are non-edible things or essential things such as water. Women are not subject to this totemic taboo but initiated men, unless they are very old, must deprive themselves of that whose name they carry: thus men of the Honey Dreaming never eat honey; men of the Kangaroo Dreaming eat this game only if they do not hunt it themselves; those of the Rain Dreaming should not take water on their own, even from sources other than their own totemic sites; and the men of the Initiated Man Dreaming may not cut the wood of the eucalyptus from which the mythical people of that name made the *witi* poles used today in initiations.

In the old days, Warlpiri men also showed a certain reserve towards their mother's totem, that is the totem naming her clan (Spencer and Gillen 1904). Parallel with this restriction on the maternal totem, it was forbidden to marry a woman from one's mother's clan who was of her classificatory generation (*kuyu-kari* for ego); women of the other generation (*kuyu-rna* for ego) are tolerated as spouses although these marriages are called *warrura* 'wrong'. The taboo on the use of food or other goods related to paternal or maternal totems may be seen as a metaphor for sexual prohibition against sexual activity with women of the corresponding clans. But it must also be related to the limits on space (taboos on places) that make everyone dependent upon individuals outside the clan. Just as the relation of an individual to his/her clanic land is that of host – who enjoys it on the condition s/he invites others home – the relation towards the animals, plants and other totemic referents is one of ritual 'producer' of these things, who offers them to others and deprives himself of them. This is a logic of symbolic exchange. The taboo on clanic totems is the ritualisation of a gift: everybody makes the symbolic sacrifice, partial or total, of what he puts at the disposal of others and he receives in exchange everything that others 'produce' and do not enjoy. The prohibition against marrying women of one's own or one's mother's clan also follows from (a) ritualising (of) exchange: the circulation of women (or men[9]) requires that clanic relatives give them to outsiders rather than maintaining exclusivity.

The language taboo, as in the secrecy surrounding the activities and knowledge related to the clanic totems, determines the basis of all exchanges, in marriage, food and terrirory. If rituals and myths were public, it would not be possible for everyone to have a role as a totemic 'producer' or the power to control the relevant sites. Finally, it is the mutual recognition of a specific role for each clan and of a power symbolised by the Dreamings of their respective sites that guarantees respect for people's territorial identification in accordance with a strategy of interdependence and of dissuasion (from transgressing each other's territory).

It is for the benefit of all the tribe that an individual is expected to control the image-forces of the Dreamings that characterise the territory of which he is the owner, *kirda*. Such control, shared by all the adults, men and women, is backed up by the ancestors with whom they share their totemic name and flesh (*kuyu*).[10] Without this sharing of the image-forces between people, the power of the Dreamings would be disorganised and non-productive, indeed malefic: there would be no more Law.

In each context of non-ritual transgression, the forces of the Dreaming do indeed become harmful: they induce sickness, followed by madness or death. That explains the danger of approaching restricted sites or even of inadvertently hearing knowledge considered secret. Warlpiri say that the Law of the Dreaming unleashes its fury against the transgressor. Men, who perform rituals to direct the generative power of the Dreamings, or to inflict magic punishment, consider themselves to be merely the mediators whose actions confirm the fate set incurred by the transgressor. The one who talks too much about what he has learnt in male ceremonies, or who has

---

[9] Especially as sons-in-law.

[10] *Kuyu* is the current word for 'meat' but it is used in kinship classification collective terms like *kuyu-wapirra*, those who belong to the same Dreaming/totem, or *kuyu-kirda*, those who belong to the Dreaming/totem of the spouse or potential spouses: see next chapter.

seen what she should not have seen, are bewitched, 'sung' to death or 'pointed' with a bone by the elders. The condemnation made public excludes the transgressor from the tribe, sometimes provoking general indifference towards him/her. Rejected in such a way, the individual withdraws into himself, sometimes refuses to eat and drink, wastes away and lets himself/herself die. To the Warlpiri, as for other Aboriginal people, this is not suicide or murder, but the effect of *Jukurrpa*, the Law of the Dreaming.

For breaches of prohibitions on food or sexuality, the threat is less severe. Food prohibitions are disappearing, but in the old days somebody who had eaten his totem might become sick and slow down the increase of that species; if a shortage followed, he would be held responsible and 'sung' to death. The man who sleeps with a woman of his own clan might also mysteriously fade away.

Failure to respect taboos implies imbalance, indeed inequality: a surplus of advantages for some to the detriment of others who lose their own goods of exchange. To prevent such a situation, everybody has an interest in respecting the Law and pressing others to do the same. In the same way, everybody has an interest in giving what he/she has so that others will reciprocate. Such an attitude, which is shared by many Aboriginal people, even those who are urbanised, explains many aspects of their relation to the objects of consumption: the refusal to accumulate and the systematic circulation of all their possessions, cars, clothes, etc.

Ritual Resolution of Transgressions Related to Sexuality and Space

Failure to respect the rules of alliance, acts of adultery, as well as the refusal of a matrimonial promise are at the heart of many conflicts. If a married woman is caught out with another man she can be punished by a collective rape and her lover may be killed, unless the husband is satisfied with a token punishment consisting in the spearing of the lover's thigh. In at least one case a husband who had been deceived died from shame. Traditionally, a non-legitimate couple who managed to run away and survive in isolation for a year was eventually reintegrated with the community and recognised as married on their return. But a punishment expedition could also end in the killing of both lovers. Nowadays, sexual transgressions often provoke public dramas and generalised fights between the kin of the respective parties, but there are no killings. Rather, social pressure induces the lovers who are in the wrong classificatory relationship to separate. In this way the threat associated with the transgression of taboos plays a dissuasive role.

It is not individual freedom that is at stake: for instance, there is a camp in Alice Springs where the Warlpiri who come to town do not hesitate to have affairs not in accordance with classificatory kinship. Dissuasion is based on the fact that all individuals have a place in the social order which, in compensation for the respect of taboos, assures status and some rights to everybody. These rights are different for each man or woman but they offer similar advantages: incorporation with a clan and the assistance of uterine kin or allies, both of which give access to lands, resources and ritual knowledge.

To occupy land without having the right to do so, that is without being invited by the *kirda*, owners of the place, is another transgression that can generate conflicts: violation of territorial rights calls for a dispute or even fighting with weapons. Such confrontations took place within the memory of the previous generation, and they are also illustrated in some myths. For the Warlpiri, this kind of situation necessarily calls for a ritual settlement, after which the distribution of territorial rights may change and a new order may be instituted: either one group assimilates another, or one site becomes their common property, on the basis of different totemic references that are justified by the relevant mythical episodes.[11]

In relation to the ethic that underlies such negotiations, I have several times heard Warlpiri say 'the ones who fought yesterday become brothers or allies today', a formula that also applies to their relations with Whites. Violation followed by a re-evalution of territorial rights is thus a traditional way of readjusting the distribution of lands according to population flux, as long as the kinship network is maintained by redefining for everybody the code of behaviour expected towards others.

To resolve conflicts, traditionally the Warlpiri used reconciliation ceremonies associated with specific clan totems. The first ceremony is called *puluwanti*, Owl. Everywhere the Owl people went, they performed a ritual which entailed burning each other with fire and burning the pubic hair of some men and women (Peterson 1970). The *puluwanti* inaugurated this ritual at Lake Surprise (sites Yinapaka

---

[11] Such a process has adapted to the new territorial changes such as sedentary life in reserves, mining and the reoccupation of land with outstations. See the introduction to this book.

and Ngarnaja), in the east of Warlpiri territory, but to do this they invited the *kurakuraja* Bird people, to whom they were related as mothers-in-law and sons-in-law. In the name of this meeting that took place in the Dreamtime, the *puluwanti* clan has the responsibility of organising this ceremony with all the clans who are *skin* brothers of the *kurakuraja* people.[12]

According to the testimony of a female custodian of Yinapaka,[13] and other women, when they were young girls the depilation of the pubis was compulsory for all the participating women and took place in a little hut built for the occasion at one edge of the ceremonial ground; at the other end, the men were getting ready for their own activities. To conclude the ceremony, which could last several days, sometimes weeks, the following ritual took place: *puluwanti* men stood in front of their *kurakuraja* mothers-in-law, actual or classificatory, for the women to tear off their hairstring headbands; the *kurakuraja* men then did the same for their *puluwanti* mothers-in-law. These hairstrings were used by women to make pubic tassels, which they later gave to their daughters who were promised to the men from whom they had received the hairstring. At the beginning of the ceremony, another ritual required the *puluwanti* men to throw little pieces of bark against the *kurakuraja* women; similarly, the *kurakuraja* men threw pieces of bark at the *puluwanti* women. The festivities culminated in a ritual fight during which *puluwanti* and *kurakuraja* joined together to throw big burning poles at the members of clans belonging to the opposite moiety.

The other three dispute settling ceremonies also simulate a fire fight which involves totems in a *kuyu-wururu* (mother-in-law/son-in-law) relationship. The *Ngajukula* is associated with the *mala* Hare-Wallaby Dreaming: it is linked to the previous one in that the *mala* hero is said to have spung from beneath the centre of the ceremonial ground of the *puluwanti* people when they were dancing with the other birds.

---

[12] Cf. May Napaljarri 1984, the birds were from the Warumungu tribe. In Glowczewski (1991), I identified them wrongly as *kuruwa*, Brolga instead of *kurakuraja* (or *taparung*), a black bird like a goose (cf. Teddy Morrison Jupurrurla, main *kurdungurlu* in charge of the ceremony for his mother, 1995). All these birds belong to Japanangka/Napanangka-Japangardi/Napangardi subsections (1–5 patricycle), which are in a 'wife's mother/daughter's husband' relationship with *puluwanti* of subsections Jungarrayi/Nungarrayi- Japaljarri/Napaljarri (3–7 patricycle).

[13] See Chapter 2, note 12, p. 99.

The latter asked who he was and he sang 'I am Warlpiri'.[14] The *mala* Dreaming belongs to a clan brother of the *puluwanti* (3–7 patricycle; Jungarrayi-Japaljarri) but also to another clan brother of the *kura-kuraja* (1–5 patricycle: Japanangka-Japangardi). The same totem here links two patriclans who exchange mothers-in-law.[15] The last two reconciliation ceremonies are called *Jardiwanpa*; one relates to the Emu (*yankirri*) Dreaming (4–6; Jangala-Jampijinpa), the other to the Wallaby (*wampana*), the Giant Snake (*Yarripiri*) and the Gecko (*yumarimari*) who slept with his mother-in-law.[16] Warlpiri people add that the Emu and Wallaby clans often used to perform their ceremonies together: in fact, their trails follow a parallel direction, from the south to the north of the tribal territory, over hundreds of kilometres.

Other classificatory relations are involved in the ritual organisation of peace-making ceremonies, but their linking element is the mother-in-law/son-in-law relationship, which symbolises par excellence the alliance between groups: ritual confirms at this collective level the importance of the mother-in-law exchange at the kinship level. These ceremonies being associated with totems, the resolution of conflict juxtaposes the two contexts subject to taboos: totemic relations and the mother-in-law/son-in-law relationship.

Depilation and the circulation of hairstrings, practised in the above-mentioned ceremonies that stage the WM/DH relation, are also found in mourning ceremonies. Widows cut their hair and depilate their pubis; the dead person's hair is cut and taken by his maternal uncles, who weave it into a string they wear in turn around the neck or the wrist until it desintegrates.

In the old days, at a person's death the corpse was exhibited on a platform erected on four poles, and a divination method was used to determine the person responsible for the death. The maternal uncles of the deceased then had the responsibility of taking revenge, either through sorcery or by organising a punishment expedition.

---

[14] Ngajukula is now the name given to both ceremonies; it was performed for the groups living in Fitzroy Crossing, Western Australia in 1995.

[15] This is an unusual situation for groups in a *kuyu-wurruru* (mother-in-law/son-in-law) relation; usually groups of the same totem are *kuyu-wapirra* (brothers). See next chapter in this book.

[16] *yankirri* is owned by Jangala/Nangala-Jampijinpa/Nampijinpa (4–6 patricycle) while the constellation *wampana, Yarripiri, yumarimari* is owned by Jupurrurla/Napurrurla-Jakamarra/Nakamarra (2–8 patricycle which exchanges mothers-in-law with 4–6).

For this occasion, they wore shoes called *kurdaija*, also the name of the 'vampire' spirits of the deceased who cannot find their way to the sky. According to Meggitt (1962), after one year of the body being exposed the maternal uncles of a man or a woman went back to this site to crush the bones and hide the powder so obtained in a termite mound. They kept the bones of the arm to pass around all their tribal brothers. Every time these remains of the dead and the string made with his hair were handed over, funeral gifts, particularly hairstrings and acacia seedcakes, were provided by the new recipients to the previous ones. Though these exchanges took place between men, women played an essential role, providing their hair and the seedcakes (Glowczewski 1983a).

Today, activities related to the treatment of the dead are a subject avoided by the Warlpiri. Bodies are buried and bones are no longer passed around. Funeral gifts are still given, but directly by the women of the 'mothers' of the dead to their 'brothers', actual or classificatory maternal uncles of the dead. They cut their hair like widows and they give food. Gifts of hairstring and gifts of food have a similar value: they are at the same time goods of exchange and symbols of reconciliation, since they mark the process of conflict resolution, the conflict arising from the loss, which occasionally requires revenge.

Hair is also cut during the stages of socialisation of boys and girls. A boy's hair is cut during initiation, and a girl's hair used to be cut at her menarche. Nowadays, girls and women like to let their hair grow and only cut it at the death of a son, a husband or sometimes a brother.[17] They still give the hair to a maternal uncle who in exchange is obliged to defend his nieces in case of a conflict with their husband. On the other hand, a woman's fathers and brothers take the side of her husband. The obligation to support uterine nieces (and not daughters or sisters) is reflected in the way reconciliation ceremonies are organised: conflict staged in bark fights sets the men in opposition to their mothers-in-law, while in another ritual they confront the maternal uncles of their wives (that is, the brothers of their mothers-in-law); but the resolution of this conflict is symbolised in the fire fight, which unites the clans who are the 'mother-in-law/son-in-law' (*kuyu-wurruru*) relationship against the clans of the other patrimoiety to which their spouses (and brothers-in-law) belong, a situation the reverse of the norm in which brothers-in-law are expected to give each other assistance in everyday life.

---

[17] Also a son-in-law.

In totemic relations, hairstrings are also used to pay for the services rendered by the *kurdungurlu* (actual and classificatory uterines and brothers-in-law). In other words, in all four contexts subject to taboo – concerning totems, socialisation, mourning and the mother-in-law/son-in-law relationship – the exchange of hairstring is the most important symbol of the alliance, which is protected by the taboos of space and sexuality.

Ritual Inversion of the Prohibitions of Speech, Body or Goods

A secret should not be revealed, but to be maintained it must be transmitted. Elders transmit their most secret knowledge to the next generation when they judge that they are ready to take their place as *kirda*, and when they believe their own lives are coming to an end. These same secrets are revealed to outsiders (affines, uterines) when they are worthy of assuming the role of *kurdungurlu*. The revelation of a secret proceeds out of a necessity determined by death and bringing about alliance. Secrecy is an object of endless negotiations, not because of a clan's protectionism but because each member of the clan in turn has to choose new allies.

In its way, the myth of the transfer of knowledge from the Digging Stick women to the heroes of the Initiated Man Dreaming illustrates this necessary revelation of the secret to the allies. It institutes order in society through exchange. Transfer between genders or between clans is also mediated by the interpretation of dreams, which are transmitted from one person to another by means outside their control. An individual may receive in a dream a revelation concerning the totems and lands of clans other than his/her own: s/he must then submit this revelation to the clans concerned who decide if they will validate this information by integrating it with their mytho-ritual heritage. Similarly, women may access some male secrets through their dream visions which result either in female ritual innovations or in a gift to the men of new ritual elements (designs, songs, dances). Men too may dream designs destined for women, who, as I have witnessed, modify them for their own use while saying they are the 'same' as were given to them by the male dreamers. This unintentional transgression in sleep plays a creative role, or rather, in the Warlpiri sense, a role of '(re)memorisation' (remembrance?) in a space-time where the difference between genders is erased.

At the ritual level, there are other trangressions with a generative power: some rituals for the increase of species require that the people who bear the name of a given totem eat some of it. This ritual transgression is intended to reverse the death that transgression implies in everyday life. The ritual assures the increase of the species and of the living *Kuruwarri* that animate it, and which give life force to the bearers of that name. The ritual reproduces a situation common to many of the mythic beings, who used to eat that which gave them their name. The men and women of the Wild Bean (*wanarri*) which grows on the Acacia coriacea (*pangkuna, kunarnturru* or *wakilpirri*), whose ashes people mix with the leaves of chewing tobacco, ate beans they grilled on a fire, and they deduced from the way the smoke blew which way they should travel; thus, they literally walked in the tracks of the Dreaming that was simultaneously feeding and guiding them. I did not find any Warlpiri myth whose heroes with the names of animals were said to have eaten those animals; on the other hand, they often kill each other, which could be a metaphor for this.[18]

Mythic beings – with names of flora, fauna or other objects and phenomena – are often shown as marrying within their own group: this model of the endogamous (actual) reproduction of species is opposed to the totemic exogamy of men. Some heroes had sexual intercourse with other species, but these acts led to the interaction between the different Dreaming paths of travel and the logic of alliance which operates today.

To consume one's own flesh (*kuyu*) – be it totems, or women of the clan – is to be in a Dreaming state that men cannot realise because the Law of the Dreaming supposes the reverse: interclanic exchange. In a ritual context, to eat one's totem, which is taboo, re-actualises the self-reproductive aspect of the totems in the Dreaming space-time; this self-reproduction is also manifest in the fact that species are endogamous for reproduction (while people of different totems are not). Women, having no alimentary taboo on their clan totem, or on those of their father or their mother, permanently symbolise self-reproduction, especially as they give birth from their own body.

It has to be remembered that sexual intercourse is forbidden to a man not only with women of his own clan – whom he calls 'sisters', 'daughters' or 'paternal aunts' – but also with women of any clan of his patrimoiety (*kirda*) that he calls 'brothers or fathers'

---

[18] See *Desert Dreamers* (Glowczewski [1989] 2016) for a story of a Cannibal Dreaming.

clans (*kuyu-wapirra*) or 'mothers-in-law/sons-in-law' clans (*kuyu-wurruru*); in the other moiety (*kurdungurlu*), which encompasses the clans who provide 'wives' (*kuyu-kirda*) or 'mothers' (*kuyu-yarriki*), he has no right of access to the women of the generation that alternates with his (*kuyu-kari*). However, it was from among these non-prescribed relations that the actors of the collective defloration of the girl he would marry were chosen.

According to Spencer and Gillen, some totemic ceremonies or male initiations also required that men have sexual intercourse with one or two women of the forbidden categories: these women, widowed or married, were volunteers and followed the men to their secret ground. Thus, the sexual transgression was accompanied by a spatial transgression, both believed to favour the rituals, that is the actualisation and the increase of the living forces which were being manipulated. This sacred prostitution seems to have disappeared except in the case of punishment: a widow accused of easy virtue or an adulterous woman may be brought to the men's camp in a ceremonial context to submit to the Law, and to be taken in turn by men normally forbidden to her. Women are scared of this ordeal and show solidarity in preventing it, but the few women who have been through it all seem proud of it and are recognised by the others as possessing a certain power through having taken part in the male ceremonies.

Although ritual sexual transgressions take place with women classified as kin, actual blood relations are excluded. Thus, even though, in particular instances, there is a ritual 'consumption' of 'sisters' or 'daughters/paternal aunts' (ego's clan and *kuyu-wapirra* clans), incest between actual siblings (and parallal cousins) or between agnatic relatives of different generations (father/daughter, paternal uncle/niece, paternal aunt/nephew) is not conceivable. Similarly, a man cannot sleep with his mother, his mother's sister, or even a blood related cross-cousin; only classificatory 'mothers' or 'cousins' ('daughters' of the father's sister or of the mother's brother) are accessible in some ritual cases. The latter are even tolerated as wives (*kuyu-yarriki* clans).

Actual and classificatory mothers-in-law seem to be absolutely forbidden. The same applies to the maternal grandmother and her sisters, or grand-nieces who are from the generation alternating with the generation of the mother-in-law in the *kuyu-wurruru* clans. Women who are classified but not actual members of these categories are possible partners in the ritual transgressions. Finally, in the *kuyu-kirda* clans, which provide the wives, some women are prohibited because they are potential wives of the man's grandfathers or grandsons; relations of the alternate generation are also prohibited, whether they are classified or blood relations (*kuyu-kirda* and *kuyu-kari*).

In other terms, the two kinship categories that escape ritual transgression altogether – uterine nieces (ego's matrimoiety and opposite patrimoiety) and potential mothers-in-law (ego's patrimoiety and opposite matrimoiety) – are the ones that characterise the exchange of nieces as the model of alliance. It seems that these ultimate prohibited relationships are identified with social incest in order to prevent the rupture of the model of alliance rather than to avoid inbreeding.

By her subsection, a mother-in-law is the 'cross-cousin' of the mother of her son-in-law, her mother is a 'sister' of the maternal grandfather of the son-in-law (DHMFZ), and her father is a 'brother' of the maternal grandmother of the son-in-law (DHMMB). The Dreamings which are *fathers* of a man's mother are therefore *mothers* of his mother-in-law (and vice versa: the *mothers* of a man's mother are *fathers* of his mother-in-law) (see Figure 1.3, p. 000). Thus, through the *Kuruwarri* that inhabit a person and are inherited from both parents, a mother-in-law is a symbolic double of the mother. As such, the mother-in-law taboo symbolises mother-son incest. To sleep with a 'daughter', a 'mother' or a 'mother-in-law' is similar: it is to replay the self-reference embodied by the Dreaming Beings who engendered themselves. One can see in the mother-in-law taboo (which prevails over all other sexual prohibitions) the symbol of this timeless self-generation, the nostalgia of a 'dream' where all kinship, and the temporality that goes with it, are negated.

Prescribed wives, through their subsection, are 'mothers' of the husband's father; a man is then in a position of 'father' of his own father, *father* of the paternal totemic Flesh, who thus engenders his own totemic Flesh. From the point of view of society, men, therefore, *self-engender* their Dreaming-totem, on condition that they marry specific women from *other* Dreaming-totems. If men had access, outside of the ritualised transgressions, to prohibited women, there would be no differentiation between the various Dreamings and all the kinship categories would be confused. Some myths illustrate the danger of such social disintegration.

Examples of Mythical Sexual Transgression

The Invincible Dreaming myth (*Wawulja*) is in its way a dream of non-differentiation and of incest, a nostalgia that is partially staged by ritual sexual transgressions.

Invincible was polygamous. He wanted all his sons to be killed so that he could marry all his daughters. His wives and daughters managed to save two newborn boys who grew up in secret. In time they took revenge on their father, by sending against him a stranger who killed him. Invincible burst into pieces and reconstituted himself straight away, but his genitals were changed. With the help of his wives and daughters, he dragged himself from place to place until one day his testes liberated secretions that accumulated into a hill since called Kurra, pus.

Invincible then disappeared underground. His wives looked for him by digging the ground with their sticks, but he came out on top of the hill and snatched their tools, which he took with him to the subterranean depths. The gigantic *Warnayarra*, Rainbow Snake, then came out from the earth and swallowed all the women. After a long, underground journey he spat them out in a place located some thousand kilometres away on the Western Australian border. Invincible followed them underground, and to the sky where all were transformed into celestial phenomena: the Snake into the rainbow, Invincible into Orion and his daughters into the Pleiades.

Nowadays, every night, Orion, subsection Jungarrayi (3), interferes between the Pleiades, his daughters, subsection Napaljarri (7), and the planet Mars, a Jakamarra (2) Crow man (*Jarntimarra*) who tries to reach them. Crow belongs to the right subsection to be the husband of Invincible's daughters. The *Warnayarra* Snake, like the Rain Dreaming he belongs to, is a member of two subsections, Jampijinpa-Jangala (4–6): Nangala (6) is the right subsection of women (from this Dreaming or any 'brother' Dreaming) that Invincible should have married instead of his own daughters (Glowczewski and Pradelles de Latour 1987).[19]

The myth tells of an incestuous aberration which turns into a tragedy of revenge. *Wawulja* cannot remain invincible like his name:

---

[19] The Rainbow Snake represents the anger of a broken alliance; as a male he embodies the allies Invincible refused to have: brothers-in-law Jangala (brothers of the Nangala potential wifes) and fathers-in-law Jampijinpa (fathers of the Nangala).

two of his sons escape his herodian law and succeed in taking revenge. Killed by a stranger, he revives but his reproductive functions are damaged. Neither sons nor father know that the boys were conceived not by Invincible but by the Wind, *mayawunpa*, a secret lover of his wives. This latter Dreaming is 'brother' of Invincible because he belongs to the same patricycle: Jungarrayi-Japaljarri (3–7). As they were growing up the two boys became cannibals who transformed themselves into whirlwinds in order to swallow the women they slept with; they also introduced shamanistic cures, and are sacred references for the medicine men not only among the Warlpiri, but also the Pintupi and Walmajarri to the west.[20]

Like all the Dreaming heroes, Invincible disappears underground and his *Kuruwarri* forces are present for ever in the sites he created on his way, but he is also a visible phenomenon in the form of Orion. The celestial trajectories of Invincible-Orion, his daughters, the Pleiades, and their pretender, Mars, are guiding people during the *kurdiji* initiation which is associated with the Initiated Man Dreaming (3–7 patricycle, like Invincible). The Initiated Man, Invincible and Wind Dreamings are owned by specific clans, but they are ritual references for the whole tribe. Everybody knows the story of the jealous father who chases the Pleiades; nevertheless, only initiated men and women know that Orion is Invincible and that he is associated with the brothers who turned into whirlwinds. Publicly, 'above' and 'below' are separated. Invincible is *below* as the ancestral principle of the patriclan that claims his name, Wawulja. As a constellation, he is *above*, a ritual and temporal mark for all the Warlpiri, only identified by the subsection Jungarrayi (3) as a possessive character, not openly incestuous, who refuses to leave his daughters, the Pleiades, with Mars, their legitimate suitor. The myth is to this discourse on the celestial phenomena, the same as a hidden, 'below' meaning is to a manifest, 'above' one.

The Invincible Dreaming is not only 'daughter and sister' of himself (*kuyu-wapirra*), which is the norm (for all Dreamings), but also, by engendering himself through his daughters, Wawulja turns his Dreaming into his own 'wife and uterine niece' (*kuyu-kirda*),

---

[20] Longer versions of the myths of Invincible and his sons were published in Glowczewski (1991b); the latter are known all across the Western Desert and the Kimberley as the 'Two-Men' who also brought different Laws to the coastal tribes; for an analysis of this transcontinental Dreaming, see Glowczewski ([1998] 2009 and 2004).

'mother and daughter's daughter' (*kuyu-yarriki*) and 'mother-in-law, uterine grand-niece or maternal grandmother' (*kuyu-wurruru*). The four types of Flesh (clans or patricycles) and the eight kinship categories (subsections) are thus confused. This Dreaming Father takes himself for the Absolute One, despising the alternation of the generations and exogamy, at the price of the murder of his sons. Insensitive to the interplay of differences, hostile to other Dreamings, he is the negation of alterity and of alliance, and so the obverse of the social order. The Dreaming he embodies, and society, are like the photo-negative of each other: Invincible transforms his wives into mothers-in-law because he marries his daughters. Similarly, a man who transgressed the mother-in-law taboo by sleeping with his wife's mother (before she gives birth to a daughter) would risk becoming the father of his own future wife.

I indicated previously that the marriage of Dreaming Beings with females from their own Dreaming was quite common. Incest, as embodied by Invincible, corresponds in other myths with a collective endogamy where the four types of Flesh (own Dreaming, mother's Dreaming, wife's Dreaming, mother-in-law's Dreaming) are also confused, although it does not prevent the members of each Dreaming from differentiating each other by kin terms. To my knowledge, this collective behaviour is not explicitly identified with incest: mythic partners of the same totemic name or of different totems are said to transgress sexually only if their kinship categories are defined as prohibited for one another. For instance, two lovers of the same totem are not said to be in an incestuous relationship if their subsections define them as 'spouses', such as with the mythic Emu couple.

One myth talks about a transgression between a youth and a woman who were permitted to marry according to their subsections. The taboo broken was not one of incest but that which forbids a young initiate from getting married or even seeing a woman.

> A young Jungarrayi (3) from the Initiated Dreaming was kidnapped by a Nangala (6) woman of the Rain Dreaming, who carried him through the air on her back before he had finished his ritual seclusion. This episode is mimed by the women during the *kurdiji* ceremony. She took him to live with her clan and looked after him as if he were her husband, but for years he refused to marry her. Finally, he gave in to love and they had a little girl. They returned to his clan whose members accepted them back.

This episode is repeated in two different sites of the Initiated Man Dreaming, whose people came out of the ground after a gigantic

Forbidding and Enjoying

windbreak (*yunta*) fell from the sky and was transformed into a long hill at Kurlungalinpa. This happened when a light in the sky (*kiiki* or *parayipilpa*), not a falling star but probably a comet, travelling at high speed, brought the night, before breaking up into small stars. After their terrestrial and subterreanean wanderings, and the fall of a new windbreak and of the night at another site, the Initiated Man people returned to the cosmos as little stars (*yanjilypirri* or *wanjilypiri*). This is secret knowledge, like the transformation of Invincible into Orion. On the other hand, the story of the woman in love who stole the initiate is a public episode told to children. So is the Willy Wagtail Dreaming which deals with another type of transgression, related to both initiation and sexuality. This is the story of a possessive mother who kept her adult son in her belly instead of giving him to the men to be initiated and to enter a marriage alliance through the promise of a mother-in-law.

Apart from the previous examples, all other episodes of sexual transgression that were told to me concern the mother-in-law/son-in-law relationship. The recurrence of this theme confirms the importance of this alliance, even when it is only virtual. It is the only relationship that is simultaneously subject to the four domains of taboo: space, language, sexuality and goods. We have seen that the Dreaming Digging Stick women were raped by their 'son-in-law', Transgressor, *wingkingarrka*: he is Jungarrayi-Japaljarri (3–7) and they are Napanangka-Napangardi (1–5). Peterson (1967) notes that before Transgressor arrived in Warlpiri country, where he met these women, he belonged to the same subsections as they: Japanangka-Japangardi (1–5).

There is also the story of the Gecko *yumarimari* who, out of shame for sleeping with a 'mother-in-law', left the path of travel of his companions from the Dreaming constellation (formed by) Wallaby (*wampana*), Giant Snake (*Yarripiri*) and Seeds (*ngurlu*) to hide himself (cf. Chapter 3). Also called transgressor, *wingki*, his story and the simple mention of the site of his transgression, Yumarimari (like his name), always provoke obscene jokes and the formula: 'This Jakamarra (2) who slept with a Nangala! (6)'. In fact, according to the myths, transgressors have various reactions.

> Two heroines of the Rain Dreaming, Nangala (6) and Nampijinpa (4), when they were crossing the country of the Plum (*marrkirdi*) and Berries (*ngardanykinyi*) Dreaming, stopped at the waterhole Kinkimularnu, where they seduced a group of men from this Dreaming: Jakamarra (2), 'son-in-law' of the Nangala and Jupurrurla (8) 'son-in-law' of the Nampijinpa.

According to Warlpiri women, the heroines did not regret this shameful (*kuntangka*) act. On the other hand, a section of the Goanna Dreaming says that a Japangardi (5) hero called himself *waji-waji*, transgressor, after he deliberately slept with a Nungarrayi (3), a potential mother-in-law. Worried about his action, he then went about inspecting his body to see whether some terrible transformation was going to afflict him. The scene is re-enacted by women in a *yawulyu* ritual (cf. annexe and Chapter 3).

A mythical episode, told by a man, shows a transgressor who, not aware of being one, was nevertheless stricken by the Dreaming Law:

> A Jangala (6) of the Rain Dreaming slept with a Nakamarra (2) without knowing her subsection nor her Dreaming. Later on, he was magically hit in the back and the killing stick went right into him. Neither he nor the men who were with him, least of all the young initiates he was leading on an initiation journey, understood why he was attacked in such a way. They carried him to his country Kalipinpa where he asked to be laid with his belly against the ground to die.

The following episode illustrates the punishment of an aggressor.

> A Jungarrayi (3) of the Initiated Man Dreaming raped a 'mother-in-law' Napangardi (5) of the Ground Honey (*nankalinji*) Dreaming, then he hit her on the neck and killed her fearing she might denounce him. Thanks to the footprints he left on the ground, he was found by the woman's people and killed in his turn. This happened at Kurlungalinpa, the site of the Initiated Man Dreaming where one of the first *kurdiji* initiations took place. The Honey people went there to participate in the promise ritual that designates a future mother-in-law for the initiate.

Relations between the two peoples would have been broken if the death of the transgressor had not been followed by a reconciliation ceremony. Kurlungalinpa had been visited previously by the Bee Honey (*ngarlu*) and Owl (*puluwanti*) people who originated such a ceremony which stages the mother-in-law/son-in-law relationship:[21] thus, the site doubly symbolises the association between this relationship and the rituals for settling disputes.

Sacred Objects: Temporality and Non-Temporality

At the end of this presentation of the Warlpiri taboos, it is clear that the four contexts they apply to relate to the same domains, both in

---

[21] See audio version in Glowczewski (2000).

the prohibitions and in their mythic or ritual inversions, through transgression or compensation. Table 5.1 summarises this: in each box, which combines a context and a domain, the first line shows the relevant prohibition or restriction and the second line shows the 'other side', the complementary practice associated with it.

The matrix, constructed with the contexts and the domains of taboos, organises the variables so that none determinates the others, although, locally, each variable may be connected to any other. The eight variables may be represented by the vertices of a cube (see Figure 5.1) which, by definition, lacks a unique polarisation: the three edges and the diagonal (not shown in the diagram) that connects each vertex to its opposite vertex (through the cube) represent the relationships that connect each context with four domains or each domain with four contexts. The relationships between the contexts are illustrated by diagonals (not shown) that run across the six faces of the cubes; and the relationships between the domains are illustrated by the opposite diagonals that also run along the six faces, but cross the previous diagonals: this is another way of visualising the interaction between the two levels of taboo.

The four contexts listed for the Warlpiri taboos correspond to their four types of collective ceremonies: funeral, initiation, totemic rituals and reconciliation through settling dispute. Other rituals exist, but they are more individual, such as magic to seduce or to keep somebody faithful, therapies to cure a pain or a state of mind, and sorcery to punish or avenge. These practices are extensions, case by case, of social and cosmological preoccupations that are addressed in the ceremonies for mourning, initiation, territorial totemism and conflict resolution. In these ceremonies, the ritualised transgression of taboos plays a very important role in the collective production of the mythical space-time and of the social temporality.

First, transgression in space is the most common catalyst in reorganising the way in which territorial rights are distributed: Dreamings are used as a mythical and ritual warranty to ensure that any reorganisation obeys a mode of land attribution acceptable to the Law. It is a way of reproducing the Law of the Dreaming. Transgression in space accompanies various ceremonial situations: women coming to the men's ground during some male totemic rituals or at the end of initiation; men coming to the women's ground at the end of mourning; mothers-in-law and sons-in-law dancing together in the ceremonies for conflict resolution. All these ritual situations oppose

Table 5.1 Contexts and domains of Warlpiri taboos

CONTEXTS:	MOURNING	SOCIALISATION	TOTEMISM	MOTHER-IN-LAW/ SON-IN-LAW
	(temporary)			(permanent)
Domains:				
Space	places avoided 'opening' rites	seclusion initiation	secret sites territorial rites	proximity avoided dispute settlement
Language	names forbidden sign language	silence of initiates reversed language	secret names, myths esoteric language	forbidden conversation restricted language
Sexuality	abstinence pubic depilation	abstinence body marking	endogamy forbidden body marking	incest prohibition pubic depilation
Goods	destruction gifts	forbidden meat gifts	regulations on totems gifts	'protected' hunt gifts

Forbidding and Enjoying

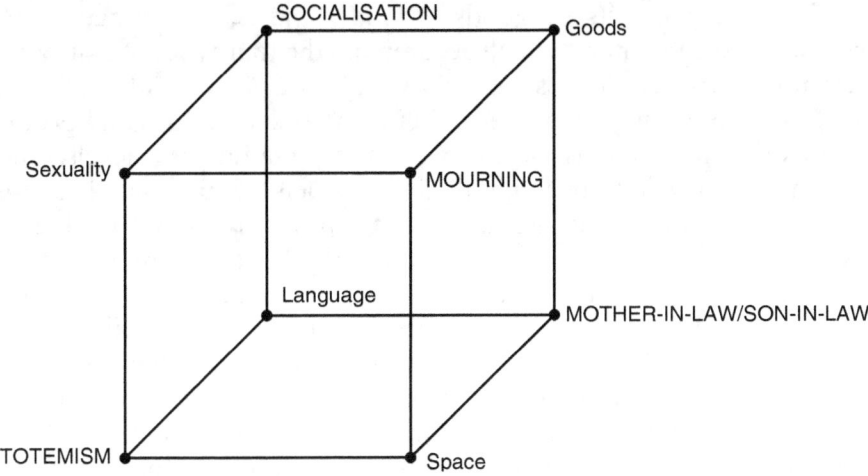

Figure 5.1 A cube for Warlpiri taboos

the two genders in a way that re-enacts the cosmological reversal (turning inside out) of 'below' and 'above'.

As a necessary revelation of secrets, transgression in language also participates in reaffirming the coming into being of any Dreaming. It is the condition for renewing the generations, marriage alliances and totemic relations. Ritual transmission changes sons into fathers, sons-in-law and husbands, daughters into mothers, mothers-in-law and wives; all agnates into affines allies, living people into dead [spirits that will join with the Dreaming and not haunt the living]. But through distinctions of access to knowledge, which are marked by the various languages of substitution (hand signs, reversed speech, esoteric language during initiation or the one restricted to mother-in-law/son-in-law), rituals are reminders that affiliation and alliance are maintained as the Law of the Dreaming beyond the interested people who actualise these links.

Similarly, ritualised sexual transgression is a reminder that kinship categories may be confounded in the Dreamtime, without cancelling the potential for social organisation that the Dreaming carries. The sexual relationship with a 'wife's mother', which is always forbidden, is mimed in ritual re-enactments of transgressing totemic heroes. This ubiquitous mythic theme – implicitly condemning both father/daughter and mother/son incest – here plays the role of an inaccessible magnet, which would fuse (and confuse) generations normally separated by rules of alliance and affiliation.

Finally, ritual gifts of goods – food, objects, hairstring, cloth, nowadays even money – which accompany the four types of collective ceremonies (which are associated with the four contexts for taboo), are a form of symbolic compensation for the deprivations and prohibitions that men impose on themselves at these different levels. The son-in-law may not consume all the products of his hunt, because he must provide his mother-in-law with meat throughout his life in exchange for the wife he enjoys, a debt of which he is reminded by the vegetable dishes his mother-in-law gives him. Similarly, young initiates may not eat meat during their seclusion because they have to learn to hunt for the elders, as repayment for the knowledge the elders reveal to them. Widows, who may not cook nor eat meat during mourning, ritualise a loss, so standing on the side of the mothers of the deceased, who provide ritual payments to their brothers for organising the funerals and the rituals that follow. Finally, restrictions on totems take symbolic value from allowing complementarity in ritual 'work', for the increase of natural phenomena for the benefit of the tribe, when the custodians, by ritually consuming their totems, re-enact the self-reproduction of the Dreamings and the conditions of fertility.

In all these contexts, ritual inversion of the various taboos relates to a mystery: how time is produced from its negation. This non-temporal time is shown in the universes of the multiple *Jukurrpa* which re-engender themselves self-referentially in the permanence of their name, outside any exchange, a situation illustrated by the endogamy of the ancestral people and of the species that descend from them. Another aspect of this self-reference is embodied in the sacred objects.

I have kept to the end the taboo on sacred objects because it seems to condense the four contexts and four domains mentioned so far. Traditionally, a stranger or a young man who was not fully initiated and who saw sacred objects without the permission of the elders was punished by death. Two Warlpiri men who disappeared in suspicious circumstances in the 1970s, were, according to some, killed because they did not respect this prohibition. Similarly, in 1984, a woman from Lajamanu who, inadvertently, found forbidden objects hidden in the bush became mad and died: her madness and death, unexplained by Western medicine, were understood by everyone to be the result of her involuntary transgression.

Women's ritual objects, handled with great care, are kept hidden by women even though most of the boards and *Jukurrpa* stones were originally given to them by men. Sometimes a ritual requires men to have contact with these women's objects, for instance during a curing ritual or at the end of a period of mourning. But apart from these ritualised transgressions, the man who thinks of stealing women's objects takes a mortal risk. Some Warlpiri men and women tell of having 'sung' to death a man who had transgressed this rule. When one day a jealous husband threw himself in anger on the women's ground pretending to grab the sacred stick erected there, immediately the women dancers hid the stick away and treated the intruder as a madman. The elders did not 'sing' him, but the ritual journey that had been planned to give another tribe the initiation cycle *Kajirri*, which was being performed, was almost cancelled. After many discussions, no novice from Lajamanu was taken to be initiated on that occasion (Glowczewski [1989] 2016).

Prohibitions are modulated nowadays by interactions with non-Aboriginal people. Children still must not touch nor see objects restricted to women's rituals, but some women have sold them to art shops. Men show a very strong resistance to the idea of selling their sacred objects, and the fact that some of these, collected by Europeans, are exhibited openly scandalises them. However, when twelve Warlpiri men invited to Paris recognised some boards at the Musée national des arts d'Afrique et d'Océanie (The National Museum of Arts of Africa and Oceania [MNAAO, 1960–2002]), and it was suggested to them that they take them back home, the Warlpiri men refused, saying it was too late. Because these objects had been exhibited, they were no longer secret, and to bring them back would have provoked conflicts about rightful ownership and the identification of those guilty of having let them go in the first place. On the other hand, elders accepted some of the sacred boards that were to be returned by the South Australian Museum in Adelaide.

The secrecy surrounding the handling of sacred objects relates to totemism, because they are connected with a specific Dreaming or are used as a medium for the actualisation of different Dreamings. But the other three contexts for taboos are also implicated: socialisation, mourning, and the mother-in-law/son-in-law relationship. It is during his initiation that a boy sees the sacred objects for the first time, and it is when a woman takes part in the initiation of her son – or the son of a co-wife or of a sister – that she is allowed to handle the women's ritual objects; as paternal aunt of a novice, she also gains the right to look at some of the men's objects while the other women have to lower their heads. While all other possessions of a dead man or woman are burnt, their sacred objects are not: these must be handed over to other members of the clan. Finally, in the context of the mother-in-law/son-in-law relationship, during reconciliation ceremonies, ritual poles and masts are made to be burnt, and wooden vessels are painted to be given to the 'sons-in-law' as part of a special dance. These vessels are of the same shape as those used for carrying babies or food, and the dance can symbolise giving daughters as wives to sons-in-law.

Through their identification with this or that totemic name, the male and female sacred objects are the transubstantiation – believed to be an effective presence – of the totemic beings. The prohibition on eating or using a clanic totem seems to be a particular case of the sacrality and secrecy that surrounds the *Kuruwarri* (as image-forces and totems-objects) that the Warlpiri say nourishes them. Nevertheless, while the eating prohibition applies principally to the father's totem (one's own), and sometimes to the mother's, the interdiction on sacred objects applies to all tribal totems: a man may not see the objects of other clans without being invited to do so in a ritual context.[22] The value attached to the objects belonging to this or that clan is strengthened by the secrecy that surrounds them. Some pass from clan to clan, but always according to a ritual and secretly coded manipulation. The exchange of such objects, or their return to their first owner after a series of transfers, symbolises confidence, fraternity or alliance which cement individual, interclanic or intertribal relationships.

Sacred objects, as living images of the totemic names and their inaccessible referents – the eternal beings – cannot be dissociated from the mythic paths of travel and the sites connected with the Dreamings. Because they symbolise totemic names, they are also taboo in language; they are to speech what the sign language is to the tongue: a way to 'say' without speaking. Finally, sacred objects are the expression par excellence of whatever is taboo in sexuality: the connection between coitus and reproduction. The mystery of life derives from the power of the Dreamings, and not from the contingency of sexual intercourse, which function is publicly disregarded in favour of the discourse about spirit-children. It is this power of the Dreaming that the (sacred) objects crystallise, as they are external to human sexuality and symbols of the cosmological androgyny: the conjunction of female and male in totemic principles.

The taboo on sacred objects condenses in itself the four contexts subject to taboo – mourning, socialisation, totemism and the

---

[22] It is the same for women's secret objects.

Forbidding and Enjoying

Figure 5.2 Women's ritual to lift the mourning taboos for the Kana Digging Stick Dreaming. The blankets are gifts for men. Lajamanu. From left to right: Liddy Nelson Nakamarra, Yulyurlu Lorna Fencer Napurrurla, Emma Morrison Napanangka, Kajingarra Maisy Napangardi, Kungariya Gladys Napangardi, Biddy Hooker Napanangka © B. G. (1984)

mother-in-law/son-in-law relationship – and the four domains to which they apply – space, language, sexuality and goods. But this taboo also implies a prohibition that transcends all that, because it is not limited to a relationship, temporary (mourning and socialisation) or permanent (totemism and WM/DH). Sacred objects reflect all possible relationships and stay taboo independent of the context or the person who handles them, and the succession of generations.

Because sacred objects are substitutes for the contingencies of space, language, sexuality and goods which make up human life, they are the warranty of the *Jukurrpa* as a space-time which is external to, but a condition of, this temporality. By extension, these taboos become a way to create human temporality, both as a vertical transmission – in the succession of generations re-enacted through socialisation and mourning rituals – and as a horizontal differentiation perpetually redefining these modalities of alliance and of ritual interdependance between the totemic groups. We will see that a similar warranty concerning the making of time is symbolised by sacred objects elsewhere in Australia.

6

A Topological Approach to Australian Cosmology and Social Organisation

I propose here to use a particular branch of mathematics, the topology of surfaces, as a means of comparing cosmology and social organisation among the Central Australian Warlpiri. After defining a topological figure for Warlpiri society, I shall try to show that topology also offers a methodology for cross-cultural comparison. In highlighting a similarity of structure between Australian social organisation and cosmology, my hypothesis will be that Aboriginal kinship neither determines nor is determined by cosmology but that the two are applied forms of a specific logic that can be accounted for by topology.

From the Land to the Dreaming

MYTHICAL PLACES AND RITUAL ROLES AMONG THE WARLPIRI

In 1978, after many hearings before the Aboriginal Land Commissioner, the Warlpiri became one of the first Australian tribes to recover most of their traditional territory.[1] This restitution was obtained by demonstrating that groups are symbolically affiliated to the geographical itineraries of journeys made by mythical heroes who bore totemic names. Each local group has rights to sites and to tracts of land connected by the itineraries of particular Ancestral Beings whom it regards metaphorically as 'fathers' to its members. During my fieldwork (1979–1984) I was able to observe a close relationship between the fluidity with which these local patrician groups are constituted and a process through which mythical stories and associated totems are ritualised. Women play an active part in this

---

[1] This text was translated from the French by Barbara Glowczewski and Kenneth Maddock and first published in 1989 in *Mankind*, 19 (3): 227–40 (following a Hunter and Gatherer conference in Darwin in 1988). Figures 6.1 to 6.4 were published in Glowczewski and Pradelles de Latour (1987) and Figures 6.5 to 6.10 in Glowczewski (1988).

interaction between cosmology and social organisation. Contrary to the assertions of Meggitt (1962) and Munn (1973), women do participate in ritual activities aimed at actualising totemic and mythical links between itineraries and sites (as has also been shown by Bell 1983). Admittedly women perform these rituals on their own, but they organise themselves in the same manner as the men. According to the totem and itinerary being celebrated, some performers act as *kirda* or owners of the rituals and sites, in which capacity they have the duty to dance; the others act as *kurdungurlu*, or managers of the rituals and sites, directing the dances and preparing the ceremonial objects and ground.

This division of ritual roles which also governs land rights is to be found in other central and northern tribes (Maddock 1981). At the first level, everyone is 'owner' of his or her father's land and 'manager' of his or her mother's land and also the land of his or her spouse (Glowczewski 1981b). In practice, the range of determination is wider than just patri- or matri-filiation. During ritual performances, the owner/manager duality of function among keepers of the land is often extended and systematised in accordance with the division of all members of the tribe into the eight subsections of the Aranda system. This system, which the anthropological literature identifies as a matrimonial classification, is above all a device for use in ritual life and in the cosmological allocation of land rights.

When analysing the spatial embodiment of myth and ritual on the one hand, and the symbolic complementarity of men and women on the other. I was led into looking for a model that would account for the inseparable articulation of territoriality with cosmology and classificatory kinship. The Warlpiri, like their neighbours, use the word *Jukurrpa* ('dream' or Dreaming) to denote the Ancestral totemic Beings, the myths that tell of their journeys and the associated itineraries. The Dreaming is not a simple mythical Golden Age annihilating time, through which Aboriginal people would be fixed in a repetitive cycle: rather it is a space-time, a kind of permanency in movement, allowing innovations to be legitimated through integration via a preexistent logic.

Such innovations, which take the form of new rituals, new geographical landmarks and new systems of alliance, are part and parcel of the reproduction of society. Consequently, the Dreaming is inducive of a dynamic social logic allowing both the maintenance of irreducible specifications and the incessant renewal of articulation between mythical and ritual elements and society. It is from this perspective that the Aborigines themselves consider the Dreaming to be their Law. It is a matter not of a set of rules but of an active process of forging social identity. The Dreaming is a programme – not a stock of remembered models for organising society, but a matrix of combinatorial possibilities.

Ritual innovation and transmission in central Australia

In 1984, two events allowed me to examine more closely the dynamic relation between cosmology and social organisation. First, I followed the process of integration of a ritual which a Warlpiri woman had dreamt two years earlier. I was thus able to measure the exceptional importance of onirical elaboration in the renewal of symbolic links between men and totemic heroes. Both the context in which she received her revelation and that in which her vision obtained tribal recognition had implicit political and territorial significance. She dreamt the new ritual at a time of negotiations with a mining company wishing to prospect in the vicinity of a Warlpiri sacred site; her dream acquired the value of a collective ritual when the Warlpiri signed a financial agreement with the company (Glowczewski [1989] 2016).

The fundamental preoccupation of Aboriginal societies seems to be to redefine the territorial eligibility of every individual and group. To this end, it is necessary to link people to the space-time reference of the Dreaming, that is, to totems and consequently to ritual and the corresponding sites. In connecting sides, with totemic itinerary and stories, Aborigines affirm distinct tribal identities expressed in different tongues while at the same time relating their linguistic and cultural differences to a common symbolic language, the Dreaming, which enables intertribal alliances to be made.

The second event through which I was able to observe the socialisation of Dreaming Law was a visit I made with sixty Warlpiri to Docker River, a settlement 1500 km from Lajamanu, the community where I was based. The purpose was to give the Pitjantjatjara ('sell' as Aborigines say in English) the *Kajirri* ceremony which the Warlpiri themselves had received from their northern neighbours a century earlier (Meggitt 1966). In addition to the ceremony a transfer was made of the famous eight subsections system which the Pitjantjatjara had not previously used (Glowczewski 1988: 398–418).

Many contributions to Aboriginal studies assume that kinship classification provides the organising model for everything else (Scheffler 1978, 1986). My example of intertribal transmission of a kinship system by means of a ceremony seems to invalidate this proposition. The eight subsections appear to be much more the formal application of an ideology conveyed through ritual activities than a model governing the exchange. I put forward the postulate that a subsection system could not have a hold on society if there were not already in operation a logic governing the construction of local identities and intertribal alliances.

To convey a ceremony (a 'business' as they say) by travelling to another tribe is to concretise, step by step, the mythical itinerary to which the ceremony refers. It is implicit in the act of transmission that the recipients take over the itinerary and extend it through their own tribal land by elaborating new mythical episodes which they add to the initial story. Thus myth, itinerary and ritual become instruments of alliance-making. In effect, the itinerary connects the two groups through places in the landscape; the myth gives their alliance an ancestral and totemic guarantee; and, finally, the ritual is both pretext and context for actualising the encounter and the exchange.

When the Warlpiri received the *Kajirri* (cycle) a hundred years ago, they elaborated an itinerary-story connecting them with the Kurintji (from whom they received the ceremony) and other northern tribes. The *Kajirri* is in fact derived from the Kunapipi fertility cults of the Roper River and Arnhem Land, which celebrate the journey of two Ancestral Beings, the Wawilak sisters (Berndt 1951). This is one example among others of the fact that over distances of hundreds of kilometres mythical itineraries can connect tribes of different languages while stimulating each of them to produce stories and rites having a local colour and conducive to a specific tribal identity.

The transmission of kinship systems reveals the same phenomenon of local differentiation. Although the Warlpiri in Central Australia, like the northern tribes of the Roper River and Arnhem Land (such as the Murngin-Yolngu), use eight subsections, they do not expand them into the same system everywhere. Now that they have adopted subsections, the Pitjantjatjara could elaborate yet another system. We shall see, however, that behind the different systems, there is always a common logic of the same order as that through which itineraries, myth and rites are intertribally communicated and particular tribal elaborations produced.

My opinion is that the diversity of Australian kinship systems can only be understood in the light of these itinerant mythico-ritual complexes, these Dreamings that trace paths between people, pathways that exist eternally yet are actualised only ephemerally.

From the Dreaming to the Hypercube

GENERALISED EXCHANGE AND HOMEOMORPHISM BETWEEN
WARLPIRI KINSHIP AND COSMOLOGY

Introduced into ethnology by Pradelles de Latour (1984, 1986) topology offers a means of defining the type of logic at work in a given society. With him I published an initial topological analysis of my Warlpiri data (Glowczewski and Pradelles de Latour 1987).

We started from the classificatory category of 'mother-in-law'. The mother-in-law is deemed taboo in all Australian tribes, her son-in-law being forbidden to talk to her or even approach her. In addition, among the Warlpiri, everybody is in a classificatory 'mother-in-law/son-in-law' relationship with a range of clans that he or she calls *kuyuwurruru* and into which he or she may not marry (Laughren 1982). We demonstrated that niece (ZD) exchange, which the Warlpiri call *kaminingi*, corresponds to mother-in-law exchange between clans related as *kuyuwurruru*. By formalising these exchanges, we proved that they cannot be reduced to the system of restricted exchange involving four patricycles (1–5, 2–8, 3–7, 4–6) that is shown in the classical subsection diagram (see Figure 6.1).

This diagram, being based on the assumption of sister exchange, implies that the classificatory second cross-cousins prescribed as wives are both matrilateral (MMBDD) and patrilateral (FFZSD). But sister exchange is incompatible with the niece (and mother-in-law) exchange valued by Warlpiri. To explain niece exchange, it is necessary to double the number of patricycles from four to eight. Instead of a restricted exchange system, we then obtain a minimal circuit of generalised exchange in which matrilateral second cross-cousins (MMBDD) are distinct from patrilateral (FFZSD), and brothers and sisters may not marry into the same patricycle (see Figure 6.2).

It should be added that among the Warlpiri (as for many Aboriginal people) one may not marry one's true second crosscousin, but only more distant women of the same subsection. As they bear the same *skin-name* as the true cousin, they are regarded as *skin*, but not blood, sisters to her.

In the early 1960s, the mathematician Guilbaud succeeded in mapping the eight subsections onto a torus (a shape like a doughnut), a figure which Lévi-Strauss adopted in *La pensée sauvage* (1962: 109). Both White (1963) and Courrège (1965) identified this system with a dihedral group and represented it by a cube that has

Australian Cosmology and Social Organisation

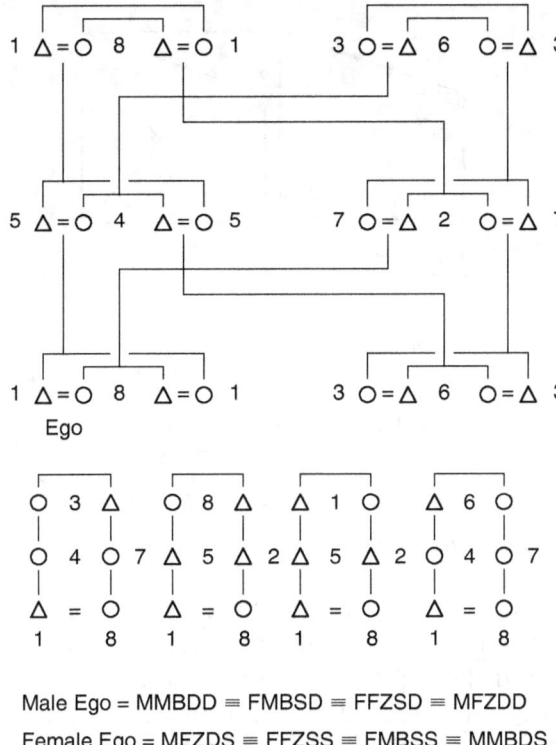

Male Ego = MMBDD ≡ FMBSD ≡ FFZSD ≡ MFZDD
Female Ego = MFZDS ≡ FFZSS ≡ FMBSS ≡ MMBDS

Figure 6.1 Eight subsections: restricted exchange

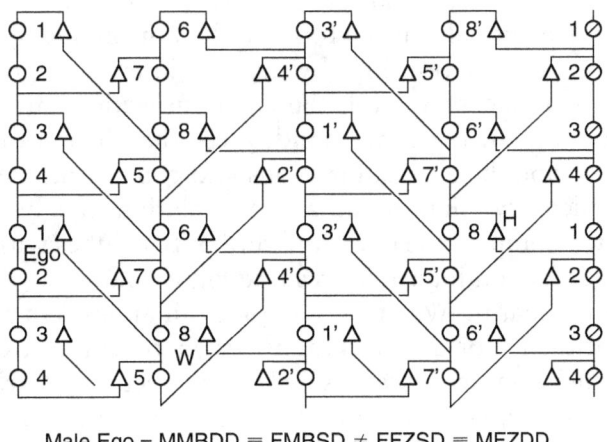

Male Ego = MMBDD ≡ FMBSD ≠ FFZSD ≡ MFZDD
Female Ego = MFZDS ≡ FFZSS ≠ FMBSS ≡ MMBDS

Figure 6.2 Eight subsections: generalised exchange

INDIGENISING ANTHROPOLOGY

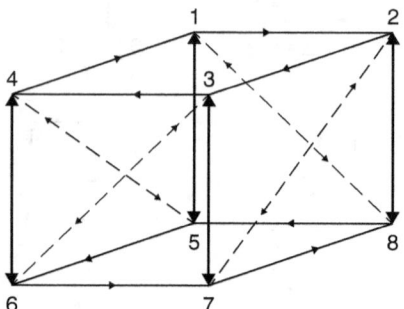

Two matricycles : 1 2 3 4
5 6 7 8

Four patricycles : 1–5 3–7
2–8 4–6

Four marriages : 1 = 8, 2 = 7, 3 = 6, 4 = 5

Figure 6.3 The eight subsections cube: restricted exchange

since become a standard way of representing subsections (Laughren 1982). In fact, the lines of Guilbaud's torus correspond to the edges of the cube, and the eight points joining them to the vertices of the cube: edges represent the relationship of agnatic or uterine filiation (real or classificatory) by which each vertex (that is, each subsection) is linked to others (see Figure 6.3).

On the cube, matrimonial relationships are represented by the four diagonals on the faces; the alternate uterine relations (to the MM or MMB) by the diagonals on the top and the bottom faces; a 'mother-in-law/son-in-law' relationships by the four interior diagonals.

If, at the classificatory level, the eight subsections are a dihedral group, the cube, on the other hand, gives the illusion of restricted exchange. By doubling the subsections and connecting them according to classificatory filiation and alliance relationships in generalised exchange, we obtained the curious figure of two cubes with interpenetrating external and internal faces (see Figure 6.4).

When investigating Warlpiri cosmology, it appears that the major postulate of their worldview is the interpenetration of external and internal, which characterises this figure. In effect, the Warlpiri define a continuous feedback relation between what they call *kanunju* 'inside', beneath, that is what is virtual, and *kankarlu* 'outside', above, what is manifest. It is precisely the interaction between these two registers which produces the space-time of the Dreaming. Thus, Warlpiri ritual life may be concisely defined as an activity consisting

Australian Cosmology and Social Organisation

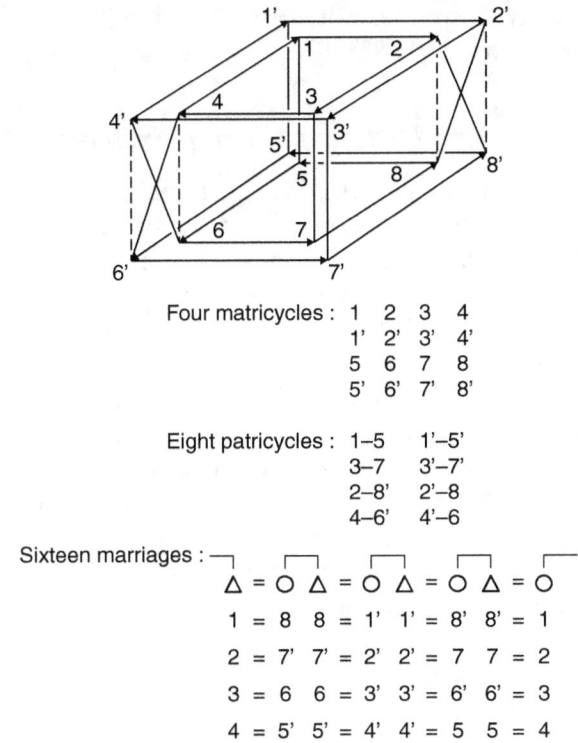

Figure 6.4 *The 8 × 2 subsections cube: generalised exchange*

in the transformation of 'beneath' into 'above' and vice versa, an activity that is different for each sex. It is a matter of making manifest what is virtual (for example, actualising totemic forces in people) and inversely of making virtual what is manifest (for example, sending the dead back to the anonymity of Dreaming Beings).

Funeral and mourning rites, which put into play the passage from 'above' (life on earth) to 'beneath' (parallel Dreaming space-time), imply the same prohibitions as are found in the mother-in-law relationship: just as space and speech avoidances exist between women and their sons-in-law, there are prohibitions on naming the dead or approaching places evocative of them. From this similarity of taboos a topological homeomorphism may be deduced between Warlpiri kinship and cosmology: 'Warlpiri kin and cosmic orders are therefore reducible to homeomorphic topological surfaces: the infinite and "open" sphere of the Dreaming where beneath rejoins above, and the cube with doubled subsections the properties of which require mapping on a hypersphere, not on a closed sphere' (Glowczewski and Pradelles de Latour 1987: 47).

A Common Logic for Different Kinship Systems

In seeking further to clarify the Warlpiri subsection system, I realised that it could also be mapped on a hypercube. A hypercube is a standard topological figure composed of eight interwoven cubes and having sixteen vertices, the same number as the doubled subsections (Glowczewski 1988: 220–3). Unlike the hypersphere, a four-dimensional sphere is hard to represent in two or even three dimensions, a hypercube, though also four-dimensional, can be suggested by multiple projections (see Figure 6.5).

On analysing other subsection systems, such as the Murinbata and the Murngin/Yolngu (see Table 6.1), I discovered that they, too, could be mapped on a hypercube, though not in the same way (Glowczewski 1988). In both cases each subsection is coupled for marriage purposes with two others, and not only with one as in the Warlpiri system (the Warlpiri do, in fact tolerate an alternative marriage into the subsection of the MBD, but this second choice has not been integrated into the formal system).

According to Stanner's data on the Murinbata (1963), matricycles follow the Warlpiri order, but each patricycle comprises four subsections, not two. In other words, the 'mother-in-law' diagonals of the Warlpiri cube (see Figure 6.3) here become segments of the patricycles (1 7 3 5 and 2 6 4 8). A Murinbata man's mother-in-law accordingly belongs to the same subsection as his father's sister (FZ).

Stanner states that the Murinbata distinguish the category of father's sister (FZ, *pipi nginar*) from that of mother-in-law which is matrilaterally defined (MBDD or MMBD, *wakail nginar*). As in the Warlpiri case, this distinction takes us from restricted to generalised exchange, making it necessary once again to double the subsections. The four matricycles and four patricycles so obtained can be perfectly superimposed on a hypercube (see Figure 6.6).

Let us now consider the famous case of the Murngin, a grouping of Arnhem Land tribes, today known as Yolngu. According to the analysis of Warner's data ([1937] 1958) by Lévi-Strauss ([1947] 1970) and Dumont (1966), Murngin matricycles are similar to those of the Warlpiri, but their patricycles are defined through two parallel systems: in each system, there are four patricycles comprising

Australian Cosmology and Social Organisation

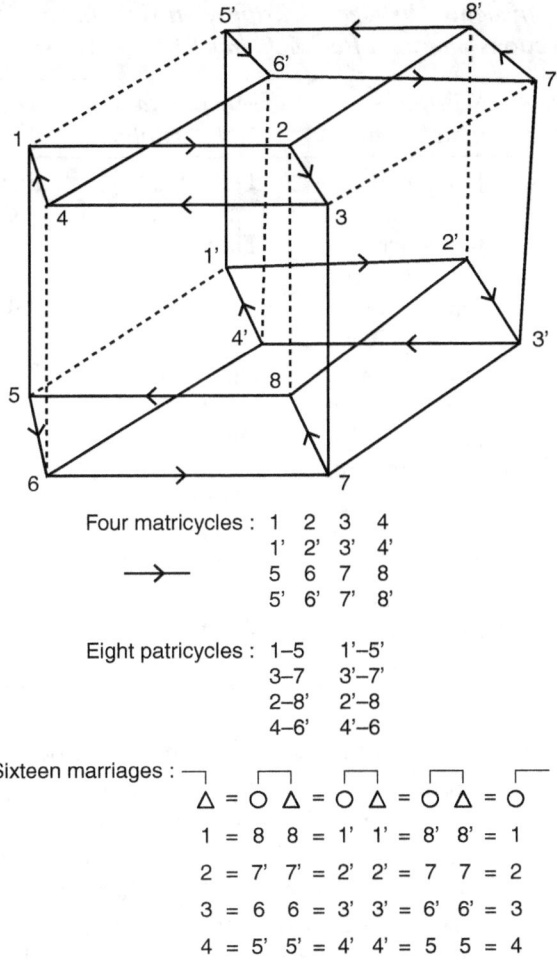

Figure 6.5 *The Warlpiri hypercube: generalised exchange*

pairs of subsections, but only two of them coincide with Warlpiri patricycles:

System I: 1–5, 2–6, 3–5, 4–8
System II: 1–7, 2–8, 3–5, 4–6

Here again the new patricycles (2–6, 4–8 or 1–7, 3–5) correspond to the 'mother-in-law/son-in-law' diagonals of the Warlpiri (see Figure 6.3). Marriage is with a classificatory MBD of the same subsection as the MMBDD: these two types of cousin are of a different subsection among the Warlpiri.

211

Table 6.1 *Equivalences between Warlpiri, Murinbata and Murngin/ Yolngu subsections' names (after McConvell 1985: 26–9)*[2]

Subsections or skin-names	Warlpiri male/female	Murinbata male/female	Yolngu (Murngin) male/female
1	Japanangka/ Napanangka	Tjanama/ Nanagu	Burralang/ Galitjan
2	Jakamarra/ Nakamarra	Tjamira/ Namira	Gadjak/ Gutjan
3	Jungarrayi/ Nungarrayi	Tjimil/ Namij	Balang/ Bilinytjan
4	Jampijinpa/ Nampijinpa	Djabidjin/ Nabidjin	Bangardi/ Bangarditjan
5	Japangardi/ Napangardi	Djangari/ Nangari	Gamarrang/ Gamanytjan
6	Jangala/ Nangala	Djangala/ Nangala	Burlany/ Burlanytjan
7	Japaljarri/ Napaljarri	Tjalyeri/ Nalyeri	Wamut/ Wamutjan
8	Jupurrurla/ Napurrurla	Tulama/ Naola	Ngarritj/ Ngarritjan

If the two Murngin systems were drawn on a cube, we would have semi-generalised exchange (brothers and sisters marrying in different patricycles) with reciprocal exchange of mother-in-law between particular clans. But Morphy (1984) has shown that such reciprocity does not exist because the Murngin-Yolngu distinguish clans that are mother-in-law givers (called *mari*) and clans that are mother-in-law receivers (called *gutharra*). That is to say, one must distinguish their respective patricycles and double the subsections, thus obtaining in each system two matricycles of four doubled and eight patricycles of two doubled subsections. All these cycles fit perfectly on a new hypercube (see Figures 6.7 and 6.8).

On the Murinbata and Murngin/Yolngu hypercubes the edges represent, as for the Warlpiri, classificatory filiation between subsections. The difference is that subsections are differently distibuted among the vertices, and uterine and agnatic cycles are differently oriented. It is precisely because different circuits can be mapped on

---

[2] For a presentation by the Yolngu of the organisation and use of their *skin-names malk* system, see: https://yidakistory.com/yolngu-malk-or-skin-names/

Australian Cosmology and Social Organisation

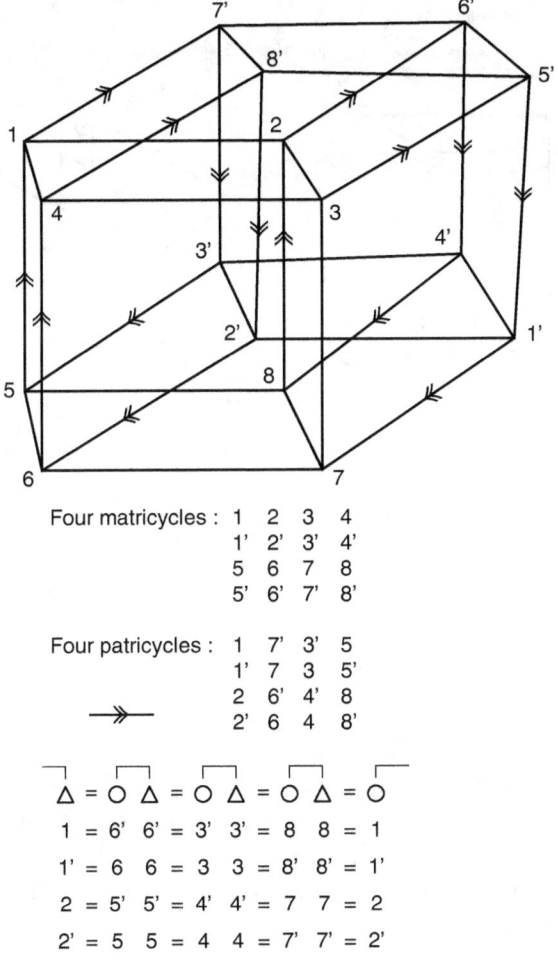

Figure 6.6 *The Murinbata hypercube: generalised exchange*

the same topological figure that the various systems can be seen as reducible to the same logic, expressed by the hypercube.

I have shown elsewhere that the hypercube can also be used for an Australian system that lacks subsections: the so-called Aluridja system practised by the Pitjantjatjara (Glowczewski 1988). White (1981) has demonstrated that, unlike the previous cases where marriage is with a classificatory MMBDD or MBD, Aluridja marriage is with a MMBSD who is not equivalent to MBD. In constructing the Aluridja hypercube, I put kin terms on the vertices: edges represent filiation cycles differentiated as male or female (see Figure 6.9).

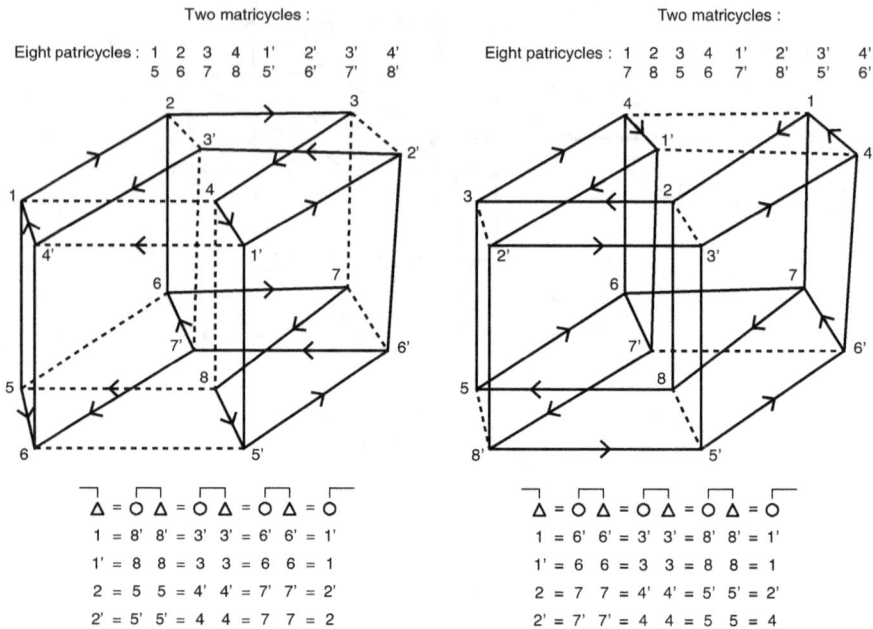

Figure 6.7 and 6.8 Two Murngin/Yolngu hypercubes: generalised exchange.

Analysis of various Australian kinship systems by resorting to the hypercube shows that their differences can be brought back to a common topological logic. From this I deduce that the transformations and innovations in these systems are inherent in Aboriginal societies, so long as they unfold according to the same logic or, as one might say, 'topologic'.

From the Hypercube to Enunciation

Topology and 'topologic'

Murngin/Yolngu social organisation has challenged generations of scholars; even on a topological approach it keeps a distinctive place. Warner's data and Morphy's rule of non-reciprocity allowed me to obtain two coherent hypercube systems. But when I applied Morphy's rule to the data reported by Webb (1933), who postulates patricycles of four subsections, I obtained two new systems with doubled subsections. These systems require a cube conceived as existing in fivedimensional space (Glowczewski 1988). The sculptor Gerd Fisher devised for it the three-dimensional representation that I show

Australian Cosmology and Social Organisation

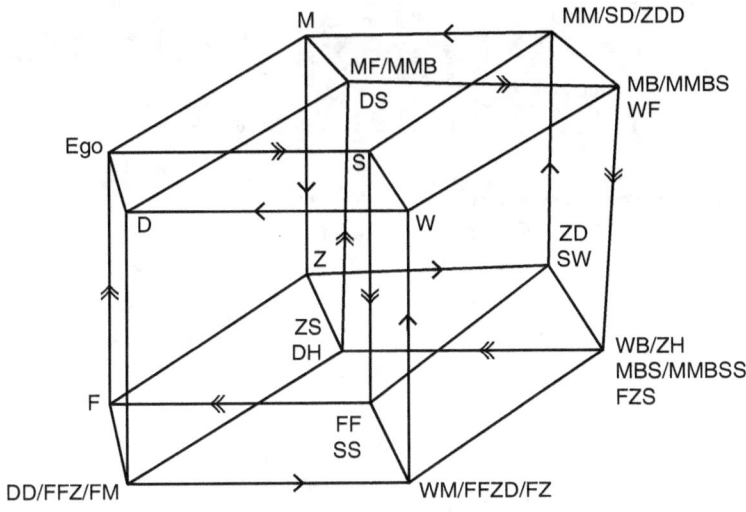

Two matricycles : M, Z, ZD/SW, SD(MM)
⟶   WM(FFZD/FZ), W(MMBSD/MBD/FZD), D, DD(FFZ/FM)

Two patricycles : F, Ego, S, SS(FF)
⟶   WF(MMBS/MB), WB/ZH(MMBSS/MBS), ZS/DH, DS(MMB/MF)

Figure 6.9 The Aluridja hypercube

here. With such a figure we reach the limits of what can be presented: it is a question that invites future research (see Figure 6.10).

Cubes in five and four dimensions, or in three (which can be used to represent generalised exchange in a simple four section system like the Kariera), may be different topological figures but they belong to the same logical set: the 3D cube is an element of the 4D cube which in turn is an element of the 5D cube. To talk about a logic that underlies the different kinship systems is to investigate the problem of structural transformations.[3] If such different systems as Kariera,

---

[3] In terms of kinship analysis, my topological approach and that of Lucich (1987) work in the same direction (Glowczewski 1989b). By showing that different kinship systems display different structures of the mathematical theory of groups, Lucich demonstrates that they are comprehensible as transformations within a logical syntax. By mapping different systems on the same topological figure, I have tried to show that they obey the same structural dynamic. In fact, cube, hypercube and five-dimensional cube are non-planar transcription of the groups drawn by Lucich (personal communication). The cube illustrates: the group $c_2 \times c_2$ or D_4 (eight subsections of Aranda/Warlpiri type) and the group $c_4 \times c_2$ (four doubled

INDIGENISING ANTHROPOLOGY

Four matricycles

Eight patricycles :
```
            1   2   3'  4'  1"  2"  3'" 4'"
            5   6   7'  8'  5"  6"  7'" 8'"
            3   4   1'  2'  3"  4"  1'" 2'"
            7   8   5'  6'  7"  8"  5'" 6'"
```

△ = ○   △ = ○   △ = ○   △ = ○   △ = ○   △ = ○   △ = ○   △ = ○
1 = 8'" = 1'" = 8"   = 1"   = 8'   = 1'   = 8   = 1
5 = 2'" = 5'" = 2"   = 5"   = 2'   = 5'   = 2   = 5
3 = 6'" = 3'" = 6"   = 3"   = 6'   = 3'   = 6   = 3
7 = 4'" = 7'" = 4"   = 7"   = 4'   = 7'   = 4   = 7

Four matricycles

Eight patricycles :
```
            1   2   3'  4'  1"  2"  3'" 4'"
            7   8   5'  6'  7"  8"  5'" 6'"
            3   4   1'  2'  3"  4"  1'" 2'"
            5   6   7'  8'  5"  6"  7'" 8'"
```

△ = ○   △ = ○   △ = ○   △ = ○   △ = ○   △ = ○   △ = ○   △ = ○
1 = 6'" = 1'" = 6"   = 1"   = 6'   = 1'   = 6   = 1
7 = 2'" = 7'" = 2"   = 7"   = 2'   = 7'   = 2   = 7
3 = 8'" = 3'" = 8"   = 3"   = 8'   = 3'   = 8   = 3
5 = 4'" = 5'" = 4"   = 5"   = 4'   = 5'   = 4   = 5

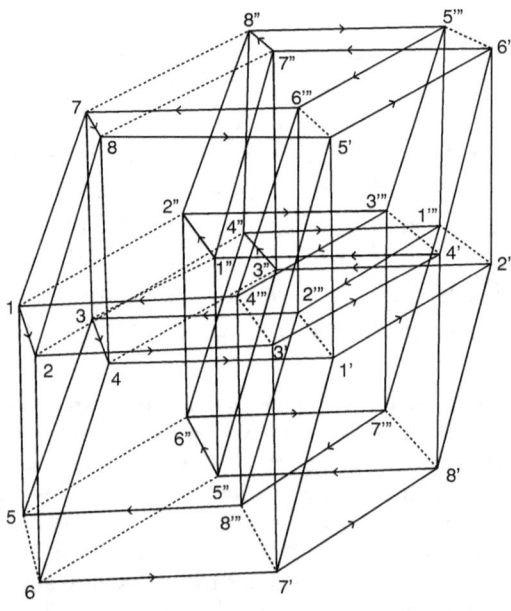

Figure 6.10 The Murngin/Yolngu 5D cube

Warlpiri (Aranda), Murinbata, Murngin/Yolngu and Aluridja are related by transformation, the fact that they obey the same logic suggests that they are capable of absorbing only those changes which are compatible with it.

My postulate is that this logical constraint is expressed not only by different kinship systems but also by particular modes of enunciation of mythical stories and ritual practices. In both cases the possibilities of transformation are limitless, as is shown by the Aboriginal creative symbolic activity. But the constraint of logic prevents kin or cosmological (mythological and ritual) systems having a structure incompatible with the topological properties of the hypercube. The question may then be posed whether the presence of different logics in the one society means that the society is 'schizoid' or whether it indicates instead that a drastic social change is taking place in the direction of a new logic, thus of a new and different society.

Pradelles de Latour (1984, 1986) has shown that the alliance systems of the Trobriand Islands can be depicted on a torus whereas the Bamileke from Cameroun follow the logic of the so-called 'projective plane'. Both figures have topological properties incompatible with those of the hypercube. Gérard (1986) has isolated yet another topological figure, Boy's surface for the Moose and Kurumba of Burkina Faso (formerly Upper Volta). With a torus, the internal and external faces are distinct, unlike a hypercube where they interpenetrate. With a projective plane, or a Boy's surface too, the faces intrepenetrate but they possess a polarity (crossing of two constitutive elements in the former, and of three in the latter figure) lacking in the hypercube. For both African societies, this polarity coincides with the pyramidal social institution of royal chieftainship, which is absent among the Aboriginal people.

The number of topological figures is limited because any object will retain the same properties even though bent, stretched, compressed or twisted. This characteristic of the 'geometry of rubber' permits an infinity of so-called 'continuous' transformations. But to tear or glue a figure is to make a transformation which changes its properties and hence the figure itself (Gérard 1989).

---

sections of Kariera type). The hypercube illustrates: the group 16T2 c_1 (eight doubled subsections, Aranda/Warlpiri), the group l6T2 c_2 (eight doubled subsections, Murinbata), and the group $c_8 \times c_2$ (eight doubled subsections, Murngin-Yolngu). The 5D cube illustrates the Abelien group $c_4 \times c_8$ (eight subsections twice doubled: Murngin-Yolngu).

The point I want to stress is that the use of a topological structure to diverse domains of a given society (kinship, power, ritual, mythology, etc.) does not mean that it is static but only that transformations of it will tend to obey a topological constraint. Consequently, when transformations are imposed from outside through contact with societies following another logic, they will be assimilated by 'translation', or else will threaten to destroy the Indigenous logic, with a new society as the ultimate result.

Towards a formalisation of Australian taboos

I have tried to show that the homeomorphism of Warlpiri social organisation and cosmology can be generalised to other Aboriginal societies. For this purpose, I have drawn up an inventory of the formal and contextual characteristics of Aboriginal taboos; it appears from documentation on some 80 tribes that, in spite of their diversity, all the taboos can be reduced to combinations of eight variables (Glowczewski 1988).

In all these societies, there seem to be only four contexts of taboo. As among the Warlpiri there is the context of the mother-in-law/son-in-law relationship and the context of mourning, to which can be added the context of the socialisation of men and women and the context of totemic relationships. Each context can give rise to taboos in four domains: language (prohibition of speech); space (prohibition on approaching a person or place); sexuality (prohibition on marriage or sexual congress); and material goods, particularly food (prohibition on consumption).

Any prohibition can occur in two apparently different modalities: it can be temporary or permanent. In the mother-in-law/son-in-law relationship and in totemic relationships, Ego is forbidden ever to speak, to approach, to have sexual congress or to consume. But these prohibitions endure only as long as necessary in the case of socialisation rites and mourning rites.

Whether permanent or temporary, the taboos give rise to similar practices of inversion by transgression, substitution and compensation: for example, both mourners and persons speaking about totemic secrets use sign language; both a funeral rite and a totemic ceremony provide the opportunity of formally resolving a latent conflict among individuals; both an initiation and an alliance ceremony (implying the mother-in-law) can include a ritual act of sexual transgression. Many other examples could be given.

Australian Cosmology and Social Organisation

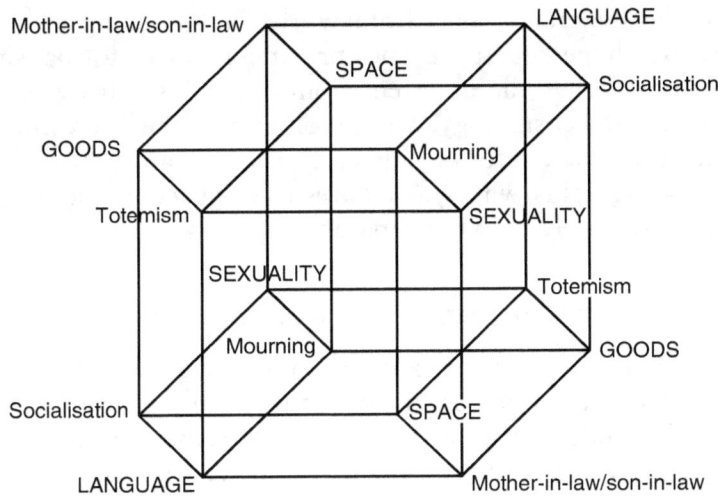

Figure 6.11 A hypercube for Australian taboos and their ritual inversion

Aboriginal people seem to strain to mark, on one hand, the difference between what is temporary and what is permanent and, on the other, to reconcile diachrony with synchrony. This quasi-metaphysical concern is also to be found in the fact that the temporal human world, the 'above', mirrors the synchronic world of the Dreaming Beings, the 'beneath'. As a characteristic of the hypercube is that an edge connects each vertex with four others, it is possible to display the connection of each context of taboo with the four domains and of each domain with the four contexts; the duplication of the eight variables shows the mirror relationship of 'beneath' and 'above' between the taboos and their ritual inversions (see Figure 6.11).

Although the Warlpiri categories of below/above (inside/outside) may not occur in all Australian societies – though they do among the Murngin [Yolngu],[4] the logic of interpretation of two universes that mirror each other is everywhere present. Dreaming Beings are always located simultaneously in a beyond (subterranean or celestial) and here on earth, in a prior time and now. The articulation of all taboos belongs to this more general logic that puts the human world in a state of feedback with a mythical world.

The identification of this cosmological vision with the topological properties of the hypercube is of a metaphorical order, but it refers

---

[4] Howard Morphy generously gave me to read the typescript of his *Ancestral Connections* that was published two years later (Morphy 1991).

back to the hypercube as a framework for modelling kinship. In other words, hypercube properties provide a way of formalising the logic that underlies the apparent homeomorphism between social organisation and cosmology. Methodologically, the interesting point is that a figure isolated for kinship can be used as an analytical device for comparing fields which to us are heterogeneous but which the Aborigines themselves do not separate.

Correspondences between Australian taboos and myths

In an attempt to carry the formalisation of behaviour still further, I examined the form and content of Australian myths. Relying on the fact that these tales constitute the Law for the Aborigines, I sought to isolate eight mythical variables that would echo the taboo variables (Glowczewski 1988) (see Table 6.2). The four contexts of Australian taboos can be found in the myths. Mourning is transposed into the journeys of Mythical Beings because these are the journeys that the dead are thought to make. The mother-in-law/son-in-law relationship crystallises the most common transgression in mythical encounters (whenever these imply conflicts or alliances between the Beings concerned). Totemism is born when Ancestral Beings attribute a specific identity to places and species. Finally, socialisation is prefigured in metamorphoses undergone by the Beings.

As to domains to which taboos are applied – space, language, sexuality, goods – they define four minimal mythical activities: Ancestral Beings form the landscape; they name places and things;

Table 6.2 Correspondences between Australian taboos and myths

Domains of taboo	Mythical domains
Space	Formation of landscape (earth and cosmos)
Language	Nomination (places and totems)
Sexuality	Differentiation (gender and kin)
Goods (food, etc.)	Institution of ceremonies

Contexts of taboo	Mythical contexts
Mother-in-law/son-in-law	Transgression (alliances, conflicts)
Mourning	Travelling (wandering, nostalgia)
Totemism	Attribution (places, names, rituals)
Socialisation	Metamorphosis of heroes (topographic features, species, spirits, sacred objects)

they differentiate by gender and alliance; and they institute ceremonies involving the circulation of goods. Accordingly, it is possible to superimpose eight mythical variables on the eight taboo variables of the hypercube.

It may be objected that the eight variables are not necessarily present in all Australian myths. I would respond that if a variable is lacking it is because the myth is in some way 'incomplete'; that is to say, the story implies another story that exists or could exist. In fact, I would go so far as to argue that this incompleteness, this 'reference back' to the Other and to that which is elsewhere, is characteristic of interpersonal and intergroup relations among Aboriginal people. The inscription of stories in space constitutes the indigenous mode of 'theorisation' of these relations – just as it is possible to make a new narrative path between two places, so a new link may be created between the people affiliated to those places.

Conclusion

In this chapter, which draws on my PhD thesis (Glowczewski 1988), I have used topology in three ways. The first, which is strictly graphic, allows different classificatory kinship systems to be transposed onto the same topological figure, in this case a hypercube, with the edges representing filiation relations and the diagonals relations of alliance.

The second use is more intuitive and, I believe, richer: it investigates the topological properties of the figure in order to find possible applications to the cosmology and social organisation of the society concerned. It appears that the absence of a univocal differentiation between the internal and external faces of the hypercube coincides with the specific interaction between 'beneath or inside' and 'above or outside'. In many Aboriginal societies these cosmic categories are perceived as simultaneously discontinuous and continuous in rituals and in the space-time of the Dreaming. They are also related to gender differentiation: the relation between the categories may be seen as expressing the interplay of male and female social roles. At another level, the absence of a single polarity on the hypercube coincides with the absence, in traditional social organisation, of a unique reference point, such as chieftainship, God or the state.

The third use proposed here for topology is metaphorical and more arbitrary: it is the attempt to articulate Aboriginal taboos with one another and to compare them with an enunciation matrix of Australian myths. Of course, it is possible to criticise my choice of variables. My defence would be that this form of ordering, far from being a final model is simply an analytical tool, with which it is possible to organise ethnographic data and to display the logic which seems to govern relationships between most aspects of Aboriginal societies.

In conclusion, Aboriginal cosmology may be regarded as homeomorphic to social organisation, not because men repeat the actions of Ancestral Beings but because, generation after generation, they interpret, according to the same logic, the virtual signs left by these Beings. Men are thus the reverse, incessantly moving and being renewed of the evanescent yet eternal images of the Dreaming, their Law, in which they see their reflections.

PART III

The Aboriginal Practice of Transversality and Dissensus

Figure 7.1 Painted Warlpiri men and women march for National Aboriginal Day carrying the Aboriginal flag (adopted by the hundreds of Indigenous language groups as an affirmation claim of their land sovereignty), Katherine, NT
© B. G. 1984

7.

In Australia, it's 'Aboriginal' with a Capital 'A': Aboriginality, Politics and Identity

Sometime in the 1960s, for both ethical and political reasons, the term 'Aboriginal' and 'Aborigine' began to be written with a capital 'A', thus becoming an ethnonym; it applied to the descendants of the first inhabitants of the Australian continent, some 500 groups speaking different languages and designated — even now — by different names.[1] Today, Aboriginal groups have not only different languages and cultural backgrounds but different histories as well — reserves, separation of children from parents, mixed descent — all of which has put more or less distance between them and their heritage. And yet many still claim that there is such a thing as an 'Aboriginality' which unites everyone under the same identity, even if not everyone can agree on its definition.

Sociologists and anthropologists generally concur that this is an ongoing process in which they themselves have a part (Beckett 1988; Thiele 1991). Nevertheless official and private discourses offer contradictory versions of this identity (Keefe 1988): on the one hand, an identity of continuity, based on language, religious beliefs and practices, and pre-contact world-vision and lifestyle; on the other hand, an identity of resistance, aimed at the revision of contact history, valorisation of national identity symbolised by a flag, land rights, denunciation of bad living conditions, analyses in terms of exclusion and exploitation. While some calls to resistance have gone out from the cities to tribal communities countrywide, the emergence of pan-Aboriginality is also accompanied by new affirmations of singular

---

[1] Adapted from translation by Nora Scott from Glowczewski 2005 in *A Changing South Pacific* (ed. Douaire-Marsaudon and Tcherkezoff [1997] 2005). A shorter version of this text was published in 1998 under the title 'All one but different' – Aboriginality: national identity versus local diversification in Australia', Chapter 14 in Jürg Wassman (ed.) (1998), *Pacific Answers to Western Hegemony – Cultural Practices of Identity Construction*, Oxford: Berg International, pp. 335–54 (from a panel of the ESFO symposium held in Basel, 1994). It was only in the mid-1990s that the French edition of the Hachette encyclopedia recognised the Australian use of the term as a proper noun.

identities partly defined by tradition. In other words: all Aboriginal people insist on their Aboriginality, but rather than advancing this claim by opposition to non-Aboriginal people as a political entity, Aboriginal people affirm themselves as different from their other Aboriginal neighbours. It is as if pan-Aboriginality itself were prompting the emergence of these identity singularities, as if the process of anthropological and social heterogenisation were part and parcel of political uniformisation. The various federal, state and regional governments regularly create royal commissions, make recommendations and pass laws and budget priorities in an attempt to find solutions for all Aboriginal descendants. It is the government which says who is legally an Aboriginal person, how he can claim his rights and what is supposed to promote Aboriginality; and it continues to enlist more and more public servants and consultants to do this – including Aboriginal people. Yet, despite this élite participation in the constant elaboration of Indigenous policy and programs, the population concerned insists on the differences of interests and opinions within the Aboriginal community, and on the need for negotiations with the 'rank and file', and not only with appointed or elected representatives. Over the course of their long struggle for the right to exist and to manage their own affairs, recognition of an initial sovereignty, which would confirm once and for all the Aboriginal people's original ownership of the land, has become a question of principle. In the 1970s and 1980s, a committee of non-Aboriginal people and the National Aboriginal Conference (NAC), an ex-body of nationally elected Aboriginal representatives, militated for a treaty with the federal government. But many Aboriginal people proved to be reticent about the idea, arguing primarily that no one body was qualified to sign on behalf of all groups concerned. Nevertheless, the idea of a treaty became a popular symbol, in particular due to a song by the Aboriginal rock band, Yothu Yindi. The 1988 bicentennial celebrations held out hope for a solution. At the Aboriginal Festival in Barunga, the Prime Minister confirmed the relevance of the issue and the necessity of negotiating a treaty or a compact aimed at 'reconciliation'.

After the bicentennial, the idea of reconciliation supplanted that of a treaty, which had been rejected by all opposition parties, who saw the two-nation distinction as a threat to Australian unity. A council for reconciliation was created in September 1991, with both Aboriginal and non-Aboriginal members. A year later, its task turned out to be highly topical. For the first time in Australian history, a native community won a Supreme Court decision, recognising their native title on lands: this was the 'Mabo case', and it concerned a group of Torres Strait Islanders. The situation was tossed about in the local and national media and aroused bad feelings and incomprehension among non-Aboriginal people, who took increasingly hostile and open positions: racist declarations, alarmist appeals and even the constitution of defence committees to counter what was felt to be a threat. Yet these first Australians now constitute less than two per cent of the population; just what kind of threat could they pose? The Mabo verdict should enable other Torres Strait Islanders and Australian Aboriginal people to command recognition of their native title; but the concrete application of such titles remains to be determined: according to some politicians, 80 per cent of Australia could be subject to such claims. What power do the Aboriginal people stand to gain by winning recognition as native land-owners? No one really knows. Except that they would become inevitable partners in most decisions involving development. In this context, Aboriginality is synonymous with a destiny rooted in the land, in the name of ancestral ties, and engaged in an alliance with the nation's future. This would be the philosophical rewards of a bond with the land traditionally defined as eternally present.

Aboriginality: Body *Versus* Spirit

Aboriginality as a pan-Australian identity is a post-contact construction with respect to non-Aboriginal people, whereas 'nativeness', as an ethnic identity, has always been the very basis of the cohesion of every Aboriginal group, through theories of conception and kinship, the organisation of society and marriage, the domain of economic survival and the religious system. It is politically correct, in today's social sciences as well as in political movements against racism and for universal equality of civil rights, to criticise all essentialist arguments attempting to justify ethnic differences or to make distinctions between peoples on the basis of racial characteristics: i.e., biological and genetic transmission, and references to blood or to skin colour. In other words, anything having to do with the body or with innate features is now taboo. It is preferable to explain differences by non-corporeal and acquired criteria, such as culture, or the length of time a group has occupied a territory conferring native or assimilated migrant status.

For Indigenous peoples, however, the notions of innate and acquired, like those of body and spirit, are inseparable insofar as the definition of what is innate and of the place of the body is cultural. Without this discourse, their culture loses a major mode of transmission. In everyday life, popular discourses on the transmission of physical features and on body marks have become more important than ever and increasingly sought after, whether as expressions of ethnic tensions or in the paramedical domain. Popular essentialism, like various Indigenous theories, is not based on innate transmission alone, however, but also on the notion of contagion or pollution from outside substances, where an individual's body is thought of as reflecting the health of the society as a whole. The same logic operates in everyday racism, which abusively amalgamates a people's identity with the ills afflicting certain of its members. In this context, criticism of essentialism should include two aspects that are often neglected: first, the ideological effects of the West's depreciation of innate features as opposed to acquired ones; and, second, the specificity and the place in discourses on identity of Indigenous essentialistic theories. In Australia – as in many other Oceanic societies – essentialism has proved to be inseparable from a certain relationship with the environment, which differentiates people according to the natural species with which they identify.[2]

Conception and Transmission: How Totemic and Linguistic Identities are Distributed

For nearly a century, anthropologists have been fascinated by Aboriginal theories of conception. The theme is well known: traditionally, Aboriginal people did not attribute conception to copulation but to a spirit-child's entry into the uterus; this conception was announced in a dream to the father, mother or a close kinsman. (I will not go into the question of whether or not Aboriginal people were aware of the connection between copulation and conception.) For decades, whenever the question has been put to them, they have replied time and again that there is no child without a spirit-child. In other words, the human being is something other than the result of what we call biological transmission. We could also say that there is

---

[2] In one work devoted to identity in the South Pacific (Linnekin and Poyer 1990), the authors raised the question of the relevance in these societies of the Western opposition between Mendel's genetic theory and Lamark's transmission of acquired characteristics: Watson (1990: 39) notes that culturally inherited ethnic differences persist only when a people identifies with its land.

no body without a spirit, and that this spirit comes from somewhere else than the body of the father or the mother.

What we are interested in here is the status of this 'somewhere else' and how it links a human being 'from the inside' with his ancestors. For this contains a paradox: the spirit transmits certain 'essences' that are going to identify the child in its spirit and its flesh with certain kinsmen, but also with certain natural species or phenomena, and with a land. Anthropologists customarily call this spiritual and physical link a 'totem'; in Australia it is known as a 'Dreaming'. Here again the many debates on whether or not totemism is a manufactured concept tend to obscure the fundamental reality: while there is no general definition of totemism, the term 'totem', and even more specifically 'Dreaming', tend to translate highly complex Indigenous concepts which differ from group to group. Although we lack a standard definition or even an adequate translation of singular concepts, we must nevertheless attempt to understand what they say about the body and the spirit that is different from Western conceptions. In the present case, they say that the identity of each person is founded on an exterior agency which internally links the person to ancestors, animals, plants and so forth, and to places.

In the case of physical transmission, the development of the foetus, which is animated by a spirit-child that comes from the land – it can be a tree, a rock, a waterhole – reacts to all outside substances that enter the mother's body. Therefore, all Aboriginal groups traditionally imposed dietary taboos on a woman during pregnancy, forbidding her to eat various foods believed to be dangerous to the child. Some taboos lasted as long as the mother breastfed the child, as her milk was also thought to be capable of transmitting harmful substances. The following example was recorded in the Kimberley in the 1930s: the mother could not eat honey received in exchange for pearl-shells, for pearl-shells being associated with Kaleru, the Rainbow Serpent, giver of spirit-children, might harm the child or make the mother sick.[3]

There are many Indigenous theories about contagion through contact with substances, but I will not go into them here. I will

---

[3] Kaberry (1939: 169). These pearl-shells circulated as wealth transmitted by both women and men, although they were used as ritual objects exclusively by men, when they would go into the desert to perform rain-making ceremonies. Among coastal groups, they were hung on the pubic tassels by both the boys, as a sign of their initiation stage, and by girls as a sign of virginity.

simply add that, in addition to food, the semen transmitted to a pregnant woman during sexual intercourse was also believed by some groups to contribute to the child's development. Whatever physical likeness the child bore to the father or mother, however, was attributed to the Dreaming, to the totemic essence; people who had the same Dreaming were also supposed to share certain physical traits stemming from their spiritual affinity with a particular species. These characteristics may be different for men and women. For instance, among the Warlpiri, I found that Possum clan men have a particular foot shape which recall this animal, while the women's lips become black when black plums are in season: the 'Plum' is a female totem associated with the Possum (Glowczewski [1989] 2016). Commonly, too, a child may have a birthmark, explained by the circumstances in which its spirit entered the mother's body. For instance, an infant may have a mark where his father shot the kangaroo that was the child's spirit before it was born. Over and above the complex symbolic elaborations each Aboriginal culture has developed in its own language, all theories about the process of conception and gestation stress one fact. The body and its substances, blood in particular, carry essences that go beyond the purely human dimension, although they are also what gives each person his human nature, his singularity, and identifies him with a place that will enrol this individual in the collective identity of the group that is tied to the same land as well as in the broader identity of all those who speak the same language.

The shared language itself is believed to come from the ancestors, for the spoken word comes from the Dreaming. For the Warlpiri, in particular, it is the spirit-child that transmits the power of speech. It has been pointed out that, for the original groups from the Western Desert that migrated northwards (south of the Kimberley) – now the majority of the Aboriginal populations, known as Wolmeri (Walmadgeri, Walmajarri), Julbaridja (Yulparija) or Wonggadjunga (Wangkajunga) – the notion of human being covered first of all those who recognised each other as *djandu*, nearby groups speaking the same language, and extended outwards to the *ngai*, distant neighbours having different languages and customs but with whom there were direct or indirect exchanges of objects or rituals (Kolig 1977). Beyond this horizon, even if objects and rituals circulated, the more-or-less 'human' status of people was debatable. The notion of *djandu* is found in different desert languages. The same study shows that the terms Walmadgeri and Yulparija were both used by the northern river peoples to designate those in the south, but when they became local culture markers, they were also adopted by new migrants from the desert (Kolig 1977).

There is a general tendency throughout Australia to use different terms, depending on whether one is designating a group from the inside or the outside. For example, north-western peoples usually call the desert peoples to the east (Central Australia) Waringari, Warmalla or Woneiga. These same groups, however, differentiate each other by the language they speak (Warlpiri, Aranda, etc.): in reality, Warlpiri use the terms Warmalla and Woneiga (Warnayaka) to designate dialectal variations that characterise Warlpiri associated with the lands on the far western edge of the tribal territory. With colonisation, certain terms came to circumscribe expanding local identities, such as Walmajarri in the Kimberley, or Warlpiri, Pintupi or Pitjantjatjarra in Central Australia. What should be remembered from all this is that traditional ethnic designation was based on local proximity and the ability, if not to speak the same language, then at least to understand each other in spite of differences. The borders between 'tribal' identities were fluid and were redefined with each new alliance that brought the various intra- or extra-tribal groups into contact for the purpose of exchanging goods and rituals. Marriages tended to be contracted within the linguistic unit, although from time to time union with outside groups would renew or inaugurate alliances between the contracting parties.

Kinship and Ritual: How Mythic Filiations and Alliances are Reproduced

I have shown elsewhere that the Warlpiri and their neighbours apply the term 'human being', *Yapa*, to all those, whatever their language, who identify each other using the same classificatory kinship system or certain equivalences (Glowczewski 1991). Of course, identification assumes encounters and alliances. But the particularity of this system of communication is that the alliances are based primarily on shared rituals before being grounded in marriage; they are founded on the sharing of certain non-human ancestors, often designated by totemic names. More specifically, it is the route travelled by these ancestors, known as a 'Dreaming', that connects one group's places to those of another, that endows them with this common, shared identity designated by the Dreaming which goes with it: Kangaroo Dreaming, Goanna Dreaming, Emu Dreaming, Yam Dreaming, Rain Dreaming, and so on. Some of these routes are more than a thousand kilometres long and run through the territories of different language groups: the ritual cycles and objects associated with the different places are also transmitted, eventually returning to their starting point enriched with new mythic episodes and rituals. Celebration of these connections by the local groups constantly renews the ties of classificatory and totemic kinship. This is not to say that the groups at either end of the chain necessarily know each other or even recognise their kinship, but that, in each place, identities are thus recomposed.

But classificatory 'kin' is by no means synonymous with consanguinity: various anthropologists have stressed this point, all too often forgotten by theoreticians. Traditional Aboriginal people speak of these relations as their *skin*, as opposed to our notion of blood, but others also speak of 'flesh' or 'body'; so to say someone is of the same 'flesh' explicitly designates an essence of the Dreaming that is shared by all members of a group, an essence that is both external and internal, corporeal and spiritual, and which is usually also a totem. The notion of being one 'body' or one *skin*, on the other hand, refers I think to the surface marked or penetrated by this essence which inhabits the body on a continuous basis (in the case of a small group) or temporarily (in the case of a bigger group) when it is painted on the body with ritual designs.

This is not the place to explore the complex connections between inside and outside that can be found at every level of ritual life, as well as in gender relations (Glowczewski 1991). Nor am I going to attempt an explanation of the classificatory kinship systems: the complexity of the Australian models is a constant source of wonder for mathematicians. But there is one fundamental rule that should be retained: traditional Aboriginal societies had a kinship system that, in many cases, divided the group into two, four or eight categories. The members of the same category regarded each other as 'brothers' and called those in another category by another kin term. This system does not use ranked classes but alternative roles: during any ritual, everyone in the same category automatically receives the same role; this role changes for the whole category when the context changes, in another ritual, for example. This applies to initiations, funerals and totemic rituals. In each case, it is the position of 'brother', 'father', 'mother', 'spouse', 'mother- or father-in-law', and so on, with respect to the initiate, the deceased or the ancestor celebrated, that determines the role the person plays. Thus, both kinsmen and direct allies are placed in a category of classificatory kinship. There is no room here for outsiders, unless they are identified with a classificatory category and thus become 'kin' in their own right.

The articulation of this form of kinship, which is still used in those communities and towns where Aboriginal groups have kept ritual alive, brings us back to the initial question of essences. A child is identified by its spirit-child with one or more Dreamings, as well as with a place. But it is the rituals that enable close kin to situate a child in a filiation which, according to the group, will give it the essence it will share with its father's line, its mother's line or with another group. Through these rituals, the child will acquire, in addition to its – let us say 'biological' or 'adoptive' – parents, yet other 'fathers' and 'mothers', together with as many potential classificatory kinsmen and allies as there are people present in a given context. This kind of generalised kinship does not encompass everyone as sharing the same essence, however. Instead, it defines a conjunction of Dreamings for each person, with the associated stories, rituals and places, for which the child will be responsible, together with a group of brothers within a broader category of *skin* brothers. Rituals constantly reaffirm these singular filiations shared between a group of people, non-human ancestors and specific places by consolidating the alliances that maintain these singular ties between all the allies. Aboriginal people call this in English 'the Law'. 'Following the Law' means first of all being initiated: passing certain tests, receiving the secrets revealed to one sex or the other, and being at the same time affiliated to one group and allied with another. Both a man and a woman are duty bound to follow and celebrate certain Laws: the term Law designates the ritual cycles that distinguish the various groups, but these can also be transmitted from one group to another.

The circulation of Laws strengthens kinship and alliance links while affirming the differences of identity. Since the 1970s, however, the southern Kimberley has been experiencing a 'Walmadgerisation', owing to the fact that the Walmadjeri (Walmajarri) desert groups have brought their Laws to the decimated groups of Fitzroy.[4] How have the Laws of one linguistic group come to supplant those of another? This can be explained by three partially linked factors: some decimated groups have been prevented from celebrating their

---

[4] Akerman (1979). Recent fieldwork by the author in the region (Glowczewski 1999, 2001) demonstrates more complex phenomena, for instance the spread of the didjeridu, a NE musical instrument, or the cultural revival of some groups of mixed descent, and the reappropriation of Indigenous data recorded in the past.

respective Laws; they have also totally or partially lost their language; and there has been increasing intermarriage between different groups. In regions with more than a century of colonial contact behind them, many people are now of mixed ancestry, not only mixed Aboriginal and European descent, but also mixed with Asian indentured labour working in the pearl-shell industry. Aboriginal people of the Kimberley have developed numerous strategies to cope with this situation. Despite the reserves and the near century-long ban on free travel, increasing numbers of rituals have circulated between coastal groups, and the western and the central deserts. Motorised vehicles have enabled tribes to extend their links with other far-away groups; some have changed kinship systems and the organisation of their rituals; new funeral rites have developed to include people of mixed descent and adapt the various changes brought in by the European settlers (Kolig 1977).

The result of the accelerated circulation of the rituals and their accompanying myths was not a uniformity of beliefs, but the inclusion of various local versions in a new mythico-historical continuity that sometimes gave rise to messianic-type cults (Glowczewski 1983b; Koepping 1988). The exchange roads travelled by the objects and the rituals, which covered North Western Australia and spanned the entire desert in pre-contact times, as well as the routes followed by the stories that linked the groups into a long chain, took on a different dimension. Increasingly, Aboriginal people on the move had the opportunity to compare local versions. In the 1950s, Petri had noticed that the coastal and the desert groups held certain pre-human ancestors known by different names to be equivalent: for instance, the Wanji peoples, who moved from the coast to the desert, are supposed to have brought with them the first Laws on the continent, while for all the desert groups, the Dingari are the first to have performed initiations.[5] Another myth runs in the opposite direction, crossing part of Central Australia and the whole Kimberley; this is the Two-Men Dreaming, also known as Watikutjarra Dreaming (Glowczewski [1998] 2009). Stories about Rainbow Serpent, Kangaroo or Dingo link other groups. Through this recognition of common Ancestral Beings, the desert groups, who have maintained their Laws, are seen by certain groups in the north, who have lost their own Laws, as custodians of the ancestrality and the authenticity of a Dreaming order in the regions where, for various reasons, these Laws have been

---

[5] Editor's annotations to the writings of Worms and Petri ([1968] 1972).

abandoned; on the other hand, ancestral heroes from the northern coastal regions continue to attest the power of these lands in certain desert cults.

People have always adopted ceremonies from neighbouring groups, but replacing one's own ceremonies by new ones means a partial change of identity, which introduces different levels. In the Kimberley, coastal or river groups – who identify with their locality and their original language – insist at the same time on their differences and on the fact that, by virtue of a given Law, they are all the same or the same as the desert peoples. There are also families who do not participate in any ceremony but believe that Aboriginal identity should be marked on the body of their boys through some aspect of the ritual initiation common to most northern and desert groups. Some therefore send their sons to be initiated in a group speaking a different language, while others have them circumcised in the hospital. In this case, interestingly enough, circumcision is no longer the sign of affiliation to a local group and of alliance with others, it has become a physical indication of pan-Aboriginality. Others still, faithful to the Christian injunction, do not practice circumcision, but found their Aboriginal identity on a different base.

Mixed Descent and Separation: How the Ban on Mixing the Colours Provided a Pretext for Taking the Children Away

At the time of the first European contacts, many Aboriginal people regarded white skin as the sign of a ghost. Europeans were therefore often thought to be spirits of dead persons. Nevertheless, the first children of mixed descent born with light skin were not identified with a European father. Their skin colour was explained by the Indigenous theory of contamination by substances: for instance, the mother must have eaten too much flour. This remark can be understood in another way, though: as meaning that the ingestion of food imported by White settlers marked the onset of a disorder in the transmission of substances or essences, in other words, identities. In the same vein, among the Worora of the north-west, the men were reported to complain that their dreams had become too 'heavy' since they had been working on the cattle stations: they dreamed of too many things from the White people's world and there was no room left to dream of spirit-children; this was the explanation they offered for the near sterility of their group (Lommel 1950). In Arnhem Land, in the 1970s, on the other hand, many women found themselves with more than four children; the unusual numbers were blamed on the fact that White people had sunk too many wells, which attracted spirit-children. These examples indicate that Aboriginal people do not view conception as a matter of biological transmission, but instead always as a relationship with the environment: the confrontation of the Aboriginal people' world with that of White people had altered the circulation of essences.

The way Aboriginal people look on people of mixed descent has varied with the region and in reaction to colonial policy, which was obsessed with preventing the mixing of colours. Until recently, administrators and settlers spoke of 'full-blood', 'half-caste', 'quadroons', and so forth. Based on the idea that Aboriginal people do not have recessive genes in the colour of their skin, the notion of a racial 'whitening' was developed. 'Half-caste' girls were separated from their families to be married to 'quadroon' boys, so that their daughters might be married to even lighter boys, until every trace of Aboriginal ancestry had vanished. In this process, the men were not to be married to a lighter girl. The theory, put into practice by the welfare services, is not without its similarities with Nazi racial rules stipulating that an Aryan woman would be permanently defiled by a single sexual relation with a Jewish man. This idea was based on the theory of impregnation that all of a woman's children would be marked by her first sexual relation. At the turn of the century, Bischofs (1908), a German Pallotine Father in charge of the Aboriginal mission at Beagle Bay in the Kimberley, expounded on this theory in a text devoted to the Aboriginal people of the north-west coast. He devoted over a page to the idea that if an Aboriginal woman had intercourse only once with an Asian, all children born thereafter would be of mixed blood. As Chief Protector of the Aboriginal people of the north-west, he therefore urged that Aboriginal people be kept away from both Europeans and Asians: mixed unions were regarded as a crime, and Aboriginal women surprised with Asians were charged with prostitution and either jailed or sent to a mission. Children born of unions with Asians or Europeans were taken away from their parents.

Many life-stories tell of the strategies used to shield mixed-descent children from the segregationist policy: they were hidden from passing patrols, or even rubbed with charcoal to hide their light skin. Today many Aboriginal people are looking for their lost families. For years they were refused access to the colonial archives, but now an Aboriginal organisation has been created to assist them in their search.

In Australia, it's 'Aboriginal' with a Capital 'A'

Numerous reports indicate that Aboriginal men and women in the north did not necessarily see these short-lived unions with Europeans or Asians as a bad thing. In the Broome region, affairs between Aboriginal women and fishermen from Malaysia or the Philippines are often presented as love stories. Maddock (1977) reports that, in Arnhem Land, Aboriginal people did not reject half-castes, but they did make fun of them and called them 'dogs' if they refused to take part in ceremonies. Unlike European settlers, Asians were not generally feared because they did no harm; instead, they brought 'good things', like curry and opium. On the northern coast, 'yellow-fella' designated people of mixed Aboriginal and European or Asian descent and their descendants. On the west coast, the expression 'coloured' was employed more explicitly for people of mixed Aboriginal and Asian descent who had developed their own community after two or three generations. Following the Second World War, many Asians were sent back to their own countries in accordance with the 'White Australia' policy; their descendants, raised by their families or in the centres reserved for people of mixed descent, were assimilated by the administration to the other Aboriginal people, unless the 'whitening' policy gave them 'European' status.

Like the administration, Aboriginal people on the reserves continued for a long time to use the expressions 'full-blood' and 'half-caste'. But these terms indicated a difference of status having less to do with skin colour than with a way of life: half-caste tended to refer to Aboriginal people, whether or not of mixed descent, who lived in town or in the White people's world. Urban militants have denounced the use of both terms and for a time used the expression 'part-Aboriginal' for people of mixed descent. Later it was decided that all persons of Aboriginal descent, whatever the shade of their skin, could identify as 'Aboriginal' and be given this status.

Jordan writes that this insistence on an Aboriginal identity stems in part from the fact that, after having been depreciated by Europeans for decades, it once again took on a positive value after the referendum granting Australian citizenship to all Aboriginal people and giving them various social advantages, such as scholarships or, more recently, the possibility of obtaining a lease to live on a land (Jordan 1988). With the new laws, many families that had maintained their 'coloured' status (as descendants of Asian settlers) to protect themselves from the discrimination against Aboriginal people began to claim their Aboriginality, and the term 'coloured' has fallen into disuse. Some people were even unaware of their Aboriginal background, kept from them by their adoptive families. The latest census figures, however, show that the majority of Aboriginal people are now proud of their roots. Although all descendants of Aboriginal people are now officially recognised as Aboriginal in all government reports and brochures concerning them, it is still not unusual for the opposition 'full-blood/half-caste' to resurface at the first sign of discord within Aboriginal organisations or even in families. Nevertheless, with the valorisation of Aboriginality, the opposition does not have the same meaning. The mention of blood does not refer to some purported racial purity but to a way of thinking: anyone who seems to betray the Aboriginal cause will be accused of being 'half-caste'; but 'full-blood' can also be used as an insult, suggesting the incapacity to understand the new issues of Aboriginality.

The desert and northern Aboriginal peoples who have survived European contact have tended, for the past twenty years, to define their way of living as following two Laws, generally opposing everything that came from the 'blackfella' to the rules imposed by the 'whitefella'. The Warlpiri thus use the term *Yapa* (humans) for all Aboriginal people – even the coloured people they now see on television. This is contrasted to *Kardiya*, which is used for 'Europeans', as non-Aboriginal Australians usually call themselves. Although the opposition between the two Laws is expressed in terms of colour – black *versus* white – as well as in terms of relations of power, I believe it also reflects acknowledgement of the impossibility of any traditional alliance, as this would require that the partners' idea of self has a common foundation. This is a directly cognitive issue: it is not so much a question of same skin colour as of sharing a certain way of thinking, which for traditional Aboriginal people is directly linked to the environment and to the reinterpretation of myths and rituals. Defining identity in terms of locality, language, totemic essence (Dreamings), classificatory kinship or ritual life (the Law) raises the question of the relationship between these identities as Aboriginal points of view and our Western categories, which, to put it schematically, oppose the identity of the self (in psychology or psychoanalysis) and cultural identity (in anthropology and classical sociology). I believe that this dichotomy does not exist in traditional Aboriginal societies. Not, as some suggest, because the notion of self is purely social, the individual being identified with society as a whole, but because society is entirely grounded in a notion of the self that defines each individual as involved in a network of identifications and self-references. These vary according to the context, but remain based on socialised internalisations of something external that is found in all manifestations of the cosmos (people, places, animals, plants, wind, rain, etc.): the notion of Dreaming, which permeates these cultures, partakes of this kind of internalisation. In a context of relative social disintegration, particularly in urban communities, Aboriginal identity, at the family or even the purely individual levels, is often based on certain characteristics that reveal a link with the traditional notion of self (Keen 1988): attachment to places and development of local Kriols, importance of extended kinship networks and duties of assistance, search for direct links between transgressions of some Law by Aboriginal people and natural catastrophes or accidents, confirmation of paranormal powers to kill or cure, visions or dreams containing messages or stimulating creativity, and above all interpretation of signs attributing a totemic and localised spirit-child to a newborn infant.

Aboriginality: Culture Versus Policy

> Aboriginal spirituality is the core part of being Aboriginal. There is a need to push for Aboriginal Spirituality (capital S) being recognised as an established philosophy by educational authorities, religious groups (...) Aboriginal Spirituality gives everyone, from infancy to old age, a sense of 'who I am'. It is Aboriginal Identity (capital I). It is respect for Elders, caring and sharing for each other and a strong connection and love of the land. Aboriginal Spirituality should be nationally registered as an Aboriginal Religion, and as such, given the recognition and status to which other recognised religions have privilege. Resources should be made available to teach Dreamtime stories to non-Aboriginal people and those Aboriginal people who were removed from their cultural heritage in infancy or as children. Aboriginal children should be given Aboriginal names at birth to reinforce their Aboriginality.

The above passage sums up the recommendations made by a delegation of Aboriginal women to a conference on the theme of 'Safe keeping: women's business'.[6] After decades of anthropological discussions on the religious or non-religious status of Aboriginal spirituality and at a time when deconstructionist tendencies are blaming traditional cultural references for freezing Aboriginality in an ideal and nostalgic image of a mythical Dreamtime, it is interesting that

---

[6] 'Australian Indigenous Women and Museums', National Conference, 6–8 March 1993, Adelaide.

the same elements are asserted by Aboriginal people, women in this instance, as the basis of a religion that should be made official like any other and as the very foundation of Aboriginal identity. Yet it is clear from various analyses that many young – or not so young – Aboriginal people, who insist on their Aboriginal identity, do not rely on religious beliefs or may even reject them. On the other hand, the call for 'caring and sharing', here used to define their religion, also frequently serves as a secular statement of Aboriginal identity. Aboriginal health organisations, among others, advance the formula to oppose risk-taking and deviant behaviours (alcohol abuse, domestic violence, etc.).

Aboriginal spirituality, it must be remembered, is part and parcel of a relation to the land. And it so happens that land claims top the list of political demands. Justification of Aboriginal people's claims as the original occupants of the land are based on people's spiritual association with places and their responsibilities as custodians. Even when these responsibilities are no longer exercised, it is with reference to the past culture as heritage that Australian law recognises the protection of Aboriginal sites. In other words, 'religion' has become synonymous with 'culture', not necessarily in the way it was traditionally practised, but in a way it can be acceptable to national, and now international, norms, such as the status of recognised religions, schooling, the art market or legislation designed to confirm the ancestral link between Aboriginal people and the land.

Between the Land and God: How Christian Churches Negotiate with the Principles of Aboriginal Spirituality

The debate over the connection between religion and ethnic identity is reminiscent of the question of Jewish identity: to what extent can a person be considered Jewish if he or she does not practise or even believe?[7] The answer depends on the branch of Judaism. Since a person is Jewish by ancestry, and more specifically through the maternal line, all that is needed for some is to acknowledge one's Jewishness and to be acknowledged by the others (which brings us

---

[7] The South Australian Jewish community officially backs the Aboriginal peoples by lending their support to an oral history project. Other ethnic minorities have also spoken out for recognition of Aboriginal rights in the name of their own religious denominations, for instance the Armenian Apostolic Church or the Greek Orthodox Church.

back to the ethnic questions raised in the first part of this chapter). For others, being Jewish is inseparable from living a Jewish lifestyle, which implies religious practice and the physical inscription it commands for boys (circumcision); this idea is also found in certain Aboriginal groups, as I mentioned earlier. In either case, Aboriginal or Jewish, the religious arguments – unlike Christianity, Islam or Buddhism – have one point in common: it is inconceivable that adopting the Jewish religion or Aboriginal spirituality is enough to make a person a Jew or an Aboriginal. Knowledge, or even practices like circumcision, cannot confer this identity. The reason for this inconceivability differs in the two cases at one level at least. Judaism is a collective and historical destiny, and a sign of a people's specificity; it is transmitted through both essence and culture. It is this memory, passed from one generation to the next in what tends to be an endogamous community, that founds the group's 'authenticity', whereas the majority of the Jewish people lives in exile (even though for some the return to the land of Israel is a necessity). Aboriginal religion lies both in the individual and in a network of connections between individuals and their respective lands and myths. But each network does not include all Aboriginal people nor does it cover the entire territory of Australia, neither historically nor geographically. Each individual exists only because he or she embodies ancestral spirits of the land, those celebrated in ritual life; in other words, spirituality is inseparable from the notion of person and place. From a traditionalist point of view, Aboriginal people who deny the link between the individual, the spirit and the land have 'lost' the knowledge of their link. But it is still present, not only through their ancestors, but in their very being, because there is no person without a territorialised spirit.

Does this mean that non-autochthonous people are without a spirit? A text by Stanner (1979) carries the title, 'White Man Got No Dreaming', according to the expression used by many Aboriginal people, for whom 'lacking Dreaming' is the sign of not being Aboriginal. In various parts of Australia, it has been reported that, when non-Aboriginal people live for a long time with Aboriginal people, their children born in that place are given a Dreaming, the sign of their implantation. Some Aboriginal people also consider that Christianity – or rather the story of the Bible and of Christ – are the White people's Dreaming. Nevertheless, most of them note a fundamental difference: Australian Dreamings are rooted in the land, whereas this European Dreaming claims to be everywhere and nowhere. In reaction, some groups in the Kimberley suggest that Noah's ark has its secret place in the Australian desert and will save them from a new flood (Kolig 1988). Similarly, Jesus (Jinimin) showed himself to some Woneiga (Warlpiri) in Central Australia: he had a black and white skin, and announced that Aboriginal people will have a white skin once they win their fight against the Europeans; he promised to protect their culture, which he took with him into the sky in the form of two cults – Wanadjarra and Worgaia – that have since spread through the Australian West (Petri and Odermann [1964] 1988). The differences in the way Dreamtime Beings and the Christian God are linked to the land invite us to rethink the whole question of 'monotheism'.

Aboriginal people who have not abandoned the beliefs of their ancestors often take a theological approach to Christianity (Mowaljarlai and Malnic 1993). The aim of their reflection is not strictly religious, however. Just as the ancestral religion was inseparable from the social and political organisation, especially the distribution of land rights enabling the people to live, so today's spiritual reflection is concerned to define the 'place' of Aboriginal people in Australian society through the respect of their land rights in an economic environment of development (urbanisation, mining, cattle stations, etc.). In other words, while Aboriginal spirituality defines Aboriginal identity, it is also a political statement. Tony Swain (1988) has defined the Warlpiri's idea of the Christian God as the 'ghost of space': he opposes the Aboriginal notion of place to that of space, an encompassing notion alien to the Aboriginal mind, which thinks in terms of relations between places but not of a spatial continuum encompassing them (Glowczewski 1996). He shows that this notion was more or less included in, or rather seen as assimilable to, an alliance between Dreamtime Beings and space, between the Warlpiri and God. The aim of this alliance was for God to 'learn the Warlpiri's language' (from the translation of the Bible into Warlpiri) so that he would understand and recognise their relation to place, thus enabling his representatives on earth – especially the governments – to do likewise and give Aboriginal people back their ancestral lands. Translations of the Bible, encouraged by several Christian groups, help preserve local languages, but not without the risk of transposing Indigenous spiritual concepts. Adaptation of traditional elements to celebrate the Christian message (song rhythms, boomerang percussion, body painting or the painting of objects, use of dreams) has also given rise to Indigenous churches with their own cults.

On the initiative of Christian groups, an exhibition was held in 1990, entitled 'Aboriginal Art and Spirituality' (Crumlin 1991). Religious paintings from various Aboriginal communities were displayed; the few Biblical themes represented were surrounded by a majority of works featuring itineraries and places from ancestral Dreamings. Mainstream churches, contrary to most of the new evangelical sects, tend to promote the spiritual importance of attachment to the land. A manifesto on land rights was published by the Catholic Commission for Justice and Peace of the Australian Council of Churches,[8] and the World Council of Churches also came out in favour of land rights.[9] In January 1988, the Australian Heads of Churches, in a declaration entitled 'Towards Reconciliation in Australian Society', called on Parliament to formally recognise Aboriginal prehistory and the continuing importance of its heritage; the counsellor for Aboriginal affairs to the Catholic bishops submitted a project to all political parties for negotiation of the terms of a 'compact'. After discussion with all the parties, the term 'reconciliation' was adopted.

The Australian churches have taken sides in the debate, but this does not mean they are leading the Aboriginal movement, or, as in other parts of Oceania, that Christians have provided activists with political training or even raised their indigenist consciousness. Although Pat Dodson, of Yawuru-Djugun descent and ex-Chairman of the Council for 'reconciliation' set up by the government in 1991, trained for the priesthood, his kinsmen had him initiated immediately after his ordination, and when he took up the political struggle after law school he left his religious functions. In fact, Aboriginal activism has often developed in reaction to mission schooling.

The Impossible Alliance: How Conversion and Allowances Contribute to Neutralising Attempts at Self-Determination

Christian conversion, with its various syncretisms, allows some groups to maintain their tribal identity, but the churches can also have the opposite effect, channelling former local and linguistic singularities

---

[8] 'Land Rights – A Christian Perspective', prepared for the Churches Task Force on Aboriginal Land Rights, set up by the Australian Council of Churches (Catholic Commission for Justice and Peace), Derek Carne, 1980.

[9] Justice for Aboriginal Australians' report of the World Council of Churches, 'Team visit to the Aboriginal people, June 15 to July 3, 1981', for the Program to Combat Racism, Geneva.

into a uniform Christian evolution (Swain and Rose 1988). Conversion to Christianity was often violently imposed in the missions, which took children away from their parents to raise and teach them in mission schools. Native languages were frequently undermined. The marriages organised by missionaries were purposely conceived to oppose polygamy and the large age difference between the spouses inherent in traditional marriage by bestowal. By opposing the marriage prescriptions, the missions destroyed the social cohesion of the traditional alliances. And by forbidding the performance of certain rituals that once marked the life-cycle, they weakened the models for becoming an adult and threw traditional sexual roles into question. Finally, by refusing to recognise European or Asian paternity, they prevented the emergence of new family structures.[10] The paternalism practised by the missions into the 1960s has been strongly criticised. In a way, the inability of many communities to manage their own affairs under the new structures of authority is directly related to decades of infantilisation. Destitution of the father's authority in particular led to a rise in the number of matrifocal homes, leaving the men without authority and drowning in grog (Hunter 1993). For lack of family models, many young people, boys and girls alike, succumbed to alcohol. Christians found an ideal source of converts among the young or older drinkers, who had resisted conversion until then. For many Aboriginal people, being a Christian became synonymous with 'no grog and no gambling', in other words with fighting the financially irresponsible attitude entailed in playing cards and drinking and thus ignoring the family's needs.[11]

The very notion of an evil inherent in humanity is fundamentally alien to the Aboriginal way of thinking; nevertheless, for Christian Aboriginal people the concept becomes a means of exploring the evil introduced by the European settlers (Rose 1988). In this new distribution of powers, many Aboriginal people see Christianity as the

---

[10] Some people of mixed Aboriginal and Malay or Indonesian descent were in contact with the Muslim religion, which, like the Aboriginal religion, was rapidly opposed by the Christian churches: the children were taken away from their parents and forced to convert.

[11] Goodale (1987) suggested, following an unpublished paper by McKnight, that, for some Aboriginal groups, card-playing was a way of redistributing resources, something like the traditional hunting ethic. But this redistribution was (is) disturbed when the winners spent all their money on grog or on paying the fines of those jailed for drunkenness, upsetting the social and physical health of the entire community (Hunter 1993).

only way to protect themselves from the harmful effects of contact – alcohol, violence, disintegration of society or new sexually transmissible diseases. Some charismatic movements hold up 'healing' as proof of the power of Christianity. In April 1993, a gathering was organised at Halls Creek to show the Aboriginal people invited from far and wide the lame being made to walk and the blind recovering their sight. Such a display of Christian 'power' does not necessarily invalidate the powers of the Dreaming, though. Instead, it becomes one of the recognised magical principles that legitimises Europe as a conqueror against whom all Indigenous powers must be mobilised. For instance, today most funerals are celebrated by the Christian Church with a religious service and burial in the cemetery. But they are also the occasion for huge community gatherings at which kin and allies, who have often travelled hundreds of kilometres, perform the traditional rituals to find the culprit.[12] It is the power of the Dreaming that is believed to bring about the punishment. In the same vein, the northern Aboriginal people tell a story, in demonstration of their Law, of some workers drowned during the construction of a dam: the site should not have been disturbed because it was the home of a dangerous serpent ancestor-spirit that lived in the sacred rock.

Is the alliance of Christianity and Aboriginal spirituality compatible with the existence of two separate laws, the Dreaming and the Australian government seen as being connected with the Bible? This is by no means clear if we consider the exclusive character of Christianity as well as that of Western economics and politics represented by the Australian government. The same question arises when traditional elements receive their only official recognition from Western institutions like art, schools and the justice system. By showing certain images of Aboriginal people yesterday and today, Indigenous writers, artists, musicians or film-makers participate in the promotion of Aboriginality and in defining this concept according to international cultural norms. The introduction of an Aboriginal school curriculum and bilingual programmes has perverse effects as well, however. The dynamism and creativity of oral literature is thus threatened by the purported 'authenticity' of the written versions of myths, which are often desacralised in the process and even made into stories for children instead of remaining knowledge acquired in the course of initiation into adulthood. A young Aboriginal boy,

---

[12] For example, a hairstring rope is passed around and, when it shakes, it is believed to indicate the person(s) responsible for the death.

who was a brilliant student at the Broome school and had been initiated according to tradition by the Bard people, maintained that the teachings of the bush did not belong in school. The concern to keep the two laws separate can also be seen in the way the elders insist on keeping their secrets, even if it means withdrawing some books from the shops. Some even refuse to transmit their knowledge to the following generations, perhaps to prevent it from being dissolved in the generalised mediatisation. This might explain why some elders have abandoned their traditional functions and have taken to drinking out of solidarity with the younger men.

A series of so-called 'Captain Cook' myths, from North Australia, tells the story of European contact. Comparing versions, Maddock (1988) has found some recurring themes such as that of White men offering gifts that are rejected by the Aboriginal people or that of White men stealing from the Aboriginal people. In the stories about the Macassans, who travelled to the north coast every season before the arrival of the European settlers, the interaction is more ambiguous: when the Aboriginal people try to accept the gifts, the exchange doesn't work.

In no case was there an attempt on either side at a balanced alliance. The elders in Broome tell of a treasure buried in a particular spot in the present-day town: they say it is a 'will and legacy' left to the Djugun, the traditional custodians of the region, by the first European navigators. According to the official history of Australia, the first to land on this shore, in 1699, were the Dutch captain, William Dampier, and his crew. However the linguist Von Brandenstein has recently suggested that, in the sixteenth century, the Portuguese established a secret colony slightly further north and cut a road as far as the present-day town of Broome; in contrast to the violence that followed the arrival of the English settlers, relations between the Aboriginal people and the Portuguese were quite peaceful. One sequence of Walungarri, an important ritual performed in the Kimberley, shows a dance evoking the gift of wine and tobacco to the Aboriginal people by the Europeans (were they the Portuguese?) as well as a grand celebration held by the latter upon arriving. Dampier, on the other hand, was unable to communicate with the natives of what is now Broome, and ultimately fired on them. So, is alliance with the order imposed by the settlers possible or not? Since Aboriginal people began receiving money, in the form of wages, allowances, pensions or mining royalties – which only dates from the late 1960s – they have often been accused of 'throwing it away' on cards or alcohol, or of running down the cars or the houses given to them by development programmes. The latest militant slogans urge rejecting the image of Aboriginal people as victims in favour of a successful image. But many families of Aboriginal men or women who have broken into politics or achieved renown as international artists (painters, film-makers, rock musicians) find it hard, in spite of their success and newfound resources, to escape the pressure of their surroundings and being sucked into 'Fourth World' living conditions. In these circumstances, Aboriginal culture is perceived as more profitable to the non-Aboriginal dealers than to the artists themselves. Could this be a replay (or demonstration) of the 'Captain Cook' myth, where White men have their gifts systematically rejected by the Aboriginal people and at the same time go on stealing from them? Is it possible to think in terms of reconciliation when there has never been an alliance? Alliance by definition supposes that each partner retains his differences, not only culturally but also and above all socially, which means keeping power of decision to manage one's own affairs. But all non-Aboriginal gifts (money, food and other consumer goods or equipment), and even the Australian laws, continue to have a perverse effect. They either destroy or assimilate, or, more subtly, do not leave room for self-determination.

Some non-Aboriginal people complain of racism in reverse, which might be explained in the following way: day in, day out, Aboriginal people are confronted with a bureaucratic machine that constantly frustrates their attempts at self-determination. They can therefore only regard with suspicion any non-Aboriginal they identify with this dominant order which excludes them by stigmatising them and at the same time alienates them while purportedly trying to seduce them. But this climate of suspicion and rejection is not restricted to relations between Aboriginal people and non-Aboriginal people; it can often be observed between Aboriginal family groups living in close proximity. In such conflicts, one group or individual typically accuses the other of making 'bad' alliances with non-Aboriginal people, or of being like 'coconuts', black on the outside but white inside. When someone is highly successful, the accusation is that they are too different to have a legitimate place with the others (the insinuation being that the accused are not genuine Aboriginal people and should not be there).

Such accusations burden everyday life with tensions and conflicts and highlight the breakdown of the traditional approaches to conflict resolution that used to enable different groups of people to cohabit seasonally on the same spot. But they also show that the massive cohabitation imposed in communities and towns is now a permanent phenomenon. Because new self-management structures are lacking, the Indigenous population has grown increasingly dependent on a bureaucratic welfare system that spawns its own contradictions. But it is also possible to see these conflicts in a positive light, insofar as they call for new forms of reconciliation and oblige all parties to constantly define themselves, thus reinforcing local singularities. In the process, the conflicts become a site for the construction of a multifaceted Aboriginality, one to which each party, through its involvement with a community, is required to contribute.

Reconciliation and Decentralisation: How Policy Makers and Bureaucrats Fight Over Aboriginal Status

> The policy of assimilation means that *all Aboriginal people and descendants of Aboriginal people* are expected to attain the same manner of living as other Australians, and to live as members of a single Australian community enjoying the same rights and privileges, accepting the same customs and influenced by the same beliefs, hopes and loyalty as other Australians. (Tonkinson 1990)[13]

Aboriginal legislation can be divided into roughly four phases. Between 1829 and 1936, in reaction to the violence committed on Aboriginal people by the settlers – sexual abuse, killings, enslavement[14] – the government set in place legislation based on a policy of 'protection'. Its purpose was to segregate Aboriginal people from the European Australian society by providing them with ration depots when they were driven off their lands by settlers. Gradually, control of the population movements legitimised the arrangements with the settlers, allotting them free Aboriginal labour on the cattle stations or sending the Aboriginal people away to work at missions or on reserves.

The Native Administration Act of 1936 marked the beginning of the 'assimilation policy', based on the idea of racial 'whitening' and

---

[13] M. E. Tonkinson (1990: 213) emphasises in italics 'all Aboriginal people and part-Aboriginal people are expected' and adds: 'The 1965 Native Welfare Conference modified the wording: "the policy of assimilation seeks that all persons of Aboriginal descent will choose to attain a similar manner of living to that of other Australians" (Reynolds 1972: 175, emphasis added)'.

[14] For example, the organised enslavement (blackbirding) in the northwest of men, women and children by pearl-masters, who made them dive for pearl-shells.

imposing specific regulations on 'quadroons' (see above). Until the 1960s, census figures divided Aboriginal people of mixed descent into different categories: they were not considered 'Aboriginal people' if they exhibited 'positive' characteristics, in the light of their character and the standard of their intelligence, according to a law passed in South Australia (1939 Act). People of mixed descent could gain citizenship rights by applying for a certificate of exemption if they could show proof of good conduct and had severed relations with their tribe; this was the only way of gaining access to paid employment and sending their children to school without separating them from the family. By forbidding Aboriginal people from different categories to mix, the policy of assimilation merely justified a form of apartheid that was already operating in public places. Until the 1960s, the Broome movie theatre had separate seating for each category as defined by the colour of their skin: white, Asian, half-caste and full-blood. The Native Welfare Act of 1963 systematised segregation by denying Aboriginal status to whoever had a quarter or less Aboriginal ancestry.[15]

The 1967 referendum giving all Aboriginal people the same rights as other Australian citizens marked the start of the policy of 'integration', bitterly summed up by many Aboriginal people as the right to get drunk. The obligation of equal pay resulted in the dismissal of the Aboriginal workforce from the cattle stations rather than their integration. A population without work or a place to live was suddenly forced to take refuge in reserves or on the outskirts of towns. It was then that the government threw its 'White Australia' policy into question by admitting migrants first from the Mediterranean countries and then from Asia. The notion of a multicultural Australia, with its cocktail of ethnic immigrants, placed Aboriginal peoples in the context of the specificity of their own culture, as a minority sharing a common identity. Aboriginal status was extended to all people descending from an Aboriginal ancestor, whatever their other ancestry. While this new attitude helped promote the idea of

---

[15] M. E. Tonkinson (1990). The policy of assimilation founded Australian citizenship on an Anglo-Saxon model which excluded all immigrants supposed to be non-assimilable: Asians, Mediterranean peoples and Jews. After the Second World War, the immigration service received confidential instructions indicating the physical characteristics – especially skin colour – to be taken into consideration for refusing applications. When Australia agreed to accept war orphans, it was stipulated in writing that they were not to be of Jewish descent.

Aboriginality, it exacerbated the opposition between those living in reserves and those living in towns. New problems were created that were further complicated by contradictions between federal legislation and the state laws which gave Aboriginal people different rights according to their region. A federal law, for example, allowed Aboriginal people to apply for native title providing their lands were on 'vacant Crown land'; but this law was valid only for the Northern Territory (Aboriginal Land Rights Act 1976), the other states having rejected it. Western Australia has the Western Australian Aboriginal Heritage Act 1972, which protects registered sacred sites; but the state only gives a 99-year lease on reserve lands. A complementary law, the Community Services Act of 1972, was passed with a view to community development on the reserves or in towns of this state.

Since the 1970s, official Australian policy has shifted from 'integration' to 'self-determination' and 'self-management'.[16] Although these promises reflect Aboriginal people's desire to manage their own affairs, the bureaucratic complications created by the measures actually set in place have led many activists and anthropologists to conclude that they were a failure (Tonkinson and Howard 1990; Hunter 1993). In 1985, the National Aboriginal Conference (NAC), an independent group of Aboriginal advisors to the Federal Minister of Aboriginal Affairs, a consultative body without any real power but having a radical impact, was dissolved and replaced by the Aboriginal Development Commission (ADC), a body of Aboriginal public servants disposing of a budget to promote community development and to buy land for Aboriginal people. In 1990, the federal government overhauled its Aboriginal services and replaced both the ADC and the old Department of Aboriginal Affairs with what was intended to be a decentralised administration, the Aboriginal and Torres Strait Islanders Commission (ATSIC), formed of a federal hierarchy with appointed members and regional councils with elected members. Its mandate was economic development. Interestingly, the name juxtaposes the term 'Aboriginal' with the expression 'Torres Strait Islanders'. The latter are distinguished from Aboriginal people because they have occupied a territory – the islands off the northeast coast of Australia – for a shorter time and because they are related to the Melanesian peoples. But the indigenist policy includes them

---

[16] 'Our Future Our Selves', Report of the Aboriginal and Torres Strait Islander Community Council, Management and Resources, House of Representatives Standing Committee on Aboriginal Affairs, August 1990.

as native peoples.[17] The ATSIC allocates federal budget resources for the Aboriginal people and Torres Strait Islanders to the different services concerned with them (development, health, housing, etc.), but it is constantly accused of being too centralised and not giving enough power to its regional councils, or of not taking local needs into account.

It was in this context of bureaucratic weight that the High Court verdict was handed down in 1992 in favour of a group of Torres Strait Islanders claiming native title on Murray Island. This was the famous 'Mabo case', after the name of one of the plaintiffs. 'Mabo' was a landmark because it invalidated for the first time the formerly legal notion of Australia as *Terra nullius* and recognised the general principle of 'native title' predating colonisation. The question now is how to recognise other claims to such titles, and what rights do they confer? The Prime Minister suggested creating a special court to decide the claims of different groups. But at a conference held in 1993 with the Premiers of the six states, the proposal was almost unanimously rejected, especially by the Premier of Western Australia, who felt not that the decision should lie with each state government but that recognition of native title would threaten the economy, in particular that it would frighten away foreign investors. Prime Minister Keating replied that recognition of native title applied only to land presently occupied by Aboriginal groups and that this could only facilitate negotiations with investors, especially the mining companies. A year later, a heated debate still divided much of Australia, and in 1997 the situation was at a standstill. The Native Title Act of 1993 was passed at the federal level, creating, among other things, a Tribunal system. But some states passed their own legislation allowing them to review or even overturn this process. Aboriginal people were caught in the middle. Nevertheless, alongside certain radicals who challenged the system by demanding native title to the entire town of Canberra, there are also communities that have already negotiated agreements with mining companies or tour operators.

The real solution, it seems to me, is not to oppose the interests of Aboriginal people to those of the nation as a whole, but to see how, as the traditional owners of the land, Aboriginal people can participate in the decisions relative to development so as to benefit

---

[17] Similarly the Australian Institute for Aboriginal Studies in Canberra was renamed the Australian Institute for Aboriginal and Torres Strait Islander Studies. ATSIC was abolished in 2004.

not only on an individual basis, but also to give their community something more to look forward to than soon joining the so-called 'Fourth World'. After decades of control and welfare, it is clear than money and services are not enough. For many Aboriginal people, who call pensions (for children, the aged and unemployed) 'sitting down money', what they need is to be able to 'stand up' with dignity, and that is only possible through a complete social restructuration, implying recognition of their links with the land and development decided by themselves.

Some Aboriginal people hold long-term leases on the land, especially in the Kimberley, where by the mid-1990s 51 per cent of the land used for cattle stations was in Aboriginal hands. This recent evolution was possible because the stations were abandonned by the settlers when the cattle industry went into decline. From the viewpoint of Aboriginal people, running these stations enables them to survive, an example of a two-speed economy which provides enough for them though seeming unprofitable to non-Aboriginal people. Many Australians feel that separate development for Aboriginal people is synonymous with apartheid (Kolig 1973) and that Aboriginal special services and rights give them an advantage over other Australians (M. E. Tonkinson 1990), an attitude echoed by the rejection of the idea of 'native title'. Yet, in view of the failure of the 'assimilation' or 'integration' policies, it is clear that both pre-colonial and colonial history have given Aboriginal people needs that are different from those of other Australians or immigrants, but that also differ according to whether or not an Aboriginal group has been alienated from its land.

A Challenge to Anthropology: Legitimising Indigenous Status to Obtain Land Rights

> Native Title to particular land ... its incidents, and the persons entitled thereto are ascertained to the laws and customs of the indigenous people who, by those laws and customs, have a connection with the land. It is immaterial that the laws and customs have undergone some change since the Crown acquired sovereignty provided the general nature of the connection between the indigenous people and the land remains.
>
> Membership of the indigenous people depends on biological descent from the indigenous people and on mutual recognition of a particular person's membership by that person and by the elders or other persons enjoying traditional authority among those people. Native title to an area

of land which a clan or group is entitled to enjoy under the laws and customs of an indigenous people is extinguished if the clan or group, by ceasing to acknowledge those laws, and (so far as practicable) observe those customs, loses its connection with the land or on the death of the last of the members of the group or clan.

This is the definition of native title given by Justice Brennan, one of the judges in the Mabo case. But another judge, Toohey, founded native title not on observation of custom, but on the plaintiff's argument of 'occupation of the land since 1788', not necessarily with constant presence but regular visits proving 'possession'. According to the lawyers who have commented on these judgments,[18] if this criterion is accepted for attribution of Aboriginal titles, it becomes possible to claim a land without having to prove current practise of customs but merely by justifying occupation of the land at the time of colonisation. The Supreme Court also ruled that a title is extinguished when the land is used for permanent public establishments such as roads. But contrary to the legislation in the Northern Territory, which restricts claims to 'vacant' lands, native title can be claimed on national or maritime park lands. The status has not been defined for land sold to private parties or under lease – most cattle or fishing enterprises – or when development activities such as mining, tourism and so forth have been started on them. The different questions of compensation also remain to be settled. In the Northern Territory, the land handed back under the 1976 Land Rights Act gave the Aboriginal owners a right of veto over future development as well as a right to royalties (4 per cent maximum) on profits from mining. Most of the mining companies, however, backed by some local governments, refuse to generalise this system to pending native title claims.

Given the knotty legal situation, many lawyers and anthropologists have been recruited to define the local content of eventual native titles. Aboriginal people themselves disagree over the question of traditional inheritance rights. With the transmission of land, for instance, what should be the rule: traditional descent reckoning, patrilineal, matrilineal, or some other? Or should the colonial history be taken into account and right to land given to all descendants? In the 1970s, at the time of the first land claims in the Northern Territory, some anthropologists criticised the systematisation of

---

[18] Declaration by Brown and O'Donnel (1992), consulted in unpublished papers giving no further reference.

unilineal transmission and the notion of patrilocality. In the Western Desert, for example, links with the land are determined primarily by the individual's conception Dreaming (totem, see above), which often differs from the father's Dreaming. Even in the Central Desert groups, who follow a patrilineal pattern of transmission, land ownership is inseparable from other ritual land rights held by the matrikin or other allies. As for the groups on the northwestern coast of the Kimberley, I am currently working with the oral history and analysis of the ritual system of custodianship of the Dreamings (partially maintained) to show that the traditional land-holding system was highly complex and in fact incompatible with generalised patrilocality (Glowczewski 1998b).

The current interest in providing an anthropological definition of the content of native titles highlights the importance of this moment of Australian history when Indigenous people are consolidating their Aboriginality, not as a shared political ideology, but as a force of local cohesion, locality by locality. Some Aboriginal activists have suggested adopting a local term, 'Koori', to refer not only to the Aboriginal peoples of the south-east, but also for all Aboriginal peoples of Australia and their descendants of mixed ancestry. The use of 'Koori' has been well accepted in the south-east, but not in other regions, where local groups prefer to use their own names, for example, Nyoongar, in the south-west includes the people of the region of the town of Perth. More important than the similarities visible in these approaches, though, is the fact that localisation carries with it a singularisation of identities which implies both continuity with local ancestral heritage and creation of new social structures. This continuity is affirmed, as can be seen in the many Aboriginal initiatives, through the maintenance or renewal of ceremonies, the creation of cultural festivals or the reconstitution of local history. The new structures are evident in the many new Aboriginal associations: tribal or family corporations for the purpose of resettling lands or negotiating their participation in the development of towns or national parks, women's groups, resource centres, and so on. As Myrna Tonkinson writes:

> While Aboriginality is developing as a political force, local and regional Aboriginal identities continue to have salience and provide, though not exclusively, some of the content of Aboriginality. And there are reciprocal influences on local attitudes. The two forms of identity help sustain each other and are therefore likely to coexist well into the future. (M. E. Tonkinson 1990: 215)

In Australia, it's 'Aboriginal' with a Capital 'A'

This polarisation between local identities and a pan-Aboriginal identity is, in my view, a particularly dynamic element in the creation of new alliances with local powers (ruling structures like the shire) or non-Aboriginal interested parties (like developers). These alliances bring both autonomy and support, owing to the political alliances contracted at the national level, which involve not only Australian interests but also a form of international solidarity with Indigenous groups from other parts of the world. This solidarity with minority groups goes hand in hand, especially among young people, with identification with a 'Black' culture, often carried by popular music from Australia or overseas. In its 1993 public report on the Mabo decision, the Commission for Reconciliation underscored, for example, treaties concluded by other governments: New Zealand with the Maori and Canada with some Indigenous groups.

In the past decade, militant groups themselves have developed exchanges with other Indigenous peoples, both political – at the United Nations – and political-cultural – the Festival of the Pacific, held in Townsville in 1990 and in the Cook Islands in 1992. Local delegations travelled to these manifestations taking with them both the specificity of their regional heritage – dancing and traditional art forms – and new forms of individual creativity – plastic arts, literature, theatre, cinema or music. National recognition of these artists and the recent fame of some Aboriginal sport champions no doubt helps to promote a respect for Aboriginal culture that makes them symbols of a new political force. Not only Aboriginal people who have remained close to their land, their language and their customs but those, too, who have been dispossessed of these are increasingly coming to identify with this many-sided Aboriginality.

Figure 8.1 Napaljarri and Nungarrayi women kneel around their sacred slabs yukurrukurru *painted with the* Witi *(Initiated Man poles) Dreaming to send the image-forces back to the virtual, inside the land of Kurlungalinpa* © B. G. 1984

8

Culture Cult: Ritual Circulation of Inalienable Knowledge and Appropriation of Cultural Knowledge (Central and NW Australia)

Indigenous People are entitled to the recognition of the full ownership, control and protection of their cultural and intellectual property. They have the right to special measures to control, develop and protect their sciences, technologies and cultural manifestations, including human and other genetic resources, seeds, medicines, knowledge of the properties of fauna and flora, oral tradition, literatures, designs and visual and performing arts. (Article 29 of the Draft Declaration on the Rights of Indigenous Peoples, United Nations, 1993)[1]

Many Aboriginal cult objects collected in unclear or even unlawful circumstances have found their way into private collections or museums in Australia and other parts of the world.[2] The South Australian Museum in Adelaide has set up a pilot program to identify sacred and secret objects in view of returning them to communities wanting to recover a portion of their heritage. Other museums have followed this initiative of collaborating with Aboriginal peoples.[3] Some groups accept restitution but draw up agreements with museums that the objects be placed in their reserves for safe-keeping. Others prefer to take back the objects but then worry about their protection. Since the 1980s, 'safe-keeping places' have sprung up throughout Australia, some in corrugated huts, others in sophisticated buildings. The Aboriginal communities regard them as 'living museums' since the traditional cult objects kept there are used in

---

[1] See: http://www.un-documents.net/dundrip.htm; see The UN Declaration on the Rights of Indigenous Peoples 2017: https://www.un.org/development/desa/indigenouspeoples/declaration-on-the-rights-of-indigenous-peoples.html
[2] This chapter was translated by Nora Scott for Carolina Academic Press, first published in *People and Things* (Jeudy-Ballini and Juillerat 2002).
[3] Anderson (1990) on exchange-relations between Australian museums and Indigenous people; see contributions to Part 2: 'Bringing people back into the collections', in Craig et al. (1999). See also Anderson (1995), Stanton (1999). More recently, see De Largy Healy (2009).

men's and women's rituals. The process of repatriating objects is part of a broader movement to reappropriate Indigenous culture and revitalise traditional practices, especially religious ceremonies.

'Safe-keeping places' are increasingly conceived as part of larger structures or of regional culture centres which require more costly technical means for the safe-keeping of objects whose access is restricted to their 'ritual custodians'. These structures serve as depositories for written, audio and visual archives accessible only to those groups considered to be the owners of this knowledge. Other, everyday objects accompanied by public audio-visual documents are carefully selected for exhibition so as to transmit an image of the culture to the younger generations and to further knowledge of the culture among non-Aboriginal people. Some of these centres also seek to keep tradition alive through the production of crafts, art and all expressions of local culture: audio-visual recording of oral history, dance workshops, bush-food collecting with children of the community, performances and guided visits of the centre and its area for schools and tourists, but also the organisation of traditional gatherings of Aboriginal groups in places which may or may not be open to the public.

After recalling the international context of the contemporary claims to cultural property, I will explain the concept of inalienability which, in Central and North Western Australia, surrounds the ritual circulation of sacred objects and the cults of which they are a part. Afterwards I will examine the elaboration of a culture centre involving the representatives of a dozen Aboriginal languages and organisations based in the coastal town of Broome; this initiative reflects an attempt to control the representation given of these cultures and to reappropriate their objects and knowledge. Finally, I will end with some thoughts on the notion of 'keeping-while-giving' (Weiner 1992).

Cultural Property, Inalienable Objects and Knowledge

Objects are repatriated to Australia on behalf of communities led by Aboriginal people who, as citizens, should enjoy moral property rights as defined in the Universal Declaration of Human Rights:

> Everyone has the right to the protection of moral and material interests resulting from any scientific, literary or artistic production of which he is the author. (Tsosie 1997: 9)

This moral right, conceived as applying to the individual and being limited in time, covers only physically tangible 'productions' of an author such as objects, patents or publications. Beyond the period stipulated (usually fifty years), the content of the novel, discovery, musical work or work of art falls into the public domain and is no longer protected by law. This law is clearly not adapted to cultural claims, for it does not recognise traditional property, which by definition dates back more than fifty years, or collective property, since it is shared by a group, often orally, and is therefore intangible. Nevertheless, Indigenous people can use incorporated bodies in order to benefit from the repatriation of objects. In the United States, the 1990 Native American Graves Protection and Repatriation Act enabled American museums to return more than 80,000 items, including human remains. But such repatriations do not go without conflict when it comes to defining entitled beneficiaries. Zuni, Hopi and Navajo, for example, dispute the ownership of pre-Colombian bones found on one site which all three groups claim as the dwelling-place of their own ancestors.[4] Bones held in museums and laboratories all over the world have also been claimed by Australian Aboriginal people, who are militating against the archaeological excavation of sites containing human remains.

> Tangible cultural resources include historic and prehistoric structures and artefacts, as well as cultural objects of importance to contemporary tribes, such as sacred objects and objects of cultural patrimony ... property may not be *alienable* outside the group. (Tsosie 1997: 5, 7)

Like sacred objects, sites bearing material indications of the ancestral presence of a culture, but also natural sites (hills, rocks, water holes) held to be sacred to the culture, were traditionally inalienable. However, in order to register a land claim in view of restitution, Australian law requires lists of owners, who must demonstrate to the court, for each geographical site concerned, the way ownership of these sites was transmitted – in these cultures without written language. Aboriginal people have often shown judges, who were sworn to secrecy, sacred objects they regarded as their 'native title,' equivalent of the Western land title. They have also invited them to listen to sacred myths and to visit the sites and attend rites – dances, songs,

---

[4] 2nd World Water Forum, Home of the Citizen and Water – Water Source of Culture, Traditions and Peace, The Hague, March 2000, communication by a Hopi/Zuni representative.

body painting, and so forth. Aboriginal people consider performance of the rite as proof of their status of 'ritual custodians' (*kirda* in Warlpiri) of this body of knowledge, practices and cult objects; they translate this status in English as 'owner,' to satisfy the Western notion of property and ownership. In the central desert, one is often the 'owner' of his/her father's land but he/she is also the 'manager' (*kurdungurlu* in Warlpiri) of the mother's or spouse's land, its rites and its objects. In other words, men and women are owners only insofar as they share a certain use and knowledge of their possession with direct kin and affines.

For Aboriginal people, sacred sites and objects materialise culture – which we regard as something non-material, intellectual or intangible – in other words the body of knowledge transmitted via oral or gestual practices, which are therefore also inalienable: languages, stories, songs, dances, medicinal plants and so on. But for Western law, once intangible knowledge is materialised in a medium, it is alienable and comes under copyright law: a work of art, a publication, a sound or a visual recording. The content then becomes the property of the author of the production, the artist, writer, photographer and, of course, anthropologist. Today anthropologists are reproached – as are museums, journalists, collectors, etc. – for appropriating inalienable bodies of knowledge or objects and commercialising them to the detriment of their original cultural owners. Aboriginal people, like other Indigenous groups, stress their need to control the distribution of their culture by recording, filming and publishing their own cultural resources. In addition to the contribution of such an approach to the patrimony and to education, the authors' materialisation of their knowledge and practices in their chosen media is supposed to protect them from dispossession by others. In many Indigenous communities and gatherings, non-Aboriginal people are not allowed to take pictures or make recordings without a permit, which may be refused. Some anthropology students even agree to sign a contract with the communities, promising they will let them read and check their thesis before they publish it, or even submit it to their university. Although many non-Aboriginal consultants are hired by Aboriginal organisations, the material they collect remains the property of their employers and they cannot use it as they wish.

Aboriginal people also claim copyright in recognition of their intellectual ownership of audio-visual productions or publications by non-Aboriginals (Janke, 1998). This position, modeled on the mining royalties, which have been in force in Australia for twenty years, was replaced only after numerous discussions with the elders, who were reticent at the idea of drawing income from their lands. Such wariness of commercial alienation has not been overcome among Native Americans either, according to Rosemary Coombe, who objects that 'copyright licenses' and other legal solutions to the problem of intellectual property alienate social relations. Indeed, Coombe appears to advocate an ethic for respecting cultural integrity, rather than a legal solution (Coombe 1997). She advocates the 'central importance of shared cultural symbols in defining us and the realities we recognise,' which seems to militate in favour of overcoming the strictures imposed by intellectual property law in favour of a free exchange of ideas and expression (Coombe 1991: 74–96; quoted by Tsosie 1997: 10).

Several proposals have been made to avoid such alienation of traditional knowledge, including the idea of taking inspiration from 'computer software licensing agreements as a potentially fruitful model for indigenous people to adopt as a means for legally protecting their right to just compensation for the acquisition and use of their intellectual products (Stephenson 1994: 182)' (Tsosie 1997: 11, note).

Much the same was said to me by young computer specialists and Internet users at a conference at the Cité des Sciences in Paris, where I explained the necessity of recognising the right of control and distribution imposed by a Central Desert Aboriginal community to whom I restored the written and audio-visual material I had gathered between 1979 and 1998 in the form of an interactive CD-ROM program. After two years of work and consultation with fifty-one Warlpiri artists from the Lajamanu community and a year of trials in their school, the Council and the artists agreed to make it available to the public. At first, some felt that the knowledge should not be commercialised inasmuch as it constituted the very essence of their culture. But after long discussion among themselves, the Council members and the community Warnayaka Arts Centre decided to accept the economic benefits, provided use of the CD-ROM was confined to settings contextualised with respect to the art and teachings of Aboriginal culture, in other words, to museums and universities.

This resistance to open commercialisation of their culture was already evident in the same Warlpiri community of Lajamanu immediately following the emergence of the acrylic painting movement among the Pintupi and the Warlpiri of Papunya, their neighbours to the south, who share similar mythic and iconographic elements associated with totemic sites and Eternal Beings (*Jukurrpa*). The Lajamanu elders decided to take up commercialised painting on canvas only several years after their neighbours' success in art galleries around the world (Myers 1994), and after a delegation of a dozen Lajamanu men had been invited to make a ritual sand-painting at the Museum of Modern Art in Paris.[5] It may be that the success they encountered as painters and dancers reassured them that the elitism of museums and the international art world would protect them against 'copy cats.' On one official visit to the Australia Room of the Musée National des Arts d'Afrique et d'Océanie in Paris, the twelve elders identified a carved wooden slab as being connected with a secret cult and not supposed to be shown in public (Glowczewski 1996). The museum withdrew the slab and ensured that it was not displaying any other objects regarded as sacred or secret. In France as well as in the other former colonial countries, where through the agency of national museums the state owns foreign collections, the prospect of repatriation challenges the very principle of national heritage, which has been largely built on the conquest of other peoples. The political issue is far from being resolved, but moral recognition of problems of intellectual property and cultural control has opened the way for protocols, which are increasingly respected by museums.

Travelling Cults, History and Secrecy

Sandra Pannell (1994) has very astutely shown the inalienability of sacred slabs, *tjurunga* (also *churinga*), and their equivalents in other desert groups. These are abundantly discussed in the literature (Moisseeff 2002) and are still the subject of speculation among collectors. For the Central Desert Arrernte (Aranda), *tjurunga* are like a spiritual and geographical ID card. Traditionally each person had his or her own slab, which was hidden and handled with the greatest care; it was a sort of spiritual duplicate, linking the person with a specific place and its totemic spirits. Slabs are said to be inhabited by a spiritual force that is animated by the esoteric design carved on

---

[5] Peter Brook's Théâtre des Bouffes du Nord and ARC, Musée d'Art Moderne, as a part of the manifestation 'D'un autre continent – L'Australie, le rêve et le réel', organised for the 1983 Festival d'Automne. See Chapter 4: p. 140.

the slab. This singular force of the slab is believed to be re-actualised from one generation to the next into its new human duplicates. In former times, when someone died, in accordance with the taboo on pronouncing the name of the deceased found in all Aboriginal groups, the name was not mentioned for the duration of the mourning period, which was two years. Similarly, the deceased's slab, his or her material double, was entrusted to a neighbouring group until the mourning period was over (Pannell 1994: 26). In other groups, the slabs are less individualised, but they are still associated with specific places, of which they are the materialisation of the life force, an ancestral and eternal singularity that is also embodied in the group which shares the same totemic name: this singularity, which is named, drawn, sung and danced, dwells in people, places, totemic species and sacred objects; the Warlpiri and their neighbours in the desert call it *Jukurrpa*: the Dreaming (Glowczewski 1991).

Other slabs are connected with initiation cults and travel from group to group, often of different languages, when these cults are transmitted over hundreds of kilometers as part of the chain of alliances, which are also manifested by the circulation of everyday goods and by marriage exchanges (Micha 1970; Ackerman 1979). After years or even decades of circulating, the rituals acquired new forms of expression and sacred objects which, having been handled by the ritual custodians of each group through which they have passed, are believed to transmit something of the power of the Dreaming. The sacred and secret objects accompanying the initiation cults can by definition be shown only to initiates. Their revelation at the time they are handed over by the initiating group to the new initiates is part and parcel of the symbolic dramatisation of the ritual.

The Central Desert Warlpiri immediately recognised the slab in the Paris museum as coming from the Western Desert and as being part of the secret cult that links them with different language groups. As the secret name of the cult must not be pronounced, it is designated by one of the public dances that is part of the cult, *Kadranya* (Moyle 1981), on the northwest coast of Broome, or by the expression 'Balgo Business' (Myers n.d.), from the name of the desert community which introduced the cult among the Warlpiri. It took the cult over fifty years to cover the 1,000 kilometers separating the coast from the Central Desert. In 1976, the Balgo elders, who speak Kukatja, Walmajarri and Warlpiri, became the 'custodians' of the objects, songs and rites that circulate with the cult and in turn passed them on to the east. However, according to these desert groups, the objects remain the spiritual property of those who, at various times, introduced them into the cult, in particular the Yawuru and Djugun from Broome.

Unlike many traditional initiation cults, which in Australia assign authority to the elders and separate the sexes in view of making the young people into men and women, this cult specifically presents itself as a new mixed Law which enables men and women of some forty years of age to assume a leadership role. It seems to deal symbolically with certain role changes imposed by colonisation, the violence of contact, the traumas of imprisonment and forced sedentarisation, the economic changes and intermarriage with Europeans and Asians. The secrecy surrounding initiation into the cult excludes – on pain of severe punishment – Aboriginal people who have not yet received the cult, on the one hand, and, on the other, non-Aboriginals, who are not invited to attend. In an earlier article, I defined it as a 'cargo cult':

> Aboriginal Law resides in sacred objects (or places) inasmuch as they are metamorphoses of the same 'essence' (life forces) which makes humans, while White Law resides in 'wealth,' which does not share any essence with human beings (wealth represents a power that people must appropriate). In the new cult, Aboriginal people do not seek to identify with White wealth, or even to integrate it into their traditional system, as they did with the circulation of the early objects from the West. Instead, an absolutely new intention is brought into play: this new power would allow people to affirm a separation from the commodities which mediate matter in the West. (Glowczewski 1983b: 12)

As symbolic work on 'cargo,' that is the Western commodity system, this historical cult is highly secret because it provided Aboriginal peoples with their own way of resisting the harmful effects of the colonial system. Many missionaries regarded it as 'devil business' on the pretext that it opposed their influence. For Aboriginal people, the accusation was inadmissible: syncretism between Christianity and traditional spirituality is found in only some regions (Kolig 1979); elsewhere it is above all a case of seeking to create the conditions for a sort of spiritual retreat in which, as in a collective psychodrama or theatrical catharsis, the ritual with its emotional charge enables new initiates to re-enact the violence experienced by their mothers and fathers, and to find ways of coping with it.

The Central Desert Warlpiri claim that part of the cult was dreamed in the small town of Broome, on the northwest coast. When I went there in 1980, I was told that the cult dated back to the wreck of the Koombana, which disappeared in 1912 off the coast of Port Hedland, a town further to the south, in the Pilbaras, where a dreamer is said to have received a message from the shipwrecked men.[6] A Broome elder told me about the cult as he had seen it in the 1920s at La Grange Bidyadanga (100 km south of Broome): he added that he was a Nyikina, raised by the Karajarri, and that he had been made the spiritual custodian of the region north of Broome which belonged to the Jabirr Jabirr, who, he claimed, had died out without descendants (see Figure 8.2). When I returned to Broome in 1991, I found that this monopoly of the custody of the land and the ritual was contested by some Jabirr Jabirr families and above all by the groups speaking the traditional languages of Broome, Yawuru and Djugun. Those local groups intermarried heavily with Europeans and Asians, but had constituted a Yawuru Aboriginal Corporation and had resumed initiation of their young men in the 1980s. The secret cult, including a dance relating the Japanese bombing of Broome during the Second World War, was probably added onto an older Yawuru-Djugun initiation ritual. In the 1970s, a Yawuru elder, custodian of the initiations in the region, transmitted a new version of the secret cult to some groups living 500 kilometers to the east, around the town of Fitzroy Crossing, who themselves adapted it in the form seen by Kolig (1979) and later transmitted these rites, together with the sacred objects they had received from the Yawuru and Djugun, to the desert groups.

The Kimberley Aboriginal groups differ in geography, culture, social organisation and language (McGregor 1988), but also in their colonial history and its consequences on contemporary politics.[7] However an exchange network, known as *Wunan*, already linked the coastal groups with the river and desert groups before colonisation:

---

[6] Swain (1993) reported a connection between this cult and the Aboriginal resistance movement in the 1940s, in which a certain Coffin, from the Port Hedland region, persuaded the Aborigines to walk off all the cattle stations in the Pilbara. I have shown (Glowczewski 1983b) that it was also a certain Coffin from the same region who, according to the Warlpiri, dreamed part of this cult. The strike movement was extraordinarily well organised thanks to another Aboriginal man, who made the rounds of the cattle stations distributing little pieces of paper divided into squares and asking the Aborigines who did not know how to read or write to cross out a square every morning until the day they were to leave their workplace. The cult reported in three regions includes several points at which little papers are exchanged: it is my hypothesis that this now-ritual act is related specifically to this historical event which, by the Aboriginal people's refusal to go on being treated as slaves, threatened the whole cattle-station system in Western Australia.

[7] See Chapter 7, this volume.

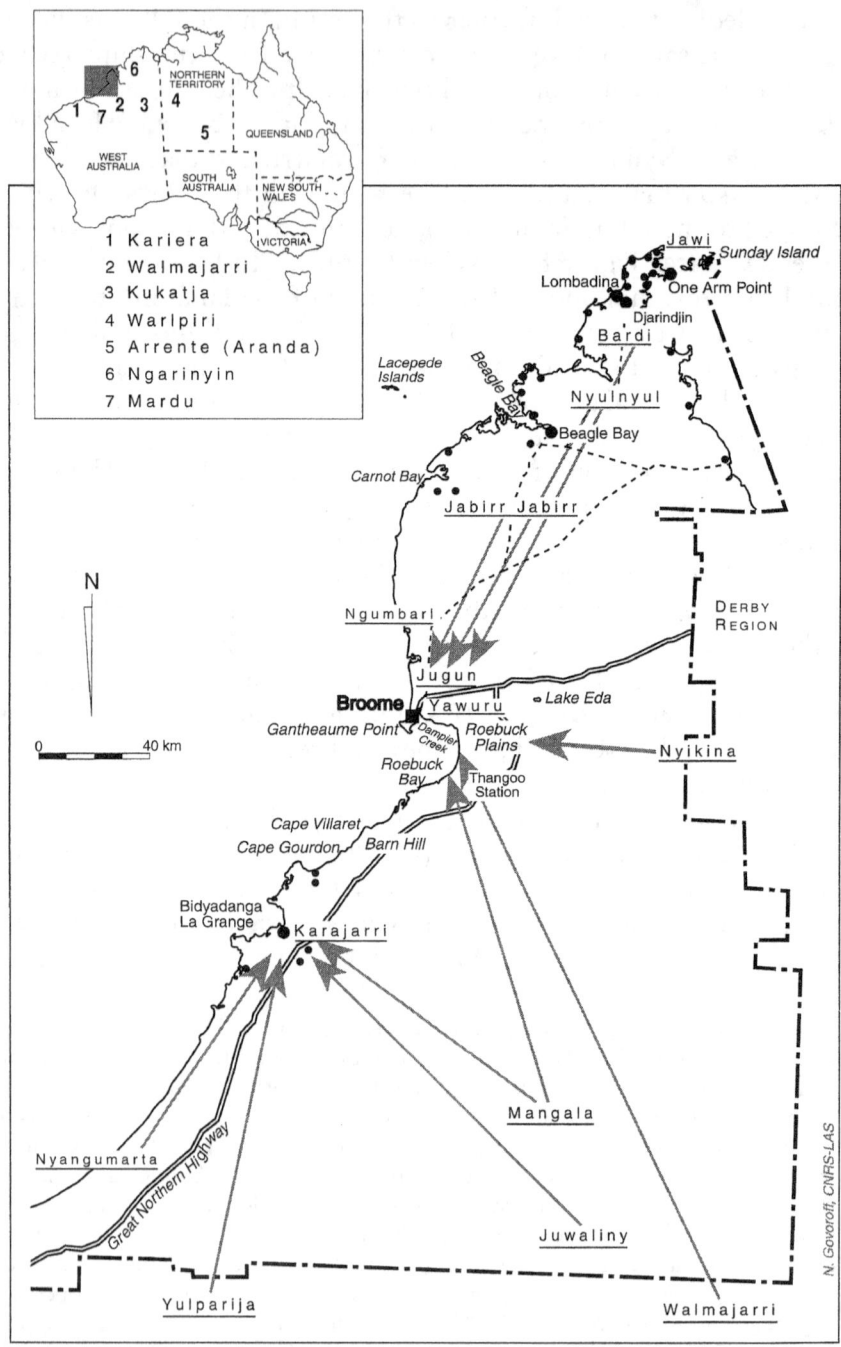

Figure 8.2 Map: some Aboriginal groups and migrations in Northwestern Australia

these exchanges involved everyday objects (shields, spears, tobacco, food, red ochre and kaolin), cult objects (pearl-shells, sacred objects, hairstrings, stone circumcision knives, objects used in love magic), and rites and their attendant myths. Phyllis Kaberry (1939) demonstrated that some of these circulations occurred in her time as chains linking together homonyms of the same sex (*narrugu*). These gendered exchange chains tied together individuals having the same first name or having only the same classificatory *skin-name*. It was then necessary for groups with different languages and social organisations (with two, four or eight *skins* or subsections) to deduce equivalences between the different *skin-names*: in this way, Aboriginal kinship systems informed and ultimately transformed each other through alliances between their respective owners. In all events, individual members of the same chain, because they bore the same name, were considered as exchange 'brothers,' or 'sisters,' which is remarkable inasmuch as the notion of exchange usually suggests alliance rather than siblingship or filiation.

There are other kinds of exchanges as well between same- or opposite-sex affines or kin, ranging from restricted family or marriage exchanges, notably with real or potential affines, to the large-scale ceremonies marking the entry of young people into the adult world or of the dead into the spirit world. Initiation, like death, entails ritual gatherings which require the presence and therefore the travel of allies from other linguistic groups: in both cases hairstrings circulate, often between men through their sisters. Ackerman (1979) has mapped the circulation of traditional objects from Western Australia, showing that the circuit extended far into the Northern Territory – which includes Central Desert groups such as the Warlpiri – and progressively integrated spear heads cut in glass from bottles or telegraph-pole insulators, fabric and money. I too witnessed the replacement of traditional artifacts by introduced materials, notably hairstrings by fabrics, clothing or blankets, not to mention the acacia-seed cakes, replaced by impressive quantities of cans of flour, sugar, tea and even cellophane-wrapped loaves of bread. The arrival of new, highly prized goods, such as video machines and four-wheel drive vehicles brought these, too, into the gift-exchange circuit. At the domestic level, it should be noted that it is still unusual for Aboriginal people who carry on ritual exchanges to hoard consumer goods for their personal use.

With the advent of pioneer pastoralism in the nineteenth century, many men and women were taken onto cattle stations as itinerant stockmen who ranged over hundreds of kilometers in the Kimberley, the Pilbaras, the Northern Territory and Queensland. Alliances between tribes intensified and expanded owing to new encounters in the course of these travels and to an apparently tacit resistance to the ill treatment suffered by all (Micha 1970). Two hundred kilometers to the north of Broome, the Beagle Bay mission, created in 1890, was used as a receiving centre for Aboriginal children forcibly taken away from their families throughout the Kimberley. Trained as domestic help, they were placed with the white pearlers of Broome, and many local women contracted unions with Asian workers, despite the prohibition on interracial cohabitation. It was against this backdrop of unlawful mixed unions and solidarity with the 'chain gangs' – prisoners chained together by the neck – that certain secret cults with their sacred objects (Worms and Petri [1968] 1972) spread from group to group: symbolic attempts to mobilise ancestral powers against the upheavals introduced by European domination.

After the 1967 referendum, which obliged cattle-station owners to pay Aboriginal workers a wage, the latter were driven off the stations and took refuge in the fringe camps around the towns. At this time, the young people around Broome were initiated among their various neighbours, who had managed to preserve their ritual life better than had the Yawuru, who had been hard hit by the pearling industry and the missions since the 1880s. Marriages bolstered the ritual alliances and gave responsibilities to members of groups from outside the region: thus, in the 1970s, it was a Karajarri man married to a Yawuru woman who was custodian of the sacred objects in Broome, which had been given back by eastern communities (like Looma) and were kept at the Broome initiation ground. These objects were stolen by a young part Aboriginal man, though some were later located in an art circuit dealing in traditional objects. The case sparked numerous disputes among local Aboriginal people, but after the culprit's release from prison, the affair was considered closed. In the 1990s, the Bardi of One Arm Point and Djarindjin, the Karajarri of Bidyadanga, the Nyikina, Mangala and Walmajarri of Looma, and other groups that initiated young Yawuru men or had received the secret cult from Broome, such as the Kukatja of Balgo, rallied to support the Yawuru when they resumed their own initiations and rituals on their traditional ground. These groups also formed a corporation which is striving to protect the sacred and secret aspects of their culture, in particular with the movement to repatriate cult objects as well as anthropological and historical archives: the Kimberley Aboriginal

Law and Culture Centre,[8] initially based in Broome and then transferred to Fitzroy Crossing, home of the Nyikina and the Bunaba, but also of many Walmajarri refugees from the Western Desert.

In 1980, when Noonkanbah, a community in this region, opposed exploratory mining in order to protect a sacred place, it received support not only from the Labor Party, the unions and the churches, but also from distant Aboriginal groups who, like the Warlpiri, had exchanged boys for initiation and marriage, and sacred objects (Glowczewski 1996; Kolig 1981). These exchanges followed the desert groups' adoption of the secret cult from the coast, transmitted via Fitzroy Crossing, and gathered strength in the 1990s, when the Warlpiri gave the communities of this town a fire ceremony for the resolution of conflicts between allies, a ceremony connected with the *Ngatijirri* Budgerigar Dreaming and the *Puluwanti* Owl Dreaming (Peterson 1970; Glowczewski 1991). Circulation of Aboriginal rites and objects thus continues to be closely connected with the political situation of a region.

The Kimberley example shows that the circulation of cult objects through the transmission of initiation-related cults is a veritable machine for producing culture(s), first by regenerating local specificities and second by asserting a common procedure which, beyond language differences, enables exchange to take place over thousands of kilometers. Each local group's identity is strengthened by this ritual nomadism, which is enriched by new religious forms wherein local variants of what Aboriginal people call their respective Laws nurture those of their neighbours. This is true of men's rituals (Wedlock 1992) as well as women's (Poirier 1992), for both help create these exchanges which reinforce the bond between each group and its sacred places, and the inalienable possession of its sacred objects. Similar identity-building can also be seen in the interregional gatherings for traditional mixed dancing, commonly called 'corroborees.'[9]

---

[8] On the history and politics of KALACC, see Préaud (2009), see also Préaud (2015).

[9] Today Australian football culture provides a stage for this affirmation of identity through travel: every Aboriginal community has its team which travels several months of the year to compete in tournaments; the players' families often follow them in great numbers. This activity is particularly valorised in eastern Victoria, where the Brambuk culture centre displays both the traditional history and the sporting history of the region's Aboriginal groups (De Largy Healy 2001).

The Bugarrigarra Nyurdany Culture Centre in Broome

When the government launched its watchwords, 'self-determination' and 'self-management,' most of the language groups of the Kimberley formed Aboriginal corporations, several of which have their headquarters or an annex in Broome: the Yawuru and the Djugun, natives of this land, the Nyul Nyul originally from around Beagle Bay, the Bardi from the northern Dampier peninsula, and the Karajarri from the south (see Figure 8.2). Some families also established themselves as incorporated associations in order to be allowed to build outstations on the land opened to them by the state, the region or the missions. After passage of the 1993 Native Title Act, which established one land claim procedure for the whole of Australia, a new organisation, Rubibi, regrouped the families of the region to help them press their Native Title applications in the face of Broome's developing tourist industry. The federation of Aboriginal groups sought to define strategies using Western law to protect traditional law, notably in the area of property rights on land and the cult objects associated with it. But this institutional centralisation of the local groups also gave rise to internal and external segmentation, against a backdrop of 'retribalisation'[10] and creolisation, which were not without their tensions and disputes, especially concerning the growing influx of Aboriginal and non-Aboriginal migrants to the towns and of tourists to the outback (Glowczewski 1998b).

Various development plans showed the local desire to create an Aboriginal culture centre that would at the same time support traditional activities and promote creation, make jobs for the Aboriginal people and protect the local communities and their natural environment (RMIT 1995; Jackson 1996). The shire and the Broome Media Aboriginal Corporation each hired an Aboriginal consultant, who put together a working party made up of delegates from Aboriginal organisations in the town as well as from two more distant communities, Bidyadanga and Djarindjin (see Figure 8.2). Numerous meetings were held to draw up a list of the activities people wanted the centre to undertake and how it was to be managed. One expert of

---

[10] Although the term 'tribe' has been rejected for some ten years by Australian anthropologists and Aboriginal militants, who complain that it lends a false connotation to the regional, linguistic and traditional political groups, it is still often used by Aboriginal people, who distinguish themselves as 'tribes' or 'clans' to accentuate their cultural and social differences.

Tamil origin, invited to speak on his experience with culture centres in North America and Southern Australia, advised first creating the centre as a network of cultural exchanges even before constructing the building, putting the argument for 'virtual museums' which would use the Internet or CD-ROMs to give back the culture and its objects without the constraints of storage, preservation and security, which are extremely costly, especially in a tropical climate.[11]

As an anthropologist married to a Yawuru man,[12] I was asked to coordinate a survey with three Aboriginal representatives. The Working Party wanted to gain a general overview, with statements from people and data that could be presented in a quantified way to the people and to the funding bodies. The main issue was: what is culture for people and what is a culture centre supposed to do in relation to different statements about culture? We had to be careful to have a representative sample of people. All the languages of the Broome region had to be represented, and we interviewed some people in their home communities away from town: one third of the 135 people in the sample identified as (D)Jugun[13] and/or Yawuru (42), another third as Bardi (40), whose traditional land lies 200 kilometers to the north, and the rest split between other coastal groups, Karajarri (23), Nyul Nyul (24), Jabirr Jabirr (11) and inland groups: Nyangumarta (7), Yulbarija (6), Mangala (4), Yamatji, Bunaba, Miriwong, Jaru, Walmajarri, Nyigina (17); three people did not identify by a language group. Some people identified to two or more languages, this is why the sum of the figures is higher than the number of people interviewed. The balance between genders was 73 women versus 62 men, and between ages: 54 over fifty, 59 between fifty and twenty, 22 under twenty. Each question listed several answers to choose from, but when, as it often happens, people answered spontaneously, the answer was written down and analyzed to fit into one or the other of the categories so as to allow statistical calculations (Glowczewski 1996). Here are some of the questions discussed in the interviews.

---

[11] Since then, virtual museums have multiplied: see De Largy Healy (2004) and De Largy Healy and Glowczewski (2014).

[12] Wayne Barker Jowandi, composer-musician and film-maker (Barker 1992, 2011, 2016). Also Djugun and Jabirr-Jabirr.

[13] In the 2000s the spelling Djugun has been adopted by this group claiming specific traditional rights on Broome which seem to have been overridden by some Yawuru people. The conflict is particularly strong in relation to fracking, which the Djugun refuse on their land while some Yawuru have signed for it.

What is Aboriginal Culture for You?

Most people defined culture as language (92), ceremonies, song and dance (91), land, attachment to place (85), old people and family (80), hunting, fishing, living in the bush (79); for less then half it was oral history (71), art and artifacts (69), and less then a third chose the common Western sense of the term 'culture' as a cumulative and creative process, expressing Aboriginality with new media (39). All people felt a 'loss' of culture and were worried by the fact that local languages are not spoken enough, even if there are some lessons in the Broome primary schools and the community schools of Bidyadanga, One Arm Point and Djarindjin.

Asked about what culture is, most old people referred to traditional practices and knowledge: stories about the relation to land, bush medicine identification and use, techniques of hunting, fishing and bush-food gathering, the body of ceremonial Law including dancing and painting. Many stressed that culture is what you eat and how you eat – by a campfire – your living style, your identity; others insisted on kinship and pleasure: 'Going to corroboree was like today people get excited for a new movie; and all the competition between the guys for dancing!' One Yawuru Karajarri woman elder identified culture with *Kunyurrung*, a traditional ritual custom common to all the Kimberley groups through the *Wunan* exchange system, where men with the same name and women with the same name can exchange goods in gendered chains (Glowczewski [1994] 2018; see also Glowczewski 1998b). (When a Karajarri child is about to be named, at around the age of four or five, an older person is chosen as his or her namesake and exchange partner. During the naming ritual, the families of the two namesakes share goods.) Other elders insisted on the fact that culture creates unity because of sharing and respecting different ceremonial Laws which connect people from different language groups: 'Law spread out and they don't jealous each other because they share. And they should *share* together.'

What Does an Aboriginal Culture Centre Mean to You?

The majority stressed: respect of men Law and women Law (78), exchange between Aboriginal people (78), resources and exhibitions (78). Less than half chose: place where generations meet (72), place where culture is maintained and alive (72), training and development of skills (71), people with cultural knowledge (68), shows, concerts and festivals (63). In their comments, people insisted on the idea that a centre was a place for activities (dance, song, crafts, teaching children) aimed at both Aboriginal children and a non-Aboriginal audience. Many elders stressed the necessity of involving different language groups, sharing culture with other regional Aboriginal groups, including Torres Strait Islanders (who have come to work in pearling), making the wider community understand about cultural differences. While the elders of the remote communities agreed on the need for a big 'sharing' centre in Broome, they also wanted to decentralise by having 'keeping-places' and 'culture-teaching places' in their local communities.

Men and women of different ages expressed concern that storage of cultural items in town might represent a spiritual danger and people would get sick. It should be noted that one culture centre in Alice Springs, which has a storage place containing sacred objects, is avoided by the local Aboriginal people, who do not want to go near them for fear of transgressing the Law that forbids approaching such objects outside the appropriate ritual context.[14] Showing culture and repatriation are all right so long as secret things are kept at a distance: they have to be protected, but people have to be protected from them as well. The same applies to sacred places.

What Should the Centre Do to Support Language and Culture in the Community?

For half of the people, protecting places of cultural heritage (72) was as important as recording, protecting, teaching knowledge and language (74); other considerations were: give resources for crafts and art (70), give cultural awareness to Aborigines and others (66), provide shop and marketing for artists (61), create programs to develop skills (58), organise exchange with other Indigenous people (53); less then a third saw a priority in facilitating creation (art, music, theatre, dance) (42). The need to market arts and create language-teaching resources was presented as a double movement to help communities develop resources themselves and to have a structure in town to host the culture custodians and organise relations with outsiders (art buyers, tourists, schools, etc.).

The protection of culture through the protection of country was expressed as the need to create a network of rangers who would be organised through the centre: a model of decentralised cultural/natural

---

[14] The Western Desert elders performed a smoking ritual at the South Australian Museum from which sacred objects were removed to a new storage place so that the room could be used with no danger to the public from spirits (Philip Clarke, personal communication).

management. Protection of country is seen as a mix of prevention of tourist vandalism or other abuses of the land: horses, boats, cars on the beach which erode the banks of the creeks and make the salt-water resources scarce. But the museum rangers also need to protect main tribal areas, secret sites, burial grounds, carved stones, places of spirit related to the reproduction of species: '*gumbali gumbali* (place of spirit), *Bugarrigarra* (Dreaming). Sometimes they dig it [the ground] and say special word, for snake, lizard, for *yarangal* (spirit) and there is plenty of them then.' Not doing this ritual 'cleaning' hampers or even blocks the renewal of that species, animal, or seafood, as can be already observed with the scarcity or even extinction of some species in the reefs and the bush. Destroying spirit places, according to a belief shared by many young people too, makes the local people, especially the ones spiritually connected with these places, feel sick.

The term *gumbali* was traditionally used by the Karajarri to designate people who have the same name, that is people who can exchange goods. In Broome Aboriginal English, *gumbali* means 'soul brother,' in the sense of pal, friend, people of the same generation that you grew up with. The relation between name, place, and spiritual brotherhood refers to an Aboriginal phenomenology which, in my experience, could be generalised to most of the desert and northwest groups: each person is the actualisation of virtual names (and often related songs) connected with places. Among the younger generations, where identification with community towns of residence tends to replace links with remote sacred places, specific sacred spots in town are still recognised, and some people still dream spiritual connections between these places and their children to be born.[15]

The existential threat to individual people from the destruction or harming of spirit-name places also applies to the wrongful manipulation of sacred objects which embody spiritual singularities: when stolen or put in the wrong place, they can threaten the community with sickness, conflict, or other disorders. If the wrong people see or touch them, not can only they themselves go mad, or even die, but their behavior also jeopardises the safety of members of the community, who can be affected in their body, their spirit, and through natural phenomena. This belief in the ancestral spiritual power common to places and sacred objects is held by many people in the community, who would rather not see the storage place be located next to where people gather and work, and even prefer not

---

[15] Glowczewski (1998b, 2004), and also last chapter.

to talk about it, for fear of unknown consequences. It is constantly stressed that the centre has to be controlled by people – elders and ritual custodians – who can protect the others from the dangerous powers involved in dealing with traditional culture.

Who Should be the Main People Involved with the Aboriginal Culture Centre?

The survey consensus gave the first voice to traditional elders (80), then people with language and other cultural skills (71); less then a third of the people favoured representatives of Aboriginal organisations (38) or people with administrative and technical skills (36). Some expressed the necessity to have representatives of each language group and community (23) and that Yawuru or Djugun should be 'first,' because they are the traditional owners of Broome (10).

The issue of who should be the main deciders is the key to the whole process of cultural reappropriation: how to write a constitution for the future incorporated body that will manage the centre. Is the centre to favour economic self-determination by becoming a place for promotion and retail, giving employment and income to Aboriginal people? Or is the centre to be a culture-sharing place without risk of 'loss' and lack of traditional control leading to social disorder and supernatural aggression, which can manifest themselves in many ways, such as a cyclone? In that dilemma, many people trusted their elders as the only ones able to protect the whole environment by protecting a culture through the circulation of rituals and sacred objects over hundreds of kilometers in the ways they had learned from their forefathers.

A year after the survey was completed, the vision of the Bugarrigarra Nyurdany Culture Centre was summarised in a conference on 'Planning Cultural and Interpretive Centres in the Kimberley' by the coordinator, granddaughter of the deceased Yawuru elder, custodian of the Broome initiations and secret cult mentioned above (Tarran 1997: 25):

- To facilitate the preservation, continuation and management of Aboriginal Law and Culture under the direction of the Old People with the strategic inclusion of Aboriginal Youth.
- To pursue sustainable economic independence through the development of employment, training and business opportunities within a supportive cultural and tourism industry environment.
- To provide appropriate cultural spaces and infrastructure support.

The notion of 'appropriate' is very sensitive in the Aboriginal context. For instance, the fact that the possible repatriation of ancient objects in a local Aboriginal culture centre and museum will give access, in terms of storage and maintenance, to other people than the traditional elders is a constant worry. At this level, even the photographic representation of such objects is considered to be inappropriate. Images, like the secret words that designate them, are believed to carry some of the power embodied in these objects. The image has this power precisely because the traditional painting of specific signs on the body, the ground, or sacred objects was aimed, like the songs, at 'nurturing' the medium. In the end such objects, which physically embody the power of the signs, *are* the culture because they are identified with the people. The whole problem of reviving the culture is to find a way of protecting these objects while allowing them to travel in the proper way, that is to stay a live sharing medium.

The Virtual Circulation of Non-Alienable Objects: Giving-Without-Losing

I used the example of northwest and Central Australia to show that, in the case of a traditional model in which cultural differences were produced by the circulation of inalienable objects and travelling rites, the question of the cultural repatriation of these objects and the accompanying knowledge to a sedentary space such as a culture centre raises political, economic, spiritual and ethical questions which challenge Western models of property. The unsuitability of the Western notion of property has also been noted in the case of Native American culture:

> The most important difference between cultural property and inalienable possessions has to do with the distinction between property and possessions ... possessions are always implicated in systems of exchange ... [the] concept of inalienable possessions provides a more inclusive and potentially more effective avenue for arriving at resolution of cultural property disputes. (Welsh 1997: 17)

We have seen that it is in the discrepancy between cultural property and inalienable possessions that the problem of restitution, not only of Australian sacred objects but of Aboriginal intellectual knowledge as well, resides. If the sacred objects which circulate between groups through rituals are inalienable, then the knowledge that goes with these rituals, in the form of stories, songs, paintings and dances, is also inalienable, as are the sacred places which, for Aboriginal people, materialise this knowledge just as the sacred objects do: they are more than a representation, they are the living manifestation of this knowledge.

One Aboriginal myth from the northern coast, in Arnhem Land, tells the story of the Djanggawul, two ancestral sisters who, after the men stole their bags and certain sacred objects, said: 'We know everything. We have really lost nothing, for we remember it all, and we can let them have that small part. For aren't we still sacred, even if we have lost the bags? Haven't we still our uteri?' (Berndt [1952] 1983: 58). The reproductive organ mentioned here is also symbolised by the mats produced by women in the north for use as pubic tassels. In an earlier article, I showed that the circulation of hairstrings which are used, among other things, to make pubic tassels, position desert women as agents of social reproduction in a way similar to that analysed by Annette Weiner (1976) for the production and circulation of mats by women in Samoa and the Trobriand Islands:

> ... hairstring transmission between men occurs through women as the sisters. This transmission is reciprocal between brothers-in-law to symbolize compensating or attaching sisters with the brother or the husband. A woman shares with her brothers the ownership of the patriclan territory and at the same time she is a ritual manager of her husband's sister's territorial ceremonies ... Hairstring circulation thus symbolizes alliances and economic exchanges (access to another person's territorial resources), affirms a certain dependence of men on women, and confirms women's responsibility not only as land owners or managers but also as producers of the value (their string made from their hair) which incarnates the ritual management relations. (Glowczewski 1983a: 238)

Ten years later, Annette Weiner, in her book *Inalienable Possessions: The Paradox of Keeping-While-Giving* (1992), referred to my analysis of Warlpiri hairstrings with respect to other work on Australian desert groups (Bell 1983; Dussart 1988–1989; Myers 1986):

> ... these recent data on women's controlling interests in the circulation of hairstrings, rope, threads, and cloth show how essential such possessions are to men as well as women and how these possessions constitute social identities as well as rights to territorial associations. Clearly, Aboriginal women had (and in some cases, still have) access to sacred objects that, infused with potency, have significant exchange value. Whether or not some of these possessions take on absolute value and become inalienable cannot be discerned from the available data. (Weiner 1992: 112)

Since my 1983 article, I have gathered new material on hairstrings, notably a myth telling how the Digging Stick women (*Kana*) wanted to acquire headbands and *makarra* ('womb') rope made by an ancestor from the hair of men in order to seduce them, and so agreed to give men their knowledge of initiations and hunting.[16] Like the women of Arnhem Land, the Warlpiri women said that they had 'lost' nothing by agreeing to this gift-exchange. In the Owl conflict-resolution ceremony – the same one the Warlpiri gave the northwest groups – men dance around with hairstrings and stop in front of the mothers of potential wives, who take these strings: mothers used them to make pubic tassels, which they wore before passing them on to their daughters when they were old enough to marry the giver of the hairstring (Glowczewski, 1991: 209). It is as though the hairstrings constantly bound up descent with alliance through a circulation of substances that were embodied and transmitted in these exchanges. Made from the hair of men or women, by men or women, hairstrings circulate between the genders, who transform them in their own way.

The hairstring pubic belt of a boy who was to be circumcised could be sent in his stead to invite distant groups – sometimes from different language groups – to participate in his initiation. In former times an initiand accompanied by his guardians could spend several months travelling hundreds of kilometers to rally various allies to his initiation. Today all kinds of vehicles, even aircraft, add many more kilometers to these initiation circuits. Peterson (2000) reports that, in 1994, a boy from a Western Desert group travelled 2,250 kilometers to the north, as far as the Lajamanu Warlpiri, before returning in a ritual convoy totaling some 600 travellers upon arrival. Novice's travels are accompanied by transfers of ritual objects, slabs and hairstrings, as well as marriage promises, the circumciser often being obliged to promise the novice one of his daughters. Similar convoys travel the east/west axis linking the Central and Western deserts to the Kimberley groups, as far as Broome. Interestingly, on this coast, boys and girls of marriageable age used to receive a hairstring belt garnished with a large pearl-shell. Once this shell, inscribed with Dreaming signs, was transmitted to the desert groups, it became a sacred object reserved for initiated men, especially rain-makers.

Desert men use hairstrings to make string crosses; these highly sacred objects are allowed to be seen by women only in exceptional

---

[16] Glowczewski (1991, 1991b); see Chapter 3 this book.

circumstances. In the northwest, wool has replaced string for the manufacture of these crosses which, here, are presented to women as ritual gifts. In desert groups, the 'womb' hairstring is extremely sacred for women; it is strung between the two meter-high sacred sticks they 'plug into' the ground; this ritual device is believed to actualise the Dreaming space-time for the duration of the ritual. Men and women alike use hairstrings and rope to wrap other sacred objects, especially wood or stone slabs. Women also use them therapeutically and at times of mourning or initiation: they rub women or men, girls or boys with them in order to infuse them with a power or to extract something from them. The purpose of touching a person with the strings seems to be the same as with the slabs. Something of the power of the Dreaming and the singular identity of all those who have ever touched these objects has become consubstantial with them in the course of the different handlings which bind together all differences: genders, kin, affines, exchangers from various language groups.

Summing up I would say, in answer to Annette Weiner, that hairstrings are alienable when they are given in payment for a ritual service, for example, when the temporary custodians of a slab return it to the original owners; but they become inalienable once they have been used in a sacred ritual function by either sex: to make ritual string crosses, to wrap up sacred objects or to rub a sick person, novice or someone in mourning. Then they become sacred objects. All circulations of men, women, objects and rites, which sometimes circulate together, sometimes one instead of another, seem to operate according to the same logic of giving-without-losing, consistent with giving to make what one gives desirable. A logic of desire imbedded in a relation of power, for it is when one succeeds in obliging the other to accept a gift that one can claim to be the strongest (Glowczewski 1991: 288). This explains the complex negotiations which lead groups to mutually impose the – temporary – adoption of each other's inalienable riches: sacred objects, rites, young people for initiation and marriage.

The idea of giving-without-losing, found in all Aboriginal ritual circulations, is in its own way like the logic of certain software designers who argue for the free circulation of their product as opposed to the principle of intellectual copyright, which benefits only the big monopolies. In what they humorously call 'copyleft,' which consists in allowing copies to be made of a program while acknowledging the creator's origin, they see a better means of controlling their creations than in the present application of the copyright laws, which transfer the original author's rights to whoever buys the product for the purpose of commercialisation. As Stephenson suggests (1994), there is certainly a parallel to be explored with Indigenous people's claims to their inalienable possessions. Such a parallel would also evoke the similarity between the non-linear synchronous nature and the hyperlinks of the Web and the Internet with the linked-up thinking and the cognitive networks of a certain kind of mythic thought.

I would like to add here that myth does not seem to me to oppose history in the way Kolig (2000) opposes the cognitive perception of the desert groups – as mythic and synchronic – to that of the Aboriginal peoples of the northwest – as historic, diachronic and post-colonial. We have seen that, over and beyond their cultural, social and geographical differences, Aboriginal groups of the two regions exchange cults which they readapt to suit themselves while reproducing local differences that go beyond simple dualism. Although it is true that north-western Aboriginal groups felt the effects of colonisation long before the desert groups did, it remains that the circulation of objects and songs as well as kinship systems between the two regions pre-dates colonisation. It is this ritualised circulation of tangible and intangible artifacts back and forth on linear journeys stretching across time which enables mythic thinking to be reproduced in the form of a living network: mythic thinking manufactures transformations and connections which singularise and reposition anchor points, sacred places, in a continually evolving structure of narrative and performance. Compared with this logic, the merely encompassing West is constantly threatening to disauthenticate those who create these anchor points. Hence the urgent need for museums, and anthropologists, not to go on 'alienating these cultures' by alienating their objects, but instead to recognise their inalienability by authenticating their creators rather than their acquirers.

9

Lines and Criss-Crossings:
Hyperlinks in Australian Indigenous Narratives

Since the 1980s, Indigenous peoples of Australia have extended their local tools of expression to global networks: exhibitions, festivals, press, radio, documentaries, short dramas, feature films and websites.[1] Many deplore the abuses of the art market which, despite the stunning success of Aboriginal paintings, still seems to benefit economically the distributors more than the artists, whose lifestyle is often subject to the miserable conditions of the Fourth World. In the era of information technology, one key to the survival of Indigenous cultures is to find ways to control the circulation and the staging of the products of Indigenous creativity in old and new media, as well as these cultures' history and current affairs.[2] In relation to such an Indigenous empowerment, the responsibility of anthropologists and other researchers is critical. Restitution of our research involves not just the return of data collected, but a 'reinterpretation' of this data in such a way that it can be used for learning, transmission and pleasure through aesthetics or entertainment, as well as for spiritual fulfilment, in a critical and ethical process. The issue of an ethical approach to pleasure does not imply a religious or moral order, but rather a constant re-evaluation of how each image or representation of any contemporary culture (Indigenous, musical, professional,

---

[1] This paper was first published in the journal *Media Internatonal Australia (MIA)* 116, August 2005, special issue on *Digital Anthropology* edited by Hart Cohen and Juan F. Salazar; it results from presentations made in 2003 at the AAA conference in Chicago and at the MIT in Boston. Special thanks to the editors for checking the author's translation and to Drew Burk for rereading the section 'Thinking in networks' which is extracted from the introduction of *Rêves en colère* (Glowczewski 2004). All my gratitude to Rosita Henry for comments on this paper and to the School of Social Sciences at James Cook University in Townsville where this paper was written.

[2] Langton (1993, 2001, 2018); Marcia Langton was the first Aboriginal Professor of Anthropology and held the Foundation Chair in Australian Indigenous Studies at the University of Melbourne in the Faculty of Medicine. She co-edited a book and film series called *First Australians* (see Perkins et al. 2009).

digital, etc.) impacts on social justice, equity, tolerance and freedom (Trend 2001). I present here two attempts of anthropological restitution developed with Aboriginal peoples for a mixed audience. The first is a CD-ROM focused on one Central Australian community, while the second is an interactive DVD film juxtaposing four regions of Australia. I developed both projects to explore and enhance the cultural foundations of the reticular way many Indigenous people in Australia map their knowledge and experience of the world in a geographical virtual web of narratives, images and performances. I conclude by discussing a number of issues relating to multiplayer online serious games.

Thinking in Networks

When I first lived among Desert Aboriginal people from Lajamanu, I was struck by the strange confluence between their traditional way of thinking and the development of artificial intelligence: this interface of ideas made me title a 1983 article 'Tribes of the Cybernetic Dream'. The Aboriginal people's perception of memory as a virtual space-time, and the way they project knowledge on a geographical network, both physical and imaginary, was in fact going to echo with the network and hyperlink programs of the first computers still stammering in those early days. The application of reticular thinking has universally expanded through the development of the Internet. It is probably not a coincidence that the contemporary art market has seized upon the explosion of Aboriginal artistic forms that precisely transpose trails weaved into networks. This phenomenon illustrates a universal connection between forms and ideas, even though this connection is not expressed by those who are seduced by such works of art. The surrounding environment allows us, Westerners, to indeed 'look at' and 'hear' cultural differnces in a very different way than a century ago. This is also one of the reasons for the current attraction of world music, and especially the didjeridu, the ancestral instrument invented by Aboriginal people, and which, for over a decade now, has come to be played by thousands of worldwide fans who are building their own sites on the Internet.

Aboriginal people also have their own websites. They use them to promote their art, their music and dance tours, or the organisation of festivals and bush trails for adventurous tourists. They also teach in various languages and share files online about their political and legal matters. Such a development was possible because Australia has equipped its schools with computers and is funding a certain number of Indigenous organisations to install such technology and provide training in its use. Nevertheless, a lot of Aboriginal people still live in Fourth World conditions and have no access to these services. As expressed by Indigenous people of the whole world, it is essential to facilitate the usage of such means of communication which seem able to facilitate, in their own way, the circulation of cultural knowledge systems. In order to be transmitted, they have always relied on oral and visual performances as well as the active practice of survival in the environment. Such transmission is often threatened nowdays by the imposing of new lifestyles dominated by writing, television and passive consumption. It is not enough to record, stock and put audio-visual data online or on digital media so that it becomes indeed a source of information and learning about a given culture. Databases and Internet sites presuppose to construct cognitive maps which would respect the way the different learning media in these societies relate with each other and also the various levels of knowledge and expertise, some of which must remain secret. It is possible to link everything a priori but, to understand the links that produce a meaning in a given social and cultural logic, it is necessary to know the rules of association that constitute the philosophy, the ethics and the priorities of survival for suc or such a group.

During the past few decades of audio-visual expansion and quasi-instantaneous circulations of information, we have seen a paradigm shift in particular in relation to the functioning of memory, or the relation between matter and spirit, actual and virtual. Such a shift forces us to consider differently what the so-called 'savage' or 'primitive' populations express about their relation to the world. Take, for instance, the debate surrounding whether or not pre-contact Australian peoples were ignorant of the consequences of sexual intercourse, under the pretext that they insisted on the necessity of the manifestation of a 'spirit-child' for the woman to be pregnant. The academic a priori opposing sperm to spirit comes under the 'dreads' of the Christian immaculate conception which cannot reconcile the body and the mind. The immaculate conception refers to the mandatory Catholic dogma (1854) stating that Mary was born free of 'original sin', and the belief that she was a virgin when Jesus was born – that is, that there was no sexual intercourse necessary for conception. The 'Virgin Mary' paradigm has informed, often unconsciously, a Western anthropological bias which continues to oppose the spirit realm and the physical one, while many Indigenous cultures combine the two. Well, for the Aboriginal people, while it's obvious that something of the man and something of the woman is needed to make a child, that alone is not enough: a virtuality of life must also make itself manifest, a desire to live which often announces itself in a dream, thus 'catching' the mother or the father. The Warlpiri of the central desert still say today that to catch their future parents, the spirits of the children wishing to be born live a virtual existence in the land and use a dream propeller to actualise their birth. Spirit-children are *ngampurrpa*, 'desirous' of life, agents in their becoming or coming into being as humans. This Warlpiri statement is enlightening and maybe appropriate for people who today fight with sterility. Since psychoanalysis has made us grow accustomed to accepting the power of the unconscious over the body, we have everything to learn from the theories of dream and the relation between matter and spirit among Aboriginal peoples. Aboriginal cosmologies can inform psychoanalytic theory and medicine in showing, for instance, more holistic ways to address sterility as well as other bodily or mental disorders.[3]

Dreaming Knowledge: Rhythm, Links and Memory

I used to have a 16 mm Pathe Webo camera – an antique today – with three turning lenses and a magazine for three-minute reels. It was mechanical, so you could only shoot 30 seconds at a time and then you had to rewind the tension spring with a handle to shoot again. I did not have a problem with that because, before I came to Australia, I made experimental films and was only interested in recording very short sequences to produce flickering effects between the information recorded on each still frame. Subsequently I brought my films to Lajamanu in 1979. After seeing a film presenting a fast flickering between different generations of my family photographed in different places in Poland and France, some old people said: 'Good one, that's your family, that's your country ...'. So, I filmed different Warlpiri women's rituals in a similar style and, after a month of fieldwork, I sent the footage to Sydney, where Ian Dunlop generously organised for it to be processed and sent back to me. I organised a screening with the Baptist mission projector and it created an uproar: 'Why do you make us look silly!', said the women. The film showed women dancing at different rhythms, with superimpositions,

---

[3] See Chapter 1 of this book.

multiple focal views of the landscape, sometimes upside down, an attempt to 'translate' the condensation effect of dreaming. I promised to film differently and then recorded the women's rituals in a more conventional way.

Image speed has considerably increased in film since the 1980s and editing convention through the production of music clips has radically changed the audience's cognitive relationship to film everywhere in the world. Video clips, for instance, use flickering effects to suggest different layers of subjectivity and to deconstruct space and time at imaginary levels. Nevertheless, beyond the convention of the tempo of film rhythm remains a question: what is the 'rationale' for this rhythm and the legitimacy to connect two images?

For the Warlpiri, rhythm conveys as much valuable information as speech or dance movement. It is culturally meaningful: one cannot just 'play' with it. Similarly, connections produce meaning so you cannot edit two images together randomly. This was my first lesson of the complexity of an Indigenous system of knowledge which conveys a whole field of meanings and codes that are not only culturally relevant but that teach us about the effect of rhythm (produced by a linear repetition) and connections (organised in criss-crossing trails). Such Indigenous tempo codes and cultural hermeneutics are not just useful for interpreting dance or guiding well-being; they are also keys to memory and survival.

For example, tracks give you both space and time information. If the footprint of an animal is a day old, you will need to evaluate whether it is worth tracking, but if the print is fresh you have the choice of taking your time or moving on to get it fast before it hides. Conception and experience of time and space in the desert are relative, almost in a non-Euclidian way. For example, a pathway linking three waterholes spread over 100 kilometres is relatively longer than another 100-kilometre pathway crossing a country with no waterholes. This relativity comes from the speed at which you need to travel at in order to survive. You need to go fast to reach the next waterhole before being too thirsty, but you can slow down or stop if there is water on the way.

So, when desert Aboriginal people sing a pathway known for its lack of water, they can sing it 'fast forward' in a ritual setting, as one way of learning how to survive in that land. People continued to perform that kind of interpretation and knowledge transmission through ritual even when they were located in government-run reserves. They continued to travel using rituals, reproducing an audio, visual and mental representation of the landscape. Thanks to these kinds of performances, embedded in a procedural and kinaesthetic memory, once the desert people moved back to their land to settle outstations, they were able to find their way.

In that sense, survival knowledge is not encyclopaedic but reticular. Data that we record from people's experiences are snapshots seen through the eye of the person who describes those experiences. It can never be a general description of a society, even if the society is holistic, because the holistic approach – accessing the whole from any part – is always related to singular places. It is like having hundreds of different eyeglasses that you change according to where you stand. Seeing the reality from this point of view is going to be different from what would be seen from another one, but you need these two, or three, or many 'points of view' to make alliances, to perform a ritual, to regenerate the society. This reticular thinking, which evokes the *rhizome* of Deleuze and Guattari, is also experienced in navigation on the World Wide Web when users chat, meet, create and link up their sites. Reticular thinking seems to articulate the Aboriginal logic of myth, kinship and land ownership, even when it is woven through other structures and topologies (Benterrack et al. 1984; Rose 1992; Rumsey 2001; Glowczewski 2004).[4] Thousands of stories and songlines stage separate entities (a Dreaming, an ancestor, a group, a person, an animal, a plant), but they criss-cross one another and the meeting points produce singularities. They can be sacred places, encounters with conflict, or alliance and the emergence of new meanings. They can be new manifestations like a spirit-child being born into a child, or a new song or painting being dreamt for that place. Non-linear or reticular thinking mostly stresses the fact that there is no centrality to the whole, but a multipolar view from each recomposed network within each singularity – for example, a person, a place, a Dreaming – allowing the emergence of meanings and performances, encounters, creations as new, original, autonomous flows.

Returning Data: Storylines and Linking Sites

Back in Lajamanu in 1984, I opted for a still camera and an analogue tape recorder. Out of this data, 500 slides and three hours of sound in Warlpiri were selected for a digital project of 'restitution' that

[4] See also Chapter 3, this volume (and note 1 of Chapter 3).

Lines and Criss-Crossings

I developed ten years later. Restitution, for an anthropologist, is not exactly the same as repatriation. When people practise their ceremonies, their dances, their songs, they don't need them 'back'. What they need is the knowledge attached to them, which many see as 'stolen' by scientists because their expression is recorded on a material medium (paper, tape, film). Anthropologists face that everywhere in the world. What are they really taking away? They are taking away the right to speak in the name of the people from whom they received the knowledge. What should be returned? Not the content as such but how it is expressed: 'I've been there, I will tell you how they live, what they do, who they are.' People we 'study' ask us: 'What are you saying about us? Give it back, because we want to know the impact it has.' It is a legitimate claim for any group, any individual, but in the case of Indigenous people this claim is a political tool for empowerment.

To return my research to the Warlpiri, I decided in 1995 to design a multimedia tool linking images of rituals and landscape, photos of acrylic paintings, and sound recordings of myths and songs. The original structure was developed in HTML, but later we converted it to Macromedia. The idea was to constitute a sort of 'mind-map' – what I call a cognitive map – that would give an insight into how elements of knowledge connect with each other in the learning process of the Warlpiri themselves. My conviction was that to invite the users to link images, dances and songs with places, storylines and trails in the way the Warlpiri do should help anybody to understand how these connections worked as a meaningful network: hyperlinks could ideally suggest how to criss-cross storylines and layers of meaning.

I drew a schematic map with 50 toponyms and superimposed 14 ways of linking some of these sites according to Dreaming stories I had recorded. Thus 14 Dreaming lines would show, but never at the same time. This virtual map – made of 14 layers of connections – became the interactive gateway to some 14 hours of audio-visual data. The user can click on any of the sites or lines to enter into the relevant constellation of Dreamings and explore them from the point of view of hundreds of proposed hyperlinks, some opening as small windows and others taking you on new pathways.

The map is an invisible web, as the criss-crossings between the lines do not show simultaneously. The links are only discovered when the narrative of a storyline which indicates links to other pathways is unfolded. In other words, each line is autonomous and each crossing or hyperlink requires the user's interaction. The *Dream Trackers*

CD-ROM (Glowczewski 2000) includes a short morphing, a photo of a sacred hill, Kurlungalinpa in the Tanami Desert, and turns into a Dreaming painting of that place by Warlpiri artist Margaret Nungarrayi Martin. The painting is showing the same place as a network of lines connecting that sacred site to five other places of the same songline, Ngarrka or 'Initiated Men'. The Warlpiri artist and other custodians of other Dreamings loved the idea that the animation conveyed the 'same' identity and power of transformation of one image into another. They were pleased because it was the right painting for the right place. A morphing with a painting of another place would not have worked. The multimedia reticular script writing has allowed me first to test with the elders (who do not read and write) whether the audio-visual links I had designed were appropriate and then to invite the users themselves to link the elements gathered through their exploration.

To respect the Warlpiri system of meaningful connections, every Warlpiri word leads to other Warlpiri concepts, every painting links to songs and stories, every artist links to other artists of the same Dreaming, and certain places link to other places. When the user travels on one storyline and arrives at a site where the heroes of one Dreaming line meet heroes of another Dreaming line, they can change the pathway by clicking on the name of the place. Multimedia allows the experience of reticular travelling as a learning process. Many things can be connected, but it should be done in such a way that every time the cultural reason for that connection is learned. Songs, dances, stories and paintings all relate to places, so the *Yapa* or *Dream Trackers* CD-ROM became a Warlpiri mind-map inviting us – as well as the young people in the Lajamanu school – to explore some of these connections. We also had to develop a device to be able to hide images showing the recently deceased and to make it adaptable over time. As pointed out by Warlpiri artist Jimmy Jampijinpa Robertson: 'The *Yapa* CD-ROM brings everybody to the mind.'[5]

Yapa, meaning Aboriginal, Indigenous people in Warlpiri (as opposed to *kardiya*, 'non-Indigenous') was the working title of this multimedia restitution process. UNESCO Publishing, after signing a partnership of distribution and intellectual copyright with the Lajamanu Art Centre, Warnayaka, asked for a more descriptive

---

[5] See Glowczewski (2001), paper reproduced in *Desert Dreamers* (Glowczewski [1989] 2016). Special thanks to all the Lajamanu artists and storytellers who participated in the *Dream Trackers* CD-ROM (1995–2000).

title. I chose *Dream Trackers* because tracking is really the core of most Aboriginal philosophy. A place marked by a track does not mean that the track is just a metaphor: it is an access to the whole, a key to investigate past, present and future actions. A track is like the imprint for a prototype – from that track you can reconstitute the performance. The track is not just a fixed moment in time, it is the trace left by something that is moving, dancing or walking – an essential dynamism in Aboriginal culture. Often the interpretation of Aboriginal art is limited because it is reduced to the semiotic view of the signs, the content and the form. It misses what is most important: the trace as the proof of the passage of something else, somewhere else. The virtual world of mythology and ritual is established in such traces. The proof of that physical track relates to all the narratives you can build out of it, which express the real relations of people to the land.

Learning through Playing with an Interactive Fiction

To try to reach further into the narrative flavour of Aboriginal storytelling and its multidimensional potential for multiple connections, I wanted to construct an interactive DVD, a film drama whose full display would require the viewer to play a series of games connected to different episodes. Each of these drama segments was to invite the user to explore an Aboriginal community from a different region of Australia in terms of landscape, art, culture and language, colonial history and the current situation. I spent weeks drawing various mind-maps to test the contents and links appropriate for the narrative of the film. The first draft was very complex, designed like a road movie criss-crossing all of Australia with built-in variations taking the user of the DVD to different places and events in the storyline. The story was constructed like a network of virtual connections which would actualise themselves according to the way the player would play a game. For instance, if the users scored well in relation to the survival quest involving recognition of animals, plants, seasons and mapping, they would be invited to explore the desert. But if the score was better in relation to the museum quest, involving identification of local art, cultural artefacts and history of urban art, the user would be invited to explore another region. If you succeeded in identifying different forms of dancing, singing and language, you were invited to go to Arnhem Land, and so on. There were also different options offered according to the choice of gender as a player.

As these various options were taking into account the user performance and learning process through games; they would require the writing of a complex series of dramas in such a way that the different localised episodes could be edited in a different order without losing the continuity of the stories and their relevant meaning.

The Aboriginal Dreaming songlines can be experienced in any given performance with similar adaptation to context. For example, segments of stories are omitted when a person dies, sometimes the same episode is repeated in two different places or more, and at other times the order of action is reversed, like a loop, even though there often is a chronology and an evolution in the characters who are the heroes of the songline: Snake or Wallaby ancestors, Rain or Plum people. The question was how to represent both human and Dreaming agents? The use of animation can unfold stories based on today's reality, but also on some aspects of the Dreaming world. Animation can integrate such elements in the learning process of a game – for instance, the help of totemic animals or the dealing with spiritual forces manifested through wind, fire and rain. But producing such a project was (and still is) incredibly expensive, especially if a team of Aboriginal people comprising experts of the different domains (art, music, dance, survival, kinship) was to be involved on location.

I thought at the time that filming with actors might be a better option than an animated film. We formed a small team contributing voluntarily to the project over three years. We selected five regions – the Western Desert, Eastern Arnhem Land, Gariwerd Park in Victoria, the city of Perth in Western Australia, and Laura in Cape York – and five topics – art, festivals, culture centres, family history and bush survival. My husband, Aboriginal film-maker and singer-composer Wayne Jowandi Barker, wrote a one-hour drama script in 2000 that intertwined the five regions and the topics. A young woman from Perth searches for the family of her mother, who was taken away as a victim of the stolen generation. She meets a Yolngu dancer from Arnhem Land at the Gariwerd culture centre. The two young people follow a different quest but they both travel through Australia and meet again in other places: a museum in Perth, the Garma festival in his home country and at the Balgo desert community, where the young woman finds her family.

The film was conceived as five episodes, each of ten minutes, which required the viewer to achieve a task in order to be able to continue to view the story. This option seemed the easiest for the user as it allowed understanding of the complexities of Aboriginal history and the cultural and personal dilemma by following one storyline. We went to Arnhem Land with a small digital camera and brought back statements from a Yolngu family from Bawaka that made us modify the storyline so as to emphasise spiritual presence as an agency animating the characters (Barker and Glowczewski 2002). A further five educational game proposals were written as interactive tools connecting the film storyline. The involvement of the user in theses games aimed at helping the main two actors of the drama to learn how to identify art, dance, music and cultural issues, family history archives and language groups, landscapes and their resources. The first game, designed by Laurent Dousset (2000–2005),[6] an anthropologist and webmaster with a long experience of the Western Desert people and kinship analysis, consisted of learning how to search family history archives to identify a given language group and kinship system. The second game, developed by John Stanton, Director of the Berndt Museum of Anthropology in Perth, invited the player to organise an Aboriginal exhibition, either by choosing from a series of topics or by focusing on one of the five regions and their people. The third game, created by Jessica De Largy Healy (2004), who was then a student in anthropology working with the Aboriginal Brambuk Cultural Centre of the Gariwerd National Park, explored the different functions of a culture centre, from a simple safe-keeping place to a big heritage and tourist precinct. The fourth game was proposed by Fred Viesner, who did fieldwork with the Anangu people for his doctorate; its aim was to introduce the user to some Indigenous systems of knowledge in relation to bush survival: tracking for hunting, identifying edible or medicine plants, facing drought but also dealing with the current economy related to mining, protection of places, management of outstations or art centres. Rosita Henry (2000), an anthropologist who has studied the Laura dance festival process for over 20 years, suggested a virtual tour of different types of cultural festivals for the last game, introducing the viewer to ethical protocols to be respected by performers and audiences.

I approached Australian and French funding agencies – in film, multimedia, science and culture – in vain: that 'interactive DVD thing' we wanted to collectively create was neither a film, nor a

---

[6] Dousset developed a kinship data base (2000–2005), see also Dousset (2011a, 2011b), and the biography of Lizzie Marrkilyi Ellis (Ellis 2016) that he edited.

game nor a database, so there was no funding corresponding to its requirements.

A small grant was eventually released by my institution in Paris, the CNRS (National Centre for Scientific Research) and the Musée du quai Branly to do a one-hour demo to showcase an interactive cultural film project. As we could not afford to shoot a new film, we used footage previously recorded by Wayne Jowandi Barker for other projects. Together we edited a 10-minute film organised in 16 sections, simulating long journeys across four regions of Australia: the Dampier Peninsula, Kimberley Plateau, Tanami Desert and Northeast Arnhem Land. There was an emphasis on the relation between different landscapes, as well as the relevant art, dance and singing. I designed a new interactive script allowing the viewer to select at any time an interactive map from which other short films could be screened with Aboriginal testimonies in relation to four themes: art, storytelling, survival and dance. This 50-minute demo, called *Quest in Aboriginal Land*, was awarded and presented in many places, but a lack of further funding prevented the completion of the original project.[7]

Curiously, even though the DVD medium has taken over the video market, there are very few interactive documentaries available on DVD. Only big production companies and TV channels can afford to pay the costs of such digital productions, including the copyright payments for distribution. This financial limitation is very damaging to the future of visual anthropology and ethnographic films because interactive DVD is the perfect format for documentation and analysis. It allows one to include on the same medium different edited versions, of different lengths, with or without a soundtrack, a comment, a subtitle in one or several languages, including thousands of pages of

---

[7] Special thanks to Jowandi Wayne Barker, Jessica De Largy Healy, Laurent Dousset, Rosita Henry, John Stanton and Fred Viesner, the Yolngu people from Bawaka and the Garma Festival who contributed to the *Quest in Aboriginal Land* DVD project (2000–2002) and to Julien Stiegler for designing the interactive animation. It was awarded as 'Best illustration of science for a wide audience' at the Festival of Researcher Film (Nancy, 2003), displayed in a loop on two huge floating screens as part of the Aboriginal art exhibition Rêves Arc-en-Ciel at the National Museum of Natural History (Lyon, 2004), and the International Union of Anthropologists Conference in Florence, 2003. The film was included on the DVD accompanying the issue of MIA where this paper was first published in 2005, and is also online but without the interactivity: https://archive.org/details/QuestInAboriginalLand

written files, photo displays, and even Internet links for further information or updates. Furthermore, it can offer cultural teaching based on simulation games to construct small events and evolving contexts based on archaeology, mythology, history or contemporary life.

Multiplayer Role Games

3D quest games on CD-ROM or DVD and multiplayer role games on the Internet have evolved considerably, both in scope and in terms of copyright. Apart from the software owners who sell licence rights or subscriptions online, players who create their own tools as part and parcel of playing such games are today recognised copyright owners of their digital creations and can sell – sometimes for an incredible amount of money – such virtual artefacts. Millions of fantasy characters and guiding hybrid creatures occupy the Internet today, with imaginary weapons and various magic tricks. Many inventors take inspiration from legends and myths, mixing all periods and regions. Some games – like *Civilization* – are based on several historical figures who provide some historical strategies as options in the playing of the game aiming at 'developing' civilisation in such a way that cities expand with enough food, money and entertainment. Such a model is very much based on an evolutionary idea of this virtual world which, in a reductive fashion, simply mixes different periods of history but very little cultural diversity. So far, the Indigenous people of Australia have not been used as an example of a digital 'civilisation'. But the trend to develop so-called 'serious' games is growing.

In 2002, I received an email from an African-American student who, as part of his degree with the MIT Comparative Media Studies Department, wanted to develop an Internet multiplayer game based on his perception of the Dreaming in an Aboriginal community from Central Australia. He entitled his project *Dream Trackers* like my CD-ROM (Glowczewski 2000), from which he had drawn ideas and data along with data from another anthropologist (Meggitt 1962), and from a linguist and a Warlpiri storyteller (Cataldi and Rockman 1994). The student's main preoccupation was to develop a game that would prove that you could learn about a culture through a gaming approach. The players were to evolve into different stages of 'initiation' to learn about Aboriginal culture. The framework of the game was MMORPG (Massive Multiplayer Online Role-Playing Game) like *Dungeons and Dragons* or other quest-type games where hundreds to thousands of players can join online disguising their personas as avatars facing different trials, trading information and virtual tools among themselves. In his written presentation, the student acknowledged the colonial history of Indigenous people, the importance of ethics, the respect of secret knowledge, the balance of gender and the specificity of Aboriginal 'Dreaming culture'. But the script of the game itself, constructed around stages of initiation, included secret rituals that should not be talked about publicly. I wrote back with strong criticism in relation to the use of the different data and insisted that no game should be developed from this project without the negotiation of a signed partnership with the relevant Aboriginal people who held the intellectual copyright to the use of their cultural information and practices applied to the game. This ethical principle was accepted both by the student and his supervisor.[8]

It is possible that young Aboriginal people, as well as other users searching the Internet might enjoy playing with avatars that have to survive in the Central Australian cultural space of the Dreaming rather than in the suburban contemporary environment. But the question that needs to be asked relates to the image such a game would circulate about Australian Indigenous peoples. A digital venture in Central Australia has just started to develop an Internet game with young Aboriginal teenagers who came to attention for their creativity in retooling bikes from recycled waste. This sounds like a 'real' cultural survival game – to learn how some Aboriginal youngsters today survive and look for fun in their ancestral environment, completely criss-crossed by the global world.

Epilogue

The main question to address in a multimedia product or a learning game about a culture is what the users or players have to 'learn' about this culture. On the *Dream Trackers* CD-ROM, I proposed an experience of Indigenous reticular thinking through navigation on the Warlpiri web of criss-crossing Dreaming stories and songlines.

---

[8] Special thanks to Zachary Nataf who granted his permission to present here his MIT cultural game project (2002–2005). His scholarship was part of a funding package for the Games-to-Teach Project that Microsoft i-campus was sponsoring at MIT in exchange for prototypes to develop out of the proposed scripts of 15 students. The *Dream Trackers of the Dream Time Community* (2002–2004) game proposal was the only one in the area of cultural anthropology: www.educationarcade.org/ gtt/proto.html

Lines and Criss-Crossings

Figure 9.1 Nampijinpa and Napanangka document Warlpiri art produced at the Warnayaka Arts Centre, Lajamanu 2011 © B. G. 2011

Figure 9.2 Jungarrayi and Jupurrurla document the Warlpiri archive on www.odsas.net, Lajamanu 2012 © B.G. 2012

In the interactive *Quest in Aboriginal Land* DVD drama project, we tried to produce virtual conditions of drama, suspense, challenge and fun, for a motivated exploration of facts presented directly on the DVD or through proposed links to existing websites with Indigenous resources like the AIATSIS library, the Family History Project in Adelaide, the Native Title Unit, the DOCIP Indigenous Centre in Geneva, other NGOs and Aboriginal organisations. The idea of both projects was to encourage exploration so the users could understand how to negotiate existing knowledge using a reticular method. Non-linear or reticular thinking mostly stresses the fact that there is no centrality to the whole, but rather a multipolar view from each recomposed network within each singularity – a person, a place, a Dreaming – allowing the emergence of meanings and performances, encounters and creations as new original autonomous flows. Reticular or network thinking, I argue, is a very ancient Indigenous practice, but it gains today a striking actuality thanks to the fact that our so-called scientific perception of cognition, virtuality and social performance has changed through the use of new technologies.

PART IV
Micropolitics of Hope and De-Essentialisation

10
Myths of 'Superiority' and How to De-Essentialise Social and Historical Conflicts

Accusations of racism can mask an ontology of superiority in which the victims of racism are themselves accused of being racist.[1] This kind of reversal is found in many domains: anti-colonialist writers are accused of racism by people who identify with the colonial power, Indigenous people or migrants are accused of racism for laying claim to their history and culture. UNESCO may have proclaimed cultural diversity as a value, but in most social interactions it is not valued. Difference is either reduced to hierarchical models – such as dominant/dominated and primitive/civilised – or denied recognition in the name of universalism as opposed to cultural relativism. Lévi-Strauss, in his second text on race and culture written for UNESCO in 1971, was accused of racism for valuing cultural diversity. Accusations of racism are often generated by the perception the speakers have of their own origin as opposed to the perception they have of the origin of the people they accuse of racism. Perception of somebody's 'origins' is in this context a subjective response to various interactions where the word 'race' encompasses social, cultural, religious and historical relationships of power. On the 60th anniversary of UNESCO (16 November 2005) Lévi-Strauss stressed his concerns about some 'recent publications produced by biologists who attempt to give a new status to the notion of race'.[2] My aim here is to show that between universalism and cultural or genetic relativism, a third option is possible. It takes into account the interactions between the global molar economic and environmental logic of the planet and the multiplicity of micropolitics or cosmopolitics redefined and

---

[1] This unpublished paper was written for the international conference Racisms in the New World Order: Realities of Culture, Colour and Identity, Cairns Institute, James Cook University, Australia. Special thanks to Mariquian Ahouansou, Estelle Castro-Koshy and Stephanie Anderson for their valuable comments.

[2] For Stoczkowski (2006), the development of medicines produced as a result of genetic diseases observed in some ethnic communities has led some scholars to question the claim of science to be 'anti-racist' if it proceeds to address sickness defined genetically.

assembled by molecular existential territories based on cultural, social, genetic and gender subjectivations.

I will speak here mainly of the French situation but I will conclude with two issues drawn from the Indigenous Australian context. Both countries, in different ways, seem to deny their citizens the right to be different. Despite this, initiatives emanating from civil society promote innovative ways of envisioning a multidimensional society in which the recognition of differences and specific rights have their place at the same time as universal human rights are respected.

Racism Battles in France

In 2010 two French lecturers at the University of Hawaii boycotted the lecture of a famous Tahitian writer, Chantal Spitz, because they judged her to be 'racist'. This accusation was a misinterpretation of the author's anti-colonial stance – voiced in her writing as well as in public forums – and her critique of nuclear testing which had been imposed on the French Polynesian population in the 1960s, and only ended in 1996,[3] leaving a legacy of pollution and illness for many people, both in the local population and among French soldiers and workers from the nuclear plant. Spitz's novel *The Island of Shattered Dreams*[4] is the story of a French woman, an engineer, who comes to Tahiti to work on the tests, but falls in love with an Autonomist activist and is fully accepted into his Tahitian family. By labelling as 'racist' the author's criticism of French colonial and interventionist power, the French academics who boycotted her lecture were demonstrating their own 'reverse racism' based on two false correlations: first, they equated 'anti-colonial' with 'anti-French' and, second, they equated the French state with French people defined as a race. Such correlations are inappropriate since the French population is not homogeneous, either in metropolitan France itself, or in the overseas territories that remain part of France.

Confusion between racism and 'anti-colonialism' or the political criticism of a state in the name of Indigenous or other cultural rights is very common in France. But a growing number of people are sensitive to the abuses of French colonial history and denounce as

---

[3] See: http://www.francetnp2010.fr/spip.php?article57
[4] See review by Sharrad (2009): 'while its positive Tahitian aspect is at odds with the disastrous French intervention, the human associations of the former make the latter seem an unnatural travesty of civilized values'.

Myths of 'Superiority'

racist the celebrations by the state of active promoters of colonisation. For example, Jules Ferry, Minister for Education at the end of the nineteenth century, made laws establishing free education and secondary schooling for girls, promoting the principle of secularism in education, but he also stated, 'I repeat that there is a right for the superior races, because they have a duty. They have the duty to civilise the inferior races.'[5] This pronouncement on the supposed racial 'superiority' of the people who colonised other people is certainly racist. But was the celebration of Jules Ferry by new French president François Hollande after his election also racist? We need to recognise that racism *is* encouraged by commemorations of national heritage when the history of what is being commemorated is not contextualised through discussion in school programmes, museums, etc., that draws on the latest historical research. For instance, students and the French population in general should be taught that voices were raised in 1885 who opposed Jules Ferry's discourse on the 'Rights and Duties of Superior Races': Clemenceau for one, stood up as an elected member of the parliament to say: 'I do not understand why we here were not unanimous in leaping to our feet to protest vehemently against your words. No, there is no right of so-called superior nations over the inferior nations.'[6] Until recently the silence in French schools and the media about this kind of critical approach has perpetuated a decontextualised vision of colonial history over several generations. In 2004, the government passed a partisan law recommending that the 'benefits of colonisation' be taught in schools. However, a strong mobilisation of Black associations in France and a petition supported by historians succeeded in having the law overturned.[7]

The myth of racial 'superiority' was revived in France in 2012 when the then Minister of the Interior, Claude Guéant, during a conference convened by UNI, a right-wing student association, declared at the National Assembly that 'Contrary to what relativist ideology of the left says, for us, all civilisations are not of equal

---

[5] See: http://www.la1ere.fr/infos/elections-2012/polemique-sur-lhommage-a-jules-ferry_95663.html

[6] See also Le Cour Grandmaison 2009.

[7] At the end of that year, 2004, the government created the HALDE (Haute Autorité de Lutte contre les discriminations et pour l'Egalité), a High Authority to Fight Against Discriminations and for Equality: http://halde.defenseurdesdroits.fr/

worth (...) we have to protect our civilisation.'[8] There followed much reaction in the media and on various blogs. A group of four French anthropologists co-signed a text against the recuperation of Lévi Strauss and misuse of ethnology by the right, such as the claim of the philosopher, ex-Minister of Education, Luc Ferry, who asserted that same year (2012) that only a 'debilitating moral' would stop him from thinking that music of Mozart is 'infinitely deeper' then the 'flute' of people that Lévi-Strauss calls the 'savage societies'. The four anthropologists responded that Lévi-Strauss's fight was to 'constantly oppose the preconceived idea that cultures different from ours would be "inferior" or "primitive", because less ' civilised'. Against Ferry's ethnocentrism, they noted that one can prefer a style but music itself does not progress, it just has different complexities. They also quoted the then deputy of French Guiana, Christiane Taubira (since nominated Minister of Justice of the new 2012 government) who explained on the television channel LCP that 'the ministerial words which suggested an inequality between human cultures, come directly from the biological racism of XIXe century, such as popularised by Gobineau (1853–1855, *Essai sur l'inégalité des races humaines*, Belfond, Paris), and later applied in eugenics and racist policies which culminated with Nazi abominations'.[9] In saying 'we have to protect our civilisation', the Minister of the Interior, Claude Guéant, was identifying himself – and French or Western civilisation – as superior to what he defined as less worthy civilisations (see this chapter, note 8). His statement revealed his belief in an ethnocentric myth deriving from his own origin as French. Emeritus Professor Françoise Héritier, who has been involved as an anthropologist in actively denouncing all forms of violence against women, commented in an interview that by claiming an implicit hierarchy of civilisations against left-wing relativism, the French minister revealed himself as a 'relativist' who judges from the civilisation he culturally identifies with.[10] Claiming that a

---

[8] Regarding the French Minister's 'civilisation' polemic, see: https://www.lemonde.fr/election-presidentielle-2012/article/2012/02/05/claude-gueant-declenche-une-nouvelle-polemique_1639076_1471069.html; Giraud (2012) revealed that the Minister's discourse was written by his neo-conservative adviser.

[9] D. Casajus, S. D'Onofrio, C. Fortier and R. Meyran (2012): https://www.nouvelobs.com/rue89/rue89-nos-vies-connectees/20120210.RUE7799/mm-gueant-et-ferry-attention-au-detournement-de-l-ethnologie.html (accessed October 2018).

[10] See: http://www.lemonde.fr/politique/article/2012/02/11/francoise-heritier-m-gueant-est-relativiste_1642156_823448.html (accessed October 2018).

civilisation or a culture is better than another denies the fact that each culture and civilisation has explored the best and the worst of human endeavour. Furthermore, no civilisation or culture is a closed and fixed entity, each is also transformed through different interactions: 1) between the members of a particular culture who live in the country of origin, but also 2) between the members of that culture who live outside of it – as in diasporas spread across the world or the travelling representatives of the culture, artists, sports people, etc., 3) through interactions with members of other cultures who are citizens of the same nation and, finally, 4) through exchanges – or conflicts – with people from other nations.

People of different origins who ask for a collective recognition of their community's shared values in heritage and cultural practices are often accused in France of '*communautarisme*', understood as sectarianism, that is in a negative sense – different from the meaning and context of British or American theoreticians of communitarianism.[11] The French understanding of 'communitarism' reflects a fear of (and moral panic about) ethnic or religious communities viewed as fundamentalists and the ghettoisation of certain communities in impoverished suburbs.[12] This fear is based on a confusion between existing forms of extremism involving terrorist threats and the African origin of many French people who practise moderate Islam or some other or no religion, many of whom – but not all – live in disadvantaged conditions. This amalgamist perception pretends to ignore that many Muslims from Arab or sub-Saharan countries who now live in France were once considered French when their countries were colonised by France: they had to learn French in their local schools, came to France to do studies, gained many members in the parliament until the decolonisation of the 1960s. Their children or grandchildren were born French on the continent. The confusion between origin, colour and religion was demonstrated in 2012 when Mohamed Merah, a young French Muslim man of Algerian origin, ex-French colony – first shot three French soldiers in the street while riding a motorbike (Imad Ibn-Ziaten, 11 March in Toulouse, Abel Chennouf and

---

[11] Although proposed in 1841 by John Goodwyn Barmby, a leader of the British Chartist movement referring to utopian socialists, the term 'communitarian' was only revived in the 1980s by certain American political philosophers putting forward common good in opposition with individualistic liberalism: https://www.britannica.com/topic/communitarianism
[12] See Lévy (2005), Lapeyronnie (2008), Revel (2008).

Mohamed Legouade, 15 March in Montauban) and four days later two children and the father of one in a Jewish school (Ozar Atorah, Toulouse). The then President Sarkozy stated that these killings were 'racist' as the targeted school was Jewish and the soldiers Muslims or rather, the President corrected himself, 'one soldier was of Muslim appearance BUT catholic ...'. Whatever the appearance (name or dark skin) and religion of the victims, the killer's motivations were probably beyond racism. He lived in a very pour district of Toulouse, mostly inhabited by families of North African origin, and was filed by the French police, since he regularly travelled to Afghanistan, Pakistan and Israel. During the funeral of the Jewish victims, Muslim representatives of Toulouse marched hand in hand with the Jewish families. After the killer was tracked down, and killed by the police in the attack, different newspapers and online sites reported the anger of many young people of North African origin who blamed the government for not intervening earlier (which could have prevented the attack on the Jewish school) and the media for reinforcing racial stigmatisation resulting from their identification – individually and collectively – be they Muslim or not – with the unforgivable crimes of a man who lost his mind.

The recognition of specific rights, including for French Polynesians or Kanaks in the Pacific – which would recognise 'cultural diversity' – is perceived by many, both on the right and the left, including scholars, as incompatible with the notion of the 'indivisibility' of the Republic based on the principle of 'Freedom, Equality, Fraternity', that is equal rights for all. Article 1 of the French Constitution says that 'France is a Republic that is indivisible, laïc, democratic and social'; indivisible is usually understood as no cultural, linguistic or religious collective can have specific rights and be recognised a sovereignty like Indigenous colonised people claim: only elected members or a referendum can express all people's decision in unity. A recent French book called *The Invention of Diversity* (Sénac 2012) talks about 'sacrificing equality as a principle to value' and asks if the claim for diversity is not 'making politically correct a larval form of sexism and benign racism?' This notion of 'benign' or 'goodwill' racism is returned against people who emphasise their cultural difference. Similarly, men and women who support the right to wear a veil claimed by many young and older Muslim women in France – where the law forbids the veil in schools although some schools do not exclude girls who do so – are sometimes accused of being sexist and jeopardising the 'principle of equality' as a condition to the human rights and freedom of women.

Myths of 'Superiority'

The fear of 'communitarism' (and Islamophobia) – added to a growing poverty and high rates of unemployment – explains the important score of the nationalist extreme right party (Front National) at the last presidential elections. At the first tour of elections, the woman candidate of the extreme right Front National reached 18.01%, with 28.63% for the socialist candidate and 27.18% for the UMP outgoing president; the second tour saw 51.64% for F. Holland and 48.36% for N. Sarkozy, reflecting a divided France which had no socialist president since 1995. Assimilation or integration is the condition imposed by the Republican French state and is equated with a myth of a uniform national identity in a relative denial of the many different origins of French citizens.[13] In response to this denial both of colonisation and the current politics of migration, a French movement protesting against the non-recognition of cultural diversity has registered itself as the *The Indivisibles of the Republic*. Equality is too often referred to in France (and in many other countries) presupposing that 'equal' is a social metaphor that can only translate similarity, homogeneity (a narcissist perception of the self), and cannot apply to a concept of society and humanity where all humans are distinct singular beings caught in various forms of intersubjectivity and constellations of multiple identities.

The denial of skin colour is currently a source of offensive discrimination and racist jokes targeting those of different ethnic origins, which are masked in cynicism, as when a colleague says to a Black PhD candidate 'you represent positive discrimination in our laboratory!' 'Positive discrimination' is the expression used in French to translate 'affirmative action' in favour of Black people as applied in the US or Brazil but not in France.[14] If many French people – in the name of the state – claim that their rejection of the collection of statistics relating to ethnicity is anti-racist, there are others who ask that cultural diversity is given recognition through statistics relating to ethnicity precisely in order to demonstrate the many negative forms of discrimination that can be experienced by members of ethnic groups, such as the denial of jobs or housing on the basis of appearance and names – especially when those names are of Asian

---

[13] See Meyran (2008) and debates on the creation of a Ministry of National Identity by Sarkozy.
[14] See: http://observatoire2.blogs.liberation.fr/diversite/2011/05/la-discrimination-positive-kesako- (The spokesperson for the CRAN, Louis-Georges Tin interviews Daniel Sabbagh).

or African origin, whether Arab, Kabyle or sub-Saharan African. A week after the election last May (2012) of the socialist president, François Hollande, who won against the former right-wing (UMP) president, I heard a boy aged 6 say: 'French people lost, Kabyle people won.' Kabyl – like Berber or Amagizh – is the name of the Indigenous population of Algeria and other North African countries that were occupied by Arabs. The French boy of Algerian origin by seeing the expression of joy of many French residents of North African origin – Muslims for many but not all – identified their joy with a loss for 'French people' because many policies and statements of the previous government expressed an anti-Islamic phobia, with a suspicion of fundamentalism and terrorism against all people of Arab or Kabyl origin, whether Muslim or not.[15]

Many Black French citizens are descendants of the population – including victims of slavery traffic – who built the economy of French island territories in the Caribbean or Indian Ocean, or were born in France into African families who migrated from former French colonies. More recent Black and Arab French citizens are children of new waves of African migrants (from North Africa or sub-Sahara) who continue to flee the violence and dire poverty of their countries that were often colonised by France, many of which gave soldiers to the French army, just like all the populations colonised by France in the Pacific, including Kanaks from New Caledonia, other Melanesians from Vanuatu (independence in 1984) and French Polynesians from Tahiti and other islands. During the 14th of July 2011 national celebration, for the first time, the French Pacific soldiers, and other Pacific members of national bodies marched together as a group and performed a haka in front of the president. The national military website expressed the 'pride of soldiers cultural diversity' but a few public comments on the website indicate how such an affirmation of a cultural identity can shock some French people.

Many young Black people – as well as those of Arab or Berber origin – are routinely harrassed by the police, under perpetual suspicion of being criminals if not illegal refugees. Not carrying an ID card can lead to a trip to the police station or mistreatment. Near my home

---

[15] See the 2012 call to the presidential candidates, with sixteen propositions from different members of the civil society compiled by the journal *Respect.mag*: http://www.fdesouche.com/271982-terra-nova-16-propositions-pour-la-france-metissee-video#. Rokhaya Diallo for instance quotes a CNRS survey and calls for developing better relations with the police (see also Diallo 2011).

in the 20th district of Paris, a young Black man, Lamine Dieng, was violently put into a police truck and died inside in 2007. Five years later his family was marching to ask for justice.[16] Some have argued that such harrassment of young people with dark skin was the cause of the tragic events in 2005 when three French teenagers ran away from the police and two of them were electrocuted after jumping the fence of a power station to hide. This incident triggered riots all over France.[17] But it also created a movement of reaction against racial discrimination and the historical process which hade made it invisible, producing its 'invisibilisation' (Ahouansou 2012a, 2012b). Many civil groups were then strengthened, the Representative Council of Black Associations (CRAN.org) was created and initiatives sprang from both the grassroots and the state in remembrance of the victims of slavery or other colonial situations by means of memorials, etc.[18]

US sociologist Crystal Fleming (2012: 488) has examined how two Black French organisations have produced a 'competing model for challenging and reversing the stigma of slavery.' The first organisation created by French Caribbeans, CM98, 'rejects both a racial and an African identity and seeks recognition for "French descendants of slaves", using the language of citizenship to criticize the French government', while the other, COFFAD (a collective of daughters and sons of deported Africans) 'by contrast, asserts an Afro-centric black identity and stigmatises White Europeans'. The author argues in her paper 'that both destigmatisation strategies unwittingly reinforce the stigma of historical enslavement'. Such a verdict of a North American researcher on a French situation is disturbing because it

---

[16] Despite annual marches of memorial and protests for justice, Lamine Dieng's and other cases have not been addressed properly and police violence continues with more harrassment and deaths. A general campaign against violence has grown accross France after protesters of all colours and age have been wounded by weapons used by the police (loosing an eye, a hand, or other terrible wounds) during the people's social movement of Gilets Jaunes, who for months since November 2018 have been marching every Saturday in many places of France to protest against various issues of social injustice. In 2019 the European Union and the UN addressed blame to the French government.
[17] See Mucchielli and Le Goaziou (2007), Kokoreff (2008), Bertho (2010) and his database Anthropology of the Present (*Anthropologie du présent*) updated every day with news of riots from all over the world: https://berthoalain.com/
[18] 27 April 1848: decreee of abolition of slavery in French colonies signed by the temporary government; 23 May in Martinique, 27 May in Guadeloupe, 10 August in French Guiana and only 20 November in the Island of Reunion.

seems to discard any possibility for the recognition of French Black history in the building of French citizenship.

French sociologist Stéphane Dufoix (2011: 125), in an excellent review essay on the usage of the word diaspora and the situation of French Black in the light of US Black movements, insists on the necessity to think about/understand identity in a non essentialist way: for instance even in the concept of the diaspora if, for some, there is a nostalgia of an 'original' place to go back to (or dream of), for others cultural identification is not based on a notion of 'origins' but a series of interconnected assemblage (*agencements*) projected in the future as 'transversality' in the sense of Félix Guattari. Such a de-essentialised position does not exclude reconstructing colonial history.

Ironically the acquisition of French citizenship is called French 'naturalisation', as if acquiring French identity were a natural process, the people 'born again' to the French state, that is receiving a new physical identity to replace the old one and to erase any other cultural traces of their foreign origins. When President Sarkozy was Minister of the Interior before his election, he had put as a condition for applying for citizenship that migrants promise not to talk their original language to their children: this was a special granting of papers to a limited selection of people who already had jobs and payed taxes and rents.[19] French history shows that France was constructed as a nation through a systematic process of eradication of local cultural identity, in forbidding, for example, the use of languages like 'Breton', which was spoken in Brittany, a Celtic region of North-West France, or Occitan, which was spoken in the south, both of which have revived thanks to the creation of special schools by regional activists. After the Second World War, the integration of refugees or cheap labour from Southern Europe (Italy, Spain or Portugal) or Eastern Europe (Poland, Yougoslavia, etc.) was difficult for the first generation, similarly for French Asian refugees after France lost Indochina.

The independence of Algeria in the 1960s is still a national wound in France, and to speak of the many Algerians drowned in the rivers in Paris during the war of independence is taboo, which is to deny an important aspect of their history to the many people from Algeria who live in France. Recently an exhibition on the subject was banned despite the popular success a few years ago of the film *Indigènes*, which portrayed the participation of African soldiers (from Sahara and sub-Sahara) in the French army during the Second World War.

---

[19] This was limited to 60,000 applications.

Myths of 'Superiority'

The film prompted a public debate, which pushed the government into finally paying the pensions that were due to the African and other Indigenous soldiers (from New Caledonia or French Polynesia) in the French army.[20]

The perception of French civilisation as resulting from ethnic mixing (*brassages*) is not shared by the majority of French people, despite the popularity of some sportsmen, like Yannick Noah (a tennis champion whose father is from Cameroon), the soccer players Zidane, of Kabyle origin, and Christian Karembeu, who is Kanak. In forging a new sense of national identity, France is still struggling to accept its colonial history and the input made by the new waves of migration.[21] Édouard Glissant and Patrick Chamoiseau, two famous French Caribbean authors from Martinique, have written after the election of Obama a little book addressed to him, *L'intraitable beauté du monde. Adresse à Barack Obama*' (The intractable beauty of the world, a letter to Barack Obama) (2009);[22] they invite the readers to create a new world beyond the discriminations produced by many states. The 'Tout-monde' is a concept Glissant proposes to understand the world as archipelic in a philosophy of relationality where creolisation is a process different from 'creolity' as it expresses a desire to come out of any form of exclusive essentialisation, Black or White.

Few French people know that Alexandre Dumas, the famous French author of the *Three Musketeeers* (1844), had a Haitian grandmother during the colonial time before Haiti gained its independence by putting in practice the emerging ideas of the French Revolution.[23] In a film about his life, the role of Dumas was recently played by a famous White actor, Gérard Depardieu, and it created a public debate. It is worth considering whether French Black or Indigenous young people who suffer discrimination on the mainland or in the overseas French territories[24] might feel better if they could identify with a French

---

[20] *Miracle in Santa Anna* by Spike Lee was refused for broadcast in France by the French/German channel ARTE. The film-maker won his case, receiving a massive compensation higher than the sales from the film (Ahouansou 2012b).

[21] Blanchard et al. ([2005] 2006).

[22] See: https://www.criticalsecret.net/the-unassailable-beauty-of-the-world-excerpts-translated-into-english-l-intraitable-beaute-du-monde,058.html

[23] See: https://aaregistry.org/story/alexandre-dumas-writer-extraordinaire/

[24] In the French hexagon and in French overseas departments (Ultraperipheral Regions [RUP] which are members of the European Union), territories and countries ([PTOM] not members of the European Union, such as New Caledonia and French Polynesia).

Black and Indigenous history and if non-Blacks might then also be able to identify with a Black and Indigenous history as part and parcel of French history. In French Polynesia, 75% of the population is of Indigenous descent, many speaking Mao'hi, the language of Tahiti and some islands, or marquisian. In New Caledonia, Kanaks represent 40% of the population with 28 languages, Whites are 23%, the others being migrants from the Pacific or Asia (Wallis and Futuna, Vietnam, etc.).[25] In French Guiana, the survivors of the physical and mental genocide that started 400 years ago are united under a common flag as six Native American nations that now represent 3% of the population and have developed a historical cohabitation with 'Maroons' or Bushinengé descendants of deported Black slaves who ran away and a creole population, descendants of various waves of people brought there as convicts who were banished from France and forced to work in prison camps (between 1854 and 1946),[26] and the Hmong refugees of Cambodgia and Laos who settled there in the 1970s.

Is promoting cultural and colonial heritage a solution? Only if all people involved can reappropriate their history and emerge from a state of collective denial. Part of this process involves the solidarity that is created when people come together for specific projects, such as the various activities – exhibitions, conferences, museum projects, memorials, etc – of the French Committee for the Remembrance and History of Slavery (CPMHE) created in 2009.[27] If social media spreads racist statements or jokes, it is also used to promote antiracist campaigns and efficient activism. For instance, when the fragrance director of Guerlain used the 'n' word on television, an immediate social media campaign across France and the Black diaspora provoked a boycott of his shops and led to his public apology,

---

[25] After the repression of the Kanak independence movement in 1984, different negotiations led to a referundum on independance taking place in November 2018.

[26] 52,000 'transported' and 16,000 'relegated' including Louise Michel and other resistants of the Paris Commune; 20,000 other convicts were 'transported' and 10,000 'relegated' to New Caledonia.

[27] CPMHE was chaired until 2011 by Françoise Vergès (2013, 2017). See also the Slavery Memorial of Nantes and the various campaigns of the group ACHAC. The historian P. Blanchard, after curating 'Exhibitions. L'invention du Sauvage' at the Musée du quai Branly in 2010 ('exhibition' in French has a pejorative meaning of objectifying exposure), co-directed the film *Savages – The Human Zoos* (2018) with examples of colonial exhibitions in Paris of Indigenous people from Australia, French Guiana and New Caledonia.

as shown by Mariquian Ahouansou (2012b, n.d.) who is working on an anthropology of Black France.

Multiculturalism and Australian Structural Racism

The French sociologist Wievorka recently advocated Kymlicka's 'liberal multiculturalism' as a way of 'favouring expressions of cultural specificities in public spaces, while guaranteeing respect for universal values. That is, for instance, by giving specific cultural rights not to groups, but to individuals in the name of multicultural citizenship.'[28] Reducing culture to individual practices is a complete denial of culture as a dynamic process, a collective heritage and shared practices that are constantly reassembled to build a becoming-in-common (*devenir-en-commun*) in interaction with others. The individual of the liberal multiculturalism evokes the impossible dialogue and love between Narcissus, who can't see anything else but himself, and the nymphea Echo, who is in love with him but cannot say anything else than the repetition of what she echoes, says Sabatier (2010), a French philosopher living in the Island of the Reunion. For him the neoliberal administrative rationality generates racial and other forms of the rejection of differences and he calls for a new politic of hospitality in France, especially towards the refugees coming from the independent Union of the Comoros, to Mayotte, an island of the Comoros archipelago, a department of France. In France the treatment of asylum seekers and other migrants is very problematic.[29] If the Greek myth illustrates in a way the way in which multicultural liberalism through individualisation of culture 'invisibilises' blackness in France and the European diaspora extended to former European colonies all over the world, this invisibilisation is now questionned by the movement of Afropeanism developed by Black people of Europe.[30]

---

[28] *Respect Mag* May–June 2012: Kymlicka's book *Multicultural Citizenship* (1995) was only translated in 2012.

[29] Amnesty International et al. (2012), Halluin-Mabillot (2012); since this was written, the situation has worsened to tragic proportions (Héran 2017). Even though many people from civil society try to help refugees and risk jail for that help, the French government has hardened its policies in accordance with the European closure of frontiers. Thousand of people drown every year in the Mediterranean Sea where saving people has become illegal. Various European organisations militate for hospitality.

[30] See Ahouansou (2012a, 2019, and her forthcoming PhD).

Underlining the global failure of liberal multiculturalism to recognise 'differential citizenship', Babacan and Gopalkrishnan (2007: 5) state: 'there is considerable debate about the policies of multiculturalism as both a preventive measure against racism and also a cause for racism by refying culture and replacing racism with "culture"'. For the Libano-Australian Ghassan Hage, anthropological research reveals the tension between a logic of domestication of 'otherness-for-us', which charactarises our world of historical and contemporary violences, and a logic of negotiation of 'otherness-with-us' which inspired most people with 'no state'. Hage (2009) criticises multicultural policies because for him to multiply laws to defend rights by forbidding 'bad relations' (like forms of racism, discrimination, anti-tabacco, etc.) is actually preventing the possibility of any relation. Interestingly in Australia, very rarely are Indigenous cultures understood under the umbrella of multiculturalism which seems mainly to address recent and older migrants who are not assimilated to the Anglo-Celtic colonial ancestry. Indigenous people are excluded from these catgories because they seem to represent a bigger threat of 'otherness' which is their potential as a collective: a declaration by an Australian minister stated that after the 'failure of collectivism in the world' there was no reason to 'favour self-government of Indigenous communities' (Glowczewski 2008). Misunderstanding of self-government, self-management and collective rights in Indigenous Australia has been widely discussed by many scholars in Australia who criticise the different waves of Indigenous policies (Sullivan 2011). The confusion between 'community' and 'collectivism' is also at stake in the fear of the French government to recognise the populations colonised by France in New Caledonia, Polynesia or French Guiana as 'Indigenous people' with specific rights to land and language.

By denying transculturality both in the nation and in the self, liberal multiculturalism and indivisible republicanism look like the two sides of the same coin in a process that essentialises differences and fixes them in the past of imagined origins rather than recognising their creative potential. It is our duty, as engaged academics, to try to dismantle the essentialism underpinning historically fabricated conflicts and fixed cultural memories, to de-essentialise them, in order to build national histories that permit the forging of a common future. Such is the propostion of the historian and archive curator Ariella Azoulay who works on different assemblages of historical photos showing both Israelis and Palestinians in alternative interactions to war. She tries to displace the violence of history to prevent both sides from being hostages of the essentialisation of a historically fabricated conflict by building dynamic archives for a potential history, which de-essentialises conflicts.[31]

Even though promoting cultural diversity or multiculturalism was – following the British model – seen as a positive policy in Australia, in fact assimilation to the European White model has been re-actualised, especially since the 9/11 2001 attack in New York that provoked a panic of terrorism and suspicion towards foreigners, across the world. In 2005 an Australian mother, Cornelia Rau, was found in an Australian detention centre where she was held by mistake for 9 months: after camping in the bush she got lost, and when found by the police she could only remember the Austrian name, Rau, that she had before becoming Australian 19 years ago. Her husband had reported her missing but it is only thanks to refugees, who saw her distress, that she was identified in the detention centre. This Kafkaian scandal led to the discovery throughout Autralia of 230 other Australians detained by mistake, after a traumatic incident, and often because of their foreign-looking appearance. In 2012 Amnesty International released a report denouncing the Australian treatment of asylum seekers as well as the Stronger Futures Bill designed to extend for another ten years the very controversial Northern Territory Emergency Intervention which was imposed in 2007 on 73 Indigenous communities for a 5-year period. Most of these communities, many Indigenous leaders and a UN Special Rapporteur have accused this policy not only being racially discriminatory and therefore racist but also of failing to achieve improvements in the living conditions of Aboriginal people – in terms of their economic situation, health and general well-being. ABC news announced, 'Launching the report, Amnesty's national director Claire Mallinson took the opportunity to criticise the Federal Government's so-called "Stronger Futures" legislation. The new bill, which is soon to be debated in the Senate, is being widely condemned by Indigenous groups as a continuation of the Northern Territory Intervention. Ms Mallinson says the legislation echoes the policies of the assimilation era.'[32] But the legislation was passed, and the Bill became law in July

---

[31] 'The artist as a citizen', conference *L'Artiste en ethnographe*, 26–28 May 2012, Paris, Musée du quai Branly.
[32] May 2012: http://www.abc.net.au/news/2012-05-24/australia-criticised-in-latest-amnesty-report/4029984/?site=indigenous&topic=latest

despite the 'Stand up for Freedom' campaign launched by the Yolngu people from Arnhem Land.

A very moving declaration was then posted on YouTube by Djiniyini Gondarra appealing to 'all people to join the fight against this paternalistic, disempowering and deceptive policy that is now spreading to other parts of Australia'; he stated that 'the government has established a war against democracy'.[33] The communities exempted from the Racial Discrimination Act 1975 with the NT Intervention of July 2007, saw their land confiscated for five years, and self-management and welfare programmes suspended by the Federal Government. On 13 February 2008, the newly elected labour Prime Minister Kevin Rudd made a historic Apology to Australia's Stolen Generations in Parliament: 'the injustices of the past must never ever happen again', promising 'a future where all Australians, whatever their origins, are truly equal partners, with equal opportunities and with an equal stake in shaping the next chapter in the history of this great country, Australia'. Despite this symbolic and moving 'Apology', a complaint was lodged by a collective of Aboriginal communities, and the UN wrote a letter in March 2009 to Kevin Rudd expressing its concern over the suspension of the Racial Discrimination Act. Kevin Rudd signed the United Nations Declaration on the Rights of Indigenous People in April 2009, and the Special Rapporteur of the UN to Australia stressed in the report of his visit the need to reinstate the protection of the Racial Discrimination Act and recommended that the government work in partnership with Aboriginal organisations. The Act was only reinstated a year later in June 2010.[34]

Other Northern Territory communities joined the fight, such as the Warlpiri from Central Australia with whom I have been working since 1979. The Intervention happened at the same as the shire centralisation which disempowered Aborignal councils and the interruption of bilingual education in Warlpiri/English which had been very successful since the mid-1980s.

The Northern Territory policies have dispossessed Warlpiri people of many jobs – councellors, teaching assistants, health workers,

---

[33] See http://www.greenleft.org.au/node/50391; http://indymedia.org.au/2012/03/18/wgar-news-responses-to-senate-committee-report-on-stronger-futures-new-nt-intervention-la

[34] See Chapter 1 on the 2017 report of the UN Special Rapporteur which denounced even more strongly the structural racism of Australia.

Myths of 'Superiority'

Figure 10.1 Warlpiri girls painted on the breast with their respective Dreamings at the end of school term, Lajamanu © B. G. (1984)

etc. – that they had gained thanks to the self-determination policies of the 1970s–1990s. At the same time, more and more non-Indigenous people now come to work in theses communities, paid high wages to supposedly take care of the local population and help them to 'find work'. The interruption of bilingual programmes saw for instance 25 Warlpiri men and women dismissed from the Lajamanu school when the teaching of Warlpiri – which is the children's first language – was reduced to half an hour a week. Warlpiri communities have created – and continue to fund with their own resources from mining – the Warlpiri Triangle to promote bilingual education – including through the Internet – as a stimulus for better school achievements. Similarly, the 40 Warlpiri who worked on part-time shifts at the shop – which they successfully managed with a profit having bought their own plane – were replaced by full-time backpackers, the plane sold, resulting in shocking private company fares that the population could not afford. Many Aboriginal people in NT have mining royalties which they invested – including in education and cultural programmes and NTIC – but the new Intervention policy has disempowered them of the control of their own resources. The building they funded partly themselves for their library and elearning was closed most of the time in 2011–2012 and they had no access to the Internet.

I have also worked with families from Palm Island, after the violent death in custody of Cameron Doomadgee sparked a riot in November 2004. I followed the Committal hearing of the 23 Aboriginal men and women charged for the riot and the long campaign for an inquest that led to the policeman held responsible being brought to trial.[35] The policeman was declared not guilty because of a lack of witnesses but there was no lack of evidence about the cause of death (Doomadgee's liver was split in two), which took place less than an hour after Doomadgee was taken to the police station for singing drunkenly in the streets. The sentences of the rioters ranged from prison terms of several months to 6 years. Lex Wotton – with whom I wrote the book, *Warriors for Peace* ([2008] 2010), about these events on Palm Island – received this maximum sentence. Wotton was released after two years in 2010, but a ban of four years was imposed on him to prevent him from speaking to the media and in public. His parole board made an exception to this ban in allowing him to speak publicly at a press conference he gave at Palm Island in July 2011 and again a few months later at a human rights convention organised by James Cook University. Former Queenslander of the Year Dr Chris Sarra drew cheers from a crowd of 130 as he labelled Mr Wotton 'his inspiration' during an opening speech at the First Nations Pathways Conference at JCU yesterday. 'It's easy for people like me to challenge injustice from the safe confines of higher education or a newspaper column', Dr Sarra said. 'You and the people on Palm Island put your lives on the line to stand up for what was right.'[36] But this year the High Court refused to lift the ban on his speaking in public or in the media. Lawyers have labelled the ban as racist: is the state afraid of an Aboriginal man who says: *'we don't want two laws, one White, one Black, we want one law for all, we want to live in peace'*? (Glowczewski and Wotton [2008] 2010). Lex Wotton triggers 'moral panic' for finding strong words and arguments to express the painful history of his stigmatised island and to criticise the difference in justice applied

---

[35] Having conducted fieldwork on Palm from 2006 till 2008, Lise Garond (2012, 2014) shows the many ambiguities in which the inhabitants – descendants of forty Indigenous languages – talk about their past and the traumatic experiences of displacement.

[36] See: http://www.townsvillebulletin.com.au/article/2011/11/29/287031_news.html

to Black and White in Australia, the criminalisation of Indigenous peoples (Cunneen 2007) and the deafness of institutions which do not listen to Indigenous propositions.

Asking for one 'Law for all' is not to deny diversity of culture or any social differences of life choices. Law and justice should be able to operate in our democracies in a way that respects the unique situation (cultural, religious, professional, political, etc.) of every citizen, without forcing all to be assimilated to the 'same' model, that is reduced to what an 'assimilated' citizen is supposed to be in each nation. In my view, positions that reject cultural or other diversity in favour of a 'neutral' homogeneity in the name of social equality and national assimilation often oppose reparation for past wrongs and reflect a dangerous and cynical ideology. By denying the existence of substantive differences in living conditions according to different cultural origins this cynicism renders the reasons for some existing social and economical inequalities invisible. Such positions also reflect a lack of imagination and inventive scholarship: we need new paradigms to combat the many forms of oppression in the current world but without destroying the uniqueness of people who are oppressed precisely because their difference threatens a certain order which reproduces the inequalities. It is the duty of social scientists to highlight the signs of creativity which offer a way of shifting the paralysing opposition between universality and cultural diversity that masks the real source of inequalities, and gives the green light to all those who prefer to deny differences and remain blind to the inequities deriving from colour and ethnicity, rather than deal with these historical and social injustices.

Academic Responsibility

One challenge for academics is to find ways to change widely held perceptions, especially to act against a global revival of eugenics and biological racism. Human safaris organised by tour operators in the Andaman Islands have recently been denounced by a campaign organised by Survival International, a London-based NGO that has offices in many countries, including France, with engaged anthropologists and members from civil society. Eugenic fantasies are also present in some TV documentaries or in literature. One recent example of this is a French novel which this year has been hailed by the media and awarded a prestigious literary prize even though it conveys a series of racist prejudices about Aboriginal people and discredits the actual Indigenous group who, in 1858, saved the life of a 14-year-old French sailor who went on to live with them for 17 years before being taken back to France against his will. An Australian researcher, Stephanie Anderson (2009), wrote an excellent essay on the story of this French sailor, Narcisse Pelletier, including a chapter by Athol Chase, the main anthropologist who had worked with the descendants of the relevant group, the Pama Malngkana or Sand Beach people, who now live in Lockhart River (Qld). Anderson sent a sound critique of the racist French novel to the French newspapers but they ignored it; only French academic websites circulated her arguments.

Creating links of transnational solidarity, through academic work and web campaigns, is one way to fight prejudice and to support the struggles of the people who militate on the ground against various forms of discrimination and injustice. Civil disobedience is another. A few years ago many French parents and preschool deans, supported by some shires, refused – at the risk of being arrested – to let foreign children be picked up by police from schools to be sent back to the countries their parents had to leave in order to survive.[37] A French law which in 2012 prevented foreign students from working even though they had contracts, or staying in France after they finish their studies, provoked a massive reaction from academics who stood as guarantors for the students and from heads of schools who objected to the law by writing letters case by case but also by a general petition 'Universal university, our grey matter bears all colours'.[38] The newly elected socialist government in May changed this law for better conditions. Another group of French academics made a call for an 'insurrection of consciousness' (Gori et al. 2009) while inspired by the 'Indignados' movement in Spain; the book *Indignate yourself* by Second World War resistant, Stéphane Hessel (2010), reached millions.[39]

---

[37] Ogien and Laugier (2010): http://www.educationsansfrontieres.org/

[38] See: https://www.huffingtonpost.fr/fabienne-servanschreiber/gueant-notre-matire-grise-est-de_b_1259351.html

[39] Other more radical actions have followed since in France, some inspired by the Invisible committee (2007/2009), others by the inhabitants of the ZAD against the airport of Notre-Dame-des-Landes who call for alternative ways of living; see also the crowds of the Nuit debout movement gathering night after night without leadership to talk for months in 2016 in the Place of the Republic in Paris, and all the people involved with Indigenous peoples in protests against extractivism or other industrial megaprojects that accelarate climate change. See note 16.

Myths of 'Superiority'

Figure 10.2 Figures painted with Aboriginal designs on the walls of the school, Lajamanu © B. G. 2017

New platforms are emerging globally where people come together to promote differences, to react against the denial of various manifestations of racism and to formulate new cultural, social and economic policies that can change the face of local and national politics. The film *The Intouchables* (2011) by Olivier Nakache and Éric Toledano made more then 19 million entries in France – partly for TV popularity of the comic show run for years by the French Black actor, Omar Sy. But some US critics found the film racist, as they did the film *Australia* with Nicole Kidman. When the audience has a different national and cultural context, other contexts are hard to understand. Probably the Australian bush with Aboriginal 'cowboys' did not make sense for Black or White American audiences, just like the humour shared by many Black French people has a different history from the African-American one. According to Randall Kennedy: 'what people reject is "pigmentocracy", a system where people are rejected because of the colour of their skin or their origin ... A lot of my students feel they are multiracial. They have parents of different origins. They build themselves differently. Their sense of allegiance is more complex ... One should not fall on the trap by slogans like "racial neutrality" that can lead to a terrifying society.'[40] There is no consensual idea on racial politics but a citizen's debate. Such a 'dissensus' is precisely what French thinkers like Guattari (1991, [1992] 1995) or Rancière (2010) have defined as a propeller [or driver] to stimulate the creation of new societal forms, forms that can respond to the poverty and injustice generated by exclusion, intolerance and the denial alterity, which is to recognise existential heterogeneity at the structural level of contemporary societies and nations.

---

[40] Interview in *Le Monde*, 2011, translated by the author. See propositions to 15 ministers by the CRAN after the presidential elections in June 2012: http://lecran.org/

11

Resisting the Disaster: Between Exhaustion and Creation

> Climate change poses the question of a human community, of a we; it points to a figure of universality that escapes our capacity to experience the world. This universality stems rather from the shared sense of a catastrophe. It calls for a global approach of politics, but without the myth of global identity, for, unlike the Hegelian universe, it cannot comprise particularities. We could temporarily refer to it as a 'negative universal history'. (Chakrabarty 2009: 199)

Thus ends a text of Dipesh Chakrabaty, responding to the thesis of Nobel Prize in Chemistry winner Paul Crutzen. The famous author of *Provincializing Europe* here takes up the concept of negative universal history proposed by Antonio Y. Vasquez-Arroyo (2008) and specifies that: 'As the crisis gathered momentum in the last few years, I realized that all my readings in theories of globalization, Marxist analysis of capital, subaltern studies, and post-colonial criticism over the last twenty-five years, while enormously useful in studying globalization, had not really prepared me for making sense of this planetary conjuncture within which humanity finds itself today.' In 2000, Crutzen and Stoermer proposed to consider that human-induced transformations of the planet and the climate since the industrial revolution constitute a new era, which he calls the 'anthropocene', where humanity as a 'species' has become a geophysical force. The consequence for human sciences would imply revising not only the separation between human and natural history but also the notions related to the classical problem of freedom.[1] Similarly, the author of *The Gaïa Hypothesis* who, twenty years ago, called for the consideration of the earth as a self-regulated living organism, has now come to insist, in his latest book (Lovelock 2009), on the

---

[1] Special thanks to Sébastien Longhurst for the translation of this paper first published under the same title by *Spheres, Journal for Digital Cultures*, 2. *Ecologies of Change* 2017: 1–19: http://spheres-journal.org/2-ecologies-of-change. It was adapted from the French version published in Glowczewski and Soucaille (2011: 23–40). Guattari's quotation p. 323 is slightly different from Goffey's translation p. 115.

responsibility of mankind and its economic choices in the future of the biosphere.[2]

These debates are stimulating all disciplines, but seem to forget that the human power of action (agency), even regarding geophysical phenomena, is not an invention of this century. Even though Western history has thought mankind as a 'prisoner of climate' (Braudel [1969] 1980: 31), anthropology shows throughout the planet that the perceptions of the world according to which humans can act on the forces of nature seem to have existed since the beginning of time. A great number of traditional societies acknowledge, on the one hand, a set of obligations – such as rituals to make the rain come or ensure that volcanoes remain dormant – and, on the other hand, a set of prohibitions: if these protocols are not respected, and if the social rules that guarantee the supposed balance between everything that exists are transgressed, then various catastrophes could occur, such as droughts, floods, plagues or famine.

Now facing global alerts and calls for degrowth that invoke man's responsibility in natural, socio-economic and technical disasters, some media and governmental or non-governmental institutions are entangled in various political and financial processes that reduce humans to a status of victims of natural forces and uncontrollable fluxes (stock exchange, markets, conflicts, etc.) without conceding them any means to intervene in those situations themselves as creators of social alternatives. However, those survival responses exist everywhere, and the collective intelligence that leads to micro-social experiments is a wave of hope for the world.

Answers to the Victimising Trap of the Humanitarian World and its Mediatisation

Thinking today's human as responsible for the global climate and environmental disaster, and for the peril of extinction that threatens humanity, invites to reflect on technical, political and economic development with a collaborative 'good use of slowness' (Nghiem 2010) looking for 'long circuits' (Steigler [2010] 2013) in order to grasp all forms of

---

[2] Having enhanced the value of the biosphere, Lovelock's hypothesis was criticised on the one hand for having served as an alibi for those considering that an active environmental policy is useless, and on the other hand for its New Age pantheism, abusively assimilated to different forms of holism or connectionism of some Indigenous peoples.

interaction and collective enunciation assemblages that emerge in situations of emergency and globalised capitalist acceleration (Rosa 2010). In *The Machinic Unconscious* the psychoanalyst and philosopher Félix Guattari defined the notion of refrain (*ritournelle*) as a 'sonorous marker of an assemblage of local desire'.[3] After his works with Gilles Deleuze, he redeveloped in his last books the notion of existential refrains as it can be found in different forms of art and other semiotic and sensory mobilisations (rituals, tattoos, automatic behaviour, etc.), as a means to create new value systems (Guattari [1989] 2013): 'These territories of the refrain make use of new individual and collective productions that enable one to survive amid deterritorializing fluxes.'[4] As an extension of Bateson's Ecology of Mind, Guattari articulated the refrains and the territories in a 'schizoanalytic' cartography, and proposed linking *Three Ecologies* ([1989] 2000), environmental, mental and social, under the name of ecosophy:

> I conceive the ecosophical object as articulated in four dimensions: those of flux, machine, value and existential territory [...] That of machine is there to give a dimension of cybernetic retroaction, of autopoïesis, meaning an ontological self-affirmation, without falling into animist or vitalist myths, such as Lovelock and Margulis's Gaïa hypothesis; for it is precisely about linking the machines of the ecosystems of material fluxes to those of the ecosystems of semiotic fluxes. Therefore, I try to widen the notion of autopoïesis, without limiting it, like Varela does, solely to the living system, and I consider that there are proto-autopoïeses in all other systems: ethnological, social, etc.[5]

Guattari's ecosophical project should be understood in relation to the transforming individual and collective assemblages (*agencements*)

---

[3] (Querrien [2008] 2011: 94). In Guattari ([1979] 2011), *ritournelle* has been translated by *refrain*, which is not the best choice: some prefer using the Italian *ritornello* (little return in Baroque music). In Guattari's further work *ritournelle* is also used in visual art and other fields of creativity.

[4] Querrien ([2008] 2011: 94); Guattari started from the *Vinteuil Sonata*, which awakens different perceptive and memory-based sensations in Proust's *In Search of Lost Time*. On Guattari's relation to anthropology and the use of *ritournelle* for Indigenous Australians, see Chapters 2 and 3 of this book.

[5] Guattari ([1991] 2013). According to the Chilean biologist, neurologist and philosopher Francisco Varela, autopoïesis is a model for the analysis of living systems that he developed with Humberto Maturana in order to oppose the notion of a black box in which the information enters and exits, with that of a system evolving in an autonomous way as it interacts with the environment: he sought to link action and knowledge together in the notion of enaction. On Lovelock, see note 2.

matrix that he constructed in *Schizoanalytic Cartographies* ([1989] 2013), in which his concepts of dimension are distributed among four transversally and temporally interrelated poles: the economy of fluxes (libido, signifier, capital, labour) corresponds to the 'actual real', the machinic phylums correspond to the 'actual possible', the incorporeal value universes to the 'virtual possible', and the existential territories to the 'virtual real'. The relation between the first two poles generates objective deterritorialisation processes while, between the other two, an enunciation (or subjective deterritorialisation) can emerge and allow the (re)creation of the virtual possible with new contents, a promise of new assemblages, against integrated global capitalism, among others. This model, commented by many thinkers since Guattari's death, is a very fruitful proposition in order to analyse the creative answers to the disasters of our world: ecosophy is at once an ethical, a political and an aesthetic paradigm (Holmes 2009).

> Guattari's discovery of Norwegian and German ecological writings, most notably Hans Jonas's *The Imperative Responsibility* [1985], moderated his belief in a post-media era in which the miniaturisation and networking of informatics devices would permit the development of a new creativity. (Querrien [2008] 2011: 93)

The lesson that can be drawn from the people, who in the most ancient traditions postulated the responsibility of human actions towards the rest of life, is that their ontologies and 'existential territories' (as Guattari would say) are not necessarily contained in a system of divine dependency but rather in a transversal way of thinking the interaction between things.[6] Many societies, such as Indigenous Australians, Polynesians, Native Americans or other groups who have lived for centuries in constant negotiations with the agency of the cosmic world – rain, wind, fire, tsunami, climate excess, etc. – do consider that any human action has an impact not only on the society but also on the forces of what the Western work considers as 'nature' as opposed to 'culture': for instance the breaking of a taboo – like colonisation destroying sacred sites for mining – can provoke people's sickness as well as a draught or a cyclone. Similarly, any catastrophy is to be traced to human excess. It is an immanent dynamism where the reticularity of interactions (such as the connections between different aspect of living beings, the

---

[6] See for example the words of Yanomami shaman Davi Kopenawa (Kopenawa and Albert [2010] 2013), and analysis by Viveiros de Castro (2007).

knowledge transmitted and updated through rituals) is simultaneously a source of links and ruptures, of solidarities and conflicts, of fusions and cleavages, of segmentations and alliances, of attractions and avoidance among people and other agents, animal, mineral, etc.

As in the relation of the Zoques Indigenous group from the Chiapas with the Chichonal volcano, on the foothills of which they live (Garcia-Acosta 2002), the villagers of Bebekan in Java refused the aid of large humanitarian agencies that urged them to abandon their village. The latter had been completely destroyed by the seismic activity of the Merapi volcano in May 2006, following the tsunami that had struck their island two years before. The villagers called on to their responsibility should another earthquake and volcanic eruption occur, but thought it could be prevented if they kept on making offerings to the volcano and living at its base. They completely rebuilt their village using the systems inherited from collective solidarity (traditionally mobilised to irrigate the fields) as well as by inventing new ways of working together. This collective work initiative has renewed the interest of the younger ones for a ritual movement of communication with spirits through ancestral trance techniques. What is at stake here is the recreation of a force of life, like a Phoenix rising from the ashes. The common experience of constant cohabitation with destruction and death brings each one back to its solitude as a survivor, but also to the possibility of a new collective assemblage implemented through a memory construction process that re-establishes a shared hope. The 2010 eruption of the volcano, which destroyed another village, taking many lives and displacing hundreds of people threatened by clouds of hot ash, recently brought up this question again. The writer, Elisabeth Inandiak, who had accompanied Bebekan's experience since 2006 (Inandiak 2007), notes in the journal in which she keeps track of the Merapi disaster since October 2010 (Inandiak 2011) that the hundred walls erected on the volcano acted as a springboard for the ash clouds, thus aggravating the impact of the catastrophe: another illustration of the need to think of technologies in time with the fluxes of the earth and of men, who precisely seek the right way to behave towards the volcano.

Another type of economic and artistic answer to the catastrophe is provided by the Brazilian city of Goiânia. In 1987, in a concrete cube in a wasteland street, scrap metal dealers found a cylinder emitting a blue glow. Even though they felt nauseous on the following day, they sheared it, thus liberating the source of the blue glow, and sold some of the pieces to other dealers. Many dwellers of the neighbourhood touched the glowing powder and even covered themselves in it, while children used it to mark the streets. A few days later, hundreds of people flooded into the hospital, their hands and bodies burning, for the powder was cesium 137, a highly radioactive substance, that had been used in the radiological equipment of a clinic that was abandoned two years before. But this diagnosis was not done immediately, but only after four deaths, including one child. The catastrophe, aggravated by this ignorance, triggered an extreme government response: the inhabitants were gathered in a stadium to sort the irradiated ones. 110,000 people were examined. The city, which was rapidly growing at the time, was temporarily removed from the list of tourist destinations thus sparking off countrywide panic. Eighty-five contaminated houses were destroyed, the population was evacuated and the area was cleaned up through the withdrawal of 3,500 m^3 of waste that had been stored thirty kilometres away. Years later, the site was converted to a storage centre for radioactive waste. It was buried under knolls of grass, and a small museum was built to tell the story that traumatised a generation. In June 2006, the annual symposium of the Brazilian Association of Anthropology gathered some 4,000 Brazilian anthropologists in Goiânia, and organised a visit to the waste storage site, and to the neighbourhood where the disaster occurred, in which some survivors with huge deformed goitres held a banner to protest against the absence of compensation to the victims.[7] During the South American Biennale, held in 2005 in Porto Alegre, the internationally renowned artist Cirone Di Franco exposed an installation of hospital beds made of blue concrete, each one bearing the imprint of a body or of an object signifying the personality of the victims of radioactivity. In those individual traces, he crystallised the collective memory of his city, which was reshaped by that disastrous event.

In France, similarly, Ariane Mnouchkine collected hundreds of stories from the refugees of Sangatte – Afghans, Chechens or Iraqis – looking to reconstruct their route throughout the world, into exile or often forced back home, in order to create a performance in 2004. The Last Caravanserai gathered around 200 scenes performed in various languages with subtitles projected on different elements of

---

[7] Telma Camargo da Silva (2009, 2015), a Brazilian anthropologist, has been studying the impact of that disaster including the non-recognised contamination of the workers who cleaned the site and whose survivors, or their children, still suffer from serious diseases.

the set, and whose order and duration could change in each show.[8] The sequences on the bureaucratic and technical treatment of the refugees were of remarkable acuteness and made that true mental torture perceptible. The show staged re-enactments of the interrogations performed on asylum seekers stranded in the north of Australia by government employees of the south of the country via videoconference. The fact that the group of actors included refugees, who took part in the elaboration of various scenes and played more or less their own characters, put immediately into practice the hypothesis of redeeming creation in the face of disaster. The theatrical process almost became a therapeutic transfer for some of them. The humanitarian morality and its technical and bureaucratic machine of emergency intervention tends to force the refugees into the constraining norms of aid, without a right to reciprocity or allowing the introduction of new rules by the refugees themselves, regardless of the fact that as a consequence of this, they may loose their humanity altogether, as social beings and actors of new communities. For some, humanitarian assistance has become a real 'business' with an 'inhuman' financial logic mostly directed to the media, who choose to cover one emergency instead of another; in order to generate the mobilisation of the public it needs passive victims and not humans trying to get back on their feet. Of course, there are journalists who defend field interventions and launch very useful alerts, but the risk that the good intentions of those ready to help could be misused for the benefit of a few, remains.

The anthropologist Jonathan Benthall has been criticising for twenty years the deforming power of the media regarding the priorities of humanitarian activities, and calls to the responsibility of anthropology to critically render disaster situations and the inner workings and power of humanitarian aid among civil society (Benthall [1993] 2010). Regarding the criticism formulated by humanitarian actors themselves – victims, volunteers, employees or agency consultants – towards the media and the institutions that limit their range of action, anthropology, as a discipline looking to understand how humans behave in society, is now challenged to address various audiences (as a counterpoint to the media machine) with comparative analyses and translocal arguments that value the freedom or the agency of man when reduced, in diverse situations, to a status of victim with no right to speak or act.

---

[8] DVD, *Le dernier Caravansérail*, 2006. On Sangatte, Courau 2007a & b.

Nature and Culture of Disasters

Whether at first natural, social or technical, a disaster ends up involving all three levels, which continue interweaving historically. Slavery, which can be seen as a social disaster for the deported populations, has become a natural and technical disaster for continental Africans who have had to reinvent their economic survival while mourning those who were taken away. While the places from where these men and women left were deeply affected economically several times since colonisation, which first forced the displacement of those hunted by slave merchants and then provoked a series of conflicts, the places through which the deported passed, and those where their descendants eventually settled still carry the impression of the technical, natural and social transformations created by this new colonial labour system (Diouf 1999, Diouf and Kiddoe Nwangko eds 2010). Such is the case of Gorée island which, for more than a century, was the embarking point to the Americas for more than 9 million future plantation workers, once their physical resistance had been drained in the narrow cells of the slave houses, often managed by the signare, the traders' African or Creole mistresses, whose brothers were in charge of human transport. Many would die there, as the guides of Gorée now explain to the African diasporas of the whole world who spend the day (rarely the night) visiting the houses that are now museums, in what is now a tourist destination. In some buildings, refurbished with international funding, specialised symposia are organised – about war in Africa, for example. The guides and the exhibitions show a history of colonisation that was rewritten by Africans, with remarkable critical distance and in sharp contrast with the hidden history of slave ancestors that surrounds the lives of some islands of the Caribbean or the Indian Ocean.[9] If Gorée, thanks to its recent commercialisation of colonial history, has become a seemingly prosperous island which hosts a competitive boarding school for Senegalese schoolgirls and the home of the famous Senegalese sculptor Ousmane Sow, it is also striking to see so many abandoned houses that their owners cannot afford to maintain anymore. Gorée also attracts women from Dakar who cross by boat every day to welcome the tourists with armloads of jewellery for sale, next to

---

[9] Vergès (2006a, 2006b); see also the texts by Boubacar Joseph Ndiaye (n.d.), in 'The House of Slaves', *Virtual Visit of Gorée Island*. Available at: http://webworld.unesco.org/goree/en/screens/25.shtml (accessed December 2018).

Resisting the Disaster

the canvases exposed in the street by young artists from all over the country who survive precariously, squatting in the bunkers connected by a network of tunnels dug under the cliffs. Oil paintings of repeated patterns, designs in coloured sands and sculptures made of used batteries, old cell phones or bottle caps: the art of recycling the waste that covers the beach has become a signature of the island.[10]

In Africa, novels, theatre and cinema have long been useful tools to change people's look on the world and propose acting on it differently. In 2009, La Tempête theatre in Vincennes received Serge Limbvani, trained in Brazzaville, who had rallied actors from various diasporas to stage *God's Bits of Wood*, a novel by Ousmane Sembène, a former Senegalese Tirailleur turned actor and film director. Through meticulous and dramatic ethnographic work, the book and the play tell the story of the railway workers' strike on the Dakar-Niger line in 1947–1948, which for five month and ten days bonded starving families together, awakened a spirit of emancipation from colonisation and modified traditional gender relations. Since 1902, Dakar was the capital of the federation of French Western Africa: on the 25th of November 1958, the Sudanese republic gained autonomy within the French community. Created on 4 April 1959, the Federation of Mali comprised Senegal and French Sudan, but broke up on 20 August 1960 due to a disagreement between the leaders and the parties. Shortly after, two independent states were created, each one with its own capital: Dakar in the Republic of Senegal (presided by Léopold Senghor) and Bamako in the Republic of Mali (presided by Modibo Keïta). A text for the preparation of the diplom Baccalauréat (inherited from the French colonial system) explained that through their 70 km march from Thiès to Dakar, 'the wives of the railway workers of the working-class town of Thiès led a very large mass-mobilisation to put pressure on the colonial administration and demand satisfaction of the worker's claims' (Africa. web),[11] such as raises, family subsidies, annual holidays, pensions and the right to conform their own union. After the shooting of the marching women, the strikers were granted part of their demands:

> [T]heir fellowship with the machine was deep and strong; stronger than the barriers which separated them from their employers, stronger even

---

[10] Especially incarnated by Djibril Sagna, an artist from Casamance, who lives in Gorée in an abandoned building that he uses as a workshop, and who sometimes exhibits in European art galleries.

[11] As at 2015, this website no longer exists and the domain name is for sale.

than the barriers which until now had been insurmountable – the colour of their skin. (Sembène [1960] 1995: 77)

After Mali and Senegal gained independence, the Bamako-Dakar line funded the tours of Malian and Senegalese musicians, thus becoming a platform to launch future stars on the world stage. Salif Keita and Mory Kanté first played in the mythical Rail Band in Bamako's rail station hotel and restaurant, which from 1970 blended the inspiration of the Mandinka griots with electro-acoustic folk music. The railway was also used to trade food crops and handicraft between stations, and to access various services along the line, such as schools or clinics (Lombard 2006). But at the beginning of the 2000s, the railway was privatised and 24 stations of 36 were shut down, leaving the railway workers unemployed, as well as many people who lived in the villages that had been created along the line. From one day to the other, the population was cut off from the world: with no decent road along the railway, the villagers were paralysed. This situation is evoked in Abderrahman Sissako's film *Bamako* (2006), the story of a popular tribunal held against the inefficiency and the abuses of the World Bank, in which Tiécoura Traoré holds the part of the owner of the family concession where the judges meet for the trial. Traoré, who studied in the USSR like many Africans, was working as an engineer at the railway when he was dismissed by his employer for being a too active trade union representative. With others he initiated in 2003 the Citizen Collective for the integrated rail development and recovery, COCIDIRAIL, which started a protest march inspired by the 1947 strike. Once again, women were in the frontline, touring with a travelling theatre play that told the problems of the villages and invited people to mobilise. Tiécoura Traoré documented the tour on film and showed goods such as grain sieves piling up in the villages, for lack of access to markets. Not only did this privatisation destroy their lifestyle, but it also turned out to be an economic and technological disaster for Mali, Senegal and the multinational company itself. Cutting stops on the line led to reduced railway maintenance and decay, even causing a deadly derailment. An audit by the Malian government confirmed the economic catastrophe, but corruption is pushing it ever deeper.[12] A historic lesson remains:

---

[12] The Declaration of the Citizen Collective for Integrated Rail Development of 24 April 2009, criticised the management of the Transrail company: 'COCIDIRAIL also denounces the whole so-called "rescue plan" including the discontinuation of the users' traffic management, a gift of 14 billion to Transrail, 376 layoffs (180

the threat of destruction of a technological adaptation such as the railway, a communication factor and a catalyst for social bonds, triggers the emergence of other networks: villagers united in a collective, but also associations and unions in Europe supported the resistance, funded sustainable agriculture and popular education projects, invited spokesman Tiécoura Traoré to address the European Parliament and organised support protests throughout France.[13] In 2010, COCIDIRAIL established a solidarity network with various African and European trade unions.

All these examples show different creations in the midst of disaster, understood as a reinvention of forms to redefine one's position in a place or a network of places, a route, both individually and collectively, and generate connections with the outside world. Reviving the past as a cultural feature is an option that can be supported by the re-emergence of ancient sacred rituals generated by trance, like in the village of Bebekan, or by generating tourism around a historical heritage site, although a painful one, as done in Gorée. What is at stake here is to find the force of life that will spark a response to the deadly force of destruction that threatened the group. Alongside structured forms, conditions for reactivated or renewed potentialities emerge, thus creating a framework for artistic work and pushing the creativity of the younger generations, who will rebuild cultural heritage based on their own common experience. This experience can in turn become a new strong foundational myth for the group, especially while it is based on shared emotions, on the redemption of survival, or rather of revival, a rebirth that offers more than just survival to the risk of dying, a very real risk as many actually died during the events.

The warranty to live lies in the fact of not being the only one who escaped death: survivors gather, forming a 'together' that will deploy into one or several communities or break up into family groups and individual units, depending on the group's responses and interactions with all the others involved in the emergency. The response of those

---

in Mali, 196 in Senegal), recapitalising the company up to 3.6 billion through investments of both countries, and a new revision of the concession agreement in order to force Mali and Senegal to start funding the heavy railway investments, which have so far been a responsibility of the company.' Ten years later, the struggle continues.

[13] Kubiakowska (2009); see also Traoré's interview: http://survie.org/billets-d-afrique/2007/160-juillet-aout-2007/article/interview-tiecoura-traore

collective assemblages can break away from inherited culture, even more so considering the impossibility to keep on living the same way if the environment has been destroyed. However, it is within a reconstructed continuity that 'culture' is redrawn as a new foundation of the survivors in a place, be it the place of the catastrophe or that where the refugees were displaced. But when the collective installation in the place of revival is hindered, the transmissions start crumbling down, culture is lost and, most of all, the collective life is threatened once again, notably in its ethical aspect. The power of action does not have a collective field of expression any longer: the existential territory erodes, there is no projection anymore, and no creation is possible. However, precisely when this exhaustion hits rock bottom, it becomes the source of a new hope. Weren't many beautiful French and Russian literary texts born in the midst of late twentieth-century melancholy? Didn't the suffering of the colonised, the deported and of the soldiers of so many wars generate countless novels and films in the Southern Hemisphere or among the diasporas of the twentieth century? As for the abundance of science fiction novels and films produced since Orwell's *1984*, they invite young generations to think utopias for the future. If novelists and film-makers can depict human resistance so well, they also make us face the current responsibility of the anthropological project: finding new ways of thinking those grounds where suffering and disasters constantly question the memory and the possibilities that would redeem human condition.

Disastrous Combinations: Racism and Exclusion

When Hurricane Katrina devastated New Orleans in 2005, the media and humanitarian treatments of the victims of the catastrophe were defined differently, based on both social and racial criteria. The poorest could not regain the city in a liveable way after its destruction and, for the most part, the Black population was excluded. During the floods, a photo by the Agence France-Presse showed a fair-skinned man and a young woman walking with water up to their chests and carrying a bag of bread. The couple was described as 'finding bread and soda from a local grocery store'. Another photo by Associated Press showed a young Black man in the same situation and was described as 'looting a grocery store' (Ralli 2005). Those two photos are circulating on the Internet and were posted by an Aboriginal professor of the Department of Aboriginal Studies of James Cook University in Australia: the sign of a new form of solidarity against colour-based discrimination as it equally affects the inhabitants of colonised countries of Africa or Asia and the descendants of slaves and deported workers dispersed throughout the three oceans, and even many Indigenous populations that became minorities in the states that colonised them.[14]

During the year 2005, at the court of Townsville, Australia, I attended the investigation of a group of twenty Palm Island Aboriginal people accused of having encouraged a riot after the death of an Aboriginal man while he was held in custody, one hour after he was arrested for public drunkenness. I have to admit that not even my twenty-five years of work on rituals, myths and identity conflicts in other regions of Australia had prepared me for the disenchantment of the Indigenous people involved in those events. I was impressed by the capacity to withstand adversity shown by the inhabitants, who were either deported on the island or the descendants of the 3,000 Aboriginal people deported there between 1918 and the 1970s, from the respective lands of about forty different language groups who spread through the state of Queensland (Garond 2012, 2014). Indigenous Australians call their displaced populations 'historical people'. Their colonial anchoring in the deportation places is thereby distinguished from the ancestral heritage of the 'traditional owners': even if both groups are opposed in land claims based on the priority of the principle of Native titles, part of their history is common nonetheless, as it is built on the same place of social belonging and life. Treated as non-humans during the colonisation of Australia by the British, Aboriginal people have suffered both a form of ethnocide and a form of apartheid: massacres, poisoning of their water supplies, deportation far away from their land, forced settlement in reservations, abduction of children of mixed descent (between 1905 and the 1970s, one child out of five was taken from its Aboriginal family, a phenomenon called stolen generations), or even the state-run confiscation of the wages that were paid by farmers or other employers (stolen wages). These

---

[14] The solidarity of Indigenous activists to denounce situations happening in other countries is not new: in 1938, William Cooper led a group of Aboriginal people of Footscray to the German consulate to protest against the destruction of Jewish homes and synagogues carried out on 9 November (the *Progromnacht*): his Aboriginal descendants were invited to Israel for a ceremony to honour his memory.

decades of traumatising history have contributed to shape a disastrous situation which – in spite of the enthusiasm of the Land Rights Movement of the 1970s and the success of Aboriginal art since that supported political and social justice claims (Cunneen 2010) – has triggered despair in the face of discrimination, suicidal behaviours and rising anger against the constant political misunderstanding towards these societies that were organised without the existence of a state before the British colonisation.[15] However, the year 2010 ended with the creation of the first Aboriginal party (First Nations Party).

The recent evolution of Australian politics towards Aboriginal people has aggravated this catastrophic logic in various regions of the continent, notably in the Northern Territory, whose 73 Aboriginal communities were put under the federal government 'Intervention' (NT National Emergency Response Act 2007) and a new centralised administrative system of city shires of the Northern Territory that suppressed their elected Community Councils. In September 2010, after a vendetta conflict opposing two groups in a desert community, an Australian colleague wrote to me: 'Yuendumu has now established a disaster community managed by the Department of Education of the Northern Territory. We now see the next step of the Intervention: the unleashed "honesty" of the new relation of power between the Australian State and remote communities. The "us and them" dichotomy is now at work. So far, the State has been treating the Indigenous people like children by managing their income and destroying its tools of governance.' Indeed, the elected Community Councils have been replaced by regional administrators who decide on municipal and individual expenses. The Aboriginal people have received debit cards to access their wages and subsidies, but they can only use them to buy food in some shops and have to request an authorisation for any other expense, such as buying a bus or plane ticket for example. This measure was trying to ban alcohol consumption and card games. 'Now the State wants to protect the Whites from the Blacks. Not only do the communities become segregated spaces, but also dangerous places for white people. We need a disaster management plan to protect the Whites from the Blacks.' This ironic testimony of Peter Stewart, who has experienced the creative enthusiasm of the 1980s as an administrator employed by

---

[15] Glowczewski and Wotton ([2008] 2010). See also Glowczewski and Abélès (2010).

the council of another desert community (and not imposed to the council), signals a dangerous turnaround in race relations. It is to be noted that about a hundred Warlpiri, alarmed by the scale of the local conflict and the security deployment, have chosen to leave Yuendumu temporarily for their relatives' place in Adelaide (over a 1,000 kms south). But what shocked the media and the politicians was that Aboriginal people would dare leave their community to 'invade' the city, and not the state's incapacity to control local violence. This reaction illustrates the Australian malaise towards the Indigenous people who, as I have described for a long time, are perceived as 'refugees from the inside'.[16]

The debates generated by the subaltern and post-colonial studies[17] are increasingly positioning themselves on those Indigenous issues (according to the definition of the Declaration on the Rights of Indigenous Peoples, adopted on 13 September 2007, by the United Nations General Assembly[18]). They inherit a violent colonial past that has destroyed their natural, social and economic environment of survival, and which continues to stigmatise the victims by characterising them as 'others'. Those debates refer to the question of power and the capacity to act – in order to exist as citizens with common rights and specific rights, or in a process seeking autonomy or independence – of these groups who became minorities within the state. Whether among the Maori or other peoples from Oceania who have not gained independence, among Indians from North and South America, Moroccan

---

[16] Glowczewski (2007), see also Glowczewski with a contribution by Lex Wotton [2008] 2010. When the Government of Western Australia and South Australia announced their intention to close many remote communities, a protest of support stormed across Australia and French scholars working in Australia supported it with a collective letter (Préaud et al. 2015).

[17] On the comments made then about those debates in France, see the online archives of the review *Multitudes* (http://www.multitudes.net/) and those of *La Revue Internationale des Livres et des Idées* (http://revuedeslivres.blogspot.fr/). In 2016 in France a network and journal of Decolonial Studies was created: http://reseaudecolonial.org/

[18] With 143 participating states, including eleven abstentions (Azerbaijan, Bangladesh, Bhutan, Colombia, Georgia, Kenya, Russia, Samoa and Ukraine) and four rejections: Australia and New Zealand (which accepted the Declaration one year later), the United States of America (accepted the Declaration with the election of Obama in 2010) and Canada (promised to ratify it in 2010 but only did so in 2017). The 46 articles of the Declaration affect more than 370 million people worldwide: https://www.un.org/development/desa/indigenouspeoples/declaration-on-the-rights-of-indigenous-peoples.html

Berbers, Touareg and Peuls in sub-Saharan states, nomadic peoples from Central Asia, everywhere indigenous leaders currently analyse their situations by proposing to 'subalternise indigenous politics' and 'indigenise subaltern politics' (Cadena and Starn 2007). On their land threatened by destruction through forestry and mining as well as in their urban exodus, Indigenous people are often confronted by social hierarchy structures that tend to dampen, and even strangle, their voices within the Nation State that surrounds them. In the 1980s, that difficulty to make their voices heard at the national level encouraged some of them to contact international bodies and to widen their networks transnationally, often by recurring to their privileged relation to nature.[19]

The rejection of Indigenous singularities and the mobilisation of transnational networks echoed the situation of the Roma and Gipsies, of which 900 settlements were dismantled in France in the summer of 2010. Can this also be considered a disaster? It can if it is included in the history of persecution through which – as with the Pogroms and the Shoah – Gipsies have been hunted down, from the concentration camps where they were tortured and gassed, to the abuses that many families experience today in Romania and elsewhere, both from non-Roma populations and Gipsy mafias. However, they have no right to asylum: as many are traditionally nomadic, their travels outside of their countries of origin are suspect. Some political leaders, the media and a portion of the public perceive them as parasites that should be sent home, as a security risk they should get rid of, even if that implies locking them up in dormitory towns and then in jail if they commit another offence on the way home.

The Right of Asylum and Refugee Rights is no clearer for people displaced from countries devastated by natural disasters. After the earthquake which devastated Haiti on 12 January, a journalist from *Le Monde* recalled that:

> Considering the increasing numbers of disasters induced by climate change, IOM has suggested the creation of an international status for the victims of natural disasters, including earthquakes. In vain. The refugee status is reserved for victims of conflicts and persecutions, even if the High Commission for Refugees (HCR) acknowledges the need for an evolution of the mechanism, and provided support to Haiti. "We provide equipment and our expertise in camp management and protection of displaced

---

[19] Bosa and Wittersheim (2009), Gagné et al. (2009), Glowczewski and Henry ([2007] 2011), Glowczewski et al. (2014).

populations", explains its spokesperson, Melissa Fleming (...?) During the violence caused by the exile of President Jean-Bertrand Aristide, the HCR had urged the international community to grant asylum to feeling Haitians. None of it has happened to this day. "The situation does not require the HCR to adopt an official position, especially since Santo Domingo has opened its border for humanitarian reasons", considers Mrs Fleming [...] The United States have decided to grant a temporary protection status to Haitians present on their soil before January 12th, but warned that they would not receive any boat people. In Europe, granting a temporary protection status in order to receive refugees is a responsibility of the European Council. Granting it to the victims of the quake is not on the agenda. "Each country should at least grant work permits to Haitian immigrants so that they can send money home", analyses Jemini Pandya. According to the World Bank, the diaspora transfers each year about 1.2 billion euros to Haiti. (Allix 2010)[20]

The key words of the humanitarian 'care' logic: manage and protect. In both cases, these concepts have become the weapons of an ideology of protectionist and interested assistance that is not new – it was at work in the colonial system, notably in the reservations imposed on Indigenous peoples in order to displace them from their land – and consists of introducing donation as a non refundable debt. The logic of 'assistancialism' which generates dependence through imposed aid, known by Australian Aborigines as 'sit down money', is dehumanising. All the victims of disasters as well as any population increasingly perceived by states as fluxes of potential commodities are transformed into resources to 'care and protect', and are no longer considered as citizens and singular beings acting in their own name. In return, populations become distrustful, and riots break out. An example of that happened last autumn in Haiti when, as the cholera epidemic affected the victims of the earthquake and the hurricane in the midst of electoral tensions, rumours were spread about water poisoning by a UN peacekeeper and its involuntary propagation through the water system.[21]

---

[20] [Translated by editors.] See also the testimonies after the earthquake archived by *Etonnants Voyageurs*, the international literature and film festival of Saint-Malo, see: http://www.etonnants- voyageurs.com/spip.php?rubrique318

[21] Estimate on 24 November 2010: 2,000 dead, 70,000 contaminated, according to the UN Coordinator in Haiti, Nigel Fisher. *Réseau Alternatif Haïtien d'Information*, AlterPresse, 24 November 2010. Available at: http://www.alter-presse.org/spip.php?article10290 (accessed 2 December 2015).

Possible Unfolding

Responding to the 2010 destruction of the Roma settlements in France, Éric Fassin (2010) noticed in the *Mediapart* online newspaper:

> The populations that represent a problem, in other words, that are constructed as 'problematic', are not so much foreigners any longer but rather those whose situation puts in question the distribution between 'us' and 'them', supposedly just as simple as the name of the new French Ministry that puts immigration and national identity in opposition [...] The same goes for Black people: some, coming from French overseas territory, have been French for many generations; others are children of the more recent waves of sub-Saharan migrants. The stigmatisation of Black people is based on this double position, both internal and external.[22]

As mentioned above, this observation can be applied to many countries in the Americas, Oceania or the Indian Ocean. Together with the descendants of Melanesian or Asian populations used as indentured labour in Australia or the Mascarene Islands, voluntary migrants stigmatised due to the colour of their skin, the Indigenous populations (whether Black or not) who are native to colonised countries (Indigenous Australians, Amerindians, Kanaks or Tahitians) are also considered 'external' to the nation that pretends to assimilate them while rejecting them.

The stigmatisation of the indigestible otherness rests on the fact that they are seen by some powers as not 'manageable' by other means than security measures, which replaces the notion of foreigner in terms of national identity with that of 'exterior' in supposedly racial terms. This shift towards a fantasied 'nature' (skin colour, ethnic, religious or ideological history, etc.) of essentialised cultures (totally denying the history of colonisation, of the persecution of semi-nomadic peoples and Gipsies, but also of the biologising evolutionism of our disciplines, etc.) sends us back to the darkest times of the birth of criminology which, echoing the racial theses of the beginnings of anthropology, intended to define a typology of natural born criminals. The current tendency to criminalise all potential victims of racial or social segregation has been denounced by many researchers

---

[22] Translated by the editors of *Inflexions* 10. See also Fassin and Fassin (2006), Fassin et al. (2014). For an update on news and campaigns about discriminations/racial profiling/slavery and reparations, see the website of the CRAN, the Representative Council of Black Associations in France: https://le-cran.fr/

in anthropology and criminology.[23] This does not mean that crime is not present in all segments of the population, but rather that the exercise of justice is not the same for all, especially in liberal states, which hide their discriminatory practices behind the Declaration of Human Rights. Through the ever-faster substitution of the social state by the penal state (Wacquant 2009), the state not only turns to humanitarian emergency NGOs and charity organisations for the provision of social care, but also strives to get rid of victims and excluded people by singling them out as potential criminals that should be jailed or sent away.

In France, when the Roma were sent back to Romania after their camps were dismantled, European intellectuals, including the French Étienne Balibar, Tzvetan Todorov, Michel Agier and Françoise Vergès, launched *A Manifesto for Another Europe*:

> Let us oppose, together, the culture of emergency management based on obsessive surveillance, control and vilification of the strange and the different. Let us create, instead, a culture of solidarity and common purpose beyond our differences. Let us declare our repulsion for the unfair and unequal society that blames its own victims and casualties. (Amin et al. 2010)

In the current evolution of the world, it seems indispensable to interrogate the meaning of our disciplines in the light of social injustices and the global mechanisms that generate it, as well as of the responses generated by populations that endure them and by activists, intellectuals or not, who respond through manifestos. The traditional academic recommendation regarding the need for a scientific distance in order to remain 'objective' in social sciences has opened curious filiation tracks in disciplines where the civic, and even political, engagement, as well as the utopic spirit that prevailed at their beginning (Graeber 2004), now seem to be frowned upon by many colleagues in France and elsewhere. As I here try to show that one cannot separate natural catastrophes from social disasters, emergency policies from long-term ones, knowledge of the present from historical memories, humanitarian responses from the agency of victims, I believe that anthropology is particularly called to engage in analyses that consider all those relations in a critical way in order to trigger local and global reflection towards new social alternatives.

---

[23] Garland (2001), Cunneen (2007, 2010), Blagg (2008). In France in 2019, like in Australia, ecoactivists are criminalised and are all people who take action to propose alternatives to the destruction of the planet and to help refugees.

12

Standing with the Earth: From Cosmopolitical Exhaustion to Indigenous Solidarities

> The humans of the Earth, those in power in the 21st century, have often been classified as naturalists ... they believed that there was continuity between all physiological processes from the most simple to the most complex ... You might say that in our historical moment, everybody knows that that is not true. For example, between HI (human intelligence) and AI (artificial intelligence), there is no continuity of physical processes, even if we may feel that there is continuity to techniques of reasoning or knowledge processing ... Conversely, Earthlings often perceived the various levels of self-experience to be discontinuous. (Bonnefoy 2010, *Polynesia*: 454)

In the science fiction trilogy *Polynesia*, an archaeologist from the future offers this analysis after exploring galactic space-time and finding a text about Descola's four ontologies (animism, analogism, naturalism and totemism) in one of its folds (Descola [2005] 2013). The conversation between him and a friend is punctuated by the commentary of their two biocoms, or biological telephones, a kind of external hard drive attached to humans which takes the form of a miniature animal that continuously changes its appearance, from lizard to small bird, for instance. When the archaeologist muses about a time when humans still lived on earth, 'Certain groups of humans could be seen as totemistic ... for them, if they had the same physiological mechanisms as their totems, which only seems rational, they may have thought they also shared a sense of self-awareness with the totem animal', his Biocom replies by asking, 'Am I your totem?' (Bonnefoy 2010: 456). In this universe, in which polymorphous biomachines reflect on their own subjectivity, the humans who discover the ontologies of days gone by begin to test – in cults – their understanding of naturalism, totemism, analogism and animism's past definitions.[1]

---

[1] Special thanks to Toni Pape and Adam Szymanski for the translation of this paper first published under the same title in *Inflexions* 10 (2017): 1–24

Standing with the Earth

In the following essay, we are going to see that the exhaustion of the earth, of certain ontologies, and of our creative forces, are all interconnected, just as the ethico-aesthetic responses to this exhaustion are inseparable from cosmopolitics.

The Reinvention of Ontologies

Polynesia's description of SF cults seems to be partly inspired by current New Age movements which draw on various Amerindian and Celtic rituals, as well as other pre-Christian practices, which some of the practitioners then recreate as pantheistic or neo-pagan in order to revalourise the Earth. The inventive reinterpretation of all these rituals is often political, as is evidenced by the yearly May Day Parade in Minneapolis which celebrates the old rural tradition of the Maypole dance as much as the working-class struggle (see Linebaugh 2016; Sheehy 1999: 79–89).

In the 2016 parade which I observed, Black families dressed entirely in purple and held placards paying tribute to Prince, a famous son of the city and singer of 'Purple Rain'. Other signs denounced racism and police violence in support of the Black Lives Matter movement. These Black families walked side by side with Amerindian families from the North and South Americas wearing dresses adorned with feathers and sequins, and sporting placards denouncing the extractive industries that threaten their land. Other families marched with their faces and clothes painted brown like the earth, green like the forest, blue like the sea, pink like crustaceans or multi-coloured like the many animal and plant species endangered by various kinds of pollution. The parade's placards and banners, some of which were full of humour, also invited participants to make like an animal and jump into the procession of witches with pointed hats and brooms, slowly advancing on stilts, scooters, bikes, floats and foot. The crowd was full of joy. The parade culminated with an immense concert on the shore of a lake. The concert opened with a tribute to Mother Earth led by ten participants who represented the cultural – and spiritual – diversity of Minneapolis: a sacred fire was carried to a site consecrated to the four winds before being thrown into the lake.

(http://www.inflexions.org/exhaustion/main.html#n2). It is the expanded version of a conference paper, 'Debout avec la terre', presented at 'Terre 2.0. Comment ne pas manger la terre?' (EHESS, Paris, June 2016) and published in *Multitudes* 65 (2016).

Then followed a dance of giant puppets among which was a Prince figure in a purple toga and others representing the Mississippi river and Mother Earth. The show, featuring classical, electronic and soul music, was interspersed with lectures conveying the repentance of civil society; admissions that it had heretofore failed to recognise the presence of Indigenous peoples, that it had abused people of colour, that it hadn't been welcoming enough towards refugees and had not taken care of the land, but that it would commit to changing things from that moment on. Thousands of people with their children gathered together to participate in these joyful festivities, bearing witness to a form of serene conviviality that went beyond mere entertainment to offer a beacon of hope.

In his dialogue with Pierre Charbonnier, Philippe Descola notes that 'one can easily sign up for a course in shamanism online or participate in New Age rituals in St. Germain forest. But that doesn't mean that naturalism has perfectly integrated animism or analogism. Because in these cases ... we're dealing with forms emptied of their content and only the most superficial elements of these cosmological dispositifs have been conserved. From this perspective, I'm not sure that this will have a profound impact on the ongoing reorganisation of naturalism' (Descola 2014a: 304). Of course, the practice of rituals is not enough to shift ontologies and modes of existence towards a transformed collective milieu. In recent years, however, more and more activist movements fighting to denounce the destruction of living environments, especially due to extractive industries that precipitate climate change and pollute the air and water, are looking for alliances and sources of inspiration among peoples, such as Amerindians, who have a vision of the Earth different from one which denies nature under the pretext that it has surrendered to human technologies. Looked at in this way, I believe that certain hybrid movements are currently reinventing at least one new form of ontology.

The accelerationist tendency of geo-engineering, so well critiqued by Frédéric Neyrat (2014, [2016] 2018), shows that Western history, by way of its colonising development of both peoples and lands rich in resources, has come to assert that nature does not exist any longer for it has been 'consumed' by the technological productions of culture. The Earth is drained, exhausted, but is perhaps not done surprising us through the descendants of those who, colonised and classified at different moments in history as animists, totemists, pantheists or pagans, today attempt to resist the technological cannibalisation of nature by inviting us to see her, nature, as living in constant spiritual interaction with human beings. Even the proposition of rewilding or renaturalising parks, which includes photo safaris of 'protected' animals, only imagines an artificialised nature. Similarly, safaris of human populations enclosed and exploited on reserves are offered in all parts of the world and illustrate the arrogance behind a conception of nature as something to be mastered or conquered (Glowczewski 2015). This sort of arrogance was further confirmed during the conversation between Bruno Latour (presented as a sociologist rather than an anthropologist) and architect Rem Koolhaas at the 'Nuit des Idées au quai d'Orsay' (Night of Ideas at Quai d'Orsay) on 27 January 2016. The two interlocutors both affirmed that the planet Earth no longer had an exteriority because it had been entirely urbanised or impacted by the conditions that allow for urbanisation. By contrast, whether it is the multinaturalist perspectivism invoked by Viveiros de Castro with regard to Amerindians, the reticular cosmogeography of Aboriginal Australians with whom I have been working for more than thirty-seven years, or those of various shamanisms from all parts of the world, these points of 'seeing', as Deligny[2] used to say, and the relation between interior and exterior they articulate, do not fall within the Western 'perspective' limited to a reappropriation of the Earth's surface as a foundation for construction and drilling.

This form of materialism, which thinks the planet as a surface to be mined, a spacecraft to continuously reconfigure, and which no longer knows any exteriority, is fundamentally different not only from shamanic ontologies, whether they be of Northern or Southern Amerindian or of Australian Aboriginal provenance, but also from ontologies that have been reconfigured by both Indigenous peoples and activists, as well as all those who try to experience the fact that we can be inhabited or traversed by exteriorities. These kinds of ontological exteriorities arise from other types of materiality which assume that spirit is not just interior to a body but multiplied across visible or invisible spaces. To accept these kinds of transversalities is the condition of a convivial relation not only with the Earth but any milieu inhabited by humans, those 'from here' and those who come from 'elsewhere', be they migrants and asylum seekers or spirits. To be inhabited or traversed by exteriorities does not speak to some

---

[2] See 'Living Networks Ecologies: Fernand Deligny in the Age of Social Networks', a filmed seminar by Drew Burk (2013): http://scalar.usc.edu/works/network-ecologies/living-network-ecologies-an-introduction

kind of transcendence. On the contrary, it means to recognise immanence within oneself. For Aboriginal Australians, this immanence of exteriority is lived in the way every birth of a human is related to the incarnation of a localised spirit of the Earth; throughout their entire lives, Aboriginal men and women actualise in themselves other spirits that are shared with different totems, or Dreamings, *Jukurrpa* as the Warlpiri and their desert neighbours say. In other words, totemism does not here resolve itself in a continuity of resemblance between an individual and an animal – 'I am like this snake which is at ease everywhere it goes, which can live both in the water and on firm ground … like the snake I avoid confrontations' (Jowandi Wayne Barker, personal communication). Instead of a unique and essentialised attribute, each person is an assemblage of several contextualised analogies, of relations that change throughout the course of life, with a singular constellation of totems or Dreamings. A given animal or plant, the rain, the wind or fire are lived as multiple virtualities in a process of becoming that is context dependent, in humans as well as non-humans, and terrestrial and extraterrestrial sites considered as a partial materialisation of a trace, an emanation or an organ of a given totem. That is why I speak of *Totemic Becomings: Cosmopolitics of the Dreaming* (Glowczewski 2015). Every man or woman is the guardian of a constellation of Dreamings for which he or she has the responsibility of regularly celebrating rituals which consist of mapping the sites and itineraries of each Dreaming through body paintings, songs and dances; a responsibility which stems from each person being recognised as a mutable manifestation of a given Dreaming which corresponds to them, either by his or her own design (as revealed in a dream), by inheritance from the family group, or through alliances created over the course of their life.

In light of this, the tragedy that constitutes the destruction of a sacred site does not only result from the fact that a totemic site is 'an ontological incubator, i.e. the site where the identity of the members of a collective is formed in very concrete ways, the common root for a group of humans and nonhumans' (Descola 2014a: 328). Each of these sites negotiates virtual relations with other sites (other humans and other beings). To destroy a site associated with any given totem amounts to endangering other sites and their guardians: all those who are connected to the same 'line' of Dreaming, the songline that links hundreds of sites spanning an ancestral totemic people, and all the sites belonging to other totemic lines which intersect the path of the endangered site. I have said elsewhere that access to the space-time of

Dreaming within those sites was 'holographic' (in the sense proposed by Roy Wagner): through each sacred site one can virtually access the other sites (Glowczewski 1991). This holographic capacity indicates that everything is related as in an open mega-ecosystem or cosmosystem: everything that affects a site or one of its human or non-human becomings can have an impact on all that is living and the forces of the universe. The rituals celebrating the Dreamtime journeys contribute to the caretaking of sites belonging to these reticulum, but also other lifelines that they encounter. To dance for the Rain Dreaming, for instance, is also to take care of animals and plants that are in need of rain. To sing to a plant is to care for the animal that feeds on this plant and for all the unborn children whose totemic becomings will be the Dreaming of this plant, or the animal that feeds on it.

It is important to note that this gigantic meshwork of Dreamlines is not fixed. Apart from the 'accidents' or events that make up the features of a rugged landscape, which do need to be considered, the ways of moving through it change according to the seasons and the climate that continuously transform the landscape. Australian mythical stories even account for transformations of a geological scale: the Fire Dreaming, for instance, refers to the ancient volcanoes and uranium deposits; the Kangaroo Dreaming evokes the marsupial megafauna that have long gone extinct on the continent; while the Emu Dreaming of the Northern Coast at the Indian Ocean accounts for paw prints recognised by specialists as belonging to diverse species of dinosaurs. Today, astrophysicists study the so-called mythical narratives about meteors that fell from the sky to leave sacred craters. Similarly, all coastal groups of Aboriginals relate stories about the continent's flooding and the subsequent separation of approximately 4,000 islands which presently surround continental Australia, a geological event that has been dated by a team of geologists as 7,000 years old (Gough 2015; Glowczewski and Laurens [2015] 2018).

This kind of interconnection between sacred sites and vital forces can also be found in the *Xapiri*'s spiderweb of shamanic spirit paths which, according to the wonderful account by Yanomami Davi Kopenawa, traverse the Amazonian forest like a network that is invisible to the naked eye but sparkles like a crystal for the shamans (Kopenawa and Albert [2010] 2013; see also Viveiros de Castro 2007). There are as many *Xapiri* paths as there are birds, plants or other forms of biodiversity. So for Indigenous people and numerous other alarmed voices, the streets and great dams which redirect rivers risk the destruction of the multiple paths that link all living forms. Stripped of its biodiversity, the forest has already been partially transformed into savannahs or deserts where human and non-human inhabitants of these lands suffer, increasingly due to the pollution of local waters with mercury (used in goldmining) and other contaminants such as oil. Scientists, for their part, have been able to demonstrate that the disappearance of oxygen due to the local destruction of the forest severely threatens the rest of our environments across the planet (Werf et al. 2009) In relation to the survival of human and non-human populations, the affirmation of the interconnectivity of sites traversed by ancestral traces and tracings that are both material and spiritual, visible and invisible can be found as a critical issue in all the ontologies that Descola distinguishes (totemic, animist, analogist or even naturalist). I for one believe that common practices make it possible to bring certain ontological traits, traits of singularity as Guattari would say, closer together in a way that doesn't deny their diversity. For instance, some groups which Descola distinguishes according to his ontological categories (Australians as totemists and Amazonians as animists) are less different when one looks at their shamanic practices. In the same way, certain Indigenous conceptions of intersubjectivity that associate the self, others (human or not) and the environment in extended relations of aliveness create a new form of ontological 'commons': such a process of subjectification can offer a response to the current challenges of global climate change and social injustice, a posture that is radically opposed to the one held by those responsible for these threats or those who speculate on accelerationism and transhumanism (Srnicek and Williams 2013).[3]

In the 1960s and 1970s, a new appreciation of Indigenous peoples crystallised in a valourisation of nature shared by the so-called hippie movement, groups advocating vegetarian and later GMO-free diets, and philosophies of organic architecture. In part, this new appreciation grew out of various Indigenous struggles to affirm a mode of existence in close spiritual relation with the environment, a struggle that passed through claims for land rights and land use. Thus in 1983 the Arrernte women of the Alice Springs region held that the construction of a dam that would destroy Welatye Therre or 'Two Breasts', their sacred site related to mother's milk, imperilled the

---

[3] See also Matteo Pasquinelli's (2014) 'The Labour of Abstraction. Seven Transitional Theses on Marxism and Accelerationism' and Frédéric Neyrat's (2014a) comment on it in *Multitudes* 56. See also Neyrat (2017).

fertility and nursing quality of not only the site's guardian women but also of women from other linguistic groups who guard the Dreamline that connects this site to other places from Southern Australia all the way to the Tiwi Islands in the north. Furthermore, these guardians of Arrernte land and law insisted that the breastfeeding and fertility of all the women living on the Australian continent would be affected by the destruction of the site. They then received massive support from other women, Aboriginal and otherwise, and well as Australian and international feminist movements.

At the time, these protests were successful in protecting the site and I evoked this example in a 1984 article entitled 'Les tribus du rêve cybernétique' ('The Tribes of the Cybernetic Dream'). New digital technologies which were then invented in California tried to combine a set of values respectful of the Earth with the notion of generalised interconnection. That is what seduced Félix Guattari and Gilles Deleuze in their writings, which were later taken up by many practitioners and thinkers of cyberspace.

SF and Slow Anthropology

> We can ask ourselves if the Aboriginal notion of the Dreaming, which links society and nature by energetic self-referential feedback loops, does not offer a philosophy adapted to our epoch in search of theories concerning matter and energy. The fascination that Aboriginal people provoke (among some people) is probably part of this intuition. We are close to a science fiction universe when we think that these peoples have survived 40,000 years of the Earth's geographical transformations and that they speak today of sacred sites where we find petroleum and uranium. Aboriginal people say that we must not destroy these energies, because they are part of a vast regulatory cycle that gives meaning to the life and death of humans. Thus it is with as much ease as detachment (which troubles our evolutionary values) that they adopt all of the material goods that our technological cornucopia proposes: houses, cars, and media can be used, they say, but the most important is to keep contact with the energies of the Earth and the Dreaming ... In American military bases isolated in the desert, engineers sometimes have peculiar visions. For example, the vision of an Aboriginal man would appear out of nowhere in the computer room, then evaporate, but not before saying in a cavernous voice, that they must cease what they are doing there ...' (Glowczewski 1984: 162)

When I wrote this in 1984, Félix Guattari suggested that I read Vico, Whitehead and Simondon, and to use the notion of 'singularity' to translate the Aboriginal understanding of energy as 'image-forces' that actualise and re-virtualise themselves through ritual in order to distinguish this from the non-renewable energies produced by humans.[4] The rumours of Dreaming voices haunting the US bases of the Central Australian desert inspired Wim Wenders to direct his 1991 science fiction film set at the end of the twenty-first century entitled *Until the End of the World*. With a nuclear satellite having lost control, the film tells of an eccentric scientist who is obsessed with controlling time through the technological visualisation of dreams, and works in a secret laboratory in the Australian desert where he experiments on the brains of his wife, his son's partner Claire and even on himself, up until the point of total exhaustion: the death of his wife, the delirious fixations of Claire and the final destruction of the research base.

The generalised interconnectivity and transversality of human and non-human, animal and machinic subjectivities that Deleuze and Guattari theorised in their writings is today – it seems to me – sometimes misunderstood by those who use them to support transhumanism and those who cite them all the while reproaching Deleuze and Guattari for legitimising a 'geo-engineering' that aims to modify the climate rather than change our modes of existence in relation to the milieu. Of course, we do not know what they would say with regards to the evolution of the world since the 1990s. But I do not think that Deleuze and Guattari would support absurd geo-engineering projects since these projects fundamentally fall outside what they valued and defended most: the responsible and ethical influence of the micropolitical on the macropolitical, creative of dissensus.[5] Evidence of this, amongst others, is the particular interest that Félix Guattari expressed in the Walpiri people's relationship to dreams when he read my thesis in 1983, which nourished his cartography of four semiotic types in mutual tension with one another.

    semiotics of subjectification (including architecture, town planning, public amenities, etc.) operate like existential territories (real and virtual).
    techno-scientific semiologies, (plans, diagrams, programs, studies, research) operate like machinic phylums (actual and possible).

---

[4] See Chapters 1 and 2 of this book.
[5] An approach very different from Bateson's consensual conflict resolution is found in Félix Guattari's late lecture 'Producing a Culture of Dissensus: Heterogenesis and an Aesthetic Paradigm' (Guattari 1991).

economic semiotics (monetary, financial, and accountancy mechanisms) operate like flows (actual and real).

juridical semiotics (property deeds, various legislative measures and regulations) operate like incorporeal universes of value (possible and virtual). (Guattari [1989] 2000: 48)

Later, Deleuze cited my book *Du Rêve à la Loi chez les Aborigènes* (1991) (From Dreaming to the Law Among Aboriginal Australians) with regards to the cartographic relation between the imaginary and the real: 'This is why the imaginary and the real must be, rather, like two juxtaposable or superimposable parts of a single trajectory, two faces that ceaselessly interchange with one another. Thus Aboriginal Australians link nomadic itineraries to dream voyages, which together compose "an interstitching of routes," in an immense cut-out [découpe] of space and time that must be read like a map' (Deleuze 1997: 63). From the perspective of transversal assemblages of singularities, the Aboriginal approach to reticular thinking allowed me to explore their multiple relations to space and time as a cosmopolitics, in the sense that Isabelle Stengers defines the term (Stengers 2005). Contrary to the cosmopolitanism promoted by Bernard Henry Lévy and Guy Scarpetta in 1981 who went to war against all claims for identity or territory,[6] for Stengers the notion of the cosmopolitical is inspired as much by her critique of scientific disenchantment as by the emergence of new alliances, such as those forged between the ecofeminists and the movement of Wiccan witches, who have revived an interest in the re-enchantment of a political world equally anchored in the body, mind and flesh, as well as in mineral, vegetal and atmospheric matter (Stengers 2011).

Wenders' film, where the scientist does not understand the creative breadth of Aboriginal dream-work, as well as the novel Polynesia, where the cults fall back onto ontological categories that become caricatural, stay within a certain science fiction tradition where science and its technological fantasies are the main motor of dramatic intrigue. Quentin Meillassoux opposes this literary tradition, in the name of a certain speculative realism, to what he calls a science fiction 'outside science', as the only path to imagine other worlds (Meillassoux 2015). In its own way, this notion of science fiction 'outside science' refuses the accelerationist logic of the sciences and echoes what Isabelle

---

[6] See Lévy's 'Le fascisme à la française' (Fascism the French Way) and Scarpetta's 'Le cosmopolitisme, encore, plus que jamais' (Cosmopolitism, Still, More than Ever) in *Art Presse* 45 (1981) and my response in *Art Presse* 47 (1981), p. 2.

Stengers calls 'slow science'. She elaborates the idea through the polysemic notion of 'SF', which for Donna Haraway can be equally read as 'science fiction', 'scientific fact', or 'string figures' (in reference to the figures made during string games) (Haraway 2013, 2015). Stengers explains that the correlations at work in 'slow' scientific reasoning correspond to the necessary correlations for passing from one string figure to another, a passage which always implies a relation, as the input of one person's hands changes the string figure held by the other. The process implied in the transformations of these figures is an image (but not a metaphor) for expressing what Stengers in her introduction calls speculative gestures that can 'slowly and softly' change reality (Stengers and Debaise 2015). I accept her invitation to think how the 'slow' social sciences could create the conditions to promote string figures as well as science fiction. 'The plea of Whitehead regarding the task of universities thus also aimed at a "slowing down" of science, which is the necessary condition for thinking with abstractions and not obeying to abstractions ... I would then characterize slow science as the demanding operation which would reclaim the art of dealing with, and learning from, what scientists too often consider messy, that is, what escapes general, so called objective, categories' (Stengers 2011: 6–7, 10). A science fiction 'outside science' joins in its own way the 'slowing down' of science: at the level of anthropology it offers one way to break out of causal and exclusive reasoning that traps us in the sciences, exhausting our power to imagine other worlds, and other ontologies for living on this Earth.

An example of a science fiction 'outside science' that invites one to think another liveable world here and now, and that changes the relationship to time and 'objective' categories of exclusion (between races, species and spiritual phenomena), seems at work in the recent television series *Cleverman*, created by Australian Aboriginal filmmaker Ryan Griffen, whose title references the Australian medicine men (see Burke 2016 and Griffen 2016). The series stars a young Aboriginal man as its hero who inherits a superpower allowing him – in spite of his initial rejection of it – to intervene in an Australia where strange beings from another dimension, called 'the Hairy people', are sequestered behind a security wall or locked in prison. These characters hark back to ancestral monsters from the Dreaming that are present in the mythology of several Aboriginal groups in Australia. But the series chooses to incarnate them in the role of a 'prehuman' minority that has been given the right to live amongst humans. In the series, the acceptance of the Hairy men and women (monsters who scared Aboriginals long before they appeared in the science fiction series) stands in for an acceptance of Australia's diverse peoples: Aboriginals, Whites, and the waves of other migrants from the Pacific, Asia or Africa, as much as the refugees and asylum seekers. The Hairy people are 'monsters' and their traits resemble the Neanderthals, the ancestors of man.[7] The fantastical cinema of superheroes has garnered extreme popularity the world over, particularly amongst youth who 'recognise themselves' in it, not just as if they share in a popular culture but more as if they themselves participate in the refounding of a veritable mythology. It is not a question of creating a monolithic culture, but of valourising possibilities for human and non-human diversity where different spaces and times intermix. We cannot underestimate the subjectifying force of these stories since they circulate across the world. The truth of their impact cannot be evaluated by separating their form (films, video games, costumes and accessories) from their content, and pretending to define this content as the basis for the ontology of a society or a religion. The popularity of superheroes and other human-nonhuman hybrids (demons, zombies, vampires, werewolves, humanoid robots or clones, aliens, etc.) must be understood beyond their symbolic efficacy or the autheniticity of their foundation. Something asignifying about them, in the Guattarian sense, puts intensities and collective assemblages of enunciation into play that act and traverse subjectivities, creating a complicity, a shared world that could elicit a new mode of collective existence. An activist mockumentary shot in black and white featured an Aboriginal man in a superman costume named Superboong – a reappropriated insult – who intervenes against racism and injustice (see 'The rise of the Aboriginal superhero'). The invention of worlds proposed by superheroes participates in the production of new myths whose wide visibility gives rise to a new 'cultural patrimony'; an SF interactive imaginary with a real role for youth, that also produces new forms of subjectification reinforced by the way the audience comments on all of this and actualises it in their lives using social media. For instance, J. K. Rowling, the author of Harry Potter is currently being criticised on Twitter for supporting Donald Trump's rhetoric on free speech and has also come under recent scrutiny from Native Americans for the way she uses their mythology in her latest book and film.

---

[7] This is far from what the Breakthrough Institute, reinforced by Latour's 'Love Your Monsters', calls for: man-made technological products.

In this context, an Aboriginal auteur's use of the TV series format to develop a Cleverman superhero, who has a White mother and refuses to accept his father's ancestry of Aboriginal medicine men until he finally decides to accept the superpowers and become an avenger of justice in a contemporary urban landscape, reflects an ontological strategy in the ecosophic sense of Félix Guattari, in that it is at once aesthetically, ethically and politically critical (a strategy that knots the mental, social and environmental ecologies, in a milieu that is equally technical and natural). If university criticism with respect to superhero films can exhaust or exhaust itself in academic rhetoric, just like many films of this genre that incessantly repeat stereotypes, this Aboriginal director's reappropriation of them invites us, rather, to imagine and produce new ontological alliances.

Ecosophy and Indigenous Alliances

> They open the door for us so that we can enter
> but they close their heart and mind and plug their ears.
> What can we do?
> Plenty of things, even a hunger strike.
> But there is one thing we must never do:
> We must never give up our rights, never!!
> ('Bonne nouvelle de l'ONU')

These are the concluding words of a text written in 2004 during a hunger strike at the United Nations by seven Indigenous delegates – including Alexis Tiouka, a Kali'na activist from French Guiana.[8] The hunger strike is yet another ecosophic type of ontological strategy that accompanies the struggles of Indigenous people. In 2007, the Declaration on the Rights of Indigenous Peoples was signed by all countries except four – Australia, the United States, New Zealand and Canada – who all later decided to support the Declaration after changes in government. In 2008, Australia and Canada held large national ceremonies to ask their Aboriginal populations to pardon the abuses they have suffered, such as the forced separation of children

---

[8] The hunger strike signatories include: Adelard Blackman, Buffalo River Dene Nation, Canada; Andrea Carmen, Yaqui Nation, Arizona, United States; Alexis Tiouka, Kaliña, Guyane Française; Charmaine White Face, Ogala Tetuwan, Sioux Nation Territory, North America; Danny Billie, Traditional Independent Seminole Nation of Florida, United States; Saul Vicente, Zapoteca, Mexico. See Tiouka and Ferrarini (2017). See also the historical 1984 statement to the French government by Félix Tiouka in Alexis Tiouka (2016).

from their families. The very same year in Ecuador, then in 2009 in Bolivia, the principle of *Buen vivir* (living well) was adopted into the constitutions of these two countries who recognise 'the rights of nature' associated with Pachamama, the name of an Andean goddess also revered by some groups of the Amazon and other citizens, including Christians. Figures such as Pachamama, 'by their political-symbolic dimension, their hybrid position between nature and culture, and their utility in spreading the revolutionary message, can be sufficiently large to hold various cosmologies within them ... A prime example is how movements which are sometimes opposed to one another, such as urban feminism and the trade unionism of rural women, or Indigenous animists and analogists, by converging around Pachamama and the rights of women, have been able to ally their positions on a number of points' (Landivar and Ramillien 2015: 36).

In 2010, at Cochabamba in Bolivia, 35,000 delegates from 45 countries signed The Universal Declaration of the Rights of Mother Earth that has for its preamble 'that we are all part of Mother Earth, an indivisible, living community of interrelated and interdependent beings with a common destiny'.[9] Mobilisation around this declaration also proposes amendments to the Rome Statute of the Criminal Court that would recognise the crime of 'ecocide'.[10] The internationalising of the concept of Pachamama as the 'maternal spirit of the Earth', like Indigenous reappropriation of superheroes in TV series, shows the impact of new mythologies and rituals as active not only during a performance at the UN, but as tools that traverse the daily lives of all of the Earth's actors. This impact of the large-scale recosmopoliticisation of ancient and local cosmological concepts stimulates the virtuality of new subjectivities and ontologies that function differently depending on the circumstances. In addition to its spiritual sense,

---

[9] For a clip with the text of the Declaration, see: https://www.youtube.com/watch?v=YU5HmTucTRg (accessed October 2018); Article 12: 'Human beings have the responsibility of respecting, protecting, preserving, and if necessary, restoring the integrity of the cycles and equilibriums that are essential to the Earth, and of putting precautionary and restrictive measures in place in order to avoid the human activities that lead to the extinction of species, the destruction of ecosystems or the alteration of ecological cycles.'

[10] In 2014 the 'Charter of Brussels' officially asked for the establishment of an International Criminal Court of the Environment and of Health: 'The Charter introduces Environmental crime as a crime against Humanity and calls for the recognition of this principle by the United Nations' (http://www.naturerights.com/site/campagne_page-10.html). See also: https://www.endecocide.org/en/sign/

for some, the Pachamama ceremony for Mother Earth or Mother Nature is a political protocol comparable to the Maori haka danced by New Zealand's sports teams (or the Ma'ohi from French Polynesia, executed by various overseas French army bodies during the Bastille Day parade in 2011) or the national anthems that reference the God of Christianity even when one part of the country's population is not Christian. But in contrast to national, and even nationalist rituals, the Pachamana ceremony is a transnational proposition that extends the recognition of the living above and beyond the human.

At the Permanent Forum on Indigenous Issues held in New York during May 2016, along with the rest of the audience I took part in the Pachamama ceremony that opened a session on the condition of Indigenous women that was followed by a number of declarations and recommendations to states, including a letter from Ecuadorian women to China, denouncing its destruction of their lands and livelihood by oil, gas and large hydraulic dam projects. Here again, the local approach of a community from Ecuador, which addresses itself to the Chinese state and a transnational company, echoes the problems faced by Indigenous Australians, particularly those from the north-west of the Kimberley where the Chinese have bought land and become the largest landowner in Australia in order to undertake a massive shale gas fracking project. As has now been revealed, not only have the two companies corrupted some Australian political representatives with astronomical sums of money, but the continent that partly depends on this region's water is under the threat of a complete drought (Cole 2016).

The Kimberley groups in Australia are engaged in a soil 'cleansing' programme, a term used to describe the traditional practice of controlled small bush fires during the wet season which prevents good plants from being overrun by weeds that are susceptible during the dry season to wildfires that destroy everything on their path for hundreds of kilometres.[11] Scientists needed time to understand the wisdom of this ancient practice that today is encouraged by all of the natural parks that hire Aboriginal men and women for their knowledge. The strategy has proven itself to be an impressive way to cut carbon emissions which are exceedingly high in Australia due to – amongst other reasons – fires that ravage the continent each year. It is promoted as a model which can be exported and it qualifies for what

---

[11] See: https://www.youtube.com/watch?v=eqqU-RNkfWk and https://www.youtube.com/watch?v=mSn2gv3tP60

is called REDD+ (Reducing Emissions from Deforestation and Forest Degradation), a form of monetary compensation for carbon emission reducers, in this case Aboriginals represented by the KLC (Kimberley Land Council), but also their sponsor, Shell, which thus appears to be cleared of the emissions caused by its extractive activities.[12]

During the COP21 (2015 United Nations Climate Change Conference), diverse official and unofficial meetings discussed the ambiguity of REDD+ and the trap of 'commodifying' nature. Certain communities don't have any choice but to participate in the REDD+ programmes that at least allow them to stay in the forest in a process of permanently negotiating with the resource extraction companies. But Indigenous peoples are increasingly looking to replace these accords with collective land-based programmes that inherently oppose extractivist industries, from fossil fuels to renewable energies, as well as large-scale dams, falsely presented by some as a 'clean' solution even though they destroy the ecosystems by diverting the river networks that maintain the forest's biodiversity. As the Alliance of Mother Nature's Guardians underline in their text, if the Indigenous peoples are the guardians of the forest, rivers and roots, their ethnocide also constitutes an act of 'ecocide' (Alliance des Gardiens de Mère Nature 2015: 163).[13]

Through these sorts of transplanetary meetings, new awarenesses are formed and new alliances forged. That is not to say that all differences are flattened in an ecumenical mould. In fact, the different Indigenous speakers at the UN insist on their respective singularities but allow themselves to compare their respective practices to build bridges and find common solutions to issues that affect the entire planet, and to call us to change our economy and lifestyles.

The political importance of these alternative modes of existence to our present ways is confirmed by the fact that Indigenous leaders are often threatened. What may appear to some to be anecdotal or exotic forms of resistance, when put into practice on the ground, become sufficiently threatening to the giants – mining companies

---

[12] 'Reducing Emissions from Deforestation and Forest Degradation (REDD) is an effort to create a financial value for the carbon stored in forests, offering incentives for developing countries to reduce emissions from forested lands and invest in low-carbon paths to sustainable development' (http://www.un- redd. org/how-we-work).

[13] See also Nidala Barker's statement about the criminal impact on life through fracking in the Kimberley, at the session on Water during the Indigenous Embassy at the Bellevilloise, in Paris, during the 2015 COP21 (Glowczewski 2016b).

and other powers – who try to get rid of these little Davids, first with money, destruction and child abduction, as recently seen in Mexico, or with assassinations, like those of the Guarani in Brazil or of ecological activists, like Berta Cáceres, leader of the Council of Popular and Indigenous Organisations of Honduras (COPINH) (see 'Environmental and Indigenous rights leader murdered in Honduras', *Euronews* (2016)). In conclusion, it seems vital that an ecosophic ontology reinvents itself from day to day, to support Indigenous peoples in their ontological becomings that they continuously redefine in synch with new transnational and transdisciplinary alliances that resist and confront other international economic and financial alliances that destroy the planet and all that lives – and stands – on and with it.

PART V
Dancing with the Spirits of the Land

Figure 13.1 An image of Exu incorporated in Father Abilio was filmed in Florianopolis by B. G., who projects it on Clarissa Alcantara dancing in Geneva. Extracted from the Cosmocolours *performance filmed by Sandra Alves 2015*

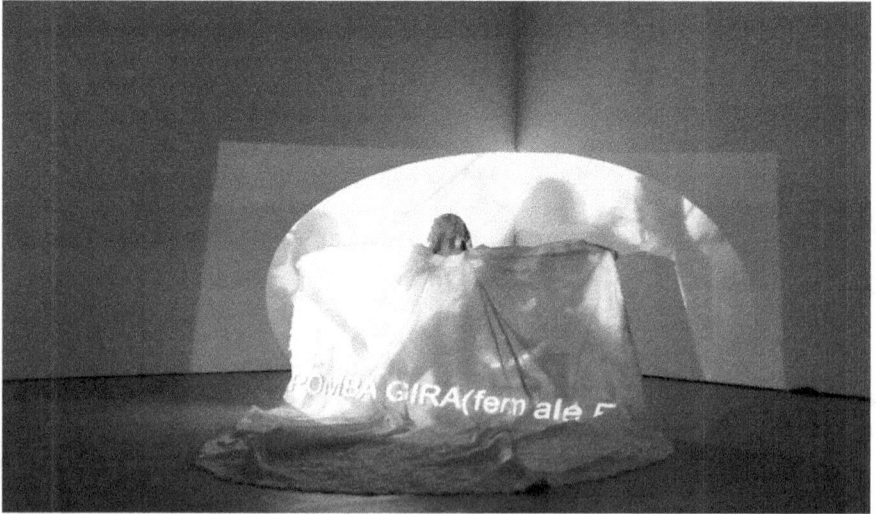

Figure 13.2 An image of a Pomba Gira incorporation is projected by B. G. on Clarissa Alcantara who incorporates in turn. Extracted from the Cosmocolours *performance filmed by Sandra Alves 2015*

13

Cosmocolours:
A Filmed Performance of Incorporation and a Conversation with the Preta Velha Vó Cirina

On the other hand (...) a more 'post-modern' position might insist that the ethnographer or anthropologist can only *hope to* 'represent' native words and life in his texts, whilst trances and possessions aim more to present a force rather than to represent a substance. In this case, it could be replied that the rapprochement between those different modes of learning could precisely help us to escape from the representationalist empire, which post-modern thinkers, themselves, have pointed out as anthropology's limit. (Goldman 2015: 24)

The performance *Cosmocolours* that I proposed for the exhibition *The Beast and Adversity* (Geneva, 2015) is a step in a long process of questioning that has haunted my work as an anthropologist since my first fieldwork in Australia in 1979, when I filmed desert Aboriginal rituals.[1] Until then I was using an intermittent mode to record frame by frame the 16 mm film strip, so as to produce experimental films working on rhythmic superimpositions and flickering pulsating lights: a music for the eyes and a visual exploration for our senses. In place of narrative, the fabrication of discontinuous images working on perception so as to interrupt the continuity of movement. Inspired by the movement of independent cinema and promoted at the University of Paris 8 in the forest of Vincennes, near Paris) by the film-makers Claudine Eizykman and Guy Fihman, this research was aiming to produce a dis-narrative effect with a material, and sensory perceptual

---

[1] This text was first published in Portugese and in English in the bilingual Brazilian online journal of visual anthroplogy: GIS, Gesto, Imageme e Som (2 (1): 274–99 [2017]): http://www.revistas.usp.br/gis/article/view/129204 (accessed October 2018). It was written first in Portugese with the help of Clarissa Alcantara and later translated into English by the author. Special thanks to Clarissa for her inspiration, hospitality and dance, and to the author's daughters, Milari Barker and Nidala Barker, for their proofreading of the English version. Milari took part in the Geneva performances and Nidala met Vó Cirina in Florianopolis in February 2015.

effect of discontinuity, by playing with the 24 frames per second scrolling of the 16 mm film roll. Personally, apart from the aesthetic and sensory dimension, I was also looking for a way to provoke altered states of consciousness arising from these subliminal stimuli. Such experimentations were echoing experimental films made at the beginning of cinema by artists like Maya Deren (1947–1953), an anthropologist, who was also questioning how to render forces at play in rituals and trances that she observed, particularly in Haïti.

To film in the Central Australian desert in 1979, I used a little Pathé Webo 16 mm camera, which only fitted 3 minute cartridges. My shots were not even longer than a quarter of a second each, and with many superimpostions created by rewinding the camera to re-film on images previously shot. This process created effects of superimposed images at different rhythms, mixing (in the same frame) close-ups with zooming movement and wide angle shots with the line of the horizon displaced as a diagonal and flickering scintillating rhythms; the Warlpiri women, whose rituals I had filmed, were not really convinced by my attempt to transpose in that way their relation to what they call *Jukurrpa* and which they translate in English as 'The Dreaming(s)'. To help the viewers to capture something of this Aboriginal cosmovision of the dreaming process, I had assumed, mistakenly, that I could suggest the condensation process characterising dreams, by 'retranslating' it through visual experimentations – constrained by the possibilities of a mechanical camera. Well, the Warlpiri specialists of dream – that is, women who use their dreams to communicate with ancestral totemic animals, plants, rain or wind – asked me to film 'normally' so as to respect the right 'rhythm' of their dances, where they are said to 'become' particular ancestral totemic forces. In those days, in the 1970s, the Warlpiri women were not familiar with films based on special effects which were going to be globally popularised later on. So, I filmed 'normally' (Glowczewski 2014) and it is 15 minutes of those 'normal' images (16 mm, silent) that I presented at the performance in Geneva.

Like Maya Deren, who did not find in the dreamlike work of surrealism a response to the transmission of spiritual experiences (Sullivan 2001), I was asking myself how to render and make feel the 'presence' of a ritual, with its affects and effects, in a way that would escape the reduction induced by any commented representation of a filmed sequence. Anna Barseghian's invitation to participate in her exhibition project *The Beast and Adversity* stimulated me to try a visual experience that would confront my images of Australian

Cosmocolours

rituals with the Umbanda rituals that I had recently filmed in Brazil.[2] I was motivated by the desire to make (others) feel that beyond the diversity of these rituals, there is something that feels 'common', that is, the specific intention of these types of cosmovisions to facilitate, through the collective assemblage, the emergence of a multiplicity of becomings in each of the participants that desires so: in Australia, totemic becomings of the Dreamings, ancestral forces shared by humans, animals, plants, wind or rain; in Brazil, ancestral becomings of African divinities, the Orixás, and spirits of Caboclo, Preto Velho, Beijada, Exu and Pomba-Gira.

> After witnessing hundreds of Aboriginal totemic rituals in which people 'become' the totems that are given as their 'dreamings' since birth or initiation, I was surprised to see in Brazil some episodes in the Umbanda rituals that seemed to present certain features that I thought were specific to Australia. In fact, both kinds of ritual respond in their own way to Guattari's definition of 'I is another, a multiplicity of others, embodied at the intersection of partial components of enunciation, overflowing individuated identity and the organized body in all directions'. (*Chaosmosis*: 83)
>
> I met many Brazilians who have been at least once to a Candomblé or Umbanda house of a *pai* or *mãe de santo* (father or mother of saint) for a divination with cowrie shells and stones to find out which Orixá (sometimes two or more) they carry 'inside' them as a virtuality that may or may not be actualized. It takes a relatively long initiation for the 'medium' to be ready for his/her Orixá to manifest during the cult. Certain people choose not to engage in this process, while others, even after initiation, may never experience it. In other words, 'becoming orixá' appears different from the notion of a body being passively possessed as the vehicle for an Orixá. People talk about being incorporated, receiving a shade or 'working' as a medium. (Glowczewski 2015: 36)

When I went back to Brazil, in 2015, I asked Clarissa Alcantara (2011) – performing artist, philosopher, schizoanalytical therapist trained in Deleuze and Guattari studies,[3] involved, for many years, in

---

[2] See: https://www.utopiana.art/en/cosmocouleurs. I was invited, from February to July 2013, by CAPES and CNPq to give a course (in anthropology) at USFC and to give conferences at other universities: USP, PUC-SP, UFRGS, UFG, UFPE, Fundação Joaquim Nabuco in Recife, UFMS, UFSCAR e UFPEL-RS. Special thanks to all these Brazilian institutions for the opportunity to carry out this research.

[3] Alcantara and Glowczewski met in Uberaba, at the International Congress of *Schizoanalysis and Schizodrama* organised by the Fundação Gregorio Baremblitt, in 2013. Alcantara was then invited to participate at the conference organised

the type of rituals I filmed in Brazil – if she would accept to collaborate with me for the presentation in Geneva. The proposition was to create a performative dance, where images made during a session of Exu (with a recording of dances by the participants in a state of incorporation by Orixás and other entities) would be projected onto her, such as might be done onto an animated screen. The movement of her body, that already had lived through and embodied different states of incorporation as a medium, would allow to 'reflect' in a real and figurative sense different aspects of the multiplicity incorporated in the filmed people. Clarissa responded enthusiastically to this proposal which brought together art, anthropology, philosophy and the sacred, an assemblage that also corresponded to her own research, as explained in her post-doctoral project:

> ... at the intersection of different fields of knowledge, taking as a motto a research started in 1988, called *Teatro Desessência*, the Theatre of 'de-essence' and my relation with the image and the oblivion, I will investigate now the framework of an anthropological perspective. This research is made of combinations rising between art, philosophy, literary theory and psychological clinic, from the invention of a practice of performance, the 'act/process' (*ato/processo*), and my devices (*dispositivos*) for producing image in the process of corporeal, visual and sound language, articulated with pragmatics of schizoanalysis, as proposed by Gilles Deleuze and Félix Guattari.[4]

We went together to talk with the Father of saints Abílio Noé da Silveira, Babalorixá of the Tenda Espírita Vó Cirina in Florianópolis, the 'Spiritual tent' located in his private house where I had filmed sessions of incorporations, every Thursday, from February till June 2013. With generosity and confidence, he accepted the project. I filmed, in February 2015, three other sessions of incorporations and called the project in French *Cosmocouleurs* (*Cosmocolours*), referring to the different colours that characterise each of the Orixás (red for Iansã, yellow for Oxum, green for Oxóssi, blue for Yemanjá, etc.), and for each of the phalanges (*falange*) of spirits: red and black

---

at the Federal University of Santa Catarina by M. Grossi and B. Glowczewski as part of her research programme, TransOceanik (an International Associated Laboratory between the CNRS and James Cook University in Australia): Blurred Interfaces: Questioning Norms, Classifications and the Primacy of Language, 27–29 May 2013, UFSC – Florianópolis, Brasil.

[4] *Teatro Desessência: imagem e esquecimento, a temporalidade do devir.* Unpublished project, 2014.

for Exu, white and black for Preto Velho (old Black people), green for Caboclos (Indigenous people and their descendants of mixed ancestry), pink and light blue for Beijada (children). The colours of the clothes of the mediums correspond to the entities that they prepare themselves to incorporate; and the fabrics that cover the *atabaque* drums also relate to specific Orixás. All these colours translate heterogeneous spaces that constitute the cosmos of those Orixás, but who manifest and multiply themselves simultaneously trough several mediums, in each terreiro, as the place for such events. The term *Cosmocolours* translates these cosmopolitics that connect heterogeneous spaces with a given place and moment. An event which has its own time, in the ritual, deterritorialising and reterritorialising the participants.

The performance *Cosmocolours* that took place in the room Le Commun (BAC – Bâtiment d'Art Contemporain) in Geneva, on 21 August 2015, unfolded over two hours and a half, in four stages. First, images were projected on Clarissa Alcantara; secondly, images of Umbanda filmed in 2013 were projected on a wall; thirdly, an image filmed in 2015 was projected on another wall, at an angle with the images of the first wall; during the whole time of the projection I told a story, standing in the dark of the room to accompany the images of the Umbanda sessions (Beijada, Preto Velho, Caboclo and Exu) and interviews with Father Abílio. During the fourth stage, I commented the Warlpiri women rituals that I had filmed, without sound, in the Central Australian desert in 1979; the images were projected alone on the first wall. Finally, there was a half an hour conversation with all the audience. After the event, back in Paris, I edited with Dominique Masson a 28' version of the performance (that she filmed): *Cosmocouleurs – Incorporations* can be seen through Vimeo, on the website of the curators of the exhibition *La Bête et l'Adversité*.[5]

For the online Brazilian journal *GIS* (Gesture Image and Sound), I chose the first part of the performance, with Clarissa Alcantara dancing for 7 minutes, as filmed by the Brazilian film-maker Sandra Alves.[6] Clarissa's white cloak, like a long veil and dress spread in

---

[5] See paper commenting the film in the exhibition catalogue, Barsaghian et Christensen (eds) 2017 and the film here: *Cosmocouleurs* (28', 2015): https://vimeo.com/173509321

[6] *Cosmocores* (7', 2015): https://vimeo.com/208347518, password cosmocores 2017*

front of her body, served as a screen for the projection. I trailed her, projector in hand. The first experimentation of this setting (*dispositivo*) was done with Clarissa, in March 2015, at the *terreiro* of Babalorixá Kabila Aruanda,[7] now called Nação Livre de Culto aos Orixás Korrente da Alegria de Aruanda, located in Embu das Artes, a couple of hours from São Paulo. Clarissa Alcantara saw my films of the Tenda Espírita Vó Cirina and selected for the performance a sequence of a session of Exu and Pomba-Gira: ancestral spirits of dead people, men and women linked with pleasure and lust, who (after death) turned themselves into messengers between Orixás and humans.

During the performance in Geneva, Clarissa kneeling head down rose very slowly to dance. In the dark, a few metres away, carrying the projector at different heights, sometimes squatting or walking closer to Clarissa, I tried to make the beam of the twirling movements (*giros*) of Exus and Pomba-Giras coincide with her own movements. Sometimes a close shot of a face would cover all her body, other times an entire silhouette would turn like her, or a group of different entities would multiply on the white outfit of the dancer, including *ogãs*, that is people who do not enter a trance, but help the entities and can also beat the *atabaque* drums. It is important to note that the film presents an angle of vision chosen by film-maker Sandra Alves, who moved around to film, creating a point of view different from the angle adopted by Dominique Masson, who was posted just behind me: these two angles are also different from the one I had, or from the diverse ones observed by the people sitting on my right or left in the room of the BAC. In other terms, the experience of projected images on the costume of the dancer that looked like a series of veils in movement – very strongly felt in each instant by myself as well as Clarissa and the audience – belongs to the moment of the performance event that filming cannot give back to feel in the same way. Similarly, according to the public, the story that I improvised along

---

[7] Clarissa Alcantara invited Kabila Aruanda with other Brazilian artists, film-maker Sandra Alves, musician Ive Luna and ten *iaôs* (sons and daughters of saints), artists of the Usina da Alegria Planetária – UAP, a collective created by Kabila – to participate in the Geneva exhibition *The Beast and Adversity*, by making together a performance Act/process-ritual Fury, on 22 August 2015. The day after, Kabila talked about his experience and collective mode of existence in Aruanda (Alcantara 2016).

Cosmocolours

the images projected on the wall stimulated a *presence effect* that would be difficult to produce with a simple commentary in the film.

In August 2016, when we worked on this paper, Clarissa summarised her experience in this way:

> The dance proposed by Barbara in *Cosmoscores* (*Cosmocolours*), did not happen, for me, only like a performative dance. Art is sacred, intensified by the proposed device/arrangement (*dispositivo*), forced a passage to another type of opening. A new dimension was introduced, developing the performance: the sacred was materialised in a subtle state of incorporation. The long white cape chosen by Kabila Aruanda, that he had made especially for a ritual of *bombogira* Dona Maria Gertrudes, the founder of his terreiro, served, not just as a screen for the projection of the Exus and Pomba-Giras images, but also as a vehicle for the vibration of a feminine Orixá, Iansã: the proper force of the winds, lightning, tempests, that also govern and guard the universe of all Exus. In the absence of a ritual symbolic mediation, it is thanks to the strange mystery of mediumnity, that Iansã, anonymous and imperceptible to the others, embodied herself there, penetrating her vibratile force in each breath of my body. During *Cosmocores*, in fact, she was the one dancing.

For me, the beauty and strength of Clarissa's performance in Geneva created a presence allowing in its own way to recreate the presence of multiple becomings, suggesting the effective co-existence and the capacity to affect those who were attending. During the performance, as images were projected on her, I felt that our interaction was lifting her breath to another space-time. I allowed myself, then, to be sucked into a sort of vortex, materialised by the luminous beams that I projected on her. She seemed to merge herself within the projected image, as much as the people that I had filmed in a state of incorporation were starting to live and animate her silhouette by multiplying her presence. I had a strange conscience of the presence of the public, a little bit as if I was feeling them not behind or next to me but from the point of view of what was animating itself in front of us, as if we had all crossed the mirror of the projection. It is only when Clarissa cowered herself in the corner of the walls (under the frame of a new film projected from the ceiling) that I recovered my own feet on the ground to carry me to give her my hand to lift her up and take her out of the dance floor. The words that came to me afterwards so to accompany the images from the *terreiro* Tenda Espírita Vó Cirina came naturally, without having been prepared in this way. During the final debate, the public expressed how they were very receptive to all that had happened.

Back in Florianópolis in September 2015, Clarissa Alcantara and Sandra Alves visited Father Abílio at the Tenda Espírita Vó Cirina to show him the filmed images of the performance and ask him if he consented to their free access on Internet. He showed genuine happiness and interest in seeing the images. Then quickly accepted their release.

A year later, on Thursday, 11 August, I went back with Clarissa to the Tenda Espírita Vó Cirina to attend a new session of Preto Velho. There I was delighted to meet the old sons and daughters of Father Abílio, as well as a big number of new participants, notably many young ones. Abílio was very busy giving consultations every day of the week. I booked an appointment for Monday to consult with the guardian spirit of the Tenda house, the Preta Velha (Black old woman) Vó Cirina. We talked for an hour and a half. I tried to ask my questions in Portuguese, though making many mistakes. Clarissa helped me to clarify my questions and translate the responses of Vó Cirina. Shortly after, Clarissa transcribed the conversation and adapted my (recorded) questions in proper Portuguese, from which I chose the various extracts proposed below.

It was a very rich teaching exchange. Most of all it showed how the Vó Cirina spirit interpreted my spiritual and anthropological questioning so as to give a response that was a non-intellectual response, but revealed to be at the same time anthropological and philosophical. Thus, from the spirit's point of view, it was obvious that my relation with religion since my childhood and my shared experience with 'índios' (Aboriginal people) of Australia, was connected to a feeling of the sacred and of socially grounded cosmological relations (cosmopolitics) with the earth and its forces – common to the experience of the sacred, revealed by the Orixás – that was different from Christianity. This declaration comes close here to a form of theoretical position that disagrees with various current theories which, since the beginning of the discipline of anthropology tend to oppose Australian totemism and cults of trance, such as Afro-Brazilian ones, as two forms of religion or ontologies with non-compatible forms of logic. It is obvious that Indigenous rituals and Afro-Brazilian ones are different. Each of them in its particular way carries its own singularity, not just as an Indigenous ritual or as an Afro-Brazilian ritual, but also with different rituals for each of the many Indigenous peoples (in Brazil as well as in Australia), or for each of the specific *terreiros* (Umbanda Angola or not, Candomblé or other) while each performance of these rituals is unique. However, a transversal trait of singularity seems to connect them.

Cosmocolours

I was deeply struck when I saw for the first time, in 2013, the incorporations of Orixás and spirits of dead in Umbanda, feeling it as something familiar. My observation was that this feeling was producing a sense of 'common' with what I had lived in Australia during the rituals (dances, songs, paintings on the body) that mapped totemic becomings of the Warlpiri Dreaming lines. I understood later that this insight of 'common' is specifically articulated around the valourisation of heterogeneity and multiplicity that manifest themselves both in Brazilian cults of African matrix and in Indigenous Australian experiences of totemic becomings.

During the discussion that followed the *Cosmocolours* performance in Geneva, several people shared their impressions in relation to this multiplicity and the experience of a 'common', which is at the same time social and spiritual.

> One thing that I found really beautiful in these Brazilian ritual dances – as you said, despite the fact that there is a type of image of the Brazilian society as perfectly mixed, that would perfect, in practice we understand that there is a blatant inequality between different populations – here (in the rituals) differences are highlighted, but in fact, without hierarchy, everybody is accepted. But, in fact, in this multitude, there is also – at least in my eyes – a type of unity because everybody is accepted, this is what touched me a lot. (Mucyo Karemara, Swiss young man, PhD candidate in Physics, *Cosmocolours* debate. Geneva, 21 August 2015)

The multiplicity in constant becoming is also at the heart of Deleuze's philosophy and the ecosophy developed by his thought companion, Félix Guattari, who accompanied my research (Glowczewski 2015). I must admit that the experience of such a transversal complicity with the spirit of the Black old woman, Preta Velha Vó Cirina (who defines herself as an Orixá, because she helps everybody) brings me joy.

It is not important if Vó Cirina exists or not as a spirit, she does exist as affect and effect in the relations with the people who consult her. Such relations are to be seen partly as the desire of each person. In this sense, she reveals a reality that cannot be proved according to a scientific mode, it is a 'real' that cannot be named. But we can try to transmit the ethnographic presence using sentences of our conversation, inviting the readers to live a subjective reading situation. An experience that reveals, beyond any image, another order that does not assume a discursive order, nor any form of symbolic language.

Figure 13.3 Cosmocolours, *Barbara Glowczewski's two-screen installation with Brazilian Umbanda rituals, BAC (Building of Contemporary Art), Geneva 2015*

Consultation of Barbara with Vó Cirina (Extract)

15 August 2016

B – *When I was 24 I went to Australia and met Australian Indigenous people.*

VC – What I am going to say for start, is that her level is the same as that of the 'Indians', I do not talk about the Indians? I talk. Because she brings an energy of persons who already left, Tupi-Guarani, Guarani ... Therefore, you have everything at the spiritual level, you can even watch (Christian ritual), but you are not going to feel well. Because Vó (the spiritual grandmother) and the Souls, Almas of Angola, which are Umbanda, have Candomblé, but the foundation of all of it comes from the source which is God alone. Only the fact that you did not accept this level (of Church), accept this spiritual level, why? Because you came over already with that mission since a little girl to assume it ... this is why it could not be done (that you become a nun).

B – *When I met these people called Warlpiri, who have a very strong spiritual relation (ligação) with animals, with the wind, with the mountain, with the water, and they call this dreamings (sonhos, sonhares). In their language, these relations/connections with animals, winds, plants, are called dreams. They celebrate, sing the travels of ancestral beings, a mixture of human and animal or plant people, wind people and rain people, and all travel from place to place. Creating places, rocks, waterfalls, springs and waterholes.*

Cosmocolours

VC – And like Vovó says: you talked about the waterfall, it's the energy of Oxum. They are Orixás that live in the waterfall. You talked about the wind. Wind, what works with the wind? It is Iansa. You talk about rocks. Xango. Xango vibrates at the beginning of the waterfall, in the middle of the waterfall where Oxum lives. Only inside our ritual of the Souls of Angola do we hold two qualities for Oxum, we have Oxum Apa Apará (...?) and Oxumaré. Why Oxumaré? Because during six months it's a man, and during six months it's a woman. You talked about the waters, there is Yemanja. All that you heard here, our talks, it all has to do with your Self it is your own spiritual level, my daughter. There is nothing wrong. You talked about the beast (*bicho*), the animal ... (Vó Cirina sings)

'Oxossi is the hunter, I love to see hunting. Oxosssi is the hunter, I love to see hunting. In the day he hunts in the forest, in the night he hunts in the sea'

Why? Because he is a hunter, he kills to eat. The forest is where Oxossi lives, who is an Orixa who never incorporated in a human being, for this (reason) he comes as Orixa. If it was like me, I already lived on the earth, I am an *egun*, evolved from light. Caboclo is *egun*, Beijada are *egun*, but they are evolved. But the rest of our saints are Orixas, they are brought they were born inside the waterfall. I have the foundations (fundamentals?) that has a Vo, I have the knowledge of a Vo, *né* (isn't that so), my daughter, there are things that I cannot answer. There are mysteries of life, that's it.

B – *For Aboriginal people, the 'índios' of Australia, every child when it is born embodies (*incorpora*) the spirit of a place that links her/him to an animal, a plant or wind, etc. all newborn children. This revelation shows in a dream.*

VC – Really! When Jurunata, who is an Indian man, who came in the head of my son the first time, the first time he incorporated in my son. Jurunata, who is an Indian man, was born in Uruguay (and lived) until 21, then for reason of fight over land they hurt him, *né*, he disincarnated. When he arrived on the strip (*terreiro*) for the first time, he asked to plant a stem of a tree, the one here on the front, *araçá*, this red *araçá*, you know? These two stems that are here, are his, they were planted in his name, because he lives from the energy of the green leaves, when he came in the head of my son for the first time, and the stem here is his. And it can be removed from here chopped only when my son is no longer here. This is his.

B –*What is the link of this spirit with Vó Cirina*

VC – when I opened my house, my son opened it with me with mother Yemanjá, and we needed another spiritual person that works with leaves. Then, in this space (*arraial=terreiro*) the Vó made a *ponto* (ponto riscado, a special 'cross out' design on the ground) of Oxalá here in the middle and sang so that he would show up and visit my house. In that prayer what showed up was this Indian (*índio*), it could have been another one, *né*, it could have been the Seven Arrows (*Sete Flechas*), it could have been Ubirajara, it could have been Pena Azul, but the one who came then, is he (Jurunata) who came to us, the Tupã who is the bigger, who is the God for them, he sent this Indian (*índio*) so he makes the work of healing (*cura*). So, a person who lies down in my *terreiro*, here in the middle – you can participate one day if there is a sick person – she is covered with leaves, and Indians and Caboclos work around that person. Many people have already been cured here, those 'balls' (*bolas*, breast nodules) here, and other things inside here (VC shows her belly). The doctor can't do it (*não deu jeito*), but he (the spirit) can.

His name is Jurunata that was given to him by his tribe. He comes just to cure. The people stay under the leaves, entirely covered, lying on a mat, under a white sheet. He already did a lot of good things. He only does it when I ask, when I request to do so, when there is a necessity. When I can cure with a candle, a prayer, he does not come. And he comes for the gyration (*gira*), then he sings (*curimba*) a little bit, he smokes his cigar. Because the cigar is to make the smoke go out, the smoke is relief, that's why Vó smokes. My son does not smoke, but when I smoke here, I puff on this pipe, relieving illness, evil, jealousy, the big eye, breakdown, all these things.

B – *Another question. I felt very well with Aboriginal people because I was feeling a familiarity with this spirituality of all places and all that exists. But in those days, thirty years ago, one family that had this religion also was Christian, because the people had translated the Bible in their Indigenous language. A 'syncretism' with the Baptist Church. They continued their old rituals of singing, dancing and painting the body. But they also sang Christian songs in their language (Warlpiri) and painted their body in the Church (with a Christian cross), only some families. Other Aboriginal people said that it is not possible to mix the spirituality of their ancestors with Christianity.*

VC – I consider it to be wrong to do so. I consider it wrong. When they paint, they trace their actual root. Now, when they go to the Church and paint themselves, they trace the root of others. I do not accept, such a division. What they are painting on themselves and dancing, is for their space (*barracão*). If they meet with another religion, it is not that it is wrong, but Vó does not accept thus, we are going to divide for this and that. It's their root, the painting that belongs to them cannot be lost, they have to continue forever.

Cosmocolours

B – *Now, after thirty years, 'índios' (Aboriginal people) of Australia are more often Christians, and, for them, the traditional religion is also important. Some Warlpiri men and women say that they hold an ancestral spirituality that is very important for life, and to maintain connections with all of nature, but they have to go to Church to experiment a connection with Jesus, because it is the religion of the Whites, which, since the colonisation of Australia, has power. It's not a mixture, it's not a syncretism, but their existence is twofold. They have a connection with nature, with dreams, but also, some people go to Churches, because for them the Bible is the power of the Whites, of colonisation, that have transformed their lives, ever changing since. With this power they have to compromise and negotiate; they understand the power of the Whites so to appropriate it for themselves to be free.*

VC – That is the case. These Whites make a brainwash of Indios, saying that their God, of the Whites, is bigger, that it is equivalent to theirs. They (Indigenous people) make their mindset and they pass over to that religion. Vó does not accept this either. If they are like that, they have to follow their father Tupã (primary figure for Guarani people, in Argentina, Bolivia, Brazil, Paraguay, Uruguay). When they were in the bush did they not cultivate father Tupã? Who is father Tupã? It's the same God. Therefore, the White is (*esta*) only today ... Many people who come here in my house to develop themselves, evolve spiritually, when they come out from here, today they are Church believers. Believers are the Assembly of God, Evangelics (Evangélicos). And when they get there, what are they going to say about us? That we are no good, only things of the demon. Everything ... These men, these pastors are completely wrong, my daughter.

They invent things, they brainwash people, because these pastors, according to Vó Cirina, make a Church to pick up money ('*patacas*') from everybody so to live from it. It's not that I do not like it. Me, I am Vó, no my son (não o meu filho), I do not accept this level. And my son does not go to this type of Church, his mission is inside my faith. Ask yourself it is not a lie that they heal people? Here came a person who had the sickness of blood (Aids – SIDA). Vó prayed for her and I removed this thing (she points to the kidney); 'your problem is serious, you have a stone of calcium and you have blood ...'. 'But how Vó? I did not even feel anything?' 'You go do an examination.' She went there (to the doctor), and it was confirmed that she has a disease. She came back here terrified, crying, having her hands burning (*ralando*), all the body Jurunata came, we did a healing work, she found herself cured of all her wounds, but it continued inside her. She went to this Church that is called Universal. 'Oh, Vó, I would like to see there if a man (the pastor) is going to cure me.' I told her, 'oh, my daughter, then go'. That's what I desire, né, I desire good for others. She went there. She gave her *bicho de fogo* (fire animal, or car), he told her not to take any more medicine, he took her house, everything ... In less than fifteen days the woman disappeared, she died. The lying took her. What cures is God, my daughter. What cures is the spiritual level. I cure, because God gives me the light to cure people. At the moment, the family is very preoccupied, she gave her fire animal (car) to him, they made a confusion, they came here to talk again with Vó. She gave because she wanted to. We did a 'head' (*mente,* made of wax) of this person. It cured her, I cured her, then she left.

People will give anything. People who give their house, who leave work ... For whom is it? And the pastor, that man, eats the best, my daughter.

B – *What is different in Umbanda de Angola from syncretism, the relation of Orixás with the saints of the Catholic Church, like Jesus and other saints?*

VC – This here (she points to the images/sculptures of the Catholic saints exhibited on the altar), nothing of it needs to be here inside. Just one cross, here in the middle (would be enough).

When it was the time of slavery (*Senzala*), and the master (*senhor*) of cane fields, in the coffee plantations (*cafezal*), we had a '*ronkó*' (ritual space), an *ibegi* (altar), there in a little corner (*cantinho*). For the master to admit that we play there our tambourines (*tamborzinho*), what did we have to do? We had to tell a lie to the master saying this is all for the Church. We would arrange those saints and place them on top of tree stumps (*tocos*). In that way the master ended up (*passou*) believing this. From this came, that to each of the Orixás we give a name of a saint. Because of this we keep them here. But at the spiritual level, in Umbanda, in Almas de Angola (Souls of Angola), Candomblé does not use these things, they are dishes, Orixás are in dishes, that Vó also accepts.

So, it is from there that we have the right to nurture (*cultivar*) for people who come from far, who come from abroad (*fora*), so they will feel good because of the saints. But if you take away everything, you put only the cross that corresponds to the Almas de Angola. The cross is the Souls, Angola is what comes from Africa. It is the difference (*defeito*) of these Almas de Angola for the Umbanda, accordingly: my son is going to lay down (*deitar*) a person for a saint, he is pure (without incorporation), he will crown the saint. The Umbanda which is done by Preto Velho, the Congo King (Rei Congo), the Vó ... The Orixá makes the saints incorporate, this is the difference, and the rest is all the same, the song, the foundation, all is same. There is an Umbanda Branca (White) also that does not beat the drum (*tambor*), does not kill animals, works only with herbs (*ervas*).

B – *And why at beginning of every session you say the prayers Our Father and Ave-Maria?*

Cosmocolours

VC – This ritual of Almas de Angola was born in Rio de Janeiro and a Caboclo, the famous Caboclo Lamparina, who was a man who started all that, that we do now in Santa Catarina, said: the Vó does not really know, she started like that, she nurtured this, the prayer. And in Umbanda before it was no like that, they do not kneel down, they make a song of Oxalá standing up, for Exu, at the opening, all standing up. Here no, here people have to kneel down for Jesus, like he humiliated himself for God. Kneeling down and humiliate oneself for Him, *né*? To make our prayer. It's better, it holds more energy. But I like to do that. But if you don't wish to do it, you don't have to do it. Like in Candomblé, it's not necessary to do it.

If you wish, it's possible just to sing for the Almas and Exu and start twirling (*tocar a Gira*). But we feel good in doing a prayer of Our father (*Pai-Nosso*) and Ave-Maria, we find it better, we vibrate more for God, and what we desire, light, truth, then, it's for this that we do the praying. But if you do not wish to do, you do not need to.

B – *Exu. There are many different Exus.*

VC – Exu, has a lot of qualities (types of Exus) and they are very different from one another. Exu, for me, is an Orixá. Exu, for me, is not like the one that is customary said to have a twig (*galho*), a bullock foot, and called '*tibinga*' the demon, not to mention ... They are not like that, my daughter, the people who invented that, people invented that; he is an Orixá of all the the less evolved, why? He drinks at night, in nightclubs, with street women, those women that are lost, others that became pregnant and took out the child, they ended up losing their own light. Thus, they became women of darkness. Thus, they come as Pomba-Gira. Each of them has her own name. Sete, who works (*trabalha*) with my sons, he got into fights in a club, so he lived from these things, in a complete mess, but his name is not only Sete, his name is Ricardo. Why is it Sete, that he brought this thing of Sete? Because in this time he does not have a place, any hole to enter, he used to enter underneath a fig tree, there he was buried. And since the matter of the earth is consumed, thus he come, he lives where it is dark. Therefore, Sete Sombras (Sete Shadows). But in one year, two years, or more, he can evolve and turn into a Preto Velho. Then he is no loger Exu, he can change. And practise good.

B – *Many Exus in Umbanda have names of demons of Christianity.*

VC – Why? This is something invented, my daughter, all invented by the priests (*padres*), invented by men of earth. They came to a house, saw an Exu drinking, with a black cape. Ah! It is a demon! They would already, this is a demon. It's a nickname, they gave a nickname and it continues like that.

B – *I was talking about demons, but there are also names in the esoteric tradition of Christianity. They have particular names, a list of first names of different demons that exist in Christianity. And priests do exorcism. Here, in Umbanda, these names appear as Exus.*

About Divination with Búzios Cowrie Shells and Pontos Chalk Designs

VC – If the drop/throw of shells (*cair*) has seven 'open' (*aberto*), this person is an ideal person. If the drop has seven 'closed' (shells turned with their opening against the table), this person is honest and sincere. If in the drop all shells are closed, it's inside a saint, you are a daughter of Obaluaê. Conform to what drops here, the quantity of them, I (then) know the names of the Orixás, the sickness, the work, the result of the entrance exam (*vestibular*). Vó discovers all that we are going to do, evoke here to see from here, thus we are going to ask ... (She gives an example) Oxóssi controls this person, who is son of Oxóssi with Iansã, and what are we going to do? Give food for Oxóssi and Iansã, this person is going to make a request and we are going to make her succeed the exam. If it is a sickness, it's the same. Each quantity of búzios that are dropped, either closed or open, thus I know the problems of the person.

I will explain. I will draw the búzios for you (on the table). I call for the Orixás, from Iansã, here talked Iansã, but I desire to know the ponto (riscado) and for me not to forget that the Vó does this (she draws a ray with a chalk), Iansã, you are a ray (of lightning), né? If Ogum gives, I make (the design of) Ogum, if for Oxóssi, I make Oxóssi. Therefore, I know what drops, and for me I do not forget what I said. Any Father of Santo is the same thing. And the stones are energies of Orixá: white Oxalá; bejada; Xangô de Nagô, Xangô da pedreira; Iansã, Oxum, Obaluaê, Oxóssi, Ossanhã, who has those leaves, Caboclo, Oxóssi is one thing, Cabloco is another thing, and those Almas (Souls). All this draws energy.

All of this is placed now Vó does not mess anymore with this, these stones are placed inside a tray with boldo, you know boldo?[8] It's a herb of Oxalá. You place all inside the boldo, let wash, wash everything real well inside the boldo, so then they can work, because if one messes with this today it's not going to work. The person has to leave this mixture moist. In other places, houses of terreiro, the owner, father of Saint, learns the búzios to play, but my son does not wish to learn. I am the one to play. He can also learn, with other people, there are books. He leaves everything in my hands.

---

[8] 'Peumus boldus', the only species in the genus 'Peumus', is commonly known as Boldo: medicinal properties. (cf. Linguee online and Wikipedia).

Cosmocolours

All people who come here always like me because I am honest with my stuff thanks to God. Some things, I cannot talk about, you know? The daughter knows that all has a mystery, not my daughter (Vó turns towards Clarissa), the spiritual level has a mystery level. But my function is to help people. They come with evil, I send them away, and I do not assist. They look for another place. Because my son does not live for this, he lives for the saint. Someone helps to do ... On October 20 it's going to be my little feast, everybody wishes to help a little bit, Vó accepts. To give added value, to charge for a work of cure, no. I came for free, I have to give for free, my daughter. Even if my son is alive, here on earth, and he is going to last many years, until he's 90 years old, I am still here, when he goes away, I have to arrange another 'equipment/device' (*aparelho*). But where? It can be here, it can be in another world. Because the world is very big.

The August 2016 consultation confirms, in its own way, how Vó Cirina actualises a multiplicity of becomings. Multiple levels of becomings cross the frontiers of life and death, the body and the spirit, the masculine and the feminine, the human and the non-human, all with blurred frontiers. The crossing (*travessia*) of these limits does not stop to actualise becomings and to virtualise possibilities (*possibles* in French), not only for the incorporations of the mediums, but more subtly for slipping movements in life which resonate (*ressoam*) in different situations. Like Clarissa in her dance in Geneva, in interaction with me and with a flow of images of incorporations of Umbanda, at the beat of drums.

During my consultation with Vó Cirina, she embodied the becoming of her Preta Velha spirit that refers to the becoming of her life as a woman of 140 anos (when she died by the sea), but also the becoming of her spiritual life after her death. When she answered my questions, she was sometimes one, sometimes the other. Vó Cirina expressed also a becoming-woman and a becoming-Black of her 'son', her medium the babalorixá Abílio, to whom she referred many times in the course of the extracts which are transcribed here and at other moments too. She also mentioned other becomings that inhabit her son, like the caboclo Jurunata, the spirit of a Tupi-Guarani man, who died in Uruguay at the age of 21, and who today is a spirit that makes healing rituals (*cura*). Similarly, his Exu Sete Sombras, called Ricardo, is a spirit of a man of the night, an outlaw (*fora da lei*) who, according to her, in one, two or more years, can evolve and incorporate as Preto Velho. 'Just practise good' ('É só praticar o bem'), says Vó Cirina.

The guardian spirit of the *terreiro* was happy with my visits in her house and also with those of the people I brought. She asks for news about anthropologists from Florianópolis, France and Australia and, also, about my youngest daughter that she knew. She showed herself satisfied with the work I did in her house and with the fact of spreading her knowledge outside. Her 'son' Abílio accepted that we perform the experience *Cosmocolours* in Geneva but was not interested in how the work was received by the public or in the artistic context. He found himself busy enough with another becoming, of the sons and daughters who, growing in numbers continue to attend every Thursday session, as well as consultations during the week. In any event, this form of virtuality drew for me a possible road to follow, which opened in respect to all those 'enchantments' (*encantamentos*, the name sometimes given to the spirits) another reality to 'present', instead of 'represent'.

The text proposed here shifts through an agency of multiple actors, human and non-human, so to experiment an 'editing' (like a photo-montage) of multiple entries: my analysis, that of Clarissa Alcantara, citations, and an interview with the spirit of Vó Cirina, my photos and those of Sandra Alves and, finally, the film *Cosmocores* of Clarissa's dance with my images of the Umbanda Almas de Angola from the Tenda Espírita Vó Cirina projected in Geneva. The blurring of frontiers, colours, languages and names accompanies the smoothness of the surface of perception upon which various spatio-temporal dynamisms are produced. A cosmopolitics of an 'indisciplined' anthropology outlines, between distant spaces and times, the design of a multiplicity of lines, a network in which some traits can be perceived to be common. Like my first experimental films, which superimposed discontinuous rhythms and pulsations to produce a rupture in perception for new emotional stimuli, so also the becoming of this current research disrupts some of the continuity of a supposed movement. The Warlpiri Dreamings, Orixás and spirits of dead, anthropology, philosophy, the sacred, art, and everything else joined in composition of the possibility of a singular dance superimposing bodies and images in a Cosmocolour-becoming.

14

The *ngangkari* Healing Power: Conversation with Lance Sullivan, Yalarrnga Healer

In April 2017, Lance Sullivan, a Yalarrnga desert healer from Boulia, a Cleverman as Aboriginal people say, based in Townsville to study at James Cook University, was part of the Australian delegation invited by the festival of shamanism in Genac, South-West France. The day before his return flight, after dinner in my flat in Paris, I showed him an art catalogue[1] with Aboriginal artists exhibited in France. He stopped on a page with a piece by Brook Andrew with an archival photo framed in a neon called *Union Jack:* the black and white photo showed a group of Aboriginal men posing for the camera, painted on the body, one displaying the design of the British flag on his chest:

> **Lance Sullivan (LS):** This is Molongo! The ceremony my great-grand-father passed to other desert groups.

Molongo was a secret cult calling for spirits to help protect the land and the people massacred and deported to reserves; this resistance ceremony travelled from group to group at the turn of the nineteenth century.[2] Lance then opened the book on a big black and white photo taken in 1894 by Spencer and Gillen near Alice Springs, the country of Arrernte people: seven men were standing facing the camera, all decorated with designs for the Rain and Emu Ceremony, four of them wearing one-metre-high headdresses made of hairstring and emu feathers:

> **LS:** This is my grandfather's *corroboree* this one, they say my grandfather took it across to Alice Spring.

The word *corroboree*, inspired by a south-eastern Aboriginal word has been generalised across the continent by the settlers to refer to

---

[1] *Vivid Memories. An Aboriginal Art History*, co-curated by Morvan and Matharan (2013), Bordeaux: Musée d'Aquitaine.
[2] About Molongo, see Glowczewski (1996, 2004).

Figure 14.1 Lance Sullivan during the filmed interview

any Aboriginal dance. Many dances, interpreted for fun or for ritual reasons were traditionnnally travelling from one language group to another, with song cycles that were sung like a trend across hundreds of kilometres. Some of the ceremonies also had ritual objects that were transmitted in that way to eventually return to their original owners after one or two generations. This was still happening oin the 1990s. Some rituals conveyed messages, like the dance of the Horns and Bumps which imitated the cattle and the camels that were brought in by the settlers. Sometimes the dance preceded the invasive arrival of these animals that were using and spoiling the Aboriginal peoples rare supplies of water.

    Barbara Glowczewski (BG): So, who was your grandfather, Lance?

LS: Wooly Sullivan. He was Poolarri, in his language name.
Poolarri is, means, man with the *nullanulla* (fighting stick) . . .
They say, that they first came to the men,
when they were out walking away.
They were trying to get away from troopers.
He sat in a cave, and all the little *Putinyjee*, the little short men came.
Them *Putinyjee* were talking to him, and did a song for that too.
(*Lance sings in his language Yalarrnga*)
That's what they sing for them short little people
(about vegetable food) . . .

Yeah, so he was sitting in the cave, and the short men came,
and they gave him the coroboree there.

The ngangkari *Healing Power, with Lance Sullivan*

Figure 14.2 Lance Sullivan during the filmed interview

For that Molongo last part, it's a five nights,
five days and five nights,
and at the last night, that's when that Molongo come in.
Molongo refers to devil devil, devil. He comes in with all.
The man comes in with all feathers,
white feathers on his head, headdress.
(*Lance puts his hands on the head and up all around*)
And he holds, forks, a fork stick,
that he uses to strike down the Aboriginal men.
But the men in this *corroboree* they come up
and kill him, with their boomerangs.

BG: That devil devil, he belongs to the land?
Or was it the devil devil from the White people coming?

LS: I think myself, that it refers to the White people shooting them all.
And that they, in the end, kill him.
Spencer, no Roth (*early anthropologist*) he said,
he called it Molonga ceremony. But we call it Butler ...

Well they say he was on his way,
he was walking towards the Alyawarre people, it's near Georgina river.
There was a lot of people fleeing,
and they ran into Georgina River because there's always water there.
And they could hide amongst those mountains and that.

BG: Your grandfather, he was from, he was a Alyawarre, or he was from another land?

LS: He was Yalarrnga. He was a boss for the Yalarrnga mob.
He lived to be 116 plus they reckon. He was oldest man in Australia.
There's a monument for him at the cemetery, that Boulia council
    put up.
But he lived on bush food.
At first when them white fella come to that country,
they were chasing him down, trying to kill him.
And they chased him from one place,
he ran into the river, further down from Boulia he dived into the water,
and as he dived all the ceremonial stuff got washed off him,
and when he got to the other side of the bank,
he said, 'look I have nothing now.
I'm not doing any coroboree or nothing now.'
So they did shoot him.
But he buried all his hairbelts and everything.
He buried everything in this one place, called One mile water hole.
There was a well there. He chucked everything in the well.
It's sealed over now. I go there.
But that's the place of the dingo, that comes from Harts Range.

He travelled from Ayers Rock, through Alice Spring,
come up through Harts Range (215km N/E),
across the border there, Georgina River, he come in our country then,
and they sing (*Lance sings in language*)
That refers to him, refers to female one (dingo),
dancing for the male one. Male one came from Harts range.
But female one, was a local one,
and from there she went up through to,
up right through our country, right up to the northern part of our country.
And she had a pup there, and the pup is Kankarri, a mountain there.
You can even find up near Townsville way,
you'll see the mountain on the side of the road.
Opposite the hospital.
And then you sing another song, you gotta dance back, hands on your hip
(*Lance bends forward on his chair to show the movement with his hands*)
that refers to the back legs of the dog.
And when she dances backward, she was singing
that song there, can't remember ...

Then that other song come in (*sings in language*).
But that song then went on to Long hills,
Long hills mob took over there,
I don't know what they say when he comes from Northern Territory.
Wanyi, they got hold of that song then ...
Wanyi people yeah, they took over for the Dingo then.

The ngangkari *Healing Power, with Lance Sullivan*

But my people they mainly Emu,
so we sit down there at Yami Yami where our great grandfather came from.
And my waterhole is right next to his. It's called Mitamara.
Mitamara refers to the shield,
where the Owl came down to strike the Snake,
but the snake put up the shield
(*Lance puts his left fingers on his forehaead while lifting his right arm*)
and the Owl hit it and left his footprint on the shield.
But the shield is a big rock, at the bottom of the waterhole,
and on the rock, there's that print imbedded of the Owl when he came down.
So a lot of cave paintings in our land, have got paintings,
footprints of the Owl or the Emu.
There the two main totems around there.
From the Emu people, but my personal *skin* is Owl, Owl Jarra.
That's where my name is from Muradjarra. Means to climb (*Lance shows the climbing gesture with his hands up*) to heavens, the Owl.
(...)

BG: Is it a different Emu from the one that in the Kimberley they call Karnananja, the big Emu?[3]

LS: There's one Emu, he come up from South,
he came up from Parajilna. He was heading down from our country.
He started at up ..., he came through there.
He went down the Burke River, feeding along the creek,
trying scratching up all the wild onions and everything.
That's why today we eat the wild onions along the bank.
Even all the way down to one place called Blue Bush Swamp,
where he dug up a nest there, to make nest,
he piled the earth up that became a swamp, Blue Bush Swamp.
In the middle of the swamp is a lot of rocks, piled up, around one tree,
that's in the shape of an emu.
They represent the eggs and the Emu.

From there, because they say there was two Emus.
There was a short neck one and a long neck one,
and we got them two Dreamings there. That male one,
he went further down, in the Parajilna, South Australia.
That's why he got speared and blood came out, it turned to red ochre.

---

[3] In Prelude Emu Song by Nakakut Gibson, see also Big Emu as dinosaur, Chapter 1, p. 00.

But our old people used to travel down there all the time to get that red ochre.

They used to follow the Watikujarra songline.
That's them Two men, them two men go all the way to South Australia, then through Kimberley's and all that then, back up through Western Australia, through all them country there, through Lurija country too, and Alice Springs and all that. Travelled all the way.
That's that painting behind you.[4]
(*He sings in Yalarrnga*)

The Two-Men Dreaming is shared by Warlpiri from Central Australia with dozens of other language groups across the desert and the Kimberley. They are considered as the ancestors of the healers ... Lance accepted then to continue the conversation, talking about healing.

> LS: Today it's all, we all, interacting a lot together.
> We got Warlpiri, Warumungu and Alyawarre, Aranda (Arrernte),
> we all sort of like allies now, we all help each other out for ceremony,
> Kaytej too and (in) Mutitjulu,[5]
> all around from Alice Spring[6] area and that,
> we all sort of join together now, cause there's not many of us left now, not many people.
>
> But I put through about 30 fellas from Hopevale community,
> put them through Law (ritual initiation)
> and another 20 from Yarrabah went through.[7]

---

[4] The painting by Bye Bye Napangardi from Balgo of Watikutjara (Glowczewski 1991), who gave the healing power to many tribes on their way, can be seen in the one-hour interview I conducted with Lance Sullivan who granted access online at: https://www.youtube.com/watch?v=bUK_OoVRpQ8. Two extracts of the transcript were published in the second issue of *Alienocene*: https://alienocene.com/2018/06/17/infra-terrestrial-journey/. See also the film *Milli Milli* by Barker (1992), with the two sacred hills that embody Watikutjarra (Two Men) near the Balgo (Wirrimanu, WA) community and the local Kukatja women's ritual dance and statement related to the Two Men who travelled from tribe to tribe, leaving their tracks in places and on their way dispensing their Law of healing and different kinship systems (McCarthy 1961; Glowczewski [1998] 2009).

[5] Mutitjulu is the name of the Aboriginal settlement near Uluru/Ayers Rock (NT) where live Ananagu people of Pitjantjatjara, Yankunytjatjara, Luritja, Ngaanyatjarra and other Western Desert languages spreading in WA and SA.

[6] Northern Territory languages: https://nt.gov.au/community/interpreting-and-translating-services/aboriginal-interpreter-service/aboriginal-languages-in-nt

[7] Queensland languages: http://www.slq.qld.gov.au/resources/atsi/languages/indigenous-languages-map?result_240451_result_page=2

The ngangkari *Healing Power*, with Lance Sullivan

> We taught them desert Law you know,
> we didn't do anything like,
> they didn't do any songs of their own people.
> We just sort of showed them our way,
> and they've been with us now, all time,
> trying to build our number back up.
> But it's hard. Unlike before back in 1985,
> down in South Australia, in Amata they had 2,000 men.
> We can't get them numbers no more,
> all the younger people not interested in the culture no more.

Hopevale is a coastal community north of Townsville where Lance went to live to study at James Cook University in the mid-2000s. Regularly working as a court translator for desert people and also during native Title proceedings, or in jail, he met a lot of Aboriginal men from Queensland. He was then asked by the men from Hopevale and Yarrabah further north to help them to revive ritual initiations that they called, as elsewhere in Australia, the Law. Lance organised for some desert elders from Boulia to come to the north to initiate these men. The ceremonial protocol was the desert one and not the coastal traditional intiation practised by these groups before it was forbidden in the missions and reserves. Some of the coastal men made boomerangs in their own coastal style which are used for fishing and they sent them as presents for the desert elders. But the desert elders sent them back, asking the coastal men to cut for them boomerangs in the desert style so that they could use them for hunting and clapping for music in the desert country. A lesson of cultural exchange...

> LS: Everything dying. Over the years, all our old men are gone.
> But over the years a lot of middle-aged men have stepped up into their
>   place.
> We sort of try to encourage each other.
>
> Like when I first started, them old men came,
> and see me there and they said:
> 'Oh you got to continue, what your uncles and that were doing,
> we remember you uncles when they were doing the coroboree with us,
> your grandfather and that.'
>
> And I said, 'oh ok, I don't really want to do it anymore,
> the people run you down and back stab you.'
>
> They said 'don't worry about what anyone says,
> you got to continue the culture, follow in it.'
> So I always try to follow it,

do what them old fellas say you know.
Keep good books with them.
But all our old men are gone, slowly. We lost many from Tennant Creek.
I think about 5 of the great leaders passed away, all our old fellas.
But now the new ones coming up there, new leaders.
I had to step in place of my uncles and do a lot of ceremonies.

BG: So Lance, would you like to tell us how you became a *ngangkari*?

LS: When I was about twelve, I went through the Law,
and the first cut they put on me was that deeper one,
(*Lance shows horizontal incision marks on his left upper arm*)
that deep one,
that was with a Stone knife.
They taught me to make stone knife, all that.
And then the next one was about fifteen,
that's when I really got into the things, like.

But, I was born into it, all the time.
When I was little, old people used to get me to rub em all the time,
cause they knew I was *Clever* (with healing powers).
So over the years,
all my old people kept on coming to me.

But then when I was fifteen it increased and they started
to ask me to do funeral rites and burn *skin*, the right *skin*,
people's clothing and swags and that,
smoke their houses out,
go around them, go through the house,
they showed me that.

During funeral rituals, some relatives of the right *skin-name* have the duty to burn the goods that belong to the person who passed away and to do a smoking ritual where they used to live to clean the place from the spirit. This is done to help the spirit to find its way away from the living but also to help the living to live around in peace.

LS: And they showed me knowledge of medicines.

But I started seeing more things then,
I started reading what they were, in dreaming,
and what they were saying and all that.
I got more and more healing people, more, rubbing them down and that,
pulling things out of them, giving them advice,
how better to look after themselves.

The ngangkari *Healing Power, with Lance Sullivan*

Anyway, after that, I was put in this cave,
and when I was, a bit older, I was put in a cave.
In that cave was all the bones of dead people, great Clevermen.
And when I . . . they came up at night,
the old people come crashing through he bushes, three of them.
One stood this side of me, and another stood next to him,
but the main one was coming up, coming up the hill,
and there's a spring in the cave.
Must have been where all the other Clevermen was,
I don't know. I never asked them.
But he came up and I thought he was going to break my neck,
    and throw me.
There was a spirit, and he . . . and he kept on like,
getting real angry with me,
and I kept on saying:
'no . . . you're my family *nyuntunyanga*
Ngaya-ka Tjupurrula',
I said like that, 'I am Tjupurrula "Ngaya-ka Tjupurrula",
you're my family and that.'
I was saying, 'Oh you my grandfather!' and all this
'We family, don't kill me!'
And then, that was a real scary night.
And I said to him,
'work through me, help me, to heal, help me to heal people.'
And he came, he laid his hand on my hand.
When he laid his hand on my hand, my fear for him went away,
(*Lance, who was talking head down, looks up*
and puts his right hand on top of his left shoulder)
and he stood behind me, with his arm over me
(*Lance slides down to his hand*)
holding my hand, on top of my hand.
From then I didn't fear him no more.
And by the time the sun came up,
I knew that something serious had happened,
and that I'll always be able to heal.

From there, nothing would stop me.
I was starting to, in that song,
(*he sings*)
came to me then.
That's for pulling out bone out of people.

When I touch people, my hand click click click all the time,
and I keep going pulling until there's nothing left, no more clicking.
(*Lance pulls with his hand and closes his eyes*)

Sometimes I close my eyes, and I see a redness where their sickness is.
(*Lance touches his forehead*)
I touch it, and I close my eyes,
and when it turns yellow, I know that it's healed.
Sometimes, it's like you can see through people.
You can see where their bloodline is clogged up.
That you have to touch it, and loosen it.
Get their blood flowing through their body again, and it works.

It's like wire, all wires going everywhere, all these different colours,
and you can see which ones need to be touched,
and which ones need to be healed.

But I had two fellas, one day, who were 'boned' (cursed)
One was from Western Australia, other from the Northern Territory
He was a Alyawarre and the other one, I don't know what tribe he was.
They brought him to me,
and I thought, they both
when they sat him in front of me,
'boned'
When I touched the Western fella,
I got a bit of worried because I could feel a real strong power ...
kurdaija on this fella.

In many parts of Australia a kangaroo bone was used to point at a distance at a person one wants to harm. The technique was used by the sorcerers or spirits called *Kurdaija*, both walking with emu feather shoes which prevent the identification of the walker by his footprints. This witchcraft technique was also used to punish people judged guilty of a crime or ritual transgression. It aimed to empty the person of his/her soul, the body then dying, slowly dying. The Cleverman can help to stop the process.

LS: I said to him, 'you stop playing around with woman now'
and he got shock.
I said 'you played around with wrong *skin*',
(*Non-respect of sexual classificatory kinship avoidance*)
that's why them old people got you.
And he got a bit of a shock,
thought I didn't know about it.
But when I touch people, I sort of know.
And I told him, I can pull this out.
And the thing is, I hit him in the back,
(*Lance claps in his hands*)

The ngangkari *Healing Power, with Lance Sullivan*

and when I hit him in the back,
that bone it came out, and he felt better.
And he went then 'how come you never pulled it from the front?'
– 'Well because it went through the back'
It was coming through the front, but it got stuck,
so when I pushed it, and it came straight through.

And that other fella,
I sucked, I had to suck it, suck
(*Lance brings to his mouth his right fist, with the left underneath like a tube*)
all that poison blood out of him,
before that thing come out

And I thought to myself,
these two fellas have the same thing, same sickness,
but they need to be treated in a different way.
And that's when I understood that each individual person,
has their own ability,
has their own power,
and own soul and spirit that you've got to use
and talk to to help heal them.

So when I sing,
I just sing through the crown of their head,
(*Lance touches the back-top of his head*)
where I believe the spirit comes from.
When someone gets a headache,
a lot of other, what people call *ngangkari*
they go for the head.
But really,
only the other day, when I did that one lady there (*in Genac – France*)
I touched her foot.
She said, 'why you doing that ey?
I got a headache.'
(*Lance laughs*)
But the headache went away, 'cause I knew she stepped on something.

And that's what happens sometimes, its a spiritual problem,
sometimes its physical.
Thats where, if you ' clap' a *ngangkari*, he could tell those things.
But you'll also get like a picture of what they've done.
So when I touched the lady
I knew she had stepped on something.
I had like a vision I guess.

I had a picture of her stepping on something,
and I see them pull her foot,
so when I touched her foot,
I knew it was the right one.
(*Lance laughs*)
Yeah, some strange things happen!
But yeah I learnt, over the years too,
I got more, over the years as I age,
I sort of slow down more,
and look more closely at people,
yeah, more knowledge.

One old fella, Marvin from Western Australia,
when I was there working, he said to me,
'I know you seek power,
but power comes only when we need it.'
I think thats true.
I couldn't understand it.
For a long time I tried to understand what he meant,
cause I knew he was talking in roundabout way.
And he was talking about power,
when you need it, it'll be there to help you.
It's not always going to be with you.
I learnt but he's ... always with us.

BG: And how did you feel when you were at this festival of shamanism in Genac?

LS: Truthfully ...? (*Lance laughs*)
There were a few odd characters there! that were a few bobs short.
But they ... a lot of the participants
they were all serious, and I knew
there was a lot of great healers there.

I always try to use the old people spirits
you know, to help heal.
I never forget what they've done for me,
so I always acknowledge them.
Every time I touch somebody,
always acknowledge that.
Cause I would be nothing without them.
I'd probably be, cause I was born to it,
but I wouldn't be able to heal as many as I could.

It drains you when you do that.
It makes you weak. You're like a sponge,

The ngangkari Healing Power, with Lance Sullivan

you suck up all the sickness of the people.
So sometimes it can wear you out and make you sick too.
You got to be careful though what you do ...
And how much you do.

BG: But there, during those four days, you treated a lot of people, how could you do that, where did you get the strength from?

LS: I felt really sorry for them,
and yeah and um, it was, when I was healing in the tent
I went into a sort of a trance[8]

I don't look at the person I'm touching,
because I see with my *mungan*.
(*Lance taps his forehead with his open right hand*)
mungan means power.
And usually call ... they call em' *munganayi* 'eye' ...
or they call em' ngangkari 'eye' (in Warlpiri) ...
I always look with my *mungan*,
so when I touch somebody, I don't see their face
and I don't see their sickness or anything,
(*Lance puts his hands forward, palms open to the camera and turns them clockwise*)

I just got like this, down them, feel, where it's hot,
and then I close my eyes and see this redness
and then I just pull! And it just comes out whatever is there
(*Lance shows the pulling gesture*)
That's how it always works,
and it just comes out, whatever's there.
I've been shocked sometimes
I get hairstring in my hand,
I've had bones, splinters, sticks.

I've had a lot of different things come out.
I can't explain it, but it just happens.
But sometimes I got like into a trance
and when I was, you might have noticed,
when I was on my knee, I might have swayed a bit?
(*Lance puts his arms forward and balances himself on the chair to the front*)

That's when I'm in that trance.
I go like that when I'm singing somebody,

---

[8] See photo of Lance in the video.

but mainly I go like that when I am healing now, I noticed.
So I was in a trance,
as quick as they could put them there, I was ready to heal them,
ready to grab another one.

But then my body starts getting weaker,
(*Lance bends his arms to this chest*)
and I start slowing down a bit,
and breathing heavy, and out of wind,
and my arms get heavy, my body, my head and that.
Sometimes I get the headache
after I've pulled it out of that other person,
I soak it up.
I get heavy and I've got to wash my arms, cool down.
When you pull poison out,
you have to take a bit of water on yourself.
If I've got no water I put dirt on my hand,
and that's what I was doing, putting dirt on,
to wipe the sickness away
(*Lance scrubs his hands*)
before I touch another person.

When you touch people too,
you get like a vision of what they've done to get sick.
Sometimes you can explain to them,
to go retrace their steps,
Or someway repay.
Like some people I've touched,
I had to tell them, you've got to put meat out at night,
for the spirits, or stuff like that, water out.
And that'll repay them.

I'm always thinking that
the more we harm the land, the sicker we get.
If we look after the land,
we look after ourselves.
And the land will look after us also.
We get stronger that way,
but if you ... not looking after land, you get sicker.
If you go to a place, wreck it
or cut a tree or something like that,
then you will get sick, because of that.

We always have to repay with a part of ourselves,
we always got to give back to the spirits,
(*Lance traces a bend up with his hand like a cup*)

The ngangkari *Healing Power, with Lance Sullivan*

not only the spirits of the land, but the spirits
but the spirits that walked the earth.
We have to repay,
with a piece of our health, so I was,
I'm always careful about that.
A lot of *ngangkari* they losing their ability, to heal,
I noticed that because in my land, there was five old Clever fellas,
there's only one left now, and me.
And that other old fella, he's asking people for payment,
(*right hand fingers squeezed, a hand sign for money*)
I said, we can't ask people for payment.
Because what we have to do is give,
(*Hand forward*)
what we do is a gift, given to us by a spiritual ...
we've got to do what is right by the people,
so I stopped associating with him.
And there was another four of them
that used to hang around him,
they're all dead now.
But I stopped associating with them,
because all they ask, been asking for is money.

Then one girl comes up from South Australia,
(*Lance points to the south*)
From Coober Pedy area, she came up
she came all the way up to Tennant Creek.
And I just happen to come into town that day,
and word was going around for the communities,
all the elders, all the camps ...
They wanted to pay some Cleverman to heal her.
None of them old fellas in that town wanted to go near her.
It ended up being me and that other fella, my cousin,
my cousin, we ended up cleaning her there,
and I sung
that stuff for her,
so that it would take the sickness away.

I said to her, 'you've been hit,
I'll take that away and turn it around,
you'll be clean now.'
And all the old men stood up behind us,
and none of them would touch her!

And I noticed that in Mount Isa too,
when another girl, niece of mine was 'boned',

went straight through her kidney fat,
and when, she was ready to die you know,
she went real skinny and everything,
and I found out I came home from hunting one day,
I said whats wrong with that girl?
nah she's caught, nobody go near her now.
I knew that they left her for dead you know.
So I told her, 'come here!'
and I put my hand straight into inside.
I can't explain how I did it,
I just went in like that,
(*Lance bends*)
and grabbed her kidney.
Grabbed that, there was a stone inside her kidney,
I could feel it and I said to this other fella:
'come here, put your hand behind
and I'll push this stone into your hand.
When I put it in your hand, you hold it tight
and I'll come around and I'll pull it out.'
He was shaking, like a leaf.

And I said 'you supposed to be Cleverman',
his father was supposed to be the Cleverman.
But his father took off inside the house, wouldn't come out.
And this young fellow was shaking,
and I said, 'don't worry about it, I'll push it in',
(*Lance leans towards the camera with his arms wide open*)
straight through the body,
and I reached around and grabbed it,
to pull it out (*the kidney stone*).

And that girl coughing up all the blood then,
(*Lance makes the gesture out of his mouth*)
but as she was coughing,
I said to her 'it's gone now, it's gone!'
And she got up, and she was better.
I can't explain how that happened.

But I noticed, that these fellas that were saying they were Clevermen,
they were afraid to do things, and I know
they drink that alcohol a bit,
and I don't associate with them sort of people.
Yeah, but um, maybe them shamans are not listening to the spirits
    enough.
I've done that a lot lately,

The ngangkari *Healing Power, with Lance Sullivan*

I've tried to listen more,
that's why sometimes you might have noticed,
I blew in the ears of the sick people,
that was so that they could hear the spirits more.
And I blew into their eyes, so that they could see the spirits more,
and listen to it, and not fear it.

You can't fear the spirit world.
There is a lot of things you can say about the spirits like,
one of the things that my old fellas told me,
they tried to scare me one time I think,
but it helped me also to understand them.
They said 'The spirits are jealous of the living,
they want the power of the living to grow strong themselves
so they will try to take your life.'
But they can't, remember that, they can't,
because the living is stronger than the dead.
They've always taught that right through
when I was about ten years old.
I've kept that memory,
and I always think about that,
(*Lance points his right finger to his right temple*)
No matter how strong the spirit is, he can never harm you.

BG: But do you think these spirits were people who were alive before, or is it something different?

LS: Some of them are spirits who were alive before,
but a majority of them were spirits from the land.
There is, I believe that ...
I've never spoken about this before but I believe that,
and I never usually look with my eye much,
(*Lance hides his eyes with his palm*)
I always look with my *mungan*,
and that's the way I can look into the spirit world.
I can talk to them when I use my *mungan*.
I can talk to them, they talk back.
And if I try and explain it to somebody,
they might think I'm crazy you know?
(*Lance smiles*)
But I, it's like this glass, someone is underneath here,
(*Lance bends to the camera*)
you can look through,
(*He stands up over the glass table*)
you can see them,

If you got your *mungan*,
but it's night now, you can't see.

There's a wall there too. But if you use your *mungan*,
you can talk to this person behind this wall, this glass.
Others, other people of today just see only the glass,
they don't see what's beyond.

So you got the little people *Putinyjee*
and you got Mugai ... Mugai is the big tall one, spirit also of the land,
he killed Aboriginal men.
But I learnt that all the spirits, even though they're fierce and that,
you can use them to help, help you.
So them little short men Putinjee we got song,
for them to bring us bread, or food.

With the Mugai, when you talk to him, introduce yourself respectfully,
then he will not harm you,
he will leave meat there for you, and go away.
A lot people fear him, first thing they do is run away,
they don't talk, stop to talk.
But, I noticed the more spirits you talk to, the more you understand
  them.

There is a lot of, like I was saying glass,
There's a lot of those glasses,
they layer them, upon layer.
The more you look into it, the more you see.
That's how I see the world today.
Like if I wanted to, I could tell you
who was here before you.
(*Lance points his arm to the wall*)

I could ask the walls, I could look beyond this time now,
you can look back and see what it was before,
by looking with your *mungan*,
and not seeing this glass,
but the others below it, with it.
It's a bit hard to explain it.
Best way I can say, that there is a line of glass,
glass walls.
(*Lance draws in space vertical parallel lines*)

Like this one time this lady went missing.
She went missing in the bush. I said to her son, 'she is there under the
  grass.'
He thought I was crazy!

The ngangkari Healing Power, with Lance Sullivan

(*Lance laughs and Barbara too*)
'She's under the grass there!'
Grass is only up to your um, halfway up your leg.

He thought I was crazy. 'How could she be hiding under that grass?'
It's only more clump of grass.
I said 'she's there, sitting with them *Putinyjee*.
I can hear them talking, and they're telling me that she's there.'
(*Hand movements from out to his body*)
I can see her there. 'How can you see?
if you can see her, grab her, bring her out!'
I said, 'she will come, when the time is right,
and the *Putinyjee* will let her go.
We'll just sit here, light a fire, put the tea on, and we wait.'

He was going off his head, carrying on, threatening to burn the grass!
'You can't burn that grass, it's the grass for them little people!'
But, when she walked out, well the next day,
the fella was making tea and he heard behind him:
'Can I have a cup of tea?'
He spun around and looked, and there she was standing up with the grass,
same grass that he wanted to burn.
(*Lance laughs*)
And, he said to me: 'How did you know she was there?'
I said 'I could see her.' I said 'tell her to explain.'
And she said, 'I could hear youse all, and I could see you, but
when I call to you, it was like a wall up, between us. I could hear you faintly.
They were holding me down and had me covered over with grass.'

BG: And what did they tell her? Why did they take her?

LS: They wanted to kill her because she walked on men land.
But they let her go. And when I went to smoke her,
they came and got me ... to clean her.
So I took her down to the creek, I smoked her and I sung her,
and blew her ears and eyes, make her feel better.
And we went back to the camp.
And this Mugai walked straight up straight into the *Marlkarri*.
Marlkarri now. *Marlkarri* is another one.
He's normal man like us, but he's wild one.
And he walked up to the house, straight into the room
and he said, 'We're not finished with her yet', and walked away.
My mother and that were going off their head.
They came and got me:

'This *Marlkarri* just come here,
he said "he is not finished with her yet".'
I said 'We've done what we can, that's that',
I knew she'd done wrong by that country.
I said to my mother 'Well, you know, that *Marlkarri* said
"she's gone *womba* now"'
(*Lance turns his finger on the side of his head*)
She's gone a bit off
because she hasn't shown respect to that country.
But it's, like that old lady explained it.
She could see us, she could hear us, but when she called out,
it was like a wall was there
(*Lance puts his right hand on top of the other*)
she couldn't, like a glass wall, she can reach, but we couldn't see her.
I could see her, because I used my mind
but none of that other fellow could.

BG: I don't know in your country ... in the Kimberley side, the Yawuru, Djugun and Jabirr Jabirr up north, they associate the, what you call that name, when you say you don't see with your eyes?

LS: *mungan*.

BG: They say the third eye, the third eye.

LS: ah yeah

BG: but they connect it with *Rayi*, which is the spirit child that everyone has, like *Kurruwalpa* for Warlpiri. Is there a relation somewhere?

LS: OK ... I always say 'look with your heart,
see with you heart, don't see with your eyes.'

BG: But you know like parents or somebody from the family before you're born, dream and see where you're coming from, which place you're coming from? And which, your dreaming, like your ... This one that they call in Warlpiri, *Kurruwalpa*, they call *Rayi* on the coast there, in Broome side. But there is a lot of *Rayi*, waiting to be born.

LS: yeah ...

BG: So for you there is a connection between those spirit children? Those little people?

LS: We call them *Tharmu*. Yeah. *Tharmu*. It refers to spirit.
They'll say, oh, when someone dies they say *Tharmuga*, that mean,
'He's returned to the spirit', returned to the spirit again, he died.
Returned to the spirit.

The ngangkari *Healing Power, with Lance Sullivan*

It's like them Arrernte mob saying *kumanjayi*[9]
and things like that, same.

They showed great respect to us when
one of our family members died.
During the funeral they called, in Yalarrnga too:
'Don't forget the Yalarrnga, he is descendant from the Yalarrnga
He is *Tharmuga*, and he is *kumanjayi*'
They said like that, they use both terms.
We were very happy with that because they showed respect to us,
to our family member who passed away.

When we are on our country,
there are places, where them *Tharmu* hang around, spirits,
where they associate with (humans).
We believe one lady walks out there,
or a man walk along, he might spear a kangaroo
or something or shoot a kangaroo,
and if he hear some child crying behind him,
he knows that he's gonna have a boy or a girl.
And he'll say, 'Oh, that *Tharmu* bin follow me,
that *Tharmu* must be that Kangaroo totem.'

Or that if he killed a turkey:
'oh that *Tharmu* must be the turkey.'
He tells his wife, and sure enough she will have a baby,
with that totem then,
with the marking where the bullet or the spear went through.
It's really powerful.

BG: So, that is the same kind of story for Warlpiri and in the Kimberley.
But what relationship with the power to heal? How do you understand
that? Is there a relationship with that spirit in you?

LS: Oh yeah, I use my *Tharmu* all the time.
I always think about my Tharmu again
and I ask it to help, work through me also.
When I'm touching someone,
I always think about where I come from,
where my spirit came from, you know?

I think about it all the time when I touch somebody.
I always ask the power of my country to help me,
my Tharmu to help me, to help me to heal.

---

[9] See Chapter 4 with regard to 'no name', the expression for names that become taboo because of a dead person whose name it was.

I never forget that.
My mother, before she was born,
her grandmother was at the creek fishing with her uncle,
and he was pulling out all the fish,
one after other, one after other,
big buggers too, yellow belly and that.
And they could hear this child crying,
peeping behind the bushes at him,
and the old lady said:
'Oh don't, our grand-daughter there,
that's our grand-daughter coming.'
And he said, 'Get away, I know you there,
I can see you there, get away from me!'
He was panicking that old man.
He was only a young boy then.
He said: 'Go away leave me alone!'
And as he's pulling in the fish,
and he gets up and packs all his stuff up, and he takes off!

And she follows behind him, crying all the way.
That was my mother, her totem was fish.
Her totem was that yellow belly that he was pulling in.
Cause she had the marking of the yellow belly (*fish*) on her.
And she, yeah that was her *Tharmu*.
But we are all born like that.
Like my brother he was born with patches all over him,
so he was like a perentie (*lizard*) so we said
'Oh you're a perentie that one there.'
Another one born was a fish too.

BG: But then, Warlpiri they say there is what you call *Tharmu, Kurruwalpa* for them, and that's that spirit that comes from one special place, that's got a special songline that is like the secret name for the person. And this is, they say, what allows a baby to walk, and to talk.
...
But they say that the spirit that travels in dream, that's different.

LS: That's a different one, yeah.

BG: *Pirlirrpa*, they call it.

LS: Yeah that's a different one that one.
You can use that one to know where to go hunting the next day.
Sometimes like, the community where I came from,
the men get up early.
We all sit out and have a cup of tea

The ngangkari Healing Power, with Lance Sullivan

(*Lance mimes drinking with his hand up and down several times*)
'Hey what did you dream about?'
'Oh I dream about a lot of kangaroos at such and such place,
Parapitri, or something like that.
What did you dream about?'
'Oh I saw a goanna at such and such place.'

We believe our dreams are more real than what reality is.
We take those dreams very seriously.
So if that man just seen this goanna,
so he's got to go there and get that.
If this man saw kangaroo at another place,
he has to go there and get them.
So we tell him, 'you take a couple of men with you,
(*Lance indicates the south*)
and you take a couple of men with you,
(*Lance indicates the north*)
and we all meet back here tonight!'
OK, and it always happens, we always come back
with what we've dreamt about.

And if someone is sick, we will dream that also,
and we take that seriously,
Like that person could be having a cup of tea good as gold,
(*Lance drinks with his hand again*)
we say: 'We dreamt you, you were sick, in such and such spot.'
So we go over there and touch them,
we heal them, and they listen,
we all think alike, like we believe in the dreams.

BG: But Lance like, Warlpiri say also that when you wake a person too quickly, that *Pirlirrpa* (soul that dreams) has no time to come back in the body,

LS: That's right.

BG: and that person can be very sick. That's when you need the *mapan* (in the Kimberley) or *ngangkari* (in the desert) to bring it back.

LS: To look for the spirit, yeah.

BG: Did you ever work that way?

LS: When someone's spirit is,
like what happened to me once,
bone went through me
and come out under my shoulder blade.
I was in Alice Spring at the time,

I got 'boned', and I crawled down into the creek,
and this Clever fellow was there,
he was an uncle to me,
and I said to him, 'Look me! I'm "boned", I'm dying,'
and he panicked, he panicked,
(*Lance laughs*)

He was making tea there,
and he look back like that
(*Lance turns himself on the chair*)
and he panicked,
'Oh no, what am I gonna do?', he must have been thinking.

And he said 'Come, sit by the fire.'
He taught me how to find my spirit,
how to find spirit of others when they left the body.
So he went looking through the grass and everything for my spirit.
And then he found it
(*Lance mimes picking up something on the floor*)
and caught it.
And he said here, and he pushed it back into my chest,
(*Lance touches his chest with a smile*)
back where the hole was in my chest.
He said 'Your spirit is back in there, I'll seal it up now.'
So he showed me how to seal it up.

And today I learnt that, a lot of people think you're crazy
if you're looking through grass and everything.
I didn't think that when I seen him doing it,
cause I knew what he was doing.
But a lot of people today's civilised society,
they would think I'm crazy.

But we believe that the spirit does leave the body sometimes
and it takes a *ngangkari* to bring it back and put it back into the person,
and we always sit that person down
and give him/her a cup of tea, water,
make him feel a bit better then,
make his spirit associate with his body again.
And we smoke him a bit more.
Eh he right then, when we sing him, he right then.

But a bit tricky that power too, a bit tricky.
It's like that, we believe at night to,
the spirit leaves the body to travel, he can travel,
if you *ngangkari* you can travel anywhere

The ngangkari Healing Power, with Lance Sullivan

and talk to your family members,
in another place you know.
And they can see you, they can hear you, just like day.
And then you're back, you come back to your body.
But sometimes, normal people dream
That, like you say, they got awoken too quick.
Then their spirit is disturbed,
and you have to make them better.

But a Cleverfella, a *ngangkari*, he can use that ability
to help heal people too.
When someone is sick long way away,
he can go there and heal them,
and people ask that sometimes:
'Can you, they ring up, can you come?'
(*Lance signs for telephone, tumb and little finger up others down*)

Today lot got mobile phone,
'Can you come here and see me please?'
But they all see, I seen a lot of, so called *ngangkari*
but I think they are kurdaija (*emu feather curse throwers*)
I've seen them using mobile phone for sorcery nowadays.
(*Barbara laughs*)
Yes! They get a picture of somebody, and they sing it,
and they poke it with knife, and they sing it,
(*Lance mimes poking with hand*)
and they say they gonna kill that fella.
I seen that happen, so today, society it's all changing ey?
They take photo of somebody, they'll take it back and sing it,
Yeah they doing that now.

BG: So before photo what did they use?

LS: They use drawing, drawing in the dirt,
they used to draw symbol of the people in the dirt,
(*Lance draws with his hand above the table*)
and sing that there.

BG: Also, the Western sorcery, antique, they would make a doll, you know, in the shape of the person or just a thing of them.

LS: Oh yeah I heard of that...
they use clothes of people.
To catch another one, they use the sweat,
Try to get the sweat part of the body, of the clothing
and they catch them with that.
They, sing that sweat, or they burn it.

Or sometimes they say like the first law women,
in creation time, dreaming time, dreaming,
there was this woman who was upset by her husband,
playing around too much with other women,
so she got his hairbelt, and put it in a,
put a hole in this tree, and stuck the hairbelt in that,
poked it in the stick, and she burnt it, and she sang,
(*Lance shows poking with his fists*)
sang some songs, and she caught him that way.
And make him swell up that way.

But nowadays they using parts of clothing
and their doing the same thing,
they putting it in a hole in the tree,
(*Lance shows poking again*)
and they burning it, they singing, they do that.
And they also burn it on a fire.

BG: And this is to harm the person, or stop him running around?

LS: Yeah, to harm them, make them sick.

BG: Last time I was in Lajamanu, a month ago, the women just happened, we went camping and, had lots of stories and they were all talking, there was a story of one woman who disappeared in the bush, a very good friend of mine. It happened Christmas, not last Christmas but Christmas before (2015).

She went missing for four days, she was sitting in a circle gambling, and walked up to answer the telephone and never came back. And they even had a helicopter to look for her, and they found her, and she was lost, but not far, like maybe a few miles from Lajamanu.

LS: Yeah.

BG: And she could not come back. And the women were saying that she was caught by a ..., I forgot the name now.

LS: *Marlkarri* (wild man)

BG: Yeah, but like a spirit that comes in dream for sex.

LS: yeah, yeah, yeah

BG: And then they were telling many more stories like that, of men who are called by a woman in dream.

LS: Yeah the *Labirinja*

BG: Yeah and the other way, woman that are ...

The ngangkari Healing Power, with Lance Sullivan

LS: Yes the *Labirinja (woman)* and *Marlkarri (man)*.
He does that now, he takes ...
(*Lance suggests with his hand holding a woman by her hair*)
he can steal a woman. Or even a child.
If they walk along, and they lag along behind,
We're going: 'Oh, they gone now!'
Then we know that *Marlkarri* took them.

And if it's a bloke, he's out hunting,
that's the story connected to the that Emily Gap,
there's a spring there, at the end of the golf course there.
And when I was young man,
we used to walk around from spring to spring hunting,
and we used to go to that spring there,
down at the end of this new golf course they got.
We used to send the dogs around to bring the kangaroo in,
and I was sitting down there one day,
and this old man said,
'You know you got to be careful there,'
– 'what are you talking about?' I'm a bit worried now,
'What are you telling me?'
– 'this is where that *Labirinja* come!
she'll hit you on the head and dance on top of you.
And she'll steal you and take you away!'
I said 'Why did you tell me that, why did we come here?'
And he said, 'She goes all the way to Emily Gap.'
Now the others had gone ahead to Emily Gap,
we best catch up to them.
I said, 'Bloody oath we should catch up to them,
shouldn't hang around here no more!'

But that *Labirinja* she's supposed to hit you on the head,
Wild woman and when you knocked out,
she dances over the top of you.
(*Lance brings his hands together on top of his head down
then mimes a dance of stomping feet with his hands*)
she is singing and then you're gone with her!

And there's another place at Heart Range,
The Tulkin Downs Area there
where a wild woman came from the mountains,
and the *Labirinja* came there from the mountain,
and the old fellas, would always sneak up from all them other camps.
And they would put on long hair,
(*Lance combs his hair*)

and they'd tie on their hairbelt
(*Lance shows putting on headband*)
and they would pretend to be women.
And the *Labirinja* would come to see their sisters,
looking to see Aboriginal women hunting and that.
And the men would act as women,
and when the *Labirinja* got close,
he would grab her, and take her for his wife.
So a lot of the wild women were caught that way but,
But them *Labirinja*, they are very dangerous, all right.

BG: Now Broome side, I was told a story of one man, everybody was saying, he likes it! he's in love with that spirit woman. He's not interested in any other woman. He's always waiting for her.

LS: Yeah, that happens.
I know one cousin of mine, he wasn't tormented,
he was sort of attracted to that one *Labirinja* again,
must be a few years ay.
About five years I think, he was used to camp on his own,
wait for her, but yeah she sing him, catch him.
He's hers, for ever then,
until someone cleanse him ... yeah

This must be a hairstring she using, pull him,
and ngangkari got to cut it, and sing him, and clean him again.
But, I heard one old man, in Alice Spring there,
he was taken away for about forty years.
He come out, he left as a young man in Heart Range.
He come out somewhere in Alyawarre country.
He walk on up to the bore,
and all them Aboriginals there, saw was a wild man coming out of the scrub,
so they cut for it. And he's calling out, water! water!

And he said the last thing he remembers, when I spoke to him,
he said he remembers going to toilet, and the next thing he remembers,
he's looking at his hand, and there's a spear and a boomerang in his hand.
And in his other hand, is a woman, and she's leading him closer to the camp.
And then she goes like that to him,
(*Lance shows the sign for going away*)
'go back to them, go back to them!'
He didn't know he was old.
When he went up closer,
all the other people were running everywhere.

The ngangkari *Healing Power, with Lance Sullivan*

And when some old man came over to talk to him,
this was in Alyawarre country.
So he was a Aranda man, he end up in Alyawarre country.
And he remembers looking back,
seeing the wild woman in the scrubs
still looking at him, going like that to him.
(*Lance signs away*)
Anyway they took him to Alice Springs,
and they brought his kids, who were old men now,
they brought his kids to him,
his wife had passed on.
And they said, these are your kids,
And he said 'Oh, I don't know them,
I only know my family in the desert.'
(*Lance points his thumb to the back of his right shoulder*)

And they couldn't really connect with him.
But that old man,
in winter time or anything, no fire, he'll be sitting in the creek,
with no shirt on, nothing, and don't get sick.
Everybody say, 'You stay clear of him'
But he was a good old man, I liked talking to him, he was good.
He told me now that story ...
He lonely too,
like he still desires to go back, bush.

There was a few men like that.
I hear there was one, near, whereabouts was that?
West I think, Western Australia.
I was there, up that way for a while, working.
Around Mongrel Down Station ... Tanami Downs!

I was working there and ... they say,
When you go, when we getting closer to these hills,
lined up hills, all the men start panicking now,
'Don't go toilet without taking another couple of fellas with you!'
I said:
'What for?'
– you'll see all the bushes shaking, that's wild people behind there,
they'll bring you, and that'll steal you!
– Oh ...'
So I had to be careful in that country, that was around Western Australia,
That's the worst place, they reckon, down Balgo Hills.

BG: *Watikutjarra* (Two-Men Dreaming)
LS: Yeah around there that's worst place, I was working there.

The Two-Men are the Dreaming ancestors of the shamans or Clevermen (*ngangkari, mapan, bapan*) from the desert and the north-west. They turned into two hills in different places from the desert to the north-west coast. In the film Lance sits in front of a painting of the Two-Men Balgo Hills painted by Bye Bye Sunfly Napangarti, a Kukatja artist. Warlpiri say that their father Invincible tried to get rid of all boys at birth and was marrying his daughters endlessly, but they took revenge on him by tricking a travelling foreigner to attack and wound his testicles, whose pus became the gold in the Tanami. He ended up following his daughters who became the Pleiades and he keeps trying to chase them as a constellation (Orion for some). The Two-Men would turn into whirlwind to seduce and swallow women on their way. But also playing with their healing colourful stones to produce many different kinship systems that differentiate several north-western language groups. For some groups they are connected to two birds that name the generation moieties, *Wir* and *Girdir*, as well as to the Rainbow Snake and the Magellanic Clouds galaxies.[10]

> **BG:** And when you used to go work in jail to help people, what would you help them with?
>
> **LS:** What problems? So of them would ... one fella was love sick with magic
>
> (*Lance laughs*)
> He was worried about his wife, that she was going to leave him
> while he was in there.
> Another one was crook in his heart, big fella.
> He was fighting with everybody this big bloke,
> but when he came to me, he showed big respect,
> he said 'would you look at me?'
> I said 'I'm not old.' He said 'Can you look at me please?'
> and I said 'Alright'. I looked at his heart, chest.
>
> See another mob get, they get anxious, and anxiety attacks, things like that
> and you have to sit down and talk to them.
> 'Don't panic now ... you'll be alright' and all this.
> Some had pains, aches and pains, some had mental problems,
> couldn't help them much them mental fellas.
> You'd try you know, talk to them.
> But I noticed all those fellas that were a bit off,
> they all still showed respect to me.

---

[10] See Chapter 2, Chapter 4 and note p. 382; see also more in Glowczewski (2004).

The ngangkari *Healing Power*, with Lance Sullivan

Yeah, they never disrespect me in any way.
A lot of, there were some spiritual problems,
some believed that they were 'caught'.
because the belief is, them Aboriginals,
they believe that if they killed somebody,
that *Kurdaija* ... gonna come for them even if they're in jail
So they would ask me to clean them, things like that.

BG: And what can you do then?

LS: You ask to clean them, I sit to clean them.
One fella there, he was next cell over from me.
I heard this (knock) on a window, near the bars.
(*Lance taps the table with his fingers*)
I knew, I thought I was going crazy first.
I looked up from my bunk like that 'did I hear that?'
(*Lance bends his head backwards*)
Then I hear glass smash,
and I got up quickly and went to my window,
I thought it was that glass smashed,
No, and I went to lie down again,
and I hear footsteps walking,
(*Lance mimes steps with his hands*)
crunching on the glass,
and next cell over, man started screaming and carrying on.
'Leave me alone!'
I thought he was going mad,
I didn't think about *Kurdaija* see, I wasn't thinking about that,
and I went back to sleep, straight to sleep.
Next morning, he wouldn't come out of his cell.
And he came out the next day after,
and he was red and raving like a loony.
Lunatic you know. And everyone say, 'He's caught.'

And then the next fella over from him,
he also come to me and said,
'Did you hear glass smash?' I said 'yeah'.
'There's no glass smashed!
did you hear someone walking on glass?'
I said 'yeah',
He said 'There is no glass on the ground ...
what the hell was we listening to?'
I said 'Hold on, don't talk about it,
people will think you're mad!',
meaning, try to forget it.
(*Lance laughs*)

To be faithful to the title of this book, *Indigenising Anthropology*, I would like, with this concluding chapter, to leave the last word to my eldest daughter, Milari Barker who, after transcribing this interview with Lance Sullivan, wrote the following comment. She had met Lance as a little girl when we were living with her sister and dad in Townsville in 2004–2005. She met him again when we all went to the festival of shamanism in Genac in April 2017. Her grandmother, Djugun healer Theresa Barker,[11] had told her when she was a child that she should nurture the healing powers she inherited. Milari was invited as a member of the Aboriginal delegation, to help the Aboriginal guests with the ceremonies they performed and the cultural and spiritual presentations they did there.

> The spiritual world, beyond and through our way, responds in waves, to our energy and willingness to listen, to see through. For ourselves, or others. To simply understand, or possibly heal. Learning from the elders how to shift shadows/energy. As Lance does with healing, when he pushes the *liyan* back in or the pain out. Sometimes, it manifests physically as a splinter or coughed up blood or bone, or maybe a part of it/the pain sticks with him. In his words, that is the cost of his gift.
>
> People over time, throughout the world have had different ways to refer and name spiritual becomings and events.
>
> Our acceptance, that something that cannot be labelled, explained or dissected, becomes a part of our reality, gives us power, as living beings, to draw from this energy, lets us tap into another dimension of our 'potential'.
>
> I believe even stronger in the fact some of us, humans, are more sensitive than others to these things. Listen harder, or are chosen to carry this weight, gift, burden. I have seen it, through my Aboriginal blood and descendance, and the weight that THAT carries. It gave me eyes to see through. Like my grandmother used to say, when I truly listen.
>
> All is network, blood, spirit, stories, land. Spirits connect it all, and have always lingered to teach us, shape us, warn us, protect us and link our dreams. We are all free to choose how to listen and see. Look without your eyes. And we can start by respecting and caring for the world we do see, we do use. If we don't, we shall get sick.
>
> It is hard to talk about spirit and not mention *Bugarrigarra*, our Dreamtime. This is what we call the popularised 'Dreaming' in Yawuru and Djugun languages, but different Aboriginal groups throughout Australia have different names for it, like for the Warlpiri it's *Jukurrpa*.
>
> Imagine our world slave to time, where the Dreamtime is all time. Past, present and future, a constellation of spiritual forces. Us, Aboriginal

---

[11] See Chapter 8 in this book, 'Culture Cult'.

The ngangkari *Healing Power, with Lance Sullivan*

Figure 14.3 Smoking ritual after Yukawala women's intertribal ceremony in Western Australia. Theresa Barker (Djugun and Jabirr Jabirr) with her son's wife, Barbara Glowczewski, and their first baby daughter, Milari Barker. Broome, WA © Wayne Jowandi Barker 1992

people, can understand, see and feel this. We use it to tell stories, draw energy and communicate with spirits. Elders have a greater understanding of this, a sensibility, which is why the passing down of knowledge is so important – why our languages, traditions, knowledge and heritage are so rich and vital to our ways, our life.

This all gives us the tools to use our *liyan*, to feel a spiritual world, and heal.

Lance is an amazing healer, I have witnessed it, felt it. His intuition guides and mends, however also draining, it has a cost. His person is a testament to his sacrifice and good. A humble and quiet man, of great respect who doesn't question what he sees, but accepts some things cannot be explained.

I have been lucky enough to observe and learn from him, as he has inspired me to listen and see, as my grandmother wanted, without my eyes, but with my *liyan* and my heart. (Milari Barker, Paris, 10 July 2017)

Bibliography

Abbie, A. A. (1969) *The Original Australians*, London and New York: Frederick Muller and Elsevier.
Abeles, M. (2006) 'Globalization, power, and survival: an anthropological perspective', *Anthropological Quarterly* (Institute for Ethnographic Research), 79 (3): 483–6.
Ackerman, K. (1979) 'Material culture and trade in the Kimberleys today,' in R. M. and C. H. Berndt (eds), *Aborigines of the West. Their Past and their Present*, Nedlands: University of Western Australia Press, pp. 243–51.
Ahouansou, K. M. (2012a) 'Aller et venir – De W. E. B. Du Bois aux âmes "Afroeuropéennes"?', *Journal Afroeuropa*. Link disappeared.
Ahouansou, K. M. (2012b) 'Internet as a tool: claiming Black French identity', 8th Biannial MESEA (The Society for Multi-Ethnic Studies: Europe and the Americas) Conference, 13–15 June, Blanquerna School of Communication, Ramon Llull University, Barcelona.
Ahouansou, K. M. (2019) 'Le devenir d'Olivia au pays de Shonda. Expérimentation de désirs et production', in A. Querrien, A. Sauvagnarguesa and A. Villani (eds), Agencer les multiplicités avec Deleuze, Paris: Hermann.
Ahouansou, K. M. (n.d.) 'Le devenir-Français noir dans les cosmopolitiques parisiennes du 21ème siècle. Entre authenticité, différence, ressemblances et creation', PhD, Paris, EHESS.
Albistur, M. and D. Armogathe (1977) *Histoire du féminisme français du Moyen-Âge à nos jours*, Paris: Éditions des Femmes.
Alcantara, C. (2011a) *Corpoalíngua: performance e esquizoanálise*, 1st edn, Curitiba, PR: CRV.
Alcantara, C. (2011b) *Corpoemaprocesso/teatro desessência*, 1st edn, 4v, Curitiba, PR: CRV.
Alcantara, C. (2017) 'Théâtre desessence en acte/processus-rituel Fureur', in A. Barsaghian and S. Christensen (eds), *La Bête et l'adversité*, Genève: Métis Presses.
Ales, C. (2006) *Yanomami l'ire et le désir*, Paris: Karthala.
Alliance des Gardiens de Mère Nature (2015) '17 propositions pour changer l'avenir de la planète', *Multitudes*, 64: 159–63.
Alliez, E. (2005) *The Signature of the World: What is Deleuze and Guattari's Philosophy?*, trans. Eliot Ross Albert and Alberto Toscano, with a preface by Alberto Toscano, London and New York: Continuum.

Bibliography

Alliez, E. and A. Goffey (eds) (2011) *The Guattari Effect*, London and New York: Continuum.

Allix, G. (2010) 'Le Séisme Repose la Question du Statut des Réfugiés de l'Environnement', *Le Monde*, 21 January. Available at: http://www.lemonde.fr/ameriques/article/2010/01/21/le-seisme-repose-la-question-du-statut-des-refugies-de-l-environnement_1294629_3222.html

Amin, A. et al. (2010) 'A manifesto for a new Europe', *The Guardian*, 14 July, Available at: https://www.theguardian.com/commentisfree/2010/jul/14/manifesto-new-europe-politics-hope (accessed September 2018).

Amnesty International France, L. Boutaleb and G. Capel (2012) *Réfugiés. Un scandale planétaire. Dix propositions pour sortir de l'impasse*, Paris: Éditions Autrement.

Anderson, C. (1990) 'Repatriation of cultural property: a social process', *Museum* 156, 42 (1): 54–5.

Anderson, C. (ed.) (1995) *Politics of the Secret*, Oceania Monograph 45, Sydney: Sydney University Press.

Anderson, S. (2009) *Pelletier: The Forgotten Castaway of Cape York*, Melbourne: Melbourne Books

Ashley-Montagu, F. (1937) 'The origin of subincision in Australia', *Oceania*, 8 (2).

Asselin, H. and S. Basile (2018) 'Concrete ways to decolonize research', *ACME: An International Journal for Critical Geographies*, 17 (3): 643–50.

Babacan, H. and N. Gopalkrishnan (2007) 'Introduction', in H. Babacan and N. Gopalkrishnan (eds), *Racisms in the New World Order. Realities of Culture, Colour and Identity*, Cambridge: CSP.

Barker, W. (1992) *Milli Milli*, documentary, 53', distributed by Ronin Films, Sydney and Jane Balfour, London.

Barker W. (2011) 'Shake-a-leg: Aboriginal festivals and the international stage', in B. Glowczewski and R. Henry (eds), *The Challenge of Indigenous Peoples*, Oxford: Bardwell Press.

Barker, W. (2016) 'Stories from the front', New Writing from Western Australia, *Westerly*, 61 (1): 188–94.

Barker W. and B. Glowczewski (2002) *Spirit of Anchor*, 53', documentary with Tim Burarrwanga Bawaka, Arnhem Land, CNRS Images/Media: http://videotheque.cnrs.fr/doc=980?langue=EN

Barsaghian, A. and S. Christensen (eds) (2017) *La Bête et l'Adversité*, Genève: Métis Presses.

Bateson, G. (1972) *Ecology of Mind*, Chicago: University of Chicago Press.

Bateson, G. (1991) 'Men are grass: metaphor and the world of mental process' in *A Sacred Unity: Further Steps to an Ecology of Mind*, ed. R. E. Donaldson, New York: A Cornelia and Michael Bessie Book, pp. 235–42 (original conference 1980).

Beckett, J. (ed.) (1988) *Past and Present: The Construction of Aboriginality*, Canberra: Aboriginal Studies Press.
Bell, D. (1983) *Daughters of the Dreaming*, Melbourne and Sydney: McPhee Gribble Publishers and George Allen & Unwin Australia Ltd.
Benterrak, K., S. Muecke and P. Roe (1984) *Reading the Country*, Fremantle: Fremantle Arts Centre Press.
Benthall, J. ([1993] 2010) *Disasters, Relief and the Media*, Wantage: Sean Kingston Publishing.
Berndt, R. M. (1951) *Kunapipi*. Cheshire, Melbourne, New York: International Universities Press.
Berndt, R. M. (ed.) (1977) *Aborigines and Change – Australia in the 70's*, New Jersey: Humanities Press Inc.
Berndt, R. M. ([1952] 1983) *Djanggawul, an Aboriginal Religious Cult in North-Eastern Arnhem Land*, New York: Philosophical Library.
Bertho, Alain (2010) *Le temps des émeutes*, Paris: Bayard. (See also his website 'Anthropologie du présent' on 'riots' and social movements: http://berthoalain.com/)
Bessire, L. and D. Bond (2014) 'Ontological anthropology and the deferral of critique', *American Ethnologist*, 41 (3): 440–56.
Bettelheim, Bruno ([1962] 1971) *Symbolic Wounds: Puberty Rites and the Envious Male*, New York: Collier Books.
Bischofs, P. J. (1908) 'Die Niol Niol, ein Eingeborenenstamm in Nordwest-Australien', *Anthropos*, 3: 32–40.
Bjerre, J. (1956) *The Last Cannibals*, London: Michael Joseph.
Blagg, H. (2008) *Crime, Aboriginality and the Decolonisaiton of Justice*, Sydney: Hawkins Press.
Blanchard, P., N. Bancel and S. Lemaire (eds) ([2005] 2006), *La fracture coloniale. La société française au prisme de l'héritage colonial*, Paris: La Découverte.
Bonnefoy, Jean Pierre (2010) *Polynesia, 2. L'invasion des formes*, Paris: Buchet/Chastel Pocket.
Bosa, B. and È. Wittersheim (eds) (2009) *Luttes Autochtones, Trajectoires Postcoloniales (Amérique, Pacifique)*, Paris: Karthala.
Braudel, F. ([1969] 1980) *On History*, Chicago: University of Chicago Press.
Burke, L. (2016) 'Meet Cleverman: our first Aboriginal screen superhero, with healing powers and a political edge', *The Conversation*, 25 May 2016. Available at: https://theconversation.com/meet-cleverman-our-first-aboriginal-screen-superhero-with-healing-powers-and-a-political-edge-59813 (accessed February 2017).
Byrd, J. A. (2011) *The Transit of Empire*, Minneapolis: University of Minnesota Press.
Cadena, M. de la and O. Starn (2007) 'Introduction', in M. de la Cadena and O. Starn (eds), *Indigenous Experience Today*, Oxford: Berg, pp. 1–30.

Bibliography

Camargo da Silva, T. (2009) *Radiation Narratives and Illness: The Politics of Memory and the Goïania Disaster*, VCM.

Camargo da Silva, T. (2015) 'La Catastrophe Radioactive de Goiânia au Brésil. Conflit sur l'Interprétation d'un Désastre, comment Vivre après', *Multitudes*, 58: 161–6.

Capell, A. (1979) 'From men to gods and back again. A review article', *Oceania*, 23 (2): 110–32.

Castro-Koshy, E. and G. Le Roux (eds) (2016) 'Introduction. Creative collaborations, dialogues, and reconfigurations: rethinking artistic, cultural, and sociopolitical values and practices with Indigenous people in Australia, French Polynesia, New Caledonia-Kanaky, and Papua New Guinea', *Anthrovision*, 4 (1), *Visual Creativity and Narrative Reseach in and on Oceania*. Available at: https://journals.openedition.org/anthrovision/2191

Cataldi, L. and P. Rockman Napaljarri (1994) *Warlpiri Dreamings and Histories: Yimikirli*, San Francisco: HarperCollins.

Cepeda, H. J. (2017) 'The problem of being in Latin America: approaching the Latin American ontological sentipensar', *Journal of World Philosophies*, 2 (1).

Chakrabarty, D. (2009) 'The climate of history: four theses', *Critical Inquiry*, 35 (2): 197–222. Available at: http://www.law.uvic.ca/demcon/2013%20 readings/Chakrabarty%20-%20Climate%20of%20History.pdf

Chamoiseau P., E. Breleur, S. Domi, G. Delver, E. Glissant, G. Pigeart de Gurbert, O. Portecop, O. Pulvar, and J.-C. William (2009) *Manifeste pour les produits de haute nécessité*, Paris: Éditions Galaade – Institut Tout-Monde.

Chomsky, N. (2016) Interview by Alexandra Rosenmann, 15 July. Available at: https://www.alternet.org/culture/chomsky-america-decline-guess-whos-blame

Cixous, H. (1976) 'The laugh of the Medusa', *Signs*, 1 (4): 875–93 (revised version from French 1975).

Clastres, P. ([1974] 1987) *Society against the State*, New York: Zone.

Coates, J., M. Gray and T. Hetherington (2006) 'An "ecospiritual" perspective: finally, a place for Indigenous approaches', *British Journal of Social Work*, 36: 381–99.

Coelho de Souza, M. (2014) 'Descola's beyond nature and culture, viewed from Central Brazil', *Hau: Journal of Ethnographic Theory*, 4 (3): 419–29.

Cole, M. (2016) '2 Chinese property developers tied to outsized Aussie political donations' *Mingtiandi*. 2 February. Available at: http://www.min gtiandi.com/real-estate/outbound-investment/2-chinese-property-develop ers-tied-to-outsized-aussie-political-donations/ (accessed February 2017).

Condominas, G. ([1957] 1977) *We Have Eaten the Forest: The Story of a Montagnard Village in the Central Highlands of Vietnam* (translated from the French by Adrienne Foulke), London: Allen Lane.

Coombe, R. (1991) 'Objects of property and subjects of politics: intellectual property laws and democratic dialog', *Texas Law Review*, 69: 1853–80.
Coombe, R. (1997) 'The properties of culture and possession of identity: post-colonial struggle and the legal imagination', in B. Ziff and P. Rao (eds), *Borrowed Power: Essays on Cultural Appropriation*, New Brunswick, NJ: Rutgers University Press, pp. 74–96.
Corn, A., S. O'Sullivan, L. Ormond-Parker and K. Obata (eds) (2012) *Information Technology and Indigenous Communities* (symposium 2009), Canberra: AIATSIS Research Publications.
Courau, H. (2007a) *Ethnologie de la Forme-camp de Sangatte. De l'Exception à la Régulation*, Paris: Éditions des Archives Contemporaines.
Courau, H. (2007b) 'Sangatte. Plus on parle de Réfugiés, moins on parle d'Hommes', *REVUE Asylon(s)*, 2, Octobre, *Terrains d'ASILES*: http://www.reseau-terra.eu/article665.html
Courrège, P. (1965) 'Un Modèle mathématique des structures élémentaires de la parenté'. *L'Homme*, 5 (3–4): 248–90.
Craig, B., B. Kernot and C. Anderson (eds) (1999) *Art and Performance in Oceania*, Bathurst, NSW: Crawford House Publishing.
Crumlin, R. (1991) *Aboriginal Art and Spirituality*, Melbourne: Colin Dove.
Crutzen, P. and E. Stoermer (2000) 'The Anthropocene', *Global Change Newsletter, IGBP*, 41: 17–18.
Cunneen, C. (2007) 'Riot, resistance and moral panic: demonising the colonial other', in S. Poynting and G. Morgan (eds), *Outrageous! Moral Panics in Australia*, Hobart, Tasmania: ACYS Publishing, pp. 20–9.
Cunneen, C. (2010) 'Framing the crimes of colonialism: critical images of Aboriginal art and law', in K. J. Hayward and M. Presdee (eds), *Framing Crime. Cultural Criminology and the Image*, London: Routledge, pp. 115–37.
De Largy Healy, J. (2001) 'Football aborigène et réconciliation nationale', *Les Nouvelles de Survival*, 40–1: 11.
De Largy Healy, J. (2004) 'The paradox of knowledge production at the Knowledge Centre: a brief history of the Galiwin'ku Indigenous Knowledge Centre', paper presented at the AIATSIS Conference, Canberra.
De Largy Healy, J. (2009) '"My art talks about link": the peregrinations of Yolngu art in the globalised world', in J. Anderson (ed.), *Crossing Cultures: Conflict, Migration and Convergence*, Melbourne: The Miegunyah Press, pp. 817–22.
De Largy Healy, J. ([2007] 2011) 'The genealogy of dialogue: fieldwork stories from Arnhem Land', in R. Henry and B. Glowczewski (eds), *The Challenge of Indigenous People. Spectacle or Politics?*, Oxford: Bardwell Press, pp. 47–69.
De Largy Healy, J. (2013) 'Yolngu Zorba meets Superman: Australian Aboriginal people, mediated publicness and the culture of sharing on

the Internet', *Anthrovision*, 1. Available at: https://anthrovision.revues. org/362?lang=fr

De Largy Healy, J. (2017) '"This Painting becomes his body for life": transforming relations in Yolngu initiation and funeral rituals', in *Anthropological Forum, Matter(s) of Relations. Transformation and Presence in Pacific life-style Rituals*, ed. P. Bonnemère, J. Leach and B. Telban, 27(1): 18–33. Available at: http://www.tandfonline.com/doi/full/10.1080/00664677.2017.1287051.

De Largy Healy, J. and B. Glowczewski (2014) 'Indigenous and transnational values in Oceania: heritage reappropriation, from museums to the world wide web', *etropics – Value, Transvaluation and Globalization*, 13 (2). Available at: http://etropic.jcu.edu.au/ET13-2/Healy_and_Glowczewski.pdf

Deleuze, G. ([1968] 1995) *Difference and Repetition*, trans. Paul Patton, New York: Columbia University Press.

Deleuze, G. ([1993] 1997) 'What children say', in *Essays Critical and Clinical*, trans. Daniel W. Smith, Minneapolis: University of Minnesota Press, pp. 61–7.

Deleuze, G. ([1983], 2003 7th printing) *Cinema 1: The Movement-Image*, trans. Hugh Tomlinson and Barbarza Habberjam, Minneapolis: University of Minnesota Press.

Deleuze, G. ([1989] 2010 9th printing) *Cinema 2: The Time-Image*, trans. Hugh Tomlinson and Robert Galeta, Minneapolis: University of Minnesota Press.

Deleuze G. and F. Guattari ([1975] 1986), *Kafka: Toward a Minor Literature*, Minneapolis, University of Minnesota Press.

Deleuze G. and F. Guattari ([1992] 1996) *What is Philosophy?*, trans. Hugh Tomlinson and Graham Burchell III, New York: Columbia University Press.

Deleuze G. and F. Guattari ([1987] 1997) *A Thousand Plateaus*, trans. Brian Massumi, Minneapolis: University of Minnesota Press.

Deleuze, G., E. Sanbar and T. S. Murphy (1998) 'The Indians of Palestine', *Discourse*, 20 (3): 25–9.

Deleuze, G. et al. ([1988–1989] 2011) *(Gilles) Deleuze from A to Z*, Pierre André-Boutang, Claire Parnet, Gilles Deleuze, Los Angeles: Semiotext(e).

Deren, M. (1947–1953) *Divine Horsemen, the Living Gods of Haiti*, B&W documentary, 50'. Available at: https://vimeo.com/140129816

Descola, P. ([2005] 2013) *Beyond Nature and Culture*, trans. Janet Lloyd, with a foreword by Marshall Sahlins, Chicago: University of Chicago Press.

Descola, P. (2014a) *La composition des mondes. Entretiens avec Pierre Charbonnier*, Paris: Flammarion.

Descola, P. (2014b) 'The difficult art of composing worlds (and of replying to objections)'. Response to Hau Book Symposium on Philippe Descola,

2013, *Beyond Nature and Culture*. Hau: *Journal of Ethnographic Theory*, 4 (3): 431–43.

Descola, P. (2016) 'Biolatry: a surrender of understanding (response to Ingold's A Naturalist Abroad in the Museum of Ontology)', *Anthropological Forum*, 26 (3): 321–8.

Diouf, M. (1999) 'Entre l'Afrique et l'Inde, sur les questions coloniales et nationales. Écritures de l'histoire et recherches historiques', in M. Diouf (ed.), *L'Historiographie indienne en débat. Colonialisme, nationalisme et sociétés postcoloniales*, Paris: Kartala, pp. 5–35.

Diouf, M. and I. K. Nwankwo (eds) (2010) *Rhythms of Afro-Atlantic World: Rituals and Remembrances*, Ann Arbor: The University of Michigan Press.

Douaire-Marsaudon, F and S. Tcherkezoff (eds) ([1997] 2005) *The Changing South Pacific*, translated from French by Nora Scott, Canberra: ANU Press ebook.

Dousset, L. (2000–2005), *The Western Desert Project*. Available at: www.ausanthrop.net

Dousset, L. (2011a) *Australian Aboriginal Kinship: An Introductory Handbook with Particular Emphasis on the Western Desert*, Marseille: Pacific-Credo Publications.

Dousset, L. (2011b) *Mythes, missiles et cannibales: Le récit d'un premier contact en Australie*, Paris: Société des Océanistes.

Dufoix, S. (2011) *La dispersion. Une histoire des usages de la diaspora*, Paris: Editions Amsterdam.

Dumont, L. (1966) 'Descent or intermarriage? A relational view of Australian section systems', *South Western Journal of Anthropology*, 22: 231–50.

Durkheim, E. ([1913] 2008) *The Elementary Forms of Religious Life*, trans. Carol Cosman, Oxford and New York: Oxford University Press.

Durkheim, E. and M. Mauss (1901–1902) 'De quelques formes de classification – contribution à l'étude des représentations collectives', *Année sociologique*, 6.

Dussart, F. (1988) 'Notes on Warlpiri women's personal names', *Journal de la Societié des Océanistes*, 86 (1): 53–60.

Dussart, F. (1988–1989) 'Warlpiri women's yawulyu ceremonies. A forum for socialization and innovation', PhD thesis, Canberra, Australian National University.

Dussart, F. (2000) *The Politics of Ritual in an Aboriginal Settlement. Kinship, Gender and the Currency of Knowledge*, Washington and London: Smithsonian Institution Press.

Elkaïm, M. (1989) *Si tu m'aimes ne m'aimes pas. Approche systémique et psychanalytique*, Paris: Seuil.

Elkin, A. P. (1939) 'Kinship in South Australia', *Oceania*, 10 (2): 196–234; 10 (3): 295–349.

Bibliography

Ellis, L. M. (2016) *Pictures from my Memory: My Story as an Aboriginal Ngaatjatjarra Woman*, edited and introduced by Laurent Dousset, Canberra: Aboriginal Studies Press.

Escobar, A. (2018) *Sentir-penser avec la terre. Une écologie au-delà de l'Occident*. Paris: Seuil, coll Anthropocène (translated from *Sentipensar con la terra* [2014] by the collective Minga).

Euronews (2016) 'Environmental and Indigenous rights leader murdered in Honduras', *Euronews.com*, 3 March. Available at: http://www.euronews.com/2016/03/03/environmental-and-indigenous-rights- leader-murdered-in-honduras (accessed June 2019).

Fals Borda, O. (2009) *Una sociología sentipensante para América Latina. Victor Manuel Moncayo Compilador*, Bogotá: Siglo del Hombre Editores y CLACSO.

Fassin, D. and E. Fassin (eds) (2006) *De la question sociale à la question raciale?* Paris: Les éditions de la Découverte.

Fassin, E. (2010) 'Pourquoi les Roms?', *Mediapart*. Available at: https://blogs.mediapart.fr/eric-fassin/blog/120910/pourquoi-les-roms.

Fassin, E., C. Fouteau, S. Guichard and A. Windels (2014) *Roms et riverains. Une politique municipal de la race*, Paris: La Fabrique editions.

Federal Court of Australia (2018) Class action settlement notice. Palm Island Residents – Queensland Police Class action. Available at: http://www.fedcourt.gov.au/__data/assets/pdf_file/0005/49523/24-Apr-2018-Settlment-Notice.pdf

Fleming, C. (2012) 'White cruelty or Republican sins? Competing frames of stigma reversal in French commemorations of slavery', *Ethnic and Racial Studies*, 35 (3): 488–505.

Fraser, C. and Z. Todd (2016) 'Decolonial sensibilities: Indigenous research and engaging with archives in contemporary Colonial Canada', L'Internationale Online and Rado Ištok (eds), pp. 32–9. *Decolonising the Archives* series. Available at: http://www.internationaleonline.org/media/files/decolonisingarchives_pdf-final.pdf

Gaard, G. (2014) 'Indigenous women, feminism, and the environmental humanities', *Resilience: A Journal of the Environmental Humanities*, 1 (3).

Gagné, N. et al. (eds) (2009) *Autochtones. Vues de France et du Québec*, Montréal: Presses de l'Université de Laval.

Garcia-Acosta, V. (2002) 'Historical disaster research', in S. M. Hoffman and A. Oliver-Smith (eds), *Catastrophe and Culture. The Anthropology of Disaster*, Santa Fe, NM: School of American Research Press, pp. 49–66.

Garland, D. (2001) *The Culture of Control. Crime and Social Order in Contemporary Society*, New York: Oxford University Press.

Garond, L. (2012) 'Il y a beaucoup d'Histoire ici': Histoire, Mémoire et Subjectivité chez les Habitants Aborigènes de Palm Island (Australie)', PhD thesis, JCU Australie/EHESS France.

Garond, L. (2014) 'The meaningful difference of "Aboriginal dysfunction" and the neoliberal "mainstream"', *etropic*, 13 (2). Available at: http://etropic.jcu.edu.au/ET13-2/Garond.pdf

Genosko, G. (2002a) 'A bestiary of territoriality and expression poster fish, bower birds and spiny lobsters', in B. Massumi (ed.), *A Shock of Thought. Expression after Deleuze and Guattari*, London: Routledge.

Genosko, G. (2002b) *Félix Guattari. An Aberrant Introduction*, London: The Athlone Press.

Genosko, G. (2017) 'Micropolitics of hope'. Available at: http://spheres-journal.org/2-ecologies-of-change/

Gérard, B. (1986) 'Entre pouvoir et terre', *Etudes Rurales*, 101–2: 121–34.

Gérard, B. (1989) 'L'abord topologique pour la recherche en ethnologie', in *Seminfor 2 – La modélisation: Aspects pratiques et méthodologie*, Montpellier, 26–28 September 1988, Paris: Colloques et Séminaires, Editions de L'ORSTOM.

Giraud, F. (2012) '"Vous avez dit civilisation …",' *L'Autre* 13 (2). Available at: https://www.cairn.info/revue-l-autre-2012-2-page-237.htm #no1

Gleyzon, F.-X. (2015) 'Deleuze and the grandeur of Palestine: song of earth and resistance', *Journal for Cultural Research*, 20 (4): 398–416.

Glissant, E. and P. Chamoiseau (2009) *L'intraitable beauté du monde. Adresse à Barack Obama*. Paris: Editions Galaade – Institut du Tout-Monde.

Glowczewski, B. (1978) 'Anthropologie des 5 sens, Mémoire de Maîtrise en Anthropologie', Master's thesis, Paris 7.

Glowczewski, B. (1981a) 'Le Rêve et la Terre – Le rapport au temps et à l'espace des Aborigènes d'Australie', PhD thesis, University Paris 7 (Jussieu).

Glowczewski, B. (1981b) 'Affaire de femmes ou femmes d'affaires', *Journal de la Société des Océanistes*, 70–1: 77–97 (translated in Arbeitsgruppe fur Ethnologie, Wien (Hg), *Von.fremden Frauen, Suhrkamp Taschen – buch wissenschaft*, 784 [1989]).

Glowczewski B. (1983a) 'Death, women, and "value production": the circulation of hair strings among the Walpiri of the Central Australian Desert', *Ethnology*, 22 (3): 225–39.

Glowczewski, B. (1983b) 'Manifestations symboliques d'une transition économique – Le *Juluru*, culte intertribal du "cargo" (Australie occidentale et centrale)', *L'Homme*, 23 (2): 7–35.

Glowczewski, B. (1984) 'Les tribus du Rêve cybernétique', *Autrement*: 161–83.

Glowczewski ([1984] 2009) 'Viol et inviolabilité. Un mythe territorial en Australie central', *Mémoire des CLO, Cahiers de littérature orale*, 66: 233–58 (reprint, CLO 14 [1984]).

Glowczewski B. (1988) 'Le Rêve et la Loi. Approche topologique de l'organisation sociale et des cosmologies aborigènes', PhD (Thèse d'État), Université Pantheon-Sorbonne, Paris 1.

Bibliography

Glowczewski, B. ([1989] 2016) *Desert Dreamers*, Minneapolis: University of Minnesota Press/Univocal (updated version with new foreword and annex of *Les Rêveurs du Desert*. Actes Sud 2006, first published 1989 Plon).

Glowczewski B. (1989b) 'Des Peintures aux structures', *L'Homme*, 110: 126–33.

Glowczewski, B. (1991) *Du Rêve à la Loi chez les Aborigènes – Mythes, rites et organisation sociale en Australie*, Paris: PUF.

Glowczewski, B. (ed) (1991b) *Yapa, Art From Balgo and Lajamanu, Yapa, peintres de Balgo et Lajamanu*, Paris: Baudoin Lebon éditeur (French/English).

Glowczewski, B. ([1991] 2017) 'Between Dreams and Myths: Roheim and the Australians', translated from French, Geza Roheim and Ernest Pichon, n.d. (collection nouveau document): 262–70.

Glowczewski, B. (1994) 'Growing up and sexual identity: a cross-cultural approach', *Anthropological Forum*, VII (1): 7–29.

Glowczewski, B. (ed.) ([1994] 2018), *Liyan – A Living Culture: Jarndu Yawuru Oral History Project*, Broome, WA: Magabala Books (unpublished manuscript see Djugun and Yawuru collection: odsas.net).

Glowczewski, B. (1995) *Adolescence et sexualité – L'entre-deux*, Paris: PUF.

Glowczewski, B. (ed.) (1996) Language and culture survey in the Kullari Region, March-April, for the Aboriginal Arts and Culture Centre Working Party, Broome, WA (conducted by Wayne Barker, Quentin Bruce, Mary Lou Farrell, Veronica Francis, Barbara Glowczewski, Brian Lee, Mary Manolis, Veronica Francis, Veronica McKeon, Mary Tarran).

Glowczewski, B. (1996a) 'Histoire et Ontologie en Australie aborigène', *L'Homme*, 137: 211–25.

Glowczewski, B. ([1998] 2009) 'Le corps entre deux-vents (nord-ouest australien)', in M. Godelier and M. Panoff (eds), *La production du corps*, Paris: Éditions du CNRS (first published by Archives contemporaines): 203–27.

Glowczewski, B. (1998b) 'The Meaning of "One" in Broome, Western Australia: From Yawuru Tribe to Rubibi Corporation', *Aboriginal History*, 22: 203–22.

Glowczewski, B. (1999) 'Dynamic cosmologies and Aboriginal heritage', *Anthropology Today*, 15 (1): 3–9.

Glowczewski, B. (2000) *Dream Trackers: Yapa Art and Knowledge of the Australian Desert*, CD-ROM with 50 Warlpiri artists from Lajamanu, Paris: UNESCO Publishing shared copyright with Warnayaka Arts.

Glowczewski, B. (2001) 'Returning research through multimedia and the internet', in 'The production and reception of contemporary media technology' symposium: AIATSIS conference 'The power of knowledge, the resonance of tradition' (18–20 September).

Glowczewski, B. (2004) *Rêves en colère. Avec les Aborigènes australiens*. Paris: Plon/Terre Humaine.

Glowczewski, B. (2007) 'Survivre au Désastre. "We Got to Move on" Disent les Aborigènes de Palm Island', *Multitudes*, 30: 58.

Glowczewski, B. ([2009] 2016) '"We have a Dreaming". How to translate totemic existential territories through digital tools', *Desert Dreamers*, Minneapolis: Univocal/University of Minnesota Press (from Corn et al. [2012]).

Glowczewski, B. (2011) 'Décoloniser l'anthropologie: agencements et réseaux existentiels des peuples autochtones', *Décolonisations de la pensée: Anthropologie, philosophie et politique (2). Leçons Deleuzo-guattariennes*, Erraphis, Université de Toulouse Le Mirail: filmed conference: http://choplair.com.free.fr/Europhilosophie/FIPS_videos/player.php?id=2011_12juil_glowczewski&auto=1 or https://www.youtube.com/watch?v=EN5NmPIGX6M (both accessed 13 October 2018).

Glowczewski, B. (2012) 'Collures: du cinéma expérimental à l'anthropologie', *L'Unebévue*, 30: 203–14.

Glowczewski, B. (2014) 'Beyond the frames of film and Aboriginal fieldwork', in A. Schneider and C. Pasqualino (eds), *Experimental Film and Anthropology*, London: Bloomsbury, pp. 147–64.

Glowczewski, B. (2014b) 'Rejouer les savoirs anthropologiques: de Durkheim aux Aborigènes', *Horizontes Antropologicos*, 41. *Antropologia e Políticas Globais*, dirigé par Ondina Fachel Leal and Guilherme Waterloo Radomsky, pp. 381–403.

Glowczewski, B. ([2012] 2014c) 'From academic heritage to Aboriginal priorities: anthropological responsibilities', *Australian Aboriginal Anthropology Today: Critical Perspectives from Europe*, 13 June: 18. Available at: http://actesbranly.revues.org/526. (From academic heritage to Aboriginal priorities: anthropological responsibilities, R@U – *Revista de Antropologia da UFSCar*: www.ufscar.br/rau, 4 (2), July–December 2012).

Glowczewski, B. (2015) *Totemic Becomings: Cosmopolitics of the Dreaming*, São Paulo: n-1 Publications.

Glowczewski, B. (2015b) 'Au coeur du soleil ardent. La catastrophe selon les Aborigènes', *Communications*, 96: 53–65.

Glowczewski, B. (2016b) 'Respecter la terre comme un être vivant', in *Le corps d'une femme, premier environnement de l'être humain*, Paris: Éditions des Femmes, pp. 13–29.

Glowczewski, B. (2016c) 'Guattari's ecosophy and multiple becomings in ritual', conference paper at 'Deleuze + art: multiplicities, thresholds, potentialities', international conference, Trinity College Dublin, April 2016 (to be published in Radek Przedpelski and Steven E. Wilmer Deleuze (eds), *Deleuze, Guattari and the Art of Multiplicity*, Edinburgh University Press).

Glowczewski (2019) 'Entre totémisme aborigène et Umbanda brésilienne: empreintes, lignes de fuites et critallisation des hétérogénéités', in

Bibliography

A. Querrien, A. Sauvagnargues and A. Villani (eds), *Agencer les multiplicités avec Deleuze*, Paris : Hermann – Les colloques Cerisy (decade Deleuze 2015): 119–29.

Glowczewski, B. with M. Abélès (2010) 'Aborigènes: Anthropologie d'une Exigence de Justice', *Vacarme*, 51, April 2010. Available at: http://www.vacarme.org/article1891.html (accessed October 2018).

Glowczewski, B. and J. De Largy Healy (with the artists of Galiwin'ku and Lajamanu) (2005) *Pistes de rêves. Voyage en terres aborigènes*. Paris: Editions du Chêne.

Glowczewski, B. and R. Henry (eds) ([2007] 2011) *The Challenge of Indigenous Peoples. Spectacle or Politics?*, Oxford: Bardwell Press (transl.).

Glowczewski B. and C. Laurens ([2015] 2018) 'Le conflit des existences à l'épreuve du climat. Ou l'anthropocène revu par ceux qu'on préfère mettre à la rue ou au musée', in C. Larrère and R. Beau (eds), *Penser l'anthropocène*, Paris: Sciences PO – Les Presses (filmed conference at the Collège de France, 2015: http://www.fondationecolo.org/l-anthropocene/video). (Also transl. in Portugese, in *Espiral* 1, 2018: http://www.iecomplex.com.br/revista/index.php/espiral/issue/view/1.)

Glowczewski, B. and B. Nakamarra Gibson (2002) 'Rêver pour chanter: Apprentissage et création onirique dans le désert australien', *Cahiers de Littérature Orale (CLO)*, 51: 153–68.

Glowczewski, B., interview with N. Petresin-Bachelez (2016) 'Guattarian Ecosophy and slow anthropology'. Available at: http://www.internationaleonline.org

Glowczewski, B. and C.-H. Pradelles de Latour (1987) 'La diagonale de la belle-mère', *L'Homme*, 104: 27–53.

Glowczewski, B. and A. Soucaille (2007) 'Introduction. Réseaux autochthones: résonances anthropologiques', *Multitudes* 30.

Glowczewski, B. and A. Soucaille (eds) (2011) *Désastres*, Paris: L'Herne.

Glowczewski, B., with a contribution by L. Wotton ([2008] 2010), *Warriors for Peace. The Political Situation of the Aboriginal People as Viewed from Palm Island* (updated translation of *Guerriers pour la Paix* [2008], with a new foreword by B. Glowczewski and a postscript by Lise Garond). Available at: http://eprints.jcu.edu.au/7286/. http://halshs.archives-ouvertes.fr/halshs-00637654/en/

Glowczewski B., L. Dousset and M. Salaün (eds) (2014) *Les Sciences Humaines et Sociales dans le Pacifique Sud: Terrains, Questions et Méthodes*, Marseille: CREDO éditions.

Glowczewski, B., E. Manning and B. Massumi (2009) 'Micropolitics in the desert – politics and the law in Australian Aboriginal communities', *INFLeXions 3. Micropolitics: Exploring Ethico-Aesthetics*: 48–68. Available at: http://inflexions.org/issues.html#i3

Glowczewski, B., J. F. Matteudi, V. Carrère and M. Viré ([1983] 2008) *La cité des Cataphiles. Mission anthropologique dans les souterrains de Paris.* Paris: ACP (with new introduction by R. Peirazeau and annex, 1st edn Les Méridiens).

Goldman, M. (2015) 'Reading Bastide: deutero-learning the African religions in Brazil', *Etudes rurales*, 196, *Multiplicités anthropologiques au Brésil-Varia*: 9–24 (trans. M. Goldman from 2011, 'Cavalo do deus', *Revista de Antropologia*, 54 (1): 408–32).

Goodale, J. (1987) 'Gambling is hard work: card playing in Tiwi society', *Oceania*, 58 (1): 6–21.

Gori Roland, B. C. and C. Laval (eds) (2009) *L'appel des appels. Pour une insurrection des consciences*. Paris: Éditions Mille et une nuits.

Gough, M. (2015) 'Aboriginal legends reveal ancient secrets to science', *BBC News*, 19 May. Available at: http://www.bbc.com/news/world-australia- 32701311?post_id=10207214797830869_10207214797790868# (accessed 10 October 2018).

Graeber, D. (2004) *Fragments of an Anarchist Anthropology*, Chicago: Prickly Paradigm Press.

Griffen, R. (2016) 'We need more Aboriginal superheroes, so I created Cleverman for my son', *The Guardian*, 27 May. Available at: https://www.theguardian.com/tv-and-radio/2016/may/27/i-created-cleverman-for-my-son-because-we-need-more-aboriginal-superheroes (accessed 1 February 2017).

Guattari, F. (1956) Clinical summary, 'Monographie sur R. A.'.

Guattari, F. (1966) 'Réflexions pour des philosophes à propos de la psychothérapie institutionnelle', *Cahiers de philosophie de la Sorbonne* 1.

Guattari, F. (1972) *Psychanalyse et transversalité*, Paris: François Maspero.

Guattari, F. ([1979] 2011) *The Machinic Unconscious. Essays in Schizoanalysis*, Los Angeles: Semiotext(e).

Guattari, F. ([1983] 1986) '1983 – La ville d'ombre', in *Les Années d'hiver 1980–1985*, B. Barrault, pp. 239–42.

Guattari, F. ([1985] 1986) '1985 – Le cinquième monde nationalitaire', in *Les Années d'hiver 1980–1985*, B. Barrault, pp. 71–9.

Guattari, F. ([1989] 2000) *The Three Ecologies*, London: The Athlone Press. (Only 17 pages here [1989]: http://banmarchive.org.uk/collections/newformations/08_131.pdf) (Continuum 2008.)

Guattari, F. ([1989] 2012) *De Leros à La Borde*, preface by Marie Depussé, postscript Jean Oury, Paris: IMEC.

Guattari, F. ([1989] 2013) *Schizoanalytic Cartographies*, trans. Andrew Goffey, London: Bloomsbury.

Guattari, F. ([1989–1990] 2013) 'L'environnement et les hommes, émergence et retour des valeurs ou l'enjeu éthique de l'écologie', in *Qu'est-ce que l'écosophie?*, ed. Stéphane Nadaud, Paris: Lignes-IMEC, pp. 523–33.

Guattari, F. ([1990] 2013) 'Au-delà du retour à zéro, interview with Toni

Bibliography

Negri' (*Futur Antérieur* 1990) in *Qu'est-ce que l'écosophie?*, ed. Stéphane Nadaud, Paris: Lignes-IMEC.

Guattari, F. (1991) 'Produire une culture du dissensus: hétérogénèse et paradigme esthétique'. Filmed Seminar in art school, Los Angeles, transcript on French website: http://www.cip-idf.org/spip.php?page=imprimer&id_article=5613. Also 29 May 2011 (standing): http://1libertaire.free.fr/FGuattari32.html (accessed 29 January 2017).

Guattari, F. ([1991] 2013) 'Qu'est-ce que l'écosophie?', interview by E. Videcoq and J.-Y. Sparfel, *Terminal* 56, 1991, reprint 1996: http://revue-chimeres.fr/drupal_chimeres/files/termin56.pdf; and 2006: http://www.ecorev.org/spip.php?article479. Also *Qu'est-ce que l'écosophie?* 2013: 73–4.

Guattari, F. (1992) 'Pour une refondation des pratiques sociales', in *Le Monde Diplomatique* (October 1992): 26–7. Translated by Sophie Thomas, revised by Brian Holmes: https://www.scribd.com/document/11320929/Felix-Guattari-Remaking-Social-Practices.

Guattari, F. ([1992] 1995) *Chaosmosis: An Ethico-Aesthetic Paradigm*, trans. Paul Bains and Julian Pefanis, Bloomington: Power Institute From p. 422 (Bloomington University Press).

Guattari, F. ([1993] 2015) 'Ecosophical practices and the restoration of the "Subjective City"', in Jay Hetrick and Gary Genosko (eds), *F. Guattari, Machinic Eros: Writings on Japan*, Minneapolis: Univocal.

Guattari, F. ([1992] 2009) 'Entretien à la télévision grecque', *Chimères*, 1 (69).

Guattari, F. ([2012] 2016) *A Love of UIQ*, trans. and ed. Silvia Maglioni and Graeme Thomson, Minneapolis: Univocal.

Guattari, F. (2013) *Qu'est-ce que l'écosophie?*, ed. Stéphane Nadaud, Paris: Lignes-IMEC.

Guattari, F. and S. Rolnik ([1986] 2008) *Molecular Revolution in Brazil*, trans. Karel Clapshow and Brian Holmes, Los Angeles: Semiotext(e). (Translated from the original Portugese *Micropolitica: Cartografias do desejo*, Petrópolis: Vozes, 7th ed. [2005] expanded and revised.)

Guesdon, M. (2016) 'Clinique, musique et expression – Le concept de ritournelle chez Félix Guattari et Gilles Deleuze (1956–1980)', PhD thesis in Philosophy and Social Sciences, EHESS.

Hage, G. (2009) 'Anthropology and the passion of the political', AAS Conference, State Library of NSW, Australia: http://www.aas.asn.au/aas_lecture.php

Hale, K. L. (1971) 'A note on a Walbiri tradition of antonymy', in D. D. Steinberg and L. A. Jakobovitz (eds), *Semantics: An Interdisciplinary Reader in Philosophy, Linguistics and Psychology*, Cambridge: Cambridge University Press.

Hale, K. (1974), *Walpiri-English Vocabulary. An Elementary Dictionary of the Walpiri Language*, Cambridge, MA: The MIT Press, mimeo.
Halluin-Mabillot, E. (2012), *Les épreuves de l'asile. Associations et réfugiés face aux politiques du soupçon*, Paris: Éditions de l'EHESS.
Haraway, D. (2013) 'SF: science fiction, speculative fabulation, string figures, so far', *Ada: A Journal of Gender, New Media, and Technology* 3.
Haraway, D. (2015) 'Sympoièse, sf, embrouilles multispécifiques', in D. Debaise and I. Stengers (eds), *Gestes Spéculatifs*, Paris: Les Presses du réel, pp. 42–72.
Harrison, N. and J. Sellwood (2016) *Learning and Teaching in Aboriginal and Torres Strait Islander Education*, South Melbourne, Australia: Oxford University Press.
Heinlein, R. (1941) 'And he built a crooked house', in *Astounding Science Fiction*, February.
Henry, R. (2000) 'Dancing into being: the Tjapukai Aboriginal Cultural Park and the Laura Dance Festival', in R. Henry, F. Magowan and D. Murray (eds), *The Politics of Dance*, TAJA, 11 (3): 322–31.
Héran, F. (2017) *Avec l'immigration. Mesure, débattre, agir*, Paris: La Découverte, coll. 'L'envers des faits'.
Hessel, S. (2010) *Indignez-vous*, Montpelier: Indigène Editions.
Holmes, B. (2009) 'Guattari's schizoanalytic cartographies, or the pathic core at the heart of cybernetics', in *Continental Drift, The Other side of Neoliberal Globalization*: https://brianholmes.wordpress.com/2009/02/27/guattaris-schizoanalytic-cartographies/
Holmes, M. C. C. and W. (S. P.) Jampijinpa (2013) 'Law for country: the structure of Warlpiri ecological knowledge and its application to natural resource management and ecosystem stewardship', *Ecology and Society* 18 (3): 19. Available at: http://www.ecologyandsociety.org/vol18/iss3/art19/
Hunt, D. and S. A. Stevenson (2016) 'Decolonizing geographies of power: indigenous digital counter-mapping practices on turtle Island', *Settler Colonial Studies*.
Hunter, E. (1993) *Aboriginal Health and History – Power and Prejudice in Remote Australia*, Cambridge: Cambridge University Press.
Inandiak, E. (2007) 'The actions of Java Bebekan Village destroyed by the May 2006 Earthquake', interview of Inandiak by Elisabeth de Pablo, 28 March: http://www.archivesaudiovisuelles.fr/949_3277_en/
Inandiak, E. (2011) 'Journal de l'Éruption du Volcan Merapi (26 Octobre 2010–12 Juin 2011)', in B. Glowczewski and A. Soucaille (eds), *Désastres*, Paris: L'Herne, pp. 41–60.
Ingold, T. (2016) 'Involving anthropology, a naturalist abroad in the Museum of Ontology: Philippe Descola's *Beyond Nature and Culture*', *Anthropological Forum*, 26 (3): 301–20.
Invisible Committee ([2007] 2009) *The Coming Insurrection*, Los Angeles: Semiotext(e) (translated from French).

Bibliography

Jackson, S. (1996) *When History Meets the New Native Title Era at the Negotiating Table. A Case Study in Reconciling Land Use in Broome, Western Australia*, Darwin: North Australia Research Unit, ANU.

Janke, T. (1998) *Our Culture: Our Future. Report on Australian Indigenous Cultural and Intellectual Property Rights*, Canberra: Michael Frankel and Co., ATSIC.

Jaulin, R. (1967), interview with Max Pol Fouchet in film by J. Pappé (dir.) (1967), *Mort et Métamorphoses des Civilisations*, Paris: INA.

Jeudy-Ballini, M. and B. Juillerat (eds) (2002) *People and Things. Social Mediations in Oceania*, Durham, NC: Carolina Academic Press.

Jonas, H. ([1984] 1985) *The Imperative of Responsibility: In Search of an Ethics for the Technological Age*, trans. H. Jonas and D. Herr, Chicago: University of Chicago Press.

Jordan, D. (1988) 'Uses of the past, problems for the future', in J. Beckett (ed.), *Past and Present, the Construction of Aboriginality*, Canberra: Aboriginal Studies Press.

Kaberry, P. (1939) *Aboriginal Woman, Sacred or Profane*, London: Routledge and Kegan Paul.

Keefe, K. (1988) 'Aboriginality: resistance and persistence', *Australian Aboriginal Studies*, 1: 67–81.

Keen, I. (ed.) (1988) *Being Black: Aboriginal Cultures in 'Settled' Australia*, Canberra: Aboriginal Studies Press.

Kendon, A. (1988) *Sign Languages of Aboriginal Australia. Cultural Semiotic and Communicative Perspectives*, Cambridge: Cambridge University Press.

Kennedy, R. (2011) *The Persistence of the Color Line: Racial Politics and the Obama Presidency*, New York: Pantheon Books.

Koepping, K. P. (1988) 'Nativistic movements in Aboriginal Australia', in T. Swain and D. Rose (eds), *Aboriginal Australians and Christian Missions: Ethnographic and Historical Studies*, Bedford Park, Australia: The Australian Association for the Study of Religions.

Kokoreff, M. (2008) *Sociologie des émeutes*, Paris: Payot.

Kolig, E. (1973) 'Progress and preservation: the Aboriginal perspective', *Aboriginal News*, 1 (4): 18–20.

Kolig, E. (1977) 'From tribesman to citizen? Change and continuity in social identities among South Kimberley Aborigines', in R. M. Berndt (ed.), *Aborigines and Change – Australia in the 70's*, New Jersey: Humanities Press Inc.

Kolig, E. (1979) 'Djuluru: Ein synkretistichen Kult Nordwest-Australiens', *Baessler-Archiv*, Neue Folge 27: 419–48.

Kolig, E. (1981) *The Silent Revolution. The Effects of Modernization on Australian Aboriginal Religion*, Philadelphia: Institute for the Study of Human Issues.

Kolig, E. (1988) 'Mission not accomplished – Christianity in the Kimberleys', in T. Swain and D. Rose (eds), *Aboriginal Australians and Christian Missions: Ethnographic and Historical Studies*, Bedford Park, Australia: The Australian Association for the Study of Religions, pp. 376–90.

Kolig, E. (2000) 'Social causality, human agency and mythology: some thoughts on history-consciousness and mythical sense among Australian Aborigines', *Anthropological Forum*, 10 (1): 9–30.

Kopenawa, D. and B. Albert ([2010] 2013) *The Falling Sky. Words of a Yanomami Shaman*, trans. Nicholas Elliott and Alison Dundy, Cambridge, MA: Harvard University Press.

Kubiakowska, J. Z. (2009) 'Zachodnia Afrykanska Bitwa o Szyny' [The Battle of the Rail in West Africa], *Le Monde Diplomatique*, 4 (38) April: 18–19.

Kymlicka, W. (1996) *Multicultural Citizenship: A Liberal Theory of Minority Rights*, Oxford: Clarendon Press. (*La citoyenneté multiculturelle*, Paris: La Découverte.)

Landivar, D. and E. Ramillien (2015) 'Reconfigurations ontologiques dans les nouvelles constitutions politiques andines', *Tsantsa*, 20: 29–40.

Langton, M. (1993) *Well I Heard it on Television*, Canberra: Australian Film Commission.

Langton, M. (2001) 'Cultural iconography, memory and sign: the new technologies and Indigenous Australian strategies for cultural survival', paper presented to the International Symposium Indigenous Identities, UNESCO, Paris. (In Glowczewski, B., L. Pourchez, J. Stanton, J. Rotkowski and the UNESCO Division of Cultural Policies (eds) (2004), *Cultural Diversity and Indigenous Peoples: Oral, Written Expressions and New Technologies*, CD-ROM, Paris: UNESCO Publishing.)

Langton, M. (2018) *Welcome to Country*, Melbourne: Hardie Grant Publishing.

Lapeyronnie, D. (2008) *Guetto urbain. Ségrégation, violence, pauvreté en France aujourd'hui*, Paris: Robert Laffont.

Laughren, M. (1982) 'Warlpiri kinship structure', in J. Heath, F. Merlan and A Rumsey (eds), *The Languages of Kinship in Aboriginal Australia*, Oceania Linguistic Monograph 24, Sydney: University of Sydney.

Laughren, M., G. Curran, M. Turpin and N. Peterson (2014) *Women's Yawulyu Songs as Evidence of Connections to and Knowledge of Land: The Jardiwanpa*, University of Queensland, University of Sydney, Australian National University.

Leach, E. R. (1961) 'Two essays concerning the symbolic representation of time', in *Rethinking Anthropology*, LSE Monographs on Social Anthropology 22, London: The Athlone Press, p. 126.

Le Cour Grandmaison, O. (2009) *La république impériale. Politique et racisme d'Etat*, Paris: Fayard.

Bibliography

Lem, S. (1984) 'Propos inoxydables', entretien de B. Glowczewski, *L'Autre Journal*, numéro 3, hiver, 1984–1985.

Le Roux, G. (2016) 'Transforming Representations of Marine Pollution. For a New Understanding of the Artistic Qualities and Social Values of Ghost Nets', in E. Castro-Koshy and G. Le Roux (eds), *Anthrovision*, 4 (1), *Visual Creativity and Narrative Reseach in and on Oceania*. Available at: https://journals.openedition.org/anthrovision/2191

Le Roux, G. and L. Strivay (eds) (2007) 'La revanche des genres' [The revenge of genre], Exhibition Bilingual Catalog, Les Brasseurs in Lièges/Cité des Arts de Paris.

Lévi-Strauss, C. ([1947] 1970) *The Elementary Structures of Kinship*, trans. J. H. Bell, J. R. von Sturmer and R. Needham, New York: Basic Books

Lévi-Strauss, C. ([1962] 1963) *Totemism*, trans. by Rodney Needham, Boston, MA: Beacon Press.

Lévi-Strauss, C. ([1962] 1966) *The Savage Mind*, Chicago: University of Chicago Press.

Lévi-Strauss, C. ([1985] 1988) *The Jealous Potter*, trans. Bénédicte Choirer, Chicago: University of Chicago Press.

Lévy, L. (2005) *Le spectre du communautarisme*, Paris: Éditions Amsterdam.

Lim, M., A. Poelina and D. Bagnall (2017) 'Can the Fitzroy River Declaration ensure the realisation of the First Law of the River and secure sustainable and equitable futures for the West Kimberley', *Australian Environment Review*, 32 (1): 18–24.

Linebaugh, P. (2016) *The Incomplete, True, Authentic, and Wonderful History of May Day*, Oakland: PM Press.

Linnekin, J. and L. Poyer (eds) (1990) *Cultural Identity and Ethnicity in the Pacific*, Honolulu: University of Hawaii Press.

Lombard, J. (2006) 'Croître ou Dépérir. Lieux Intégrés, Lieux Oubliés sur l'Axe Dakar-Mali', in J.-L. Chaléard et al. (eds), *Le Chemin de Fer en Afrique*, Paris: Karthala, pp. 69–86.

Lommel, A. (1950) 'Modern culture influences on the Aborigines', *Oceania*, 21 (1): 14–24.

Lovelock, J. (2009) *The Vanishing Face of Gaia: A Final Warning*, New York: Basic Books.

Lucich, P. (1987) *Genealogical Symmetry – Rational Foundations of Australian Kinship*, Armidale NSW: Light Stone Publications.

Lupasco, S. ([1960] 2003) *Trois matières*, Paris: Éditions Cohérence.

McCarthy, F. D. (1961) 'The story of the Mungan or Bagadjimbiri Brothers', *Mankind*, 5 (10): 420–5.

McConvell, P. (1985) 'The origin of subsections in Northern Australia, *Oceania*, 56: 1–33.

McDuffie, M. (2016) 'Jimbin Kaboo Yimardoowarra Marninil: Listening to Nyikina women's voices. Film as a strategy of resistance', Anthrovision 4.1

Visual Creativity and Narrative Research in and on Oceania: https://journals.openedition.org/anthrovision/2220

McGregor, W. (1988) *Handbook of Kimberley Languages, V.1: General Information* (Project of the Kimberley Language Resource Centre), Canberra: The Australian National University (Pacific Linguistics, Series C, 105).

Maddock, K. (1977) 'Two law in one community', in R. M. Berndt (ed.), *Aborigines and Change – Australia in the 70's*, New Jersey: Humanities Press Inc.

Maddock, K. (1981) 'Warlpiri land tenure: a test case in legal anthropology', *Oceania*, 52 (2): 85–102.

Maddock, K. (1988) 'Myth, history and a sense of oneself', in J. Beckett (ed.), *Past and Present, the Construction of Aboriginality*, Canberra: Aboriginal Studies Press.

Manning, E. (2009) *Relationscapes: Movement, Art, Philosophy* (Technologies of Live Abstraction), Cambridge, MA: The MIT Press.

Mariotti, H. (1999) 'Autopoiesis, culture, and society'. Available at: http://www.oikos.org/mariotti.htm

Massumi, B. (2002) 'Sur le Droit à la non-communication des différences', *Ethnopsy. Les mondes contemporains de la guérison*, 4 (April), special issue, ed. Isabelle Stengers and Tobie Nathan, *Propositions de paix*: 93–131.

Massumi, B. (2002b) 'Introduction', in B. Massumi (ed.), *A Shock of Thought. Expression after Deleuze and Guattari*, London: Routledge.

Martin, J.-C. (2010) *Plurivers – Essai sur la fin du monde*, Paris: PUF.

Mathieu, N.-C. (1985) *Arraisonnement des femmes, essais en anthropologie des sexes*, Paris: Édition de l'EHESS.

Maturana, H. and F. J. Varela (1980) *Autopoiesis and Cognition: The Organization of the Living*, Boston, MA: Reidel.

Maturana, H. and Varela, F. (1987 [revised 1992, 1998]) *The Tree of Knowledge: The Biological Roots of Human Understanding*, Boston, MA: Shambhala Press.

Mauvaise Troupe Collective (2018) *The Zad and NoTAV. Territorial Struggles and the Making of a New Political Intelligence*, translation from French (*Contrées*) and preface by Kristin Ross, London and New York: Verso Books.

Meggitt, M. (1954) 'Sign language among the Walbiri', *Oceania*, 25: 1–16.

Meggitt, M. (1962) *Desert People*, London: Angus & Robertson.

Meggitt, M. (1966) *Gadjeri among the Walbiri' Aborigines of Central Australia*, Oceania Monograph 14, Sydney: Sydney University Press.

Meillassoux, Q. (2015) *Science Fiction and Extro-Science Fiction*, trans. Alyosha Edlebi, Minneapolis: Univocal.

Melitopoulos, A. and M. Lazzarato (2010) 'Machinic animism', *Animism*, catalog: 45–56. (And related video film *Assemblages: Félix Guattari et*

Bibliography

l'animisme machinique [55', long version 2012] https://www.youtube.com/watch?v=4L_m5vPQoaY)

Mercier, C. (2019) *En un éclair. La troisième proposition d'octobre de Jacques Lacan*, Paris: Cahiers de l'Unebévue.

Meyran, R. (2008) *Le mythe de l'identité nationale*, London: Berg International.

Miano, E. (2008) *Afropean soul et autres nouvelles*, Paris: Flammarion.

Micha, F. J. (1970) 'Trade and change in Australian Aboriginal cultures: Australian Aboriginal trade as an expression of close culture contact and as a mediator of culture change,' in A. R. Piling and R. A. Waterman (eds), *Diprotodon to Detribalization*, East Lansing: Michigan State University Press.

Moisseeff, M. (2002) 'Australian Aboriginal objects or how to represent the unrepresentable', in M. Jeudy-Ballini and B. Juillerat (eds), *People and Things: Social Mediations in Oceania*, Durham, NC: Carolina Academic Press, pp. 239–64.

Moore, H.(ed.) (1988) *Feminism and Anthropology*, Cambridge: Polity Press.

Morphy, H. (1984) *Journey to the Crocodile's Nest*, Canberra: Australian Institute of Aboriginal Studies.

Morphy, H. (1991) *Ancestral Connections*, Chicago: The University of Chicago Press.

Morvan, A. and F. Matharan (2013) *Vivid Memories. A History of Aboriginal Art/Mémoires Vives*, bilingual exhibition catalogue, Musée d'Aquitaine, Bordeaux, Paris: Éditions de la Martinière.

Mountford, C. P. (1968) *Winbaraku and the myth of Jarapiri*, Adelaide: Rigby.

Mowaljarlai, D. and J. Malnic (1993) *Yorro Yorro – Everything Standing up Alive – Spirit of the Kimberley*, Broome: Magabala Books.

Moyle, A. M. (1981) *Songs from the Kimberleys*, companion booklet for a 12-inch LP disc and tapes recorded in 1968, cat. no. AIAS/13, Canberra: Australian Insititute of Aboriginal Studies.

Mozère, L. (2007) 'Deleuze et Guattari: Territoires et devenirs', *Le Portique*, 20, 2e semester 2.

Mucchielli, L. and V. Le Goaziou (2007, édition revue et augmentée), *Quand les banlieues brûlent. Retour sur les émeutes de novembre 2005*, Paris: La Découverte.

Munn, N. (1964) 'Totemic designs and group continuity in Walbiri cosmology', in M. Reay (ed.), *Aborigines Now. New Perspectives in the Study of Aboriginal Communities*, Sydney: Angus and Robertson.

Munn, N. (1970) 'The transformation of subjects into objects in Walbiri and Pitjantjara myth', in R. Berndt (ed.), *Australian Aboriginal Anthropology*, Nedlands: University of Western Australia Press.

Munn, N. (1973) *Walbiri Iconography*, Ithaca, NY: Cornell University Press.

Munn, N. (1973b) The spatial representation of cosmic order in Walbiri iconography, in A. Forge (ed.), *Primitive Art and Society*, London: Oxford University Press.

Munn, N. (1992) 'The cultural anthropology of time. A critical essay', *Annual Review of Anthropology*, 21: 93–123.

Myers, F. (1986) *Pintupi Country, Pintupi Self. Sentiment, Place, and Politics among Western Desert Aborigines*, Washington, DC: Smithsonian.

Myers, F. (1994) 'Culture-making: performing Aboriginality at the Asia Society Gallery', *American Ethnologist*, 21 (4): 679–99.

Myers, F. (2002) *Painting Culture. The Making of an Aboriginal High Art*, Durham, NC: Duke University Press.

Myers, F. (n.d.) 'What is the business of the 'Balgo business'? A contemporary Aboriginal religious movement', unpublished manuscript.

Ndiaye, B. J. (n.d.) in 'The house of slaves', *Virtual Visit of Gorée Island*. Available at: http://webworld.unesco.org/goree/en/screens/25.shtml (accessed 2 December 2018).

Neyrat, F. (2014) 'On the political unconscious of the Anthropocene: interview by Elizabeth R. Johnson and David Johnson', *Society and Space*, 20 March. Available at: http://societyandspace.org/2014/03/20/on-8/ (accessed 10 October 2018).

Neyrat, F. (2014a) 'Critique du géo-constructivisme. Anthropocène and géo-ingénierie', *Multitudes* 56. Available at: http://www.multitudes.net/critique-du-geo-constructivisme-anthropocene-geo-ingenierie/

Neyrat, F. ([2016] 2018) *The Unconstructable Earth: An Ecology of Separation*, New York: Fordham University Press (translated by Drew Burk from *La Part indestructible de la terre*, Paris: Seuil).

Neyrat, F. (2017) 'Faster, stronger, more than human: accelerationism, transhumanism, and existential risks', in *The Unconstructable Earth: An Ecology of Separation*, New York: Fordham University Press, pp. 120–4.

Nghiem, T. (2010) *Des Abeilles et des Hommes. Passerelles pour un Monde Libre et Durable*, Paris: Bayard.

O'Donnell, E. (2018) *Legal Rights for Rivers*, London and New York: Routledge.

Ogien, A. and S. Laugier (2010) *Pourquoi désobéir en démocratie?*, Paris: La Découverte (coll. 'textes à l'appui').

Ong, A. and S. J. Collier (eds) (2005, online 2008), *Global Assemblages: Technology, Politics, and Ethics as Anthropological Problems*, London: Blackwell Publishing.

Ortner S. B. and H. H. Whitehead (eds) (1981) *Sexual Meanings. The Cultural Construction of Gender and Sexuality*, Cambridge: Cambridge University Press.

Pál Pelbart, P. (2017) 'Modes of existence, modes of exhaustion', *Inflexions* 8. Available at: http://www.inflexions.org/exhaustion/main.html#n8

Bibliography

Pannell, S. (1994) 'Mabo and museums: the indigenous (re)appropriation of indigenous things', *Oceania*, 65: 18–39.

Pasquinelli, M. (2014) 'The labour of abstraction. seven transitional theses on Marxism and accelerationism', *Fillip* 19. Available at: https://www.academia.edu/12509291/The_Labour_of_Abstraction_Seven_Transitional_Theses_on_Marxism_and_Accelerationism

Perkins, R., M. Langton and L. Nowra (2009) *First Australians: An Illustrated History*, Melbourne: Melbourne University Press. (The seven episodes of the series are accessible online at: http://www.sbs.com.au/firstaustralians/)

Peterson, N. (1967) *Walbiri Ritual at Gunadjari*, film and documentation, Canberra: Australian Institute of Aboriginal Studies.

Peterson, N. (1970) 'Buluwandi: a Central Australian ceremony for the resolution of conflict', in R. M. Berndt (ed.), *Australian Aboriginal Anthropology*, Nedlands: University of Western Australia.

Peterson, N. (2000) 'An expanding Aboriginal domain: mobility and the initiation journey', *Oceania*, 70 (3): 205–18.

Peterson, N., P. McConvell, S. Wild and R. Hagen (1978), *A Claim to Areas of Traditional Land by the Warlpiri and Kartangarurru-Kurintji*, Alice Springs: Central Land Council.

Petri, H. and G. Odermann ([1964] 1988) 'A nativistic and millenarian movement in North West Australia' (translated from German), in T. Swain and D. Rose (eds), *Aboriginal Australians and Christian Missions: Ethnographic and Historical Studies*, Bedford Park, Australia: The Australian Association for the Study of Religions, pp. 391–6.

Poirier, S. (1992) 'Nomadic rituals: networks of ritual exchange among women of the Australian Western Desert', *Man*, 27 (4): 757–76.

Poirier, S. (1996) *Les Jardins du nomade. Cosmologie, territoire et personne dans le désert occidental australien*, Münster: Lit Verlag (from 1990 PhD).

Poirier, S. (2005) *A World of Relationships: Itineraries, Dreams, and Events in the Australian Western Desert*, Toronto: University of Toronto Press.

Polack, J. C. and D. Sivadon (2013) *Intimate Utopia*, São Paulo: n-1 Publications.

Povinelli, I. (1993) *Labor's Lot. The Power, History and Culture of Aboriginal Action*, Chicago: The University of Chicago Press.

Povinelli, I. (2002) *The Cunning of Recognition: Indigenous Alterities and the Making of Australian Multiculturalism*, Durham, NC: Duke University Press.

Povinelli, E. (2016) *Geontology, A Requiem for Late Liberalism*, Durham, NC: Duke University Press, 2016.

Pradelles de Latour, C.-H. (1984) 'La parenté trobriandaise reconsidérée', *Littoral*, 11–12: 115–36.

Pradelles de Latour, C.-H. (1986) 'Le Champ du Langage dans une chefferie bamilekée', PhD (Thèse d'État), Ecole des Hautes en Sciences Sociales, Paris.

Préaud, M. (2009) 'Loi et culture en pays aborigènes: anthropologie des réseaux autochtones du Kimberley, nord-ouest de l'Australie', PhD, JCU/EHESS.

Préaud, M. (2015) 'Indigeneity behind the scenes: invasion and kriolisation', *etropic*, 14 (2): 11–21. Available at: https://journals.jcu.edu.au/etropic/issue/view/165

Préaud, M. and B. Glowczewski and 20 signatories (2015) 'Aboriginal communities should not be closed', *The World Post*, 21 July. Available at: http://www.huffingtonpost.com/martin-preaud/australian-aboriginal-communities-should-not-be-closed_b_7161392.html (accessed 2 December 2015).

Prigogine, I. and I Stengers ([1979] 1984) *Order Out of Chaos: Man's New Dialogue with Nature*, New York: Bantam New Age Books (translated from French).

Prober, S., M. O'Connor and F. Walsh (2011) 'Australian Aboriginal people's seasonal knowledge: a potential basis for shared understanding in environmental management', *Ecology and Society*, 16(2): 12.

Querrien, A. ([2008] 2011) 'Maps and refrains of a Rainbow Panther', in É. Alliez and A. Goffey (eds), *The Guattari Effect*, London and New York: Continuum, pp. 84–98.

Querrien, A. and A. Goffey (2017) 'Schizoanalysis and ecosophy: scales of history and action', in C. Boundas (ed.), *Schizoanalysis and Ecosophy: Reading Deleuze and Guattari*, London and New York: Bloomsbury Press.

Rainbird, P. (2001) 'Deleuze, turmeric and palau: rhizome thinking and rhizome use in the Caroline Islands', *Journal de la Société des Océanistes*, 2001 (112): 13–19.

Rajkowski, P. (1995) *Linden Girl – A Story of Outlawed Lives*, Nedlands: University of Western Australia Press.

Ralli, T. (2005) 'Who's a looter? In storm's aftermath, pictures kick up a different kind of tempest', *The New York Times*, 5 September. Available at: http://www.nytimes.com/2005/09/05/business/whos-a-looter-in-storms-aftermath-pictures-kick-up-a-different-kind-of-tempest.html

Rancière, J. (2010) *Dissensus: On Politics and Aesthetics*, New York and London: Continuum International.

Reece, L. (Rev.) (1975) *Dictionary of the Wailbri Language of Central Australia, Part 1: Wailbri-English*, Oceania Linguistic Monograph 22, Sydney: University of Sydney.

Reuter, T. (2006) 'Land and territory in the Austronesian world', in T. Reuter T. (ed.), *Sharing the Earth, Dividing the Land. Territorial Categories and Institutions in the Austronesian World*, Acton, Australia:

Bibliography

ANU Press: chapter 1. (Ebook: http://epress.anu.edu.au/austronesians/sharing/mobile_devices/index.html)

Revel, J. (2008) *Qui a peur de la banlieue ?*, Paris: Bayard.

Ribeiro, G. L. (2014) 'World Anthropologies: Anthropological Cosmopolitanisms and Cosmopolitics', *Annual Review of Anthropology*, 43: 483–98.

Ribeiro, G. L. and A. Escobar (eds) (2002), *World Anthropologies – Disciplinary Transformations within Systems of Power*, Oxford: Berg Publishers.

RMIT (Royal Melbourne Institute of Technology) (1995) *Keeping Country – A Draft Report Submitted to the Rubibi Working Group*, Melbourne: Royal Melbourne Institute of Technology.

Roheim, G. (1945) *The Eternal Ones of the Dream*, Oxford: International Universities Press.

Roheim, G. (1974) *Children of the Desert: The Western Tribes of Central Australia*, vol. I, ed. and introduction W. Muensterberger, New York: Harper and Row.

Rosa, H. (2010) *Social Acceleration: A New Theory of Modernity*, New York: Columbia University Press.

Rosaldo, M. Z. and L. Lamphere (ed.) (1975) *Women, Culture & Society*, Redwood City: Stanford University Press.

Rose, D. B. (1988) 'Jesus and the Dingo', in T. Swain and D. Rose (eds), *Aboriginal Australians and Christian Missions: Ethnographic and Historical Studies*, Bedford Park, SA: Australian Association for the Study of Religions, pp: 361–75.

Rose, D. B. (1992) *Dingo Makes us Human: Life and Land in an Australian Aboriginal Culture*, Cambridge: Cambridge University Press.

Rose, D. B., T. van Dooren, M. Chrulew, S. Cooke, M. Kearnes and E. O'Gorman (2012) 'Thinking through the environment, unsettling the humanities', *Environmental Humanities*, 1:1–5.

Rubin, G. S. (1975) 'The traffic in women: notes on the political economy of sex', in R. R. Rapp (ed.), *Toward an Anthropology of Women*, New York: Monthly Review Press.

Rumsey, A. (2001) 'Tracks, traces, and links to land in Aboriginal Australia, New Guinea, and beyond', in A. Rumsey and J. E. Weiner (eds), *Emplaced Myth: Space, Narrative, and Knowledge in Aboriginal Australia and Papua New Guinea*, Honolulu: University of Hawaii Press.

Sabatier, A. (2010) *Critique de la rationalité administrative. Pour une pensée de l'accueil*, Paris: L'Harmattan (coll. 'Des hauts & Débats', Préface de R. Fraisse, Postface de J.-Y. Mondon).

Sansot, P. (2000) *Du Bon Usage de la Lenteur*, Paris: Payot & Rivages.

Scheffler, H. (1978) *Australian Kin classification*, Cambridge: Cambridge University Press.

Scheffler, H. (1986) 'Kin classes as cultural categories: the Walbiri case', in D. Barwick, J. Beckett and M. Reay (eds), *Metaphors of Interpretation*, Canberra: Australian National University.

Sembène, O. ([1960] 1995) *God's Bits of Wood*, Oxford: Heinemann.

Sénac, R. (2012) *L'invention de la diversité: Le lien Social*, Paris: PUF.

Sharrad, P. (2009) 'Island of shattered dreams', *The Contemporary Pacific*, 21 (1): 190–2. Available at: http://muse.jhu.edu/login?auth=0&type=summary&url=/journals/contemporary_pacific/v021/21.1.sharrad.html

Sheehy, C. J. (ed) (1999) *Theatre of Wonder: 25 Years in the Heart of the Beast*, Minneapolis: University of Minnesota Press.

Sibertin-Blanc, G. (2005) 'État et généalogie de la guerre: l'hypothèse de la "machine de guerre" de Gilles Deleuze et Félix Guattari', *Astérion*. Available at: http://journals.openedition.org/asterion/425

Spencer, W. B. and F. J. Gillen ([1899] 1968) *Natives Tribes of Central Australia*, London: Macmillan.

Spencer, W. B. and F. J. Gillen (1904) *The Northern Tribes of Central Australia] London*, London: Macmillan.

Spitz, C. ([2003] 2007) *The Island of Shattered Dreams*, Huia, Wellington: Te Aotearoa (translated from French).

Srnicek, N. and A. Williams (2013) '#Accelerate manifesto for an accelerationost politics', in J. Johnson (ed.), *Dark Trajectories: Politics of the Outside*, Miami: [NAME] Publications.

Standing Rock: https://www.independent.co.uk/topic/standing-rock-sioux

Stanner, W. E. (1936) 'Murinbata Kinship and Totemism', *Oceania*, 7 (2): 186–216.

Stanner, W. E. (1963) *Aboriginal Religion*, Oceania monograph 11, Sydney: Sydney University Press.

Stanner, W. E. (1979) *White Man Got No Dreaming, Essays 1938–73*, Canberra: Australian National University Press.

Stanton, J. (1999) 'At the grass-roots: collecting and communities in Aboriginal Australia', in S. Toussaint and J. Taylor (eds), *Applied Anthropology in Australasia*, Nedlands: University of Western Australia Press, pp. 282–94.

Steiner, C. E. (2015) 'A sea of warriors: performing and identity of resilience and empowerment in the face of climate change in the Pacific', *Contemporary Pacific*, 27 (1): 147–80.

Stengers, I. (2005) 'The cosmopolitical proposal', in B. Latour and P. Weibel (eds), *Making Things Public*, Cambridge, MA: The MIT Press, pp. 994–1003.

Stengers, I. (2011) '"Another science is possible!" A plea for slow science'. Inaugural Lecture for the Willy Calewaert Chair 2011–2012 (ULB), held 13 December. Available at: http://we.vub.ac.be/aphy/sites/default/files/stengers2011_pleaslowscience.pdf

Bibliography

Stengers, I. and D. Debaise (eds) (2015) *Gestes spéculatifs*, Dijon, France: Les Presses du Réel.

Stephenson, D. (1994) 'A legal paradigm for protecting traditional knowledge', in T. Greaves (ed.), *Intellectual Property Rights for Indigenous People*, Oklahoma City: Society for Applied Anthropology, pp. 179–89.

Stern, D. (1985) *The Interpersonal World of the Infant: A View from Psychoanalysis and Development*, New York: Basic Books.

Stiegler, B. ([2010 2013) *What Makes Life Worth Living. On Pharmacology*, Cambridge and Malden, MA: Polity Press.

Stoczkowski, W. (2006) 'L'anti-racisme doit-il rompre avec la science?', *La Recherche*, 46. Available at: http://acatparis5.free.fr/html/modules/news/print.php?storyid=142

Strehlow, T. G. H. (1964) 'The art of circle, line and square', in R. Berndt (ed.), *Australian Aboriginal Art*, Sydney: Ure Smith.

Sullivan, L. (2005) *Ngiaka Yalarrnga* (with a preface by Rosita Henry, James Cook University), Townsville, Queensland.

Sullivan, M. (2001) 'Maya Deren's ethnographic representation of ritual and myth in Haiti', in Bill Nichols (ed.), *Maya Deren and the American Avant-Garde*, Berkeley: University of California Press.

Sullivan, P. (2011) *Belonging Together. Dealing with the Politics of Disenchantment in Australian Indigenous Policy*, Canberra: Aboriginal Studies Press.

Swain, T. (1988) 'The ghost of space: reflections on Warlpiri christian iconography and ritual', in T. Swain and D. Rose (eds), *Aboriginal Australians and Christian Missions: Ethnographic and Historical Studies*, Bedford Park, Australia: The Australian Association for the Study of Religions, pp. 452–69.

Swain, T. (1993) *A Place for Strangers. Towards a History of Australian Aboriginal Being*, Cambridge: Cambridge University Press.

Swain, T. and D. B. Rose (eds) (1988) *Aboriginal Australians and Christian Missions: Ethnographic and Historical Studies*, Bedford Park, Australia: The Australian Association for the Study of Religions (Special Studies in Religions, 6).

Tarran, M. (1997) 'Overview of the Bugarrigarra Nyurdany Aboriginal Culture Centre', in Kimberley Culture and Natural History Centre Steering Committee Inc. (ed.), *Planning Cultural and Interpretative Centres in The Kimberley*, Regional Confrence, Broome, pp. 23–7.

Tauli-Corpuz, V. (2017), *Report of the Special Rapporteur on the Rights of Indigenous Peoples on her Visit to Australia*, United Nations General Assembly, Human Rights, 36th Session, 11–29 September 2017. Available at: https://digitallibrary.un.org/record/1303201/files/A_HRC_36_46_Add-2-EN.pdf

Teaiwa, K., (2018) 'Our rising sea of islands: Pan-Pacific regionalism in the age of climate change', *Europe and the Pacific*, special issue of *Pacific Studies*, 41 (1/2): 26–54 (guest edited by Toon van Meijl).

Thériault, S. (2015) 'Justice environnementale et peuples autochtones: les possibilités et les limites de la jurisprudence de la cour interaméricaine des droits de l'homme', *Revue québécoise de droit international*, hors-série: https://www.sqdi.org/wp-content/uploads/RQDI_HS201503_7_Theriault.pdf

'The rise of the Aboriginal superhero' (2016) *ABC.NET.AU*, 4 June 2016. Available at: http://www.abc.net.au/radionational/programs/awaye/the-rise-of-the-aboriginal-superhero/7458888 (accessed 1 February 2017).

The UN Declaration on the Rights of Indigenous Peoples (2017): https://www.un.org/development/desa/indigenouspeoples/declaration-on-the-rights-of-indigenous-peoples.html

The Universal Declaration of the Rights of Mother Earth (2010): https://www.youtube.com/watch?v=YU5HmTucTRg Earth's Rights

Thuram, L., Diallo, R., Cheb Sun, M. and P. Blanchard (2009), *Appel pour une république multiculturelle et postraciale – suivi des 100 propositions pluricitoyennes*, Paris: Respect Magazine.

Tiouka, A. (2016) 'Stratégies amérindiennes en Guyane française', *Multitudes*, 64 (autumn 2016): 199–210.

Tiouka, A. with H. Ferrarini (2017) *Petit Guerrier pour la paix. Les lutes amérindiennes racontées à la jeunesse (et à tous les curieux)*, Matoury, Guyana: Ibis Rouge Editions.

Todd, Z. (2015) 'Indigenizing the Anthropocene', in H. Davis and E. Turpin (eds), *Art in the Anthropocene: Encounters Among Aesthetics, Politics, Environment and Epistemology*, London: Open Humanities Press.

Todd, Z. (2016). 'An Indigenous feminist's take on the ontological turn: "Ontology" is just another word for colonialism', *Journal of Historical Sociology*, 29 (1): 4–22.

Tonkinson, M. E. (1990) 'Is it in the blood? Australian Aboriginal identity', in J. Linnekin and L. Poyer (eds), *Cultural Identity and Ethnicity in the Pacific*, Honolulu: University of Hawaii Pressp, pp. 191–218.

Tonkinson, R. and M. Howard (eds) (1990) *Going it Alone: Prospects for Aboriginal Autonomy*, Canberra: Aboriginal Studies Press.

Traoré, T. (2007) interview: http://survie.org/billets-d-afrique/2007/160-juillet-aout-2007/article/interview-tiecoura-traore

Trend, D. (ed.) (2001) *Reading Digital Culture*, Oxford: Blackwell.

Trimble, A. Y. (2013) 'Settler sovereignty and the rhizomatic west, or, the significance of the frontier in postwestern studies', *Western American Literature*, 48 (1): 115–40.

Tsing, A. L. (2015) *The Mushroom at the End of the World: On The Possibility of Life in Capitalist Ruins*, Princeton, NJ: Princeton University Press.

Tsosie, R. (1997) 'Indigenous people's claims to cultural property: a legal perspective', *Museum Anthropology*, 21 (3): 5–11.

Bibliography

Vasquez-Arroyo, A. Y. (2008) 'Universal history disavowed: on critical theory and postcolonialism', *Postcolonial Studies*, 11 (4): 451–73.
Vergès, F. (2006a) *La Mémoire Enchaînée. Questions sur l'Esclavage*, Paris: Albin Michel.
Vergès, F. (2006b) 'The African slave trade and slavery. Blind spots in French thought', *Transversal*. Available at: http://eipcp.net/transversal/1206/verges/en (accessed 2 December 2015).
Vergès, F. (2013) *Exposer l'esclavage: méthodologies et pratiques*, Paris: Africultures.
Vergès, F. (2017) 'Racial Capitalocene', in G. T. Johnson and A. Lubin (eds), *Futures of Black Radicalism*, London: Verso.
Viveiros de Castro, E. (1998) 'Les pronoms cosmologiques et le perspectivisme amérindien', in E. Alliez (dir), *Gilles Deleuze: une vie philosophique*, Le Plessis-Robinson, Institut Synthélabo.
Viveiros de Castro, E. (2004) 'Le don et le donné: trois nano-essais sur la parenté et la magie', *ethnographiques.org*, 6: 1–30. Available at: http://www.ethnographiques.org/2004/Viveiros-de-Castro.html
Viveiros de Castro, E. (2007) 'The crystal forest: notes on the ontology of Amazonian spirits', *Inner Asia*, 9: 13–33.
Viveiros de Castro, E. ([2009] 2014) *Cannibal Metaphysics. For a Poststructural Anthropology*, trans. from French by Peter Skafish, Minneapolis: Univocal.
Wacquant, L. (2009) *Punishing the Poor: The Neoliberal Government of Social Insecurity*, Durham, NC: Duke University Press.
Warner, W. L. ([1937] 1958) *A Black Civilisation*, Chicago: Harper and Brothers.
Wassman, J. (ed.) (1998) *Pacific Answers to Western Hegemony*, Oxford: Berg International.
Watson, J. B. (1990) 'Other people do other things: Lamarckian identities in Kainantu Subdistrict, Papua New Guinea', in J. Linnekin and L. Poyer (eds), *Cultural Identity and Ethnicity in the Pacific*, Honolulu: University of Hawaii Press, pp. 17–42.
Webb, T. T. (1933) 'Tribal organization in Eastern Arnhem Land', *Oceania*, 3 (4): 406–11.
Wedlock, T. (1992) 'Practice, politics and ideology of the "travelling business" in Aboriginal religion', *Oceania*, 63: 114–36.
Weiner, A. (1976) *Women of Value, Men of Renown: New Perspectives in Trobriand Exchange*, Austin: The University of Texas Press.
Weiner, A. (1992) *Inalienable Possessions. The Paradox of Keeping-while-Giving*, Berkeley: University of California Press.
Welsh, P. (1997) 'The power of possession: the case against property', *Museum Anthropology*, 21 (3): 12–18.
Werf, G. R. van der, D. C. Morton, R. S. DeFries, J. G. J. Olivier, P. S. Kasibhatla, R. B. Jackson, G. J. Collatz and J. T. Randerson (2009)

'CO2 emissions from forest loss', *Nature Geoscience*, (November): 737–8.
White, H. C. (1963) *An Anatomy of Kinship*, Englewood Cliffs, NJ: Prentice Hall.
White, I. (1981) 'Generation moieties in Australia: structural, social and ritual implications', *Oceania*, 52: 6–27.
Whitehouse, H., F. Watkin Lui, J. Sellwood, M. J. Barrett and P. Chigeza (2014) 'Sea country: navigating Indigenous and colonial ontologies in Australian environmental education', *Environmental Education Research*, 20 (1): 56–69.
Whitehouse, H., M. Taylor, N. Evans, Doyle, J. Sellwood and R. Zee (2017) 'A sea country learning partnership in times of anthropocenic risk: offshore coral reef education and our story of practice', *Australian Journal of Environmental Education*, 33 (3): 160–70.
Wild, S. (1977–1978) 'Men as women: female dance symbolism in Walbiri men's rituals', *Dance Research Journal*, 10: 14–22.
Worms, E. A. and H. Petri ([1968] 1972) 'Les religions primitives d'Australie', in H. Nevermann, E. A. Worms and H. Petri (eds), *Les religions du Pacifique et d'Australie*, Paris: Payot, pp. 153–388. (Translated from *Australischen eingeborenen-Religionen*, Stuttgart: W. Kohlhammer Verlag [1968], in v. 5 (2) of Die Religionen der Menschheit series.)
Young, A. T. (2013) 'Settler sovereignty and the rhizomatic west, or, the significance of the frontier in postwestern studies', *Western American Literature*, 48 (1): 115–40.

Index

Ackerman, Kim, 267
activism, 11, 20, 30, 33, 49, 56, 59, 74–6, 237, 243, 250, 254–5, 300, 308, 310, 318n, 333n, 338–9, 342–3, 351–6
actual *see* virtual
Africa, 372, 7, 60–1, 75–6, 93, 199, 217, 303–4, 306–9, 330–3, 351, 361, 367, 372
  Gorée island (Senegal), 328–9
  Indian Ocean, 306, 328
  Mascarine Islands, 338
  Mayotte (French), 311
  Reunion Island (French), 33–4n, 307n, 311
  Union of Comores, 311
  see also Americas; diaspora; Europe; racism
Ahouansou, K. Mariquian, 310–11
Alcantara, Clarissa, 358, 361, 364–6
alliances, 16, 20, 45, 49, 57, 76, 118, 126, 131, 146, 149, 159–61, 166, 277–8, 286, 325, 342, 349, 352; *see also* activism; conflict; marriage
Alliez, Eric, 14, 103, 111, 124
Aluridja, 214–15, 217
Alyawarre (Yalyuwari), 156, 379, 382, 386, 404–5
Americas, 7, 24, 32, 46, 50, 53–4, 58, 61, 75, 259, 271, 303, 307, 310, 328, 335, 338, 341, 347
  African-American, 43–4, 56, 58, 76, 293, 319–20
  Bolivia, 21, 353
  Brazil, 7, 11, 44–5, 53–4, 59–60, 305, 325–6, 356, 359, 361–76
  Canada, 21, 59, 255, 335n, 352
  French Caribbean Islands, 306–7, 309, 328
  French Guiana, 34n, 44, 59, 76, 302, 307n, 310, 312, 352
  Haiti, 309, 336–7, 360
  Native Americans (NA), 21, 28, 45, 59, 76, 82, 352, 114, 116, 125, 259, 261, 276, 310, 324, 341, 351–2

Anderson Stephanie, 318
anthropology, 7–8, 12, 37, 55–6, 61, 77, 85, 119, 260, 311, 322, 327–8, 338–9, 347, 350, 366, 376
  indigenise, 4, 26, 77, 116, 252, 285–7, 359
  restitution, 31, 36, 257, 276, 281–2, 286–7, 291–2, 295
  urban, 1314, 307n, 326, 336
  see also ontological; sacred objects
Arrernte (Aranda), 22, 156–7, 203, 215, 217, 231, 262, 346–7, 377, 382, 397, 405
Asia, 32, 50, 75, 234–7, 244, 249, 263, 268, 305, 308, 333, 336, 338, 351
  Andaman Islands (India), 317
  China, 354
  Israel, 333n, 241
  Japan, 58
  Java (Indonesia), 325
  Macassar (Indonesia), 30, 246
  Palestinians, 12, 75, 114, 312
  Vietnam, 308, 310
  see also Australia
assemblage, 48, 54, 70, 102, 106, 108, 115, 120, 122–4, 308, 312, 323–5, 332, 344, 349, 351, 361–2
Australia, 20–1, 29, 30–1, 33–4, 41–3, 45–6, 48–9, 50, 96, 119, 125, 225–7, 237–8, 240, 243, 248–52, 268, 282, 311–14, 316–17, 319, 345–6
  'Afghan' cameleers, 32, 69, 108, 378
  Asian indentured labor, 32, 234, 338
  asylum seekers, 47, 313, 327, 343, 351
  'Intervention' (Act 2007), 43, 50, 313–15, 334
  Melanasian indentured labor, 338
  Muslims, 32, 244n
  Noonkanbah 1980 protest, 97, 269
  Palm Island, 42–3, 48, 316, 333
  Referendum 1967, 249, 268
  'Refugees from the inside', 335
  Stolen generations, 33, 41, 314, 333

Australia (*cont.*)
  Stolen wages, 33, 49, 333
  Torres Strait Islands, 31, 37n, 44, 122, 227, 250–1, 273
  see also language; racism
Azoulay, Ariella, 312–13

Barker, Jowandi Wayne, 29, 36, 271n, 290–2, 344, 409
Barker, Milari, 29, 359n, 408–9
Barker, Nidala, 3, 355n, 359n
Barker, Theresa, 408–9
Bateson, Gregory, 71–3, 115, 323, 348n
becoming, 7, 10, 12–13, 15, 23–4, 59, 77, 91, 117, 120, 126, 131, 146, 162–4, 284, 344–5, 361, 375, 408
  becoming-Black, 375
  becoming-in-common, 311
  becoming land, 4–5, 69, 74, 161–2
  Cosmocolour-becoming, 61, 365, 376
  ontological becoming, 356
  totemic becomings, 16, 54, 60, 65, 73, 81n, 119, 367
  vampire, 169, 185
  see also Dreaming; totemism
Benthall, Jonathan, 327
Black affirmation, 301, 305, 307–11, 319, 338n; *see also* racism
boundaries, 37, 51, 61, 82; *see also* limits

capitalism, 6–7, 11, 40, 48, 56, 62, 76, 113, 120, 321, 323–4, 331n
  capitalistic subjectivity, 105–9
  refusal to accumulate, 118, 181, 264
  see also colonisation; mining
cartography, 16, 27, 51, 62–5, 72, 86, 91, 109–10, 114, 122, 126, 323, 348–9; *see also* map
Certeau, Michel de, 8
Chakrabarty, Dipesh, 321
Chomsky, Noam, 21
Christianity, 32, 152n, 235, 240–5, 264, 283, 353–4, 366, 368, 370–1, 373–4
cinema, 6, 13, 62, 255, 281, 292, 308–9, 319, 329–30, 332, 337n, 351–2, 348–9, 350–1, 359–60; *see also* experimental films
Cixous, Hélène, 6
Clastres, Pierre, 7, 116, 118
colonisation, 7, 9, 13, 20, 30–1, 35, 48, 52, 54, 64, 69, 76, 85–6, 88, 109, 118, 120, 122, 231, 251–3, 264, 280, 301, 305, 312, 324, 328–9, 333–4, 338, 342, 371
  decolonial, 53–4, 56, 116, 303, 335n
'communitarism', 303–4
conflict, 3, 16, 20–1, 32, 35, 43, 51, 116, 161, 181, 199, 218, 220, 247–8, 259, 274, 286, 299, 303, 312–13, 322, 325, 328, 333–6
  settlement, resolution, 69, 182–5, 195, 269, 271, 278, 348n
Coombe, Rosemary, 261
cosmologics/cosmological, 12, 38, 63, 69, 125, 169–70, 73, 195, 197, 200, 217, 219, 342, 353, 366; *see also* space-time; time-space
cosmopolitics, 56, 63–4, 299, 341, 344, 349, 363, 366, 376
  recosmopolitisation, 353

dance, 2, 4, 9, 11, 16, 18, 24, 35, 58–9, 61, 73, 84, 101, 108, 118, 121–3, 138–9, 157, 161, 165, 200, 242, 258–60, 265, 278, 282, 285, 288, 292, 345, 360, 378, 380, 382n, 403
  Brazilian, 362, 364–6, 367, 375–6
  Japanese, 58, 265
  Kimberley, 246, 263, 268, 272–3, 275
  Laura festival, 291
  May day, 341–2
  Warlpiri men ritual, 140–7, 153, 261, 278
  Warlpiri women *yawulyu*, 132–8, 146–7, 150–1, 154–6, 174–5, 186, 199, 201, 203, 363
  see also ritual
De Largy Healy, Jessica, 58n, 269n, 271n, 291
death, 13, 23, 27, 34, 42, 63, 93–4, 100, 120, 137, 144, 149, 158, 169, 172, 181, 184, 197–9, 220, 235, 245, 253, 267, 316, 325–6, 384–5, 391–3, 397
  Brazil, 61, 364, 367, 374–6
  France, 304
  Indonesia, 331
  see also funeral; spirits
Deleuze, Gilles, 5–7, 11, 14, 27–9, 39, 42, 53, 57, 60–1, 64, 67, 71–3, 75, 114–15, 125, 286, 323, 347–9, 361–2, 367
Deligny, Fernand, 71–2, 343
Deren, Maya, 360
Descola, Philippe, 38, 52–5, 117n, 340, 342, 344, 346

Index

deterritorialisation (deterritorialization), 28, 63–4, 73, 75, 120, 119–21, 323–4, 363
diaspora, 35, 61, 76, 303, 308, 310–11, 323, 328–9, 332, 337
digital, 36–7, 57, 63, 73, 75, 281–3, 286–7, 291–4, 295, 347
  copyleft, 279
divination, 184, 361, 374
Djugun (Jugun), 3, 35, 243, 246, 264–6, 270, 271n, 275, 396, 408–9
Dousset, Laurent, 291
dream, 1–3, 8, 18, 72, 81, 83–4, 90, 123, 349, 360, 399, 401, 408
  condensation, 284, 360
  Dreamland, 85
  dreamscape, 101
  Dreamtime, 37, 87, 197, 239, 242, 408
  images, 167, 151, 186
  interpretation, 121, 162, 186, 235
  revelation of songs, paintings, 13, 19, 101, 106, 117, 119, 135–6, 140–3, 149–50, 186, 197, 204, 263, 274, 286
  of spirit-children, 167, 228, 235, 284
  see also Dreamings; images; spirits: spirit-child
Dreamings (*Jukurrpa*), 10–11, 25–6, 37–8, 63, 73, 81–2, 97–9, 102, 116–17, 119, 131, 133–4, 137–8, 145, 151, 153–4, 161, 163–7, 198, 203–4, 231–2, 239, 241, 245, 262–3, 290, 344, 348, 360, 384
  Birds, 99, 137, 139, 142, 159–60, 170, 182–3, 193–4, 269, 381, 406
  Bugarrigarra, 269, 274, 275, 408
  Bush Bean, 130, 187
  Digging Stick, 24, 63, 117, 137, 153–5, 156–60, 166, 193, 201, 278
  Emu, 1–4, 19, 63, 69, 134, 140, 184, 192, 345, 377, 381, 386
  Fire, 143, 345
  Gecko, 184, 193
  Goanna, 154–5, 157, 160, 194
  Honey, 99, 157, 179, 194
  Initiated Man (*Witi* tree), 137, 146, 154–7, 161, 179, 186, 191–4, 256
  Invincible and Two-Men, 97, 190–2, 386, 406
  Kangaroo, 160–1, 173, 345
  Plum and Possum, 4, 193, 230
  Rain, 140, 151, 166, 193–4
  Seeds and Wallaby, 134, 138, 142, 159–60, 183–4, 193, 381, 406
  Snakes, 24, 158, 160, 177, 184, 190
  Yam, 15-18, 21, 126, 135–6, 141
  see also dream; space-time; time-space; totemism
Dumas, Alexandre, 309
Durkheim, Emile and Marcel Mauss, 21–2
Dussart, Françoise, 137, 150

ecocide, 353, 355
ecofeminism, 7, 56, 349
ecology, 7, 14, 39–40, 73, 90, 115, 323
ecosophy, 27, 40, 47–8, 51–3, 57, 74, 115, 127, 323–4, 352, 367
Eizykman, Claudine, 6, 359
Elkaïm, Mony, 73
ethnocide, 7–8, 32, 115, 333, 355
Europe, 6, 30, 32, 51, 199, 245, 308, 309n, 313, 321, 331, 337, 339
  Afropeans, 76, 311
  Basques, 12, 114
  France, 13–14, 23, 25, 34n, 43–4, 49–51, 59, 75, 70, 72, 74–6, 262, 300–12, 317–18, 326, 334, 338–9, 352, 354, 377, 387
  Muslims, 303–6
  Roma and Gipsies (Gypsies), 50, 114, 336, 338
  Russian consortium, 44
  see also diaspora
exchange network (*Wunan*), 265, 267–9
experimental films, 6, 9, 36, 284–5, 292, 359–60, 363, 376

fire, 6, 16, 20, 97, 119, 135–6, 141–3, 146, 157, 182–3, 185, 269, 272, 341, 344, 354, 371–2, 395, 402, 405
Freud, Sigmund, 18, 22–3, 87, 119
funeral, 100, 171, 185, 195, 198, 209, 218, 232, 234, 245, 304, 384, 397
  mourning, 13, 93, 131, 149–50, 153, 172, 177, 184, 186, 196, 199–201, 219–20, 263, 278–9

game, 30, 36, 109, 118–19, 125, 282, 289–91, 293–4
Garond, Lise, 316n, 333
gender, 24, 84n, 131, 144, 150–1, 155, 158, 161, 165–8, 173, 178, 186, 197, 220–1, 278–9, 289, 294, 329, 404
  androgyny/two- or double-gendered, 24, 159, 167, 176, 200, 151

441

gender (*cont.*)
  gendering, 167–8, 267, 272
  indeterminate gender/non gendered, 161, 167, 186
  sexual bias, 7, 22, 26, 132
  see also virtual/actual
Genosko, Gary, 47, 277
Glissant, Edouard, 309
Godelier, Maurice, 12
Goodale, Jane, 244, 347–8
Guattari, Félix, 5–7, 11–15, 18, 22–3, 27–9, 34, 39, 42, 44, 54, 60–1, 71, 73, 75, 81–3, 87, 90–4, 102–3, 106, 108–9, 111–13, 114–26, 323, 361–2
  asignifying, 104–5, 109, 351
  dissensus, 320, 348
  metamodel, 40, 62, 64–5, 348–9
  ordology, 103, 124, 346
  SF, cyberspace, 61–2, 347
  see also ecosophy; refrain
Gumbula, Joe Neparrnga, 58

Hage, Ghassan, 312
Haraway, Dona, 350
Hau'ofa, Epeli, 56
health, 11, 23, 35, 100, 123, 177, 228, 240, 244n, 251, 313–14, 353n, 391
  Cleverman, 70, 350–1, 377, 384, 385–6, 391–2, 400–1, 406
  healers (*ngangkari, mapan, mungan*), 38, 70, 350, 352, 377, 388–90, 393–4, 396, 401
  healing, 69–71, 90, 132, 134, 245, 370–1, 375, 382–8, 397, 399, 408–9
  healing stone, 374, 406
  see also sorcery
Henry, Rosita, 291
hunter-gatherer, 69, 86, 90, 116, 120–1, 137, 139n, 148, 156–9, 161–3, 172–3, 179, 196, 198, 244n, 272, 278, 291, 369, 383, 392, 398–9, 403–4

identity, 11, 29, 31, 35, 38, 56, 58, 61, 68, 82, 95–6, 98, 106, 110, 114, 119, 147, 150, 162, 166–8, 204–5, 220, 226–55, 269, 272, 278–9, 288, 305, 321, 338, 349, 361
  French, 305–9
  of resistance, 225
  see also gender; totemism
images, 8–9, 36–8, 72, 100, 115–16, 162, 245, 275, 282, 285, 287–8

images (16mm), 359, 360
images-forces, living images (*kuruwarri*), 15, 26, 69, 152, 164, 167, 174, 178, 180, 189, 200, 222
  sculptures, 372
  see also dream; Dreamings; dancing; painting; singing; spirits
imprint, 138, 151, 161, 163, 289, 326; *see also* line
inalienability, 34–5, 117n, 126–7, 257–60, 262, 269, 276–7, 279–80
incest, 22, 97, 171, 188–92, 196–7; *see also* taboo

Jampijinpa, Jimmy Robertson, 288
Jampijinpa, Wanta Steve Patrick, 63–9
Jangala, Abe, 112
Japaljarri, Paddy Gibson, 66
Jaulin, Robert, 7–8, 115–16
Jupurrurla, Maurice Luther, 121

Kaberry, Phyllis, 267
Kariera, 215
Kennedy, Randall, 319–20
Kinship, 107, 118–20, 125, 131, 146, 189, 191–2, 197, 202–5, 209, 214–15, 220, 231–3, 291, 382n, 406
  matriline, 67–9, 146–8, 152, 253–4
  niece exchange (*kainingi*), 25, 189, 206
  patriline, 148, 152, 175, 206, 253–4
  see also skin-name(s) (subsections)
Kukatja, 263, 268, 382n, 406

Lacan, Jacques, 26–7, 120–1, 125
land, 4–5, 69, 74, 101, 162
  claims, 19–20, 48, 87–8, 92, 95–6, 116, 132, 227, 240, 251–3, 333, 346, 349
  holding, 162, 252, 254
  management (*kirda/kurdungurlu*), 20, 118, 137, 143, 260, 277, 291
  Native title, 31, 88, 122, 227, 250–4, 259, 269, 296, 333, 383
  restitution, 31, 202
Langton, Marcia, 281n
language, 10, 22, 25–7, 38, 42, 43, 48, 53, 61, 81, 95, 116–17, 119, 122, 150, 205, 219–20, 224–5, 230, 234–5, 242, 244, 258–9, 282, 308, 326, 378, 382n, 406, 409
  bilingual education, 34n, 245, 273, 314–15

Index

Breton, 33, 83, 308
Kimberley, 35, 235, 263, 265–75, 279, 315
Kriol, 30, 239
sign language (*rdaka-rdaka*), 90, 171–2, 177, 197, 200, 218
'upside-down" (*ngudalj-kitji-rni*), 172, 197
Warlpiri, 18, 29, 63–4, 69, 161–3, 172, 231, 238, 242, 259–60, 288, 315
see also Americas; Oceania; taboo
Latour, Bruno, 55–6, 343, 351n
Laughren, Mary, 168
Lazaratto, Maurizio and Angela Melitopoulos, 54
Lévi-Strauss, Claude, 25, 53, 116, 119–21, 125, 206, 210, 299, 302
limits, 52, 72, 82, 86–7, 151, 179, 259, 292, 323, 327, 375
limitless, 100, 121, 217, 289
lines, 17, 27, 36, 39–40, 52, 58, 61, 67, 72, 89, 102, 125, 138–9, 187, 208, 290, 294, 344, 367–8, 376, 394
path of travel, 10, 11, 13, 15, 31, 37, 73, 101, 111, 116, 118, 126, 132–3, 137–8, 152–3, 166–9, 187, 193, 205, 221, 285, 345
songline, 16, 20, 25, 63, 123, 131, 151, 286, 290
storyline, 86, 287–9, 291
track(ing), 2, 4, 22, 36, 53, 63, 69, 117, 119, 151, 187, 285, 289, 311
trail, 1–3, 98, 131, 133, 139, 184, 285
see also Dreamings; kinship; totemism
love, 6, 8, 23, 27, 32–3, 61, 173, 176, 181–2, 191–3, 237, 300, 404
love magic (*yilpinji*), 70, 132, 156, 157, 159–60, 195, 267
love sick, 406
Lupasco, Stéphane, 26

Mabo, Eddie, 31, 122, 227, 251
Manning, Erin and Brian Massumi, 40–1
map, 36, 71–2, 88, 89, 96, 110–11, 125, 266, 292, 349, 367
mapping, 81, 206, 210, 212, 215n, 267, 282, 289, 344
mind-map, cognitive, 283, 287–9
painting-maps, 73
totemic, 116
see also cartography; paintings
marriage, 95, 107, 109, 118, 147–8, 159–60, 165, 171, 174, 206, 210–13
bestowal (promise), 146, 148, 160, 174–5, 181–3, 193–4, 244, 278
endogamy, 192, 231
exogamy, 187, 192, 234, 263, 268
polygamy, 244
polygyny, 160
wrong marriage (*warrura*), 179
see also kinship; taboo
Meggitt Mervyn, 151–2, 156, 159
memory, 10, 16, 37, 39, 41, 71, 90, 98, 100, 104, 111, 119, 163–4, 182, 241, 282–6, 323, 325–6, 332, 333n, 393; *see also* refrain
mining, 1, 3, 19–20, 44, 70, 76, 96–7, 125, 204, 242, 246, 251, 253, 260, 269, 291, 315, 324, 336, 346, 355
fracking, 20, 35, 74, 271n, 354, 355n
Mnouchkine, Ariane, 326–7
Morvan, Arnaud, 377n
Mudpura (Mudbura), 3, 150
Munn Nancy, 133, 150, 161
Murinbata, 210, 212–13, 217
museums, 11, 121n, 199, 257, 259–63, 270, 272n, 273, 275, 280, 289–92, 301, 310, 326, 328
Myers Fred, 262–3
myth, 82, 99, 107–8, 126, 155, 160–1, 163, 187, 189, 350
male/female versions, 157, 155–61, 166, 168
mythic network, 117, 241, 279, 280, 287–8
mythico-ritual complexes, 205, 234
'payback', 101
transgressors, 192–3
see also Dreamings; lines; ritual

Nakamarra, Janjiya Liddy Herbert, 11, 130, 135–6, 140–3
Nakamarra, Nakakut Barbara Gibson, 1–4, 19, 123
Napaljarri, Peggy Rockman, 293
Napanangka, Nelly Morrison, 15–16
Narcisse Pelletier, 318
nature/culture, 38–40, 46, 52–4, 57, 63, 98, 119, 123, 166, 322, 324, 328, 338, 342–3, 346–7
Pachamama, 353–4
renaturalising, 343
New Age, 37, 322n, 341–2

Neyrat, Frédéric, 342
Nungarrayi, Betty Jamanawita, 17–18

Oceania, 50, 57, 59, 97, 115, 125–6, 199, 243, 335, 338
  Banaba Island (Kiribati), 56–8
  Festival of the Pacific Arts, 58, 255
  Kanak (New Caledonia), 111, 304, 306, 309–10, 312
  Ma'ohi (French Polynesia), 41, 75, 300, 304, 306, 309–10, 312, 324, 354
  Māori (New-Zealand), 46–7, 50, 255
  Palau, 58, 126n
  Papua New Guinea, 126
  Trobriand Island, 22, 34, 37, 117n, 217, 277
  Vanuatu, 126, 306
  Wallis and Futuna (French), 310
  see also Australia
ontologies, 40–1, 46, 52–3, 54–7, 77, 103, 115, 117, 120, 123–4, 299, 324, 340–4, 346, 349, 350–3, 353, 356, 366
Orixàs, 61, 361–7, 369, 372–4, 376; see also becomings, spirits

painting, 5, 16, 64, 73, 132, 161–3, 168, 242–3, 275, 329
  with acrylics, 37, 66–7, 116, 261, 281, 287–8, 382
  body, 2, 103–4, 108, 116, 133–5, 137, 154, 174, 315, 344, 367
  'looking after the country', 122, 131
  of objects, 135, 137
  rock (cave), 125, 151, 381
  sand, 11, 121, 140, 165, 262
  see also dream; Dreamings; inalienability; ritual
Pal Pelbart, Peter, 59
Pannell, Sandra, 262
Peterson, Nicolas, 132, 157–9, 182, 193, 269, 278
Pintupi, 162, 191, 231
Pitjantjatjara, 161–2, 204–5, 213, 382n
pluriverse, 15, 38, 53, 59, 69, 70, 76–7
Polack, Jean-Claude, 84–91, 109–11
pollution, 46, 54, 228, 300, 346
Povinelli, Elizabeth, 24, 54–5, 57

Querrien, Anne, 62, 83–4, 91, 93n, 97, 120

racism, 32, 41–4, 47, 57, 75, 227–8, 243, 247, 299, 301–5, 307, 310, 316–17, 319, 332, 335, 338, 350–1
  apartheid, 236, 249, 252, 268, 333
  Black Lives matter, 43–4, 341
  and multiculturalism, 311–13
  Racial Discrimination Act 1975 (Australia), 43, 314
  reverse racism, 247, 300
  slavery, 33, 45, 49, 59, 76, 248, 306–7, 310, 328, 333, 338, 372, 408
  structural racism, 311, 313–14
  'whitening', 32–3, 237
refrain (*ritournelle*), 15, 71, 73, 323n, 323–4; see also memory; singing
refugee, 50–1, 269, 306, 308, 310, 311, 313, 326–7, 332, 335–7, 342, 351
rhizome, 6, 14, 39, 73, 76, 125–6, 286
reticular cosmogeography, 343
reticular thinking, 36–9, 282, 286, 294, 296, 349
reticular travelling, 288
reticularity, 324
ritual, 121, 147, 153, 155, 165, 168, 201, 341, 205, 230, 267–8
  Cargo cult, 264
  depilation, 150, 183–4
  female camp (*jilimi*), 151
  female innovations, 132–3, 135–6, 138, 149, 186
  hairstring exchange, 144, 277–8
  Kajirri, 107–8, 136, 172, 199, 204–5
  male, 23, 139–40, 143, 147, 159, 165, 178
  'smoking' (fumigation), 70, 146–7, 273n, 384
  Umbanda, 60, 361, 363, 366–8, 372–6
  see also conflict; dance; funeral; painting; sacred objects; singing, taboo
Roheim, Geza, 22
Roth, Walter, 379

Sabatier, Arnaud, 311
sacred objects, 131, 194, 199–200, 263
  female (*kuturru, yukurrukurru*), 1–4, 86, 137–8, 154–5, 199, 201, 256
  hairstring, 267, 276–9
  male (*tjuringa or churinga*), 139, 262
  pearl-shells, 229, 234, 248n, 266, 278
science-fiction, 13, 26, 28, 52, 61–2, 125, 169n, 340, 347–51
secret, 149, 151, 155, 167–8, 180, 186
  'below' meaning, 191

Index

mangaya, 1, 3, 137, 149–51, 167–8
maralypi, 150–5, 167–9, 178
mungamunga, 123, 135, 136, 141, 143, 149–51, 167
  see also virtual
self, 27, 48, 238–9, 305, 312, 340, 344, 346, 369
self-affirmation, 40, 115, 323
self-appropriation, 105
self-constructed, 74
self-determination, 30, 44, 243, 247, 250, 250, 270, 275, 315
self-generation, 189
self-management, 3, 12, 248, 250, 270, 312
self-penetrate, 169–70
self-referential, 71, 73, 111, 163, 189, 198, 238
self-regulated, 321
self-reproductive, 198
self-sufficient, 52
Sembène, Ousmane, 329
sense of 'common', 367
sexuality, 7, 23, 92, 165, 154–5, 157–61, 165–6, 168, 171–2, 174–9, 181–2, 402; *see also* love
shamanism, 12, 38, 52, 53, 70, 100, 116, 169, 191, 324n, 342–3, 345–6, 377, 388, 406, 408; *see also* health
singing, 1–2, 16–17, 19, 93, 101, 108, 116, 122, 131, 135, 137–8, 144–5, 153n, 156, 161, 316, 380, 389, 402–3; *see also* lines
singularity, 12, 28n, 35–6, 40–1, 52, 106, 124, 161, 230, 263, 286, 296, 346–8, 366
  maralypi, 152, 154, 167, 169, 178
site, 25, 31, 46, 48, 73, 85, 90, 96, 98–100, 103, 131, 155, 180, 287, 344
  of conception, 17–18, 95, 98, 236
  sacred, 12–14, 16, 19, 70, 116, 124, 136, 151, 250, 266, 288, 344
  see also Dreamings; land; map; mining; spirits: spirit-child
skin-name(s) (subsections), 15n, 18, 24, 67–8, 95, 107, 118–19, 135, 183, 206, 208, 211–12, 232, 233, 267, 381, 384, 386; *see also* kinship; land; marriage
sorcery, 184, 195, 239, 401–3
  kurdaija, 165n, 185, 386, 401, 407
  singing to death, 199
  see also health; soul

soul (*pirlirrpa*), 99–100, 137, 147, 151–2, 169, 386–7, 399
  almas (Brazil), 368–9, 372, 374
space-time, 10, 14, 15, 117, 119, 126, 137–8, 149, 163, 168–70, 176, 186–7, 195, 200, 204, 209, 221, 279, 282
  holographic, 345
  of images, 364–5
  relativity, 37–8, 69, 169n, 340
  see also Dreamings; virutal
Spencer, Walter Baldwin, and Francis James Gillen, 22, 174, 179, 188, 377, 379
spirits, 13, 15–17, 30n, 38, 61, 99, 135, 140–3, 151–2, 169, 197, 200, 227, 235, 241, 245, 267, 273–4, 344, 353, 361–7, 377, 387–8, 390–6, 398, 402–4, 407–9
  consultation, 368–75
  incorporation or trance, 60, 93, 182, 325, 331, 358–66, 375, 389–90
  path, 345
  place of, 273–4
  spirit-child (*Kurruwalpa, Tharmu, Rayi*), 18, 64, 69, 92, 95, 98–100, 125, 150–1, 165, 167–9, 200, 228–30, 235–6, 283–4, 286, 395, 396–8
spiritual cleansing, 384
spiritual danger, 272–3, 385–6, 399–401
spiritual forces, 290–1, 343
spirituality, 19, 21–2, 38, 59, 60, 63, 100, 116, 229–30, 239–43, 245, 262–4, 276, 281, 283, 341, 343, 346
  see also Christianity; death; Dreamings; Orixàs; soul; totemism
Spitz, Chantal, 300
Stanner, W. E., 210, 241
Stanton, John, 291
stars, 14, 16, 66, 74, 97, 193
  Magellanic Cloud galaxies, 100, 147, 152n, 169, 406
  Milky Way, 68–9, 102, 169
  Orion and Pleiades, 190–1, 193, 406
  Southern Cross, 16, 63, 67, 69, 147
Stengers, Isabelle, 28, 56, 349–50
sterility, 235, 284
Sullivan, Muradjara Lance, 69–70, 378–9, 408–9
survival, 13, 119, 227, 281, 283, 285–6, 289–94, 317, 322, 328, 331, 335, 346
Swain, Tony, 152n, 242–3, 265n

taboo, 13, 47, 153, 178, 193–7, 201, 206, 209, 218–21, 227, 229, 308, 324
  on food and water, 171, 177–9, 187, 198, 200, 229
  incest, 22, 97, 171, 188, 189, 192, 196
  inversion, transgression, 182, 192, 198
  mother-in-law/son-in-law, 22–3, 158, 171, 193
  sacred objects, 198–201
  totemic, 178–81, 186–8
  on words, song (*kumanjayi*), 13, 17, 95, 153, 170–3, 178, 95, 180, 193, 196–7, 200–1, 218, 263, 397
  see also death; ritual; totemism
Taubira, Christiane, 302
Teaiwa, Katerina, 56–8
time-space, 4, 91, 98, 153, 164, 285; *see also* Dreamings; space-time
Tiouka, Alexis, 352
topology, 24–7, 41, 124–5, 202, 206, 209, 218
  5D cube, 216
  Boy's surface, 217
  Hypercube, 25, 64, 125, 210, 213–15, 217, 219, 221
  Klein Bottle, 25, 125
  Torus, 217
totemism, 39, 82, 95, 106, 118–19, 119, 166, 199, 229, 290, 340, 344, 346, 361, 366
  conception totem, 18, 94–5, 98, 254
  totemic forces, 360
  totemic kinship, 232
  totemic marks, 230, 398
  totemic name, species, 125, 200, 231, 263, 381
  totemic sites, 262
  totemic spirits, 239, 254, 262, 397
  totemic territory, 120
  see also becoming; Dreamings; image-force; lines; ritual; spirits: spirit-child; taboo
transversality, 28–9, 37, 41, 46, 74, 102–3, 124, 127, 308, 324, 343, 348–9, 366–7
Traoré, Tiécoura, 330–1
Tsing Anna, 56

UN Declaration on the Rights of Indigenous Peoples 2007, 257n, 335

virtual/actual, 7, 37, 47, 61–2, 71–3, 117, 119, 121, 125, 165, 167, 173, 193, 222, 274, 279, 283–4, 289, 324, 344–5, 348–9
kanunju/kankarlu, 169, 176, 208–9, 219, 256, 284, 361, 375–6
Viveiros de Castro, Eduardo, 53–4, 124n, 343, 345

Walmajarri, 159n, 191, 231, 263, 268, 271
'Walmadgerisation', 233
Warlpiri, 11–12, 19, 29, 36, 64, 68, 98, 104, 131, 155, 182, 202, 267, 382, 314, 382, 408
  in Alice Springs, 182
  in Docker River, 204
  in Katherine, 144, 224
  in Lajamanu, 140–2, 148, 150, 153, 261–3, 278, 314–15
  map, 88–9, 288
  new system, 107, 159
  in Noonkanbah, 148, 268
  in Paris, 140, 199, 262
  system of knowledge, 285, 288
Walpirised, 107
Woneiga (Warnayaka), 231, 242
  in Yuendumu, 1, 3, 29, 132–3, 135, 137, 150, 334–5
  see also language
Warumungu, 150, 183n, 382
Weiner, Annette, 34, 117, 276–7, 279
Wenders Wim, 348–9
Wild, Steven, 144–5
Wotton, Lex, 42–3, 316, 333
Wurundjeri, 45–6

Yalarrnga, 69–70, 377–8, 380, 397
Yanuwana Christophe Pierre, 44
Yapa/Kardiya (Aboriginal/White), 29–30, 36, 231, 238, 288
Yawuru, 35, 263, 268, 270–2, 396, 408; *see also* Djugun
Yolngu (Murngin), 58, 205, 210, 212, 214, 216–17, 219, 290–1, 292n, 314
Yulparija (Yulbarija), 230, 271

ZAD (zone to defend) of Notre-Dame-des-Landes, 59, 74–5, 318

EU representative:
Easy Access System Europe
Mustamäe tee 50, 10621 Tallinn, Estonia
Gpsr.requests@easproject.com

www.ingramcontent.com/pod-product-compliance
Lightning Source LLC
Chambersburg PA
CBHW071824230426
43672CB00013B/2757